Authority

A Sociological History

MW01070135

Concern with authority is as old as human history itself. Eve's sin was to challenge the authority of God by disobeying his rule. Frank Furedi explores how authority was contested in ancient Greece and given a powerful meaning in Imperial Rome. Debates on religious and secular authority dominated Europe through the Middle Ages and the Reformation. The modern world attempted to develop new foundations for authority – democratic consent, public opinion, science – yet Furedi shows that this problem has remained unresolved, arguing that today the authority of authority is questioned. This historical sociology of authority seeks to explain how the contemporary problems of mistrust and the loss of legitimacy of many institutions are informed by the previous attempts to solve the problem of authority. It argues that the key pioneers of the social sciences (Marx, Durkheim, Simmel, Tonnies and especially Weber) regarded this question as the one principal challenges facing society.

FRANK FUREDI is an Emeritus Professor of Sociology at the University of Kent in Canterbury, and Visiting Professor in the Institute of Risk and Disaster Reduction, University College London. Dr Furedi has published widely on controversies relating to issues such as health, parenting children, food and new technology, and his books and articles provide an authoritative yet lively account of key developments in contemporary cultural life that have been widely debated in the media.

Authority

A Sociological History

Frank Furedi

CAMBRIDGE
UNIVERSITY PRESS

University Printing House, Cambridge CB2 8BS, United Kingdom

Published in the United States of America by Cambridge University Press, New York

Cambridge University Press is part of the University of Cambridge.

It furthers the University's mission by disseminating knowledge in the pursuit of education, learning and research at the highest international levels of excellence.

www.cambridge.org
Information on this title: www.cambridge.org/9780521189286

© Frank Furedi 2013

This publication is in copyright. Subject to statutory exception and to the provisions of relevant collective licensing agreements, no reproduction of any part may take place without the written permission of Cambridge University Press.

First published 2013

Printing in the United Kingdom by TJ International Ltd. Padstow Cornwall

A catalogue record for this publication is available from the British Library

Library of Congress Cataloguing in Publication data
Furedi, Frank, 1947–
Authority : a sociological history / Frank Furedi.
  pages   cm
Includes bibliographical references and index.
ISBN 978-1-107-00728-4 (hbk.) – ISBN 978-0-521-18928-6 (pbk.)
1. Authority.   I. Title.
HM1251.F87   2013
303.3′6 – dc23   2013016238

ISBN 978-1-107-00728-4 Hardback
ISBN 978-0-521-18928-6 Paperback

Cambridge University Press has no responsibility for the persistence or accuracy of URLs for external or third-party internet websites referred to in this publication, and does not guarantee that any content on such websites is, or will remain, accurate or appropriate.

Contents

vi   Contents

Preface

During the past two decades I have been preoccupied with the difficulty that Western culture has in giving meaning to authority. In a number of studies I explored the different manifestations of this problem in relation to issues such as disputes over child-rearing, scientific advice or who to trust in public life. From these studies I became aware of the absence of a serious account of the cultural devaluation of an idea that once constituted a central category of philosophy, political theory and of my own discipline of sociology. This study attempts to find answers through the sociological investigation of the concept of authority.

During the past five years I have attempted to understand how authority emerged, evolved and changed through different historical periods. This work of historical sociology represents an attempt to mobilise the experience of the past to help explain why authority today has such an elusive quality. The story begins with the Homeric legend and leads up to our present day predicament. Hopefully, through providing a historical context for the constitution of the problem of authority, it will allow twenty-first-century readers to interpret the relation between society and authority in a new way. I believe that history provides a unique vantage point for understanding the different symptoms of the crisis of authority. Studying and maybe diagnosing those symptoms will be the subject of my next book on this area.

Despite the length of this study, it was impossible for a single author to do justice to the history of authority. The wealth of historical and philosophical scholarship devoted to all the periods and debates covered in this book is truly impressive. Any sociologists attempting to familiarise themselves with Socrates' Athens or Hobbes's England will find the task a truly humbling experience. They will also be surprised by the important sociological insights that can be gained from the study of the historical literature.

I used this journey into history as an opportunity to reflect on what can be learned from old intellectual friends and enemies. After all, some of the most influential figures in the humanities and social sciences – Hobbes, Hume, Mill, Marx, Durkheim and Weber – were deeply concerned about the question of authority. And even when their views appear incompatible they have something important to add to our understanding of the problem. No doubt many readers will note the influence of Hannah Arendt on the way that the problem of authority is conceptualised. It was not until I finished the book that I came to appreciate her extraordinary intellectual courage of going down a road where others fear to tread. At a time when many of her colleagues abandoned this journey, Arendt remained committed to completing it.

I am grateful to the many colleagues who have helped me to navigate around the intricate and complex scholarly debates that surround all the subjects covered in this book. In the course of researching and writing *Authority: A Sociological History* I have had the pleasure of encountering a variety of thinkers whose work is often hardly known and therefore underappreciated. The historian Leonard Krieger has written what are arguably the most important reviews of the history of authority.[1] His all-too-brief monographs demonstrate an unparalleled capacity to capture the movement and evolution of authority in history. His unexpected contribution has significantly influenced the direction taken by this study. Towards the completion of this book, I encountered an article 'Towards a Sociology of Authority' published by a young American sociologist, Jeremiah Wolpert in 1950. Unfortunately Wolpert passed away a year before the publication of his immensely suggestive contribution to this subject and therefore did not have the opportunity to make a significant impact on the discipline. I hope that some of my readers will feel stimulated to revisit these ideas as well as those of some of the other scholars mentioned in this book, for their ideas can help encourage a much needed rethink on the meaning of authority.

My close collaborator Jennie Bristow served as a constant sounding board and her comments have helped to clarify many of the arguments in this book. I thank her for patience and her friendship.

[1] See Krieger (1968) and Krieger (1977).

Introduction: always in question

When the word 'authority' in its original Latin form was used as a form of self-description by Augustus, the Emperor of Rome, his aim was to communicate the possession of something far more important than mere military or political power. His self-conscious reference to his unique *auctoritas* sought to draw attention to a far more compelling attribute, which was a dignified moral authority. Augustus's implied distinction between power and *auctoritas* spoke to a world that had begun to understand that something more than force was needed to maintain order and cohesion.

Since Augustus's time there have been continual attempts to claim the possession of something more than power. Yet time and again, societies have found it difficult to find an adequate way of conceptualising this. In England at least, it was not until the seventeenth century that a new language was created to respond the unsettled political realities sought to distinguish conceptually between authority and power. One pamphleteer in 1642 drew attention to the distinction between the two terms which, he claimed, were 'commonly confounded and obscure the whole business'.[1] However, the absence of a language to contrast power and authority does not mean that the distinction itself was absent from Western political culture. The historian Leonard Krieger has argued that what was significant and distinct about 'the Christian dimension of authority' was its independence from political power: while 'medieval men' would use the terms 'interchangeably in many contexts', a 'context was established for the separation of authority from power'.[2] And certainly, the distinction between authority and power has been an integral component to Western political theory for well over two millennia. 'The most fundamental of all distinctions in political thought is the distinction between 'force' or 'violence' and 'authority'; between *potential*, which is physical, and *potestas*

---

[1] William Robinson's 1642 statement in *The People's Plea* is cited by Tuck (1974) p. 42.
[2] Krieger (1968) pp. 146 and 147.

or *auctoritas*, which is mental; between 'might' and 'right''', argues the political theorist, Michael Oakeshott.[3]

In the present era, the discussion of authority has become even more confused than it was in the seventeenth century. Despite the frequent use of the phrase 'moral authority' as a cultural ideal, authority has an uneasy relationship with morality. Matters are complicated by the prevailing sensibility that authority has become an elusive force. People ask: 'who is *in* authority?', 'who is *the* authority?', 'who can speak *with* authority?' or 'on whose authority do you *act*?' Every controversy surrounding an act of misfortune – whether it is an outbreak of a flu epidemic, an environmental problem, a natural disaster, an accident or a financial crisis – creates a demand for authoritative solutions. Yet this aspiration for authoritative answers coincides with a cultural sensibility that is profoundly suspicious of the exercise of authority.

Unmasking authority has become a fashionable enterprise that resonates with popular culture. Those who hold positions of responsibility and power – politicians, parents, teachers, priests, doctors, nursery workers – are regularly 'exposed' for abusing their authority, a feature of life that is symptomatic of Western society's disenchantment with the so-called authority figure. It appears that we have become far more comfortable with questioning authority than with affirming it. Consequently, even those who are formally in authority hesitate about openly exercising their influence. In businesses and public institutions, this objective is accomplished through the now widely practised custom of outsourcing authority to consultants and experts.

Though the question of authority constitutes one of the most significant issues facing our world, society finds this question difficult to acknowledge and explicitly confront. From time to time, queries are raised about the authority of science, religion, the media or the political class. But such concerns tend to respond to a particular dimension of authority and overlook its more fundamental and general features. More specifically, there appears to be a lack of interest in reflecting on the question of why Western culture finds it difficult to give a positive meaning to authority. Most serious studies of this subject have as their focus the political and philosophical debates that surround deliberations on political and religious authority, and related topics such as legitimacy, obedience, freedom, autonomy and consent. In my own discipline of sociology, topics that bear upon the question of authority tend to be represented as the question of trust.

---

[3] Oakeshott (2006) p. 293.

Contemporary social theory also often signals the idea that authority no longer constitutes a significant problem. The French sociologist Pierre Bourdieu has hinted that consumer society has transformed the mode of domination to the point that public relations, advertising and needs-creation have displaced the necessity for authority,[4] while the eminent social theorist Zygmunt Bauman contends that the authority of the state is no longer a pressing matter: 'authority has become redundant, and the category specializing in servicing the reproduction of authority has become superfluous'.[5] One influential variant of this argument, put forward by Anthony Giddens,[6] is that we live in an age of 'multiple authorities' where their commands are no longer 'taken as binding'.[7]

Historically, authority has frequently served as a focus of struggle; even when authority itself was beyond question, its meaning and institutional expression was often an object of dispute and political contestation. Powerful lords resisted the demands of absolute monarchs, kings reacted to claims made by the Church on behalf of Papal Supremacy, and subordinate classes resisted the authority of their rulers. As one historian recalls, such challenges 'helped to keep alive the habit of interrogating the most basic principles of authority, legitimacy and the obligation to obey, even at moments when social and political hierarchies were at their most rigid'.[8] That is why authority served as a central category of Western political theory since the days of the Roman Empire. However, as we note in the chapters that follow, the relation of authority to society has undergone important mutations and its contemporary role arguably has little in common with the way it worked in the past.

History is implicated in representation of authority. Religious, cultural, nationalist and political movements have continually mobilised a narrative of history to justify their objectives and worldview. In times of social and political crisis, competing interests attempted to gain validation through drawing on myths of origin, tradition and precedent. But the consciousness of history that emerged with modernity altered the relation of authority to society. As society became sensitised to change and alteration, the past lost some of its authorising role. The idea that societies are subject to variations in custom and government encouraged a conventional perception of authority, and fostered a climate where authority can be contested, either implicitly or explicitly. The most important outcome of this process was the gradual dissolution of the authority of tradition – which is the authority of the past.

---

[4] See Bourdieu (1984).   [5] Bauman (1987) p. 122.   [6] Giddens (1994) p. 87.
[7] Giddens (1994) p. 42.   [8] Wood (2008) p. 25.

How authority emerged, gained shape and meaning, sought to reconcile itself to the loss of the past, and attempted to reconstitute itself in modern times is the principal focus of this book. Our aim is not to provide a history of authority, but to examine its shifting meaning from Ancient Greece to the contemporary era, and the beliefs, customs and conventions that provide a foundation for justifying authority.

History and sociology

Sociological accounts of authority, order and trust often suffer from their detachment from history. The powerful presentist imagination that dominates sociology means that often it ceases to have any serious engagement with the concepts that influenced proceedings in the past. Donald Kelley, the historian of ideas, believes that 'few other fields of intellectual endeavour have taken so restricted a view of the past' as sociology.[9] There are some honourable exceptions to the anti-historical orientation of contemporary sociology; but as George McCarthy points out, the utilitarian turn of particularly Anglo-American sociology encouraged an ahistorical temper: 'In the end, both philosophy and history were lost in a sociology geared to measure what is, but unable to understand what was or what could be'.[10]

Yet, the rise of sociology is indissolubly linked to the historical examination of the problem of order and authority. All of the discipline's founding figures regarded authority as a key concept for inquiry, and in the nineteenth century, sociology embraced authority as its cause. Durkheim's project of a 'science of morality' is underpinned by a concern with the relationship between authority and morality: for him, moral authority is central for the regulation of human behaviour and for mandating action. In developing his well-known typology of authoritative domination, Weber drew attention to the important relationship between authority and social action.

Weber's theory of rationalisation and domination is based on a major historical investigation of the subject. But his attempt to reconstruct the changing forms through which authority was expressed and validated was integral to a wider conversation that social and political theorists conducted with the past. His peer, the Italian political theorist Gaetano Mosca, developed the idea of an authoritative ruling class as one that is 'independent of those who hold supreme power and who have sufficient means to be able to devote a portion of their time to perfecting their culture and acquiring that interest in the public weal – that aristocratic

[9] Kelley (1984a) p. 134.   [10] McCarthy (2003) p. 2.

spirit' which 'alone can induce people to serve their country with no other satisfaction than those that come from individual pride and self-respect'.[11] Ancient Rome was his model for authority. The laws of society presented by Vilfredo Pareto's *The Mind and Society: A Treatise on General Sociology*, published in 1916, are almost exclusively based on historical examples that go back to Biblical times.

Arguably one reason why sociology has become detached from history may be due to the loss of authority of the past. As Harrison states, 'since Aristotle, thinkers have posed their problems with an eye to history of their past answers'.[12] However, as I discuss elsewhere, the past has lost much of its capacity to validate the arguments conducted in the present. Indeed, past answers are frequently interpreted as irrelevant precisely because they have become de-authorised in contemporary times.[13]

Conceptualising authority as a problem

Max Weber's sociology of domination exercises a powerful influence on the conceptualisation of authority in the social sciences: a point illustrated by the philosopher Alasdair MacIntyre's statement that 'we know of no justification for authority which are not Weberian in form'.[14] One well-known introductory text for sociology undergraduates published in the 1960s claims that Weber's 'account for the history of authority and power in the West' and his 'sociology of authority' informs the 'bulk of inquiries into the subject'.[15] Weber's writings indicate that he was profoundly interested in, but also deeply troubled by, the problem of authority. As Turner argues, in 'Weber's sociology of law and in his political writings, the disenchantment of capitalist society precludes the possibility of any normative legitimation of the state'.[16] The question that haunted Weber was how the prevailing order could be legitimised, yet his theory fore-closes the possibility of providing impersonal formal authority with moral content. That is why, in his political writing, Weber places his hope in the charismatic authority of individual leaders.[17]

The question of 'normative legitimation' constitutes what I charac-terise as the problem of foundation. Rules, procedures and laws possess no intrinsic authority; as the legal scholar Harold Berman states, the law 'in all societies . . . derives its authority from something outside itself'. That 'something' which is separate from and logically prior to the formu-lation of a rule or the codification of a law, is the *source* or the *foundation*

---

[11] Mosca (1980) p. 144.   [12] Harrison (1994) p. 9.   [13] See Furedi (2009a).
[14] MacIntyre (2007) p. 109.   [15] Nisbet (1979) p. 142: originally published in 1966.
[16] Turner (1992) p. 185.   [17] See Potts (2009) p. 114.

of its authority. When 'a legal system undergoes rapid change', notes Berman, 'questions are inevitably raised concerning the legitimacy of the sources of its authority'.[18]

The social theorist David Beetham provides an important insight into the problem of foundation in his discussion of the relationship between legitimacy and the law. He contends that legality on its own 'cannot provide a fully adequate or self-sufficient criterion of legitimacy'. Conflicts of interpretation about the meaning of law invariably attempt to justify their claims by 'reference to a basic principle', which refer to 'norms or an authoritative source that lies beyond existing rules'. What Beetham suggests is that the compelling power of rules, their moral authority, requires that they are 'normatively binding' and based upon a 'common framework of belief'. The problem of foundational norms constitutes one the fundamental questions facing public life:

> What is the ultimate source of law and social rules, from whence do they derive their authority, what provides the guarantee of their authenticity or validity – these are questions that concern the most fundamental of a society's beliefs, its metaphysical basis... which cannot itself be questioned.[19]

The 'ultimate source' that validates society's laws and conventions has been subject to historical variations. In the past it has been served by tradition and custom, divine command, popular will and consent and the doctrine of science.

Weber's sociology of domination attempts to analyse the foundation of authority as consisting of different sources of legitimation. He argues that it is 'rare' for rulers to rely merely on 'one or other' of the pure types, and reminds us that 'the basis of every authority, and correspondingly of every kind of willingness to obey, is a *belief*, a belief by virtue of which persons exercising authority are lent prestige'. This focus on belief raises the question of 'belief in what?' It is evident that Weber is referring to is some kind of foundational norm. Weber states that 'the composition of this belief is seldom altogether simple', and that, in the case of '"legal authority" it is never purely legal'. Moreover, 'belief in legality comes to be established and habitual, and this means that it is partly traditional'; and consequently, 'violation of the tradition may be fatal to it'. Weber also asserts that authority even has a charismatic dimension, 'at least in the negative sense that persistent and striking lack of success may be sufficient to ruin any government to undermine its prestige, and to prepare the way for charismatic revolution'. In the same way, 'entirely pure charismatic authority' is rare.[20]

[18] Berman (1983) p. 16.   [19] Beetham (1991a) pp. 67, 69 and 70.
[20] Weber (1978) pp. 263–4.

While Weber's discussion draws attention to heterogeneous foundations for people's belief, there is a tendency to conflate the manner in
which authority is exercised with its source. Although he writes of a
'legitimacy derived from the authority of a "source"', he does not reflect
conceptually the relation between source and its authority.[21]

Authority is a relational concept, and its study inevitably touches on
the question, what makes people perceive commands and institutions
as authoritative? The one relationship of authority that appears to have
existed in 'all historically known societies', which is that of parents over
children, has frequently served as a model in political thought.[22] Aristotle, in claiming that 'every community is composed of those who rule and
those who are ruled', used the example of inter-generational authority to
substantiate his point, writing that 'nature itself has provided the distinction' between 'the younger and the older ones, of whom she fitted the
ones to be ruled and the others to rule'.[23] However, this form of simple
and non-political relationship expresses the relationship of authority in
only an embryonic form. Authority is a both a social and cultural accomplishment that presupposes a consensus on the norms through which it
gains both meaning and force.

Some critics claim that Weber tended to focus on the command
side of the authority relationship at the expense of studying how it
was accepted and internalised. As Turner remarks, 'Weber was more
concerned with the problem of how authoritative commands were produced than with the conditions which made them socially acceptable'.[24]
This focus on the relationship between command and obedience meant
that he was distracted from analysing the social and cultural forces that
could authorise commands. In this respect, compared to the work of
some of his contemporaries, Weber's work on early twentieth-century
authority comes across as narrowly political. Ferdinand Tonnies's conceptualisation of authority provides an interesting counterpoint, representing authority as a relational concept that is not merely or even
principally political but that also has a cultural, social and symbolic
significance.[25] In more recent times, the point has been stressed by
Michel Foucault, who argued that 'power is not something that can be
possessed, and is not a form of might, power is never anything more than a
relationship'.[26]

---

[21] Weber (1978) p. 1124.   [22] See Arendt (1956) p. 403.
[23] Aristotle *Politics 1332b12* cited in Arendt (1956) p. 403.
[24] Turner (1992) p. 188.   [25] See Tonnies (1955).
[26] Foucault (2004) p. 168. Foucault sometimes uses the term power to connote authority but it is evident that his focus is on the relationship between command and its
internalisation.

Although authority is a relational concept, its 'claim made to adherence depends on the antecedent authentication of the speaker'.[27] Genuine authority possesses a compelling power to motivate and gain obedience. It is closely associated with power and particularly the power to persuade, yet remains distinct from it. As Arendt and others have argued, persuasion through the use of argument is alien to the concept of authority. The very need to persuade is usually a testimony to authority's absence.[28] Authority's capacity to guide people's behaviour is an outcome of a moral influence which, when allied to the power to compel, can gain obedience without either having to argue or to threaten the use of force.

The tendency to conceptualise authority as merely a relationship of power encourages a lack of clarity on this subject. Authority also gives cultural meaning to power, and provides the intellectual and moral resources through which authoritative acts and behaviour gains definition. When De Grazia argues that 'authority is a communal matter', he is attempting to point to its fundamental and foundational dimension.[29] The American sociologist Dennis Wrong focuses too closely on authority as a relation of power; however, he is also sensitive to the workings of its foundational dimension. Wrong states that it is the '*source* rather than the *content* of any particular command' which 'endows it with legitimacy', and recognises that the 'source' is, at least in part, distinct from the exercise of 'command and compliance'.[30]

Authority should not be equated with, or reduced to, the act of justification. It already contains a warrant for influencing and directing behaviour and does not have continually to justify itself: Once authority has to be self-consciously justified it is well on the way to losing its unquestioned status. Authority rests on a foundation that warrants its exercise and for the right to expect obedience. Throughout history, such foundational norms – divine authority, tradition and customs, reason and science, popular consent – provide the resources for narratives of validation. Weber appeared less than certain whether political rule in his time could be underpinned by a form of foundational authority, and as we discuss, the absence of any explicit engagement with this question represents a conspicuous gap in his sociology of domination.

The problem of foundation demands an engagement with history. As Quentin Skinner, the pre-eminent historian of political thought, observed, political theory and action continually draws on the legitimation of the past since 'what is possible to do in politics is generally limited by what is possible to legitimise'. In turn, 'what you can hope to

[27] Miller (1987) p. 29.   [28] Lincoln (1994) p. 5.
[29] De Grazia (1959) pp. 321–2.   [30] Wrong (1979) p. 49.

legitimise' depends on 'what courses of action you can plausibly range under existing normative principles'.[31] The principles essential for legitimation constitute the foundation for authority. That is the subject of this book.

So what is authority?

Hannah Arendt, one of the leading political philosophers of the twentieth century, has argued that, 'if authority is to be defined at all it must be in contradistinction to both coercive power and persuasion through argument'. From this perspective, authority is not reducible to a relation of power; when governments force an issue through the exercise of power they inadvertently draw attention to their inability to act authoritatively. Nor can authority simply rely on persuasion to gain public endorsement for a specific objective. Persuasion through debate presupposes a relation of parity between competing but equal parties, and Arendt suggests that the use of coercion and of persuasion is symptomatic of non-authoritative behaviour. In writing that a 'father can lose his authority either by beating his child or by starting to argue with him, that is, either by behaving to him like a tyrant or by treating him as an equal',[32] Arendt means that when authority relies on coercion or persuasion it is forced implicitly to concede that it has lost the trust of those whom it seeks to influence.

Lincoln explains that coercion and persuasion exist as 'capacities or potentialities implicit within authority', which are 'actualized only when those claim authority sense that they have begun to lose the trust of those over whom they seek to exercise it'.[33] Historically, the meaning of authority was associated with the acknowledged capacity of certain people to gain the voluntary obedience of people to commands and beliefs. As the historian Leonard Krieger remarks, authority has the ability to place 'pressure upon men to conform in ways' in which 'they could not be ordered or compelled by the possessor of power'.

The *Oxford English Dictionary* indicates that the term authority encompasses the exercise of influence and pressure in a variety of relationships. In its starkest form, it expresses 'the right to command' and the 'power to influence action'. Those in authority are presumed to have 'power over the opinions of others', they have power to 'inspire belief' and a 'title to be believed'. According to the *OED*, those in authority enjoy 'moral or legal supremacy'. They can be people 'whose opinion or testimony is accepted'. Through its different usage this term evokes political, moral

---

[31] Skinner, Q. (1998) p. 105.   [32] Arendt (1970) p. 45.   [33] Lincoln (1994) p. 6.

and intellectual qualities. The Latin term *auctoritas*, from which the word 'authority' is derived, was not a political term but had more in common with the meaning captured by phrases like 'being in authority', 'speaking with authority' or 'moral authority'. The root of *auctoritas* is *augere* – to initiate, set in motion, to found something or to make something grow. This usage of the term communicates the ideal of a foundational authority which someone develops (augments) and takes forward into the present. According to Hopfl, *auctoritas* 'is a capacity to initiate and to inspire respect', and in this respect the moral quality of authority is emphasised.[34]

It is useful to remind ourselves of the historical relationship between *auctoritas* and authority for it helps highlight its foundational aspiration. As Friedman points out, from the perspective of *auctoritas*,

> a person with authority has been understood to be someone to whom a decision or opinion can be traced back as the source of that decision or opinion or else as someone who carries forward into the present, continues or 'augments' some founding act or line of action started in the past.[35]

Studying authority in history

Situating authority in history is essential for understanding its distinct modern features. A review of the different ways in which the problem of authority has been conceptualised in the past shows an attempt to answer very different questions at different times. So, whereas in the post-Reformation era the demand for authority was fuelled by conflict and rivalry among the European secular and religious elites, in the nineteenth century it was activated by the imperative of containing the threat from below. Consequently questions to do with the relation of religious to political authority, obedience, individual conscience and resistance gave way to concerns about the status of public opinion and the role of democratic consent. In the sixteenth century, debates and conflicts were fuelled by competing visions of what constituted the source of authority; by the nineteenth and especially the twentieth centuries, the very possibility of constructing a normative foundation for authority was put to question.

Analysing authority in history is a strategy that emerges from the constitution of this concept. Since the time of Aristotle, political thinkers have 'posed their problems with an eye to history of their past answers'.[36] Even future-oriented modern revolutions – those in America, France and

---

[34] Hopfl (1999) p. 219.   [35] Friedman (1990) pp. 74–5.   [36] Harrison (1994) p. 9.

Russia – have relied on the language of the past to endow their claims with authority. Current rational-legal claims to authority, based on the law or science, still need to appeal to some form of precedent to validate their claim.

Since the beginning of modernity, the main impulse driving philosophical and sociological interest in this question is the perception that society faces a crisis of authority. Hannah Arendt put matters most starkly when she declared that 'authority has vanished',[37] arguing that 'most will agree that a constant, ever-widening and deepening crisis of authority has accompanied the development of the modern world in our century'.[38] The political theorist Terence Ball has questioned Arendt's diagnosis of the vanishing of authority, claiming that Arendt's conceptualisation of authority is tied 'to one historically specific experience', and that 'a more adequate conceptual history would show how "authority" has been repeatedly reconstructed by being relocated in different conceptual schemes or theories'.[39]

No doubt Arendt's writings on this subject are dominated by her idealisation of Roman authority and of its subsequent influence on Western civilisation, and Ball is right to argue that authority has not stood still but has been recast into different political forms. Nevertheless, our study suggests that, at least in one very important sense, Arendt's interpretation captures authority in history more adequately than that of her critics. Authority based on a normative foundation has become very weak; and as our study explains, the very modest role that contemporary social thought has assigned to authority is testimony to its diminishing significance. The pluralised system of authority outlined by Ball lacks the cultural depth of Arendt's concept of *auctoritas*. In this book I follow Arendt who, as Villa stated, sought to 'rethink authority in a "disenchanted" age'.[40]

Weber believed that rationalisation and scientific advance lacked the capacity to generate 'ultimate' values.[41] His analysis indicated that capitalist modernisation had unleashed a process of rationalisation that undermined custom and habit. Implicitly, Weber also understood that the erosion of tradition was not paralleled by the emergence of a mental outlook disposed towards accepting values that bound them to the prevailing order. According to his theory of domination, belief in the legitimacy of the political order grounded in legal and rational norms displaced the justification provided by tradition. However, he had little faith in capacity of rationally devised rules to influence and inspire

---

[37] Arendt (2006, originally published 1954) p. 1.   [38] Ibid.   [39] Ball (1987) p. 39.
[40] Villa (2008) p. 97.   [41] Weber (1919a) pp. 139 and 144.

the public – which is why he tended to bank on the charismatic and inspirational potential of leaders to legitimate order.[42]

Weber's discovery that the process of modernisation and rationalisation has tended to diminish authority's foundation has not stopped social and political thinkers from searching for new ways of validating authority. Our study argues that this quest has frequently led to the conceptualisation of a negative theory of authority. Such negative theories bypass the problem of foundation and through a critique of mass culture and society justify domination through the need to keep in check the irrational and non-rational behaviour of the public.

Authority in Question attempts to parallel the practice of the pioneers of sociology, who attempted to gain insight into the shifting meaning of authority through a conversation with history. More specifically, this study can also be seen as the outcome of a critical dialogue with Max Weber. During the century following the publication of Weber's theory of domination, the meaning of authority has undergone a profound transformation. That is why, from the vantage point of the twenty-first century, it becomes necessary to revisit the history of authority. But what kind of history is adequate to the study of this subject matter? Weber was rightly critical of those who use history instrumentally, and those who fail to recognise the distinct and unique characteristics of different historical moments. He warned against making too much of historical comparisons, and counselled against chasing after '"analogies" and "parallels" in the presently fashionable general schemes'. History should 'be concerned with the *distinctiveness*' of what is compared.[43]

Our focus is on the distinct ways that authority has been asserted and problematised in history. The study of social problems often has only a limited temporal dimension; yet without a sense of temporality it becomes difficult to grasp the contemporary manifestations of a social problem in its specificity. To bring sociological inquiry into a dynamic relation with the past we have opted for a historical-logical reconstruction of the problem of authority. To carry out this investigation we have relied on a synthesis of constructionist social problems theory and the resources of intellectual history, history of ideas and conceptual history. Sociology's sub-branch of social problems theory has focused on the dynamics of competitive claims-making in an era where authority is habitually contested. Every claim about a social problem seeks validation from some form of foundational principle. As Hannigan wrote, warrants,

---

[42] Weber's 1919 lecture 'The Profession and Vocation of Politics' clearly shows this preoccupation. See Weber (1919), especially pp. 312–13.
[43] Weber (1978) p. xxxvii.

which are 'justifications for demanding that action be taken' are central to the rhetoric of claims making – yet warrants must be linked to some form of authority for legitimating the claim.[44] Since such warrants refer to previously established precedents, they must also be linked to the history.

Though the act of claiming authority has a historical dimension, it is far from evident what has been claimed and contested in the past and what is meant by it today. Are we talking about the same phenomenon when very different historical experiences are compared? Hobbes was preoccupied with the absence of consensus about the meaning of words like 'good', 'evil', 'just' and 'unjust' in the era following the English Civil War.[45] When it comes to a concept like authority, matters are further complicated by the fact that its meaning is often expressly contested. Assumptions on authority are informed through cultural narratives about how a community perceives the past, its institutions and the uncertainties it faces. Moreover, historically, attitudes towards authority are often formed and gain clarity in their relation to the values that society gives to related concepts such as freedom, obedience and anti-authoritarianism.

The chapters that follow provide an account of the historical moments when authority was not simply confronted with physical resistance but its claim to legitimacy was also put to question. Our focus is on the key historical experiences when authority was forced to account for itself, and when the normative and cultural foundation on which it rested underwent modification. In particular the focus of the study is the shift in historical meaning and context within which the concept altered and acquired different cultural connotations.

The final shape of this study is very different from its original intent. Our initial plan was that the study would have extended discussions on the experience of the Concilliar Movement and the French Revolution and pass through the Middle Ages relatively swiftly. However, on closer inspection it became evident that the Middle Ages provided an ideal focus for a historical sociology of authority, and that its influence had disproportionate impact on modernity's imagination of this subject. The English Civil War demanded that the issues raised by Hobbes be dealt with at length, distracting attention from the important philosophical debates leading up to the revolution in France.

As a sociologist, I felt much more at home reviewing the debates in the modern era. The questions raised from the late eighteenth century onwards have already been subjected to sociological inquiry and the

[44] Hannigan (2006) p. 35.   [45] See Ball (1985).

language used to express the problem of authority became more and more akin to our own. At this point it was also possible to use instruments of sociological inquiry such as textual analysis of newspapers and periodical literature to interpret the meaning of authority. Through an examination of such texts it was possible to explore what the conceptual historian Melvin Richter has referred to as the semantic struggle that surrounds key political concepts. As Richter reminds us, 'political language in situations of conflict is characterized by fundamental disagreements about usage and rules'.[46] Our discussion of the concept of 'principle of authority' and of the term 'authoritarian' indicates that they provided a rhetorical resource for the protagonists in the nineteenth- and early twentieth-century debates about the role and influence of democratic consent.

The study relies on the insights gained through a review of the contribution of historians of ideas and of scholars working in the field of conceptual history. It reinterprets the work of historians and of political theorists and philosophers who contributed to the discussion of authority over the centuries. In the last six chapters of the book, the analysis has sought to integrate a broader sample of texts – such as periodical literature of the nineteenth century, and newspaper accounts – to explore contextually the terminology used to express and interpret the problem of authority.

Although the study has as its focus the shifting meaning of authority in Western culture, its range and focus is restricted by the fact that it mainly relies on sources written or translated into the English language. To minimise the possible distortions imposed on the analysis, an attempt was made to integrate the historical experience of European societies through the engaging with some of the key debates through which ideas on authority were clarified. The aim of this study is to contribute to the revitalisation of the sociology of knowledge. Back in the 1960s Alvin Gouldner, in his magisterial contribution titled *Enter Plato: Classical Greece and the Origins of Social Theory*, stated that in his 'judgment there is hardly a serious history of social theory'. He wrote that the sociological literature was 'deficient in the virtues of both history and sociology' since it usually lacked 'the historian's grasp of documented detail and the sociologist's analytic thrust or imagination', and concluded that the 'history of social theory has failed' in part because contributors have been unable to 'resolve the crisis of intellectual identity' that a genuinely critical engagement with the past required.[47]

---

[46] Richter (1995) p. 42.   [47] Gouldner (1965) p. 167.

Enter Plato was published in 1965. Since that time, the estrangement of sociology from history has become even more profound. The orientation of *Authority: A Sociological History* towards history is motivated by the conviction that a more self-conscious and active relationship to the legacy of the past is necessary in order to move beyond the limits set by the presentist intellectual culture that dominates our time.

1 Thersites and the personification of anti-authority

Storytellers have been fascinated with the subject of authority since the birth of Western literature. The model of authority that prevailed in Homer's great epic the *Iliad*, written in the eighth century BC, is one where the authority of the king was 'anchored in the authoritative decree of the king of Gods', Zeus, who 'commissions an earthly king to share his sovereign rule'.[1] A king represented his rule as authorised by divine forces. The exercise of royal leadership required creativity and intelligence: it was not sufficient to be commissioned for the role of king by a divine power; the king had to demonstrate that his leadership could benefit the community and win favour with the gods. Consequently the king could increase or decrease his personal authority through the quality of his leadership.

The dominant influence of the aristocratic-warrior code ensured that acts of courage and prowess on the battlefield formed the foundation of individual authority. When the Greek hero Achilles derides Agamemnon's record as a warrior, he reminds the assembled gathering of prominent warriors that their leader did not earn his authority through a display of courage: 'never once have you taken courage in your heart to arm with your people for battle'. Agamemnon's position of kingly authority rests on his wealth and command over a large body of warriors, but his behaviour indicates that he lacks valour and rhetorical skills, the qualities that the Greeks associated with authoritative leadership. From this point onwards we all know that the angry exchange of insults between these two men will not be the last time that Agamemnon's authority will be contested.

Achilles openly calls into question the individual authority and moral status of King Agamemnon. In a world in which 'authority relations are first and foremost personal',[2] his criticism of Agamemnon can have a profound impact on the morale of the army. In any case, the contrast between his legendary authority and the insecure position of Agamemnon as the head of the coalition of Greek forces is evident to the

---

[1] Launderville (2003) p. 25.   [2] Hammer (1997) p. 353.

army. The soldiers also resent Agamemnon's selfish behaviour towards the distribution of the booty of war, believing that he has abused his royal position by claiming a disproportionate share of the plunder for himself. Agamemnon, conscious of his isolation from the rank-and-file soldiers, cannot be sure that he possesses sufficient power for commanding the loyalty of his troops. Achilles pointedly asks Agamemnon: 'with your mind forever on profit', why would any of the soldiers 'readily obey you'?[3]

Faced with the disintegration of his army, Agamemnon adopts a desperate measure to restore its fighting spirit, and tells his closest advisors that he will test the courage of the Greek forces through using a rhetorical trick that nowadays would be called reverse psychology. He will hold an assembly and deceive the army by telling them to leave the field of battle and return home. The goal of this act of deception is to provoke a sense of embarrassment and shame among his troops so that they would be jolted into action and renew their will to fight. Agamemnon's inspiration for this stratagem is a dream in which Zeus, the supreme god of gods, promises him that victory and the capture of Troy will soon follow this course of action. In effect, his plan was 'to test the troops by demoralizing them still further'.[4] In his speech to the soldiers, Agamemnon blames Zeus for betraying the army and failing to deliver on his promise to the Greeks that Troy would be conquered. Knowing that there is a serious possibility that rank-and-file soldiers would take flight, Agamemnon decides to limit this risk by instructing his generals to stand ready to restrain their men from fleeing the camp.

Agamemnon's attempt to consolidate his authority through a brazen act of deception only serves to expose his precarious hold over the Greek army. His decision to test the loyalty and morale of his troops by telling them to board their ship and return home has all the hallmarks of an act of desperation. But on this occasion, the assertion of royal authority works only too well, as Agamemnon's speech provokes the soldiers to flee to their ships and turn their back on their king. Even the generals are overwhelmed by this climate of demoralisation and instead of rallying the troops they appear passive and immobilised. According to one interpretation of this scene, 'it is less the troops' flight than the elders' failure to check it quickly that threatens the war'.[5]

As thousands of soldiers rush towards their ships, it appears that the Greek army lacks an 'inherent sense of order and authority'.[6] The divine intervention of the goddess Athene is required to restore a semblance of

---

[3] Cited in Hammer (1997) p. 4.   [4] Cook (2003) p. 168.
[5] McGlew (1989) p. 293.   [6] McGlew (1989) p. 290.

order, by instructing Odysseus to intercede. Odysseus openly confronts the problem of authority, engages with it, and succeeds in tackling it. He takes hold of Agamemnon's royal sceptre and strikes out at fleeing soldiers as he rebukes them for their cowardly behaviour. At the same time he appeals to the noble generals to assume their leadership role and shepherd the men back to the assembly. As he moves through the army, calming the nerves of the soldiers he encounters, it becomes evident that he is a man capable of restoring faith in the authority of the king's office, if not in Agamemnon.

Odysseus chooses his words carefully. He is careful not to embarrass the generals and is firm and forceful in his handling of the rank and file. In his speeches he emphasises the importance of restoring and obeying authority, appealing to and affirming the 'divine legitimation of kingly authority'.[7] Through his decisive intervention, Odysseus succeeds in gaining the army's obedience: with one notable exception. Described graphically as the 'ugliest man at Troy', the malcontent Thersites takes the floor in the assembly of Greek warriors and proceeds to denounce and expose Agamemnon's all-too-apparent failings.

The personification of anti-authority

Homer provokes a powerful sense of revulsion towards Thersites. He is 'bandy-legged and lame in one foot'; 'his humped shoulders were bent inwards over his chest' and 'his head rose to a point, sprouting thin wisps of wool'.[8] No other character in this epic poem has his physical appearance described in such graphic detail. It is evident that Homer is not simply describing this character, but morally condemning him: as one commentator notes, Thersites' 'grotesque ugliness... seems to play on the Greek tendency to regard physical appearance as a correlate of moral worth'.[9] The idealisation of beauty and the stigmatisation of ugliness had explicit moral connotations in Homeric Greece, and even before Thersites opens his mouth his deformed appearance is used to convey the message that he is a malevolent figure who threatens the moral integrity of the assembly.

Homer reinforces this point by warning us not to take this malcontent's words seriously: Thersites is 'loose-tongued', his 'head was full of abuse' and his 'reckless insubordinate attacks on the kings' were motivated by the impulse of raising a laugh among his fellow soldiers. Homer points out that he is a widely hated figure, especially by Achilles and Odysseus – the two heroes who are described as the 'best of the Achaeans', while

[7] Donlan (1979) p. 60.   [8] Homer (1987) p. 69.   [9] Thalmann (1988) p. 15.

Thersites is the 'most base'. We are told that the assembled soldiers 'felt furious anger and resentment at him' as he shouted his taunts at Agamemnon.[10] Yet his speech echoes Achilles' earlier criticisms of Agamemnon, accusing the king of poor leadership and greed. Assuming the role of a spokesman for rank-and-file troops, Thersites reminds his audience that, without the contribution of ordinary soldiers, the king would be reduced to a state of powerlessness.

Thersites does not possess the heroic status of Achilles, and he is certainly no match for Odysseus. But he is not without courage. Despite the anger and hatred directed at him by members of the assembly, he refuses to shut up. In the end, Odysseus reasserts order: not through responding to his criticisms, but through denouncing Thersites, questioning his right to speak, and proceeding to beat him with the king's spectre. Homer concludes this scene by drawing attention to the assembled soldiers' positive approval of Odysseus's action. Homer informs us that the crowd laughs at Thersites' humiliation and hails the 'best' deed that Odysseus has accomplished.

And yet the silencing of Thersites does not resolve the profound issues to do with leadership, obedience and authority in the *Iliad*. Silencing Thersites through the application of physical force exposes the precarious status of relations of authority. Arguably it serves as a reminder that questions about the nature of how rule is authorised and exercised are far from resolved. As one recent scholarly commentary notes: 'Odysseus' beating-up of Thersites draws attention to the exercise of authority which, paradoxically, opens it up to analysis'.[11] While Odysseus could easily force Thersites into submission, the questions raised by this subversive figure could not be answered. That is why, in the centuries to come, Thersites's defiance of the Homeric aristocratic code would often be interpreted by observers as relevant for the very different historical circumstances that they inhabited.

There is something unusual and unsettling about this rebel and his challenge to royal authority. Although Thersites is widely despised and derided, he has clearly spoken to the assembled warriors before, and his reputation for mendacious oratory precedes him. Homer regards Thersites's rhetorical skills as a menace to the authority of the Greek leadership. One of the ways in which a Homeric poem communicated authoritative behaviour was through *mythos*, which is characterised as a 'speech-act indicating authority, performed at length, usually in public'. It expresses views on the actions that a community should take; and through speech the personal authority of the individual gains strength.[12]

---

[10] Homer (1987) p. 69.   [11] Barker (2009) p. 60.   [12] Launderville (2003) pp. 57–8.

Odysseus is able to raise the morale of the Achaean army through numerous rhetorical interventions. In contrast, Agamemnon is a poor rhetorician, and his exercise in reverse psychology almost proves fatal to the Greek army's cause.

Through Odysseus' swift response to Thersites' challenge, authority is apparently restored and, as Thalmann notes, the outcome of this episode is the re-establishment of the Greek army's morale – 'authority and its accompanying ideology have been reinforced'.[13] In the hands of Odysseus, the sceptre – the symbol of royal power – is transformed into a weapon, indicating that those who refused to accept the king's authority would be cast out of the assembly.[14] From this perspective, the episode can be seen as part of a process of political healing through which the authority lost because of the dispute between Agamemnon and Achilles is restored.[15] But that it is the authoritative behaviour of Odysseus that saves the day exposes feeble foundation of Agamemnon's authority as king. The centrifugal tendencies contained within Homer's warrior culture will continue to pose problems for the assembled nobles.

Although the spectre serves as a mark of royal authority, in the hands of a man who lacks the quality of leadership it is merely an object with little intrinsic power. Possession of the spectre is not sufficient to compensate for the weakness of Agamemnon's character. Through having Odysseus take temporary possession of the spectre, Homer invites his audience to consider the meaning of royal leadership. As one important study asserts, Homer 'created scenes in which the character of particular kings and the relationships among them raised questions about the viability of this form of leadership'.[16]

Homer's dramatisation of an issue that would in subsequent centuries be called the problem of authority has raised questions that continue to be debated to this day. Thersites is portrayed as a repulsive, almost subhuman figure who would be represented as an ape in some of the visual art of classical Greece. Yet as Rankin notes, 'it is strange that this abject person is allowed to speak at all' and 'even more remarkable that he is given some telling points to make against the army's royal leadership'.[17] This paradox is also noted by Donlan, who observes that even though he is described in 'odious terms' by Homer, the 'impact' of Thersites words is 'significant'.[18] Whatever Homer's intention, the voice of Thersites raises important questions.

[13] Thalmann (1988) p. 2.   [14] McGlew (1989) p. 292.
[15] See Donlan (1979) on this point.   [16] Launderville (2003) p. 62.
[17] Rankin (1972) pp. 38–9.   [18] Donlan (1973) p. 150.

What is Homer doing?

Given his dramatic intervention in the assembly of the warrior chiefs, it is not surprising that Thersites has become a subject of controversy. Unlike the other protagonists in the *Iliad*, we know very little about Thersites's ancestry or background, which underlines his identity as an isolated outsider. He is not only different to the *Iliad's* heroes, but their moral opposite. Thersites is the personification of anti-authority.

It is possible that Homer self-consciously constructs an unambiguously repulsive character who can be disowned while also permitted to voice criticisms about the irresponsible way that nobles and warrior-heroes discharge their duties to their community. The American literary theorist Kenneth Burke has drawn attention to a literary strategy he characterises as 'Thersitism': a tactic used by authors to raise criticism and protest 'voiced in a way that in the same breath disposes of it'. Burke observes:

> If an audience is likely to feel that it is being crowded into a position, if there is any likelihood that the requirements of dramatic 'efficiency' would lead to the blunt ignoring of a possible protest from at least some significant portion of the onlookers, the author must *get this objection stated in the work itself*. But the objection should be voiced in a way that in the same breath disposes of it.[19]

However, while Thersitism can be detected as a device in modern literature, it is unlikely that such a motive can account for the construction of this character in an ancient epic poem. The authorship of the *Iliad* is a subject of controversy and it is likely that Thersites is as much a product of folklore and legend as of self-conscious literary construction.

There are numerous theories about how to interpret Thersites' very public challenge to royal authority. In an important sense, the *Iliad* is a story about war and leadership in circumstances where the 'workings of the authority-system were neither precisely defined nor clearly stated'.[20] When the soldiers flee their camp and attempt to return their ship it is evident that royal authority has been lost. The introduction of a morally dubious character, who dares openly to challenge the king, serves as a warning of what can happen when authority is lost. According Poslethwaite, 'it is to emphasize his distance from the established order that Homer endows Thersites with by far the most extraordinary description in the entire poem'.[21] He is cast in the role of someone who is outside the camp's moral universe – someone who is sufficiently alienated from the prevailing warrior ethos to remind the army of some uncomfortable truths about their leaders. That is one reason why Homer draws an

---

[19] Burke (1966) pp. 110–11.   [20] Donlan (1979) p. 51.
[21] Poslethwaite (1988) p. 125.

unambiguous moral contrast between Thersites and the rest of the Greek camp. At the same time, through providing an obvious target for moral outrage, Homer provides a dramatic ritual for the re-establishment of harmony and order.

Thalmann advises against seeing the 'issue that divides Thersites from Odysseus and Agamemnon as simply one between legitimate authority and the challenge of an upstart'.[22] Rather, he suggests that the poem 'portrays a challenge to authority' and then chronicles its restoration. Through the removal of Thersites from the scene, harmony and authority are restored, along with the Greek army's resolution to carry on the war.

Interpretations of Thersites' criticism of Agamemnon are frequently influenced by a tendency to read the *Iliad* in the light of subsequent ideas about the working of relations of authority. Consequently this encounter is often represented as the precursor of the kind of conflict between plebeians and aristocrats that characterised subsequent centuries in Greece and Rome. Many critics appear to read history backwards and treat Homer as an ideologue of the aristocracy. One study of the role of Thersites takes the view that 'Homer's prime contribution was in tailoring this figure to provide a hostile image of those who protested against the rigid aristocratic dominance of the Archaic Age'. According to this analysis, Homer 'thereby created a person who points forward to other radicals and dissenters in subsequent times',[23] and the very fact that Homer introduced this disturbing character into the drama indicates his concern with the fragility of the prevailing aristocratic order. In one important commentary on this scene, Donlan contends that 'the savage caricature, the beating with the spectre, and the acquiescence of the rank and file to his silencing serve to underscore the seriousness of the conservative reaction to that kind of anti-aristocratic display'.[24]

Other commentaries on his denunciation of Agamemnon argue that Thersites did not only challenge the status of the king but also called into question the authority of the norms and values that prevailed in Homeric Greece. 'Thersites did not show what the Greeks called *aidos*, shame, respect, for those in positions of authority or for the norms that governed the community of the Achaeans laying siege to the city of Troy', notes Saxonhouse.[25]

In modern times, Thersites's rhetorical challenge to Agamemnon is often interpreted as the first recorded contestation of elite authority. According to one account, 'we can say that the birth of democracy in

---

[22] Thalmann (1988).   [23] Rankin (1972) p. 59.   [24] Donlan (1973) p. 150.
[25] Saxonhouse (2008) p. 1.

ancient Athens is marked by the entrance of Thersites into the delib-
erative circle' of the Greek nobles.[26] Donlan believes that Homer's
'Thersites incident' is 'the first recorded instance of anti-aristocratic,
anti-heroic sentiment'.[27] The representation of Thersites as the pioneer archetypal democratic rebel is sometimes associated with the tendency to reconstruct Homer as a self-conscious apologist for reactionary
aristocratic authority. One historian dismisses the scene as an example
of 'anti-democratic propaganda' and describes Thersites as a 'popular
"agitator"'.[28] The representation of Thersites as an opponent of aristocratic values tends to eternalise the kind of social conflicts that will
emerge centuries later in the city-states of Greece. Thersites' outburst
is directed at the behaviour of an individual king, not at the status of
aristocratic leaders.

For all its sympathies with the aristocratic heroes fighting one another
in the Trojan War, and the negative depiction of Thersites, the *Iliad* is not
an ideological tract committed to the upholding the authority of the rich
against the poor. This is a story of a society where relations of authority
have not yet been institutionalised. In circumstances where authority
has a predominantly personal and unstable character, rivalries between
individuals can become a threat to the well-being of the entire community.
Homer's epic is not so much about the questioning of authority from
below as it is about the loss of confidence in the exercise of authority by
the chiefs, particularly Agamemnon. It appears that Homer is concerned
with the confused and arbitrary manner with which rule is exercised. In
an important analysis of this problem, Hammer writes that according to
the *Iliad*, Agamemnon's 'mistakes are not simply those of an individual
whose personality is ill suited to kingship': rather, 'Homer is engaged in a
more general critique of the nature of authority upon which Agamemnon
premises his leadership'.[29]

There are numerous theories about who Thersites was – whether this
man was based on a character known from other legends and poems,
or whether he was simply an invention of Homer's imagination. But
however his role is interpreted, it is unlikely that either folklore or Homer
cast Thersites in the role of a common man standing up against his social
superiors. Even his depiction as someone consigned to the lower rungs
of the social hierarchy is open to interrogation: he may not have been
the equal of the heroes Achilles or Odysseus, but he was not a marginal
commoner consigned to the bottom of the heap. Feldman reminds us

---

[26] Saxonhouse (2008) pp. 1–2.   [27] Donlan (1973) p. 150.
[28] De Ste. Croix (1981) p. 413.   [29] Hammer (1997) p. 4.

that Thersites was a 'freeman, a warrior, bearing his own arms', sharing in the fruits of fight 'according to the value of his prowess'. Moreover, 'he has freedom of speech in the assembly of his fellow warriors'.[30] Feldman argues that the dispute between Thersites and Agamemnon takes place in an assembly of warriors who enjoy relative prestige compared to their social inferiors. He notes that:

> Greeks who might with reason be designated as members of inferior classes, the *demioergoi* (peasants, artisans) and *thetes* (labourers for hire) were not present on the Homeric battle field. The fact of the matter is that Thersites belonged to the *aristoi* rather than *hoi polloi*.[31]

Drawing on other poems and legends that refer to this character, Feldman goes so far as to argue that Thersites was portrayed as a son of a warrior chief and of 'divine stock' related by lineage to the Greek hero, Diomedes. Even if this interpretation is misplaced, it is evident that Thersites was not a lowly figure who had no right to address the assembly of warriors. The dramatic exchange between he and Odysseus ought to be seen as an example of elite 'rivalry for relative status within a class of highly ranked, nominal equals'.[32]

To interpret Thersites' challenge as an integral part of the dramatisation of competition for authority among the elite does not preclude recognising that the simmering discontent of rank-and-file soldiers contained a threat to the prevailing aristocratic order. As Stuurman observes, the *Iliad* serves as testimony to the co-existence of different forms of social tension. For Stuurman, the *Iliad* is a story of 'failed leadership and infighting among the elite' and, as he suggests, 'these are precisely the circumstances that frequently occasion criticisms of aristocratic and kingly authority and the emergence of popular dissent'.[33]

The absence of authoritative leadership is particularly damaging during the course of a war. When Odysseus argues that the rule of the 'many' is not a 'good thing', he is not so much attacking democracy as attempting to uphold the necessity for leadership at a perilous moment of military discord. In centuries to follow, Odysseus's denunciation of the rule of the many would be interpreted as a critique of democracy; but this interpretation is fuelled by historical experiences that postdate the Homeric era. Homer was not so much interested in devaluing the moral status of the many as in attempting to draw attention to the need to resolve the conflict between the personally motivated authority figures that dominated the battlefield.

---

[30] Feldman (1947) p. 20.   [31] Feldman (1947) p. 20.
[32] Marks (2005) p. 5.   [33] Stuurman (2004) p. 173.

Competing representations of authority

How Thersites is represented is influenced by historical experience and often by prevailing perceptions about the role of authority. People in Elizabethan England were familiar with his 'rhetorical mode of violent railing',[34] and he makes a memorable appearance as a vile common fool in Shakespeare's tragedy, *Troilus and Cressida*. In early modern times and well into the nineteenth century, conservative caricatures of Thersites depicted him as an envious malignant rebel against the moral order. Numerous nineteenth-century commentators who were worried about the widespread tendency to question the authority of tradition reacted to Thersites as if he was a precursor of the agitator for parliamentary reform. The 1879 comments of the English classical scholar F. A. Paley express this sensitivity to the challenge from below. 'This celebrated episode gives a sketch of one of the turbulent and insolent malcontents in an army, who use their best efforts to misrepresent the authorities and to incite sedition in others', concludes Paley.[35] The future Prime Minister, William Ewart Gladstone, wrote in 1858 that Thersites is 'in all things the reverse of the great human ideals in Homer'.[36]

However, by the time Gladstone dismissed Thersites and his 'vein of gross buffoonery', there were numerous critics who were prepared to adopt a more positive interpretation of the man. Some Enlightenment thinkers were uncomfortable with accepting the association of the physical appearance of ugliness with morally depraved characteristics. The eighteenth-century German writer, philosopher and dramatist, Gotthold Lessing, criticised what he took to be the devaluation of Thersites's humanity. In his 1766 essay *Laokoon*, Lessing reveals that the 'intemperate murderous Achilles becomes more hateful to me than the spitefully growling Thersites', and 'I feel that Thersites too is my relative, a human being'.[37] With the rise of Enlightenment humanism, attitudes towards Thersites became increasingly sympathetic. In an era where the questioning of authority was perceived as a legitimate form of public duty, Thersites could no longer be depicted as the moral opposite to the social norm. In the early twentieth century the Austrian novelist Stefan Zweig, inspired by Lessing, recorded his personal identification with Thersites, who presented a 'certain trait of my inner attitude that inevitably never takes the side of the so-called "heroes", but can see tragedy always only in the vanquished'.[38] In an era where Homeric heroes are perceived as

[34] See Kimbrough (1964) p. 173.   [35] Cited in Rankin (1972) p. 36.
[36] Cited in Rankin (1972) p. 36.
[37] I am grateful to my friend Sabine Reul for translating this passage for me.
[38] Zweig (2006).

impossible caricatures, it is the anti-hero who is more likely to resonate with the cultural imagination.

Nietzsche regarded Thersites as the cultural antithesis of the heroic age of Greek civilization, which he so much admired. He took exception to the rationalism and what he took to be the sentimentalism of the Enlightenment for devaluing the values and ethos associated with the aristocratic character, and regarded the softening of attitudes towards Thersites as symptom of the demise of the age of heroes. Nietzsche bemoaned the loss of an age when 'there was no disposition on anyone's part to pretend that the difference between an Achilles and a Thersites was anything but the difference between noble and base and no sentimental drawing back from the implications that difference carried'.[39] In his imagination, Homeric heroes exercised authority without having to justify themselves, and dealt with the like of Thersites by beating him into submission. In conservative circles Thersites stood for the anti-heroic and pacifist sentiments that swept Europe in the inter-war period. Typically Erich Maria Remarque, author of the famous anti-war novel *All Quiet on the Western Front,* was compared by a German critic to Thersites.[40]

The rehabilitation of Thersites, which gained momentum with the emergence of the Enlightenment, acquired greater significance in the nineteenth century, when he often assumed the shape of a pioneer spokesman for the people. George Grote's magisterial and democratic interpretation of Ancient Greece was critical of the 'degradation of the mass people before the chiefs'.[41] Grote treats the scenes depicted in the *Iliad* as a historically accurate portrayal of the ancient Greek assembly, and the treatment of Thersites as proof that the 'feelings of personal dignity' was 'yet underdeveloped in the time of Homer'.[42] From this point onwards, a growing number of commentators have idealised Thersites as a progressive anti-authoritarian figure. J. P. Mahaffy's *Social Life in Greece* (1874) is paradigmatic in this respect, seeking to rehabilitate Thersites through questioning Homer's reliability as a witness and challenging the historical accuracy of the *Iliad.* Instead of engaging with the *Iliad* as an epic poem influenced by folklore and legend, Mahaffy treats it as an inaccurate historical text, and Homer as an ideologically motivated historian.

In effect, Mahaffy criticises the *Iliad* as if it were an apology for the domination of the poor by the ruling class. The tendency to reduce this epic poem to an ideological tract is dominated by an anachronistic

---

[39] These comments are made by Olafson (1991) p. 564.
[40] Eksteins (1980) p. 353.   [41] Grote (1857) vol. 2, p. 12.
[42] Cited in Rose (1988) p. 7.

tendency to rediscover one's ideological commitments in ancient times. As Rose comments,

for those who view the Thersites passage as evidence of the *poet's* ideology there is an almost irresistible temptation to stand up and be counted for or against, and the line between the characterization of views attributed to the poet and the critic's own views becomes imperceptibly thin.[43]

Mahaffy certainly stands up in defence of the downtrodden Thersites, and treats Homer as an ideological adversary. He takes the 'epic poets' to task for ignoring the 'importance of the masses on the battlefield', and refuses to accept the Homeric poems as a 'safe guide to the political life of Greece in the poet's own day'.

Mahaffy writes as if he regards the 'special spite and venom' directed at Thersites as an insult to himself. He therefore attempts to correct the apparent distortions of the truth conveyed by Homer. 'We may be sure the real Thersites, from whom the poet drew his picture, was a very different and a far more serious power in debate, than the misshapen buffoon in *Iliad*', insists Mahaffy, who regards Thersites as one of history's first critics to rise up 'among the people' to question 'the divine right of kings to do wrong'.[44]

Many liberal and democratic critics appear to find it difficult to read the *Iliad* for what is was: one of the first recorded poems from ancient times. Instead they interpret it as a very old political tract defending aristocratic privilege and authority, with 'Thersites, cruelly caricatured and ruthlessly manhandled, [as] the beginning of a democratic opposition to aristocratic misuse of power'.[45] In such interpretations, Thersites is reborn as a genuine historical figure whose reputation needs to be defended from Homer's poisonous polemic.

What Feldman has described as the tendency to deify Thersites can be interpreted as a symptom of a cultural mood that affirms anti-authoritarian sentiments. Rankin pointed to this trend when he observed that 'our democratically-minded age is more sympathetic to Thersites than preceding ones have been, and if Thersites is not praised by modern commentators, he is not automatically scorned as he is in the *Iliad*.'[46] From this perspective the hierarchical ethos of Homeric warrior culture is regarded as harsh and authoritarian, and its ancient critic embraced as the champion of the new world. As Constable indicates, 'the seriousness with which modern Thersites get taken today' is linked to an 'age' that 'some characterize precisely by its so-called crisis of

---

[43] Rose (1988) p. 11.   [44] Mahaffy (1925) p. 13.   [45] Ferguson (1973) p. 11.
[46] Rankin (1972) p. 41.

authority'.[47] The twentieth-century apotheosis of Thersites is clearly elaborated through Kenneth Burke's poem:

> And what of Thersites,
> Despised of all his tribe
> (Whipped by power, wisdom, and heroic love, all three;
> By Agamemnon, Ulysses and Achilles),
> Loathed by the bard that made him,
> Ultimate filth, speaking against epic war?
> What of Thersites?
> Salute –
> To Saint Thersites.[48]

The canonisation of Thersites highlights modern culture's unease with its cultural and intellectual legacy. According to one contemporary account, the scene where Thersites appears in the *Iliad* is likely to be interpreted by a modern audience in ways that are antithetical to Homer's intent. 'For the modern democrat', we are told, 'Thersites' complaint is reasonable, and it is equally reasonable whether it is made by Thersites or Achilles'. So although the 'scene would appear to reaffirm aristocratic power for Homer's near contemporaries', for the 'modern reader it fails to achieve its objectives'.[49]

Of course every era is drawn towards reinterpreting the meaning of classic texts in light of its own experience and values. But blindness to historical context can only encourage the confusion of the present with the past. Indeed the tendency to evaluate mythical Greek heroes according to twenty-first-century cultural sensibilities prevents us from understanding what is distinct about our current predicament. It also distracts readers from gaining some of the interesting and important insights provided by a study of the classics. From our perspective the *Iliad* offers a very early account of the search for a form of authority that exists independently of the individual and is not intertwined with personal qualities.

Our dialogue with Thersites

Too often the historical imagination falls prey to prejudices of the time. Like his democratic opponents, Nietzsche interpreted the epic poems of Homer as a call to take sides. But in his case the heroic warriors fighting for honour in the Trojan War are seen as exemplars of the noblest virtues. Nietzsche embraces these heroes as authoritative figures who possessed

---

[47] Constable (1994) pp. 558–9.   [48] Burke (1966) pp. 1101–11.
[49] Stefanson (2004) p. 38.

the noble qualities lost in his apparently decadent times. From his standpoint, the rehabilitation of Thersites by some of his contemporaries was symptomatic of the slave mentality that afflicted his era. Nietzsche had no problems with the way that physical force was used to silence Thersites: he would have interpreted this act as an illustration of authoritative behaviour. Nietzsche took the view that the need to persuade was inconsistent with the exercise of authority: 'wherever authority still belongs to good usage', men 'do not prove but command'.[50]

In one sense Nietzsche was right to point out that real authority does not have to enter into a debate to justify itself. Authority is more than persuasion. But Nietzsche's conceptualisation of authority as simply 'command' is one-sided. Authority is not synonymous with the arbitrary exercise of power: as we noted in the Introduction, authority stands between persuasion and the use of force. In the *Iliad*, the act of command often conveys the open implication of force. Agamemnon relies on using fear to gain 'silent obedience',[51] and even Odysseus risks undermining his considerable personal authority through his violent behaviour towards Thersites. Through this act, order is restored but questions on the nature of kingly authority linger on. 'One possible reading of the Thersites episode focused especially on this use of the spectre is as a demonstration that Agamemnon's hierarchy of power has retained domination, but lost hegemony' states Rose.[52] That Thersites had to be physically repressed with the royal spectre exposes the fragile status of authority relations.

Arguably what Odysseus and certainly Agamemnon possessed was not authority in the sense that it was understood in subsequent times. In Homeric times the status of leadership was closely associated with personal qualities. The *Iliad* is about many important themes – one of which is the destabilising consequences of the absence of authority. Although individuals might be referred to as kings, as an institution kingship had a very weak existence in the Homeric epics. Some scholars argue that in fact there were no kings in the Dark Age or the Archaic Age.[53] The oral tradition on which this legend is based took on a fixed shape between the eighth and sixth centuries BC, and it is possible that this poem sought to use what was a well-known story about the capture of Troy to engage a 'Greek audience in the city-states of the Archaic Age to imagine how a king might exercise authority'.[54] It was in this period that the nature of political leadership confronted people living in the city-states of Greece. 'The dialogues of the epics repeatedly raise questions about the king's

---

[50] Nietzsche (2007) p. 13.   [51] On this point see Hammer (1997) p. 4.
[52] Rose (1988) pp. 16–17.   [53] Launderville (2003) p. 71.
[54] Launderville (2003) p. 70.

use of power and authority, the means for sustaining collective action, the role of public assembly, and so forth', concludes one study.[55] These epics communicated a view of the world that touched on most of the issues confronting Greek political and public life, including the meaning of authority. These are questions that would continue to exercise the imaginations of communities for centuries to come, and it took more than a few centuries for authority to gain a stable and institutional reality.

That a relatively minor character like Thersites continued to excite the imagination of thinkers and philosophers in the centuries to follow is testament to the enduring significance of the issues associated with his act. Thousands of years after the writing of the *Iliad*, Nietzsche could not help but associate Thersites with what he perceived as his cultural and historical nemesis, the Greek philosopher, Socrates. Nietzsche, who took the view that Socrates destroyed Greek culture, represents this philosopher as the revenge of History for the death of Thersites.[56] His reaction and description of Socrates has striking parallels with the manner that Homer depicts Thersites. Nietzsche argues that Socrates was the 'lowest of the low'; 'ugly' and of the 'mob'. 'Was Socrates really a Greek?' asks Nietzsche, since his ugliness appears to refute the standards of this refined ancient culture. Yet this 'decadent' man, this 'clown', succeeded in making men take him seriously. He is a dialectician who 'cripples the intellect of his opponents'.[57] The authority of traditional Greek culture appeared to be no match to the questions posed by Socrates. And Nietzsche is deeply disturbed by the premonition that Socratic reasoning may have the last word.

[55] Launderville (2003) p. 16.   [56] Cited by O'Hear (1977) p. 85.
[57] Nietzsche (2007) pp. 12–14.

2   Socrates and the quest for authority

Like the trial of Jesus, the proceedings against Socrates represented more than the prosecution of one man. This was a classic show trial: staged events that serve to dramatise moral and political uncertainties faced by a community. Show trials provide an opportunity for those who initiate criminal proceedings to make a statement about what values ought to be affirmed by society, and offer the accused the opportunity to confess, recant or at least apologise. Socrates made no attempt to play the game. 'Do not be angry with me for speaking the truth', he told the jurors, before stating his awareness that 'No man will survive who genuinely opposes you or any other crowd'.[1] Through his denunciation of the intolerance of the gathering, Socrates sought to affirm that it was he, and not his persecutors, who occupied the moral high ground.

Socrates's trial, in a packed court and before a jury of 501 Athenian citizens in 399 BC, was the outcome of a protracted period of social anxiety and unrest. The Peloponnesian War between Athens and Sparta had ended just four years previously, having lasted for almost three decades and resulted in the catastrophic defeat of Athens and the demise of her powerful navy and empire. The surrender of Athens was followed by the forced dismantling of her powerful fortifications, and conflict was unleashed within the walls of the city. Many citizens blamed the city's open-air democratic institutions for allowing demagogues to manipulate people's emotions and create a feverish atmosphere hospitable to military adventurism. They claimed that leading public figures lacked integrity and were devoid of attributes associated with responsible leadership. These partisans of the oligarchy blamed Athenian democracy for her military defeat, and attempted to establish a more elitist hierarchical government in the immediate aftermath of the war. On one point, democratic politicians were in agreement with their oligarchic foes: Athens's predicament was caused by the enemy within. But from their standpoint, a significant factor contributing to Athens's defeat was the betrayal of

---

[1] *Apology* (31e–32a) in Cooper (1997) p. 29.

the city by sections of the oligarchy. Although these charges of betrayal were unspecific, it was widely claimed that members of the Athenian oligarchy had frequently expressed sympathy for the more hierarchical and conservative constitution of Sparta.

Sparta sought to secure her power over Athens by imposing a government consisting of a group of 30 powerful and wealthy collaborators, known as the Thirty Tyrants, who unleashed a reign of terror against the supporters of the previous regimes. Although this regime lasted barely a year, its violent and heavy-handed police state tactics helped to destabilise everyday life in the city. In 403 BC the Thirty Tyrants were overthrown by an army of exiles and a new regime of democracy was established in Athens. But although peace and stability were restored, Athens faced a profound moral crisis. A mood of confusion and disorientation about the upheavals of the previous three decades fostered a climate where there was a constant search for scapegoats. It was in the middle of this moral crisis that Socrates was accused of corrupting the city's youth and of undermining the community's religion.

It is unlikely that Socrates set out to challenge the way of life of his Athenian citizens. He did not have an alternative way of life to advocate and he self-consciously avoided getting involved in what he saw as the political process. Nevertheless, he succeeded in provoking the hostility of many people through his constant probing of the views that he encountered. Socrates believed that his mission was to enter into dialogue with his fellow citizens and, through questioning, to force people to account for their views. His questions often led to the exposure of other people's ignorance. Socrates may have believed that he provided a public service in highlighting the distance between everyday opinion and real knowledge, but many experienced their interrogation as a form of intellectual humiliation. From their perspective, Socrates represented a destructive force that had to be contained. The ruling political elite resented Socrates's philosophical activity and dismissed him as a subversive hair-splitter. Political insecurity readily interprets criticism as a form of malicious subversion. As one contemporary commentator remarks, if we 'take account of the no-holds-barred criticisms of Athenian democracy', the 'popular perception' of Socrates as a 'crypto-oligarch and dangerous corruptor of youth becomes eminently understandable'.[2]

Throughout the trial and in the period leading up to his execution, Socrates appeared almost indifferent to his fate. It is his commitment to his vocation and the lack of interest he displayed in trying plead for his life that impressed so many observers. Socrates personified the principle

---

[2] Villa (2001) p. 13.

of pursuing the truth regardless of its consequences. The romantic poet John Keats wrote to his brother George in 1818 that only 'Socrates and Jesus' possessed 'hearts completely disinterested'. Shelley too was drawn towards this link and described Socrates as 'the Jesus Christ of Greece'.

Why Socrates?

The decision to prosecute and execute Socrates still constitutes something of a historical puzzle. Why would a relatively free and open society like Athens seek to eliminate an elderly philosopher for propagating unconventional views, when he had been allowed to pursue his teaching most of his adult life? The most probable answer lies less in Socrates's own words and actions, than in the context surrounding them. There is little doubt that the trial was motivated by the desire to settle scores with a critic of Athens in an attempt to restore the stability that appeared to have been lost in the previous decades. Socrates's trial 'reflected a generalized distrust of his unconventional intelligences and even more unconventional activity during a period when Athenian democracy was still struggling to recover from traumatic defeat, betrayal and virtual civil war'.[3] Uncertainty and anxiety about the role of custom and religion encouraged a nervous Athenian officialdom to look for ways of restoring belief in the city's traditional way of life.

In the years before Socrates's trial, the Athenian regime launched a project to revise the city's laws and attempt to promote the concept of public piety. There was a concerted attempt to codify the legal system and gain support for the authority of the law. A revised calendar of public sacrifices and rituals were published in the same year that Socrates was condemned on the charge of impiety. In this context the prosecution of Socrates served the purpose of reminding the citizens of Athens of the 'state's newfound authority to regulate religion' and uphold the authority of customs and law.[4]

It is important to recall that Socrates was charged with impiety rather than heresy. In Athens the concept of heresy made little sense since there were no sacred texts and doctrines to profane. Religion in Athens involved participation in a community's rituals – performing traditional sacrifices and rites. The notion of impiety referred to transgression against customs and unwritten religious and moral norms: evidence would be, for example, the reluctance to participate in community festivals. In his dialogue with Socrates, the philosopher Protagoras described impiety as behaviour 'opposed to civic virtue'.[5] What the vague charge of impiety conveyed was

[3] Villa (2001) p. 13.   [4] Munn (2000) p. 273.
[5] *Protagoras* 324a, in Cooper (1997) p. 513.

the indictment of unconventional behaviour at a time that many felt that the survival of Athens depended on the affirmation of its conventions. The trial itself can be seen as a dramatic ritual through which the rulers of the city sought to consolidate tradition, law and piety. Socrates, who had little regard for this traditionalist project, was brought into a 'fatal collision with the emerging definition of legal authority in Athens'.[6]

Throughout recent history, the attempt to restore lost traditions is often associated with insecure elites who, fearing a threat from below, yearn for stability and order. No doubt sections of the beleaguered Athenian oligarchy felt threatened by the unstable conditions that prevailed in their city. But the main force behind the search for authority and the restoration of old customs and law were the political leaders of ordinary citizens, who felt anxious and confused by the uncertainties they faced. This was a movement of traditionalism from below.

To be sure, members of the aristocracy sought to strengthen their position by restoring Athens's ancient constitution. A commission was set up to compile the ancestral laws with a view to eliminating some the procedures introduced to promote popular participation in the previous half century. This was also the approach adopted by the Thirty Tyrants, whose vision of the ancestral constitution involved the elimination of institutions of popular participation and the removal of 'statutes by which the sovereignty of jury courts had been affirmed'.[7] The Thirty Tyrants appealed to the ideal of an ancient past that preceded the institutionalisation of democratic procedures and which therefore invalidated them. In a sense they sought to counter the customs and traditions of post Periclean Athens with their version of an older and therefore apparently purer tradition.

Yet what is interesting about Athens's aristocracy was not its aspiration to restore ancient customs but its hostility to the tradition of their city's more recent past. Many young aristocrats looked to new ideas brought to Athens from abroad and adopted a sceptical, if not hostile, orientation towards the traditions of their city.[8] Some of the ideas that attracted their attention called into question the authority of prevailing moral norms. The Sophist Thrasymachus argued for a theory that claimed that all laws, including moral ones, were 'mere conventions'. Along with other Sophists, he claimed that laws were simply the invention of the weak, 'by which they tried to deprive the strong of their natural right and prerogative'.[9] So aristocratic dissent towards *nomos* – a concept that encompasses both the idea of law and of custom – led to a situation

---

[6] Munn (2000) p. 204.   [7] Munn (2000) p. 223.
[8] Fritz (1941) p. 54.   [9] Fritz (1941) p. 57.

where its authority was attacked and undermined by the educated elite but 'generally accepted by ordinary people'.[10]

Competing claims about the status of moral values and the law expressed a profound social conflict between the elites and the leaders of the demos. The prosecution of Socrates was seen as a blow against those who sought to undermine the authority of law and custom in Athens. But ironically, Socrates was no less concerned with the problem of authority than those who persecuted him. Contrary to the charges laid against him, he was critical of Sophist arguments against the authority of law. However, he could not go along with the regime's attempt to legitimise its rule through the codification of past traditions and customs. Socrates did not seek to overthrow the prevailing moral and cultural norms: his concern was to challenge the tendency for convention to turn into dogma and prejudice. J. S. Mill took the view that Socrates challenged the dogma of tradition to an extent unheard of before.[11]

Socrates personified the ambiguous attitude that Athenian culture possessed towards what would subsequently be conceptualised as authority. His response to the competing projects to construct authority was to promote an ideal of moral authority through the celebration of moral expertise. Does that mean that he was opposed to the democratic ethos that prevailed in his time? In one sense he was. His exalted view of the moral superiority of the expert makes him potentially indifferent to the opinion of others. Indeed he seems to assume that such opinions are erroneous precisely because they are held by many people. Yet he was not uninterested in people's opinions. It was precisely because he believed that through dialogue people's opinion could be clarified that he spent so much time conversing with his fellow Athenians. As noted previously, for Socrates, dialogue was akin to the art of midwifery – what he called *maieutic* – and his aim was to assist others to give birth to what 'they themselves thought anyhow'; to find the truth in their opinion.[12] According to Arendt, Socrates invested his hope in the potential for persuasion to forge a genuine consensus and he therefore did not see the need for a distinct group of rulers.[13]

The importance that Socrates attached to dialogue and the pursuit of the truth suggests that his statements about experts reflected an attempt to give meaning to a form of moral authority where wisdom and truth authorise public behaviour. He was hesitant about pushing the idea of a moral expert too far, and in numerous dialogues, as Villa notes, the 'claim of statesmen and citizens alike to moral expertise is repeatedly

---

[10] See note 54 in Ober (1998) p. 146.   [11] See Giorgini (2009).
[12] This point is well argued by Arendt (2004) p. 434.   [13] Cited in Villa (2001) p. 150.

revealed as fiction'.[14] Socrates's belief in the value of dialogue did not contradict his belief that some people's opinions were worth more than others. However, before we examine his views on expertise, it is necessary to answer the question of why the Greeks had such difficulty in developing a concept of authority.

The curious absence of authority

It is tempting to perceive the uncertainties surrounding the meaning of tradition in Athens as an early version of the crisis of authority experienced by modern societies. One study of the Sophist movement draws attention to the reaction against traditional values and morality, and observes that 'the revolt against nineteenth-century values' in the twentieth century 'may serve as an analogy'.[15] Sociologists have drawn attention to the parallels between Plato's *Republic* and Durkheim's sociological classic, *The Division of Labour in Society*, suggesting that 'both works were written by their authors in periods of perceived dislocation'.[16]

However, this is an analogy that may lead to overlooking what was distinct about the Athenian experience. Outwardly it bears a striking resemblance to the numerous episodes in the post-eighteenth-century era, when anxieties about the potentially destructive consequences of the loss of tradition were raised. To this day, commentators lament the loss of traditional ways of life, and sometimes even propose the restoration of traditional customs and values. Although there are some interesting parallels between the contemporary concerns about traditional values and those of Athens in the fourth and fifth centuries BC, it is important not to overlook one fundamental difference, which is that in ancient Greece the meaning of tradition and of authority were not clarified in the first place. The meaning of the idea of tradition or the ancestral way of doing things was not codified or expressed in a systematic manner. Even religion – which in many ancient civilisations acquired a systematic character – was not codified. In contrast to the Egyptian or Hebrew cultures, the Greeks did not have a centrally co-ordinated and organised religion. Numerous Greek cults competed against one another, and the Greeks did not subscribe to a 'single orthodoxy of belief'.[17]

Although the Greeks and their leading thinkers were interested in exploring ideas about who had the right to lead, what role should be assigned to the role of an expert, and what the status was of the

---

[14] Villa (2001) p. 304.   [15] Kerferd (1981) p. 122.
[16] Inglis and Robertson (2004) p. 171.   [17] Havelock (1957) p. 31.

law and of public opinion, they did not develop a concept of authority. Hannah Arendt notes that the Greek language lacked a concept of
authority, as in Greek life 'there was no awareness of authority based on
immediate political experience'.[18] Arendt claims that it was the failure
of Socrates to persuade his fellow Athenians of his innocence that forced
Plato to embark on a philosophical quest for an elaborated concept of
authority, perceiving Socrates's demise as the consequence of the failure of the politics of persuasion. She believes that Plato and Aristotle
'in quite different ways but from the same political experience, tried to
introduce something akin to authority into the public life of the Greek
polis'.[19]

There is little doubt that in the aftermath of Socrates's death, Plato
became preoccupied by authority's absence. Gouldner states that 'the
problem of authority was among the most crucial with which Plato is
concerned'. Plato blamed the political conflict that afflicted the Athenian polis and wider Greek disunity on the absence of a power that could
compel citizens to behave in a proper manner without resorting to violent force. He interpreted conflict and disunity in Athens as 'deriving in
important part from the failure of authority – from the double failure of
natural rulers to rule correctly and of the subordinates to obey'.[20] Plato
himself was more aware of authority's absence than how it could develop
from the experience of Greek city states. It appears that Plato could only
imagine authority in a utopian form as it would work in the idealised
society that he expounded in his *Republic*.

The absence of a concept of authority in ancient Greece does not
mean that communities and individuals did not attempt to influence
people's behaviour through appeals to traditions, customs and precedent.
It was generally agreed that it was right to conform to the ways of the
ancestors and to the old customs. But the question was, 'which ancestors,
and what were their customs?'[21] Competition between oligarchs and
democratic leaders was often expressed through accusing the other side of
violating the dictates of the (unwritten) ancestral constitution. Aristocrats
argued for the restoration of the customs of the pre-democratic past and
their opponents responded 'by making Solon and even Theseus into
democrats'.[22] But the very intensity of political conflicts over custom
and tradition indicated that public life in Athens lacked foundational
authority.

The limited weight of authority in Greek city-states is emphasised by
the German Neo-Kantian philosopher Wilhelm Windelband, through

---

[18] Arendt (1958) pp. 105 and 119.   [19] Arendt (1958) p. 104.
[20] Gouldner (1971) pp. 133–4.   [21] Ober (1998) p. 146.   [22] Ober (1998) p. 146.

contrasting its significance with medieval times. He acknowledges that 'the *appeal to authority* often makes its appearance in Greek and Hellenistic philosophy in the sense of a confirmation and strengthening of an author's own views, but not as a decisive and conclusive argument'. However, in medieval times the appeal to authority was 'regarded as quite different as a type of argument from what it was taken to be by the Greeks', since it worked as a 'much more ultimate, finalistic type of argument that is not open to critical questioning in the way the Greeks would have thought appropriate'.[23]

What Windelband describes is a situation where authority lacks an institutional underpinning and a cultural foundation and is therefore open to continual critical questioning. And the evidence of history indicates that Greek culture was unusually hospitable to those who critically questioned the authority of its customs, religion and tradition. Ideas about the sacred status of tradition, the law, and religion were questioned and demystified at a relative early stage of historical development. From Homer's times onwards 'there was a continuous process of intellectual discussion and reinterpretation of everything concerning the gods'.[24] Many thinkers associated with the Sophist movement drew a clear distinction between natural laws and forces – *physis* – and humanly constructed laws and customs – *nomos*. This distinction between *physis* and *nomos* provided the intellectual foundation for questioning the divine or traditional validity of law and custom.[25] Sophists like Antiphon and Hippias expressed scepticism towards positive law; others agreed that the laws were conventional – man-made – but claimed that nevertheless there were still valid reasons for obeying them.[26]

The development of a Greek natural science and the tendency to counterpose *physis* to *nomos* occurred precisely at a time when sections of society had become conscious of the need to affirm tradition. Through what one scholar characterised as the 'reasoned rejection of tradition', the concept of authority was questioned even before it was consolidated and endowed with a coherent form.[27] *The questioning of authority as a foundational concept that guides a community's behaviour actually preceded its conceptual elaboration.*

Sceptics called into question the status of traditional custom by arguing that whereas natural laws were universal, those of the city were specific to that community.[28] Consequently they concluded that 'the qualities of this universal nature diminish the authority of everything associated with

---

[23] Cited in Walton (1997) p. 43   [24] Kerferd (1981) p. 163.
[25] See Chapter 4 in Guthrie (1971).   [26] See discussion in Mulgan (1979).
[27] Guthrie (1971) p. 17.   [28] See Ostwald (1990).

nomos'.[29] If laws and traditions were culturally specific, transient and subject to human modification, then their status as unquestioned authority was put to question. A striking illustration of this sceptical intellectual culture is the boldness with which sceptics interrogated the workings of religion. It appears that even the existence of God was contested. In his book *On the Gods*, Protagoras indicated that he could not decide whether or not gods existed. Prodicus attempted to explain the origin of religious belief in gods in 'psychological and naturalistic terms'.[30] In his play *Sisyphus*, Critias went so far as to portray religious belief as a 'deliberate imposition by government to ensure an ultimate and universal sanction for the good behaviour of its subjects'.[31] This was probably the first time that a theory of religion presented gods as a deliberate political invention designed to gain the acquiescence of people.

The radical questioning of custom and religion could not but undermine the moral and political foundation of the Greek polis. Once the values of the community were represented as the product of human convention, its capacity to motivate and compel citizens to act in accordance with its dictates were significantly undermined. It was this fundamental questioning of the sacred character of law and customs that incited figures like Aristophanes, Euripides, Thucydides and Aristotle 'to defend traditional society against those who encouraged the casting off of political and social chains in order to listen to a nature which demanded the gratification of private desires'.[32] Thucydides, the author of *History of the Peloponnesian War*, took the view that *nomos* had to be accepted as if 'they were natural and supported by divine authority'.[33]

Thucydides' account of Pericles's famous funeral speech provides a case study of a very public attempt to rhetorically affirm political authority. Pericles, the democratic statesman and leader of Athens, gave this speech at the end of the first year of the Peloponnesian War. The aim of his speech is to celebrate Athens' democratic tradition and political system. His speech begins with paying his respect to Athens' ancestors and their customs and traditions which are represented as of divine origin. He attributes the great achievement of Athens to its democratic traditions, which combine tolerance with equality before the law. He praises the people for obeying 'the authority of the laws, whether they are written or unwritten, that is, those which the polis has codified as well as those which remain at the moral foundation of the city, not needing the sanctions of authoritative approval.'[34] As far as he is concerned, the respect of

[29] Ostwald (1990) p. 299.   [30] Kerferd (1981) p. 40.   [31] Guthrie (1971) p. 243.
[32] Saxonhouse (1978) p. 463.   [33] Saxonhouse (1978) p. 463.
[34] Saxonhouse (1978) p. 468.

the people for their customs and law is one of the defining characteristic of Athens.

Yet Pericles's speech comes across as an exercise in promoting propaganda for an undefined way of life. One perceptive analysis of this speech discusses of the 'self-serving description of Athens', which 'portrays a polis which accepts the traditions of the past' in a way that overlooks the prevailing insecurities afflicting the community. What is interesting about Pericles's idealised portrait of Athens is that the authority of the law is affirmed only pragmatically, and not based on any foundational principles. As Arlene Saxonhouse observes, 'nowhere in Pericles' funeral oration is implied that the *nomoi* are natural, that the unwritten laws come from the divine order, or even that these laws are the very best that could be made; what is suggested is that the *nomoi*, the *politeia*, and the polis must be accepted and defended as if they were the best and worthy of the individual's full devotion if the society is to continue to enjoy the civilization which currently exists'.[35] Thucydides is also aware that respect for the authority of the law was tested and found wanting as a result of the upheavals caused by the war and the plague that afflicted Athens.

Thucydides' *History* provides an important account of how Athens experienced the moral and political uncertainties surrounding its attempt to give meaning to the authority of *nomos*. However, the issue that he could not successfully engage with was to account for the curious questioning of law, custom and religion in Athens. It is to this question that we now turn.

Why authority failed to flourish in ancient Greece

From a sociological perspective, Athens serves as a paradigm of a community that was uniquely disposed towards the acceptance of change. Communities that are open towards change have a characteristically relaxed orientation towards their customs and tradition. They are ready to embrace new ideas and to try out novel ways of organising their life. Athenian society was also unusually bold in taking risks and seizing opportunities. It promoted ideals of fame and heroism that were underwritten by an unusually enthusiastic attitude towards risk-taking. In his path-breaking study of Athenian culture, the sociologist Alvin Gouldner writes that its people were not conservative and security-minded, and demonstrated what he calls 'total-commitment rationality' in their war against Persia. This was a rationality that demonstrated a 'low degree of attachment

[35] Saxonhouse (1978) p. 470.

to objects' and by implications to customs. According to Gouldner, an illustration of Athens's total commitment was the decision to evacuate the city in order to concentrate on defeating the overwhelming Persian forces in a sea battle. The willingness of this community to abandon its land and possessions is illustrative of an attitude that was alien to a traditionalist people.

Gouldner states that total commitment strategy undermines traditionalism since it implicitly assumes 'a readiness to depart from traditionally received forms and to find better ways of realizing certain objectives'.[36] According to this analysis, an ethos of total commitment, which also encourages individuals to win at any cost, leads to a pragmatic outlook that is unlikely to be deterred by the 'claims of established morality'. Gouldner argues that characteristically, individuals with low object attachments are likely to make choices about their personal goals rather than 'having these imposed by unexaminable tradition and rather than being bound to them by deeply affective sentiments or by a fear-laden belief in their sacred character'.[37] Most important of all, what Gouldner characterises as the Greek 'contest system' served to fuel 'rationality' because it did not hesitate to 'depart from traditionally received forms' and because it eroded the 'traditional properties of interpersonal relationships'.[38] The cumulative effect of these cultural influences was to create an Athenian character that was uniquely prepared to be persuaded by reason rather than tradition.

Gouldner's analysis of the Athenian character and individual values not only helps us to understand this community's remarkable disposition to change, but also throws light on its relatively weak adhesion to custom and tradition. A community oriented towards change is unlikely to be dominated by an ethos that insists on obedience and respect for the customs and traditions of the past. In such communities 'authority and public officials are held in scant esteem, let alone awe'. One consequence of this irreverent attitude towards authority is the relative absence of formal institutions and hierarchical structures. Whether bold, risk-taking sentiments led to Athens's democratic political culture or the other way around is not entirely clear. However, in a world 'for whom established tradition and its interpreters have lost authority', individuals are less likely to see themselves as inferior to others. In such circumstances, ideas about right and wrong are not communicated through the received wisdom of tradition but are crystallised through discussion and debate with others. And when the views and opinions of others become important, a more argumentative political culture emerges.

---

[36] Gouldner (1965) p. 65.   [37] Gouldner (1965) p. 71.   [38] Gouldner (1965) p. 65.

The emergence of a dynamic and argumentative political culture was also the outcome of the significant social change experienced by Athens in the fifth century BC. Economic and political expansion and war served to open people's imagination to new ideas and ways of doing things. According to some accounts, travel and foreign contacts led to the spread of new ideas.[39] One reason why many 'traditional norms came under attack was the process of social and political change that was in fairly full flow in Athens in the latter part of the fifth century B.C.'[40]

However, the creative potential of a culture that affirms the embrace of change and opportunity is seldom realised without undermining social stability. Numerous scholars have alluded to the intensely competitive and envious side of the Greek character. As Gouldner concludes, 'the social cohesion and integration of a society is precarious indeed where object attachments are thin, where loyalties and sentiments fade easily under the rational scrutiny of short-range self-interests, where envy is permeative, where human relations are strained constantly by the contest system, and where class conflicts frequently border on violence'.[41]

Political fluidity and instability was an integral part of Athenian culture. Whatever its downside, its openness to change encourages a relatively free attitude towards new ideas. Its critical spirit was personified through Socrates – but it is important to note that he himself and his ideas were products of a culture that he so often criticised. There is little doubt that Athens's disposition to change encouraged a democratic ethos which in turn made it difficult to consolidate and institutionalise tradition and authority. Peter Euben puts it well in stating that 'uniquely among political regimes, democracy calls attention to the conventional quality of its own conventions, generates a cultural logic that demystifies the authority of its own practices'.[42] One of the remarkable features of Athenian society was that it called attention to the 'conventional quality of its own conventions'. This questioning had not only a political but also a profound intellectual dimension. In such circumstances, institutions of rule and laws cannot be endowed with sacred or transcendental qualities. Without a moral, intellectual or political foundation for external authority that was independent of people's decision-making, laws and institutions appear as just conventions. This meant that in Athens the concept of authority was demystified before it was developed.

Of course, the failure to establish a concept of authority was not simply an intellectual problem. A highly fluid society that was open to risk-taking and change was not one where social and political hierarchies

[39] Guthrie (1971) p. 17.   [40] Waterfield (2009) pp. 128–9.
[41] Gouldner (1965) p. 74.   [42] Euben (1997) p. 35.

could be stabilised. This created continuous problems for those interested in the institutionalisation of elite rule. Ober claims that the 'failure' to 'settle into a stable political hierarchy' in effect 'delegitimated many forms of aristocratic privilege'.[43] That is another way of stating that the lack of cultural affirmation for hierarchy undermined the consolidation of authority.

Unable to consolidate elite rule and authority, sections of the oligarchy became hostile to the laws and conventions of Athens. They adopted forms of anti-democratic dissent that called into question the legitimacy of the prevailing institutions and system of laws. Precisely the section of society that is usually is in the forefront of the construction and elaboration of authority lacked the institutional framework and coherence to promote this project. On the contrary, sensitive to its relative lack of political weight it adopted a hostile orientation towards the kind of institutions – for example, the law – that are usually deemed essential for the emergence of the concept of authority. The failure to consolidate elite authority led the oligarchy to adopt a hostile orientation to the attempts to institutionalise other forms of authority.

Ober argues that elite dissent directed against popular participation and democratic institutions was the inevitable outcome of the failure to establish a non-democratic regime in Athens. The elite's criticism of Athenian democracy was promoted systematically and led to the emergence of what can be characterised as the first coherent elaboration of political theory. '[T]he Western tradition of formal political theorizing originated in the work of an informal, intellectual and aristocratic community of Athenian readers and writers,' writes Ober.[44] Here was a group usually associated with the celebration of authority calling the prevailing authority of the law and tradition into question. Since they could not validate their authority, pro-elite dissent became focused on undermining the authority of Athens's conventions. Plato's uncle Critias denounced laws as simply the inventions of the weak to protect themselves from the strong and to 'deprive the strong of their natural right and prerogative'.[45] In light of this elite hostility towards the authority of the law, defenders of law and custom were far more like to come from below than above.

Opinion and expertise

Despite the underdeveloped state of the idea of authority, Athens, like any society, required institutions and conventions that could gain

---

[43] Ober (1998) p. 4.   [44] Ober (1998) p. 5.   [45] Cited by Fritz (1941) pp. 56–7.

people's support and acquiescence. Athenian society worked most of the time because its people identified with their city. This was a community where authority was invested in the people and the opinions they expressed through the Athenian assembly and other public venues. There is considerable truth in Ober's claim that 'Athenian political culture was specifically based on collective opinion, rather than on objectively verifiable, scientific truths'.[46] The legitimacy enjoyed by public opinion and its democratic culture was reinforced by historical events such as the defeat of the Persians by the Athenian navy at the battle of Salamis. It was the poor sailors of the Athenian navy rather than heroic upper-class warriors who were identified with the glory of Athens. Euben notes that the victory at Salamis 'helped open the public arena in both size and substance beyond anything known in the Hellenic world by legitimating the claims to power and authority of the poor whose courage and steadfastness had won the victory'.[47]

Athens provides an early example of the authorisation of public opinion. Socrates regarded the authority of public opinion as far too wedded to custom and dogma to be able to engage with new challenges and experience. J. S. Mill believed that Socrates stood up to the tyranny of tradition and custom – King Nomos – and supported the attempt to engage critically with public opinion.[48]

But the growing authority of public opinion was paralleled by the development of a more formal and professional orientation to the management of economic and social life. As Athens grew and expanded its rule over diverse groups of people, the demands of public life became more complex and there was a need for the establishment of a more specialised division of labour and a greater permanency of function. The 'increasing emphasis on professionalism' also expressed a 'claim to cultural authority'.[49] The centuries-old debate about the relationship between public opinion and expertise first acquired significance in Athens, in the fifth century BC.

Socrates was preoccupied by the authority enjoyed by public opinion, and concerned by the insufficiency of opinion to point the way to the truth. In some of the comments attributed to him in the *Apology*, what he seeks is not opinion but 'opinions that are better informed and more completely thought through'.[50] Socrates argued that society was ready to defer to the views of experts and ignore the opinion of ordinary folk on technical matters such as shipbuilding and architecture, and was at a loss

---

[46] Ober (1998) p. 35.   [47] Euben (1997) p. 65.   [48] Mill (1978) p. 410.
[49] Euben (1997) p. 47.   [50] Euben (1997) p. 107.

as to why the same approach was not adopted in relation to political life. In his dialogue with Protagoras, Socrates states that 'when it is something to do with the government of the country that is to be debated, the man who gets up to advise them may be a builder or equally well a blacksmith or a shoemaker, a merchant or ship owner, rich or poor, of good family or none'.[51] As far as he is concerned 'what most people think' on political matters is far less important than the views of the one man who really understands the issues at stake – the expert.[52] In the case of politics, the experts needed to possess the wisdom to understand the truth.

Although Socrates upheld the authority of the political or moral expert, he was at a loss to explain how that individual could be found. Moral expertise can be interpreted as an ideal to strive for rather than as a fixed role.[53] He found it much easier to devalue the authority of public opinion than to give meaning to the authority of the moral expert. However, he implicitly raised a problem that continues to be a focus of controversy to this day. How wisdom can be attained, authorised, recognised and institutionalised were issues that preoccupied Socrates at a time before the concept of authority could have real meaning. At the same time his advocacy of the idea of moral expertise can be understood as his attempt to find some kind of an answer to what would, in subsequent centuries, be seen as the problem of authority. Athens was not ready for the authorisation of the moral expert because it represented the negation of so much of its public life. It is likely that it was the excessive faith that Socrates placed in the status of moral expert rather than his oligarchical sympathies that earned him a reputation for being a *misodemos* – an enemy of the people.

But possibly Socrates was killed because he rejected the moral authority of the customs and convention of Athenian society. Through his behaviour Socrates clearly communicated the idea that he wasn't interested in what his fellow citizens thought of him. He therefore appeared as beyond society and the law, and by his very being called into question the conventions of Athens. Even democratic Athens could not handle this challenge to its way of life.[54]

Through the story of Socrates, one generation after another sought to make sense of the meaning of political obligation, the relationship between freedom and authority, and the role of individual conscience. It is ironic that someone who did not write a single line of philosophy

---

[51] Protagoras 319b–d.   [52] See *Crito* (47b10–11).
[53] See the discussion in Bostock (1989).   [54] Saxonhouse (2008) p. 5.

is nevertheless often called the father of philosophy. Cicero stated that Socrates had brought down philosophy from heaven to earth; his trial has become a point of reference for many of the leading political theorists and philosophers of the West. St Augustine, Hegel, Mill, Kierkegaard, Nietzsche and Arendt are just some of the thinkers working in response to this influence.

3   Rome and the founding of authority

The idea of political authority gained shape and definition during the evolution of the Roman Republic. Although the meaning of political concepts are subject to historical variations, it is in Rome that many themes and problems associated with the modern understanding of authority – tradition, religion, morality, competing visions of the past – emerged with force. As one review of the history of this idea concluded:

> There is common agreement that the idea of authority, in the full range of meanings that have given it an integral intellectual life to the present, has its origins during the Roman Republic with the coinage of the distinctive term, *auctoritas*, to cover several kinds of primarily, albeit not exclusively legal relationships.[1]

Roman society was no less subject to the upheavals brought by change than the Greek city states. However, as Arendt notes,[2] while Greek philosophy tended to take change for granted, the Romans expressly attempted to consolidate a powerful sense of tradition and continuity. The Romans continually wrote about their past and were self-consciously devoted to their ancestors, traditions and customs.[3] This played an important role in the construction of a unique Roman sensibility towards authority.

But the social upheavals brought about through imperial expansion, competition and rivalry within the ruling elites and unrest from below meant that Romans could not take authority for granted. Questions to do with who had authority and how it should be exercised dominated public life during the final two centuries of the Republic. Such questions were posed with increasing urgency during a series of civil wars that threatened the very integrity of Roman political institutions.

At least in part, the elaboration of a Roman idea of authority represented an attempt to avoid the perils of instability that were associated with the Greek *polis*. The Romans never tired of pointing out 'the weaknesses of the Athenian political system in comparison to their own'.[4]

---

[1] Krieger (1968) p. 163.   [2] Arendt (2006) p. 18   [3] Rawson (1985) p. 322.
[4] Roberts (1994) p. 98.

The construction of a distinct Roman tradition and way of life required that the influence of Greek culture should be kept in check, and the Romans were 'intensely anxious about what it meant to be Roman and not Greek'.[5]

Cicero's conversation with Greece

The writings of the political philosopher Marcus Tullius Cicero (106–46 BC) are dominated by a concern with the preservation of Rome's ancient customs and the upholding of its traditional authority. Cicero regarded the welfare and stability of Rome to be inextricably linked to the resilience and influence of its customs and traditions, and was intensely worried about the cultural and social influences that had the potential for diminishing the authority of Roman tradition. For Cicero the upheavals that led to the demise of Greek city-states were, to a significant extent, the outcome of cultural forces that prevented them from consolidating a stable and authoritative traditional way of life. Thus his idealised representation of the founding of Rome stressed the importance of avoiding Greek societies' exposure towards foreign culture. Cicero praised Rome's founder, Romulus, for establishing the city inland and not on the coast, claiming that he possessed an 'exceptional imagination' and understood that coastal sites were exposed to 'unforeseeable dangers'. Such dangers consisted of not merely military threats but also of cultural and moral ones.

Cicero's prescription for the founding of a city comes across as a call for cultural autarchy. He warned that the 'moral character of coastal cities is prone to corruption and decay' from the foreign influences to which a coastal city was exposed: 'Foreign customs are imported along with foreign merchandise; and so none of their ancestral institutions can remain unaffected'.[6] This Roman philosopher also believed that the environment of a coastal city was ill-suited for the cultivation of the right type of public spirit. He complained that 'the inhabitants of those cities do not stay at home' for 'they are always dashing off to foreign parts, full of airy hopes and designs'. Worse still, even when 'physically, they stay put, they wander abroad in their imagination'. Pointing to the danger represented by people's psychic mobility, Cicero claimed that 'no factor was more responsible for the ultimate overthrow of Carthage and Corinth' than the 'restlessness and dispersal of their citizens', who had become too fixated with adventure and commercial profit to 'attend to their land and army'. This lack of commitment to the ancestral home

---

[5] Roberts (1994) p. 177.   [6] 'The Republic', Book 2, 6–9 in Cicero (2008) p. 37.

is compounded by the temptations of 'luxury in the form of booty and imports', which leads to 'sensual indulgence' through 'extravagance and idleness'. 'What I have just said about Corinth could be said with equal justice, I suspect, of Greece as a whole', Cicero intimated.[7]

In line with the prevailing Roman political culture, Cicero upheld the importance of being bounded by place. Tradition was rooted in a specific physical environment and both served as the foundation for authorising a way of life. Unlike the Greeks, who readily moved from one place to the next to find new homes and colonies, the 'Romans were bound to the specific locality of this one city'. 'Not the Greeks but the Romans were really rooted in the soil and the word *patria* derives its full meaning from Roman history,' observes Arendt.[8] Although the Romans possessed unprecedented expansionary ambitions, the sacred and eternal character of Rome as a place was beyond question.

Cicero's lamentation of the corrosive influence of a mobile and a culturally exposed environment is informed by a keen sociological sensitivity to the influence of cultural contact between people. As we noted in our discussion of Athens, numerous Greek philosophers perceived laws and customs as mere conventions. Cicero blamed such foreign influences for this lack of respect for tradition: 'Seafaring was clearly the cause of Greece's misfortunes, including her political instability'.[9] Cicero's exposition of the evils afflicting Greece can be interpreted as an indirect commentary on the disintegration of the institutions of the Roman Republic. It should be noted that foreign influences were arguably no less evident in Rome than in numerous Greek city states; and paradoxically, it was the powerful influence exerted by the Greeks on Roman life that informed Cicero's anxiety about the contact of cultures.

Cicero personified the ambivalence that many Roman thinkers and statesmen held towards Greece. One interpretation of his essay on *The Republic* notes that Cicero comes across as a 'Socratic thinker' – but with the important difference that Cicero anchors the dialogue in political tradition.[10] As Hathaway points out, 'Cicero was fully conscious of a tension between the native virtues of Rome and foreign arts'.[11] His response to the allure of foreign influence was self-consciously to cultivate a Roman identity, and in *The Republic* he thus minimises the influence of the Greeks on Roman political culture. The voice of the heroic general, Scipius Aemilianus, expresses outrage at the suggestion that Numa Pompilius, one of Rome's early kings and founding religious leader, was a

---

[7] 'The Republic', Book 2, 6–9 in Cicero (2008) p. 37.   [8] Arendt (1958) p. 98.
[9] 'The Republic', Book 2, 9 in Cicero (2008) p. 37.   [10] Hathaway (1968) p. 4.
[11] Hathaway (1968) p. 5.

pupil of the Greek thinker Pythagoras. Upon hearing this statement and expressing a palpable sense of relief, one of his interlocutors, the youthful Manilius, replies: 'I am happy to learn that we got our culture, not by importing foreign expertise but through our native qualities'.[12] At this point Cicero reassures his audience that 'our ancestors' wisdom' continues to shape the evolution of Rome's constitutions and institutions: to the point that 'even the features borrowed from elsewhere have been made much better here than they were in the places where they originated and from which we derived them'.[13]

What is remarkable about Rome's uneasy relationship with the influence of the Greeks is that, despite cultural tensions, it nevertheless opted to integrate the Homeric past into its tradition. While distancing itself from the 'corrupt' and 'degenerate' customs of latter-day Greek city-states, Rome appropriated the heroic Homeric era into its founding myth. In this way Rome could claim the inheritance of the best of the Greek past while also boasting a superior political wisdom to that possessed by the Hellenic world. The Romans adopted the myth of descent from Aeneas and 'through the *Aeneid*'s foundation legend the Roman populace bound itself to Greek history'.[14] In this way Rome came to be represented as the inheritor of the legacy of Greek culture. In Virgil's *Aeneid*, the founding of Rome is depicted as the culmination of a prophecy and through this act 'the spirit of the best of the Greek ancestors lives on through its resurrection on Italian soil'.[15]

Although Cicero's celebration of the ancient ways was written more than 2000 years ago, his constant concern with their survival sounds distinctly modern. 'Oh, if only we could maintain the fine tradition and discipline we have inherited from our ancestors!' he wrote, before remarking that 'somehow it is now slipping out of our hands'. Holding up the example of Athens as a city that departed from practising its customs, Cicero sought to cultivate a sense of Roman traditionalism.[16] Through his writings Cicero communicates the kind of plea for the preservation of tradition that one associates with the traditionalism of modern times:

Long before living memory our ancestral way of life produced outstanding men, and those excellent men preserved the old ways of life and the institutions of their forefathers. Our generation, however, after inheriting our political organization like a magnificent picture now fading with age, not only neglected to restore its original colours but did not even bother to ensure that it retained its basic form

---

[12] 'The Republic', Book 2, 29 in Cicero (2008) p. 44.
[13] 'The Republic', Book 2, 29 in Cicero (2008) p. 44.   [14] Arendt (2005) p. 48.
[15] Arendt (1958) p. 99.   [16] Roberts (1994) p. 102.

and, as it were, its faintest outlines. What remains of those ancient customs on which he said the state of Rome stood firm? We see them so ruined by neglect that not only do they go unobserved, they are no longer known.[17]

However, unlike the twenty-first-century traditionalist who intuitively understands that there is no return to the pre-modern ways, Cicero did not give up on the project of revitalising of ancestral wisdom. Indeed Cicero's writings can be seen as an attempt to contribute to the revitalisation of the relevance of tradition. An unambiguous orientation towards preserving traditions was explicitly endorsed by Roman political culture. For example, Scipio Aemilianus, destroyer of Carthage, in 142 BC 'astonished his countrymen by asking, in his official prayer, no longer that the possessions of the state might be extended but that they might be "preserved"'.[18] Cicero too insists that 'for everyone' who has helped preserve and extend their state, 'a sure place is set aside in heaven where he may enjoy a life of eternal bliss'.[19] From his standpoint the act of safeguarding and perpetuating the customs of the city represents a source of moral authority.

The act of preservation is upheld as a form of virtuous behaviour that enhances the personal influence of the preserver. The pursuit of preserving tradition and its formalisation reached its most consistent expression with the ascendancy of the Principate of Augustus. In his rise to power, Augustus carefully cultivated the reputation of upholding the traditions of Rome, reminding the people that he would not 'accept any office inconsistent with the custom of our ancestors'.[20] Augustus consistently presented himself as a restorer of the ancient ways, someone whose policies were devoted to the restoration of the ancient laws and customs, the traditional morality, religion and rituals and the old Republic. He was sensitive to the traditions of the old Republic and, throughout his 57 years of imperial rule, 'resolutely' opposed the 'appearance of being a monarch'.[21] That Augustus succeeded in achieving many of his objectives indicates that Roman society possessed considerable flexibility for institutional adaptation, which allowed for the preservation or reinvention of ancient customs. Moreover, through this reinvention of tradition Augustus succeeded in constructing a multi-dimensional system of political authority.

[17] 'The Republic', Book 5, 1–2 in Cicero (2008) p. 80.
[18] Joseph Wells (1966) 'The Spirit of Republican Rome', Chapter 58 in *Universal History of the World, Vol. 3*, p. 1712.
[19] 'The Republic', Book 6, 13 in Cicero (2008) p. 88.
[20] Eder (2005) p. 14.   [21] Eder (2005) p. 14.

Founding authority

The need for a concept of authority only emerges when communities are forced to contend with uncertainty about questions about who to believe, trust, follow or obey. Sheldon Wolin argued that the 'problem of political obligation emerges when conflicting considerations are recurrent, when it is seen that the acceptance of authority involves the individual in real choice between competing goods, as well as competing evils'.[22] Competing claims for loyalty and trust acquired a systemic character in the Roman republic from around 150 BC onwards. Concerns about the nature of political, military and religious leadership and power, and the relationship of different groups of people to the state, encouraged Romans to reflect on the institutions of their city. The transformation of Rome from a small city-state to a powerful empire demanded institutional and intellectual innovation. 'The attempt to govern this enormous space while retaining the values and institutions of a small political community imposed severe strains on the system,' notes Wolin.[23]

Until the middle of the second century BC, the Roman political order rested on a carefully crafted system of checks and balances. Public life in the city was managed through a system of countervailing influences that was referred to as a mixed constitution. Power was dispersed and carefully calibrated. Its executive branch consisted of elected magistrates, of whom the two consuls elected annually were the most powerful. The consuls possessed military or supreme power. But this power could be exercised only in the provinces and not in Rome itself, where the magistrates had to share influence with the people's tribunes and also heed the advice of the senate. In this way the three components of the machinery of government – magistrates, senate and the people – existed in an uneasy relationship with one another. This system aimed to minimise the tension between conflicting interests and, in particular, sought to reconcile the plebeian masses to the preservation of a hierarchy dominated by an elite group of aristocrats. Accordingly the plebeians gained the right to elect their own officers, the people's tribunes, which according to one account 'made the plebs almost a state within the state'.[24] The emergence of parallel institutions and rival jurisdictions ensured that the constitution of public life was a regular subject of debate. With the gradual breakdown, from around 134 BC, of this finely balanced political arrangement, the question of what constituted the foundation of political life and authorised decisions could not be avoided.

---

[22] Wolin (2004) p. 48.   [23] Wolin (2004) p. 65.   [24] Wolff (1987) p. 10.

As Shotter states, 'it is difficult, in any description of government, to capture its spirit adequately; the three elements – magistrates, senate and people – were not independent from or equal to each other'.[25] It is likely that in this uneasy and fluid relationship, the aristocracy through the senate was the dominant influence over the running of public life. Despite periodic expressions of plebeian dissent and even rebellion, the aristocracy was able to retain control over the running of government. The elite preferred to rule through an informal system of aristocratic rule that emphasised the importance of custom and precedent rather than a formal process of government.

It is widely acknowledged that there are formidable barriers to understanding the complexities of the early Roman Republic's political arrangements. Historians constantly draw attention to the 'the notorious unreliability of our sources',[26] and there is a gap of almost three centuries between the establishment of the Republic and the first written historical accounts of the era. Commentaries on the emergence of legal and political institutions often retrospectively impose a coherence and order that was likely to have been absent. Indeed the attempt to conceptualise these arrangements is complicated by the absence of any systematic codification of its practices, theory and laws in the early Republic.[27]

The political life of Rome was dominated by custom and tradition, and the day-to-day decisions were often shaped by the tacit knowledge possessed by its political and cultural elite. Yet Roman political life possessed an impressive capacity for institutional adaptation and innovation. The Roman constitution – or, to put it more accurately, constitutional arrangement – expressed a powerful sense of continuity with the past as well as an open orientation towards further development in the future. It offered a synthesis of tradition with a willingness to adapt to new experience. Cicero claimed that association of the values of origins, preservation and continuity with the constitution accounted for its superiority to others, because it 'had been established not by one man's life but over several ages and generations'. The virtue of this arrangement was that it was not simply based on 'one man's ability' but 'by that of many' over a long period of time. He noted that since 'no collection of able people at a single point of time could have sufficient foresight to take into account of everything; there had to be practical experience over a long period of history'.[28] This was depicted as a collective endeavour that integrated the contribution of diverse generations and individuals to a common project, and succeeded in evolving through assimilating new experience.

[25] Shotter (2005) p. 5.   [26] Oakley (2004) p. 15.   [27] See Wolin (2004) p. 65.
[28] 'The Republic', Book 1, 70 and Book 2, 2, p. 35, in Cicero (2008).

The ancient constitution should not be conceptualised as a legal document or a code but as a set of informal guidelines based on custom and precedent and transmitted from one generation to the next. Its lack of formality possessed the virtue of adaptability which allowed it to evolve in line with the shift from Rome as a city-state to becoming a vast empire. The emphasis that Cicero and others placed on foundation as a sacred moment in the constitution of the community was motivated by the understanding that a consensus on common origins and a way of life was essential if the city was to cope with the internal tensions and external pressures that confronted it. From 250 BC onwards, a series of major foreign wars and imperial expansion irrevocably transformed the Roman world in a way that began to expose the 'weakness of a governmental system that relied upon respect for authority and adherence to tradition'.[29] In such circumstances tradition needed be nurtured and cultivated.

As one overview of this period notes, 'constant expansion required a basic consensus at home'.[30] Cicero's emphasis on the 'foundation and preservation' of the state represented an attempt to endow custom and tradition with life.[31] Through this construction of a dialectic of foundation and preservation, the story of Rome's origins served as a source of validation for subsequent events. The preservation of tradition was represented as the obligatory duty of all; every generation was bound to the previous one and, through this process of interaction, to the foundation of the city.

For Cicero the foundation for belief was tradition; and religion was focused less on gods than on the affirmation of the past. In the Roman case religion 'literally meant *religare*: to be tied back, obligated, to the enormous, almost superhuman and hence always legendary effort to lay the foundations, to build the cornerstone, to found for eternity'.[32] The founding of Rome was presented as the culmination of historical events that could never be re-created; it was an authoritative event that contained within itself the potential to authorise. In her reflections on this process Hannah Arendt posits the act of foundation as the source of authority; a unique experience which Roman tradition developed to authorise belief and behaviour.[33] From this perspective, authority meant 'fundamentally the wisdom of the ancestors, the *mos maiorum*, in the form of the necessity of religious belief for the solidarity, loyalty, cooperation and dynamism of the citizenry'.[34]

---

[29] Shotter (2005) p. 10.   [30] Flower (2004) p. 9.
[31] 'The Republic', Book 2, 65, p. 56.   [32] Arendt (1958) p. 99.
[33] See Arendt (2006), Chapter 5.   [34] Wood (2008) p. 60.

Rome was by no means the only society that took its founding myth and traditions seriously. Yet it went further than most in its cultivation – indeed, politicisation – of tradition. Arendt writes of the Romans' 'indefatigable search for tradition and authority'.[35] The historian Helen Flowers wrote how the 'sense of a shared set of values was cultivated for a surprisingly long time' despite the upheavals experienced by the Republic.[36] The Romans expended considerable resources on this project, and frequent outbursts of conflict and civil war indicated that the ancient constitution could not always provide a foundation for solidarity. Arguably that is why the rulers of Rome devoted so much energy on promoting visible and tangible expressions of their authority. Given the extent of competing claims for loyalty, it 'is not surprising that the 'Romans found the need for a large number of authority symbols'.[37]

Roman traditionalism was far from dogmatic: indeed, some Roman thinkers possessed a pragmatic attitude towards tradition and religion. The scholar Marcus Terentius Varro (116–27 BC) wrote that it is useful 'that the crowd believe great men to be of divine origin', and the poet Ovid stated that 'it's expedient that there be gods, as it is expedient, let us believe so'. Such cynical sentiment towards the role of religion indicates that there was a general awareness that this institution was essential for the maintenance of order and stability. These instrumental attitudes did not mean that Roman customs and traditions were not taken very seriously; rather, that the sacred existed in an uneasy relationship with the pragmatic. Galinksy throws light of this relationship when he states that Roman religion was 'not a matter of faith, but the Roman state was unthinkable without it'.[38]

The Roman state was underwritten by the authority of its custom and law, which was 'rooted in the *mores maiorum*, the ways of the forebears'. These rules could be 'added to and moulded into something new, they might be allowed to fall into disuse when obsolete, but they could not be simply and arbitrarily abolished and replaced by something else'.[39] The imperative of conserving the traditions of the past ensured that innovation and new proposals required the validation of ancestral law, thus making the ways of the old formally binding for future generations. Arguments required the sanction of the *mores maiorum* if they were to persuade. Even Augustus, whose rule brought about a fundamental transformation of the way that Rome was ruled, was careful to present the objectives of his radically new policies as the restoration of the old ways.

---

[35] Arendt (1958) p. 98.   [36] Flower (2004) p. 9.   [37] Wolin (2004) p. 69.
[38] Galinsky (1996) p. 291.   [39] Wolff (1987) p. 63.

From the standpoint of the development of the idea of authority, the Roman Republic can be perceived as a laboratory for ideas. The period showed a 'characteristic Roman energy for innovation and the complex interplay between inherited tradition and bold invention'. In this era, 'times of great innovation repeatedly alternated and overlapped with typically Roman phases of conscious archaism and of the (re)invention of traditions'.[40] Roman society was continually under pressure to adapt to changing circumstances, making its institutions responsive to social pressures created by the 'dynamics of class conflict, group rivalries and personal ambitions'. Wolin claims that during the two centuries leading up to the establishment of the Principate in 27 BC, the Romans 'tested and perfected' almost every technique of political management', such as the manipulation of political and religious symbols, and the organisation of mass spectacles to gain the acquiescence of the masses.[41] Although these attempts failed to resolve the crisis of the Republic, they helped to stimulate the clarification and emergence of the idea of authority.

The loss of tradition

The anxiety expressed by Cicero and other leading Roman public figures about the loss of tradition was precipitated by the perception of political crisis. From around 133 BC onwards, the Roman Republic faced a series of social and political upheavals. The old political order could no longer contain the social division between the landowning senatorial aristocracy, the rich business class of the equestrians and the plebeian masses. Rivalries among the elites led to a series of civil wars and the assumption of dictatorial power by ruthless leaders culminating in the regime of Julius Caesar. Remarkably these conflicts did not inhibit Rome's foreign expansion and cultural and economic development.[42] Nevertheless the crisis of the Republic exposed the fragility of the institutions and values that gave definition to what it meant to be a Roman.

To many observers the crisis of the Roman Republic appeared as one of institutional decay. The system of countervailing power and carefully constructed balance between the magistrates, people and senate broke down. According to one account, 'the situation changed during the second century BC when the consensus on political guidelines and standards started eroding and *mores* (customs) were increasingly being replaced by *leges* (laws)'.[43] Formal laws could not serve as a substitute for consensus and the continued polarisation of society was paralleled

---

[40] Flower (2004) p. 4.   [41] Wolin (2004) p. 78.   [42] Wolff (1987) p. 13.
[43] Eder (2005) p. 15.

by the diminishing of the strength of the bonds of tradition. The ruthless pursuit of self-interest by ambitious members of the Roman elite led to displays of indifference, if not outright contempt, towards traditional customs and religion. 'Imperial expansion, the enormous flow of wealth into Rome, the seemingly endless opportunities for political ambition intensified the pace of politics and made men impatient with traditional restraints and customary procedures' concludes Wolin.[44] Paradoxically it was the uncontained conflict between the main beneficiaries of the system that was responsible for the slow disintegration of the Republic. As Wood explains:

Yet the very success of the republic as an instrument of aristocratic gain proved its undoing. The irony is that it was the triumph of the aristocracy which eventually led to the fall of the republic, as the weakness of the threat from below deprived the ruling class of any unity it might have had in the face of a common enemy . . . With no strong state to keep the warring aristocracy in check the republic descended into chaos.[45]

The cumulative effect of the chaotic reign of naked self-interest was to diminish the moral authority of Rome's elites and republican political institutions. It was this that led for a call for the revival of ancient values by figures like Cato and Cicero. Probably the greatest institutional casualty of this crisis was the senate. Although the senate was arguably the key institution of governance in the Roman Republic, it lacked formal and legal powers. As Shotter observes, to Romans, 'the prestige and authority of the senate (*auctoritas senatus*) were real and effective – and indeed the more impressive because the senate required no legal formulae to enable it to exercise control'.[46] Although strictly speaking the senate possessed only an advisory role, it 'emerged as the truly governing body of Rome'.[47] Its ability to play this central role was due to its capacity to represent the 'accumulated experience and wisdom' of Rome, and even powerful generals and magistrates 'seldom dared to take steps involving questions of general policy without consulting the Senate, or to disregard its advice'.[48] However by the beginning of the first century BC, the weakness of a governmental institution that depended upon respect and adherence to custom and tradition stood exposed.

Individual proconsuls were able to overcome the conventional constitutional restraints and consolidate their influence and power to the point that they could bypass the senate. Such powerful individuals formed alliances and coalitions with groups of senators and 'for the first time,

---

[44] Wolin (2004) p. 81.   [45] Wood (2008) pp. 116–17.   [46] Shotter (2005) p. 9.
[47] Wolff (1987) p. 43.   [48] Wolff (1987) p. 43.

individual senators and the factions into which they formed themselves began to see their sectional loyalty as more important than the senate's corporate authority'.[49] The senate lost its ability to govern, and during the four decades leading up to the Civil War of 49 BC, power was grabbed by dictators on at least five different occasions. It was evident that the Roman Republic had become ungovernable and that senatorial authority had broken down.

What is noteworthy about the crisis of the Roman Republic is that, despite the disintegration of its institutional arrangements, the customs and practices associated with the ancient constitution remained uncontested and retained a significant degree of moral influence. Although the elite consensus that underpinned the Republic's political order had fallen prey to conflict and rivalry, the customs and principles associated with the ancient ways still continued to define what it meant to be a Roman. In part the ability of the ancient constitution to endure was a testimony to its flexibility. As Eder writes, this was a 'system of traditional concepts and principles that could be adapted time and again to changing realities'.[50] But it also served to define Roman identity, way of life and political culture; and whatever reservations people had about the workings of the Republic its foundational values and constitution remained hegemonic.

At the time, and in subsequent decades, the crisis of the republic was interpreted as the cumulative outcome of individual greed and weakness, and the failure to preserve the old ways. The corrosive impact of foreign influences and the temptations offered by imports of luxury goods were held responsible for the moral corruption of society, and the failure of the republic perceived as the 'failure to adhere to a traditional value system that placed the common good, the *res publica*, ahead of private interests'.[51] Christian Meier's important essay on this subject notes that 'the legitimacy of the existing constitution was not questioned',[52] and even the senate, which had clearly lost its way, was perceived as central to the maintenance of a legitimate political order. That is why Augustus Caesar, who in effect overthrew the republic and assumed the power of an imperial ruler, carefully cultivated the image of a traditionalist and represented himself as the saviour of the ancient constitution.

Through the deeds of ancestors, the sacred beginnings of Rome provided people with a compelling story about their life and gave meaning to their existence; and with so much of Roman identity being bound up with the wisdom of the past, alternatives to the ancient constitution could not be conceived. Individual customs could be ignored and even

[49] Shotter (2005) p. 10.   [50] Eder (2005) p. 15.   [51] Galinsky (1996) p. 6.
[52] Meier (1993) p. 55.

violated but the tradition itself was beyond question. 'Such a discrep-
ancy between continuing confirmation and acceptance of the old order
on the one hand and its weakness and manifold failures on the other
presents a difficult (and, for many today, hardly comprehensible) problem', observes Meier, before going on to ask why the causes of the crisis
were 'not recognised', and why any solution was seen to lie 'in restoring
the traditional constitution rather than in changing it'.[53]

From the standpoint of today, where the term 'traditional' often conveys a pejorative connotation, it is difficult to grasp why it was held beyond
question in the antiquities. The links that bound community to its origins and customs could not be ignored or replaced without undermining
the sense of place that Romans possessed. Thus despite all the changes
experienced by Rome, ancient societies could not regard their institutions entirely instrumentally. Such institutions could not be divested
of their sacred and therefore binding character without putting into question virtually every dimension of social and cultural experience. Even the
defiance of the existing order required that it should be expressed through
the idiom of custom and tradition. This was the problem facing anyone
who sought to resolve the crisis of the Republic. Augustus could not
simply get rid of the republic and establish a new political regime – 'he
had no choice but to style himself the defender of the old system and to
fight for the *causa senates* – if necessary even against the senators'.[54]

In retrospect, the crisis of the Roman Republic can be understood as a
historical moment when authority required justification and conceptual
elaboration. Informal customs and traditional practices could no longer
contain the destructive impulse towards civil war and the fragmentation
of the elites. Individual political and military leaders did not simply lay
claim to power, but also sought to usurp the power of the constitution
while demanding recognition for their dignity and moral authority. One
attempt at a provisional answer was provided by Cicero's elaboration of
tradition and the authority of ancient customs. It was left to Augustus
Caesar to revitalise tradition and establish a political order that succeeded
in finding a place for the individual authority of the leader while also
revitalising authority.

Reflections on *auctoritas*

Before we consider the contribution of Augustus Caesar to the elaboration of the concept of authority, it is necessary to explore the meaning of
the concept of *auctoritas*. There is widespread agreement that this concept

---

[53] Meier (1993) p. 55.   [54] Meier (1993) p. 69.

played an important role in the public life of Rome, but precisely because it was used in a variety of different contexts, its meaning for Roman political life remains a subject of controversy. 'The problem with the ancient Roman origins of authority, indeed, is an embarrassment of riches: it is the problem of inferring a characteristic and coherent Roman idea from the welter of literal usages developed for the term,' states Krieger.[55]

Retrospective interpretations of culturally specific concepts invariably require sensitivity to context and attention to detail. To understand an important cultural and political concept such as *auctoritas*, it is necessary to explore what questions it tried to answer and what problems it tried to solve.

Writing at the turn of the third century, the Greek historian Cassius Dio referred to the *auctoritas* of the Senate and, in passing, remarked that 'it is impossible to find a word in Greek which will have an equivalent meaning'.[56] Cassius Dio used his words carefully. His emphasis is not the untranslatable quality of the word but its unique meaning. According to one commentator, Dio 'acknowledges that the Romans have a word that subsumes a span of meanings not captured in any individual Greek equivalent, and he may hint that the existence of a word with such a semantic range may speak to a uniquely Latin quality about it'.[57] There has been a tendency to emphasise the untranslatable quality of what one English classicist terms the 'notoriously indefinable word'.[58] One German lexicographer warns that:

The word *auctoritas* belongs to the most significant and lasting coinages of the Latin language. Its meaning is not always easy to ascertain, and attempting to translate it causes even more trouble. A wise person will do better to refrain from the effort.[59]

The nineteenth-century classicist Theodor Mommsen wrote that *auctoritas* was 'an indefinite word, evading strict definition'.[60] Mommsen sought to conceptualise the term as a force that was 'more than advice' and 'less than a command' – an 'advice which one may not safely ignore'.[61]

In retrospect, it appears that the problem of giving meaning to the Roman concept of *auctoritas* is not so much a linguistic one but an inevitable consequence of the difficulty of capturing contested relations of power in a historic setting. As a Roman political concept, *auctoritas* is frequently contrasted with the word *potestas*, which can be defined as power, and with *imperium*, which refers to military power. Cicero, who

[55] Krieger (1968) p. 141.   [56] Cassius (1987) Book 55.3, p. 191.
[57] Ziolkowski (2009) p. 442.   [58] Grant (1949) p. 98.
[59] Wolfgang Hefler cited in Ziolkowski (2009) p. 442.
[60] Cited in Balsdon (1960) p. 43.   [61] Cited by Arendt (1958) p. 100.

took the idea of *auctoritas* very seriously, claimed that in an ideal state, *potestas* lay with the people and *auctoritas* with the state.[62] Cicero not only drew a distinction between the two concepts – he also endowed *auctoritas* with moral meaning and authority. Galinsky argues that the concept possesses 'strong moral connotations', suggesting 'material, intellectual and moral superiority' and conveying the idea of moral leadership.[63]

Originally *auctoritas* worked as a pre-political cultural term that communicated the possession of highly valued moral attributes. The root is *auctor* – an agent that validates or guarantees a translation. It is also linked to the word *augere*, which can be translated as 'augment' but which also suggests the act of beginning, initiating, causing or founding something. Arendt argues that what is augmented through the transmission of tradition is the 'foundation': that 'those endowed with authority were the elders, the Senate or the *patres*, who had obtained it by descent and by transmission from those who laid the foundation for all things to come'.[64] However, *auctoritas* encompassed a wide range of experiences and attributes and can be more generally expressed as the 'capacity to initiate and to inspire respect'.[65] In line with Roman custom, old age itself constituted to a claim to authority, which is why Cicero writes of the '*auctoritas* of old age'.[66]

In terms of its pre-political or private meaning, *auctoritas* expressed the capacity to hold responsibility for a variety of relationships and transactions. The most overt link between private and public authority was expressed through the notion of patriarchal authority (*auctoritas partum*), which in Rome was directly linked with the authority of the Senate (*auctoritas Senatus*). As Krieger points out:

Denoting the Senate's function, as a council of elders, of approving the resolutions of the popular assemblies before they could become law, the patriarchal authority of the Senate was obviously the public analogy of the private authority inherent in the certificatory function of the trustee.

Krieger characterises this function as the 'incremental or tutelary idea of authority', one that is 'additional to regular legal sanctions' and is based on the status of special trust enjoyed by the individual.[67]

Auctoritas was also widely used to communicate the personal quality of individuals who 'spoke with authority', were perceived as 'being in authority', or possessed the inner quality of 'moral authority'. This emphasis on personal authority or 'doing something by someone's

---

[62] See discussion in Balsdon (1960) p. 43.   [63] Galinsky (1996) p. 12.
[64] Arendt (1958) p. 100.   [65] Hopfl (1999) p. 232.
[66] Galinsky (1996) p. 16.   [67] Krieger (1968) p. 142.

authority' are frequently mentioned in Roman literature. In classical Latin, the 'author' is an authority;[68] and in that capacity, an author an individual poet, philosopher or scholar serve as a source for authoritative statements and proposals. However, the moral or personal authority of the individual played an important role in the constitution of public authority. The authority attributed to personal qualities 'often shaded insensibly into the incremental authority of public office', writes Krieger.[69] Individual prestige and influence mutated imperceptibly into reinforcing and enhancing public standing. Such qualities served to enhance the influence of the senate, where the quality of membership was regarded as an essential component of the prestige enjoyed by this body of elders. For Cicero and other public figures, 'much of the prescriptive force that was imputed to the "counsels" of the Senate stemmed from the personal attributes of lineage, propertied wealth and character associated with the Senators'.[70]

One important and distinct connotation of *auctoritas* was the capacity to create and initiate. This ability continues to be expressed through words such as 'author' and 'authorise'. In the Roman context, it also carried the implication that the *auctor* served as the *source* or the *origin* of an act, a statement or a proposal. From this perspective the original authority of the individual was expressed as form of public leadership that endowed the individual with the right to initiate. In the senate, the idea of authority as initiatory was expressed through the practice of allowing individuals with the greatest *auctoritas* to speak in the debates before those with less. In the same manner, the *auctoritas* of the Senate was expressed through the 'sort of approval' that preceded the enactment of important executive decisions. Galinksy's discussion of this form of senatorial authorisation points to the potentially foundational status of *auctoritas*, meaning the 'kind of substance on which real influence is based'.[71]

It is likely that the attempt to capture the spirit of *auctoritas* through a definition is doomed to fail. The Romans themselves used the term in an expansive sense in order to make sense of a variety of different relationships and experiences. This was a politically contested and protean term that could be harnessed to assist a variety of projects. However, despite its multiple usages, *auctoritas* represented a claim to influence, respect and esteem. What is interesting about this concept is that its claim for influence is often self-consciously contrasted with holding of a formal office or the possession of executive, military or physical power.

---

[68] Hopfl (1999) p. 220.   [69] Krieger (1968) p. 143.   [70] Krieger (1968) p. 143.
[71] Galinsky (1996) p. 15.

In this sense it is a claim for influence that goes beyond the formal power associated with an office or position. Wirszubski observes that:

The practical implications of supremacy by virtue of *auctoritas* are far-reaching. Unlike *potestas*, *auctoritas* is not defined, and therefore whereas *potestas* is confined within certain limits, there is, in theory at least, no limit to the scope of *auctoritas*: it can be brought to bear on any matter.[72]

It was the creative potential of a claim for an influence that could be not confined to formal limits that encouraged so many leading Romans to promote their *auctoritas* so seriously.[73] As we shall see in our discussion of Augustus, the emphasis on *auctoritas* represented a claim to something more than the office of leadership. Although it was expressed through a claim about individual achievement, a person's *auctoritas* was expressed through an ability to preserve the tradition of Rome and to build on its foundation. In this way, the claim for individual influence was expressed through a constant affirmation that tradition remained a living force.

The Roman Revolution

Res Gestae Divi Augusti ('The Deeds of the Divine Augustus') is the most important document of the Augustan Era, and represents an extraordinary contribution to the historical construction of the concept of authority.[74] Written by Augustus shortly before his death, *Res Gestae* offers a clear statement of what Augustus regarded as his important attainments and historical legacy. In this succinct account of his reign, what is fascinating is the purposeful manner with which Augustus elaborates what he takes to be the principal features of his authority.

Augustus draws attention to his numerous deeds – his political and military triumphs, his financial and material contribution to the city of Rome, his great popularity with the people and the respect that he enjoyed from the leading elites. But the statement is not simply a boastful listing of battles won and honours received. He continually reminds posterity of the effort and resources he devoted to securing the welfare of the people of Rome, underlining his role as the protector of Rome's customs and traditions. He claims that he not only restored the republic but also Rome's traditional way of life: 'By new laws, passed on my advice, I have revived many exemplary practices of our ancestors, which in our age were

---

[72] Wirszubski (1950) p. 166.

[73] In the inter-war period of the twentieth century, the limitless scope of *auctoritas* would excite the interest of political theorists drawn towards this concept's potential for authorising authoritarian rule and domination. See the following chapter.

[74] For a translation of this document see Takacs (2003).

about to fade away, and myself transmitted to posterity many models of conduct to be imitated'.[75]

Augustus's focus is moral authority, and in the penultimate paragraph of *Res Gestae,* he outlines what he considers to be his principal accomplishment. During his sixth and seventh consulships (28–27 BC), after 'extinguishing civil wars' and gaining total control over the destiny of Rome, he transferred his formal powers to the senate and the people of Rome, upon which a decree of the senate bestowed upon the man formally known as Octavian the name of 'Augustus'. The name had important moral connotations, 'an honour which linked its owner with the "august augury" which had accompanied the foundations of Rome, and which was etymologically connected with *auctoritas*',[76] and which implied that he was in 'some way above ordinary human standards'.[77] It is important to stress that that Octavian gained this honour as a reward for his act of restoring the republic. Augustus was a 'word often associated with sacred objects and phenomena, and suggested something venerable, an embodiment of power';[78] if the senate's decree did not quite imply his deification, it certainly endowed Augustus with the status of moral supremacy.

The claim to moral authority is emphasised by Augustus when he states that, after receiving the recognition of the Senate, 'I excelled all in *auctoritas,* although I possessed no more official power than others who were my colleagues in the several magistracies'.[79] Augustus's focus on his *auctoritas* reveals his commitment to the construction of an idea of authority that is distinct from physical and military power. The juxtaposition of *auctoritas* to *potestas* represents a clear statement of how Augustus wanted his rule to be interpreted by history. It does not wish to represent his military, political or financial power as the distinctive mark of his rule – indeed, he appears to understate his formal powers, in claiming that these were no greater than those enjoyed by his fellow magistrates. His intention is to differentiate himself from other members of the Roman elites by drawing attention to his unique personal influence, qualities and moral authority. As Galinksy writes, 'by emphasizing *auctoritas* as his governing concept Augustus makes it clear that he does not want to be just a functionary or magistrate but that he aims to provide a higher kind of moral leadership'.[80]

The different elements of Augustus's powers have been a subject of continual historical debate, which is inextricably linked to the

---

[75] See translation by Takacs (2003) p. 137.   [76] Shotter (2005) p. 33.
[77] Wirszubski (1950) p. 15.   [78] Grant (1949) p. 27.
[79] This translation is cited in Galinsky (1996) p. 11.   [80] Galinsky (1996) p. 12.

controversy surrounding the so-called Roman Revolution. After trans-
ferring his powers to the Senate, Augustus claimed that he had restored
the Republic. But the formal restoration of the Republic coincided with
the establishment of a new form of institutional arrangement – the Principate – which gave Augustus supreme imperial power. His title *princeps
senates* – leader of the senate – rendered formal the traditional meaning
of *princeps*, which was traditionally that of 'leading statesman' or 'first
amongst equals'. Traditionally the term *princeps* was used to refer to the
leaders of the city, of whom there could be several at once. However with
the establishment of the Principate, Augustus emerged as the personification of both leadership and authority. As Wirszubski explains, whereas
previously 'there might be several statesmen of outstanding *auctoritas* at
a time, there was to some extent a free choice between various *auctores*',
with the establishment of the Principate '[t]hings changed completely':

> since the *auctoritas* of the Princeps was permanently pre-eminent, just as he was
> permanently supreme; it overshadowed and dwarfed all other *auctoritates*, and
> since it had no equal, the only course open to the Romans was to accept the
> *auctoritas* of the Princeps or defy it at their own risk.[81]

There is little doubt that the establishment of the Principate represented
a phase of transition from the Roman Republic to the establishment of
an Empire. Less clear are the motives and objectives of Augustus, and
the extent to which this transition was the conscious design of the careful
calculation of a far-sighted leader.

Numerous critics have questioned Augustus's account of his achievements in the *Res Gestae*, including his claim that it was his moral authority that constituted the unique foundation of his regime. According to
Salmon, 'the *auctoritas* of the Princeps and what has been called his
charismatic significance, so it seems to me, have been very much overem-
phasized of recent years'.[82] Ronald Syme, the influential historian of the
Roman Revolution, dismisses Augustus's claim to moral authority by
insisting that 'contemporaries were not deceived', and that 'the convenient revival of republican institutions, the assumption of special title, the
change in the definition of authority, all that made no difference to the
source and facts of power'.[83] Syme depicts Augustus as dictator whose
power was founded on his control of the military.

However, such interrogations of Augustus's legacy overlook the
broader historical significance of this Roman leader. *Res Gestae* should
not be assessed on the basis of its historical accuracy, but as a statement
through which the Augustan project is framed – that is, how Augustus

---

[81] Wirszubski (1950) p. 114.   [82] Salmon (1956) p. 459.   [83] Syme (2002) p. 2.

wanted to be seen by subsequent generations. *Res Gestae* may not be a rigorous and accurate depiction of past events, but it provides a radically new representation of authority. Through its claim to restore the republic and its constitution, it binds together the custom, religion and tradition of Rome with the personal authority of the supreme leader. The juxtaposition of *auctoritas* to *potestas* serves as a prelude to indicating how they reinforce one another, and formal office gains its meaning through the authority of the leader in the way that *auctoritas* lends meaning to power. Thus, Salmon accepts that what underlay Augustus's rule was the 'interdependence between office and *auctoritas*'.[84]

Res Gestae can be seen as an attempt to integrate the diverse strands of authority into a generic concept through which Augustus's actions could be interpreted as continuous with Rome's founding and traditions but also their restoration in a new form. In this document, individual authority is fused with the power of tradition, religion and Roman identity. *Res Gestae* concludes with the reminder that Augustus was awarded the title of *pater patriae* – 'Father of my Country' – co-joining the pre-political authority of the father with that of the nation. A new form of authority is under construction, personified through the individual figure of Augustus. Galinsky remarks that 'few cultural periods in the history of the world have taken their name from their rulers for intrinsic rather than convenient reasons: political power and cultural creativity are not often related'.[85] The Age of Augustus or the Augustan Era served as a prelude for two centuries of order and stability.

An unresolved question

Like other leading Romans, Augustus was sensitive to the necessity for validating his actions and the use of power on the basis of recognised customs and norms. Max Weber concluded that, in societies where *imperium* was clearly specified and 'particularized as distinguished from unlimited domestic authority', one finds the 'beginnings of the distinction between "legitimate" command and the norms by which it is "legitimated"'.[86] The *imperium*-holder is forced self-consciously to seek authorisation through custom and law. From this perspective, the Principate can be interpreted as an attempt to extend the jurisdiction for the exercise of legitimate authority.

Disputes about whether the act of establishing the Principate was an act of cynical deception, or a genuine impulse to restore Rome's tradition, can be understood as a variant of history's perennial debate about

---

[84] Salmon (1956) p. 460.   [85] Galinsky (1996) p. 10.   [86] Weber (1978) p. 764.

the meaning of authority. In this case, the preoccupation with the nature of Augustus's power can be seen as an attempt to conceptualise the relationship between individual influence, the use of force, persuasion and moral authority. Such concerns invariably focus on the question of where power lay in the Principate. Syme believes that Augustus gave the senate only a semblance of power, and that 'behind the nominal authority and government of the Roman Senate the real and ultimate power needs to be discovered'.[87] Numerous accounts reduce the 'real' power of Augustus to naked coercion. 'Augustus had really secured his rule by fear,' writes one American political scientist.[88] Others concede that Augustus may have possessed some *auctoritas*, but it was his control of the military that underpinned his power.[89]

The issue here lies with the ability to conceptualise the problem, rather than with the behaviour of an individual leader. Eder may have a point when he asserts that, 'Augustus made it no simple matter to identify clearly "the real and ultimate power on which his position in the *res publica* rested"'.[90] But the difficulty of conceptualising the workings of ultimate power is inherent to the task, and appears to emerge in a wide variety of historical contexts. In Rome, the different strands of *auctoritas* existed in an ambiguous relation with one another. The Romans did not develop one generic concept of *auctoritas* because they regarded it as having an indeterminate relationship with different forms of power. It is in Augustus's *Res Gestae* that the historically specific rendition of authority was clarified. Drawing on his own experience, Augustus was striving to develop an idea that explained how the coercive threat or use of power was not always necessary to gain obedience.

Historical context is everything, and it is true to say that Augustus was the right person in the right place at the right time. After decades of bloody civil war, Rome was exhausted and its people yearned for stability and order. Octavian was seen as a strong military commander who combined political intelligence with potential statesmanship. This was a moment where a dominant figure could harness a people's readiness to exchange obedience for security, and develop the institutionalisation of a new form of authority. As Krieger suggests, the 'principate initiated, under personal auspices, the process which would be completed under institutional auspices, in the later Empire: the compression of loose-jointed authority, in response to the needs of official political organs, into a compact legal basis of constitutional power'.[91]

---

[87] Syme (2002) p. 406.   [88] Starr (1952) p. 6.   [89] See Salmon (1956).
[90] Eder (1993) p. 71.   [91] Krieger (1968) pp. 144–5.

The process of unifying various strands of Augustus's authority helped to sensitise Romans to the relationship between *auctoritas* and power. The different fragments of *auctoritas* served to validate the exercise of power. *Auctoritas* provided a moral foundation for the exercise of power. The idea of foundation served as a metaphor for giving meaning to what would, in subsequent centuries, serve as *foundational authority*. Hannah Arendt's emphasis on 'the sacred binding force of an authoritative beginning to which one remained bound through the strength of tradition' seeks to turn the metaphor of founding into a durable political concept.[92] That may be going a step too far: the very fact that Romans tended to use a metaphor for something they sensed to be very real indicates that the clarification of a fundamental concept requires the passage of time.

The question of a foundation, or source, for authority was raised abstractly by Cicero in his discussion of natural law. He explained that the law – by which he meant customary and statutory law – was 'not thought up by the intelligence of human beings' nor by a 'resolution passed by communities', but 'rather an eternal force which rules the world by the wisdom of its commands and prohibitions'. Cicero added that the 'original and final law is the intelligence of God, who ordains or forbids everything by reason'.[93] This 'original and final law' had universal applicability and exercised moral authority over the conduct of public life. However, the clarification of the meaning of this 'original' source of custom and tradition required the institutional innovation associated with the Augustan era. It is at this point that we see the 'actualization of the coherent idea of autonomous authority'.[94]

Disputes about the relationship between power and *auctoritas* are sociologically significant because they provide valuable insights about who or what is really valued. In a different context, Tuck has noted that unlike the claim to power, the claim to possess authority contains a 'highly problematic element'. A claim to power can be 'substantiated in the last resort by a pitched battle' while the meaning of authority is more elusive and mysterious'.[95] He adds that 'what is clear is that claims to authority occur in a wide variety of situations, and that there is no *prima facie* reason to suppose that the nature of the claim is in each case the same (though there will presumably be at least a tenuous connection between them)'.[96]

A century after the death of Augustus, the Roman historian Tacitus took it upon himself to expose the author of *Res Gestae* as an unscrupulous and power-hungry manipulator of Rome. The representation of

[92] Arendt (2005) p. 49.   [93] Cicero (2008), *Laws*, 2.7, p. 124.
[94] Krieger (1968) p. 164.   [95] Tuck (1972) p. 194.   [96] Tuck (1972) p. 194.

Augustus as a morally repellent precursor of modern totalitarian dictators remains an influential theme in the literature on the Augustan Era.
However, neither Tacitus nor his later critics could deny the impressive
achievements of this man. In subsequent centuries, numerous thinkers
and leaders sought to learn the meaning of Augustan authority.

4   Augustus: a role model for authority through the ages

Rome provided the intellectual resources for rendering authority meaningful. It is frequently observed that *auctoritas* is a 'uniquely Roman idea'.[1] This does not mean that the Romans discovered authority, but that they self-consciously reflected on it and attempted to conceptualise its different dimensions. In particular, through distinguishing between *potestas*, the power to command, and *auctoritas*, the Romans succeeded in representing authority 'in terms of a procedure of authorization'.[2] Moreover, the Romans turned their political experiences into a durable legacy that others would draw on. As the political philosopher Michael Oakeshott notes,

> this political experience generated a legend of itself in which actions and events acquired poetically universal significance – a legend unmatched until quite modern times, in which the Romans expressed their beliefs about themselves as a community and about what they were doing in the world.[3]

Over the past two millennia Rome has served as source of authority for a variety of political rulers, religious leaders, revolutionaries and philosophers. The influence of Rome did not only transcend national boundaries but also the political divide. Conservative thinkers dreaming of a restoration of order were no less drawn towards finding inspiration from the legacy of Rome than were radical revolutionaries aspiring to the building a new world. 'Law, order, reverence for authority, the whole framework of political and social establishment, are the work of Rome on the lines drawn once for all by the Latin genius', noted the Scottish socialist and Virgil scholar, John William Mackaill, in his address to the Classical Association in 1904.[4] Similar thoughts were expressed by his more conservative-thinking colleagues, who equated Rome with permanence, stability and order.

---

[1] Oakeshott (2006) p. 229.   [2] Oakeshott (2006) p. 229.
[3] Oakeshott (2006) pp. 206–7.   [4] Cited in Edwards (1999) p. 3.

To this day, diagnoses of political issues and problems are often medi-ated through reflections on the experience of Rome. It is as if the appropriation of Roman legend, ideals and symbols is necessary for re-discovering the meaning of authority in very different circumstances, and in line with different historical and cultural sentiments. Those whose focus is the representation or consolidation of authority have frequently turned to Augustus for guidance. It is a testimony to the accomplish-ment of Augustus that the historical quest for validation and legitimation has time and again sought to clarify its own views and learn from the experience of the Principate.

A cultural resource for authority

The Romans were uniquely self-conscious in the construction of their own foundational myth. The project of developing a legend of origins acquired an interesting twist around the third century BC, as the Romans decided to trace their descent not from Romulus but from the Trojan hero, Aeneas. In this way, Rome could draw on the authority of Greek foundational myths to give greater historical depth to its own tradition. According to one account, it was the traumatic effects of the outburst of Roman expansionary energy from 300 to around 200 BC that dis-posed this society 'to accept so eagerly an Hellenocentric vision of their origins'.[5] Whatever the immediate influences, the Trojan legacy offered Romans a powerful and compelling heritage, which was 'superior' to the pre-existing story of origins. Moreover through incorporating this legend, the cultural heritage of the Greeks was utilised to lend greater historical depth to the way that Romans understood themselves.[6]

The transformation of the story of Rome into a durable legacy was of course not unconnected to the capacity of this civilisation to project order, stability, power and authority over an exceptionally long period of time. *Pax Romana* created a sturdy foundation for reflection on the meaning of order, leadership and political authority. In contrast to the quick succession of ruling dynasties and violent upheavals of medieval and early modern Europe, Rome appeared as a model of a sturdy orderly empire. In centuries to come, Augustus's Principate would be seen as a Golden Age of prosperity, order and stability. It is important to note that it was during the Age of Augustus that the myth of Roman origins was further recast and incorporated into the emerging culture of authority. In the *Aeneid*, Virgil not only rewrote the founding legend of Rome

[5] Donlan (1970) p. 113.   [6] See the discussion in Donlan (1970).

but also depicted his patron, Augustus, as a latter-day Aeneas. Thus, the founding of Rome was recreated and preserved through the action of the author of the Principate.[7] But the *Aeneid* is not just a work of invention: it speaks to a well-established and recognised centuries-old Roman tradition, which Augustus carefully cultivated and promoted. As Galinsky remarks, '*Aeneid* is Augustan without sacrificing any of its timelessness'.[8] It is above all a statement about what it means to be a Roman: yet it would go on to serve the demand of numerous subsequent cultures for a story of origins.

The translation of Roman political ideas to a wider global and historical audience was assisted by their capacity to transcend cultural and national boundaries. From its Roman inheritance, Europe acquired the common language of Latin, and a political vocabulary through which the experience of the ancients acquired relevance. 'With the language, that medieval Europe acquired from Rome was a past-relationship with a Roman civilization in terms of which they came to understand themselves,' notes Oakeshott.[9] Cultural inheritance is rarely embraced indiscriminately – societies adapt their cultural legacy to their circumstances, and develop them in line with the preoccupations of their era. However, it is striking how Roman ideas about foundational and other layers of authority influenced deliberations on this subject throughout most of European history. 'The disappearance of the Roman empire in Western Europe did not bring with it the eclipse of the imperial theme in political reflection', notes one review of medieval political thought, claiming that Roman political ideals 'remained firmly embedded in the language of Western writers and were to find new application when a Western Empire once again became a real political possibility'.[10]

For example, sixteenth-century proponents of England's imperial cause traced the origins of the British Empire back to the fall of Troy. This claim was based on Geoffrey of Monmouth's *Historia Regum Britanniae* (1136). *The History of the Kings of Britain* links the origins of the British Empire to the Trojan diaspora that was created after the fall of this city. The story focuses on Brutus, a refugee from Troy who is destined to become the leader of Britain. According to Geoffrey, Brutus founded the city of *Troia Nova* (New Troy), later called London. This legend posits a common ancestry with the people who founded Rome and through the construction of a connection with the civilisation of the Mediterranean, this national myth endows the British Empire with legitimacy.[11] In a

---

[7] See discussion in Galinsky (1996) p. 250.   [8] Galinsky (1996) p. 253.
[9] Oakeshott (2006) p. 253.   [10] Burns (1991) p. 90.
[11] See the discussion in Armitage (2009) pp. 37–51.

similar way, the representation of authority by Romans provided a historical legacy that succeeding societies could adopt as part of their tradition and adapt to their own circumstances. 'Since the *Imperium Romanum* at its height had encompassed the whole of the world known to the Romans, the authority of the emperor was *ipso facto* universal', writes Armitage.[12] The universal appeal of this authority was reinterpreted by the Christian Church and integrated into its new doctrine. The new Christian church could represent the resurrection of Christ as a form of rebirth, and project its new community as the re-creation of the foundation of Rome. Arendt contends that,

> thanks to the fact that the foundation of the city of Rome was repeated in the foundation of the Catholic Church, though of course, with a radically different content, the Roman trinity of religion, authority, and tradition could be taken over by the Christian era.[13]

The Christianisation of Rome's political and spiritual heritage can be understood as representing its preservation and development. Through this process of cultural borrowing and adaptation, the authority of foundation gained further definition and relevance to a new community of people. The Christian Church was believed to have been 'founded' in a manner not remotely different from the legendary foundation of Rome itself'. Moreover, 'there was an attachment to this "foundation" at least as strong as the attachment to this "foundation" of Rome'.[14] The Church was 'new' but what it represented was the New Rome.

This transmission of a historical legacy is illustrated through the influence exercised by the idea of *imperium* in European societies. As noted in the previous chapter, with the emergence of the Principate, the transformation of *imperium* into the idea of an indivisible *Imperium Romanorum* ensured that the emperor now carried supreme authority throughout the empire. This language of power and authority was an inheritance that the rulers of medieval and early modern European rulers were ready to embrace. Armitage argues that this legacy of *imperium* was to prove important to medieval and early modern European political thought in three important respects: 'it denoted independent authority; it described a territorial unit; and it offered an historical foundation for claims to both the authority and the territory ruled by Roman emperors'. *Imperium* thus provided a foundational precedent for the exercise of authority: '*Imperium* in the sense of independent and self-sufficient authority offered a more generally applicable precedent for later polities and, especially, their rulers'.[15]

[12] Armitage (2009) p. 31.   [13] Arendt (1958) p. 104.   [14] Oakeshott (2006) p. 220.
[15] Armitage (2009) p. 30.

Although claims for authority were invariably contested by competing factions and interests, their meaning and association with Rome was taken for granted. 'In the struggle for *imperium*', observes Armitage, 'all roads led back to Rome, though they did not necessarily lead back to the same conception of Rome'.[16] Competing European powers and interests would have their own stories to tell about Rome but the legacy of this empire was a cultural resource upon which they could all draw. The recovery and revival of Roman law in 1070 at Bologna provided potential claimants to the crown of the Holy Roman Empire with a legal foundation for the imperial title.[17] That Roman law 'became one of the greatest intellectual forces in the history of European civilization, because it provided principles and categories in terms of which men thought about all sorts of subjects and not least about politics' is recognised by students of the history of political theory.[18] The language, concepts and symbols of the post-Augustan Roman Empire 'provided early-modern monarchies with the resources for the legitimation of their independence, just as it originally allowed Italian city-states in the fourteenth century to assert their juridical independence from the Empire'.[19]

This point is stressed by the historian Frances Yates in her discussion of the idea of Empire in medieval Europe. In the twelfth century, Frederick II emerged as one of the most formidable Holy Roman Emperors. Through his writings on the role and authority of the emperor, Frederick sought to revive the idea of *Divus Augustus*. According to one account, Frederick's 'imperial "theology of rulership"' no longer depended 'on the idea of a Christ-centred kingship'; rather, his authority as ruler was founded upon Roman law.[20] Dante's *De Monarchia* (circa 1310–13) advanced a clear argument for imperial independence from the spiritual authority of the papacy. Drawing on the experience of Rome, he claimed that the emperor has no human superior and that he was the 'heir to the universal authority which had rightfully belonged to Rome'.[21] Dante sought to develop this tradition, and his theory of the Monarch emphasises the supreme authority of the ruler. For Dante the Holy Roman Emperor is 'the true successor of Caesar and Augustus'.[22]

The Holy Roman Empire was a pale imitation of its predecessor, and the Emperor a far less authoritative figure than the Pope. Most of the time the Emperor's rule did not extend beyond territories in Germany. Yet, as Yates notes, 'ineffective though he may seem, his very existence

---

[16] Armitage (2009) p. 33.
[17] It was in 1070 that the newly discovered Roman code of Justinian was first taught in Bologna University. See Canning (1996) pp. 114–16.
[18] Sabine (1961) p. 168.   [19] Armitage (2009) p. 34.   [20] Kantorowicz (1997) p. 102.
[21] See discussion in Sabine (1961) pp. 257–61.   [22] Yates (1985) p. 11.

witnessed to the truth that all Europe was descended from one root, the Roman Empire'.[23] The idea of a universal source of authority was often sacralised through the association of 'the tradition of the providential role of Rome as a historical preparation for the birth of Christ'.[24] From this standpoint, the legacy of the Divine Augustus was not simply the supreme authority of empire but of a Christian *imperium*. 'The age of Augustus was the supreme example of a world united and at peace under the Roman Empire, and to that age had also belonged the supreme honour of witnessing the birth of Christ', observes Yates.[25] The birth of Christ during the era of Augustus in a world dominated by Roman law was interpreted a sign of divine approval for this order. It is from this perspective that 'Virgil's *Aeneid* with its glorification of Augustus' became 'a semi-sacred poem glorifying the historical framework of the Saviour's birth'.[26]

The *Aeneid* would be continually reinterpreted as not just simply a story about the foundation of Rome, but as a prophecy – about the birth of Christ, or the origin of a new nation.[27] It has been argued that one of the legacies of Augustus was the creation of the conditions for a flourishing partnership between classical culture and Christianity. Had it not been for the achievement and personality of Augustus, it may be questioned whether classical culture would have been preserved by Christianity and handed down to the Middle Ages in both east and west, eventually to fructify the renaissance and hence the culture of the modern Western world writes Hammond.[28]

The quest for authority, particularly the authority of a new order, has frequently led revolutionaries on a journey of the rediscovery of ancient Rome. Cola di Rienzo (1313–54), the medieval visionary and leader of the people of Rome and symbolic hero of modern Italian national-ism, sought to restore the glories of his ancient city. His goal was to re-establish the Roman Empire led by an Italian Emperor. Through his popular appeal to the masses, in May 1347 he overthrew the rule of the barons and the Pope. His triumph proved short-lived and seven months later he was forced into exile; nevertheless, through his ability to com-municate a powerful vision of the values of ancient Rome, he succeeded in exercising influence on the poet Francesco Petrarch and other renais-sance humanists. Petrarch's desire for the rebirth of Rome was widely shared by his contemporaries, and the tradition of Rome was embraced by humanists as their very own.

[23] Yates (1985) p. 3. [24] Yates (1985) p. 3. [25] Yates (1985) p. 4.
[26] Yates (1985) p. 4. [27] Yates (1985) p. 4. [28] Hammond (1965) p. 152.

Karl Marx, in *The Eighteenth Brumaire of Louis Bonaparte*, famously wrote that 'the tradition of all dead generations weighs like a nightmare on the brain of the living'. He observed that at a time when they are engaged in,

creating something that has never yet existed, precisely in such periods of revolutionary crisis they anxiously conjure up the spirits of the past to their service and borrow from them names, battle cries and costumes in order to present the new scene of world history in this time-honoured disguise and this borrowed language.

As examples of this trend, Marx wrote that 'Luther donned the mask of the Apostle Paul, the Revolution of 1789 to 1814 draped itself alternatively as the Roman republic and the Roman empire'; and the leaders of the French Revolution – Danton, Robespierre, Saint-Just, Napoleon – 'performed the task of their time in Roman costume and with Roman phrases'.[29] The power exercised by the legacy of Rome even influences revolutions 'which we commonly regard as radical breaks with tradition'.[30] The French Revolutionary Republic, like the Ancient Regime that it overthrew, could not take its authority for granted. Appropriating the symbols of the ancient Romans made sense to French radicals who were educated in the Classics.

However, the revolutionaries of the eighteenth and early nineteenth centuries did not simply turn to the 'tradition of all dead generations'. They turned to antiquity, and specifically to Rome, in search of answers to the problems of their time. Centuries after the physical collapse of the Roman Empire, its political concepts and symbols could still convey a paradigm of authority. According to one account of eighteenth-century British cultural life, 'allusions to Roman political history were instinctive among men brought up on the classics'. Such men also believed that a 'knowledge of the past provides an infallible insight into the affairs of the present'.[31] The wisdom of the ancients provided an alternative source of authority to the prevailing order. 'Rome then could function in the late eighteenth century as a revolutionary alternative to the existing order', argues one study on the reception of Rome in European culture.[32]

In one sense Marx was right to point to the almost staged manner with which various protagonists of the French Revolution worked to a script that they imagined was written in ancient Rome. Napoleon I energetically transformed himself into the persona of, first, a Roman Consul and then an Emperor. He self-consciously sought to cultivate the myth

[29] See Marx (1970) p. 96.   [30] Arendt (1958) p. 110.
[31] Johnson (1958) pp. 512 and 516.   [32] Edwards (1999) p. 9.

of being a 'natural heir' to the Roman Empire and exploited its art and culture to glorify his rule.[33] But his calculated display of the traditions of Rome should not be interpreted as simply a disguise for a hidden agenda. As Arendt has observed, the 'Roman pathos for foundation' worked to inspire a new generation of revolutionaries.[34] It is a testimony to the durability of the Roman legacy that successive generations of revolutionaries drew on it to authorise their actions. And the tendency to draw on the legacy of Rome was not confined to revolutionaries: numerous liberal and conservative British observers of the drama unfolding in France regarded Napoleon's disciplining of the Directorate and his subsequent imposition of order as acts worthy of 'comparisons with Caesar'.[35]

The creation of the Consulate after the coup of Eighteenth Brumaire (18–19 November 1799) appeared to follow a script written by Augustus. 'What is striking about the constitution is the use of terminology drawn from the Roman Republic', notes one account of how Napoleon constructed his own identity in the image of a latter-day Augustus.[36] Outwardly, the first consul, Bonaparte, shared power with two other consuls. Laws were debated by a tribunate and senate. But this was a military dictatorship masquerading as a republic. Following the path of Augustus, Napoleon refused the offer made by the senate to become consulate for life, thus seeking to assure the people of his loyalty to the French Republic: 'Bonaparte, just as Octavian had done, required a power that was legitimate'.[37]

Octavian Augustus carefully cultivated the people of Rome and, according to Galinsky, 'became the ultimate champion of the vast majority'. Indeed one of the few formal powers 'by which he chose to rule for most of his reign was the *tribunica potestas*, the power of the tribune, that "bastion of liberty"'.[38] Through holding the power – though not the office – of a tribune, Augustus signalled his claim to be the leader of the people. Napoleon too was careful to project the image of the champion of the people. It was only after a plebiscite of people – where a small majority voted to make him life consul – that Napoleon made his move to become Emperor of France. As Huet notes,

Octavian's brilliance had lain first in prolonging his consulship, then in becoming *imperator* for life, an Augustus. The genius of Bonaparte was to redeploy this model but not in every particular; first a consul for life, then emperor for life with the full meaning implied by the title 'emperor' *after* centuries of imperial Roman power.[39]

---

[33] See the interesting discussion on this point in Huet (1999).
[34] Arendt (1958) p. 109.   [35] Turner (1993) p. 248.   [36] Huet (1999) p. 54.
[37] Huet (1999) p. 55.   [38] Galinsky (1996) p. 56.   [39] Huet (1999) pp. 55–6.

Napoleon, like his Roman role model, also claimed the legitimation of a divine inheritance. Augustus traced his lineage through his adoptive father, Julius Caesar, to the lineage of Romulus, Mars Aeneas, and Venus. Napoleon presented himself as the successor of Charlemagne, the Holy Roman Emperor and the 'founder' of France.

Napoleon Bonaparte's adoption of the trappings of a Roman emperor did not mean that he was simply acting out an ancient script. Indeed, through his consolidation of personal power and the expansion of the French Empire, Napoleon himself succeeded in becoming a model of nineteenth-century authority, and the entry of the term 'Bonapartism' into the lexicon of politics indicates he, too, became an exemplar of a form of political rule. It was the capacity of a Bonaparte to claim legitimacy through expressing the will of the people that attracted the interest of numerous figures concerned with the problem of order. This sentiment also extended to his nephew, Louis Napoleon Bonaparte, who was elected as President before transforming himself into the Emperor of the Second French Empire. Louis Napoleon modelled himself on the Romans, writing a book about Julius Caesar and often portrayed by his supporters as a nineteenth-century Roman imperial ruler. As one study points out, 'the Second Empire apologists stressed the need for redeeming Caesar and an Augustus, who had to seize power in order to restore order and reform a society fallen into anarchy and corruption'.[40] Writing in the early twentieth century, Weber represented the two Napoleons as the 'classical examples' of what he called *plebiscitary leadership* – leaders who gained 'the legitimation of authority by plebiscite', despite the fact that this legitimation 'took place only after they seized power by force'.[41]

Louis Napoleon was widely regarded in by the British political class as a man who restored order to France. An article in *The Times* referred to him as 'the man of our choice' who 'can most effectively consolidate the principle of authority'.[42] On numerous occasions he was cited by *The Times* as 'the representative of the principle of authority'.[43] Such a positive evaluation of a Caesarist ruler expressed a suspicion towards the workings of mass party politics and its potential for undermining order. The rule of a strong leader – preferably acclaimed through election – was perceived as the ideal guarantor of stability in the mid-nineteenth century. This outlook was clearly expressed by the English historian, James Froude, who in *Caesar: A Sketch* (1879) portrayed him as a 'genuinely

---

[40] Richter (2004) p. 100.   [41] Weber (1978) p. 267.
[42] 'The State of the Continent', *The Times*, 28 February 1849.
[43] See for example 'The State of Europe', *The Times*, 14 June 1850.

democratic leader overcoming the bungling and selfish machinations of politicians'.[44] In the early twentieth century, Max Weber would have Napoleon in mind as one of those charismatic individuals who could claim authority through a plebiscite of citizens or what he called 'Caesarist acclamation'.[45] Although initially Weber saw Caesarist influences as dangerous to public life, the political upheavals experienced by Germany in the aftermath of First World War changed his views, and by 1919 he was arguing for the virtues of a plebiscitary leader.[46]

Napoleon's use of referenda to demonstrate that his rule enjoyed the authority of popular consent followed the approach adopted by Augustus in the course of consolidating his power. In the late nineteenth and early twentieth centuries, numerous historians of antiquity were drawn towards the Augustan formula of combining imperial rule with the acclamation of popular consent. As the English historian Charles Merivale points out in his eight volume *History of the Romans Under The Empire*, 'it was the policy' of Augustus to 'rest his authority on the presumed will of the nation'. Instead of ruling as a king – 'a dictator by the authority of a privileged order' – Augustus opted for tribunitian power, which endowed his authority with the consent of the people. That is why, Merivale states, 'Augustus and his successors always carefully inscribed the tribunitian title on their coins and monuments'.[47]

Of course the Napoleonic project of constructing a myth of a modern Roman Empire pales into insignificance in comparison with Mussolini's promotion of the cult of *Il Duce*. If anyone 'performed the task of their time in Roman costume and with Roman phrases', it was Benito Mussolini. One of his many classical scholar admirers, Kenneth Scott eulogised that 'Ancient Rome had already aroused the admiration of the future leader of the blackshirts when on March 23, 1919, he assembled at Milan his first group of sixty-three men'. Scott noted how Mussolini,

called to the remembrance of his little group of ex-soldiers the symbol of the Roman power, the fasces, the staves of the lictors. He gave them the ancient Roman salute and made for them a scheme of military and political organization on the model of the old Roman legions; his Fascisti were divided into principi and triari, into maniples, centuries, cohorts, legions; and when they were marching on Rome, he made this solemn affirmation to them at Civitavecchia: 'I swear to lead our country once more in the paths of our ancient greatness.' The ideal has always remained the same, for he says, 'We represent the spirit which once carried the legions of the consuls to the farthest limits of the earth'.[48]

---

[44] Turner (1993) p. 252.   [45] Weber (1918) pp. 220–1.
[46] Kennedy (1988) p. xxii.   [47] Merivale (1896) pp. 446–7.   [48] Scott (1932) p. 645.

Mussolini's imitation of a rising Caesar was underwritten by a passionate commitment to the project of harnessing the legacy of Rome for the consolidation his authority.

Fascism is steeped in the mythology of Rome. The word's etymological root is the Latin *fasces*, meaning a 'bundle', which contained an axe. In ancient Rome, the *lictors* or bodyguards of a magistrate carried *fasces*, which thus came to serve as the symbols of power and authority. The *fasces* and other symbols of the Roman Empire were re-appropriated and prominently displayed throughout Fascist Italy. One study notes that 'fascist symbolism, as it developed in the 1920s, located the Roman legacy at its core', adding that the 'fascist imaginary which dominated Italian visual culture between 1922 and 1943 mobilised an endless array of *fasci*, eagles, Romulus and Remus she-wolves, Roman battle standards, soldiers, triumphal arches and columns'.[49] Mussolini also sought to adopt all the trappings of military authority, such as the *passo romano* (Roman march) and the Roman salute. For Scott, the rule of Mussolini represented the rebirth of a modern Augustus:

> The leader of Fascist Italy has found a parallel for our own times, it seems, in the Italy of Augustus and of the Empire, and his deeds and words are a proof of his reading of Roman history and drawing of parallels. Symbols of the past and its significance for modern Italy are everywhere in Italian life today – even on postage stamps, where we find Julius Caesar, Augustus, and the wolf of the Capitoline. Perhaps Fascist theory is correct, and the Roman Empire never really died but goes on in the New Italy and its premier.[50]

The representation of Fascist Italy as the re-founding of Rome, along with the redeployment of ancient symbols and legends, was constantly promoted to assist the construction of a foundational authority for a new order. Mussolini explained, in an interview in December 1929, that the 'entire practice of Latin virtue is here in front of me', and 'it represents a heritage which I try to make use of': a heritage whose 'nature never changes', it is 'out there, eternal – Rome'.[51] One study observes that 'from the start, fascist ideology looked back to the Roman Empire as a source of stability and tradition',[52] which was regarded as a counterweight to the chaos and disorder of inter-war Italy. From this perspective, the Roman Empire represented 'an organic and stable society, in striking contrast to the disorder and individualism represented by liberal democracy'.[53] Given Mussolini's concern with the restoration of order in inter-war Italy, it is not surprising that his psychic journey back to the Roman Empire led him to the Principate. Like other men of order, he came to model

---

[49] Stone (1999) p. 207.   [50] Scott (1932) p. 657.
[51] Cited in Gentile (1990) p. 245.   [52] Stone (1999) p. 206.   [53] Stone (1999) p. 207.

his public persona on Augustus – or at least, the fascist reinvention of Augustus.

Augustus: the personification of order

Throughout the past couple of millennia, Augustus has proved to be an ideal interlocutor for those seeking to clarify and affirm authority. As noted in the previous chapter, Augustus succeeded in re-founding the Roman state. Moreover, his success in institutionalising the authority of the state through the Principate was paralleled by his success in personifying authority. 'For the first time in Roman history, *potestas* and *auctoritas* were joined in one person' states Oakeshott.[54] His was an authority that appeared as both supreme and legitimate. But history has not always accepted the authenticity of the authoritative status of Augustus's legacy. Augustus has been denounced for his naked pursuit of power, condemned for replacing the Roman Republic with the Empire, and accused of manipulating Roman institutions to give the appearance of taking seriously the aspirations and welfare of the people.[55] Some have dismissed his claim to *auctoritas* and insist that his rule depended simply on military power and coercion.[56] Augustus has also suffered from comparisons with his adoptive father, Julius Caesar, who for many represented the heroism of Rome.

However, even Augustus's hostile critics could not entirely detract from his historic achievements. The Principate (27 BC – 284 AD) endured for over three centuries and provided an unprecedented degree of stability and prosperity for the Roman Empire. This is one reason why Augustus's reign has been frequently perceived as a Golden Age: Dante maintained that 'the world had been at its best when mankind was guided by Divus Augustus, after all a pagan emperor, under whose reign, Christ himself chose to become a man'.[57] Voltaire represented the reign of Augustus as one of the four Golden Ages of history, alongside the Ages of Pericles, Medici and Louis XIV. Subsequent rulers sought the validation of their position through an association with Augustus; so when Charlemagne was crowned Holy Roman Emperor in 800, he used the title 'Emperor and Augustus'.[58]

The reign of Augustus also enjoyed a significant degree of cultural authority. Roman literature flourished, through the work of Virgil,

---

[54] Oakeshott (2006) p. 203.
[55] For a review of some of this critical assessment of Augustus, see Carter (1983).
[56] See Mason (1965) for a discussion of Augustus's sincerity.
[57] Kantorowicz (1997) pp. 465–6.   [58] Fox (1960) p. 133.

Horace, Ovid and Livy, and veneration for the Roman Classics often coincided with an appreciation for Augustus as the patron of such great men of letters. There was a widespread belief among educated Europeans of the eighteenth century that the 'time of Augustus was the point at which Roman literature attained its fullest expression'.[59] The term 'Augustan' was often used as a 'common synonym for literary achievement', and the period 1700–1740 was referred to as the Augustan Age in Britain. According to one account, 'as a designation for a period of English literature, it was in the main, complimentary, implying a high standard of linguistic and stylistic accomplishment'.[60] During this period the term was also used to emphasise the authoritative qualities of a political ruler, with rulers such as Cromwell, Charles II and George II at various times dignified with the name of Augustus.

It is important to point out that the construction of a positive image of an Augustan Golden Age was not uncontested. The fierce eighteenth-century political struggle between Whigs and Tories led to bitter disputes about the status of Augustus. The Whigs, who dominated the press and cultivated the association of the Hanover kings with Augustus, were challenged by the Tories with an alternative representation of Augustus as a despotic, absolute monarch. Instead of serving as a term of eulogy, Tory satirists endowed the term 'Augustan' with a sense of irony.[61]

Interest in Augustus gained new momentum in the nineteenth century – a time of rapid change, institutional instability and the growing perception that the old order lacked legitimacy. Although the word 'tradition' had not yet become a pejorative term, there was a growing perception that it no longer worked to validate people's behaviour. 'In our days', wrote Tocqueville,

men see that that the constituted powers are crumbling down on every side; they see all ancient authority dying out, all ancient barriers tottering to their fall, and the judgment of the wisest is troubled at the sight . . . they imagine that mankind is about to fall into perpetual anarchy.[62]

The Principate of Augustus appeared as a heroic era of stability where tradition was celebrated and even sacralised. It could serve as a historical counterpoint to the uncertain world of a modernising Europe. In a school essay on Augustus, the 17-year-old gymnasium student Karl Marx expressed admiration for this Roman leader. He wrote that 'the greatness of Augustus, the institutions and laws of the men he selected in order to put the troubled state in a better condition, did a great deal to end

---

[59] Johnson (1958) p. 507.   [60] Johnson (1958) p. 5.   [61] Johnson (1958) p. 522.
[62] Tocqueville (1998) vol. 2, p. 314.

the disorder which had been evoked by the civil wars'. He further noted that this was an authoritative and well-ordered era, when 'arts and letters flourished', and added that Augustus should be 'held in high esteem' because although he was omnipotent, he used his power to realise 'only one aim', which was 'to ensure the safety of the state'.[63] The young Marx was expressing a widely held sentiment that Augustus was the kind of leader required to restore order through the building of a strong state.

At a time when authority and order faced serious challenge throughout the European continent, interest in the experience of Augustus began to grow. In this era Julius Caesar was frequently perceived as a heroic strong man who succeeded in putting Rome's messy house in order. According to a study of Victorian intellectual life, mid-century concern with order and disillusionment over the working of 'liberal democracy' provided the 'foundation for the Victorian apotheosis of Julius Caesar'.[64] Interest in Julius and Augustus Caesar was shared by commentators and public figures who were perturbed about the loss of authority of traditional hierarchy and felt threatened by the democratisation of public life. According to a study by the intellectual historian Frank Turner, 'mid-century authoritarian and pro-Caesar interpretations of the late Roman Republic reflected impatience with a number of contemporary political matters voiced in other contexts by various writers' in Britain. Political clashes between conflicting interests over the Corn Laws, Electoral reform and social reform led to 'intellectual criticism of the liberal state'.[65]

Around the turn of the twentieth century, interpretations of Augustus celebrated his ability to uphold imperial order and authority. These were troubled times for the British Empire and the disturbances afflicting the European overseas empires encouraged officials to look to *Pax Romana* for lessons. In 1910, H. F. Pelham, Professor of Ancient History at Oxford, expressed the dominant British view on Augustus in an entry to the eleventh edition of the *Encyclopaedia Britannica*. Pelham acclaimed Augustus as one of the world's great men, 'a statesman who conceived and carried through a scheme of political reconstruction which kept the empire together, and secured peace and tranquillity and preserved civilization for more than two centuries'.[66]

In the Edwardian Era, British commentaries on Augustus were less interested in his charismatic personality than in his role as reformer and builder of institutions. The classical scholar Evelyn Shuckburgh writes:

---

[63] Marx (1975a) pp. 641–2.   [64] Turner (1993) p. 247.   [65] Turner (1986) p. 594.
[66] Cited in Turner (1986) p. 595.

He found his world, as it seemed, on the verge of complete collapse. He evoked order out of chaos; got rid one after the other of every element of opposition; established what was practically a new form of government without too violent a breach with the past; breathed fresh meaning into old names and institutions, and could stand forth as a reformer rather than an innovator, while even those who lost most by the change were soothed into submission without glaring loss of self-respect . . . He and not Julius was the founder of the Empire, and it was to him that succeeding emperors looked back as the origin of their powers.[67]

Here was a man whose qualities served as an idealised antidote to the uncertainties facing the early twentieth-century Empire. According to Shuckburgh's verdict, Augustus not only consolidated and renovated the old institutions of Rome but also laid the foundation for the power of subsequent emperors. For Shuckburgh it was this man of order rather than Julius who succeeded in providing a solution to the problem of authority.

While in the British context, Augustus could be reinterpreted as an effective administrator who got on with the job of efficiently running the Empire, in continental Europe he was increasingly acclaimed as an authoritative charismatic leader who was able to uphold law and order and curb the excesses of popular democracy. It was in the aftermath of the First World War, when revolution and the disintegration of the old older accentuated the dramatic erosion of political authority, that the new authoritarian political movements reached out to Augustus. According to the Italian political philosopher Giorgio Agamben, it was at this point in time that Europe saw the 'rediscovery of the concept' of *auctoritas*.[68] Authoritarian intellectuals embraced this concept and reinterpreted it as a form of unbounded personal/dictatorial power. Writing in this vein in 1939, the German legal historian Leopold Wenger remarked that *auctoritas* 'that is, the fundamental concept of public law in our modern authoritarian states, can only be understood – not only literally but also as regards the content – starting from Roman law of the time of the principate'.[69] From this standpoint Augustus embodies an extreme form of personal authority not unlike those of the 'total' dictators of the inter-war period.

The rediscovery of *auctoritas* by anti-liberal authoritarian movements was influenced by a political agenda that sought to develop an ideological critique of parliamentary democracy. This movement was hostile to liberal democracy and claimed that effective authority was rooted in the personality of the leader rather than in popular consent. They

[67] Cited in Turner (1986) p. 597.   [68] Agamben (2005) p. 81.
[69] Cited in Agamben (2005) p. 81.

conceptualised *auctoritas* in a way that made it indistinguishable from power. One of the most systematic advocates of this cult of the leader, the German political philosopher Carl Schmitt insisted that what counted was the right to 'command'.[70] Weber's sociology of domination expressed this sentiment in a more muted form. But as Melvin Richter, a historian of ideas, reminds us, 'the Bonapartist dictatorship originated in the seizure of power by military violence did not, in Weber's view affect its legitimacy'.[71]

Agamben argues that 'to understand modern phenomena such as the Fascist *Duce* and the Nazi *Führer*, it is important not to forget their continuity with the principle of the *auctoritas principis*'.[72] Whether there is indeed a continuity between the Augustan Principate and the twentieth-century authoritarian state is a matter of debate. However, what is evident is that the opponents of liberal democracy did seek to reinterpret *auctoritas* as an authoritarian principle that could justify personal dictatorial rule. Augustus was presented as a prototype of the modern authoritarian leader whose authority was personal and based on his capacity to express the will of the people. Inter-war authoritarian thinkers seized on an interpretation which personalised the authority of Augustus and recast his *auctoritas* in the totalitarian form of the cult of the leader.[73]

A tradition turned into a myth

The resurrection of Augustus as the heroic precursor of fascist Italy represents the zenith of the mythologising of the tradition of the Principate. Although at the time the revival of Rome was perceived as the rebirth of a classical form of imperial authority, it can also be seen as a symptom of a desperate attempt to plunder the Roman past for its authoritative cultural resources.

Even before the emergence of fascism, Italian nationalists had sought to define their identity through the legacy of Rome. The unification of Italy in 1861 gave impetus to the growth of nationalist ideology. An important component of this ideology was a renewed interest and celebration of the Roman past. Guglielmo Ferrero's *Greatness and Decline of Rome* (1907) praised 'the pacifier Augustus, who is able gradually by cleverness and infinite patience to re-establish peace and order in the troubled empire'.[74] During the years of the *Risorgimento*, the cultivation of the values, ideals

---

[70] Schmitt (2008) p. 55.   [71] Richter (1982) p. 211.   [72] Agamben (2005) p. 84.
[73] 'The authority of the *doctor* or the *Fuhrer* can never be derivative but is always originary and springs from his person'. See Agamben (2005) pp. 84–5.
[74] Carter (1983) p. 12.

and symbols of Rome was transformed into an ideology that is described as the 'cult of Romanita'.[75]

The promotion of Italian national identity, and particularly the advocacy of its imperial ambitions through the cult of Romanita, was widely communicated through literature and popular culture. Parallels were frequently drawn between the expansion of the Roman Empire and the legitimacy of modern Italy's ambition for possessing colonies in Africa. An illustration of this form of Romanita propaganda is Enrico Guazzoni's 1913 film *Marcantonion e Cleopatria*, in which Octavian's triumph over the tyranny of Cleopatra communicates a 'founding myth of Western culture'. In her analysis of this film, Maria Wyke draws attention of the final shot, of 'Octavian high up beneath a statue of winged Victory, standing and saluting the cheering crowd', on which image is imposed the Latin motto '*Ave Roma Immortalis*' (Hail Rome the Eternal City).[76] Wyke concludes that if 'Rome is indeed eternal, then the cinematic language of justification for Octavian's conquest of Egypt can easily translate into a justification for and celebration of the more recent conquest of Libya' – from this perspective, Italian imperialism is 'doing nothing less than carrying on the civilising mission of Augustus Caesar'.[77] From the launch of his fascist movement, Mussolini's rhetoric was devoted towards a celebration of Romanita, and sought to present his era as the direct successor of the Roman Empire. He wrote:

For the Italian people all is eternal and contemporary. For us it is as if Caesar was stabbed just yesterday. It is something proper to the Italian people, something which no other people have to the same extent.[78]

In effect, as Melograni states, the 'the myth of Romanita, was able to find unrestrained expression' during Mussolini's regime.[79]

The mythical, quasi-religious calling of Mussolini's Romanita expressed a self-conscious attempt to share in the glories of the past. 'Rome is our guiding star; it is our symbol – or if you prefer, our myth', he declared in April 1922.[80] Part of the myth was Mussolini's attempt to project himself as a new Augustus, and the high point of the mobilisation and the performance of this myth was celebration of the bi-millennium in 1938 of the birth of the Emperor of Augustus.

An exhibition titled the *Monstra augustea della romanita* provided a focus this celebration. Visitors began their journey in rooms devoted to the foundation of Rome. Maps of Aeneas's travels, drawn according to Virgil's *Aeneid*, greeted the visitors, and other exhibits displayed key

[75] See Visser (1992).   [76] Wyke (1999) p. 199.   [77] Wyke (1999) p. 199.
[78] Nelis (2007) p. 396.   [79] Melograni (1976) p. 229.   [80] Melograni (1976) p. 245.

moments in Rome's history, culminating in a very detailed presentation of the accomplishments of Augustus. As one study of this exhibition argues, 'this creation of mythical history was key not only to Augustus, but to Mussolini as well', since the show provided a 'legendary background for fascism so that Mussolini, too would appear as "divinely appointed"'.[81] According to another account, 'in 1938 when the Augustan Exhibition of Romanita was opened the official orator, a professor of the day, let it be understood that in Mussolini were summed up the gifts of both Caesar and Augustus: of the one who had subdued disintegrating factions and the other who had founded the empire'.[82]

This year-long exhibition depicted the Italian fascist state as the glorious culmination of a millennia-old adventure that began with the founding of Rome. In effect this exhibition 'transformed the contemporary Fascist empire under Mussolini into the modern day incarnation of Augustus' empire'. A statement from Mussolini at the entrance stated, 'Italians, make certain that the glories of the past are surpassed by those of the future'.[83]

Authority as myth

As we shall see in our discussion of the crisis of nineteenth-century order, the turn of the quest for foundational authority towards mythology was a relatively hesitant response to the early growth of mass society. In the nineteenth century the politicisation of mythology existed in a relatively underdeveloped form. However, with the breakdown of the old order in Europe following the First World War, the legitimacy enjoyed by constitutional democracy diminished in many parts of the continent. In this context, the self-conscious politicisation of myths, such as that of Augustus, should be interpreted as evidence of the exhaustion of both pre- and post-Enlightenment foundational norms, leading to an increasing tendency literally to construct myths around which political communities could be forged.

Liberals, Conservatives, Royalists, Socialists and Communists were all preoccupied with gaining authority for their social and political outlook. Some looked to the restoration of the monarchy, others to religion or traditionalism, while still others claimed that reason or science of popular consent was the true foundation for a legitimate political order. Fascism was sufficiently modernist to understand that society could not 'return' to tradition or religion. But it also felt uneasy with the consequences of

---

[81] Lewine (2008) pp. 7–8.   [82] Melograni (1976) p. 229.   [83] Stone (1999) p. 214.

the process of rationalisation, to the point where it regarded the authority of science and reason with suspicion. It was the French philosopher Georges Sorel who gave the most consistent expression to the radical anti-rationalist impulse of the inter-war era. Sorel claimed that a civilisation based on myths was superior to the materialist rational culture that prevailed in Europe, and regarded myths as possessing a great power to motivate people. At a time when politics appeared to have reached an impasse, Sorel's emphasis on the will to act appeared to some as a positive alternative to paralysis, and his myth of violence and struggle succeeded in attracting intellectuals looking for radical solutions.[84] Sorel was not so much interested in elaborating a content for myth as in popularising the *idea* of myth: what was important about the myth was its unleashing of an emotional and volitional drive, which could give a group cohesion and a common will.[85]

Since Sorel's myth lacked any specific content, the idea of fighting for a myth could appeal to a politically heterogeneous audience. The Hungarian Marxist philosopher Georg Lukács remarked that 'Sorel's myth was so exclusively emotional, so empty of meaning that it could pass without difficulty into the demagogically exploited myth of fascism'.[86] However, the myth through which fascists sought to project a symbolic foundation for the constitution of a community was no more meaningful than that of Sorel. What was important about a myth was precisely the quality that Lukàcs decried – its emotional power. In a speech given in Naples in October 1922, Mussolini represented myth as a form of passion:

We have created our myth. The myth is a faith, it is passion. It is not necessary that it shall be a reality. It is a reality by the fact that it is a good, a hope, a faith, that it is courage. Our myth is the Nation, our myth is the greatness of the Nation! And to this myth, to this grandeur, that we wish to translate into a complete reality, we subordinate all the rest.[87]

Carl Schmitt regarded this speech as the first significant political affirmation of the authority of the myth. Referring to this speech, Schmitt stated 'until now the democracy of mankind and parliamentarism has only once been contemptuously pushed aside through the conscious appeal to myth, and that was an example of the irrational power of the myth'. He added that the 'theory of the myth' offered the potential for establishing an 'authority based on new feeling for order, discipline, and hierarchy'.[88]

[84] See discussion in Sternhell (2010) pp. 330–6.
[85] See discussion on Sorel in Sabine (1961) pp. 717–18.
[86] Lukàcs (1980) p. 32.   [87] Cited in Finer (1935) p. 218.
[88] Schmitt (1988) pp. 75–6.

Mussolini believed that myths possessed the capacity for unleashing action and passion. In a lecture titled 'The Political Doctrine of Fascism', Mussolini's Minister of Justice, Alfredo Rocco argued that 'fascism is, above all, action and sentiment and such it must continue to be'.[89] Rocco along with Mussolini and other fascist thinkers hoped that through the projection of a myth of historical destiny a foundation for authority could be forged. 'For fascism, the life of society overlaps the existence of individuals and projects itself into the succeeding generations through centuries and millennia,' stated Rocco.[90] Thus through the process of generational transfer, the past gains the immediacy of the present. In this way, continuity with the traditions of the Roman Empire constituted the guiding myth of Fascist Italy. According to this myth, the high point of human history was the Roman Empire which was followed by a protracted period of disintegration and, after the French Revolution, liberal decadence. 'If Fascism can be said to look back at all it is rather in the direction of ancient Rome whose social and political traditions at the distance of fifteen centuries are being revived by Fascist Italy', explained Rocco.[91] One of the key messages communicated through the myth of Rome was the pre-eminence of the authority of the state.

The principal driving force of the fascist myth was the project of constructing a viable form of authority. Preoccupation with its loss encouraged an obsessive impulse to recast authority as a force that stands in its own right. From this perspective – the power to compel, which is how authority was perceived – became a virtue in its own right, and the fascist future was depicted as the era of authority. Rocco prophesises that the 'period of authority, of social obligations, of "hierarchical" subordination will succeed the period of individualism, of state feebleness, of insubordination'.[92] In effect, Rocco's forecast for the future recast authority into a myth about authority and order. However, the abstract idea of authority needed to be given shape and meaning, in order to resonate with the Italian public. This was accomplished through the myth of the cult of the leader. What counted was the personal qualities of great leaders rather than popular sovereignty or the rule of law: 'natural intelligence' was required, but 'still more valuable perhaps is the intuitiveness of rare great minds, their traditionalism and their inherited qualities', explained Rocco.[93] In a sense, what this myth of the great leaders expressed was an extreme form of personal *auctoritas*. According to this mythologisation of authority, authority is not simply personal but actually comes from the person.

---

[89] Rocco (1926) p. 10.   [90] Rocco (1926) pp. 18–9.   [91] Rocco (1926) p. 24.
[92] Rocco (1926) p. 23.   [93] Rocco (1926) p. 21.

Unlike Weber, who tried to reconcile charismatic leadership with the continuation of some form of parliamentary democracy, fascist ideologues had no hesitation about negating the values of democratic accountability and popular sovereignty. What they took from Rome was not so much Augustus, the consummate political operator, but the idea of an omnipotent dictator. Adopting this approach, Schmitt developed the concept of a sovereign dictatorship that was based on the 'traditional role played by the Roman commissarial dictators'.[94] As Galinsky commented, 'on the Continent there was adulation and more as Augustus emerged as the prototypal *Fuhrer* and *duce*'.[95]

The adulation directed at Augustus by authoritarian right-wing activists invited anti-fascist scholars to present a mirror-image of this Roman leader as a brutal and cynical tyrant. Few questioned the myth of Augustus constructed by authoritarian and fascist writers. Ronald Syme's 1930s classic, *The Roman Revolution*, betrays the political preoccupations of its author, with chapter titles such as 'First March on Rome' indicating how the establishment of the Principate was interpreted from the vantage point of 1930s Europe. Accordingly, Augustus is depicted as a dishonest 1930s dictator who is hiding his power behind a veil of mystification:

The convenient revival of republican institutions, the assumption of special title, the change in the definition of authority, all that made no difference to the source and facts of power. Domination is never the less effective for being veiled.[96]

Syme directly called into question Augustus's claim to *auctoritas*, which 'his enemies would have called ... *potentia*' – 'and they were right'.[97] In other words what Augustus possessed was not authority but *potential* – power or force. In this way, the premise of Mussolini's myth of Augustus as a precursor of totalitarian dictatorship was accepted though criticised.

In the inter-war period, the politicisation of the myth of Augustus encouraged a partisan historiography of Rome. Very few were prepared to adopt a nuanced multi-dimensional interpretation of the man. One exception was American classic scholar, Dorrance White, who took exception to Mussolini's rewriting of the history of the Principate. In response to Mussolini's aggressive militaristic philosophy, White asked, 'Does this modern Roman think that he is expressing the sentiment of his more illustrious ancestors?'; 'does he think that this *bellum Romanum* is a worthy match of the *pax Romana* instituted by the great Caesar Augustus?' White argued that Mussolini's exaltation of foreign aggression and

---

[94] See Cristi (1997) p. 193.   [95] Galinksy (1996) p. 3.
[96] Syme (2002) p. 3.   [97] Syme (2002) p. 3.

war had little in common with Augustus: 'It is a matter of history that the foreign policy of Octavian Augustus was one of extreme conservatism'.[98] However, in the highly charged political climate of the 1930s, polarised views about the new Roman Empire made it difficult to have a detached conversation about Augustus.

The triumph of charisma

The one person who did not have much of a conversation with Augustus was Max Weber. Weber's writings refer to Augustus surprisingly rarely, given his pursuit of a historical-sociological investigation of the problem of authority. His study of authority also drew him to the problem of leadership, and from around 1910 onwards he became particularly interested in the potential of charismatic leadership for dealing with the problem of order.[99] Weber defined charisma as 'a certain quality of an individual personality, by virtue of which he is considered extraordinary and treated as endowed with supernatural, superhuman or at least specifically exceptional powers or qualities'.[100] If anyone, Augustus, whose very name conveyed a divine quality and who came to symbolise an imperial cult, can be seen as a personification of charisma.

The most important reference that Weber makes to Augustus is in his discussion of 'The Genesis and Transformation of Charismatic Authority'. It is in context of the routinisation of charismatic authority that Weber draws attention to one of Augustus's most significant achievements: the institutionalisation of impersonal authority through the Principate. Weber does not deal directly with the emergence of Augustus's charismatic authority, but the possession of this form of authority is assumed when he writes:

To have established the principate as an office was the achievement of Augustus, whose reform appeared to contemporaries as the preservation and restoration of Roman tradition and liberty, in contrast to the notion of a Hellenistic monarchy that was probably on Caesear's mind.[101]

In fact Weber's idea of charismatic authority overlaps with the Roman conception of *auctioritas*. So when Weber discusses the charismatic features of an 'extraordinary man', he implicitly touches on that person's *auctoritas*.

According to a study of Augustus's charisma, 'there was no "objective fact" involved in Octavian's rise to power': he 'inherited the title

[98] White (1936) pp. 466 and 475.   [99] See Adair-Toteff (2005) p. 191.
[100] Weber (1978) p. 241.   [101] Weber (1978) p. 1125.

Divi filius and used his own personal charisma, combined with the critical circumstances of the time, to bring about an irreversible change in Roman government'.[102] Here the term charisma refers to attributes that Augustus would have defined as his *auctoritas*. While Augustus's authority was not reducible to his personal attributes, his prestige and influence strengthened his claim to supreme authority. The concept of *auctoritas* expresses many dimensions of authoritative rule and should not be seen as merely a Roman version of charisma. As Galinsky contends, 'Augustus's leadership was not simply "charismatic" but was defined in terms of traditional virtues'.[103]

It is likely that Weber's charisma represents a reconceptualisation of the previous notions of Bonapartism or Caesarism. As Beetham states, the underlying assumptions of the Weberian category of charisma were 'already a commonplace of political text books under the more specifically political label of "Caesarism", a category developed to characterize the Bonapartist regimes'.[104] Despite its claim to value neutrality, this category is fundamentally a political concept which conveys the positive qualities of the charismatic leader. Weber's writings on charisma draw on the nineteenth-century German theologian, Rudolf Sohm, who was concerned with the problem of order and regarded charismatic authority as an antidote to popular sovereignty.[105]

One reason it is puzzling that Weber did not engage in a dialogue with Augustus is because of his fascination with the charismatic authority of great leaders. In his political writings, Weber expressed a lack of faith in the capacity of rationally devised rules to influence and inspire the public, and emphasised the charismatic and inspirational potential of leaders to legitimate order.[106] In Weber's theory, charisma, 'in some shape or form', had become 'the source of all authority'.[107] As McIntosh stated, charisma for 'Weber is the legitimating principle behind any authority'.[108]

Weber sought to bypass the problem of foundational authority by opting for the personal authority of the leader. From this perspective,

---

[102] Edwards (2003) p. 4.

[103] Galinksy (1996) p. 80. Weber would have been aware of the complexity of the authority of this Roman leader. Augustus' principate can lay a claim to be associated with all three of Weber's ideal types of legitimate domination. A man of charisma, a restorer and preserver of tradition, he also succeeded in institutionalising a form impersonal office – the principate.

[104] See Beetham (1977) p. 177. This point is also echoed by Baehr P. (1999).

[105] See Smith (1988) p. 38.

[106] Weber's 1919 lecture 'The Profession and Vocation of Politics' clearly shows this preoccupation. See Weber (1919), especially pp. 312–13.

[107] Baehr (1998) p. 248.   [108] McIntosh (1970) p. 909.

legitimation becomes a fragile episode associated with the acclamation of the leader. He wrote that:

Regardless of how its real value as an expression of the popular will may be regarded, the plebiscite has been the specific means of deriving the legitimacy of authority from the confidence of the ruled, even though the voluntary nature of such confidence is only formal or fictitious.[109]

Drawing on the widely held nineteenth-century interpretation of Bonapartism or Caesarism, Weber stated that 'plebiscitary democracy – the most important type *Führer-Demokratie* – is a variant of charismatic authority, which hides behind a legitimacy that is *formally* derived from the will of the governed'. Weber had no inhibitions about endorsing legitimation gained through manipulation. Such authority was underwritten by the emotional bond between the ruled and the individual ruler. Drawing on the examples of Gracchus, Cromwell, the two Napoleons and Robespierre, he concluded that 'it is characteristic of the *Führerdemokratie* that there should in general be a highly emotional type of devotion to and trust in the leader'.[110]

Whatever Weber's intentions, his writings on charismatic leadership were interpreted by some of his followers as a prescription for the political malaise afflicting inter-war Europe. The leader capable of developing an emotional bond with the masses was projected as possessing the will to overcome political *stasis*. While Weber presented charisma as a neutral category, his follower, the sociologist Roberto Michels, depicted it as a positive attribute of leadership, using this to justify his conversion to Mussolini in 1922.[111] Unlike Weber, Michels naturalised the idea that people need leaders, and cited with approval Rousseau's statement that it is 'against natural order that the great number should govern and that the few should be governed'.[112] Michels extolled Mussolini's charisma, writing that when 'Mussolini speaks, he translates in a naked and brilliant form the aims of the multitude', and 'the multitude itself frantically acclaims, answering from the profundity of its own moral beliefs, or even more profound, of its own subconscious'.[113]

Carried away by what he perceived as charisma-in-action, Roberto Michels wrote about the virtues of the charismatic dictator:

The charismatic leader does not abdicate, not even when water reaches to his throat. Precisely in his readiness to die lie one element of his force and triumph. He will abdicate only when he is seized from within by extreme bitterness and repugnance: in such a case it means he has lost his charisma. For the charismatic

---

[109] Weber (1978) p. 267.   [110] Weber (1978) p. 266.   [111] Mommsen (1981) p. 115.
[112] Michels (1927) p. 760.   [113] Michels (1965) p. 126.

leader does not beseech the multitude; rather, when occasion arises, he will know how to chastise it, and he takes for granted, in his mission, the adaptability of the masses to his plans.[114]

For Michels, the capacity to contain and discipline the masses expresses the main virtue of charismatic authority. His celebration of the arbitrary dictatorial powers indicates that in the eyes of many, the fascist leaders of inter-war era were the true embodiment of charismatic authority; and that is why many sociologists in the inter-war period saw the rise of dictators as a vindication of Weber's idea of charisma.

It is worth recalling that Weber's most important American populariser, Talcott Parsons, interpreted the rise of fascism and of political instability the 1930s and 1940s as analogous to the problem of order faced by Weber in the early twentieth century. He wrote that Weber's 'sociology of authority' can 'when applied to the present situation, make a most important contribution to the understanding of the deeper nature of the crisis in which we have become involved'.[115] Parsons regarded Weber's theory of authority as an attempt to account for its feeble state in the inter-war era. In particular, Parsons regarded Weber's concept of charisma as relevant for understanding the rise of fascist parties. For example he characterised the Nazi movement 'as anti-traditional "charismatic" movement', which was 'peculiarly dependent on success to maintain its internal prestige'.[116]

Through an authoritarian (mis)interpretation, the Roman idea of *auctoritas* was transformed into an unbounded idea of charisma. The concept both described and, in some cases, justified the emergence of a twentieth-century Augustus. Agamben pointed to the links that brought together otherwise unconnected strands, noting that although 'there cannot be some sort of eternal human type periodically embodied in Augustus, Napoleon, or Hitler', nevertheless 'the power that Weber called "charismatic" was linked in 1930s Germany (and elsewhere) to the concept of *auctoritas* and elaborated in a theory of *Führertum* as the originary and personal power of the leader'.[117]

The authoritarian anti-liberal project of constructing a mythical foundation for authority became far too discredited to survive World War Two. After the 'age of dictators', Western societies became weary of charismatic authority, at least in its overt dictatorial form. At least temporarily the conversation with Rome was suspended.

---

[114] Michels (1965) p. 130.   [115] Parsons (1942b) p. 166.
[116] Parsons (1954) p. 251.   [117] Agamben (2005) p. 84.

5   Medieval authority and the
       Investiture Contest

The disintegration of Roman civilisation in the fifth century had a devastating impact on European societies. Warfare and instability were endemic between 500 and 1000 AD, and economic, urban and intellectual life declined and stagnated. Constant military incursions by Germanic tribes unleashed a process of political and institutional disintegration. The unified system of administration institutionalised during the Roman Empire gave way to fragmentation and a highly unstable form of rule. In the absence of a recognised ethos of authority, no stable institutions of governance emerged to provide a focus for cultural unity. Latin Christianity was the only institution that could contain or at least minimise the tendency towards political fragmentation. The Church itself lacked unity and it took centuries for the establishment of an effective papal monarchy which could serve as a focus for spiritual unity. The Pope served as figurehead of a medieval Europe that shared a common religion.

One of the principal questions confronting Europe in the Early Middle Ages, traditionally described as the Dark Ages, was how to establish and give meaning to authority. As Oakeshott states, the 'problem of government was how to impose and maintain the rudiments of law and order in a world in which the *Pax Romana* had been destroyed . . . [and] in which a single, recognized "law of territory" had not yet emerged'.[1] The Church of Rome sought to claim authority on the grounds that it was responsible for the spiritual guidance of Christendom. Although the Church was militarily weak, the 'Popes were enormously influential as custodians of ideational bonds that continued to hold medieval society (*populous christianus*) together'.[2] Despite the absence of order, medieval Christian culture could draw upon the legacy of the past, and possessed an idealised version of how authority worked in previous times.

The defining feature of medieval authority was the idea of divided lordship. As one detailed study of this historical epoch observed, the principle 'that human society was controlled by two authorities, a spiritual

---

[1] Oakeshott (2006) p. 257.   [2] Damaska (1985) p. 1813.

95

as well as a temporal, represents the development of what is one of the most characteristic differences between the ancient and the modern world'.[3] The development of a dual system of authority occurred through the emergence of the Christian Church in a pagan Roman Empire. The early Christian Church could make claims on its congregation but not over the others members of society, and thus developed a sense of separation from the public institutions of Rome. This claim to a limited or differentiated jurisdiction was far more restrained than the authority proclaimed by Augustus, who presented himself as the possessor of a multi-dimensional authority – *imperium*, *auctoritas* – and also a protector of Rome's religious tradition. Unlike other religions, Christianity accepted what sociologist Talcott Parsons has characterised as a 'fundamental *differentiation* between church and state'.[4]

One consequence of the differentiation of society into a spiritual and temporal sphere was that Christianity was prepared to provide a '*relative legitimation of the temporal*' so long as it lived up to the Greco-Roman standards of natural law. Even with the ascendancy of Christianity and its focus on gaining universal adherence to the Church, the differentiation between the two spheres persisted after the fall of the Roman Empire. All that changed was that the Church now looked to the temporal ruler to play the role of a Christian monarch.[5] So the initial differentiation between the (Christian) spiritual and the (Pagan) temporal jurisdictions turned into the institutionalisation of dual spheres within Christianity itself.

In medieval doctrine, Christendom was represented as consisting of two distinct jurisdictions – the *sacerdorium*, or priesthood; and the *imperium*, or empire. This principle was spelled out by Pope Gelasius I in 494, when he told the Emperor Anastasius I that,

> The world is chiefly governed by these two: the sacred authority of bishops and the royal power. Of these the burden of the priests is greater in so far as they will answer to the Lord for the kings of men themselves at the divine judgment. For you know, most merciful son, that although you rule over the human race in dignity, you nevertheless devoutly bow the neck to those who are placed in charge of religious matters and seek from them the means of your salvation; and you understand that, according to the order of religion, in what concerns the receiving and correct administering of the heavenly sacraments you must subject rather than command.[6]

When Gelasius wrote of the emperor's duty to submit to the 'sacred authority of bishops' in religious matters, his main emphasis was on

---

[3] Carlyle and Carlyle (1957a) p. viii.   [4] Parsons (1963a) pp. 42–3.
[5] Parsons (1963a) p. 43.   [6] Cited in Robinson (1991) pp. 288–9.

limiting the priestly ambitions of the emperor.[7] His aim was not the political subordination of temporal power to a theocratic pope, but the affirmation of the papacy's moral authority over the empire. Gelasius's view was implicitly rejected by the Christian Roman Emperor Justinian (482c–565), who established a clear legal distinction between *imperium* and *sacredotium*. And unlike Gelasisus, Justinian 'saw the emperor as uniting in himself not only the supreme temporal power (*imperium*) but also the highest spiritual power (*sacerdotium*)'.[8]

The tension between the formulas adopted by Gelasius and Justinian would influence developments for centuries to come; but on balance it was the former whose views prevailed over the medieval conceptualisation of the relation between the two spheres. According to this political theology, ecclesiastical and temporal hierarchies 'coexisted within the same territory and claimed allegiance from the same persons'.[9] This was a system based on institutional independence but an allegiance to a shared Christian doctrine. The tension – creative and destructive – between these two jurisdictions was to play a significant role in influencing the elaboration of medieval ideas about authority.

Under the shadow of Rome

Despite the fall of the Roman Empire, its legacy continued to have a significant impact on the cultural and political life of medieval Europe. Latin served as the language of European intellectual discourse and legal and religious thought. 'With the language, that medieval Europe acquired from Rome was a past-relationship with a Roman civilization' which supplied people with the intellectual legacy through which they 'came to understand themselves'. The influence of this legacy is demonstrated by the fact that even for the recently arrived Germanic migrant tribes, their newly 'acquired past-relationship with Rome became far more important than their relationship with their own past'.[10] Rome provided both the foundation and the model for the dominant institutions of medieval Europe. This durable appeal of the Roman past to medieval Europe underlines the historic significance of the culture of authority established by this civilisation.

The survival and continuing appeal of Roman universal ideals was assisted by the absence of any territorially based interests opposed to them. Territorial fragmentation provided a geopolitical and cultural context for the reception of the ideal of imperial unity. It was not until the

---

[7] See Markus (1991) p. 102.   [8] Stein (1991) p. 46.
[9] Damaska (1985) p. 1813.   [10] Oakeshott (2006) p. 253.

emergence of relatively powerful and coherent territorial units in the late fourteenth and early fifteenth centuries that the authoritative status of universalism would be challenged.

The application of the customs and traditions of the past always involves an element of reinterpretation and innovation. As Canning notes, although the political ideas of the ancient world 'conditioned the development of those of the Middle Ages', the process of assimilation was 'a highly complex one involving reinterpretation and innovation as these ideas were applied in the context of medieval conditions radically different to those of ancient times'.[11] Important elements of the Roman legacy were reinterpreted in a Christian form. The conversion of the Roman Empire to Christianity was paralleled by the assimilation of Roman cultural and institutional practices into Christianity. As Ullmann indicates, the Bible and pagan Roman law could 'effortlessly penetrate into the very matrix of the rapidly growing Christian doctrinal body'.[12] This process involved 'infusing the very language, substance and method of Roman law into Christian ideology', so 'at the cradle of what later became known [as] Christian dogma stood the Roman law, swiftly to become part and parcel of Christianity itself'.[13] In effect, the 'fundamental trusteeship' of the classical heritage was 'built into the basic structure of the Christian church itself and in a Christian form' was 'rediffused into the secular world'.[14]

'In basic Christian thinking, the Roman Empire as the secular order of the world had never ceased to exist,' states Talcott Parsons. The idealisation of this Empire as the symbol of universal order led to the construction of a Christian variant, the *Holy* Roman Empire. After the crowning of Charlemagne as Holy Roman Emperor in 800, the Empire offered the 'normative framework of a universal Christian society'.[15] Although the Holy Roman Empire rarely acquired a serious geopolitical reality, it possessed great symbolic significance.

The Roman Empire provided an inspiration for the medieval European ruling and educated classes. At a time of confusion and instability, an aspiration for the certainties of tradition and continuity found its locus in ancient Rome. For the medieval mind, Rome came to constitute a central dimension of the European traditionalist sensibility. Writing before the outbreak of the First World War, the historian Alexander Carlyle noted that 'we can without difficulty recognize' not only 'the survival of the tradition of the ancient empire' but also a 'form of the perpetual aspiration to make real the dream of the universal commonwealth of

---

[11] Canning (1996) p. 1.   [12] Ullmann (1975) p. 32.   [13] Ullmann (1975) p. 33.
[14] Parsons (1963a) p. 47.   [15] Parsons (1963a) p. 47.

humanity'.[16] The literature of this period resonates with testimonies to the glory of Rome; and it was the aspiration for universal community and peace that inspired the Italian humanist poet, Dante (1265–1321) to look forward to the rebirth of the Roman Empire as heralding a new golden age. One of the central themes of his *Divine Comedy* is the 'longing for the restoration of a universal empire, and its necessity for the attainment of human happiness'.[17]

In part, Dante's enthusiasm for the Empire was motivated by the hope that this institution could contain what he perceived to be the destructive consequences of papal ambitions in Italy. But Dante's work, particularly his treatise *Monarchia*, was not simply an anti-theocratic text directed against papal theocracy. Living in a divided Italy and facing the threat of papal expansionism, Dante saw 'no hope for peace except in the unity of the empire and under the all-embracing authority of emperor'.[18] For Dante, monarchy or the empire represented the foundation for the exercise of enlightened authority, signifying 'the command directing all other commands, the jurisdiction embracing and authorizing all other jurisdictions, the will uniting all other wills'. For Dante, the 'primary meaning' of empire was 'universal authority'.[19]

Dante's writing also expresses an idealisation of the Roman era as a golden age that established the normative standards for the conduct of a good life. Dante's idealisation of the Roman *imperium*, particularly as it was perfected by Augustus, rested 'primarily on memory and desire, memory of an alleged golden age under Augustus, a universal peace' that he believed 'existed only once in history'. It was also motivated by a 'desire for a savior, evidently a new Augustus, who would restore this unique and vanished order to the modern world'.[20] In Dante's thought, Rome's successes were represented as the outcome of divine providence. Dante closely followed Virgil's *Aeneid* narrative, which has Jupiter saying, 'To them I have given empire without end'.[21] The idea of an empire without end provided Dante and his co-thinkers with a sense of continuity and permanence that lent Rome a sacred character. As Davis remarks, 'Dante's sacralising of Roman history continues with his exposition of the theory that the legitimacy of Rome's rule was affirmed by both Christ's registration in the Roman census under Augustus and his execution at the hands of the Roman governor Pilate under Tiberius'.[22]

Dante argued that society required a 'single directing will' and in order to 'keep the subordinate societies at peace, imperial authority is

---

[16] Carlyle (1913) p. 1.   [17] See Davis (2007) p. 258.   [18] Sabine (1961) p. 257.
[19] Davis (2007) p. 258.   [20] Davis (2007) p. 263.   [21] Cited in Davis (2007) p. 261.
[22] Davis (2007) p. 267.

essential'.[23] But of course imperial authority in the way it was exercised in *Pax Romana* did not exist in medieval Europe. Dante's absorption with a world that was lost represented an attempt to transcend the problems confronting his era. In this respect, he was very much the product of his time: as Swanson points out, the 'theorising about the political implications of the Roman past was both impressive and fundamental, but there was one major weakness: it concerned a lost world'.[24] The conceptual vocabulary derived from Rome, which dominated medieval intellectual thought, necessarily possessed an abstract character. The German legal historian Franz Wieacker noted that, in the Early Middle Ages, 'Western civilization was still incapable of expressing its own identity and ideals; it was restricted to assimilating disparate antique elements'.[25]

The abstract quality of medieval discourse was particularly evident in relation to the discussion of empire. Although the idea of the Holy Roman Empire existed in some form or another from the time of Charlemagne's assumption of the title *imperator augustus* in 800, it bore little relationship to the imperial entity that served as its model. Nevertheless the legacy of Roman *imperium* was sufficiently robust to continue to inspire the medieval imagination. Roman law and the idea of empire survived in the sense of the 'soul of a man might survive the body'.[26]

The Church self-consciously modelled its own claim to authority on the Roman experience. The claim to universal authority by the Papacy was often represented as the continuation of the traditions of the Roman *imperium*, and the Roman tradition 'was critical for the Church because every essence of its self-identity derived from the past'.[27] As Oakeshott contends,

Here, as in so many other respects, the Christian church in the West reflected the beliefs of the ancient Romans: the pope in respect of doctrine was like an emperor, who had succeeded to the *auctoritas* of the senate; the general council of the church itself corresponding to the senate.[28]

Through claiming an authority that derived from God through St Peter, the Pope often sought to assert his *auctoritas* not only over the spiritual but also over temporal rulers. The church played an important role in reviving the idea of empire: it took the initiative in the crowning of Charlemagne as Holy Roman Emperor, and in 875, Pope John crowned Charles the Bald, an act that emphasised the unique authority of the Pope. Canning

---

[23] Davis (2007) p. 261.   [24] Swanson (1999) p. 99.   [25] Wieacker (1981) p. 272.
[26] Berman (1983) p. 7.   [27] Swanson (1999) p. 98.   [28] Oakeshott (2006) p. 274.

notes that for the first time, 'the pope took the initiative as the sole, constitutive creator of the emperor'.[29]

The influence of Rome's legacy actually increased during the so-called twelfth-century Renaissance, when Europe experienced a period of cultural and commercial revival. The recovery and study of the Justinian Code had a significant impact on political and intellectual life and was widely interpreted as the definitive source of legal authority. Reflections on the past were oriented towards providing the newly emerging medieval political entities with the authorisation of the ancient world. In line with this trend, there was an explosion of interest in reviving the foundational myths of Rome. The Trojan Wars were widely discussed and following the path outlined by Virgil, medieval writers showed an interest in tracing national origins. A belief in the continuity of the Roman imperial tradition was linked to the assumption that even imperial power might be reactivated.[30]

The flourishing of Roman law in the twelfth century was testimony to its unusually influential character as a source of authority: although the very fact that so much cultural and political capital was invested in the legacy of Rome can be interpreted as a symptom of the insecurity of Medieval Europe's own self-awareness. However, with the rise of canon law in the eleventh century, medieval Europe was beginning to gradually reinterpret the legacy of the past and to develop its own idea of authority. Western civilisation was gradually beginning to mature 'to the point where it was capable of congenial and creative confrontation with the legacy of Roman classical jurisprudence, because it had created its own theological philosophy and political ideology'.[31] By the twelfth and thirteenth centuries it had become evident that a distinctly medieval interpretation of the past influenced society. Despite the association of this era with superstition and dogma, medieval Europe was continually in the business of developing new interpretations of authority. Thus it is difficult to disagree with the observation that 'the political experience of medieval Europe is an experience of continuous inventiveness and improvisation'.[32]

The self-conscious construction of authority that evolved in ancient Rome provided an important political and cultural legacy for medieval Europe. From a sociological point of view, the legacy of Rome served as a warrant for claims-making.[33] A warrant authorises claims for some form of recognition or entitlement, and in its capacity as a form of a

[29] Canning (1996) p. 72.   [30] Swanson (1999) p. 86.
[31] Wieacker (1981) p. 272.   [32] Oakeshott (2006) p. 264.
[33] On the concept of claims-making see Best (1999) p. 164.

foundational statement, a warrant certifies the authority of a claim or an argument.[34] In effect, when institutions and individuals sought to validate a claim for authority, particularly for one that was new, they drew on the warrant provided by antiquities, especially Rome. For example, from the eighth to the eleventh centuries the papacy sought to justify its claim for supreme authority by 'insisting on the continued presence of St Peter' in Rome.[35] Such claims-making activity involved a constant search for precedents, and the formulation of new arguments. It also sometimes involved the literal construction of customs and precedents that could serve as warrants for authority.

Thus the claim that the papacy held exclusive and supreme authority above all the churches of the world was frequently justified through appealing to the *Constitutum Constantini*, known as the 'Donation of Constantine'. This document, forged in the eighth century, claimed that the Emperor Constantine had donated the Western Roman Empire to the Church. In the centuries to follow, the document served as a warrant for monarchical interpretation of the papacy; and consequently, at times, the 'Roman pontiff was represented as a Caesar and the College of Cardinals was remodelled after the ancient Senate'.[36] The forgery served to justify the papal claim to possess not only spiritual but also imperial authority. Through appealing to the Donation of Constantine, Pope Gregory VII (1015c–1085) could claim that the 'pope alone can use the imperial insignia'.[37]

Dictatus Papae

One of the most interesting documents in the history of claiming medieval authority is the *Dictatus Papae* (Dictates of the Pope) of Pope Gregory VII, drawn up around 1075. The significance of this papal statement for the historical sociology of authority is comparable to Augustus's *Res Gestae*. Although its authenticity has been questioned, the weight of opinion 'attributes it to Gregory VII and regards it as probably a private memorandum'.[38] Whatever its provenance, this document can be interpreted as a comprehensive list of prerogatives claimed by the papacy. Consisting of 27 claims, the *Dictatus Papae* expressed the aspiration to establish the supremacy of papal authority, advancing an unambiguous claim to a form of universal authority that trumped that of temporal lords and kings. It insisted that the Pope was above all rulers and that he could

---

[34] See the discussion in Toulmin (2008) pp. 91–3.   [35] Robinson (1991) p. 279.
[36] Luscombe (1991) p. 169.   [37] Robinson (1991) p. 281.
[38] See Lewis (1954a) p. 380.

not be judged by anyone. Moreover it proclaimed that the Pope's 'decisions ought to be reviewed by no one, and that he alone can review the decisions of everyone'. In this memorandum, Gregory VII also claimed that the papacy possessed doctrinal infallibility. He declared that the 'Roman church has never erred nor will ever err, as the Scripture bears witness'.[39]

Dictatus Papae left little to chance. The memorandum included the claim that the 'Roman bishop alone is by right called universal', and by implication asserted possession of universal authority. As the Pope, Gregory declared that he had the right to judge secular rulers and could 'depose emperors'. This statement also contends that in effect the Pope is the source of new laws, for 'him alone is permitted' the right to 'make new laws according to the needs of the times'. This papal memorandum constituted an explicit attack on prevailing temporal authority and political arrangements. Its most radical claim was that the Pope has the right to dissolve the customary bonds of loyalty between lord and vassal, stating that 'he may absolve subjects of unjust men from their [oath of] fealty'.

The implications of this claim were far-reaching, for in assuming the power to release vassals of their obligations to their lords, the papacy directly threatened the status of temporal authority. Aside from the assertion of such formidable powers, the *Dictatus Papae* also focused on the Pope's symbolic authority, stating that 'the Pope alone is the one whose feet are to be kissed by all princes', and that 'no chapter or book may be regarded as canonical without his authority'.[40]

Unlike Augustus's *Res Gestae*, the *Dictatus Papae* was not a testimony based upon an individual ruler's record of achievement. It was a wish-list for power and authority that lacked precedent in the medieval experience. The division of the old Roman Empire between Rome and Constantinople provided the basis for the division between emperor and papacy, but the division of the government of Christendom between the temporal and the spiritual did not endow the papacy with the authority claimed by Gregory. Indeed, when the Pope crowned Charlemagne as the Holy Roman Emperor in 800, it was evident that the secular ruler was the dominant figure. Prior to the tenth century, 'neither clergy nor laity questioned that it was royal responsibility to direct the church in creedal, liturgical and administrative matters'.[41]

As a ritual, the crowning of Charlemagne symbolised the ambiguity of shared lordship. The head of the church legitimated secular authority and, in return, Charlemagne accepted his obligation to rule on the basis

[39] This document is reproduced in Lewis (1954a) pp. 380–1.
[40] Berman (1983) p. 96.   [41] Garrett (1987) p. 5.

of shared Christian values.[42] Charlemagne was not simply a political ruler but a Christian monarch. Moreover, in temporal affairs he was the Emperor – with powers superior to the Pope.

The demands of the *Dictatus Papae* are striking in their aspirational quality. The memorandum proclaimed adherence to a form of authority not yet recognised. It is worth noting that when the document was written, 'the control of the emperor over the papacy was more conspicuous and effective' than the other way around,[43] and this memorandum in effect demanded a 'massive shift in power and authority both within the church and in the relations between church and secular polities'.[44] Gregory depicted kings and princes as laymen who could be deposed by the Pope. Through desacralising the status of temporal rulers he called into the question the validity of the prevailing traditions of rule, which were based on the premise that secular princes were invested with not just political but also spiritual authority. According to custom, such temporal rulers were defenders of the Church and played an active role in the religious institutions of their territory. Until this point, the two jurisdictions were 'thoroughly intermingled'. As Strayer recounts, 'Kings had been considered semi-religious personages and had extensive influence in Church affairs', while at the same time, 'bishops played an important role in secular affairs, as advisors to kings, as administrators, as rulers of ecclesiastical principalities'.[45]

Gregory's project was to ensure that temporal power was, to use McCready's term, 'despiritualised'.[46] By attempting to divest temporal rulers of their spiritual mission, Gregory was going against the grain of established custom. His determination to challenge custom represented a radical departure from the prevailing conventions, and for this reason the legal scholar Harold Berman concludes that Gregory's 'document was revolutionary'. Berman goes so far as to argue that, at least implicitly, this revolutionary document sought to abolish 'the previous political and legal order'.[47]

The Gregorian reforms can be seen as an attempt to deprive secular rulers of spiritual authority. In previous centuries, the differentiation of church from society co-existed with the belief that this dualism was essentially within the same ecclesia. Consequently, 'the king was a member of the *ordo clericalis*, or, in the terminology applied to Charlemagne, *rex et sacredos*'.[48] Gregory's aim was to widen the prevailing differentiation between the two jurisdictions and alter its meaning. The motive for this

---

[42] Parsons (1963a) p. 43.   [43] Sabine (1961) p. 227.   [44] Berman (1983) p. 100.
[45] Strayer (1970) pp. 20–1.   [46] McCready (1973) p. 662.
[47] Berman (1983) p. 104.   [48] Leithart (2003) p. 11.

policy was to ensure that the Church was protected from the attempt by temporal rulers to interfere in ecclesiastical matters.

Although many of the claims made in this memorandum represented a radical departure from the prevailing traditions and authority relations, Gregory 'ultimately managed to find some legal authority for every one of its provisions'.[49] His self-conscious construction of supreme papal authority was paralleled by a systematic attempt to elaborate an authoritative foundation for papal supremacy. One important outcome of this project was to unleash an unprecedented era of claims-making about the source of authority. These activities touched on the origins of authority, the legacy of Rome and of Christianity, and the source and meaning of law. Moreover, his quest for the legitimation of supreme papal authority provoked secular rulers to search the ancient texts for arguments with which to fight what they perceived to be an attempt to usurp their power. This conflict, known as the Investiture Contest (1075–1122), initiated a political struggle and debate that was to last for half a century. It also played a crucial role in the development of the medieval conceptualisation of authority.

The Investiture Contest

In the early middle ages, lords and princes possessed considerable power in the appointment of the clergy, including bishops. The lay investiture of appointments within the church was based on a tradition that originated in a ceremony in which the lord transferred land to his vassal in exchange for an oath of loyalty. The adoption of a similar ceremony at the installation of a bishop was testimony to the influence of feudal custom on the rituals of ecclesiastical appointments: it 'encouraged greater loyalty to the local lord than to the pope or to the Church as a universal communion'.[50] Such an arrangement promoted a tendency towards the regionalisation of the clergy and therefore threatened the integrity of the Church. That is why the ceremony, whereby the king or his representative handed the newly installed bishop the insignia of his new office, was resented by supporters of the so-called papal party, who regarded it as a threat to the integrity of the institution of the Church.

It is likely that the practice of lay investiture was not so much the cause but served as the pretext for the conflict. In his analysis of this conflict, the historian Zachary Brooke contends that the real question at stake was a 'struggle for supremacy' between 'the heads of the secular and ecclesiastical' jurisdictions, with 'each side claiming that its power derived from

---

[49] Berman (1983) p. 96.   [50] Wilken (1999) p. 27.

God and that it has the right to judge and depose the other, while itself subject to no human judgement but to god alone'. Brooke states that if this disagreement about who possessed supreme authority had been settled so would 'all minor issues such as lay investiture' – which apparently the Pope barely mentioned 'save for a brief reference' in a letter to the German King Henry IV in December 1075.[51] Brooke's analysis appears to correspond to the unfolding of events during Gregory's papacy. At the outset of his reign, Gregory appeared to be reconciled to accepting this practice, but in the course of attempting to assert his authority, he began to focus on challenging this outward symbol of secular influence over ecclesiastical appointments. It was two years after acceding to the papal throne before he issued a decree prohibiting this lay investiture.

Gregory's hostility to lay investiture was motivated by the wider objective of eliminating secular political influence over church appointments and thus protecting its institutional independence. It was the project of reforming the church through centralising the authority of the papacy that drove Gregory to challenge the prevailing traditions of authority. Before his election as Pope in 1073, Gregory had been concerned with the fragmentation of ecclesiastical organisation along the lines of existing fiefdoms and political jurisdictions, and to counter this trend strove to contain what he perceived as secular interference in the management of ecclesiastical affairs. Moreover, Gregory believed that it was secular authority, particularly in the Empire and in France, that stood in the way of Church reform.[52] Hence this conflict can be seen as a result of 'an increased self-consciousness and sense of independence on the part of churchmen and in a desire to make the church an autonomous spiritual power'.[53]

Initially the German King Henry IV, who hoped that Gregory would crown him as the Holy Roman Emperor, sought to defuse the conflict. But matters came to a head when Henry IV attempted to consecrate his nominee, the newly appointed bishop of Milan. Gregory responded by accusing Henry of disobeying not only the Pope but also God's will, and threatened him with excommunication and deposition unless he accepted the decree on lay investiture. Gregory's threat to depose a king was without precedent. Until this point it was widely accepted that medieval rulers possessed both a spiritual as well as a political role, and were regarded as the supreme leaders of their community, not as the political inferiors of the Pope. In this context the call to abolish lay investiture represented a radical reconceptualisation of relations of authority. Gregory not only

---

[51] Brooke (1964) p. 26.   [52] See Carlyle and Carlyle (1962) p. 388.
[53] Sabine (1961) p. 231.

sought to divest kings of their spiritual authority but also to reduce them to a status that was politically subservient.

Not surprisingly, Henry IV responded to Gregory's attack by mobilising his own supporters. In January 1076, at the assembly in Worms, Henry and a group of German and Northern Italian bishops called for the abdication of the Pope. For his part, Henry denounced Gregory as a 'false monk' who had incited rebellion against properly appointed prelates, and urged the Pope to resign from his office. In turn Gregory responded by excommunicating Henry and his ecclesiastical supporters and declared that the king was deposed.[54] While he lacked the power actually to depose the king, he succeeded in undermining his support among the German princes. This objective was accomplished through absolving Henry's vassals from their feudal oaths, thereby providing the moral and ideological justification for German princes to rebel against the king. It also struck at the confidence of the King's own bases of support. Many of these supporters were concerned about the consequences of being excommunicated from the Church and demanded that the King seek absolution from the Pope.

Facing a rebellion by a powerful alliance of German Princes and isolation from his ecclesiastical supporters, Henry had little choice but to ask for forgiveness. At a famous encounter in the northern Italian town of Canossa, Henry was forced to stand barefoot in the snow for three days, waiting for Gregory to respond to his plea. In effect, by 'coming to Canossa and submitting to Gregory, Henry acknowledged the Pope's right to judge kings'.[55]

The Investiture conflict of the eleventh and twelfth centuries indicated that Pope Gelasius's fifth-century division of the world into secular and spiritual spheres was far too vague to avoid conflict between these two powers. Gelasius's doctrine of the two swords – the co-existence of temporal and spiritual authorities – became an integral part of the received wisdom of the early Middle Ages. But although the idea of a society guided by a dual authority made sense in the abstract, it did not deal with the practical problem of managing the tension between two competing hierarchies.

For its part the papacy was continually testing how far it could expand its influence. It had always assumed that its moral authority was far greater than that of secular rulers: Gelasius himself stated that although the world is ruled by two great powers, the authority of the pontiffs is far greater than that of kings since 'they must give account to God of

---

[54] For an account of this conflict see Wilken (1999) and Williams (1964).
[55] Wilken (1999) p. 31.

the souls of Kings'.[56] This formulation of the primacy of ecclesiastical moral authority led to a 'logical extension of existing papal governmental claims'.[57] By the late twelfth century, theocratic claims-making accelerated and papal claims to authority over temporal matters became less and less restrained. Innocent III claimed that royal power itself 'derives from pontifical authority'.[58] This radical claim can be seen as an expansion of the arguments formulated by Gregory. The Investiture crisis represented a crucial moment in the unfolding of the drama of a contest of authority. As one study states, 'the controversy in the eleventh and twelfth centuries served to show the instability and vagueness of the relation between the temporal and spiritual powers in the Gelasian tradition'.[59]

In retrospect, it is evident that the ill-defined boundary between the two jurisdictions always contained the potential for transforming an uneasy and unstable balance of power into an overt conflict. In this instance the conflict was precipitated by the determination of the church to gain greater autonomy and greater institutional independence. The pursuit of institutional autonomy necessitated the systematic elaboration of the church's claim to authority. However, in the very act of affirming the greatness of the Church's authority, Gregory could not help but draw a sharp moral contrast with that of secular power. The superior moral status of the Church's authority was clearly spelled out by Gregory during his speech to a council in Rome in 1080:

So act, I beg you, holy fathers and princes, that all the world may know that, if you have power to bind and loose in Heaven, you have power on earth to take away or to grant empires, kingdoms, principalities, dukedoms, marches, counties, and the possessions of all men according to their merits . . . Let kings and all the princes of the world learn how great you are and what power you have and let these small men fear to disobey the command of your church.[60]

This statement clearly expressed the spirit of papal supremacy that was codified in the *Dictatus Papae*. The claim to possess the power to 'take away or to grant empires' represented an explicit challenge to the status of imperial authority. What has been described by Harold Berman as the Papal Revolution inexorably led to the elaboration of a doctrine that justified the subordination of secular rule to the moral authority of the Church.

The response of Henry IV and his supporters was to reiterate the validity of traditional customs and the accepted doctrine, which was that the power of a king was derived directly from God and that God alone

---

[56] Cited in Kamen (1976) p. 15.   [57] Canning (1996) p. 35.
[58] Canning (1996) p. 36.   [59] Sabine (1961) p. 242.
[60] Cited in Carlyle and Carlyle (1962) p. 201.

could judge a monarch.[61] This was a defensive position that attempted to validate the imperial position on the basis of tradition and custom. The papacy, too, claimed that its campaign to reform the Church was based on tradition. However, Gregory's elaboration of papal authority ought to be seen as a self-conscious attempt both to use and reinterpret traditional custom and doctrine. Consequently, as one historian remarked, 'in the struggle which ensued the monarchists were the conservative, the Gregorians the revolutionary party'.[62] 'Like all revolutionaries he convinced himself that he was only restoring the old law; but the principles he enunciated fell like a bombshell on the traditional thought of the age, which they challenged at every turn', writes Barraclough.[63] There is little doubt that the project of negating prevailing customs with older traditions represented a radical form of innovation. However, what is particularly fascinating about Gregory's reinterpretation of tradition is the self-conscious manner with which he tackled the problem. He was by no means the first person to reinterpret custom and tradition; but he also sought to subordinate custom to what he perceived to be an even more important source of authority which was the Truth – that is, the doctrinal authority of the teaching of the Church.

Although Gregory sought carefully to validate his claims with the authority of precedent, he was also prepared to demand the right to overturn unjust custom. Responding to a letter from Wimund, the bishop of Aversa, who criticised him for overstepping the traditional authority of the papacy, Gregory wrote: 'Christ did not say "I am custom" but "I am truth"'. This aphorism, originally associated with the early church fathers Tertullian and St Cyprian, was applied by Gregory in a radically new fashion. Gregory had not only called into question the status of custom, but also of traditions that had evolved in the Christian era.[64] In claiming a warrant for pronouncing the Truth, Gregory endowed the papacy with unprecedented authority to judge all other powers and jurisdictions.

The *Dictatus Papae* provided a radically new orientation towards the law. Until the late eleventh century the law was perceived as a legacy that could be reaffirmed, reinterpreted and very occasionally revised. Gregory asserted, 'for the first time the power of the pope to "create new laws in accordance with the needs of the times"'. These new laws – decretals – were not represented as 'simply incremental additions to the pre-existing canons but as something new'.[65] One legal scholar argues

---

[61] See discussion in Carlyle and Carlyle (1962) p. 186.   [62] Barraclough (1964) p. 62.
[63] Barraclough (1964) p. 56.   [64] See the discussion in Wilken (1999).
[65] Berman (1983) p. 202.

that the legal revolution initiated by the Investiture Contest created a crisis for the customary system of feudal Europe.[66]

Richard Southern characterises the Investiture Contest as 'the first major dispute in modern history'.[67] At least in outline, this contest resembles the kind of ideological debates and conflicts that are far more characteristic of the modern era. The Gregorian offensive initiated a process whereby some of the most fundamental traditions of medieval society were put to question. Probably the single most contentious issue raised by Gregory was the claim that he had 'the authority to free subjects from their oaths of allegiance and depose kings'. As Canning remarks, 'the papacy was here on its most insecure ground and its claims most shocking', and 'fundamental questions concerning obedience to authority and the justifiability of rebellion were at issue'.[68]

The numerous claims made in *Dictatus Papae* forced medieval society to respond and find new ways of justifying competing claims. It initiated a public debate about the nature of authority. Both sides of the debate sought to undermine each other's authority, and through calling into question the status of each other they ensured that very few of the prevailing assumptions would remain beyond question. Although the parallel powers of temporal and spiritual were universally accepted, the relation between them became a permanent subject of controversy. As Walter Ullmann, one of the leading authorities on this era, observes, 'the issues of the Investiture Contest had brought into the open problems which had not been perceived before'. As a result, the 'unquestioned assumptions upon which society and government rested came to be questioned and scrutinized'.[69]

The debate surrounding the Investiture Contest had repercussions throughout European society. For the first time in the history of the West, an attempt was made to 'enlist public opinion on either side, and a war of treatises and pamphlets was carried out in which the most fundamental questions concerning the relation of Church and state and the right of resistance to unjust authority were discussed exhaustively'.[70] This point is also echoed by Ullmann, who writes of a 'deliberate attempt to create and shape and influence public opinion', adding:

'Political' literature as such became part of public life; it was an instrument by which the warring parties appealed to larger sections of the populace. It was the first time in European history that literature had been put to this use, and it has never lost this function... This literature, aiming as it did at broad sections of the public, is rightly called publicistic – in pamphlets, tracts and monographs it

---

[66] Van Caenegem (1981) p. 22.   [67] Southern (1967) p. 129.
[68] Canning (1996) p. 105.   [69] Ullmann (1975) p. 245.   [70] Dawson (1964) p. 53.

pursued the intention of moulding public opinion by a severe scholarly analysis of governmental matters . . . every statement and assertion had to be supported by 'authority'. The more ancient 'authority' the greater its weight.[71]

Ullmann's reference to the importance of validating competing statements with 'authority', particularly that of ancient authority, reminds us that this Europe-wide public dispute was about the nature of foundational authority and the source of medieval authority.

But the Investiture Contest was also a struggle about *whose* authority would prevail. The Papal Revolution challenged secular rulers throughout Europe. Almost a century after Gregory's death, Thomas Beckett challenged King Henry II's authority, which was exercised through the upholding of old customs, and claimed that Truth should prevail over custom. Although Henry managed to get rid of Becket, he was forced to make significant concessions to the authority of the Pope.[72] According to Strayer's interpretation, kings 'lost their semi-ecclesiastical character and some of their control over Church appointments'. From this perspective, the Gregorian reformers had won a 'partial victory'.[73]

Elsewhere the Investiture Contest led to unexpected outcomes. It created a space for the northern Italian cities to weaken the control of both the German Emperor and the papacy over their affairs, allowing them to acquire new legislative power and develop a form of authority that was at least indirectly based on public consent.

The Investiture Contest also stimulated the evolution of medieval kingdoms. The papal campaign against the authority of the Emperor encouraged the emergence of new territorially based political units. It was in the context of the 'territorial consolidation and institutional maturation of medieval kingdoms' that feudal ideas about the people consenting to be ruled emerged. Ideas about the popular basis of authority were crystallised in the Italian communes, but it is important to recall that the medieval idea of consent was a very limited one: 'little more than the rationalization of a hierarchic construction of power and some check against its abuse'.[74] Max Weber argued that 'the separation of state and church in the wake of the Investiture Struggle' led to the withdrawal of the clergy from administrative institutions of Venice, and their eventual replacement by a 'salaried lay officialdom' – a kind of secular bureaucracy that would constitute the backbone of the yet-to-emerge nation state.[75] Clearly, the claims formulated by Gregory in the *Dictatus Papae* continued to have both a moral and a practical significance in the centuries to follow.

[71] Ullmann (1975) p. 245.   [72] See Brooke (1928).   [73] Strayer (1970) pp. 21–2.
[74] Lewis (1954) p. 158.   [75] Weber (1978) p. 1272.

Sociological reflections on the meaning of the Investiture Contest

Medieval Europe was continually preoccupied with the fragility of authoritative institutions, and consequently drawn towards constructing, elaborating and innovating ideas about authority. All the main disputes, including the Investiture Contest, were expressions of the impulse to seek a resolution to this problem. 'Twelfth-century political thought was preoccupied with the legitimacy of political institutions and of governing authority' states one study of this period.[76] Nor did the outcome of the Investiture Contest resolve this problem. Throughout the medieval era, the relationship between religious and secular institutions was one of tension; but it was a form of tension that contained the potential for both conflict and harmony.

This tension was immanent in the uneasy relationship between spiritual and temporal authority, and expressed through a ceaseless attempt to assert, claim and contest authority. As a result, every assertion of supreme authority was challenged by counter-claims. In this period many of the arguments about authority from the past were rehearsed and elaborated. At the same time arguments that would be raised in centuries to come were raised in a hesitant and tentative form.

Weber's sociology of domination drew on his extensive study of the medieval era, and his analysis of the conflict between what he characterised as hierocratic and caesaropapist power. According to Weber, a 'hierocractic organization' like the papacy is an organization that enforces its order through psychic coercion by distributing or denying religious benefits ('hierocratic coercion'). He added that a 'compulsory hierocratic organization will be called a "church" insofar as its administrative staff claims a monopoly of the legitimate use of hierocratic coercion'.[77] Once that monopoly is questioned, its capacity to work as 'system of spiritual domination over human beings' becomes compromised. The 'extreme opposite' of any kind of hierocracy, Weber characterised as caesaropapism, which is 'the complete subordination of priestly to secular power'.[78] Both of these concepts attempted to capture a trend towards the assumption of spiritual authority. In this epoch, a close association with the will of God as expressed through Christian doctrine was essential for the legitimation of all forms of authority.

Weber's concepts of hierocracy and caesaropapism do not correspond to the modern contrast between religious and secular authority. Indeed, caesaropapist rulers attempted to position themselves as possessing some

---

[76] Benson (1991) p. 339.   [77] Weber (1978) p. 54.   [78] Weber (1978) p. 1161.

form of power over ecclesiastical affairs. English and German kings, who adopted the role of head of church, expressed an aspiration to dominate ecclesiastical affairs in their own country; and during the Investiture Contest, it was the monarch's influence over ecclesiastical appointments that was one of the principal targets of the papal revolution. During the decades following the end of the Investiture Contest, Frederick I assumed that his role as Holy Roman Emperor gave him 'supreme jurisdiction over the ecclesiastical body'.[79] Throughout Europe, kings sought to sacralise their authority through practising rituals of healing. That was why, in 1081, Pope Gregory VII's letter to Herman bishop of Mainz justifying the excommunication of Henry IV, 'stripped emperors of any magic'.[80]

Although the medieval church 'tried to minimize the sacerdotal function of the monarchy', it could not dispense with 'the act of consecration itself'. This coronation ceremony 'not only put the final stamp of legitimation on the rulers and formally inaugurated the reign, but it was also held to convey certain magical properties to the person of the ruler notably the power to cure scrofula, the "King's evil" by the laying on of hands'.[81] The Royal Touch, whereby a pious king laid his hands on people suffering from scrofula, was widely practised by European monarchs;[82] the practice was abandoned in England in 1714, and continued in France for a further century.

As the experience of the Gregorian reform movement indicated, a hierocracy has a tendency to attempt to subordinate secular power to itself. At the very least a hierocracy needs to possess and assert moral authority over secular rulers. That is why, as Weber explained, a 'hierocracy must forestall the rise of secular powers capable of emancipating themselves'.[83] Drawing on the experience of the medieval era, Weber concluded that a hierocratic power seeks to 'degrade' political authority. The Gregorian reform movement attempted at times to 'negate completely' the religious claims of political power, but it was not 'permanently successful' in the realisation of this project.[84]

The inconclusive outcome of the Investiture Contest was, to a considerable extent, the inevitable consequence of the structural interdependence between the protagonists. The differentiation of the two spheres and their independent jurisdiction was underpinned by a common set of values and norms that tended to mediate the intensity of conflict. Moreover, in the medieval era, the relationship between the two powers was not only of conflict but also of interdependence. So alongside the

---

[79] Canning (1996) p. 95.   [80] Barlow (1980) p. 14.   [81] Zaller (1998) pp. 757–8.
[82] See Huntington (2007) and Barlow (1980).   [83] Weber (1978) p. 1160.
[84] Weber (1978) p. 1162.

tendency towards conflict is a perceptible tendency to compromise. The medieval Church found it expedient to compromise with secular rulers in order secure some of its interests and defend itself from its religious opponents. The 'political power can offer exceedingly valuable support to the hierocracy by providing the *branchium saeculare* for the annihilation of heretics and the exaction of taxes', wrote Weber.[85] In turn, medieval rulers were dependent on the Church for endowing their power with moral authority. Weber contends that as 'a legitimating power hierocracy is almost indispensable even (and especially) to the caesaropapist ruler', and that the hierocracy is the most effective institution for 'domesticating the subjects in things great and little', helping secure 'internal control'.[86]

Despite the temporary victories scored at the expense of the other power, conflicts like the Investiture Contest usually result in a stalemate. Weber concluded that:

> It is very rare that the antagonism between political and hierocratic power finds simple solution in the full victory of one side or the other. The history of all churches demonstrates that even the most powerful hierocracy is continuously forced to compromise with economic and political realities; and in general, the caesaropapist ruler cannot afford to intervene into question of dogma and even less, of sacred rites. For every change in the ritual endangers its magic efficacy, and thus mobilizes all the interests of the subjects against the ruler.[87]

The tendency towards compromise should not obscure the underlying and irresolvable tension between the two powers. Indeed, one of the most significant features of medieval Europe was the strength and durability of the conflict between temporal and spiritual power.

The Investiture Contest played an important role in deepening the differentiation between the two powers. In the period that followed, as Parsons noted, the 'differentiation of the church *from* secular society has become more clearly marked'.[88] The institutionalisation of the differentiation of the medieval world is one of the distinct features of Western socio-cultural development. The historian Brian Tierney characterises this 'unusual duality of structure' as the 'most obviously distinctive feature' of medieval society.[89] For Weber, the differentiation of society into two independent spheres represented a significant contrast with the workings of other cultures. He wrote that 'at least from a sociological viewpoint, the Occidental Middle Ages were much less of a *unified culture* than those of other societies', and was particularly struck by the remarkable tendency to contest authority. His statement 'in the Occident authority

---

[85] Weber (1978) *Branchium saeculare* (Translates as secular branch), p. 1175.
[86] Weber (1978) p. 1176.   [87] Weber (1978) p. 1174.
[88] Parsons (1963a) p. 49.   [89] Tierney (1982) p. 10.

was set against authority, legitimacy against legitimacy' can be interpreted as, in part, a conclusion based on an assessment of the conflicts surrounding the Investiture Contest.[90]

The differentiation of the two spheres was underwritten by Christian doctrine, which placed great emphasis on the Church's institutional autonomy and moral authority. This led to the development of what has been described as 'Christian dimension of authority', which, based on the separation of the Church from temporal rule, introduced a 'source of authority independent of political power'.[91] The very institutionalisation of Church independence created an actual or potential source of alternative authority to that of the feudal ruler.

In the long run the consolidation of the idea of an authority that was independent of political power served to contain the absolutist tendencies of medieval monarchs. One influential study of the Middle Ages concludes that dualism and the belief that 'life on its spiritual side is not subject to the temporal authority, but independent of it' provided the foundation of a 'new conception of liberty'.[92] This point was echoed in the nineteenth century by Lord Acton, who stated that to the conflict between the two powers 'we owe the rise of civil liberty'.[93] Weber echoed this point when he remarked that the requirement to obey God and his worldly representatives has 'been the most ancient check on all political power'.[94] It may be reading history backwards to link the emergence of the modern idea of liberty directly to the medieval theory of divided lordship. However, there is little doubt that this dualism served to restrain the power of the ruler. Tierney points out that there was 'never one structure of government presided over by an unchallenged theocratic head', but two powers, 'always jealous of each other's authority always preventing medieval society from congealing into a single monolithic theocracy'.[95] The conflict immanent in the division of power served to restrain the tendency towards the consolidation of absolutist power.

The contest between the papacy and temporal rulers did not exhaust the possible configuration of conflicts. As the Investiture Crisis indicated, neither side could rely on the unquestioning loyalty of the members of their jurisdiction. Internal disputes were endemic within the two hierarchies; feudal barons were happy to gain the backing of the papacy for their rebellion against their king, and many ambitious bishops sought to evade papal centralisation. During the Investiture Contest the papacy provided arguments for the German feudal princes against the idea that

---

[90] Weber (1978) p. 1193.   [91] See Krieger (1968) p. 146.
[92] Carlyle and Carlyle (1957a) p. 385.   [93] Cited in Tierney (1982) p. 10.
[94] Weber (1978) p. 1175.   [95] Tierney (1982) p. 10.

royal power should be hereditary. At the assembly in Forcheim in March 1077, where a group of Saxon and South German princes elected Rudolf, Duke of Swabia, as king of the Germans, there was a self-conscious 'repudiation of the hereditary nature of kingship'. This sentiment would lead to the elaboration of the idea that the princes possessed a right to choose their own king 'unfettered by any tradition of hereditary succession'.[96] In effect, the German princes who challenged Henry VI implicitly claimed that their consent, through an election, constituted the source of royal authority – a claim that also implicitly questioned the Gregorian conception 'which claimed the role of judge for the Church, and in particular the pope'. Thus, alongside assertions of papal and imperial supremacy were claims that depicted consent as a source of authority.

Another unintended consequence of this conflict was the emancipation of the north-Italian city-states, which were able to manoeuvre to win important concessions, including the right to legislate.[97] While the papacy encouraged Italian city-states and feudal rulers to assert their independence from the Henry IV, the imperial party helped local clergy to resist the imposition of centralised power by the Pope. In turn, many bishops supported temporal rulers in order to preserve local church autonomy.[98]

Possibly the most important unintended consequence of the papal revolution was that it forced secular leaders to set about the task of constructing an independent form of secular authority. Gregory's project of desacralising kings and his claim that the Pope had the right to depose them 'left emperors and kings with no basis for legitimacy'. At the time of the Investiture Contest, the idea of a secular kingship without any ecclesiastical role had not yet been born.[99] Commenting on the dilemma facing temporal power, the German historian Wilhelm Komel stated that the Investiture Contest was:

expressly a struggle for the correct understanding of the *regimen christianum*, or, in any case, this was what it necessarily led to in its consequences. It was of decisive significance for the relationship between *regnum* and *sacerdotium*. It reduced the civil power to its secular essence, namely a *gladius materialis*, in order to deprive it of the ecclesiastical prerogative of lay investiture.[100]

In the short run, the reduction of civil power to its secular essence would be resisted by temporal rulers; but in the long run it forced them to elaborate a secular political theory that would legitimate their authority. Moreover, as papal arguments became increasingly audacious in claiming

---

[96] Robinson (1979) pp. 721–4.   [97] See Van Caenegem (1981) p. 22.
[98] Lewis (1954a) p. 359.   [99] Berman (1983) p. 98.
[100] Cited in McCready (1973) p. 662.

supreme authority, they moved beyond matters spiritual and acquired a political form. 'The supreme irony of this development was that it helped prepare the way for the emancipation of political theory from its servitude to theology' asserts Wolin.[101] So the strategy of despiritualising civil authority forced temporal rulers to elaborate a political theory that was independent of church influence. Paradoxically, the pursuit of Church independence would in the end result in the autonomy of the political.

Some accounts of the consequences of the Investiture Contest go so far as to suggest that it 'prepared the way' for the emergence of the modern state. According to Joseph Strayer:

> By asserting its unique character, by separating itself so clearly from lay governments, the Church unwittingly sharpened concepts about the nature of secular authority. Definitions and arguments might vary, but the most ardent Gregorian had to admit that the Church could not perform all political functions, that lay rulers were necessary and had a sphere in which they should operate. They might be subject to the guidance and correction of the Church, but they were not a part of the administrative structure of the Church. They headed another kind of organisation, for which there was as yet no generic term. In short the Gregorian concept of the Church almost demanded the invention of the concept of the State. It demanded it so strongly that modern writers find it exceedingly difficult to avoid describing the Investiture Conflict as a struggle of Church and State.[102]

From a sociological perspective the main significance of the Gregorian reform movement was that it forced temporal authority to account for itself in terms that can be best described as secular and political. Ironically, through the pursuit of institutional independence and spiritual supremacy, the Church created the conditions for the emergence of secular institutions: a process of institutional differentiation that would, eventually, effectively negate the authority of the papacy.

The (rationalising) and universalising impulse

The Investiture Contest represents an important historical moment in both the contestation and the construction of authority. One important legacy of this conflict was that it accelerated the tendency to elaborate legal rules and procedures for supporting authoritative claims. Until the late eleventh and early twelfth centuries, the legal form was virtually indistinguishable from tradition and custom and, as Berman states, 'law was not consciously systematised'. The Gregorian revolution played a central role in the evolution of a new legal tradition,[103] which was principally

---

[101] Wolin (2004) p. 125.   [102] Strayer (1970) p. 22.   [103] Berman (1983) p. 50.

fuelled by the aspiration of the Church to establish a 'legal identity independent of emperors, kings and feudal lords'.[104] As Weber noted, one of the outcomes of the Investiture Contest was to establish the foundation for the 'separation of state and church'.[105]

One of the most significant legacies of the Gregorian reform movement was the consolidation of the dualism of medieval social life. The aim of this movement was to remove secular influence over ecclesiastical affairs and to separate layman from the clergy. 'When Gregory defrocked the emperor and other political leaders, he removed most of the laity's remaining priestly vestments and confirmed the clerical monopolization of "real" priesthood,' concludes Leithart.[106] Talcott Parsons took the view that it was the reform programme associated with the Cluniac order and led by Gregory VII that was responsible for the 'firm establishment of the principle that priesthood was an office with powers and authority clearly separable from the person of the individual incumbent, or any particularistic network of relationships in which he might be involved', and argued that these reforms 'served to consolidate and extend the independence of the church from secular influences'.[107]

From the available evidence it appears that it was the imperative of institutional autonomy that encouraged the rationalisation of the Church. Although caesaropapism –'the complete subordination of priestly to secular power' – has never existed in a pure form, it acquired a significant degree of influence during the Carolingian Empire (800–888).[108] In this period 'theocratic notions were deliberately fostered by the monarchy as part of its programme for legitimising and consolidating the power of the dynasty'.[109] But even in the later medieval era, kings tended to claim spiritual powers and express theocratic aspirations. Such theocratic ambitions were contained by the Church through assuming responsibility for king-making through administrating inauguration rituals – anointing and crowning the king. Through the act of unction, the Church asserted its spiritual authority and, by the eleventh century, felt sufficiently confident to go a step further and develop its own institutional autonomy. It was through the establishment of its independent administrative organisation that the church succeeded in countering 'caesarpapist tendencies'.[110]

The consolidation of institutional independence was underwritten by the reform movement's conception of a priesthood as an office with powers and authority clearly separable from the person of the individual incumbent, or any parochial or family relationship in which he

---

[104] Berman (1983) p. 51.   [105] Weber (1978) p. 1272.   [106] Leithart (2003) p. 10.
[107] Parsons (1963a) p. 45.   [108] Weber (1978) p. 1161.   [109] Canning (1996) p. 47.
[110] Weber (1978) p. 1175.

might be involved. Moreover, through a renewed emphasis on enforcing the doctrine of celibacy, the reform programme 'served to consolidate and extend the independence of the church from secular influence'.[111] Parsons argued that the institutionalisation of clerical celibacy played an important role in the establishing a separation between office and person. Through separating clergy from family and particularistic ties, celibacy turned out to have a special significance in providing a universalistic basis for role allocation. Through this institutional innovation the Church also sought to give meaning to the ideal of universalism associated with the Roman tradition. The construction by the Church of an authority that claimed to be universal represented an attempt to maintain continuity with the Roman tradition. This project was mirrored through a parallel attempt to formulate an imperial universality. Murvar writes of 'two universally competing ideologies – papal and imperial universality in Western Europe', and contrasts this development to the rest of the world, where a 'monistic identity' appears to be the norm.[112] However, it is important to note that this competition looked to the same foundational legacy to validate itself, and at times co-existed with attempts to forge unity between the two jurisdictions. Ladner contends that until the twelfth century, a degree of Christian unity prevailed and Empires and Kingdoms were in the Church and 'not *beside* the Church' and not above.[113]

Ullmann's study of medieval law indicates that the tension between German kings with pretensions to the title of Emperor and the Papacy was inseparable from a mutual aspiration for claiming the status of successor to the universal authority of Rome. The German kings perceived themselves as 'successors of the ancient Caesars' and attempted to emulate the behaviour of Roman emperors. Between the sixth and eighth centuries the Roman ideal was symbolised by the papacy, which acted as the 'transmitter of Roman law and of Roman principles of government'. According to Ullmann, at this time the Church became an 'effective bridge builder between the mature, ancient Roman civilization and the virgin, fallow youthful Germanic societies'. Ullmann claims that,

the 'imperial' idea fostered and consistently advocated by the papacy in the West concretely expressed the fusion between the old and the new, between the papacy as the symbol of the ancient Roman world, and the Franks as the most gifted people of the Germanic peoples.[114]

The 'discovery' and diffusion of Roman law played a significant role as a *source* of medieval authority. 'The most effective preparatory

---

[111] Parsons (1963a) p. 45.   [112] Murvar (1967) p. 72.
[113] Ladner (1947) p. 419.   [114] Ullmann (1975) pp. 63, 71, 72.

circumstance in the diffusion and influence of Roman law as a source of governmental conceptions was the imperial idea with which the papacy began to operate from the late eighth century onwards', states Ullmann.[115] The association of the Roman Empire with universalism ensured that the Roman law was in course of time to be raised to the level of a universally applicable law'.[116] Roman law was particularly attractive to temporal leaders who required a form of validation that was independent of Church doctrine. During the Investiture Contest, Roman law was frequently upheld by German kings to legitimise their imperial claims.

The competition between papal and imperial universality can therefore be interpreted as a contestation for the authority of the tradition of Rome. The theologian and polemicist Manegold of Lautenbach (1030c–1103c), who was a strong supporter of the Gregorian reforms, not only attacked the pretensions of kings to a divine authority but also asserted that that it was the papacy 'which was the real heir of the Roman tradition of universalism and international order'.[117] However, the Church did not confine its attempt to validate its claim to universal supremacy to appealing to Roman law. The invention and elaboration of Church canon law can be seen as an attempt to develop a source of legal authorisation that need not be shared with secular society. Ryon Lancaster states that canon law, which was 'principally an administrative law for the church', helped to establish 'jurisdictional boundaries with other groups, notably the family and secular rulers'.[118] Canning indicated that 'the beginnings of a canonistic school at Bologna are directly connected with the reverberations of the Investiture Contest, when many of the assumptions which society had taken for granted came to be rather effectively questioned'.[119]

Universalism gained force and meaning through the development of canon law, which, unlike customary and Roman law, was based on the universalistic principles of the Christian faith: 'on belief in a God of justice who operates a lawful universe, punishing and rewarding according to principles of proportion, mercifully mitigated in exceptional situations'.[120] The universalistic claims of a document like the *Dictatus Papae* acquired a legal form through the work of Church jurists.

The elaboration of the Roman tradition of universalism into a Christian-based legal form represents the forging of an important dialectic between religious doctrine and rationality-based institutions. As Lovin argues, law was 'the principal instrument by which moral convictions and basic beliefs receive institutional form'.[121] Both historically and also

---

[115] Ullmann (1975) p. 72.   [116] Ullmann (1975) p. 72.   [117] Dawson (1964) p. 54.
[118] Lancaster (2010) p. 31.   [119] Canning (1996) p. 164.
[120] Berman (1983) pp. 529–30.   [121] Lovin (1984) p. 210.

logically, there is a close connection between the authority of religious tradition and its instrumentalisation into a rational legal form of authorisation. Behind the rationality and universality of modern Western law lie the theological assumptions that provided the foundation for the innovations of canon law. That is why Harold Berman could put forward the provocative thesis that modern history began with Gregory VII's papal revolution.

The rationalisation of the Church, which was closely associated with the construction of new legal forms, provided a model of social organisation that would exercise a significant influence over the thinking of secular administrators. The rationalisation of Church affairs had a significant impact on other institutions, as secular lords and princes and the emerging urban corporations were 'obliged to define themselves in relation to the new, powerful institution of the universal church and to develop their own system of law in order to retain jurisdiction over the questions that were crucial to them'.[122] What followed was a period of constant borrowing of ideas and practices between the two jurisdictions. In a sense, the unintended consequence of the attempt to elaborate a universal authority was to encourage the process of rationalisation, first within the Church and later more widely in society.

During the Middle Ages the conflicts between temporal power and the papacy led to the development of a situation where competition was mediated through the common acceptance of the principal of universalism. It 'led to a recognition that though the *principles* of law may be universal, the *jurisdiction* of each legal authority is restricted'.[123] Competition encouraged both jurisdictions to devote considerable energy to the systematisation of the law. But whatever the ambiguity of medieval dualism, in the end both of the jurisdictions drew on a shared source or foundation of authority. Cicero's idea of a universal law of nature and the principles of government associated with it became a legacy that was virtually unquestioned, and the formidable authority of Roman universalism and law proved to be a powerful heritage. There were differences about how to interpret and apply these laws, but not about issues of substance.[124] The Latin Bible, which was 'suffused with notions, ideas and quite specific linguistic expressions which had been taken from Roman constitution and law' served to transmit the legacy of the past to the medieval mind. It is important to note that the role of law as foundational in medieval times was linked to its association with widely held traditions of beliefs. As Van Caenegem points at, 'Roman Law, like the Bible, was not seen as the product of a particular and transient historic phase, but as an

---

[122] Lovin (1984) p. 207.   [123] Lovin (1984) p. 208.   [124] Sabine (1961) p. 167.

eternal paradigm, a treasure-house of timeless wisdom and a revelation for all time'.[125] Van Caenegem's emphasis is shared by other scholars, who underline the formidable influence of the Bible as a 'source of governmental conceptions', which conferred 'permanency, stability and order' on societies that were ruled by it.[126]

The durability of medieval foundational authority is demonstrated by the fact that, despite the frenetic claims and counter-claims made in the Investiture Contest and other disputes, it remained essentially unquestioned until the late fourteenth and early fifteenth centuries. It is because of the shared acceptance of foundational norms and values that medieval dualism was able to survive attempts by temporal and especially papal forces to expand their claims for monolithic authority. Papal claims for *plenitude potestatis* (fullness of power) – supreme authority in temporal affairs – still recognised the sphere of the temporal and did not or could not 'wish to destroy the working distinction between the two realms'.[127] What was at issue was the 'relative authority of the two powers', rather than the total displacement of one by the other.[128]

Although Weber recognised the unique development of a dual system of authority in medieval Europe, he tends to generalise from this specific experience to develop a more general model of the relationship between hierocratic and caesaropapist authority. Statements that describe aspects of this relationship in medieval Europe – for example, that the antagonism between the two jurisdictions rarely leads to the 'full victory of one or the other' – are expressed as possessing a more universal character.[129] This impulse to generalise occasionally leads to a loss of clarity about the concepts used. Thus, on occasion, Weber uses the contrast between hierocratic and caesaropapist as the equivalent of religious and secular power, writing about the 'anatagonism between political and hierocratic power' or of the relationship between 'otherwordly and the thiswordly powers'.[130] However, the relationship between the two jurisdictions should not be confused with modern couplet of 'secular and religious'. Despite the attempt by the Gregorian reform movement to de-spiritualise temporal power, feudal kingship retained a spiritual dimension; it was 'not exclusively temporal'.[131] It would require the attainment of a degree of confidence before kings and princes could develop political theory that could help them to gain greater independence from the Church and transform themselves into secular rulers.

[125] Van Caenegem (1981) p. 15.   [126] Ullmann (1975) p. 48.
[127] McCready (1973) p. 671.   [128] Carlyle and Carlyle (1962) p. 386.
[129] Weber (1978) p. 1174.   [130] Weber (1978) pp. 1174, 1175.
[131] McCready (1973) p. 671.

Weber on transition

The durability of medieval foundational authority rested on the relatively uncontested status of a tradition based on a synthesis of Roman law, the Latin Bible, and local custom. The stability of this form of authority is, as Weber wrote, 'ultimately determined by the power of tradition, that is the belief in the inviolability of what has always been'.[132] However, although outwardly the inviolability of 'what has always been' was rarely questioned, the Gregorian movement was prepared – at least implicitly – to question custom in the name of the Truth. Moreover, the pursuit of institutional autonomy encouraged a process of rationalisation where rules rather than custom served to validate behaviour. So alongside custom and tradition emerged rational rule-bound norms. The papal claim to the right to make new laws led to the consolidation of legal-rational practices within an institution that represented itself as sacred.

It is in an era of transition, such as the eleventh and twelfth centuries, that Weberian ideal types are truly tested. In his own assessment of this period, Weber warned against presenting the evolving structures of domination as corresponding to one of his ideal types of authority, stating that 'on the contrary, the great majority of empirical cases represent a combination or a state of transition among several such pure types'.[133] Weber opted to develop concepts like 'patrimonial bureaucracy' in order to highlight the synthesis of traditional and rational forms of domination. Aware of the difficulty of imposing pure ideal-type categories on the historical process, he explained that 'we do not wish to force schematically, the infinite and multifarious historical life, but simply to create concepts useful for special purposes and for orientation'.[134] Certainly in this period of transition, it is the blending of different sources of authority that needs to be captured through historical-sociological analysis.

In the medieval era the construction of authority co-existed with its contestation. This was a time when the papacy self-consciously sought to divest kingship of spiritual power and when feudal rulers called into question the temporal ambitions of the Church. The very character of such contestation encouraged a cycle of claims and counter-claims that would eventually expose the assertion of any authority to unprecedented scrutiny.

---

[132] Weber (1978) p. 1008.   [133] Weber (1915) pp. 299–300.
[134] Weber (1915) p. 300.

6 Medieval claim-making and the sociology of tradition

Medieval political life during the twelfth and thirteenth centuries was dominated by the problem of the constitution of authority. According to one account, the twelfth century felt this concern with a 'new intensity, rarely matched during the centuries intervening since the death of Augustine in 430'.[1] Old dynasties searched for a new foundation for their authority, papal officials sought to expand the role of Rome in Europe's temporal affairs and advocates of city autonomy were busy constructing arguments for their independence. Within medieval urban centres, noted Weber, 'numerous claims to authority stand side by side, overlapping and often conflicting with each other'.[2] The authority of Roman law competed with that of feudal Germanic custom and Christian doctrine, and medieval lawyers had to integrate these 'three systems of thought' and reconcile their potentially contradictory claims to authority. As one study of medieval law observes:

Perhaps their most difficult task was to accommodate a conception of kingship that rested on divine foundations, derived in part from Roman and in part from Christian thought, with Germanic and feudal kingship, which based its claim to legitimacy on the relationship of the king to his barons and people.[3]

In the prosperous commercial centres of Italy, rapid social and economic change created a condition of fluidity and instability that tested the influence of traditional authority. In such 'relatively unstable circumstances with competing authority claims', the traditional ruler's authority was often displaced or 'usurped' by popular associations led by a new class of prosperous merchants. This urban revolution was frequently legitimised by the construction of legal precedents and procedures.[4] The Italian jurist Bartolus de Saxoferrato (1314–1357) developed the idea of popular consent from customary law, representing custom as an expression of people's consent and an important constituent of legitimation.

[1] Benson (1991) p. 339.   [2] Weber (1978) p. 7.
[3] Pennington (1991) p. 434.   [4] Weber (1978) p. 1254.

Bartolus's main innovation was his attribution 'to the independent city-*populus* within its territory the jurisdictional powers which the emperor possessed within the empire as a whole'.[5] Although he recognised parallel jurisdictions derived from imperial and papal sources, his development of the role of consent helped to consolidate the idea of city-state sovereignty.

Feudal barons were no less interested than urban political leaders in harnessing the status of custom to assert their independence from kings and popes who claimed an authority based on divine power. In England, the knights and barons who forced King John to enact the Magna Carta were 'fighting for the restoration of the traditional laws', which, they claimed, were perverted by 'king's arbitrary rule'.[6] In turn, kings sought to uphold their independence from papal authority by appealing to precedent and custom. In this environment of competing jurisdiction and claims-making, it is easy to overlook the fact that the foundational norms and doctrines of medieval Europe proved to be remarkably resilient until well into the fifteenth century.

Historical consciousness and law

Marc Bloch, the famous French historian of this era, summed up the orientation of the medieval imagination as one of 'vast indifference to time'.[7] According to Le Goff, at 'the level of the collective mentality, past, present and future were mixed together in a fundamental confusion. The past was highly valued, indeed its authority was so influential that references to it 'were almost obligatory in the middle ages'.[8] However, by the twelfth century it was possible to detect a more questioning approach towards the past and a greater sensitivity towards change.

One of the effects of competing claims-making was the development of an increasingly conscious orientation towards the interpretation and reinterpretation of precedent and customary traditions. When Henry II insisted that old principles of English jurisdictional customs be written down, he in fact developed them beyond old precedent in order to expand royal justice.[9] His attempt to reinterpret custom occurred at a historical moment when the relationship between custom and newly created law had become a subject of controversy and discussion. Some legal scholars went so far as to argue that the construction of new law was a 'natural function of society', and the Italian jurist Johannes Bassianus declared

---

[5] Canning (1991) pp. 470–1.   [6] Van Caenegem (1981) p. 18.
[7] Cited by Le Goff (1994) p. 174.   [8] Le Goff (1994) pp. 174 and 326.
[9] Van Caenegem (1991) p. 191.

that 'nature creates many new things daily' and for a 'new situation new responsibility is needed'.[10]

However, the recognition that new laws were sometimes required to respond to unprecedented developments was tempered by the recognition that custom was still the principal source of authority. Medieval lawyers 'defined law as being the will of the prince, promulgated for just and necessary reasons, and tempered by custom that could represent the will of the people'. The idea that new laws could be promulgated was expressed by canon lawyers through the term *ius positivium* (positive law) towards the end of the twelfth century.[11]

The evolving relationship between law-making and custom and tradition had important implications for the way that medieval society conceptualised authority. One outcome of this new orientation towards law was that tradition had become a subject of explicit disputation, and its representation as an immutable legacy had to be reconciled with the requirement to adapt custom to new circumstances. The necessity for reconciling these potentially contradictory imperatives raised questions about how innovations could be authorised, and required the emergence of a disposition that was open to perceiving custom as a practice that could be modified, improved and even tempered by reason.

It appears that some medieval thinkers in the twelfth century gained a degree of confidence in applying 'rational principles' to choose between 'authorities which occasionally seemed to contradict one another'.[12] The clearest statement on the 'indeterminancy of authorities' and the need for applying reason is offered in the well-known statement of Alan of Lille (c1130–1203) – 'because *auctoritas* has a wax nose, which means that it can be bent in any direction, it must be fortified with *rationes*'.[13]

It is important to note that until the twelfth century, 'law was largely undifferentiated from custom' and did not exist as autonomous institution. 'Until the great upheavals of the twelfth century the law was not viewed as an adaptable instrument of social regulation, bound to be changed regularly by the lawgiver,' argues the legal scholar R. C. Van Caenegem.[14] On the contrary: 'Law was considered an unwritten and unchanging eternal norm, dominating the lives and actions of all members of society, including crowned heads', and 'Kings might declare the law, as judges "found" the law and hence the right judgment, but they certainly did not make it'. Moreover, the law was,

---

[10] Cited in Pennington (1991) p. 425.   [11] Pennington (1991) p. 425.
[12] Ziolkowski (2009) p. 4443.   [13] Cited by Ziolkowski (2009) p. 446.
[14] Van Caenegem (1981) p. 21.

not to be meddled with by human action – an occasional addition or clarification was the furthest one could go, and even then the aim was to discover more precisely and fully what the law was and always had been, not to innovate.[15]

According to some accounts, 'law for medieval people was primordial' or a product of a 'common conscience'. It was the unwritten way of doing things – something that was inherited and 'its authority was believed to spring from its antiquity'. In this era the belief in 'the good old law' proved to be pervasive throughout medieval Europe. As Canning wrote, its 'implications were to deny the possibility of true legislation, and certainly of innovative legislation' and precluded 'legislative sovereignty on the part of rulers'.[16] Until the twelfth century, the idea that law was something that could be made – the 'notion of legislation, was far out of sight'.[17] The German historian Fritz Kern argues that law-making as such was alien to this period, that instead 'law was held to be something eternally valid, and unchanging which was "found" or "discovered" by rulers, judges and those experts in law'.[18]

As against the modern practice of permanent legislation, with its devotion to novelty and legal change, the medieval sensibility based on custom and tradition can appear to be entirely static. This tendency is reinforced in some of the social science literature, where the conceptual contrast between 'traditional' and 'modern' lends itself to a one-sided reading of the working of custom in the Middle Ages. The conviction that law was eternally valid did not preclude rulers and legal experts from acts of innovation through interpreting the meaning of old custom for contemporary times; however, such innovations were expressed and understood through a language that stressed continuity with the past. Before the twelfth century, notes Berman, 'although kings issued laws, they did so rarely, and largely to reaffirm or revise pre-existing customs'. A similar pattern was evident within the Church, where 'the lawmaking authority of popes, metropolitans and bishops was also largely restricted to occasional reaffirmance or revision of pre-existing rules laid down in Scriptures or by church fathers or church councils'.[19]

'Of course the men who used authorities stretched their meanings to the point where they barely impeded personal opinions', writes Le Goff.[20] So the traditionalist orientation towards custom co-existed with the recognition that the law had to be interpreted and sometimes revised. In numerous disputes the act of interpretation extended into a search for precedent, or for what Weber characterised as 'law finding'. Findings of

---

[15] Van Caenegem (1981) p. 21.   [16] Canning (1996) p. 24.
[17] See Oakeshott (2006) pp. 295–7 and Berman (1983) p. 69.
[18] See Canning (1996) p. 24.   [19] Berman (1983) p. 76.   [20] Le Goff (1994) p. 326.

law 'can refer only to documents of tradition, namely to precedents and earlier decisions'; and although in such circumstances it is 'impossible for law or administrative rule to be deliberately created by legislations', innovation is still possible: 'Rules which in fact are innovations can be legitimized' but 'only by the claim that they have been "valid of yore" but only now been recognized'.[21] The unearthing of 'lost' documents and customs helped endow legal innovations with the authority of the past. For example, before 1140 many papal claims were based on appeals to traditional custom. Some of these precedents were collected in the ninth-century *Pseudo-Isidore*, which also included a large number of forgeries which were used to support papal claims such as the Donation of Constantine. In the Middle Ages, law was fundamental to the constitution of authority: as Oakeshott observes, 'so important was this that laws were forged in order to substantiate claims'.[22]

Arguably the discovery of Roman law in the eleventh century can be interpreted as an example of innovation through the re-appropriation of the legacy of the past. The rediscovery of Justinian's *Digest* in 1070 led not only to the revival of Roman civil law but also to a legal revolution that would ultimately assist the emergence of the institutionalisation of jurisprudence.[23] The newly discovered Roman law had a significant impact on legal thinking in medieval and even modern Europe, serving as a new form of authorisation that provided a level of sophistication that went beyond the prevailing legal theory.[24] It also assisted the shift from law-finding to law-making – consciously constructed law.

The discovery of Roman law should not be interpreted as an example of a historical accident, but rather as an act of innovation in response to the circumstances of the time. Ullmann states that the assertion that law in the Middle Ages was 'found' is 'one of the myths that dies hard'.[25] The discovery of Roman law should be construed as a by-product of a quest for an authoritative precedent. 'Roman Law, like the Bible, was not seen as the product of a particular and transient historic phase, but as an eternal paradigm, a treasure-house of timeless wisdom and a revelation for all time', writes Van Caenegem.[26] It provided a provisional answer to the demand for foundational norms at a time of conflict between competing claims to authority.

Van Caenegem writes that the 'deliberate creation of new laws, breaking through the primeval "crust of custom", this conscious and calculated policy of changing the law to renovate society according to new social,

---

[21] Weber (1978) p. 227.   [22] Oakeshott (2006) p. 296.
[23] See Luscombe and Evans (1991) pp. 315–16.   [24] See Ullmann (1975) pp. 53–5.
[25] Ullmann (1975) p. 30, ln. 1.   [26] Van Caenegem (1981) p. 15.

intellectual and political needs, was started in the twelfth century'.[27] However, it is likely that the intensification of legal innovation was more hesitant and outwardly less revolutionary than Van Caenegem outlines. Gregorian reformers were careful not to be seen to violate the authority of the past. Gregory himself claimed to be attacking only the bad customs that had emerged in recent centuries, and his denunciation of evil custom co-existed with appealing to the 'principle of revitalizing primitive, neglected norms rooted ultimately in the early Jesus and Apostles'.[28] In acclaiming the old custom of early Christianity against the legacy of subsequent ecclesiastical corruption, Gregory represented himself as the preserver of the real tradition. 'The ideological emphasis was on tradition, but the tradition could only be established by suppressing the immediate past and returning to an earlier one', explains Berman.[29]

The discovery of Roman law needs to be situated within this context of intense competition for precedents that could serve as warrants for contrasting claims. 'It was highly convenient, and not wholly accidental, that a manuscript of Justinian's Digest turned up in a library in Florence in the 1080s,' states Berman.[30] Justinian's codification of Roman law was just what the Church needed in its attempt to rationalise custom to underwrite its authority. Roman law provided jurists with the legal instruments to sift through precedent and reform custom in line with the Church's agenda. The aim of this project was not to destroy custom and tradition, but to reform them in line with reason and conscience.

Krieger believes that the cumulative effect of the Gregorian reform programme was to diminish the independent status of traditional authority, writing that as:

the set of religious practices and beliefs hallowed by long usage and predicated upon the universal consensus of the faithful over the generations, tradition took its place during the early Middle Ages alongside Scripture, official administrative position, and canon law as a separate, frequently competing, subheadings of authority.[31]

However, this status of tradition was undermined by the papacy and the hierarchical official order within the Church, until by 'the end of the Investiture conflict' the 'idea of tradition as an explicit kind of authority had all but disappeared'.[32] Customs were absorbed into other doctrines.

The absorption of custom and tradition into doctrine occurred in the context of a debate between different claim-makers for authority.

---

[27] Van Caenegem (1981) p. 22.   [28] Preus (1972) p. 13.
[29] Berman (1983) p. 112.   [30] Berman (1983) p. 528.
[31] Krieger (1968) p. 147.   [32] Krieger (1968) p. 148.

Although this development had a significant impact on the way that competing authorities sought to validate their status, it is difficult to evaluate its significance for everyday practice. Le Goff contends that 'customs ruled society long after Gregory's time. According to Le Goff, conflicts between peasants and their lords continued to be expressed through arguments about traditional and customary rights'.[33] It is unlikely that the doctrinal appropriation of custom fundamentally affected local practices in feudal Europe, where the taken-for-granted persisted and the traditionalist imagination continued to shape people's attitudes.

In retrospect, this era appears as one of slow transition from traditional custom to a legalistic orientation. Although this process took centuries to evolve, the main catalyst for its emergence was the Investiture Contest. Carlyle and Carlyle point to the twelfth and thirteenth centuries as the time when the idea took hold that the source of law was not simply custom but the outcome of 'some conscious authority'. They add that in the thirteenth century, 'the conception of law as custom was being modified by another – that is, by the conception of law as the expression of a conscious will and determination' a 'transition towards making laws'.[34]

The emergence of a conscious orientation towards law-making was a product of political instability caused by the conflict between ecclesiastical and lay claims-makers. In this situation of political ferment, 'law could no longer continue to be regarded as an immutable entity'.[35] The transition towards legalism was expressed through a form of legal consciousness that had become sensitive to the demands of changing times. Some historians suggest that in this era emerged an unprecedented awareness of different historical periods; the so-called twelfth century renaissance has been associated with an 'intensified consciousness of historical period' and an awareness of a 'break between antiquity and middle ages'.[36] Others are more circumspect: 'It is not quite true to say that medieval minds were not aware of historical growth and change, but they had no elaborate consciousness of history', contends Lewis.[37]

The instability fuelled by competing authority claims invariably touched on the status of custom and traditions. These developments were most pronounced in commercial centres of Europe, particularly in the Italian city states, where urban citizens succeeded in challenging traditional authority. Weber developed the concept of 'non-legitimate domination' to account for the tendency to displace traditional rule with new forms of domination authorised from below, and argued that this urban revolution led to important legal innovations including the 'codification

[33] Le Goff (1994) p. 328.   [34] Carlyle and Carlyle (1962a) pp. 51–3.
[35] Damaska (1985) p. 1814.   [36] Melve (2006) p. 235.   [37] Lewis (1954) p. 140.

of a special rational law for urban citizens'.[38] In such an environment, the immutability of law was put to question by the needs of a fluid and changing urban environment. Bartolus took the lead in questioning the old assumption that facts must be adjusted to fall in line with the literal interpretation of the law, holding the view that 'where the law and the facts collide, it is the law which must be brought into conformity with the facts'.[39]

The sense of change in the urban commercial centres of Europe sensitised jurists to the need to revise the law in line with new conditions. In other parts of Europe this sensibility was less developed, but nevertheless an awareness of difference between the customs of the past and the claims made by twelfth- and thirteenth-century rulers indicated that at least among the main protagonists in the key controversies, a sense of historical consciousness had emerged. Ullmann's study of the changing landscape of jurisprudence notes that as a result of the 'reverberations of the Investiture Contest', many of 'the assumptions which society had taken for granted came to be rather effectively questioned'.[40]

Nevertheless the authority of tradition, especially in its form as a legacy from the distant past, was not in question. Specific customs could be challenged but tradition remained intact. Gregory VII assaulted evil custom through proclaiming the superior virtue of a more authentic older custom; the Gregorian reform movement drew on the authority of the ancient past in order castigate the evil customs of a more recent past and in turn, Gregory's enemies within the Church accused the Pope of a 'violent attack on the traditional rights of the episcopate'.[41] Nearly 20 years after Gregory's death the pro-imperial clergy of Liège, with Sigebert of Gembloux as their spokesman, proclaimed their allegiances in these terms: 'We adhere to our bishop, our archbishop, our provincial and our provincial synod, according to ancient tradition'.[42]

The quest for origins

One of the most important ways of attempting to resolve the paradox of challenging custom with ancient traditions was through elaborating the *origins* of authority. Through the centuries that followed the Investiture Contest, debates surrounding the source of authority were expressed through contrasting views about its historical origins. The significance attached to origins indicates that the legacy of the past still

---

[38] Weber (1978) pp. 1234 and 1254.   [39] See Skinner (2009) p. 9.
[40] Ullmann (1975) p. 164.   [41] Robinson (1978) p. 106.
[42] Cited in Robinson (1978) p. 106.

possessed a sacred character in the medieval imagination. As Coleman explains,

the various hypothesis on the origins of government as legitimate jurisdiction and the nature of political obligation were posed when they were precisely because medieval corporative structures had developed out of custom and sought legal justification in canon and Roman civil law.[43]

The sacralisation of origins co-existed with an openness to law-making, which was accomplished through a doctrine that reconciled the origins of authority to rule with the right of that authority to make rules.

The debate on origins should be interpreted as an attempt to theorise about politics but within a traditional form. With its emphasis on continuity, the quest for origins was based on the premise that the authority of a law was determined by its age. The 'goodness of a good custom can be inferred from the fact of its preservation', and the 'longer it had been in existence, the greater the presumption in its favour', states Pocock.[44] Le Goff adds that 'references to the past, however, were almost obligatory in the middle ages'.[45] It was believed the original source of the power to rule could provide a foundation for medieval authority; Ullmann notes that implicitly the debate about law was about its source and origins, raising questions about 'nothing more or less than the location of original power'. This question about the 'seat of final jurisdiction, that is law creating power and competency' was the medieval equivalent of locating what 'today would be called political sovereignty'.[46] The gradual acceptance of the idea that laws could be made would eventually lead society to embark on a search for the original source of authority of the right to legislate.

The main driver of the search for the origin was the need to find an answer to the question of political obligation. Tierney asked 'how did tradition begin addressing the real problem of political obligation through the pseudo-problem of origins?'[47] Competing claims about who had jurisdiction over what created a situation where questions about who had the right to change customs and in what conditions encouraged a search for precedent. The emergence of independent urban corporations was paralleled by the rise of new communities – secular and religious – often through 'acts of voluntary consent'. In Tierney's opinion, 'men living in a society with so much experience of this sort' may 'readily approach the problem of political obligation by considering the original constituting point of political societies'. However, the most important driver of the

---

[43] Coleman (2000) p. 45.   [44] Pocock (2003) p. 15.   [45] Le Goff (1994) p. 326.
[46] Ullmann (1961) p. 20.   [47] Tierney (1982) p. 36.

search for origin was the conflict between the papacy and temporal power, where it was necessary to state 'how legitimate governments first came to be constituted'.[48]

In his attempt to 'explain why so much subsequent political thought became focused on the question of the origin of jurisdiction', Tierney claims that this was a problem 'bequeathed to political theory by the canonists', who had developed the concept of jurisdiction as a power of ruling that was independent from the individual office holder. The concept of jurisdiction as the power of ruling gradually gained influence and would in the early modern era help clarify the idea of sovereignty. However, the question that remained unresolved was how 'jurisdiction first began'.[49] This was a question posed by Pope Innocent IV in 1250, and his answer clearly did not satisfy him: 'I do not know unless perhaps God assigned some person to do justice . . . or unless in the beginning the father of a family had complete jurisdiction over his family by the law of nature'. Another possibility he raised was that 'a people could have princes by election as they had Saul and many others'.[50] Tierney observed that Innocent IV 'posed very clearly the problem of origins and hit nearly on the three possible sources of legitimacy that would be discussed for centuries – patriarchal authority, direct divine right, or government by election and consent'.[51]

That Innocent raised the possibility of diverse sources of legitimacy was influenced by the changing social contours of feudal society. With so much institutional innovation it was inevitable that the source of authority would become a focus of debate. Competing jurisdictions existed alongside corporations – universities, professional guilds, urban associations – whose identity was established through common consent. 'From at least the thirteenth century onwards some began to speak of consensus as the *cause* of legitimate government, a consequence of medieval society being saturated with consensual practices', writes Coleman.[52] In such circumstances, corporate rulers and kings could claim consent as the basis for their authority, and they too could find the origins of this authority in the practice of the Roman Empire, where the people allegedly transferred their power to the emperor.

The quest for origins represented the project of finding a source of authority that could validate the prevailing jurisdiction or ruling office. As we noted in our discussion of Rome, this was an old problem; and Augustus was by no means the last ruler to recognise the importance

[48] Tierney (1982) p. 38.   [49] Tierney (1982) pp. 32–4.
[50] Cited in Tierney (1982) p. 34.   [51] Tierney (1982) p. 35.
[52] Coleman (2000) p. 45.

of the myth of origins for the revitalisation of tradition and authority. It appears that what is crucial to innovation within tradition is that adaptation and change occurs under the influence of what Durkheim characterised as 'ancestral approval': that is, the authority of the past.[53] In this way innovation is both experienced and represented as not a violation of the customs of the past, but as an act of preservation and continuity with their origins.

The modification of tradition

The medieval experience suggests that conserving the form of tradition can coincide with changing its content. During the Middle Ages, tradition was constantly tested through acts of interpretation and innovation, and it is difficult to disagree with Ziolkowski's verdict that 'the long twelfth century is also a phase of extensive forgery and misattribution',[54] where laws and customs were sometimes invented and in some cases, such as the challenge to lay investiture – directly challenged. But nevertheless, even in the course of constructing new customs, medieval thinkers and claims-makers believed that they were acting in accordance with tradition. 'They believed themselves to believing within a tradition but actually were in the extended process of constructing one', asserts Coleman.[55]

Since the concept of tradition conveys so many after-the-event assumptions in the modern imagination, it can often be caricatured as a static dogma. But the medieval experience indicates that tradition is not so much a stand-alone doctrine as an orientation towards the world where the consciousness of history exists in a relatively restricted form. Within this context, there was scope for change and innovation but in a way that was consistent with what the sociologist Edward Shils has characterised as substantive traditionality, which is 'the appreciation of the accomplishments and wisdom of the past and of the institutions especially impregnated with tradition, as well as the desirability of regarding patterns inherited from the past as valid guides'.[56] Unexpected threats, opportunities and problems confronted medieval Europe no less than in modern times, and people had to engage in acts of interpretation and construct solutions to the problems of the time. This process is most usefully conceptualised as one of change within a traditionalist setting, where individuals drew on their understanding of the legacy of the past

---

[53] Durkheim (1984) p. 233.
[54] Ziolkowski (2009) p. 439. He added that the twelfth century 'teems with pseudonymous texts and pseudosources'.
[55] Coleman (2000) p. 3.   [56] Shils (1981) p. 21.

and attempted to reconcile it with their own experience. They used reason to attempt to resolve the tension between the received wisdom of eternal truths and the experience that confronted them. By the thirteenth century, medieval men were 'decreasingly afraid' of change.[57]

In the relationship between tradition and custom, it is useful to perceive the former as a foundational orientation towards the world and the latter as specific practices through which those foundational norms are applied to specific circumstances. This understanding offers an interpretation that is consistent with the 'Invention of Tradition' paradigm proposed by Eric Hobsbawn, who writes that the 'object and characteristic of "traditions", including invented ones, is invariance' and the past 'to which they refer imposes fixed (normally formalized) practices, such as repetition'. In contrast, custom does not 'preclude innovation and change up to a point, though evidently the requirement that it must appear compatible or even identical with precedent imposes substantial limitations on it'. Hobsbawn writes that custom gives any 'desired change (or resistance to innovation) the sanction of precedent, social continuity and natural law as expressed in history'.[58]

It is important to understand that, despite its constant exposure to interpretation, tradition and custom retained their status as warrant for claims to authority. The answers provided by the traditions of the past were still seen as providing the normative principles that were necessary to deal with what were perceived as the unchanging questions faced by Europe in the Middle Ages. Political ideas and practices continued to draw on the Old and New Testaments, Roman Law, the writings of the Church Fathers, especially Ambrose, Augustine and Gregory, and on rituals and conventions associated with feudal custom.[59]

In his discussion of the role of tradition, Weber emphasised people's reluctance to violate custom. The power of tradition is based on 'the belief in the inviolability of what has always been', and the,

Talmudic maxim, 'man should never change a custom' derives its practical significance not only from inherent power of the custom which is rooted in fixed attitudes, but originally also from fear of undefined magical evils which might befall an innovator or an approving group who violate the interests of the spirits.

Later, 'as the idea of god develops, this belief is replaced by one which holds that the gods have posited the traditional as norm, to be protected as something sacred'.[60] However, the sacred status of traditional norms does not preclude their meaning altering through the cumulative impact

[57] Le Goff (1994) p. 348.   [58] Hobsbawn (1992) p. 2.
[59] See Luscombe (1991) pp. 169–70.   [60] Weber (1978) p. 1008.

of interpretation, and the meaning attached to practices and custom is influenced by historical context and culture. Hence, the way that ideas drawn from antiquities were interpreted and applied to the conditions of the Middle Ages would have been incomprehensible to people living in the city-states of Greece or Rome.

In medieval Europe, a traditionalist outlook could be expressed in a variety of ways, and custom and tradition was absorbed into other doctrines such papal jurisprudence or corporation theory.[61] According to one account, 'as the 12th century progressed, more and more claims were made on the basis of the law, and less on the basis of tradition'; but 'appeals to tradition never disappeared, many of them were brought into the rubric of the canon law'.[62] Indeed, a legal judgment made on the basis of canon law served to prove a 'custom's existence and lawfulness' and 'a custom, once judged, led a life of its own'. In this way the act of legal judgment became a source or validation of custom.[63]

Tradition could also be expressed through new and diverse forms. The Stoic notion of natural law, which posited the idea that there was a divinely ordained law common to all of humanity, was readily Christianised and could serve as an authoritative form through which traditional norms could be communicated. 'The law of nature was the law of God; it was absolute in its authority, above kings and emperors and even popes', states Oakeshott. Moreover, given its ancient pedigree, natural law provided an ideal foundation for the expression of traditional norms.[64]

With the rediscovery of Aristotle in the thirteenth century, the idea of a law rooted in Nature and comprehensible through reason appealed to the medieval imagination.[65] The law of nature offered the stability of an immutable and eternal foundation for claims-making. As far back as the fourth century BC, Antigone, in Sophocles's tragedy, responds to Creon's demand for obedience to man-made laws by appealing to the authority of natural law. She stated that these 'laws are not for now or for yesterday, they are alive forever; and no one knows when they were shown to us first'.[66] In the late Middle Ages, argues Oakeshott, 'when the authority of ancient custom was beginning to be lost', the 'notion of a "natural law" as the touchstone of justice took the place of the notion of ancient custom'.[67] So natural law became one of the forms through which the authority of the old was recast in a manner that was consistent with previous tradition.

---

[61] Krieger (1968) p. 147.   [62] Lancaster (2010) p. 22.   [63] Cheyette (1963) p. 379.
[64] Oakeshott (2006) p. 303.   [65] See Sabine (1961) p. 245.
[66] Sophocles (1973) pp. 38–9.   [67] Oakeshott (2006) p. 303.

In contemporary times, the tendency to represent the Weberian category of the 'rational-legal' as the polar opposite to tradition may obscure the historic tendency of the latter towards adaptation and transformation. Friedrich has put up a strong argument for modifying this contrast, especially when it is presented in the form of rational versus the irrational. His argument is that 'neither authority nor tradition is unrelated to reason and reasoning, and more particularly that tradition is often the very basis of reasoning and rational argument'.[68] The glossators – medieval legal scholars commenting on canon law – 'recognized that custom was part of the basic legal tradition of the Church', taking the view that one of the characteristics that 'made a custom valid' was that 'it be reasonable, that is not be contrary to natural law'.[69] In the medieval era, it seems that the tendency towards rationalisation could co-exist with tradition. It was only much later, with the detachment of politics from religion and science from the domain of the sacred, that the apparent irreconcilability between tradition and reason would resonate with the prevailing intellectual climate.

The transformation of tradition

Once tradition had to be reconciled with law-making, the location of the foundation of this activity became crucial. As the authors of an influential study of medieval political theory remark, in the thirteenth century 'the conception of law as custom was being modified by another – that is, by the conception of law as the expression of a conscious will and determination'.[70] The question that needed to be answered now was what constituted the foundation for the will to legislate; and in medieval Europe the answer inevitably assumed a traditional form.

The idea of tradition has in any case conveyed the idea of consensus and acceptance if not consent. As Macdonald explains, the term tradition (*traditio*):

signified generally any idea or set of ideas, any statement or explanation, placed on record, which had received wide acceptance at the time it was codified, and was accepted by later generations partly on the ground of its recognition in previous times. 'Tradition' was authoritative not merely because its content was ancient and had been handed down, but because the latter had been accepted and approved by faithful men in past days.[71]

The linkage of tradition with acceptance and approval provided law-making with the legitimacy of consent. However, it did not offer an

---

[68] Friedrich (1972) p. 13.   [69] Cheyette (1963) p. 379.
[70] Carlyle and Carlyle (1962) p. 81.   [71] Macdonald (1933) p. 5.

answer to the question of how law-making was authorised or whose approval was required.

Once the notion that laws could be made gained influence, society was forced to account for the source of those laws. One answer was provided by Gregory VII when he declared that the Pope alone is permitted to make new laws. Others replied that consent or approval of the community was necessary for a new law to be legitimate. Ullmann has outlined an approach that contrasts the two main ways to conceptualise the creation of the law, and thereby of the authority of the law based on it. One is the 'ascending theme of government and law', which presupposes that 'law-creative power is located in the people itself' and assumes an element of consent and representation. In this case the ruler is a representative of the people and 'power ascends' upwards, and some version of 'the right of resistance is built into this theme'.[72] As an example of the ascending theme, Ullmann cites ancient Greece and republican Rome and Germanic communities and tribes. The alternative to this model of consensual law-making power is the descending theme, 'according to which original power is located not in the broad base of the people, but in an otherworldly being, in divinity itself which is held to be the source of all power, public and private'. In this instance, rulers are not representatives but 'delegates of the supreme Ruler',[73] and consent 'plays no role within this framework'. The theocratic ruler personifies this model.

Ullmann argues that these themes are expressed through the creation of law. A key moment is the Principate in ancient Rome, when the 'ascending theme came to be supplanted by its descending counterpart'. He adds 'to be specific this descending theme was clothed in the Christian garb which was to set the tone and complexion of society from the early fourth century onwards'.[74] According to his analysis, Christianity had already internalised a great deal of Hellenism, oriental law and ancient philosophy, notably Platonism. It also absorbed Roman institutional ideas, of which 'none was more important than the very concept of law'. Consequently the Bible and pagan Roman law could 'effortlessly penetrate into the very matrix of the rapidly growing Christian doctrinal body'.[75]

The transformation of tradition in the twelfth and thirteenth centuries bore all the hallmarks of the tension between perceiving the construction of law as involving consent and the will of the people, or perceiving it as the outcome of the will of the ruler. The attempt to answer the question

---

[72] Ullmann (1975) p. 30   [73] Ullmann (1975) p. 31.
[74] Ullmann (1975) p. 32.   [75] Ullmann (1975) p. 32.

of who had the right to legislate provoked conflicting interpretations that emphasised a range of arguments, from upholding legislation by rulers to law-making by the people. From the twelfth century onwards, both the descending and the ascending trends were visible. During the century following the *Dictatus Papae*, the number of decretals grew in number, and there were some 2000 during the period between the papacy of Alexander III (1159–1181) and Gregory IX (1227–1241). When Boniface VIII (1294–1303) declared that 'all laws rest in pope's bosom', he gave a clear expression to the doctrine that law-making was the prerogative of the ruler. This ambition was not confined to the papacy: as Van Caenegem notes,[76] temporal rulers – Kings and territorial princes – emulated the Church hierarchy and began to legislate. Royal law-making was actively pursued in England, Normandy, France, Flanders, Germany, Northern Italy, Sicily, Spain, among other regions. However, even the more radical exponents of the descending theory of law tended to recognise that custom and tradition could not be ignored. So Boniface VIII, one of the most radical advocates of papal supremacy, stated in his decretal *Licet Romanus* that 'no papal constitution could override local custom' unless that custom was '*specifically* mentioned in the constitution'.[77]

The descending conception of law-making co-existed with ascending conceptions. In some of the cities, communal organisations developed their own constitutions and constructed laws that were often in conflict with the views of their rulers. In the northern Italian city-states, such as Milan and Pisa, these organisations were also able to wrest significant concessions from their rulers, in particular gaining the authority to modify and 'improve' 'their customary laws, which soon led to a full-fledged legislation promulgated by the town magistrates'.[78] In England, where customary law possessed a unique influence, the idea of consent was important. The thirteenth-century English jurist, Henry de Bracton (1210–68), stated that customary laws had a legal force because they 'have been approved by counsel and consent of the magnates and the general agreement of the *res publica*'.[79] Some historians go so far as to argue that the role of consent in some shape or form underpinned medieval law-making. The Carlyles conclude that: 'the feudal concept in of law is first that of custom: and secondly, that so far as men began to recognise the necessity of actual legislative action, they conceived of the law as deriving its authority not from the will or command of the ruler alone, but also from the counsel and consent of the great or wise men,

---

[76] Van Caenegem (1981) p. 24.   [77] Cheyette (1963) p. 379.
[78] Van Caenegem (1981) p. 24.   [79] Stein (1995) p. 342.

and the assent of the whole community'.[80] Tierney states that nearly every important legal tract of the medieval world referred to the idea of consent.[81]

Co-existence of different forms of authority

As the potential for contradictory interpretation of Roman law indicates, there was considerable latitude for competitive claims-making in relation to authority. These contradictions reoccurred in relation to other dimensions of law-making. Monarchical authority drawn from Germanic custom, and feudal law had to reconcile the king's contractual relations with the people with his right to make a new law. As Pennington contends: 'To reconcile these conflicting ideas, the lawyers had to solve two problems: to understand and define the sources and functions of law in society, and to integrate three systems of thought, Roman, Christian, and Germanic'.[82]

Custom, theology and law provided competing and sometimes mutually reinforcing warrants for claims. In retrospect, what is striking about the co-existence of different accounts of authority is that they constantly influenced one another.

Kantorowicz's insight into the 'theology of kingship', the use of theology to validate monarchy, points to the ceaseless borrowing of concepts and practices by competing jurisdictions and claims-makers.

'The *quid pro quo* method – the taking over of a theological notions for defining the state – had been going on for many centuries, just as, vice versa, in the early centuries of the Christian era the imperial political terminology and the imperial ceremonial had been adapted to the need of the Church', he writes.[83] 'This transfer of definitions and arguments from one sphere to the other was a feature of the development of distinctively medieval political ideas'.

The continuous exchange of ideas and arguments between the different jurisdictions led to the emergence of a medieval synthesis of political principles. Tierney writes:

The history of phrases like *plena potestas* and *quod omnes tangit* provides a good example of the interplay between secular and ecclesiastical idea on government that characterised medieval thought and practice. The typical process that occurred was the assimilation of a text of Roman private law into church law, its

---

[80] Carlyle and Carlyle (1957) p. 51.   [81] Tierney (1982) p. 42.
[82] Pennington (1991) p. 426.   [83] Kantorowicz (1997) p. 19.

adaptation and transmutation there to a principle of constitutional law, and then its reabsorption into the sphere of secular government in this new form.[84]

Although this process of exchange can be construed as a deliberate act of imitation, it is likely that the different claims to authority were 'all drawing on a common pool of legal doctrines that they found both persuasive and useful'.[85] The general acceptance of a shared pool of doctrines ensured that despite the intensity of competitive claims-making, the foundational sources of authority were not in question.

The un-making of the universalist legacy

During the Middle Ages the law – whether unwritten or codified – provided the warrant for authorising claims across all jurisdictions. 'Anyone who made a claim whether he were a pope, emperor, king "vassal", or merchant' always 'tried to show that it was a claim based upon *law*', notes Oakeshott.[86] Ullmann writes that the creation of the law was the 'central problem' of this era, and that 'the law has at no other time played such a pivotal role in society as in the Middle Ages'.[87]

Despite its foundational significance, the traditional normative structure of medieval Europe could not always be enforced. Moreover, it was always tested by the law-making activities of various rulers and by the construction of positive law. However, despite such tensions, claims-making activity had to pursue its objectives through idioms and ideas that were consistent with the normative structures. Legal expertise was essential for claims-making, and medieval jurists played a central role in this activity. The Investiture Contest stimulated the growth of universities and legal scholarship, and canon and civil lawyers provided arguments that were used to validate competing claims to authority. According to one study of medieval legal culture, 'at no other time did pure scholarship affect society and government to the degree that the civilians – and later canonists – did in the centuries between the Investiture Contest and the reformation'.[88]

Petrus Crassus, the eleventh-century Ravenna jurist, sought to use Roman law to promote Henry IV's case against Gregory. His tract *In Defence of King Henry* introduced 'the Roman law into the arena of "political" conflicts from which it was not to disappear until long after the Reformation'.[89] Lawyers at Bologna University were at the forefront of advocating the imperial cause against the papal party, and there

---

[84] Tierney (1982) p. 25.   [85] Tierney (1982) p. 25.   [86] Oakeshott (2006) p. 296.
[87] Ullmann (1975) p. 29.   [88] Ullmann (1975) p. 79.   [89] Ullmann (1975) p. 77.

were close links between Bologna and the German Emperors during the eleventh and twelfth centuries. As secular rulers gained confidence and established a more effective system of government, they came to rely on a group of professional lawyers, who were professionally trained and 'professionally employed in the royal courts or the royal council'.[90]

One of the principal objectives of medieval civilian jurists was to develop a 'theory of secular kingship for secular kingship'. To counter the arguments of papal claims-makers they had to show that 'the king or emperor derived his authority directly from God in spiritual matters'.[91] They used a variety of arguments to realise their objectives. Aristotelian political theory was deployed to substantiate the claim that the rule of the king was underwritten by popular consent; later, natural law 'added another source of legitimation for secular sovereignty alongside incipient "divine right" doctrine'.[92]

Canon lawyers played a crucial role in the elaboration of the arguments used by the papal party. They were the 'technicians who worked the machinery by which Christian society in the high Middle Ages was to be guided',[93] and provided intellectual support for the 'accentuation of the monarchic powers of the Pope' through the 'doctrinal clarification of his function as vicar of Christ'.[94] Theological leadership was closely associated with legal expertise. Every Pope from 1159 to 1303 was a lawyer, and some, such as Alexander III and Innocent IV, made a significant contribution to the scholarship of canon law.[95]

Throughout most of the medieval era, the claims elaborated by the papal party played the decisive role in influencing the conceptualisation of authority. This was a time when, in terms of organisational efficiency and doctrinal coherence, papal government appeared more developed than its temporal counterpart, and the papacy's 'claims to an authority which outshone that of any lay ruler did not seem unrealistic'.[96]

In the twelfth century, the papacy's claims for supreme power over temporal affairs were elaborated by theologians. Honorius of Augsburg (1106c–1135c) was one of the first theologians to argue that the authority of secular power was derived from that of the Church. Honorius, along with John of Salisbury, advanced a theory which 'in contradiction to the traditional view of the Church, would have reduced the conception of authority in the Church to one'. The Carlyles claim that this was a minority view that had little influence of the policy of the Church.[97]

[90] Sabine (1961) p. 266.   [91] Garrett (1987) pp. 9 and 10.
[92] Garrett (1987) pp. 10 and 11.   [93] Ullmann (1975) p. 165.
[94] Canning (1996) p. 182.   [95] Nielsen (1988) p. 222.   [96] Keen (1967) p. 92.
[97] Carlyle and Carlyle (1962) p. 392.

Nevertheless, in subsequent centuries there was a perceptible trend towards widening the claim for papal powers. Canning notes that by the time of Innocent III in the late twelfth century, 'theocratic pretensions were at their peak'. Innocent III argued that the authority of the Pope was not human but divine: the 'Pope has this authority because he does not exercise the office of man, but that of the true God on earth'.[98] The trend towards the assertion of papal absolutism is evident in the claims made by theologians and popes in the fourteenth century. In his edict *Unam Sanctum* (1302), Boniface VII claimed that all authority was based on the Church. This position, described as the 'most advanced ground on papal imperialism that was ever written into an official document', assumes that the Pope is the 'vicar of Christ'.[99]

During his struggle with King Phillip IV of France, 'Boniface called into action every piece in the hieroctratic armoury in an attempt, as he saw it, to reduce the king to filial obedience'.[100] During this dispute, papal intransigence acquired an unusually unmediated dimension. As Watt writes, 'Boniface VII personally, his curia collectively and his loyal theologians and canonists, produced a hierocratic dossier of unprecedented proportions and ingenuity, whose general trend was to assail or abandon every moderating or qualifying tenet about papal omnipotence suggested by past theory and experience'.[101] Figgis's important study of medieval political theory observes that 'Boniface VIII strained the medieval theory of Papal domination to breaking point in the *Unam Sanctum*'.[102] In his tract *On Eccclesiastical Power*, Boniface's champion, Giles of Rome (1296–1303), invested the Church with supreme authority. This has been described by Sabine as the 'most thorough-going presentation of the argument for papal imperialism', which claimed that the Pope's power was 'unique and supreme'; an argument that was 'substantially similar to that used in the sixteenth century to support the monarchy by divine right.[103]

Boniface's claim for a unique sovereign authority, and his justification for such absolute power on the basis of divine right, provoked a powerful counter-reaction. Arguably it was responsible for encouraging the development of political theories that sought to displace papal with secular sovereignty. Phillip raised an army to arrest Boniface and remove him from his office, and in September 1303 his mercenaries attacked the papal residence in the Italian town of Anagni. After capturing the Pope and plundering the palace, Boniface was kept in prison for three days

---

[98] Cited in Pennington (1991) p. 427. See Canning (1996) p. 36.
[99] Sabine (1961) p. 273.   [100] Watt (1991) p. 399.   [101] Watt (1991) p. 400.
[102] Figgis (1960) p. 22.   [103] Sabine (1961) p. 277.

without food and drink and humiliated by his captors. It is claimed that he was also slapped by one of his Italian opponents. Although eventually the townspeople rallied around and expelled the mercenaries, Boniface could never regain his authority. His humiliation expressed an important shift in the relationship between temporal and ecclesiastical power. Figgis observes that 'as has been well said "the drama of Anagni must be set against the drama of Canossa"'.[104] This incident, referred to as 'The Slap of Anagni', is symptomatic of the gradual unravelling of the moral authority of the papacy.

One of the paradoxes of papal claims-making is that in its more extreme forms it invited scrutiny of its own authority. Indeed, in its attempt to extend its influence into the domain of the temporal, it risked undermining its own claim to sacred authority. Hegel pointed to this danger when he remarked that the 'secular possessions of the Church brought it however into a relation to other secular princes and lords, which was alien to its proper nature'. Since in this relationship, the behaviour of the Church resembled that of a temporal power, it exposed to criticism its claims to sacred status. Hegel contends that in 'these proceedings the Church brought to bear against opponents only a force and arbitrary resolve of the same kind as their own, and mixed up its secular interest as an ecclesiastical, i.e. a divinely substantial power'. Hegel's analysis concludes that 'what the popes acquired in point of land and wealth and direct sovereignty, they lost in influence and consideration'.[105] Hegel's point is further elaborated by Sheldon Wolin, who remarks that 'theology had become compromised by its politicalness'. Moreover, the very attempt to subordinate temporal matters to the sacerdotal had the effect of encouraging the development of secular orientation towards political life.[106]

In early medieval times, the fiction of the *translatio imperii* was developed to account for the continuity of the Roman Empire and its universalistic authority. According to this myth, Constantine had deliberately abandoned Rome and transferred the empire's capital to Constantinople. It was claimed that this shift of empire to Constantinople was followed by a succession of transfers until the establishment of the Holy Roman Empire.[107] This myth, which helped to render conscious a historical sense of continuity with the legacy of Rome, proved to be surprisingly resilient. However, with rise of territorial sovereignty and a diversity in the form of political rule, the universalist ideals lost some of their force. With the decline in the salience of universalist doctrines,

---

[104] Figgis (1960) p. 22.   [105] Hegel (2004) pp. 376–7.
[106] Wolin (2004) pp. 125–6.   [107] See Nicol (1991) p. 59.

the myth of continuity with previous empires also lost some of their influence.

Arguably the decline of the universalist idea of empire was an indirect outcome of the success of papal diplomacy. During the thirteenth century the papacy succeeded in undermining the status of the Hohenstauffen German Emperors, and the imperial ideal consequently lost some of its cultural force. Figgis claims that while the papacy was focused on checking the influence of the imperial party, it was not alert to the emergence of potentially powerful territorially based secular powers: 'Owing to a variety of causes of which not the least important was the success of the Popes in undermining the Imperial authority, the national states has been left to develop in their own way'.[108]

The main responsibility for the rising tide of criticism of papal authority lay with the Church itself. In one sense the papacy overplayed its hand, when it claimed such widespread power and authority. The politicisation of the Church made matters worse by encouraging a scramble for power and influence at all levels of this institution. Rivalries and in-fighting wreaked havoc within the Roman Church and led to the corrosion of its institutional foundation. Criticism of papal authority and ecclesiastical corruption came to a head in the aftermath of the disputed papal election of 1378, which led to the Great Schism that lasted until 1417. In this period, the spectacle of rival popes manoeuvring for influence seriously undermined the Church's moral authority.

The crisis of papal authority was expressed through a growing tendency to demand curbs on the power of the Pope. In the late fourteenth and early fifteenth centuries, criticism of the abuse of papal power was led by the conciliar movement, which sought to contain and limit the arbitrary power of the Church. It demanded the reform of church institutions and a shift in the locus of authority from the Pope to a General Council. One of the 'fundamental doctrines of the conciliar movement was the principle of common consent of the governed'.[109] This questioning of the Church hierarchy can be seen as an explicit attempt to curb the power of despotic authority. Representatives of the conciliar movement, such as Nicholas of Cusa, argued that power and authority was based upon consent and upheld the role of community and representation as a source of ecclesiastical authority.

The significance that conciliar thinkers attached to consent was influenced by their attachment to local, territorial and national causes. 'What the principle of consent does contribute,' writes Nederman, is 'a powerful justification for localized variations in political rule'. He adds: 'because

---

[108] Figgis (1960) p. 22.   [109] Watanabe (1972) p. 222.

political order and law depends upon human volition, at least in its temporal applications, valid systems of government must always be traced to public consent apart from spiritual authorization'.[110]

The conciliar concept of consent should not be confused with the way it was understood by republican and democratic theorists in subsequent centuries. The consent of the many was taken for granted, and it was assumed that the masses would submit to the rule of the wise. It was argued that the rule of the few over the many was based on the rational foundation of natural law, which only a small number of wise leaders could understand and uphold.

The conciliar movement reflected the emerging interests and outlook of the national. Although its historical significance is often linked to its contribution to the shift in emphasis from papal sovereignty to the principle of consent, it also contributed to the desacralisation of universalist ideal. Universalism was integral to the legacy of tradition that validated medieval authority, and its desacralisation threatened to weaken that legacy by drawing attention to the conventional quality of rulership. The desacralisation of the legacy of universalism occurred gradually, in an unsystematic manner. For example, Nicholas of Cusa upheld the ideal of medieval imperialism in theory, while implicitly recognising that this political institution, based on the foundation of political consent, had a conventional quality.[111]

Gradually tradition was unmade. Some of the legacies of the past that provided medieval authority with the continuity of tradition were slowly losing their cultural appeal. One ideal in particular – the universal empire – always possessed an abstract quality. For a time, its very abstract quality helped to construct a foundational myth that could be appropriated by secular and ecclesiastical rulers alike. But in the end the geopolitical reality of a territorially fragmented continent – the break-up of Christendom – led to the demystification of this ideal.

Conclusion

Despite the intensity of the contestation of authority, all sides more or less accepted the foundational norms that validated rulership. McCready's study of the doctrinal positions of competing claim-makers concludes that 'the major papal theorists and at least some of the antipapalists had much in common'.[112] Figgis reminds his readers of 'the permanence of fundamental notions amid the most varying forms of expression and argument'.[113] The co-existence of bitter conflict with a shared source of

---

[110] Nederman (2005) p. 11.   [111] See the discussion in Nederman (2005) pp. 8–13.
[112] McCready (1975) p. 273.   [113] Figgis (1960) p. 26.

foundational norms meant that debates about authority were conducted within a common moral framework. Gray writes that,

> in the medieval period, the two centres faced one another as enemies, and yet both claimed authority from the same source, both acknowledged some force behind the enemy's claim of legitimacy, and both governed subjects who maintained loyalty to both.[114]

Even when in the ascendancy, the anti-papalist secular thinkers were careful not promote doctrines that fundamentally challenged medieval tradition. During this era, 'even in the midst of imperial and papal disputes, there remained a mutual acknowledgement of the necessity of balance between the spiritual and temporal concerns'.[115] In response to the papal offensive, argues Krieger, 'the intellectual defenders of the secular rulers sought in the main to make a cogent doctrine out of traditional pluralism in the medieval attitude toward authority'.[116] This involved the realignment of the relationship between the temporal and spiritual realm in a way that conceded the Church authority in the domain of the spiritual while consolidating regal authority in the temporal. The establishment of parallel lines of authority implied an equivalence in function, though royal authority was 'superior in power to pontifical authority'.[117]

The rulers of the emerging territorial states understood that the cultivation of their own authority required the validation of the Christian Church. So in the short run the question confronting them was how to curb papal power while retaining an essentially Christian idea of authority. Debates about power and authority continued to be expressed in the language of religion, and power struggles between secular rulers were often expressed through religious doctrine. This tendency was evident even in the early modern era. 'Yet when all reservations have been made, there can be little doubt that it is right to treat the growth of political ideas, during the fifteenth and sixteenth centuries, as a branch of ecclesiastical history', declares Figgis.[118] Until the sixteenth century, kings and rulers lacked the confidence to express their authority in a new secular form. Later, some monarchs sought to resolve this problem by adopting the papal doctrine of plenitude of power. As Oakeshott notes, 'when some kings in the sixteenth century claimed a *plenitude potestas* they were aping a claim made centuries before on behalf of the popes'.[119]

From the standpoint of the sociology of authority, the medieval era appears as a world where taken-for-granted norms prevailed outwardly while their meanings were tested and modified by competing claims-makers. Contrary to the manner in which traditional societies

---

[114] Gray (2007) p. 197.   [115] Gray (2007) p. 195.   [116] Krieger (1968) p. 149.
[117] Krieger (1968) p. 149.   [118] Figgis (1960) p. 26.   [119] Oakeshott (2006) p. 276.

are represented, medieval Europe demonstrated a surprising degree of openness to doctrinal development and innovation. This suggests that, rather than counterposing tradition to change, conceptual clarification is required to elaborate how change is expressed and experienced in a traditional context. In this context, it is difficult to disagree with Berman when he contends that Weber may have overlooked the 'creative role of historical consciousness in the development of new legal institutions'.[120] Again a measure of historical specificity is called for. Historical consciousness in medieval times existed in an embryonic form and was preoccupied with reconciling modification to custom with the legacy of tradition.

In retrospect one is struck not by the antithesis but by the synthesis between traditional and legal-rational norms. Tradition could be expressed through natural law and appeals to reason and in turn, tradition played an important role in the validation of the law. Although conceptually distinct, these Weberian ideal types were often mutually reinforcing sources of authority. Weber of course recognised that his ideal type of domination could not be placed 'into a simple evolutionary line' and that 'they in fact appear together in the most diverse combinations'.[121] However, it is necessary to go a step further and look at the combination through which authority is validated. Our discussion of medieval claims-making suggests that it was the mutually reinforcing influence that custom and rational/legal imposed on one another that gave foundational norms such resilience.

The normative foundational unity on which medieval authority was based could survive the divisive effects of territorial fragmentation. Although the legacy of universalism was implicitly and sometimes explicitly questioned, the normative foundation of authority remained relatively coherent. What led to its demise was the expression of territorial divisions through the medium of religious conflict. Whereas papal imperialism only undermined the moral status of the papacy, the religious wars unleashed by the Reformation had a far graver consequence for the standing of tradition and authority. In the early modern era, the problem of authority became the problem of order.

[120] Berman (1987) p. 768.   [121] Weber (1978) p. 1133.

7 Reformation and the emergence of the problem of order

The sixteenth-century Reformation Movement helped to create the conditions for the final unravelling of medieval authority. This movement can be interpreted as at once a cause, a response and expression of the moral crisis of the Roman Church. That Luther's break with the Roman Church coincided with the emergence of soon-to-be nation states ensured that controversies over religious doctrines would intersect with secular political conflicts. The ferocity of theological conflict and its destructive divisive impact had the long-term effect of forcing European society to look for an authoritative solution to the problem of endemic disorder and insecurity. Since violent conflicts of interests were expressed through religious disputes, the search for order was drawn towards secular solutions; and as Hegel remarked, 'states and communities had arrived at the consciousness of independent moral worth'.[1] As a result authority gradually divested itself of its outward religious appearance and assumed a political form. In the post-Reformation era, authority became increasingly politicised and gradually attached itself to the sovereign nation state.

Unintended shattering of authority

The gradual erosion of the Universalist foundation for medieval authority was the inevitable consequence of the growing salience of national, or at least territorial, consciousness. Until the sixteenth century this consciousness lacked the confidence to express its aspiration through an explicit claim for secular sovereignty. But from the late medieval period onwards, trends towards the weakening of the papacy over temporal matters, the centralisation of territorial institutions, and the crisis of the universal Church were working towards the demise of the medieval idea of authority. The most significant influence at work in the late fifteenth and early sixteenth centuries was the rising criticism of the moral standing of the

---

[1] Hegel (2004) p. 406.

Church, which ultimately led to the demise of Christian unity and papal authority.

The Reformation, which began with the publication of Martin Luther's Ninety-Five Thesis in 1517, had the effect of totally unsettling authority. Luther's defiance of the papacy, which eventually led to the disintegration of a united Christendom, also provoked an irresolvable debate about the locus of religious authority. Luther's claim that Christians could have direct access to God without the need for an intermediary called into question the role of the clergy and the Church hierarchy. In effect he raised 'the dominant question which still exercises us today: where does religious authority lie'?[2] Luther also opened up a wider debate on obedience and resistance to political rule. In the sixteenth century, the political and religious spheres were so intertwined that 'no reformation of religion could take place without a transformation of the public order of the commonwealths'.[3]

Until this time authority as such had not been subject to a powerful intellectual and political attack; and the Reformation itself did not set out to undermine authority. It is unlikely that when Luther nailed his Ninety-Five Thesis on the door of the Castle Church in Wittenberg he sought to fundamentally weaken the Roman church: as Davies notes, at this time 'Luther seems unconscious of having contravened the Church's doctrine of authority'.[4] At most what Luther sought was the constitution of a different locus for religious authority. Indeed it can be argued that the leaders of the Protestant churches wanted to preserve ecclesiastical authority, but in what they claimed was a more spiritual and moral form.

However, through challenging the moral integrity of the Roman Church, Luther set into motion a chain of events that would lead to fundamental questions being asked. 'Do I obey my conscience, the established religious creed, my government or the larger claims of mankind?' were the kind of queries raised by Luther's actions.[5] 'Here I stand, so help me God, I can do no other' – Luther's response to the demand that he recant his views at the Diet of Worms in April 1521 – gave voice to a sentiment that would eventually provide legitimation for the act of disobeying authority. The English historian Christopher Hill goes so far as to state that the 'essence of Protestantism – the priesthood of all believers – was logically a doctrine of individualist anarchy'.[6] Writing more than three centuries after Luther's remarkable statement, Marx observed that

[2] Hurstfield (1965) p. 6.   [3] Hopfl (1991) p. VII.   [4] Davies (1945).
[5] Hurstfield (1965) p. 6.   [6] Hill (1986) p. 38.

in effect Luther had 'shattered faith in authority'.[7] What Marx implied was that the sensitising of European society to the sanctity of individual conscience would inevitably render problematic an unquestioned obedience to external authority. Hegel's formulation that the 'essence of the Reformation' was that 'Man is in his very nature destined to be free' also drew attention to this significant development.[8]

The idea that individual conscience could stand in opposition to authority, or at least diverge from it, often led to the view that these were principles that were potentially or actually antithetical. In subsequent centuries the tension between conscience and obedience would acquire a more systematic expression in the elaboration of the polar opposite principles of freedom versus authority.

Thomas More, in his polemical tract *Responsio ad Lutherum* (1523), predicted that criticism of Church corruption would lead to a turn against all forms of authority. More, along with most leading public figures of his day, had become preoccupied with the threat posed by the fragility of authority over the 'masses of the ignorant and destitute',[9] and regarded those who questioned the authority of the Church as not simply heretics but as a threat to the maintenance of order. The outbreak of the Peasants' Revolt in Germany in 1524 appeared to vindicate More's prediction that Luther's doctrine inexorably led to chaos.

Luther himself shared More's violent hatred of rebellion. His violent denunciation of the Peasants' Revolt and his call for its bloody repression indicated that he was no less concerned with preserving order than his Catholic opponents. But Luther could not quite comprehend the momentous consequences of his challenge to papal power. Since the different dimensions of early sixteenth-century authority were intimately interconnected, the attack on the political institutions of the Church could not leave other constituents of authority untouched. Arendt writes that 'whenever one of the elements of the Roman trinity, religion or authority or tradition was doubted or eliminated, the remaining two were no longer secure', and that 'it was Luther's error to think that his challenge of the temporal authority of the Church and his appeal to unguided individual judgment would leave tradition and religion intact'.[10]

The problematisation of authority in the sixteenth century was not merely the outcome of the logic inherent in the doctrines of the Reformation. The Peasants' Revolt was inspired by the ideas raised by reformers, but it was also the product of socio-economic upheavals that were

---

[7] See Marx's 'Contribution to the Critique of Hegel's Philosophy of Law. Introduction', published in 1844, in Marx (1975) p. 182.
[8] Hegel (2004) p. 417.   [9] See Marius (1985) p. 303.   [10] Arendt (2006) p. 128.

transforming Europe. This was a moment of intense social and economic change, and the rise of the Reformation was closely linked to the powerful impulse towards political centralisation. Indeed the pre-existing tension between the papacy and nationalist aspirations within the Catholic Church proved crucial for the spread of influence of Protestantism.

For its part, religious divisions diminished the moral and political influence of Christianity overall, which in turn encouraged the desacralisation of authority. Once authority lost the validation of the divine it had to account for itself in the secular language of political theory and philosophy, and new secular arguments had to be developed to justify the claim to authority and obedience to it. From this point onwards, authority became increasingly conceptualised as conventional and political. It is in the sixteenth and seventeenth centuries that the 'modern idea' that authority as a 'consciously constituted or legitimate power to command and to secure obedience' was forged.[11] The debate could no longer be confined to issues such as what constituted the origins of authority or how it could be restored: polarised questions were now raised about how to restrain and justify authority. As Berry states, 'the central problem of post-Reformation Europe was legitimacy'.[12]

The anti-authoritarian tendencies inherent in Protestant doctrine were offset by the predominant mood of fear and anxiety about the destructive consequences of religious conflict in Europe. As Allen writes, 'people in the sixteenth century, when they thought politically, were above all preoccupied with the problem of establishing and maintaining order'.[13] This period brought the emergence of what sociologists characterise as the modern *problem of order*. With the erosion of the normative foundational unity on which medieval authority rested, the very constitution of social order became a subject of discussion and concern. 'It was very manifest that above all what was needed was a profound recognition of the duty of obedience to duly constitute political authority', argued Allen, adding that 'the question how such authority is derived, on what rests the obligation to obey and how far and in what sense it is limited, was, above else, the question of the century'.[14]

The answer to 'the question of the century' increasingly sought to posit the capacity to enforce order and social consensus as the source of authority. Thus religious disunity encouraged a pragmatic turn from divine, moral and traditional authority towards a more conventional and consensual model. By the end of the century, authority was 'conceived to be the voluntary creation of natural individuals for the expressly political

[11] See Krieger (1977) p. 253.   [12] Berry (1997) p. 30.
[13] Allen (1964) p. 512.   [14] Allen (1964) p. 512.

function of providing the coercive power of governments with an origin and a purpose which transcended this power but was directly relevant to it'.[15]

Over the course of this period, obedience to authority itself became an issue, since the supposition that the authority of individual conscience was logically raised prior to the idea of resistance as a permissible option. So although Luther adopted an authoritarian stance in relation to secular politics, he also 'contended that the papacy might be forcibly resisted'.[16] Luther wrote that 'the Church has no authority except to promote the greater good', and that if any Pope fought against reform, 'we must resist that power with life and limb, and might and main'.[17] Gradually the idea of religious liberty gained traction. With time, the refusal to obey a corrupt Church hierarchy hardened into a principled demand for freedom for the individual conscience.

Today, when obedience enjoys little cultural valuation and when questioning authority is interpreted as a duty of a responsible citizen, it is difficult to appreciate the dramatic significance of the reconceptualisation of authority in the Reformation era. It is worth reminding ourselves that until the post-Reformation period, authority was rarely questioned explicitly: the authority of individual rulers or the legitimacy of a particular claim to authority was challenged, but not authority as such. In this respect, the contrast between Renaissance humanism and the Reformation is striking. The anti-clericalism of the Dutch humanist theologian Erasmus, or the French humanist monk Rabelais, was 'contained within the limits of inherited thought and values'. As one study notes, 'for all their mighty efforts the men of the Renaissance were cautious and reverent of authority'.[18]

The aim of Renaissance humanists was to re-appropriate the traditions of ancient times and make them relevant for their society. The Renaissance was 'not anti-authoritarian; its most strenuous labours led to substituting one authority for another, all safely within the framework of the Christian tradition without which nothing had meaning'.[19] This was a very different mood to that of the restless seventeenth century, whose 'anti-authoritarian impatience was so powerful, its hopes for a great instauration so pervasive, that it could not, like the Renaissance, be content merely to rediscover the past; it had to push on'.[20]

The impulse of anti-authoritarianism evolved in a hesitant and gradual manner. During the early phase of the Reformation, religious and

---

[15] Krieger (1968) p. 151.   [16] Wolin (2004) p. 132.
[17] Cited in Wolin (2004) p. 132.   [18] Baker (1952) pp. 1–2.
[19] Baker (1952) p. 3.   [20] Baker (1952) p. 4.

political leaders were reluctant to explicitly raise fundamental questions about the status of authority or about the duty of obedience. Luther's personal act of disobedience was not directed against religious authority as such, but its transfer to its rightful place; and until 1550, Lutherans and Calvinists were consistent in adhering to a doctrine of non-resistance to the powers that be. This approach was modified only later, in response to political persecutions and the exigencies of physical survival. Faced with a threat to their survival, Lutherans and then Calvinists felt compelled to develop arguments that justified resistance to an ungodly tyrannical ruler.

During the 1550s Calvinist theologians John Ponet and John Knox developed a theory of popular resistance. Ponet argued that since authority was a unique gift from God to the community, those rulers who abused it should be disobeyed and dispossessed of their power.[21] Indeed, from their perspective, resistance to idolatry and tyranny had become a religious duty. Skinner wrote that this enabled them finally to 'reverse the most fundamental assumption of orthodox reformation political thought', so that they can,

reassure the people not that they will be dammed if they resist the powers that be, but rather that they will be dammed if they fail to do so, since that will be tantamount to breaking what Knox calls the 'league and covenant' which they have sworn with God himself.[22]

Calvinist theories of justified resistance were vociferously articulated by Huguenots facing persecution during the religious conflict that prevailed in France in the second half of the sixteenth century. Such theories were exported by Calvinists to the Netherlands and eventually made their way to England, where they provided intellectual sustenance to the English Revolution of the 1640s. Jesuit theologians were no less busy constructing Catholic versions of resistance theory.[23] The Jesuit theologian Suarez anticipated the liberal theories of social contract, arguing that people invested their ruler with the power to rule over them. By the closing decades of the century, 'resistance theorists on both sides of the religious divide provided scriptural grounds for regicide, when conditions warranted'.[24]

Although the early expressions of individual conscience, the quest for religious liberty and resistance theory solidified into coherent principles over time, at their inception they could be interpreted as pragmatic responses to perilous conditions. Thus, the Huguenots developed

[21] See Allen (1964) pp. 118–19.   [22] Skinner (2004) p. 238.
[23] De Jouvenel (1945) p. 35.   [24] Spellman (1998) p. 35.

doctrines of resistance in the first half of the French religious wars, and in the second half it was the turn of Catholic writers: what determined how a religion represented duties of obedience and resistance was its relationship to political power. Although this was a 'period of intense religious belief', shifting attitudes towards obedience and resistance indicated that 'the real priorities in political ideals were all too human'.[25]

A paradoxical marriage of doctrine and pragmatism

The movement for reforming the Church was a response to the apparent moral exhaustion of this powerful institution. Anti-clerical sentiments were widespread among thinking people in the early fifteenth century; a hundred years later, the institutionalised corruption of the Church of Rome had become an object of widespread cynicism. In many people's eyes the Church's devotion to the expansion of its material possessions and political power fostered a climate of spiritual malaise and corruption. Abuses such as the peddling of indulgences – the granting of full or partial remission of the punishment of sin – by the church were regarded as deviations from the doctrine of Christianity.

The rise of anti-clerical sentiment was inversely proportional to the decline of the spiritual authority of the papacy. 'Anticlericalism was built partly on disappointment that the church had not lived up to the high moral standards that clergymen were supposed to exemplify', writes Marius.[26] Anti-clericalism also served as a vehicle through which the ascending secular powers could assert their independence from the influence of Rome. Secular rulers who wished to restrain the influence of the Church were frequently sympathetic to the anti-clerical sentiments promoted by the early reformers, and often adopted the policy of embracing Reformation doctrine in pursuit of their territorial ambitions. In turn, the leaders of the Reformation frequently turned to secular governments for protection, so that religious disputes became inextricably linked with political ones. By the end of the sixteenth century, both Protestant and Catholic parties throughout Europe 'had fallen under the dominion of secular authorities'.[27]

Although the leaders of the Reformation were motivated by the duty to uphold what they perceived to be the religious truth, pragmatism dictated that they had to be closely involved in secular affairs. By calling into question the authority of the Pope and the special status of the Roman Church, Luther had implicitly invited the intervention of secular rulers in ecclesiastical affairs. The religious dispute between reformers

---

[25] Salmon (2008) p. 253.   [26] Marius (1985) p. 352.   [27] Marius (1985) p. 254.

and Rome was therefore politicised from the outset. The balance of doctrinal influence between Roman Catholics and Protestant within a particular region was invariably expressed through the relative weight of political power. Since religious conflict undermined the integrity of domestic political stability, secular rulers, no less than the leaders of competing churches, sought to enforce a homogeneity of belief in the territories they dominated. The security of secular powers was 'seriously compromised by the intensity of contemporary ideological and religious conflict'.[28] In the end, such religious disputes in Germany, France, the Netherlands and England were only resolved through war.

At this time religious disputes were pursued through wars and political conflict was expressed through rivalries between competing faiths. All the main religious leaders believed that theological purity had to be enforced by public authority. For their part, political leaders assumed that the 'unity of religion was an indispensable condition of public order'.[29] In practice, the outcome of religious disputes was determined by the balance of political power in the region concerned. In the short run the Reformation encouraged the 'amalgamation of religion and politics'.[30] The politicisation of the cause of religious reform meant that competing claims and arguments about the right to resistance and about the nature of authority were presented through the language of political theology. Kings wrote treatises on theology and religious leaders were often at the forefront of arguing the case for centralised royal power. According to one account, the church became the 'most vocal – and influential – supporters of the King's absolute power'.[31]

The amalgamation of politics and religion had the effect of strengthening the power and authority of secular rulers. The decline of Christian unity, which coincided with a powerful momentum for national territorial centralisation, meant that a 'new model of authority was surfacing'.[32] The disintegration of religious unity led to the formation of hostile factions, which often resulted in the outbreak of violent internal conflicts; and when one faction's Truth was another's Heresy, religious rivalry invariably posed the threat of permanent bloodshed and disorder. With so much irreconcilable tension surrounding religious authority, temporal rulers were frequently forced to become final arbiters of such disputes. A pervasive sense of fear and disorder dominated sixteenth-century European society. Paradoxically, the era that saw the first hint of cultural affirmation for the need for the freedom of conscience was also the time when Europe was plagued by an outbreak of panic about heresy and

---

[28] Spellman (1998) p. 35.   [29] Sabine (1961) p. 355.   [30] See Sabine (1961) p. 357.
[31] Spellman (1998) p. 44.   [32] Spellman (1998) p. 2.

witchcraft. An explosion of witch-hunting fuelled by mass hysteria about alleged malevolent satanic plots erupted around 1550, which continued well into the seventeenth century.

The threat of endemic violence forced Luther and other reformers to rely on secular rulers to enforce order and stability. 'It was not surprising that men as diverse as Luther and Bodin had voiced the same warning that only a powerful coercive authority spelled the difference between anarchy and order', writes Wolin.[33] In response to the disintegration of religious unity and the emergence of mass unrest, Luther was prepared to empower secular authority with unrestrained and absolute power of coercion. As Hopfl writes,

what is crucial given Luther's Augustinian cast of thought, is not that power should be exercised legitimately and by duly authorized office-holders (*potestates*), but that someone should use force (*gewalt*) to prevent the ungodly from tearing each other to pieces.[34]

In all but name the secular ruler was charged with becoming the supreme head of political power; and imperceptibly, the doctrine of papal absolutism was revived in the form of political absolutism.[35] Figgis observes that, 'had there been no Luther there could never have been a Louis XIV', and concludes that after Luther, the 'religion of the State superseded the religion of the Church'.[36]

Through his reliance on temporal rulers Luther set in motion a process through which the locus of authority would shift from the religious to the secular. There was an apparently contradictory dynamic at work here. The intersection of religious and political conflict unleashed a tendency towards the contestation of authority; however, such trends were initially vigorously contained by the doctrine of the Reformation. Luther may have taken a stand in accordance with his individual conscience, but he also insisted on absolute obedience to external authority, and was ruthless in his advocacy of repressing resistance to secular authority. His denunciation of Anabaptists and the Peasants' Revolt revealed Luther's unambiguously authoritarian streak. Hill argues that this 'not a logical consequence of the reformers' teachings', but rather that it was borne of a 'political necessity';[37] Wolin, by contrast, claims that Luther's deference to temporal rulers flowed logically from his religious doctrine. He contends that 'Luther's attachment to temporal authority . . . was not the particular stage in his development, but was rooted in the conviction that the fallen world of man was fundamentally orderless', and cites

[33] Wolin (2004) p. 218.   [34] Hopfl (1991) p. xv.   [35] See Sabine (1961) p. 331.
[36] Figgis (1960) p. 51.   [37] Hill (1986) p. 39.

in support of this thesis Luther's statement: 'let no one think that the world can be ruled without blood; the sword of the ruler must be red and bloody; for the world will and must be evil, and the sword is God's rod and vengeance upon it'.[38]

Luther's demand for unquestioned obedience to secular power was shared by most leading reformers. Calvin asserted that even an unjust tyrant could not be resisted. His willingness to turn Geneva into theocracy was matched by an inflexibility towards people's moral life, which 'led him to claim, in practice, for his Church, far more intensive and oppressive rights of interference than were ever, practically, claimed for the Roman clergy'.[39] Nevertheless, despite their fervent religious commitments, reformers were ready to engage with the exigencies of *realpolitik*.

However one interprets the relationship between doctrine and pragmatism, it seems that Luther's approach to political and religious authority was inconsistent. Wolin writes that Luther 'was willing to raise fundamental questions about every form of religious authority, but towards political institutions he was quite unsceptical, even when he doubted the morals and motives of rulers',[40] adding that 'although Luther adopted an authoritarian stance in relation to secular politics, he also contended that the papacy might be forcibly resisted'.[41]

One significant consequence of Luther's uncritical advocacy of absolutist political rule was that it helped erode the linkage between morality and power of the ruler. Hopfl reminds us that this is 'hardly surprising, given Luther's 1523 view of the proper function of government as repressive and punitive; repressing and punishing can be done as well by those whose power is illegitimate as by those with legitimate power'.[42] Such an instrumental attitude towards the use of coercion worked towards the separation of political authority from religious validation; indeed, the call for unqualified obedience to secular rulers made the 'Christian ethic appear irrelevant to the logic of political order'.[43] One legacy of this instrumental turn towards secular rule was to establish a relation of tension between moral authority and power.

In the midst of the religious wars and conflicts of the sixteenth and seventeenth centuries, the gradual disassociation of the validation of Christianity from the logic of political order was not strikingly apparent. Religious opinion was inherently political and theological disputes had direct political ramifications. Religious persecution in France and England was directly shaped by the political calculations of the protagonists, while kings, princes and secular rulers still looked to religious

---

[38] Cited in Wolin (2004) p. 142.   [39] Allen (1964) p. 68.   [40] Wolin (2004) p. 147.
[41] Wolin (2004) p. 132.   [42] Hopfl (1991) p. xxxvii.   [43] Wolin (2004) p. 146.

sources for the authorisation of their power. Even in seventeenth-century England, faced with a civil war, the diverse forms of political thought looked to the authorisation of religious faith for validation. Nevertheless, the steady ascendancy of political order and the subordination of the Church to that provided the conditions for the emergence of a secular form of ultimate authority.[44]

The interweaving of religion and politics fostered a public culture where the intensity of doctrinal and religious conflict co-existed with political pragmatism. It is striking how both sides of the religious divide could shift from demanding unquestioned obedience to secular rulers to calling for resistance to their authority. The imperative of survival and political expediency dictated attitudes towards resistance: as one study of sixteenth-century political theory argues, 'The struggle between religious parties or between governments and religious dissidents, was the chief factor in breaking down, here and there and more or less completely, the belief in the wickedness of overt resistance to authority'.[45] Thus, 'whereas in the 1570s resistance theory and concepts of limited monarchy had usually served protestant interests, in the 1590s they were increasingly adopted by militant Catholics'.[46] However, it is worth noting that the justification for resistance was still posed as a matter of religious duty. The tyranny of a king was represented as a form of heresy and Calvinists construed 'the lawfulness of resistance as a religious duty'.[47]

The growth of religious conflict and affirmation of theological orthodoxy was paralleled by the tendency towards political pragmatism. Allen points out that calls for 'obedience to constituted authority' and doctrines of non-resistance to authority was decreasingly presented as a 'duty to God' and increasingly argued for to pre-empt disorder.[48] Similarly the hesitant abandonment of the doctrine of non-resistance was an outcome of circumstances where the conflict between religious dissidents and governments forced participants to question the authority of their oppressor. Once religious authority could be challenged, it was only a matter of time before political necessity would lead to a similar orientation towards the secular. Resistance theories were often expressed in the language of religious reform though the issues at stake were at least as political as religious ones.[49]

The cumulative outcome of the religious wars and disputes of the sixteenth century was to accelerate the shift in influence from the papacy to the authority of royal power. The dispersal of power that characterised the medieval era gave way to the process of centralisation, and royal power

[44] See Davis (2003) pp. 377–8.   [45] Allen (1964) p. 513.   [46] Smuts (2003) p. 273.
[47] Skinner (2004) p. 240.   [48] Allen (1964) p. 513.   [49] Sabine (1961) p. 357.

grew 'at the expense of competing institutions, whether nobility, parliaments, free cities, or clergy'.[50] The tendency towards the establishment of nationally based churches co-existed with territorial centralisation, and anticipated the gradual emergence of state authority in the seventeenth century. The convergence of the religious and the political on the site of the national played an important role in providing the preconditions for the development of the State as the locus of supreme authority.

In a sense, the acquiescence of competing churches to the subordination of their institutions to the authority of the territorially based sovereign provided doctrinal preconditions for the emergence of the modern state. According to Skinner, the precondition 'for arriving at the modern concept of the State is that the supreme authority within each independent *regnum* should be recognised as having no rivals within its own territories as a law-making power and an object of allegiance'.[51] Reflections on royal power and the nation state represented an attempt to provide answers about the nature of authority at a time when disputes among churches rendered problematic the validation of rulership by religion, and the very theorisation of the state and its authority was underpinned by a sense of insecurity about prevailing disorder. Allen astutely observes that the 'amount and the seriousness of the thought devoted to the nature of the State seems to tend to vary inversely with the sense of security'.[52] Not surprisingly it was in France, where religious wars between Catholic and Huguenot forces threatened to undermine the integrity of the emerging state, that theorisation of sovereign authority, the duty of obedience to a political ruler, and the right of resistance, was most developed. In the 'latter half of the sixteenth century France became a great factory of political ideas', and the foundations for the monarchy became an important subject of theoretical reflection.[53] A century later, the growing sense of political fragility in England ensured that it was this country that was in the forefront of developing ideas about the state and the workings of authority.

So it was in the context of the religious wars in France between 1562 and 1598 that some key issues associated with modern political theory gained definition. In particular, the unresolved tension between freedom of conscience and the demand for absolute obedience contained within Reformation thought were externalised as polarised claims to the duty of resistance and absolute sovereignty. In the struggle for religious hegemony in France, the defence of the right to resist a heretical ruler was

---

[50] Sabine (1961) p. 331.   [51] Skinner (2004) p. 351.
[52] Allen (1964) p. 273.   [53] Allen (1964) p. 280.

met with the affirmation of the divine right of the monarch to absolute authority. The most significant contribution to the theorisation of
sovereign authority was made by the French political philosopher Jean
Bodin, whose *Six Books* (1576) explicitly challenged the revolutionary
ideas put forward by Huguenot resistance theorists. Bodin concluded
that since the role of government was to secure order, any resistance
to the ruler had to be outlawed to 'preserve the fragile structure of the
commonwealth'.[54]

Bodin's theory of the sovereign state represented an important departure from the previous conceptualisation of absolute authority. Unlike
the medieval theorists, Bodin did not provide a religious foundation
for the ruler's unlimited authority to make law. Sabine notes that he 'took
the idea of sovereign power out of the limbo of theology in which the theory of divine right left it'. Allen concurs, contending that the originality
of Bodin was that he represented sovereignty as a 'creation of man' and
not the will of God. Sovereignty 'came into existence because the ends
and the nature of human co-operation logically require its existence'.[55]
Bodin recognised that the state ought to serve as a moral force, but the
main priority of this institution was the capacity to exercise power.[56] His
elimination of the mandate of God in his theory of absolute sovereignty
expressed an important trend that would have enormous consequences
for the modern conceptualisation of authority – *desacralisation*.

The Luther paradox

It is one of the great paradoxes of history that a man who was so devoted
to the pursuit of Christian morality helped unleash a chain of events that
led to the desacralisation of modern authority. Luther was unwavering
in his pursuit of what he perceived as the Truth, and his passionate
commitment to his dogma at times led him to become an enthusiastic
advocate of a violent persecution of heretics and rebels. But in the very act
of demanding absolute obedience for his dogma, he inadvertently helped
foster a theological and intellectual disposition towards the contestation
of authority. His demand for answers from the papacy contributed to
the evolution of a cultural climate where authority was forced on the
defensive and had to justify itself.

Luther did not simply claim the authority of individual conscience on
his own behalf: he put forward an argument that all but negated the
capacity of external authority to exercise power over the inner life of

---

[54] Skinner (2004) p. 287.   [55] Sabine (1961) p. 399 and Allen (1964) p. 423.
[56] See Krieger (1968) p. 151.

people. His *Treatise on Good Works* (1520) stated that 'the power of the temporal authority, whether it does right or wrong, cannot harm the soul'.[57] Luther's separation of external authority from the soul helped to create the potential for the emergence of a parallel authority: that is, the authorisation of the self.

In his fascinating study *On Authority*, the literary critic Thomas Docherty writes that the 'present-day modes of thought stem, in some respects, from a crisis of authority at a very specific historical moment'. According to his interpretation, modern thought is the product of a crisis that led to the consolidation of an aspiration of autonomy from the influence of tradition. 'This modern thought' begins 'in the Renaissance and comes to fuller self-consciousness in the seventeenth century, when in England at least, the crisis of authority realised itself in the Civil War'.[58] For Docherty, a key moment in the unfolding of this drama was the crisis of authority raised by the divorce proceedings begun in 1527 by Henry VIII – which were not just about the separation of husband and wife, but a divorce between king and Pope. Until this moment, authority 'did not mean the personal initiatives of individuals': it was a 'power, sanctioned by tradition, to which one submitted'.[59] The process that Docherty explores is one where authority is contested by individuals who are prepared to question tradition. This involved a 'measure of the subjective power of initiation', as a result of which 'the meaning of the word "authority" undergoes transformation, coming closer to our understanding of it: to have authority now implies a power of instigation or innovation on the part of an individual capable of choice'.[60]

The transformation of the concept of authority from its association with divine or traditional origin was to a considerable extent an accomplishment of the freeing of the inner person from the power of external authority. Luther's protection of the soul from secular imposition led to the paradox of the co-existence of inner freedom with external domination. Nevertheless, the co-existence of apparently contradictory relations to domination could not indefinitely survive without one giving way to another. The recognition of a sphere of freedom where political rule could not legitimately coerce the individual ultimately undermined status of absolutist authority. As Marcuse wrote, the inner freedom of person must 'mean an "internal" weakening and breaking of authority relationship, however completely the individual may submit externally to earthly power'. So no matter how pervasive is the system of secular domination, its authority over the individual self was likely to diminish

---

[57] Cited in Marcuse (2008) p. 9.   [58] Docherty (1987) p. 47.
[59] Docherty (1987) p. 47.   [60] Docherty (1987) p. 49.

in the post-Reformation era. Marcuse concluded that the 'simultaneous recognition and transcendence of the whole system of earthly authorities announces a very important element in the Christian-bourgeois doctrine of freedom – its *anti-authoritarian tendency*'.[61]

Yet while the Reformation gave rise to anti-authoritarian tendencies, creating the conditions for the restraint of external power in people's inner life, it also sanctioned the use of unrestrained power in public life. In the course of the next century the contradiction between inner freedom and external domination would gain definition through the evolution of competing arguments about the nature of authority.

Arguably, the immediate impact of the Reformation was to strengthen absolutist forms of power, as 'the disruption of the universal church, the suppression of its monastic institutions and the ecclesiastical corporations, and the abrogation of the canon Law, removed the strongest checks upon secular power that had existed in the Middle Ages'.[62] This point is also stressed by Gray, who blames the Reformation and Luther in particular for subordinating the Church to the state: 'The effect was to atomize society, rendering the individual naked before the state, without a strong, institutional church to act as a check on the state'.[63] Gray adds that during the 'medieval period, even in the midst of imperial and papal disputes, there remained a mutual acknowledgement of the necessity of balance between spiritual and temporal concerns'; however, 'by the time of the Reformation and the subsequent wars of religion, this mutual acknowledgment had dissipated'.[64]

Gray's emphasis on the authoritarian consequences of the Reformation has been echoed by commentators in recent centuries. From their standpoint, Lutherism is not so much defined by its anti-authoritarian impulse as by its opposite. During the twentieth century Luther has been frequently caricatured as the historic ancestor of the modern authoritarian dictator; thus in 1944, William Ralph Inge, the former Dean of London's St Paul's Cathedral, wrote that,

if we wish to find a scapegoat on whose shoulders we may lay the miseries which Germany has brought upon the word – I am more and more convinced that the worst evil genius of that country is not Hitler or Bismarck or Frederick the Great, but Martin Luther.[65]

In historical accounts, Luther the authoritarian competes with the image of a man who is responsible for the liberation of the inner man. The

---

[61] Marcuse (2008) p. 9.   [62] Sabine (1961) p. 362.
[63] Gray (2007) p. 185.   [64] Gray (2007) p. 195.
[65] See Inge's article in *Time Magazine*; 6 November 1944, www.time.com/time/magazine/article/0,9171,803412,00.html#ixzz1iU0H3lGw (accessed 30 April 2013).

English historian Geoffrey Elton emphasises the importance of the Reformation for encouraging the rise of individualism and secularism, and for its encouragement of 'self-reliance and self-determination'. Elton writes that a,

more serious problem lay in wait for a religion which placed complete confidence in the work of God upon the individual soul, and from the first the new churches found themselves doing battle with the constant divisions they had invited by rejecting the authority of the one universal church;[66]

and concludes that,

on balance one can say no more than that the failure of Luther and Calvin to capture all Christendom strengthened those parts of their teaching which denounced authority and led man to seek the ultimate reality within himself, at the expense of those which counselled submission to the established order.

The legacy of the Reformation is most usefully conceptualised as the positing of a contradictory relationship between the imperative of order and the aspiration for individual liberty. More specifically, through solidifying this contradictory relationship, freedom and authority would be increasingly interpreted as the polar opposite of the other. The pre-Reformation consensus, which regarded authority as essential for the realisation of freedom, now gave way to a radically new interpretation. 'The problem of authority versus liberty in the determination of ultimate religious truth, would to be sure, develop into a perennial and provocative concern of Protestant theology', writes Krieger.[67] It would also constitute a serious problem for modern political theory.

The paradoxical legacy of Luther expressed itself in the crystallisation of apparently contradictory political trends: the growing validation of the freedom of inner life alongside the entrenchment of absolutist rule. One important legacy of this paradox has been construction of the modern antithesis between freedom and authority.

The post-Reformation model of authority

From the late sixteenth century onwards, authority increasingly assumes a political form. A significant section of the upper classes and of the rising commercial elite recognised the need for institutions that could minimise the disruptive effects of religious conflict and enforce order and security. In France the *politiques*, a group of Catholic elites, argued that religious 'uniformity was no longer worth preserving, however valuable it might

---

[66] Elton (1973) p. 279.   [67] Krieger (1968) p. 150.

be itself, if the cost of enforcing it seemed liable to be the destruction of the commonwealth'.[68] Pragmatically they opted for an authority that was political and whose strength was underwritten by powerful national institutions.

The detachment of religious validation from power lent authority an increasingly secular character. This desacralisation of authority stood in stark contrast to the previous medieval model. Authority was now perceived as conventional and frequently represented as the voluntary creation of consenting individuals. The validation of authority on the basis of ancient origins and tradition also weakened. The disintegration of Christian unity and the growth of the nation state meant that authority could rarely be presented as an expression of universal norms.

The desacralisation of authority

In Western history until the sixteenth century, theologically informed norms constituted the principal validation of authority as such. Thus, disputes about the authoritative source of religious truth had consequences that went way beyond the institutional interests of the Roman Church and its Protestant competitors. Once the disputes escalated and doctrinal differences became irresolvable, the search for the source of authority could no longer be contained within to the domain of the religious.

All the religious factions, 'whether they were Catholics, Lutherans, Anabaptists, Zwinglians, Calvinists, Socinians, or whatever they were, agreed with one voice that there is an authoritative source of religious truth; the question that divided them was: what was it?'[69] However, the relentless pursuit of theological conflicts had the effect of diminishing overall the universalistic claims of religious foundational authority. The decline of the institutional influence of Christian universalism coincided with the ascendancy of secular territorial and political forms of authorisation, and by the end of the seventeenth century, universal Christendom 'had been replaced by separate and sovereign states whose claims to power were derived from inside the political community, not from external and transnational authority'.[70] These new institutions enjoyed moral authority in their own right and did not require the continuous affirmation of divine sanction.

The gradual separation of religious validation for claims to power worked towards undermining the influence of the Church on practical political matters. The primacy of secular rulers and their order was most strikingly expressed through the steady desacralisation of authority:

---

[68] Skinner (2004) p. 250.   [69] Davies (1945) p. 12.   [70] Spellman (1998) p. 135.

Hegel wrote that 'perfect moral validity' presented 'itself to secularity in the formation of states'.[71]

Some political rulers in the seventeenth century carried through the logic of the territorialisation of Christianity by formally assuming leadership of their national Churches. This was consistent with Luther's own outlook: the reformers had insisted on the primacy of the Word and, by implication, called into question the status of priestly authority. The enthronement of the Bible as the source of religious truth led not only to the repudiation of the papal authority, but also to the empowerment of its secular interpreters. Philip Melachton (1497–1560), one the most respected Protestant leaders of the sixteenth century, summed up this attitude when he stated that 'there is nothing on earth more noble than the state'. Melachton, like Luther, still insisted that it was the Church and the magistrate who decides what is 'true doctrine and heresy',[72] kings and princes increasingly took the view that religion was too important an issue to leave to chance. The supremacy of the political ruler over religious affairs was explicitly formulated in the phrase *cuius region ejus religio*, which in practice meant that the religion of a principality or nation must follow that of its ruler.

Advocates of Reformation contributed to the process of secularisation through developing doctrines that reconciled theology with political pragmatism. Calvin integrated political concepts into his theology. In England, the Anglican theologian Richard Hooker (1469–1527) helped to provide arguments for the establishment of a national church led by a supreme monarch. His treatise, *The Laws of Ecclesiastical Polity* (1594), sought to refute Puritan critics of an established national church by arguing that 'in refusing obedience to the established church' the Puritans were 'implicitly denying the foundations of all political obligation'.[73] His argument for the royal supremacy in ecclesiastical affairs expresses the general trend towards the rise of national political institutions. The secularisation and politicisation of power was welcomed by many public figures who were sensitive to the destructive consequences of religious conflict.

The centralisation of political power required that the newly established nation state would enjoy indivisible authority. This standpoint was systematically expressed by Thomas Hobbes, in his insistence that a political sovereign should enjoy absolute power; and seventeenth-century European society was prepared to accept the desacralisation of authority implicit in Hobbes's political philosophy. As Hill points out, Luther's acceptance of the dominant position of the political ruler led to Hobbes,

---

[71] Hegel (2004) p. 406.   [72] Allen (1964) p. 32.   [73] See Sabine (1961) p. 439.

and though Hobbes's 'insistence that the sovereign and only the sovereign could interpret the Bible was unpopular among theologians', it 'proved more acceptable to ordinary citizens'.[74]

The separation of power and authority

The desacralisation, or secularisation, of authority required that its relationship to power be reformulated. The outcome of this reformulation was to recast the meaning of authority as principally a political attribute of the sovereign state. Despites religious differences, both Catholic and Protestant societies gave way to the ascendancy of lay political power. Although the Reformation set in motion a powerful current of thought critical of the imposition of external authority, a generalised sense of insecurity predisposed European societies to embrace the politics of order. By the early seventeenth century, the idea of political authority linked to the emergence the state, 'its nature, its powers, its right to command obedience', had become 'the most important object of analysis in European political thought'.[75]

The unquestioned moral foundation of medieval authority could not survive the loss of Christian unity in the post-Reformation era. It is likely that, at least in part, the loss of moral authority of the Church encouraged reliance on more explicit forms of absolutist coercion. It also led to the clarification of the secular distinction between the moral and the political and between authority and power. The process of clarification occurred in a roundabout way through the unconscious convergence of advocates of religious reform and secular rulers seeking to consolidate national sovereignty. Through this convergence, churches became increasingly territorially differentiated and subordinated to the imperatives of national sovereignty. But the cumulative outcome of the convergence of church and state was to establish the precondition for the crystallisation of political autonomy and the detachment of the moral from political authority.

The argument for this eventuality was already rehearsed in the writings of Nicolo Machiavelli (1469–1527). Machiavelli's writings express a single-minded focus on the political; as Russell states, he 'never bases any political argument on Christian or biblical grounds'.[76] Machiavelli's separation of the pursuit of political interest from morality represented a clear argument in favour of the autonomy of the political. The exhaustion of old medieval institutional arrangements was evident in the Italian city-states before anywhere else, and Machiavelli's writing can be interpreted

---

[74] Hill (1986) p. 47.   [75] Skinner (2004) p. 349.   [76] Russell (1947) p. 469.

as an attempt to reconstitute authority on a self-conscious political foundation. It would take more than a century for Machiavelli's separation of morality from politics to become clarified as a separation between power and authority.

The distinctions between power and authority had an important cultural salience in ancient Rome, captured by concepts such as *imperium*, *potestas* and *auctoritas*. However, these distinctions tended to play a relatively minor role in the medieval era. Even the leaders of the Reformation did not quite make a sharp separation between power and authority. Weimann notes that in Calvin, like Luther, 'there is a distinctly traditional, medieval refusal to differentiate between *potestas* and *auctoritas*'. As proof he refers to the last chapter of Calvin's main work, where '*potestas* stands not for imperial might and authority, but for that of the church, while "civil government" is rendered as *administratio*'. He adds that 'there is an undifferentiated connotation of legitimacy in his uses of both *potestas* and *autoritas* [sic]'. Similarly, his French version of 1560 fails to 'differentiate the semantic field marked by *Puissance* and *authorite* as well as, again, by *domination*'. The vocabulary of Calvin and Luther is still steeped in the language of the past and 'in its lexical order clearly precedes (even while it helps bring about) modern differentiations among socio-cultural locations of authority'.[77]

Richard Tuck's fascinating study of the birth of a new political language in the seventeenth century provides a vivid account of the development of a vocabulary that is sensitive to the distinction between power and authority. He cites numerous writers who, in contrast to earlier times, explicitly distinguished between the two concepts. For example, William Robinson's *The People's Plea* (1642) stated that 'the King hath his power from the Kingdome, and therefore his Authoritie', and adds 'I must crave leave here to distinguish these termes [sic], which commonly are confounded and obscure this whole business'.[78] In his review of seventeenth-century English political writing, Tuck states that the 'distinction between *power* and *authority*, which has been a familiar concept with which to analyse politics since the seventeenth century, could not be found (they claimed) in the writings of their predecessors'.[79]

The elaboration of a new political language was influenced by the emergence of the belief that not all rulers were entitled to obedience. Prior to this, the 'almost universal conviction among sixteenth-century European political theorists that no individual subject could be allowed

[77] See Weimann (1996) pp. 43–4.   [78] Tuck (1974) p. 43.   [79] Tuck (1974) p. 43.

a right of resistance against even a tyrannical ruler' meant that the dis-association of power from authority did not have to be conceptualised.[80] However, the elaboration of the thesis that an evil ruler need not be always obeyed led directly to the contention that coercive power could in some cases lack legitimacy. As events unfolded in the rapidly changing political landscape of the seventeenth century, the need to distinguish power from authority became more pressing.

The conceptual distinction reflected the growing disposition towards differentiating between a form of rule that relies on physical coercion to gain acquiescence and one that 'succeeds in exacting obedience' when 'its "right" to be obeyed is recognized to be legitimate and is acceded to'.[81] Once power and authority are expressed as polarised conceptions, the relationship between them, and with the rest of society, becomes a subject of reflection and debate, and the focus of constant evaluation. With the desacralisation of obedience as a political theological duty, power needed to be justified. As natural or religious claims ceased to serve as credible foundational norms, new questions about the right to resist, liberty and obligation become increasingly difficult to answer. Power was now exposed to critical inquiry. Even a thinker of an authoritarian mould, such as Hobbes, needed to claim that the authorisation of the absolute sovereign had a voluntary basis.

Authority becomes perceived as increasingly conventional/artificial

The seventeenth and eighteenth centuries are frequently ascribed the label of an age of absolutism. This was a time when insecure rulers responded to the uncertain conditions created by the Reformation by elaborating the doctrine of absolute royal power which, they claimed, was validated by divine right. Louis XIV's declaration in July 1652 that 'All authority belongs to us', and 'We hold it of God alone', is often cited as an example of the powerful assertion of divine right kingship.[82] The rise of powerful absolutist monarchs, such as Louis XIV, Frederick II of Prussia or Peter the Great, was the outcome of a protracted process of political and military consolidation. The doctrinal influence of divine right kingship sought to provide this new form of rule with intellectual legitimation.

The ascendancy of the claim of divine right was outwardly an expression of royalist certainties about nature of supreme kingly power. But its very explication can be interpreted as a pragmatic response to the

---

[80] Tuck (1974) p. 45.   [81] Oakeshott (2006) p. 293.
[82] Cited by Kamen (1976) p. 474.

uncertainties posed by the unsettling of authority in the post-Reformation era. As David Parker argues in relation to French Absolutism, this was a conservative philosophy – a 'pragmatic, frequently *ad hoc* and contradictory attempt to *restore* royal authority in the context of a rapidly changing world'.[83] From a sociological perspective the elaboration of the doctrine of divine rights of kings can be conceptualised as an initial response to the early modern problem of order. Political chaos in post-Reformation Europe, particularly in France, created a demand for absolute certainty. Divine right kingship was part of a project designed to contain the destructive effects of religious civil strife and conflict in nations such as France and England.

Divine right theories can also be understood as a defensive reaction against the threat posed by the influence of resistance theories. Proponents of this doctrine, such as Jacques-Beninge Bossuet (1627–1704), sought to validate royal authority through elaborating the ancient claim that monarchs were divinely chosen. In England, Sir Robert Filmer's (1588–1653) attempt to defend this doctrine relied on the rather clumsy tactic of tracing political authority back to the Garden of Eden. 'Sir Robert implicitly claimed that the standards established by God at the very beginning of the world were the ones by which subsequent acts and institutions were to be judged', comments an important study.[84]

Divine Right theories possessed little intellectual substance and their attempt to resurrect Biblical arguments about God-chosen rulers went against the temper of the times. As Sabine explains, the problem with these theories was not so much that they were theological – resistance theories were too – 'but that the peculiar legitimacy attributed to royal power defied analysis or rational defense'. Often, as in Filmer's case, they were based on a forced analogy with the authority of the patriarch over his family.[85] Advocates of Divine Right were frequently uncertain how far to push their claim to absolute authority. James I wrote extensively on the subject of royal authority and sought to defend it as an absolutist; nevertheless he acknowledged that 'though he did derive his title from the loins of his ancestors, yet the law did set the Crown upon his head', and added that 'it was dangerous to submit the power of a king to definition'.[86]

James appeared to possess an instinctive understanding of absolutist authority. He grasped that once it had to be spelled out in detail, its legitimacy would be compromised. His warning that it was dangerous to 'submit the power of king to definition' exposed an underlying insecurity about the desacralisation of royal power and other forms of authority.

---

[83] Parker (1973) p. 90.   [84] Schochet (1975) p. 7.
[85] Sabine (1961) pp. 393 and 394.   [86] Cited in Smuts (2003) pp. 278–9.

The seventeenth century may have been an era of absolutism, but it was also a time that was subject to a crisis of belief and a new consciousness of historical transience. In his path-breaking study, Paul Hazard characterises this period as one which led to questions like 'what was man to believe?' and 'what is truth?'[87] Authority now had to account for itself through arguments rather than relying on faith. The French philosopher Pierre Bayle (1647–1706) summed up the mood of questioning that characterised European intellectual life: 'I have said it before, and I say it again; it is the purest delusion to suppose that because an idea has been handed down from time immemorial to succeeding generations, it may not be entirely false'.[88] In such a cultural climate, political and social arrangements were increasingly interpreted as artificial and conventional.

The Reformation itself played an important role clarifying the social character of community life and political arrangements. The sociologist Adam Seligman underlines the shift towards what he described as the 'deification' of society through pointing to the Reformation's 'this-worldly' sensibility. He points out that Calvin in particular stressed the voluntary nature of Christian community, which was expressed in 'the conventional or consensual nature of the ties assumed by its participants'.[89] By the early decades of the seventeenth century, the intimate connection between Christian theology and political thinking had been sufficiently loosened for the emergence of new conventional theories of authority.

Conventional conceptions of authority, which emphasised consent as it its foundation, emerged in parallel with the rise of absolutist theories of the divine. According to some accounts, one of the accomplishments of the assertion of divine right was to stimulate its opposite, which 'made the consent of the governed a necessary element in government'. Clark added that 'it was inevitable, if unforeseen and undesired consequence of the Protestant revolution, that where the individual had loosened the power of ecclesiastical authority, he should shake that of secular authority'.[90]

The project of formulating a viable theory of authority could not avoid providing a role for popular consent. In his book *Politica Methodice Digesta* (1603), the German jurist and Calvinist philosopher Johannes Althusius (1537–1638) offered an early attempt to elaborate an anti-monarchical social contract theory. His argument that sovereignty resided in people as a corporate body represented a coherent alternative to the absolutist state theory of Bodin.[91] This political theory 'was both interesting and

---

[87] Hazard (1973) p. 35.   [88] Cited in Hazard (1973) p. 188.
[89] Seligman (1990) p. 163.   [90] Clark (1947) pp. 224 and 225.
[91] Clark (1947) p. 226.

important, because it depended logically upon the single idea of contract and owed substantially nothing to religious authority'.[92]

Authority as the product of convention and consensus was not inconsistent with the elaboration of absolutist model of authority. Thomas Hobbes explicitly rejected the attempt to construct the authority of the state on the foundation of theology or natural law. His representation of the crystallisation of political authority as a covenant based on people's willingness to exchange their freedom for security offered a coherent attempt to reconcile absolute sovereignty with popular consensus. As Wood remarks, Hobbes is 'the most striking example' of an absolutist determined to uphold authority on the basis of popular consent:

> for he set out to accomplish nothing less than a defence of absolutism on the basis of the most democratic principles current in the revolutionary period. He adopted the radical idiom of natural right, the natural freedom and equality of all individuals (at least all male heads of households), and the doctrine that no principle of nature sanctions the division between ruler and ruled, so that there can be no legitimate authority except that which is ultimately based on consent.[93]

Hobbes's attempt to reconcile principles of consensus with absolutism was possibly one of the most thoughtful attempts to resolve the problem of order.

The corollary of the strengthened perception that political arrangements were conventional was the weakening of the power of tradition. Yet tradition did not simply vanish. Its capacity to link the present to a common cultural origin played a crucial role in the historical evolution of authority in early modern Europe. In England, resistance to James I's absolutist claims of royal prerogative was mounted by Chief Justice Sir Edward Coke (1552–1634): Coke's assertion that it was the common law that assigned the king his powers found adherents in Parliament, who used it to establish a countervailing power to Royal authority.[94]

In England, customary law and the Ancient Constitution drew on such precedents as the nobles' revolt against King John and the granting of the Magna Carta to unsettle the claim of Divine Right kingship. The radicalisation of Parliamentary opposition to the Stuart Dynasty was based on claims about the relevance of tradition and historical precedent, with liberty upheld as a right based on ancient precedent. On 22 May 1610, the jurist Sir James Whitelocke attacked the claim to royal prerogative by stating that 'the ancient frame of the commonwealth' would be 'much

---

[92] Sabine (1961) p. 417.   [93] Wood (1991) p. 56.   [94] Smuts (2003) pp. 278–9.

altered', and Parliament, 'the storehouse of our liberties', would be seriously threatened.[95]

Arguments about ancient traditions and liberties were regularly mounted by the Parliamentary opponents of Charles I in the years leading up to the outbreak of the Civil War. However, on their own, purely historical arguments claiming to uphold ancient tradition lacked the capacity to uphold the authority of Parliament: they required more sophisticated philosophical arguments about the foundation of sovereignty. In an era of massive social and political transformation, when the conventional character of institutional arrangements was difficult to ignore, the explanatory status of tradition was significantly compromised.

The detachment of political theory from theology created a demand for a normative foundation for authority. One provisional solution put forward in the seventeenth century was to propose the law of nature, with its emphasis on reason and rationality, as the basis for political authority. Natural law theory tended to express itself through positing a contract between the ruler and ruled, and from this standpoint the duty of obedience to the ruler was based on some form of chronologically prior consent. As with Hobbes's theory of the absolutist sovereign, contract theory could be used to uphold the power of the ruler as well as to justify acts of disobedience. However, because such a pact was inherently linked to the act of individual consent, supporters of royal authority regarded contract theory with hostility; and in England, because of the 'dangers inherent in contract theory almost all royalists firmly rejected the notion that civil society is the product of individual wills and pacts'.[96]

Hostility towards contractual theories of political authority and the assumption that civil society was conventional was countered by the doctrine of Patriarchy, which contended that everyone from Adam had been the 'natural subject of his father' and therefore political authority was 'natural, not conventional; men had not created the state and were powerless to change or control it'.[97] However, the attempt to establish patriarchialism as a validation for absolutist authority failed to counteract the influence of consent-based contract theory. The demand for conventional explanations for authority was fostered by a climate where cultural and intellectual life had developed a fundamentally novel orientation towards the past.

The Reformation did not merely challenge religious and political authority, but also the intellectual outlook that preceded it. Religious

---

[95] See Sommerville (1999). Whitelocke is cited by Sommerville (1999) p. 142.
[96] Goldie (2008) p. 604.   [97] Schochet (1975) p. 55.

conflict unleashed a cycle of intense debate which led to the exposure of the fallacies of opponents, and 'the next generation to doubts as to the dogmas themselves'. Hurstfield believes 'that is one reason why, in the late sixteenth century, we notice the rise of sceptical humanism among educated men',[98] and 'theologians, having discredited each other in their bitter quarrels, found to their dismay that they had brought discredit upon the very fundamentals of their religion and thereby helped to open the door to scepticism, free thinking and rationalism'.[99] In turn the 'spread of scepticism' was 'slowly eroding belief in traditional values and traditional hierarchies'.[100]

In this climate of debate all claims, including appeals to the past, were subjected to forensic criticism. The Reformation did not simply disorient theological thought; it called into question the fundamentals of European intellectual life.

The loss of the authority of the past

The growth of historical consciousness is itself a major influence in the transformation of the idea of authority. As society becomes sensitised to change, the past loses some or much of its authorising role. The idea that societies are subject to variations in custom and government encourages a conventional perception of authority, and fosters a climate where authority is open to contestation – either implicitly or explicitly. The most important side-effect of this process is the gradual dissolution of the authority of the past. Hints of this process are already discernible in ancient Greece, but it acquired an irreversible dynamic in the seventeenth century.

The authority of the past was exposed to powerful criticism by philosophers who regarded reason, rather than tradition, as the source of the truth. A variety of cultural influences – religious upheaval, scientific discovery, overseas travel, the impact of printing, rapid social change – had the cumulative effect of undermining allegiance to tradition. Hazard notes that this era saw the rise of a fascination with novelty, leading to the enthronement of the present at the expense of the past.[101] 'Probably in no century before or since was there so self-conscious a break with the past or so resolute an effort to win freedom from the dead hand of custom and tradition', notes one review of seventeenth-century political

[98] Hurstfield (1965) p. 16.   [99] Hurstfield (1965) p. 16.
[100] Stone (1986) pp. 108–9.   [101] See Hazard (1973) Chapter 2.

theory.[102] Even the authority of tradition a source of historical truth was contested.[103]

Sceptical thinkers argued that claims based on tradition were likely to be misrepresentations of the past. Michel Montaigne (1553–1592) was a key figure in the deconstruction of the knowledge of the ancients, reducing the 'authority of antiquity' to a 'collection of moral and epistemological exemplars'.[104] History itself was derided as possessing little truth. Rene Descartes (1596–1650), in his *Discourse on Method* (1637), 'dismissed historical writings as misleading on account of their grand style'.[105] Descartes's scepticism towards historical writings was linked to his rationalist commitments. The growing valuation of reason and science meant that what counted was first-hand experience, rather than an authority handed down from the distant past.

The development of theories of contract and sovereignty were a political response to the post-Reformation problem of order, and were intellectually shaped by the scientific revolution of the time. Hobbes, whom we shall discuss in greater detail in the next chapter, wrote his momentous contribution to the philosophy of authority in the context of the Civil War in England and the unfolding revolution in science. As Wolin indicates, 'Hobbes wrote from the midst of a scientific revolution which seemed to snap the continuity between the present and the past, exposing the wisdom of the ancients as convenient targets of sarcasm'.[106]

The loss of universal validation

Arguably the most irresolvable problem faced by theorists of authority was the loss of its Universalist validation. This was not simply a doctrinal issue. The decline of the medieval traditions and loyalties during the Reformation meant that European societies no longer shared or accepted any Universalist claims to authority. The new ideas about sovereign authority enunciated by Bodin and Hobbes could not subject kings and rulers to any higher or universal laws. Without the validation of Universalist foundational norms the uneasy relationship between the will of the sovereign and popular consent could always erupt in conflict.

Arendt notes that 'it was the error of Hobbes and the political theorists of the seventeenth century to hope that authority could be saved without tradition'.[107] However, an equally significant (and generally unremarked) problem faced by political theorists of authority was the loss

---

[102] Sabine (1961) p. 431.   [103] Cited in Hazard (1973) p. 188.
[104] Sedley (1998) p. 1082.   [105] Cited in Burke (1998) p. 4.
[106] Wolin (2004) p. 217.   [107] Arendt (2006) p. 128.

of universal norms for validating it. The detachment of authority from an unquestioned claim to universal validity would erupt into periodic crisis of legitimation in modern society. In the short run, it unleashed an unprecedented process of contestation and the elaboration of contradictory versions of authority. Competing claims and theories about legitimacy – Divine Kingship, Sovereignty of the State, Patriarchal Rule, Natural Law, Tradition and Ancient Constitution, Contract Theory of Consent and Popular Consent – exposed the absence of consensus about the meaning of authority in Europe.

The loss of a Universalist foundation for authority would continue to preoccupy political philosophers in the centuries to come. In the nineteenth century Hegel would turn to the state as the instrument through which the particularistic perspectives could be overcome by a richer universalistic one. He wrote that the,

principle of modern state has the deep-seated ability of allowing the principle of subjectivity to work itself out to the current extreme limit of independent individual particularity and of bringing it back simultaneously to the main unity; and so maintaining this unity in the midst of this principle of licence.[108]

But the secularisation of the search for the source of truth could not provide an answer accepted by all. In that sense, the contestation of religious authority of the Reformation anticipated the modern paradigm of an authority that lacks universal validation. As the English political theorist Harold Laski remarked in 1919, 'the notion of a single and universal authority commensurate with the bounds of social life was utterly destroyed when Luther appealed to the princes in the interests of religious reform'.[109] Laski's remark is not an overstatement of the significance of the Reformation for the subsequent fate of authority. This was a unique moment when the 'question of authority came to the front more prominently' than 'at any other point of history before or since'.[110] The forces unleashed by the Reformation worked towards the consolidation of a new model of authority, which by the end of the seventeenth century came to dominate European political endlife and thought.

Contestation for intellectual authority and the striving for freedom

The religious disputes initiated by Luther had a significant impact on the wider lay public. The claim that the authority of the Word was absolute

---

[108] Cited by De Jouvenel (1945) p. 58.
[109] Laski (1919) p. 21.   [110] Davies (1945) p. 11.

called into question priestly monopoly over the interpretation of Christian doctrine. Accordingly, members of the Church hierarchy could no longer maintain their positions as sole interpreters of the scriptures since the 'laity were just as well authorized to interpret' the Bible as were they.[111] Opponents of Luther and his ally William Tyndale were not simply concerned about protecting the status of the clergy: they feared that if ordinary folk were allowed to interpret the scripture, the integrity of Christian doctrine would be compromised. Thomas More, who was initially open to the idea of translating the Bible to the vernacular, eventually became hostile to it because he feared that it would 'stir up disputation rather than piety among the common people'.[112]

Instinctively the Catholic Church grasped the challenge posed by the destabilising consequences of providing common people with direct access to the vernacular Bible. In the theological disputes that followed, Catholic theologians deployed a variety of arguments against the authority of the scriptures, of which the most important was the necessity of defending the integrity of the Christian tradition. Thomas More argued that these traditions were based on 'common consent' and precedents and customs which he claimed were far more authoritative than the written text. As his biographer wrote, 'More located the inspiration of custom in oral tradition, Christ had spoken and done far more things than had been written down'.[113] More insisted that 'whatever has been practised for so long by the Church must be correct because God would not allow His Church to remain in error'.[114]

Although More's defence of custom and tradition failed to check arguments supporting the expansion of the Bible's availability, his premonition about the destabilising potential of its loss proved prescient. Through encouraging the bypassing of the professional clergy, theological interpretation and controversy now gained a far wider public. The popularisation of religious disputes had the potential for forcing all forms of authority under scrutiny. As Hill states, the Bible 'proved a time-bomb which humbler protestants used against their betters'.[115] The subversive implications of encouraging people to make a direct appeal to God was recognised by the royalist thinker, Sir William Sanderson (1586–1676), who pointed out that if man possessed '"direct warrant from the written Word of God" for everything they do "all human authority will soon be despised"'.[116]

[111] McCutcheon (1991) p. 44.   [112] Marius (1985) p. 428.
[113] Marius (1985) p. 284.   [114] McCutcheon (1991) p. 100.
[115] Hill (1986) p. 41.   [116] Hill (1986) p. 42.

Protestantism, with its emphasis on the priesthood of all believers, created the condition where the questioning of conventional truths became more widespread and common. It is in this period that intellectual authority became a target of permanent questioning. The difficulty in maintaining theological and intellectual consensus was further complicated by the growing availability of printed pamphlets and texts. Hill claims that printing 'ruined Protestantism as a single coherent creed, because the reading of books is even harder to control than the reading of manuscripts'.[117] Hill's statement is echoed by Weimann, who insists that,

> what the inward scriptural location of authority presupposed and helped bring about was not simply the emancipation of knowledge from the coercion of outside authority, but a state of affairs in which knowledge could achieve a kind of 'autonomy' by judiciously governing (and) guarding itself.[118]

In a sense the authorisation of the text weakened the domination of external authority on the intellectual life of the post-Reformation era.

The emergence of a reading public had a significant impact on the conduct of public affairs. Seventeenth-century England brought a massive increase in the quantity of printed material, from 22 pamphlets published in 1640 to 1966 published in 1642.[119] A significant section the wider public became involved in public life and the authority of Royalist Power came under severe criticism. The expansion of literacy itself had a radicalising outcome: Lawrence Stone writes that it was 'dangerous', because it 'aroused expectations of political and religious participation and exposed large numbers of humble people to heady egalitarian wine of the New Testament'.[120]

One account writes of this 'extraordinary period of freedom as authority withered away'.[121] The cumulative effect of this process was the entry of common people into the political life of the nation.[122] That arguments about the nature and source of authority now had to be played out in front of an ever-expanding audience of politically interested and literate people would ensure that in the future popular consent could rarely be taken for granted. Two important events – the English Revolution of 1640, leading to the declaration of a republic and the execution of a monarch, and The Fronde in France from 1648 to 1653 – served as testimony to the destabilising consequence of the forces unleashed by the religious conflicts of the previous century.

Ideas about the right to resist despotic authority converged with those of the freedom of the inner person and the acknowledgement of

---

[117] Hill (1986) p. 25.   [118] Weimann (1996) p. 4.   [119] See Zaret (1996).
[120] Stone (1986) p. 96.   [121] Wilson (2009) p. 16.   [122] See Lake and Pincus (2006).

consent as the source of sovereignty to forge a cultural sensibility towards valuation of the authority of the self. This trend was more widely reflected in the rising influence of the conceptual distinction between subject and object, and between the internal and external world. The political theorist Kenneth Minogue claims that this reorientation towards psychology constituted a 'fundamental blow to authority', since it freed the inward-oriented individual from the duty to obey external rule.[123] Minogue's observation is echoed by Weimann, who regards the shift of authority from the clergy to the scripture as intimately linked to the growing autonomy of the inner person. According to Weimann, the Reformation 'provided an efficacious impetus to internalize authority, "to shift the basis of its verification from external and public modes to internal and private ones"'. Although the logical outcome of the divergence between the authority of the inner conscience and that of the external ruler was far from evident in the seventeenth century, it was only a matter of time before it led to a conflict between 'one mode of authority whose source is external "other-directed"' and 'another mode which claims internal, self-directed authority' in the self.[124]

According to Hill, the significance that Reformation thought attached to individual conscience 'leads logically to anarchism'; and 'once a constraining authority exists, be it state or bishops or presbytery, it is bound at some stage or another to come up against dissenting consciences'.[125] As the English Civil War demonstrated, the tension between individual protestant conscience and prevailing forms of secular authority proved to be explosive. These dramatic events in England proved to be the precursor of a series of clashes over the constitution of authority. Unlike the pre-modern disputes, these clashes came directly to involve and affect an ever-widening constituency of the public. In effect, the unravelling of authority, which 'expressed itself with peculiar fervour of entrenched religious dogma', mutated into the modern problem of order.[126]

In his important account of the 'general crisis of the 17th century', the historian Hugh Trevor-Roper notes that 'to contemporary observers it seemed that society itself was in crisis, and that this crisis was general in Europe'.[127] Contemporaries 'tended to find deep spiritual reasons' for the crisis. But one of the important developments that lent the crisis a special intensity was the preparedness of a growing constituency of people to question authority itself. As Spellman asserts, 'maintaining order in the face of desperate disturbance from below was one of the

---

[123] Minogue (1963) pp. 33–4.   [124] Docherty (1987) p. 49.
[125] Hill (1986) pp. 37–8.   [126] Hurstfield (1965) p. 2.
[127] Trevor-Roper (1959) p. 1.

paramount concerns of writers from across the ideological spectrum in the seventeenth century'.[128]

The challenge raised by ideas of popular sovereignty and theories of resistance led to the elaboration of the idea of the sovereign nation state. The development of the idea of an impersonal institution and autonomous object of loyalty in the form of the state represented the most significant and creative response to the problem of authority. Political theorists like Hobbes recognised that order required that sovereignty should be expressed through an impersonal form of authority that was 'distinct from both rulers and ruled'.[129] Skinner characterises the authors of this theory as the founders of the 'earliest major counter-revolutionary movement within modern European history', which reacted to the challenge posed by the ideas of popular sovereignty that developed in the course of the religious wars in France and in the English revolution.[130] The constitution of the problem of order, and Hobbes's response, is the subject of the next chapter.

---

[128] Spellman (1998) p. 24.   [129] Skinner (1989) p. 120.   [130] Skinner (1989) p. 121.

8   Hobbes and the problem of order

The problem of establishing a compelling foundational norm for authority has haunted modern society since the seventeenth century. Virtually every political crisis has been accompanied by a sense of uncertainty about how to secure a legitimate grounding for power. The clarity with which Thomas Hobbes grasped the meaning of this issue, and his understanding of the need for a fundamentally novel form of authorisation, endows his contribution with an enduring legacy. Hobbes's *Leviathan* (1651) represents one of the most ambitious attempts to rethink the relationship between power and authority, and time and again it would be looked to for inspiration.[1] As the political scientist Richard Flathman writes:

IF there is a single most perspicuous account or analysis of the concept of authority, and IF there is a single most compelling normative conception of authority, then that account and that conception find their origin and one of their most forceful articulations in the writings of Thomas Hobbes.[2]

Unlike most of his contemporaries, Hobbes comprehended the scale of the socioeconomic and political change that divided his era from medieval times. The upheaval of European society, particularly that of his own strife-ridden England, forced Hobbes to understand that previous varieties of traditional authority could not be revived.

What is particularly interesting about Hobbes's political theory is that, as well as constructing a new argument for the validation of a stable order, he offered a critique of the failure of previous foundational norms on which authority was based. Although dominated by the issues that directly confronted him, the very attempt to distance his *Leviathan* from past conceptions of authority illustrates a very modern sensibility. Hobbes's historical critique of authority is directed at the 'orthodoxy

---

[1] A striking illustration of this tendency is provided by Schmitt's conversation with Hobbes during the inter-war crisis. See Schmitt's (2008) *The Leviathan In The State Theory Of Thomas Hobbes*.

[2] Flathman (1997) p. 3.

developed by the Christian tradition' that made 'the rightness of opinion' the foundation for authority. Hobbes claimed that such opinions,
which were interpreted by groups of priests, intellectuals and lawyers,
inevitably led to conflicts of dogma, with destructive consequences.
Kraynak notes that 'the conclusion of Hobbes's historical writings, therefore, is that civilization had been characterized by the establishment of
authoritative opinions and the disputation of these opinions, rendering it
not merely unstable but positively self-destructive'.[3]

Critics of Hobbes are often taken aback by the uncompromising realism with which he pursued his argument for the institutionalisation of
absolute power. Hobbes did not mince his words and left no one in doubt
that he regarded indivisible authority as the *sine qua non* for the maintenance of order and stability. But he did not worship power for its own
sake: he recognised that the obedience of the people could not be gained
through coercion alone. His farsighted appreciation of the power of opinion was based on the social turmoil of his era. The conclusion he drew
from his assessment of the upheavals of the seventeenth century was that
absolute authority could only be effective it could demonstrate that its
power was based on the consent it ruled. As he wrote in *Behemoth*, the
'power of the mighty hath no foundation but in the opinion and belief of
the people'.[4]

Hobbes's theory was oriented towards resolving the tension between
the necessity for a form of absolute, unquestionable authority, and the
need to validate authority with the consent of the ruled. *Leviathan*
offered an unambiguous case for an absolute sovereign, rejecting
medieval notions of parallel or divided authority and insisting that unless
sovereignty was indivisible, society would be doomed to permanent conflict. Hobbes also argued that the effectiveness of an absolute sovereign
was contingent on the capacity to claim the authority provided by
consent.[5] His synthesis of the sovereignty of absolute power with the
consent of the individual can be seen as an attempt to solve Luther's
paradox. That is why he is sometimes seen as a liberal consent and contract theorist, whilst also denounced as an authoritarian advocate of the
unrestrained absolutism.[6]

Despite the enduring influence of his work, Hobbes was very much
a man of his time. His support for absolutist authority was a response
to the fragility of order in England, at a time when the old institutions
and customs appeared to be overwhelmed by the scale of social and
political change. The experience of the English Civil War was decisive:

[3] Kraynak (1982) p. 841.   [4] Cited in Lloyd (2002) p. 39.
[5] See Oakeshott (2006) p. 293.   [6] See Flathman (1973) p. 234.

in a Dedicatory Letter to *Leviathan*, Hobbes writes of a country divided between 'those that contend, on one side for too great liberty, and on the other side for too much authority'.[7] Hobbes knew that one of the most divisive drivers of the conflict was precisely what legitimated authority in former times – religion.

Since the nineteenth century, conservative thinkers have tended to regard religion as the saviour of authority, rather than a threat. Consequently, the contribution that religious conflict made to the weakening of medieval authority is minimised. However, back in the seventeenth century numerous thinkers realised that religion had to depoliticised and its power curbed if some viable form of authority was to be preserved. Thus Hobbes makes no attempt to harness the power of theology to the construction of authority; writing from the 'bitter experience of sectarian controversy', he 'could see religion only as a potential source of political disunity'.[8] The political theorist Tracy Strong goes so far as to suggest that the absolute sovereign, the 'mortal God', of the *Leviathan* serves as a secular equivalent of the 'God of Scriptures'.[9]

The challenge facing Hobbes was to elaborate an authority that resembled some of the attributes of an earthly God but without drawing on the resources of religion to justify it. This quest for a mortal God would be taken up by others in the centuries to come. Some interpreters of Hobbes regard his pursuit of the secularisation of politics as an 'eschatological project'.[10] In the early twentieth century, the search for an extraordinary sovereign ruler led Max Weber to invest his hopes in the charismatic authority of the exceptional leader.[11] That the most influential theorist of the sociology of authority proposed such a solution is testimony to the durability of the unresolved question confronting Hobbes. Arguably, the pursuit of a mortal God continues to this day.

The political turn

Leviathan should be read as an attempt to contain and transcend the religious divisions of its time. For Hobbes, religious explanations for human affairs lacked plausibility and were inconsistent with the secularisation of reason; accordingly, he adopted the project of taking religious divisions out of politics. In line with the wider post-Reformation trends discussed in the previous chapter, Hobbes's political theory avoided the custom of grounding laws and authority on pre-existing norms. His break with the validation of moral norms was decisive and far more thoroughgoing than

---

[7] Hobbes (1998) p. 3.   [8] Wolin (2004) p. 245.   [9] Strong (1993) p. 148.
[10] Goldie (2008) p. 615.   [11] See Bertman (1997) p. 92.

any of his contemporaries. What he appeared to be stating was that justice was not established through a pre-given norm but through the exercise of political authority. As Letwin explains, 'justice was transformed by Hobbes from a quality of law to a quality defined by law, and the only meaningful question one could ask about law became whether it had been made by someone authorized to make it'.[12]

Hobbes offered a conception of political authority that is autonomous, not grounded on moral or religious norms. *Leviathan* directly questioned the power of tradition and upheld a rationalist orientation towards the subject of sovereign rule. De Stier writes that 'When it comes to the issue of authority, as in many others, Hobbes wishes to take distance – and he actually succeeds in his purpose – from the treatment given to the issue in the Middle Ages';[13] he has 'as an objective to displace the divine origin of authority as conceived by scholasticism' and wishes to 'make politics immanent and to secularize the notion of power'.[14] Through clarifying the necessity for a new form of authorisation, Hobbes directly contributed to the discrediting of traditional approaches to this subject. His argument coincided with the growing understanding among educated Europeans that the old sources for authority were 'incapable of providing internal peace and stability'.[15]

Hobbes's detachment of political authority from religious or moral validation is sometimes interpreted as the act of someone whose *realpolitik* was underwritten by an amoral temperament. Talcott Parsons took the view that 'Hobbes is almost entirely devoid of normative thinking'. This observation overlooks the fact that Hobbes's *realpolitik* is mediated by his attempt to validate authority through claiming consent for a contract with the ruler. Moreover, Hobbes understood that obedience to the Leviathan needed to be justified as a *moral* obligation. Through associating what he saw as the fundamental imperative in human society – that of individual self-preservation – with the security provided by the state, he attempted to recast morality on both a secular and individualistic basis. It can be argued that Hobbes's political theory was grounded on certain basic norms, such as that of the primacy of human security: a point that Parsons implicitly recognised, in noting that Hobbes has people giving up their natural liberty in exchange for security.[16] From this standpoint, the imperative of self-preservation constitutes the basis for the institutionalisation of a stable social order, under the rule of an absolute sovereign.

[12] Letwin (2008) p. 94.   [13] Lukac De Stier (1997) p. 67.
[14] Lukac De Stier (1997) p. 67.   [15] Heineman (1994) p. 39.
[16] See Parsons (1968) pp. 89–94.

ration of this ideal contract was part of Hobbes's attempt to establish a
normative foundation for rule.

Hobbes also, as Bernard Gert indicates, 'appeals to morality', through
emphasising the duty of obedience imposed by the assent to the covenant:
'Hobbes's discussion of contracts and covenants leaves no doubt of his
view that we ought to keep our promises, and not merely because it is to
our benefit to do so'.[19] A careful reading of his work indicates that Hobbes
was in no doubt that the absolute sovereign had to possess moral power.
Contrary to the widely held interpretation, Hobbes's mortal god did not
rely merely on coercion and the instinct of individual self-preservation
to gain obedience; he recognised that people had to possess a sense of
moral obligation to obey. As Lloyd points out, the maintenance of stable
authority could not rely simply on self-interest. Hobbes stated that 'it
may be necessary for the maintenance of effective social order for people
to defend their political authority' even though it meant 'risking their
preservation'.[20]

What de Jouvenel describes as Hobbes's 'obsession' with the 'fragility
and worth of social order' can be interpreted as a moral commitment to
security.[21] His main criterion for justifying a sovereign's right to rule was
the capacity to protect the security of his subjects. Hobbes's autonomisation of political authority expressed not so much a rejection of normative thought as a belief in the rationality of the political. Despite
his description of a precarious human existence in a state of nature,
Hobbes's conviction that human beings could transcend this condition
suggests that he took political rationalism seriously. As Heineman points
out, 'Hobbes believed that men are at least sufficiently rational to remove
themselves from this condition by granting absolute power to a sovereign
authority'.[22] Hobbes also believed that people could change their views
and that, through educating them, a sovereign could achieve consensus
and consolidate order.[23]

The political turn

185

Parsons also grasped that the 'immediate practical animus of Hobbes'
social thought lay in the defense of political authority on a secular basis'.
He added that 'a strong government, justified by the social contract, was
a necessary bulwark of the security of the commonwealth, threatened as
it was by the imminent danger of the resurgence of force and fraud'.[17]
A strong government is 'justified' by a social contract. Such a contract
symbolised 'the kind of commitment which members of society must
have towards the political arrangements which they accept'.[18] The elabo-

---

[17] Parsons (1968) p. 94.   [18] See Malcolm (2008) pp. 538–9.
[19] Gert (1967) p. 557.   [20] Lloyd (2002) pp. 56–7.   [21] Jouvenel (1957) p. 232.
[22] Heineman (1994) p. 35.   [23] See Lloyd (2002) p. 2.

Hobbes's political theory, despite its absolutist and authoritarian tendency, acknowledged the potential for human agency. That is why Hobbes's political realism was regarded with such hostility by so many contemporary theorists of absolutist and royalist authority. Edward Hyde, the Earl of Clarendon (1609–74), attacked what he called Hobbes's 'pernicious and dangerous' errors for undermining the religious and traditional foundation of monarchical authority. Clarendon took exception to Hobbes's claim that sovereign power lies in people, who consent to transfer it to a ruler. Significantly, Clarendon was also uncomfortable with the realism and absolutism of Hobbes's theory of authority; as one study of this debate notes, he stressed 'that Hobbes has gone too far in emphasizing the sovereign's complete independence from the laws that have been made'.[24] For royalist theorists it was not enough that the absolute authority of the sovereign be affirmed – absolutism also needed to justified on the ground of divine right. Clarendon objected to Hobbes's mortal god because it was a form political authority that was validated through a convention rather a divinely ordained truth.

Hobbes's elaboration of a specifically political authority had important implications for the subsequent development of ideas about equality and independent choice. His suggestion that people in a state of nature might possess equal capacities challenged prevailing hierarchical thinking. As Krieger notes, through 'positing a natural equality of human capacities, wants and necessities which abolished the natural and moral hierarchies behind traditional authority', Hobbes 'developed an explicit definition of political authority which was both consistent with the presumption of extra-political authority and indispensable to the establishment of a distinctively political – that is, of transferred – power'.[25] Political authority established through the voluntary transfer of power gave recognition to the initiating role of individual judgment. According to some political theorists, the significance that Hobbes attached to the transfer of power helped the subsequent clarification of liberal principles in relation to the exercise of individual judgment. Heineman states,

With this conceptual move, the possibility of a standard for political judgment based on the desires of the subjective individual was raised, an occurrence that in retrospect can be seen as a logical outcome of the individualized judgment encouraged in the religious sphere by the protestant Reformation.[26]

Hobbes himself did not go that far, and, as we shall see, he sought to limit the exercise of judgment because he feared its potential for destabilising society.

[24] Curran (2002) p. 17.   [25] Krieger (1968) p. 151.   [26] Heineman (1994) p. 35.

The exercise of individualised judgment leading to the transfer of power to the ruler offers a secular and political road to the constitution of authority. This transfer of power is integrated by Hobbes into one of his most original concepts – that of *authorisation*.[27]

Authorisation

Hobbes's elaboration of the concept of authorisation represented an attempt to define authority in terms of an act of human will and agency, which would serve as the foundation for an authoritative act. According to this concept, it is through the transfer of an original right to a 'represen-ter' that the sovereign's authority to act comes into being. Authorisation implies that individuals are 'authors' of a mutual covenant that under-writes the sovereign's right to act, and the concept constitutes an attempt by Hobbes to establish the act of voluntary consent as the origin of polit-ical authority. The act of voluntary consent both validates authority and obliges those who consent to obedience. So when a sovereign declares that a particular act is 'done by authority', the people as the authors are implicated and made responsible for the action. The act of authorisation plays a critical role in the legitimation and preservation of authority. As Lloyd argues, 'subjects must *regard themselves* as having authorised all of the actions of the government if a commonwealth is to function reli-ably and to be capable of ensuring perpetual stability'.[28] To be a durable institution, sovereignty requires that people continue to believe that they authorised it.

Authority always derives its status from something outside itself. The concept of authorisation attempts to provide a pre-existing source of validation, offering an alternative to natural or religious authority. The authorised sovereign is Hobbes's alternative to previous models of foun-dational authority: as Letwin notes, 'any order in human life rests on abiding by rules made by an authorized legislator'.[29] For Hobbes, the 'rules which we recognize as obligation to obey can never be ultimately justified by reference to any universal necessary truth that all rational beings are obliged by reason to accept', rather, obligation is founded on the voluntary transfer of rights to a sovereign ruler.[30]

The concept of authorisation involves the conversion of individual aspirations into a single unifying force – ultimately, the secular state. The willingness of people to give up power and allow another to act on their behalf is principally driven by the fear of death and aspiration for

---

[27] Lukac De Stier (1997) p. 67.   [28] Lloyd (2002) p. 67.
[29] Letwin (2008) p. 95.   [30] Letwin (2008) p. 95.

security: people 'agree to create a sovereign because they are afraid of one another'.[31] The relationship between authorisation and the establishment of authority is outlined by Hobbes in the following terms:

> *I authorize and give up my right of governing myself, to this man, or to this assembly of men on this condition, that thou give up thy right to him, and authorize all his actions in like manner.* This done, the multitude so united in one person, is called a COMMONWEALTH, in Latin CIVITAS. This is the generation of that great LEVIATHAN, or rather to speak more reverently, of that mortal god, to which we owe under the immortal God our peace and defence. For by this authority, given him by every particular man in the commonwealth, he hath the use of so much power and strength conferred on him, that by terror thereof, he is enabled to perform the wills of them all, to peace at home, mutual aid against their enemies abroad.[32]

The act of authorisation presupposes that people are in some sense authors of the 'mortal god' that they obey. It is 'an act by which every member of the multitude makes himself the author of whatever is said and done in his name by his sovereign representative'.[33] The mortal god is thus born through a collective act through which people give up the right of governing themselves to realise a common end – their existential security.

People are able to possess a capacity to will and choose because they are by nature free. The capacity to act in accordance with individual interests connects choice with authority. Flathman observes,

> Arguably the fundamental normative proposition of Hobbes's thinking, this Right is at least the proximate and in my view the ultimate or final source of his conviction that all obligations arise from voluntary acts on the part of those whose obligations they are.[34]

At least in principle, through the act of authorisation the self-interest of private individuals acquires political definition in the Leviathan. Arendt writes that through this distinct approach to authority, Hobbes,

> exposed the only political theory according to which the state is based not on some kind of constituting law – whether divine law, the law of nature, or the law of social contract – which determines the rights and wrongs of the individual's interest with respect to public affairs, but on the individual themselves, so that 'the private interest is the same with the publique'.[35]

The individual pursuit of self-interest, as expressed through the imperative of self-preservation, provides the impulse to come together and transfer power to the sovereign.

---

[31] Lively and Reeve (1991) p. 14.   [32] Hobbes (1998) p. 114.
[33] Skinner (2006) p. 159.   [34] Flathman (1997) p. 7.   [35] Arendt (2009) p. 139.

Hobbes's social theory has been described as 'almost a pure case of utilitarianism'.[36] Implicit in the act of authorisation is a pragmatic calculation about the achievement of order and security. From this standpoint, authorisation presupposes an end for which authority was willed. This is an authority that is directed towards transforming conditions of uncertainty to one of security, and it expresses the future-oriented sensibility of a new modernity. Unlike pre-modern authority, which was validated through its relation to foundational norms, Hobbes's authority is realised through its relationship to the commitment to protect order. Thus, what emerges from the Leviathan is a voluntaristic conception of authority which is created for the express purpose of establishing a coercive power capable of realising an end for which it was willed.

The impulse behind the act of authorisation is not the aspiration to establish a just regime, but to validate sovereign power. As Lukac De Stier concludes, 'we can say that if political authority in Hobbes is legitimized by the consent given by those who empower the civil person, his notion of authority is voluntarist', adding that this 'opposes the classic notion of political philosophy which bases the legitimacy of political authority on the just character of its norms and laws'.[37] In Hobbes's political theory, the origin of the state is the conversion of individual wills through a covenant into a singular sovereign power. Once this conversion is realised, a distinct and autonomous power emerges. 'A body politic or "real unity" as distinct from a multitude is created when this authorization has been given, thus imposing the obligation of obedience on all of those who have "authored" the relationship', states Flathman.[38] The conversion of the multitude into one sovereign also means its transformation into a more coherent and stable entity.

As a sociological concept, authorisation can be understood as the idealisation of the political process through which a stable society and culture is forged. As Wrong writes, for Hobbes the precondition for the evolution of a stable society was the establishment of political authority. Political authority helps transpose people from the state of nature into a society where order prevails.[39] This is a highly politically charged version of authority, where the political takes chronological and logical precedence over the social.

Arguably, Hobbes lived in an era where the sense of the social still only existed in an undeveloped form. Politics itself had only recently separated from theology to acquire a heightened sensibility of its own significance. Political philosophers such as Jean Bodin and Hobbes regarded the key

---

[36] Parsons (1968) p. 89.   [37] Lukac De Stier (1997) p. 52.
[38] Flathman (1997) p. 18.   [39] See Wrong (1995) p. 16.

division as lying between the political and the natural, not between the political and the social. Numerous supporters of monarchy sought to present this form of authority as a variant of the natural and unlimited power of the father. However at a time when authority had become de-naturalised, patriarchal theories could not compete with conventional ones.

Hobbes's concept of authorisation has been the subject of conflicting interpretation. Flathman has argued that 'much of Hobbes's thinking about authority is grounded in respects in which human beings are and should be regarded and treated as equals'.[40] From this standpoint, Hobbes's theory can be grasped as an attempt to ground obligation to the sovereign on consent and voluntary agreement. Other interpreters present Hobbes as a cynic who was disingenuous in his use of the language of voluntary consent and authorisation. Wood charges Hobbes with elaborating 'his defence of absolutism' through turning 'radical and egalitarian principles against itself'. To illustrate her point, Wood notes how Hobbes's recognition of the natural right of individuals turns into its submission to 'an absolute sovereign power'.[41]

Quentin Skinner takes the view that Hobbes self-consciously appropriated some of the language used by advocates of popular sovereignty in order to legitimise absolute rule. Skinner usefully recalls that variations of the concept of authorisation were circulated through the writings of radical and parliamentarian writers in the 1640s, and cites the radical pamphleteer, Henry Parker (1604–52), whose *Observations* (1642) declared 'that man not God is "the free and voluntary Author" of whatever powers are "derived" into the hands of kings and magistrates'.[42] Skinner adds that parliamentarian thinkers frequently argued that the 'people must *authorise* their kings and magistrates to rule and thus that governments are lawful only to the extent that they have been duly authorised'.[43]

It is possible that Hobbes appropriated the vocabulary of his parliamentary foes in order undermine their arguments. However, it is necessary to point out that Hobbes's use of the concept of authorisation was very different to the manner in which it was elaborated by advocates of popular sovereignty. Hobbes rejected the belief that it was the people who authorised a ruler, on the ground that the 'people' did not have a political existence. According to Hobbes's argument, the starting point for the act of authorisation was an atomised multitude that transfers its rights to the individual sovereign. It is through the loss of rights that sovereignty acquires its existence.

---

[40] Flathman (1997) p. 7.   [41] Wood (1991) p. 56.
[42] Cited in Skinner (2006) p. 159.   [43] Cited in Skinner (2006) p. 160.

What was distinct about Hobbes's concept of authorisation was that it claimed to mediate consent with the logic of coercive power. Hobbes's realism compelled him to grasp the fact that order could not be maintained unless authority could claim the legitimacy afforded by popular consent. At the same time, Hobbes was no democrat and he feared that anything less than absolute sovereignty would lead to conflict and disorder. Nothing less than a mortal god would do. Hobbes hoped that the transfer of individual power to such a mortal god would create an irreversible moral obligation to obedience: once they agreed to the covenant, individuals are 'obliged by their action to accept the sovereign's decision even when they dislike it'.[44]

Authority versus freedom

For Hobbes, sovereignty was indivisible and authority was absolute. But he also recognised that competing individual interests could not be ignored and that self-interest had to be reconciled with obedience to the sovereign ruler. One of his aims was to attenuate this tension through associating liberty with the right of the individual to preserve his life, thus positing a form of liberty that was consistent with authority. Hobbes suggested that since the conditions for the preservation of life required order and stability, obedience to the absolute sovereign was the precondition for the exercise of this liberty.

Hobbes defined liberty as simply the 'absence of external impediments',[45] and insisted that the words 'free' and 'liberty' could not be applied to anything other than 'bodies', which are subject to motion and impediment. A 'freeman' is '*he, that in those things, which by his strength and wit he is able to do, is not hindered to do what he has a will to do*'.[46] But once the 'freeman' becomes the subject of a sovereign ruler, his liberty becomes more limited. Through the covenant drawn up upon leaving the state of nature, much of people's natural liberty is lost through their transfer to a sovereign. Hobbes explains that, at this point, the liberty of the subject is determined by what the sovereign has permitted, such as 'liberty to buy and sell, and otherwise contract with one another, to choose their own abode, their own diet, their own trade of life, and institute their children as they themselves think fit; and like'.[47]

Although liberty becomes contracted in the aftermath of authorising a sovereign, Hobbes maintains that the 'liberty of the subject' is protected by the 'the unlimited power of the sovereign'. A measure of individual

---

[44] Letwin (2008) p. 95.   [45] See Hobbes (1998) p. 86 and Chapter 14.
[46] Hobbes (1998) p. 139.   [47] Hobbes (1998) p. 141.

liberty is made consistent with its loss. It is at this point in the argument that the absolutist dimension of this theory of authority manifests itself. Hobbes asserts that 'nothing the representative can do to a subject, on what pretence so ever, can properly be called injustice, or injury, because every subject is author of every act the sovereign doth'. He even goes so far as to argue a case for the legitimacy of putting to death an 'innocent subject'. Hobbes notes that true liberty is not that of 'particular man' but of the sovereign commonwealth.[48]

Hobbes's insistence on obedience to the demands of the sovereign ruler is qualified in relation to instances that touch on matters of the direct survival of the individual. For example, the subject cannot be expected to obey a command to kill or wound himself, or to abstain from eating or taking essential medicine: in such instances the subject has 'the liberty to disobey'.[49] Although Hobbes does not accept the right to freedom of religion, he is prepared to restrain the sovereign ruler from intervening in the internal and private faith of the individual. So while rulers have the right to forbid a Church from teaching a certain doctrine, they cannot prevent people from believing what they were taught.[50] In other words, the sovereign possesses an authority over religious matters but 'inquisition into the private belief of his subjects is no part of his rights'.[51] In any case, Hobbes believed that strongly held religious sentiments could not be suppressed out of existence.

The tension created by the Reformation doctrine between the authority of conscience and that of the authority of order remains unresolved in Hobbes's political theory. Hobbes looked to 'vindicate the authority of the civil order over conscience', and suggested that through the voluntary submission to sovereign authority 'individuals gave up the right of individual judgment'. He claimed that, as the authors of the sovereign, the judgment of the rulers was actually individuals' own. According to the logic of this argument, authorisation led to the loss of legitimacy of the public expression of private judgment.[52]

More specifically, Hobbes acknowledged the right to private belief and the right of people to judge the diktat of their sovereign as wrong. What he did not allow was the right to act on such beliefs. Stanton states that:

formally Hobbes conceded that subjects might retain privately the judgement that what an authority commands is wrong while nevertheless doing what it commands – just how much of a concession this was in his own terms is a different

[48] Hobbes (1998) pp. 141 and 142.   [49] Hobbes (1998) p. 144.
[50] Malcolm (2008) p. 543.   [51] Oakeshott (1975) p. 53.
[52] See Stanton (2010) pp. 13–14.

matter – but he insisted that any subject who acted out of conscience against the demands of authority *eo ipso* was acting unreasonably: for right judgement and the demands of authority, on Hobbes's view, were necessarily coincident.[53]

The abstract harmony between the demands of authority and individual judgment constructed by Hobbes co-existed with the understanding that rulers should desist from intervening in the realm of private thought.

Nevertheless, Hobbes's political theory had to acknowledge the possibility that in exceptional circumstances individuals ought to be permitted to disobey their rulers. As noted previously, when people's self-preservation was directly threatened, authority could be repudiated. Thus despite its absolutist tendency, Hobbes's recognition of the right of individuals to repudiate authority in extremely exceptional circumstances has been interpreted by some as the precursor of liberal theories of sovereignty:

Now Hobbes conceded (infamously) that in the most extreme case . . . individuals were able to repudiate . . . authority and to disown its actions if, but only if, their self-preservation was immediately threatened. To many this concession has seemed to open a crack in the edifice of authority that threatens to destroy it from within – for one individual may ally himself with others who judge that their lives also are in danger, and their alliance may threaten others again, who judge that their own self-preservation is now threatened, until eventually the whole, as Hobbes balefully put it, 'must assuredly fall upon the heads of their posterity'. In a sense this is obvious enough. If authority necessarily involves a claim to know better, it is hard to see how it could long survive the usurpation of that claim by every individual.[54]

Hobbes's willingness to allow for the disobedience of a ruler's command, albeit in rare and exceptional circumstances, signified the difficulty that he had in reconciling the conflicting pressures of freedom and authority.

Hundreds of years later, during the inter-war crisis of the twentieth century, Carl Schmitt stated that the modest concession that Hobbes made to the individual freedom of belief jeopardised authority altogether. Schmitt wrote that this concession contained the 'seed of death that destroyed the mighty leviathan from within and brought about the end of the mortal God'.[55] The lesson that Schmitt and other reactionaries drew from the experience of post-Reformation era was that the liberal principle of individual freedom was inconsistent with authority and order. Despite his enthusiastic praise for *Leviathan*, Schmitt was critical of Hobbes for not making religion the business of the state and denounced him 'for

[53] Stanton (2010) p. 16.   [54] Stanton (2010) p. 14.
[55] Cited by Stanton (2010) p. 10.

allowing the privacy of belief'.[56] Reading between the lines, it seems that Schmitt wished for a Hobbes that remained steeped in a medieval political theology that had no room for individual belief.

However, the seventeenth-century Hobbes grasped better than the twentieth-century Schmitt that the genie of individual belief could no longer be contained in the bottle. He understood that with the expansion of the political public, people's beliefs and conscience could not be policed and repressed by a centralised inquisitorial institution. His response was to attempt to manage the conflict of individual opinion, rather than banish it out of existence.

The search for a common language

Living through an era where disputes over religion and politics threatened to disrupt normal life, Hobbes was unusually sensitive to the power of individual opinion to unsettle the social order. His hostility to the free expression of individual opinion and judgment was motivated by his concern with its divisive effect on social consensus, perceiving debate not as a means of clarification but as an invitation to strife and civil war. For Hobbes the contestation of truth by competing voices was antithetical to the realisation of order and stability. He had no doubt that without consensus about fundamentals, the very validation of authority would be rendered problematic.

Hobbes believed that appeals to private reason and the competing claims that arose from this were at least partly responsible for undermining the established institutions in England in the 1640s, and viewed the expression of individual opinion as a corrosive influence on public life. That is why he asserted that private reason 'could not be tolerated because it bred a confusion of meanings which destroyed the body politic as a communicating whole'.[57] He regarded the failure of communication as one of the defining features of the state of nature, where 'every man is his own judge and differeth from other concerning the names and appellations of things, and from those differences arise quarrels, and breach of the peace'.[58] The question posed by Hobbes was, how could society survive 'when its members disagree, often quite radically, about basic moral principles' – 'not only about the meaning of good and evil, but also the ground upon which to make such distinctions'.[59]

For his time, Hobbes possessed an unusual degree of sensitivity to the contribution that consensus on values and ideas made to the forging of

---

[56] See Strong (1993), 'Foreword' in Schmitt (2008) p. xii.
[57] Wolin (2004) p. 231.   [58] Cited in Robin (2004) p. 6.   [59] Robin (2004) p. 6.

order and stability. One of the key lessons that he drew from his study of history was that a shared understanding of the world was a precondition for the emergence of effective authority. The lesson that Hobbes, the author of a book on the ancient Greek historian Thucydides, learned from the past was that:

[a] destructive crisis was caused by inaccurate understanding and correspondingly inappropriate behaviour on the part of men in power. The appropriateness of political behaviour comes from the right understanding of the principles on which sovereignty rests, which depends in its turn on the accuracy of the language used to teach these principles to the men who rule and to those who are ruled. The dissolution of commonwealths is the fault of the men who misunderstand the foundations of authority.[60]

For Hobbes, a correct understanding of the past expressed accurately through a common language was essential for creating a shared culture of meaning.

Hobbes explicitly drew on the experience of the past in *Behemoth*, a study devoted to exploring the cause of and the lessons from the Civil War. The book places great emphasis on the role of opinion, ideas and the manner of their communication in creating the conditions for civil conflict. The first two parts of *Behemoth* can be read as a historical sociology of opinion and of opinion makers. Part I, which is devoted to looking at the causes of the revolt, focuses on 'certain opinions in divinity and politics'; Part II then 'exposes the artifices of the rebels, specifically the techniques of indoctrination and rhetoric by which they incited the people against the king'.[61]

For Hobbes, the principal instigators of the collapse of social order were the Presbyterian ministers, whose preaching undermined the authority of the monarchy and the established Church. One consequence of their activities was to encourage the proliferation of competing religious sects, which in turn endowed the prevailing conflict with an uncompromising zealousness. Although these groups differed on matters of doctrine, they all agreed that the state had no legitimate authority in the domain of religion. Hobbes blamed universities for producing men who take their ideas so seriously that they disregarded their disruptive consequences. Lloyd notes that Hobbes believed the education that 'men received in the universities of his day' to be a 'tremendously destabilizing force', and that the support that the Reformation gave to the private interpretation of the Scripture enhanced the climate of dissent, conflict and, ultimately, violence.[62]

---

[60] Borot (2006) p. 312.   [61] See Kraynak (1982) p. 838.   [62] Lloyd (2002) p. 201.

Hobbes blamed university education and the pursuit of private interpretation of the Scripture for fostering a climate where conceited individuals who believe that their ideas are divinely inspired entitle them to
cause grievous mischief:

Pride, subjecteth a man to anger, the excess whereof, is the madness called
RAGE, and FURY. And thus it comes to pass that . . . excessive opinion of a
man's own self, for divine inspiration, for wisdom, learning, form, and the like,
becomes distraction, and giddiness: the same joined with envy, rage: vehement
opinion of the truth of any thing, contradicted by others, rage.[63]

Hobbes experienced the contestation of intellectual and theological
authority as a destructive process whereby conceited learned individuals, afflicted by 'spiritual madness', become obsessed with their opinions
to the point where they lose sight of their destructive consequences.
Although this analysis one-sidedly psychologises the issues at stake,
Hobbes eloquently captures some of the intellectual constituents that
are involved in the contestation of authority in the early modern setting.

There is some evidence that Hobbes's analysis of the contestation
of intellectual and religious truth pointed to an important destabilising force in seventeenth-century England. Stone interprets Puritanism
as representing the 'generalized conviction of the need for independent
judgment based on conscience and bible reading' and therefore as a
'major threat to order', which threatened established beliefs and made a
significant contribution to the emergence of a 'real crisis of confidence
in the early seventeenth century'.[64] Wolin believes that 'one of Hobbes's
most original yet least noted contributions to political theory' was his
recognition that political order depended on a 'system of verbal signs,
actions, and gestures bearing generally accepted meaning'.[65] One of the
lessons that Hobbes learned from the English Civil War was that it represented not simply a conflict over power but also a dispute about whose
system of meanings would prevail.

The Civil War was a remarkable period, in which competing schools of
philosophy and political theory competed with one another for intellectual and ideological hegemony. Moreover, these debates about the fundamental issues facing society were played out in front of an ever-increasing
politically educated public. According to some accounts, it was during
this era that we see the 'first appearance of public opinion as an important
factor in politics'.[66] The Civil War began as a war of words and showed the
destructive potential of the absence of generally accepted meaning. Thus

---

[63] Hobbes (1998) p. 49.   [64] Stone (1986) pp. 99 and 110.   [65] Wolin (2004) p. 231.
[66] Sabine (1961) p. 477.

the early modern period was not simply subject to religious and dynastic strife, but also to a contestation of cultural and intellectual authority.

Paralleling the violent dissent characteristic of the Civil War, Hobbes's state of nature is dominated by linguistic discord. Ball attributes to Hobbes the analysis that thinks that what is '*wrong* with the state of nature' is that 'words like "good" and "evil", "just" and "unjust" have no agreed-upon meaning, other than of signalling approval and disapproval'.[67] This linguistic confusion stands in contrast to a commonwealth, where 'moral concepts do have a single fixed, agreed-upon meaning'.[68] The transition from the state of nature to the founding of sovereign authority involves not simply the unification of individual wills around an individual ruler, but also the forging of a consensus around a commonly accepted language and system of meaning. Hence the call to submit individual liberty to singular power also implies the necessity to unite behind one language of communication.

'Through the act of submission men had exchanged the uncertainty of nature's code for a set of "common rules for all men"', writes Wolin, who adds that 'in endowing a sovereign with an absolute legislative power they had erected a Great Definer, a sovereign dispenser of common meanings, a "publique reason"'.[69] One of the clearest expressions of sovereign authority is the establishment of social consensus and order around a system of meanings. As Ball notes: 'The sovereign supplies nothing less than the common coin of political communication, the conceptual currency that makes civil society possible'.[70] Hobbes also claimed that through education and propaganda the sovereign could socialise his subjects into a common set of values and beliefs, and to realise this objective, he accorded the sovereign far-reaching power. Heineman states that,

the sovereign has the right to control the doctrines and opinions of his subjects, for 'the Actions of men proceed from their Opinions; and in the well governing of Opinions, consisteth the well governing of mens Actions; – absolute power of sovereign is dependant on the 'government of doctrines'.[71]

Hobbes's determination to empower the sovereign to control and regulate language and intellectual life was motivated by his concern regarding the divisive consequences of the pursuit of private opinion. He was realistic enough to understand that what was at issue was not enunciation of an abstract truth. The man who wrote that 'no discourse whatsoever, can end in absolute knowledge of fact, past, or to come' was not so much

[67] Ball (1985) p. 759.   [68] Ball (1985) p. 759.   [69] Wolin (2004) p. 232.
[70] Ball (1985) p. 759.   [71] Heineman (1994) p. 38.

interested in an inner Truth but in order and stability.[72] According to one interpretation, for Hobbes, political truth was not an 'intrinsic quality, but a function of the requirements of peace and order'.[73]

It would be one-sided to characterise Hobbes's realistic theory of power as simply amoral. According to the interpretation advanced by Gert, Hobbes never underestimated the formidable influence that views about what is right and wrong had on people's behaviour. Gert reminds us that his *De Cive*, Hobbes 'laments the lack of a true moral philosophy and says that mistaken doctrines of what is right and wrong have been responsible for a great amount of bloodshed'. One of the arguments that Hobbes proposes for 'the necessity of a coercive power is that men may be misled in their opinion of good and evil, right and wrong'.[74]

In the context of the epidemic of disorder that was sweeping Europe, Hobbes's justification for the absolute sovereign made sense to many. However, what Hobbes provided is a negative form of validation for the *Leviathan*. The political philosopher Leo Strauss wrote that 'it is striking that Hobbes prefers the negative expression "avoiding death" to the positive expression "preserving life"'.[75] Experience indicates that fear only provides a provisional solution to the maintenance of order, and does little to mobilise support for authority. In the long run, the absence of a positive rendition of moral norms would ensure that the mortal god would face a crisis of legitimacy.

Hobbes's *Leviathan* sought to provide a thoroughly political solution to the problem of order thrown up by the Reformation. The emphasis on the role of individual will and on voluntary consent shows a modern sensibility towards the role of human agency in the shaping of customs and institutions. But according to W. G. Runciman, Hobbes is 'not a sociologist as we would now understand the term': he was interested in pursuing a 'prescriptive position', rather than unravelling the 'causes and effects at work within the fabric of civil society'.[76] Runciman is right to emphasise the prescriptive focus of Hobbes's political theory. But his heightened sense of agency, as well as his representation of institutions as the product of human convention, leads him to pose some of the fundamental question that sociology was forced to confront in the nineteenth century. In particular, Hobbes's work was directed towards the question posed by Georg Simmel in 1907: 'how is society possible?' His answer is that this 'artificial' construction is a product of a political will and that order and consensus is forged through education and the exercise of sovereignty of the absolute ruler.

[72] Hobbes (1998) p. 42.   [73] Wolin (2004) p. 233.   [74] Gert (1967) p. 557.
[75] Strauss (1966) p. 15.   [76] Runciman (1971) p. 26.

Although Hobbes communicated his theory of authority in a self-consciously political form, he implicitly granted the *Leviathan* a significant socialising function. Society, particularly in the form of sovereign authority, possessed significant potential for influencing the behaviour of its citizens. In *De Homine*, Hobbes explains the character-forming influence of authority:

I call authorities anyone on any matter whose precepts or example one follows, because of one's estimation of their wisdom. From them, if they are good, good inclinations of youth are fashioned, and bad inclinations if they are bad; whether they are teachers or fathers or anyone else whom they, the youths, hear commonly praised for their wisdom; for youth honors those who have been praised, and regard them worthy of imitation.[77]

Lloyd goes so far as to assert that, for Hobbes, education is 'the key to the maintenance of social order'. To support this claim he cites what he takes to be the central contention of Hobbes's theory, which is that 'the actions of men proceed from their opinions; and in the well governing of opinions, consisteth the well governing of men's actions, in order to their to their peace and concord'.[78] Lloyd's emphasis on re-education as a central feature of stable authority tends to go against the grain of a consensus that regards coercion and fear as Hobbes's preferred solution to the problem of order.[79] However, there is little doubt that Hobbes took the education of opinion seriously, because he regarded its diversity as a serious threat to order. The experience of modernity would confirm that opinion is indissolubly linked to the problem of order.

Sociology's encounter with the problem of order

Sociology's engagement with the problem of order sometimes lacks sensitivity to historical variation. The problem is frequently attributed to the social upheavals unleashed in the aftermath of the French Revolution, and which came to the fore only in the early nineteenth century. The paucity of a historically informed sociological analysis is also demonstrated by a tendency to eternalise the problem of order as an issue that exists in its own right, and to adopt narrow technical interpretations.[80] This transhistorical account of the problem of order is explicitly advanced by the American sociologist Dennis Wrong, who states:

---

[77] Cited in Gert (1967) p. 520.   [78] Cited in Lloyd (2002) p. 219.
[79] See for example Lukes (1979) pp. 651–2.
[80] For a recent variant of ahistorical naturalistic accounts of order, see Fukuyama (2011).

The problem of order arises out of the dual circumstance that human beings have limited (though not nonexistent) capacities for sympathy with their fellows and that they inhabit an environment that fails to provide them with sufficient resources to satisfy fully the needs of all of them. The problem of order is therefore a genuinely transhistorical problem rooted in inescapable conflict between the interests and desires of individuals and the requirements of society: to wit, the pacification of violent strife among men and the secure establishment of cooperative social relations making possible the pursuit of collective goals.[81]

The confusion of the problem of order with the scarcity and the relative absence of empathy overlooks the important changes that occurred in the sixteenth century. The problem of order is not reducible to a conflict over resources; it is an expression of a crisis of authority and the weakening of its classical forms of validation. Moreover, a conflict between individual interests and that of society only gained political and expression through the emergence of the authority of the self, in the aftermath of the Reformation. Wrong's projection of an 'inescapable conflict' across time and space betrays a fatalistic teleology that reduces history to an individualised struggle for survival.

It is important to recall that the Reformation and the movement it unleashed led to the explicit rejection of the normative foundations of the prevailing order. The fracturing of Christian unity undermined the role of religion as a source of foundational authority. The subsequent ascendancy of secularism and the recognition that institutions and laws are conventional led to a historical moment where medieval ideas about the origin or foundation of authority gave way to ideas based on consent. The Reformation movement impacted on all sections of society. Its revolt was 'directed against an established order, a revolt whose success depended upon radicalizing the masses into disaffection with existing authorities and institutions'.[82] From this point onwards, disputes about authority could not be confined to small coteries of aristocrats, theologians and philosophers. With the emergence of competing socio-economic groups, religious communities and national conflicts, the maintenance of order become more problematic. The expansion of education, secularism and mobility fostered a climate where people became more questioning. In this new environment, the force of tradition and rule based on unquestioned authority became far less effective, and authority was exposed to the scrutiny of an ever-growing constituency of individuals. As Hobbes insisted, opinion became a potentially destabilising force.

The transformative impulse of the Reformation, the subsequent religious and civil wars afflicting Europe, and the emergence of historical

---

[81] Wrong (1995) p. 36.   [82] Wolin (2004) p. 173.

consciousness in the seventeenth century are often overlooked in sociological accounts of the problem of order. Thus the conservative sociologist Robert Nisbet states that 'the fundamental ideas of European sociology are best understood as responses to the problem of order crated at the beginning of the nineteenth century by the collapse of the old regime under the blows of industrialism and revolutionary democracy'.[83] Other sociologists accept the proposition that 'sociology was shaped by the nineteenth-century conservative reaction to the Enlightenment, the French Revolution and the Industrial Revolution'.[84] This sentiment is often expressed through perfunctory statements of conventional wisdom. For example, a student's guide to sociology explains that 'it is often said that social sciences are mostly understood as responses to the problem of order that was created in men's minds by the weakening of the old order under the blows of French Revolution and Industrial Revolution'.[85] A standard *Dictionary of Sociology* echoes this interpretation, when it asserts that the 'Hobbesian problem of order' preoccupied 'those classical sociologists faced directly with the apparent consequences of industrialization . . . and general instability associated with the rapid social change in the nineteenth century'.[86]

The inconsistency of referring to the 'Hobbesian problem of order' in relation to the nineteenth century is rarely reflected upon. Yet back in the 1930s, when Talcott Parsons credited Hobbes with first stating the problem, he had no doubt that its origins ought to be traced back to the Reformation. Parsons rightly linked the emergence of the problem of order to the secularisation of social and political thought:

Thus when social thought became secularized about the seventeenth century its central problem was that of the basis of order in society, in the particular form of the sphere of individual freedom from authoritarian control in relation to the coercive authority of the state.[87]

The origins of the 'breakup of the old order in Europe' were already visible in the religious conflict of the sixteenth century, and it was the Reformation that unleashed the forces that resulted in the problem of order.

Hobbes's writings can only make sense as a response to the religious and political conflicts that culminated in the Civil War. The question of liberty of conscience, which was one of the key political issues of the

---

[83] Nisbet (1979) p. 21.   [84] Dawe (1970) p. 207.
[85] See www.sociologyguide.com/introduction-to-sociology/impact-of-revolutions-on-sociology.php, accessed 17 January 2012.
[86] Scott and Marshall (2005) p. 613.   [87] Parsons (1968) p. 88.

seventeenth century, raised elementary questions about alternative foundations for authority.[88] Debates about such fundamental issues gained
a large audience and contributed to the emergence of public opinion as
a powerful new force.[89] It is also worth noting that the significance of
the Reformation for the constitution of the problem of order was not
lost on some of the leading thinkers associated with the conservative
reaction to the French Revolution: Louis de Bonald (1754–1850) and
Joseph De Maistre (1754–1821) singled out Protestantism as the principal force responsible for the decline of medieval authority.[90] However,
with the passage of time, the option of reclaiming medieval political values appeared increasingly anachronistic, and the problem of order was
pushed forward to the nineteenth century.

One reason why the problem of order was decoupled from its linkage
with the crisis of the sixteenth century was that it was associated with the
threat of mass movements from below. This phenomenon existed only
in a relatively undeveloped state, when the conflict was mainly driven
by intra-elite rivalry. It was in nineteenth-century Europe that the threat
from below became an inescapable feature of life. By this time, the threat
to order appeared to have little in common with the points of conflict
in the sixteenth and seventeenth centuries. One of the principal causes
of disorder identified by Hobbes – that of intense religious conflict and
violence – had become relatively muted by the time of the Industrial
Revolution, and many social philosophers regarded the problem as too
little religion, rather than too much.

It is likely that the problem of order came to be located in the nineteenth century because it was at this point that some of its manifestations
– decline of tradition, religion, deference to authority – came to dominate public discourse. In this context, Hobbes himself was condemned by
some conservative sociologists as bearing responsibility for the decline of
order. Nisbet blamed the politicisation of authority by Bodin and Hobbes
for its subsequent devaluation in public discourse. He argued that the
distinction 'between social authority and social power' led to the elaboration of a doctrine of sovereignty that became abstract and hostile to
traditional associations. As a theorist devoted to community and traditional associations, Nisbet was critical of Hobbes for contemptuously
dismissing such institutions as similar to 'worms in the entrails of natural man', and portrayed his philosophy as the precursor to the French
Enlightenment's 'distaste for traditional authority' and 'traditional
community'.[91]

---

[88] See Davis (2003) p. 384.   [89] Atherton (2003) p. 98.   [90] Zeitlin (1997) p. 62.
[91] Nisbet (1979) p. 116.

The animosity with which Nisbet condemned Hobbes for being 'utterly ruthless' in his exaltation of power exposed the bitterness that this upholder of tradition bore towards the author of *Leviathan*. Nisbet stated that it was probably Hobbes who Edmund Burke had in mind when he wrote that 'nothing is harder than the heart of a metaphysician'.[92]

From Nisbet's standpoint, the very attempt by Hobbes and others to provide a response to the loss of medieval authority through developing a theory of sovereignty is responsible for the subsequent marginalisation of tradition. Yet it was precisely the weakening of medieval tradition that created a demand for the elaboration of a new foundation for authority. Accordingly, the attempt to solve the emerging problem of order is confused with its cause. Nisbet claimed that the 'result of two centuries of preoccupation with sovereignty had thus been to make political power appear as something either independent of or antithetical to moral tradition and authority'.[93] For Nisbet, one of the principal virtues of nineteenth-century sociology was its 'rediscovery of custom and tradition, of patriarchal and corporate authority, all of which, it is argued, are the fundamental (and continuing) sources of social and political order'.[94]

Parsons's work provides an important contrast to the approach of Nisbet. In particular he grasps the significance that the desacralisation of authority represented for the emergence of the problem of authority. Parsons notes that Christian thought 'during the Reformation period was directed toward the jealous safeguarding of the sphere of religious freedom of the individual'. He makes the important observation that the 'problem of religious freedom tended to become identified with that of political obligation, because the only authority that could threaten this sphere was the state'.[95] Pointing to the consequences of the desacralisation of the state, he remarks:

From a protestant Christian point of view the general trend of thought on this question was unfavourable to the state, for in contrast with its status in pagan antiquity the state had been robbed by Christianity of its intrinsic sanctity it had enjoyed.[96]

Thus the loss of sanctity of the state and the possibility that this institution would not 'enjoy religious approval' had important implications for the constitution and locus of moral authority.

Parsons also draws attention to the implications of the way that Protestantism 'settled the locus of religious values in the individual'. As a result, religious freedom tended to be represented as a matter of individual

[92] Nisbet (1974) p. 137.   [93] Nisbet (1979) p. 116.   [94] Nisbet (1979) p. 116.
[95] Parsons (1968) p. 87.   [96] Parsons (1968) p. 87.

conscience: 'The arguments for freedom from authority tended to become predominantly normative, only with freedom of conscience could even the opportunity for a truly Christian life be guaranteed'.[97] Parsons's analysis bears a striking resemblance to the argument pursued by Hobbes in *Behemoth*, in which he claimed that it was Presbyterian ministers who incited people to interpret the Bible by themselves who 'instigated the collapse of social order'.[98]

Since Parsons is the person most associated with the rediscovery of Hobbes's problem of order as a key issue for social theory, it is not surprising that his theory has been subject to critical scrutiny. Parsons has been criticised for both taking normative solutions to the problem of order too far, and also for not taking them seriously. Burger writes that Parsons naively assumes that 'the solidarizing dispositions of individuals is sufficient to ensure the authority of values', and indicts Parsons for imagining that the problem of order 'consists in nothing else than the postulate of the natural identity of normative interests'.[99] In contrast, Van Krieken states that the way that Parsons interprets Hobbes is to emphasise the 'coercive force of sovereign authority' in holding society together.[100] An inspection of Parsons's reading of Hobbes suggests that it is possible to detect both the theme of the coercive power of sovereign authority alongside of a normative solution to the problem of order. What particularly concerns Parsons is the dichotomy between individual and society. His orientation to the problem of order sought to address the issue of how conflicting individual interests could be reconciled. He asks, 'How could the relational structure of a market economy be expected to have even a minimum level of stability when the individual participants were in the first instance bound to that structure only by "self-interest"?'[101]

For Hobbes, self-interest turns into a disruptive force when it is politicised and expressed through disruptive religious doctrines. Hobbes's formulation of the problem is directly shaped by his discovery of the formidable power of opinion. It is the politics of competing individual judgments and beliefs that influence so much of Hobbes's theory. He writes at a point where religious doctrine had become compromised and when politics appeared to possess an autonomous existence. Accordingly, the act of political will was conceptualised as the instrument for restoring order, and the consolidation of the right political belief was seen as the

---

[97]   Parsons (1968) p. 87.
[98]   This interpretation is forcefully developed by Lloyd (2002) p. 193, see also pp. 193–223.
[99]   Burger (1977) p. 322.   [100]   Van Krieken (2003) p. 3.
[101]   Parsons (1974) p. xvii.

precondition for maintaining it. Hobbes hoped that his formula could settle matters, but experience would show that the politicisation of authority merely highlighted its conventional quality and invited challenges to it.

Hobbes's strategy of privileging the political was motivated by this conviction that religion could no longer serve as a stabilising influence in society. Along with a significant section of the educated elites, Hobbes saw the violent upheavals of his time as a consequence of the zealous and intolerant behaviour of the Protestant sects. 'The problem of sectarianism led to a shift in the thinking of educated elites on the relationship between religion and society', argues Zaret. These elites drew the conclusion that 'it was no longer possible to assume that religion would stabilize the social order'. Zaret has put forward the view that the very development of 'liberal-democratic ideology was a response to the radicalism and intellectual dissonance generated by conflicts internal to Protestanism'.[102] It is likely that Hobbes's engagement with the problem of authority represented an important contribution to the elaboration of a liberal construction of authority.

Through highlighting the political dimension of authority, Hobbes succeeded in successfully breaking with previous traditional and religious conceptions of authority. But the highly politicised representation of order drew attention to necessity for foundational support. It was not sufficient to declare that what was required was a uniformity of opinion. The question that remained to be answered was what would constitute the basis of this consensus. Since Hobbes's time, many have struggled to come up with a plausible answer, and even more have opted for the strategy of evading the question altogether.

[102] Zaret (1989) pp. 163 and 172.

9   The rationalisation of authority

Hobbes sought to address the problem of order through reconciling the aspiration for individual liberty with the reality of absolutist rule. Despite his realistic advocacy of absolutist sovereignty, his recognition of the natural liberty of the individual situates him as one of the key influences on modern liberalism. Hobbes grasped that in his time, competing versions of authority made the task of gaining consensus about its meaning problematic. He provided a very early account of the threat that dissident intellectuals and ideologically inspired religious groups could represent to the maintenance of order, and in this sense his criticism of the role of intellectuals and universities during the English Civil War anticipated the subsequent tendency to blame the *philosophes* and other intellectuals for the breakdown of authority in the eighteenth and nineteenth centuries.[1]

One of the unique features of Hobbes's political philosophy was its realistic representation of domination and authority as the accomplishment of the political will. Although Hobbes was conscious of the need to ensure that his *Leviathan* provided security and order for individuals and their property, his absolutist emphasis was not quite congruent with the demands of the rapidly expanding commercial society. The modernising economies of Europe required new freedoms for the pursuit of commerce and trade and its advocates demanded restraints on the activities of the state.

Even supporters of a strong and centralised monarchy recognised the necessity for restraining government regulation of trade and commerce. In France the Physiocrats, a group of economists, combined their demand for maximum individual freedom in the domain of economics with supporting the ideal of an enlightened absolute monarchy. However, such sentiments contradicted the spirit of the times, which regarded the powers of the absolute ruler as something to be limited by the rule of

---

[1] It is worth noting that since the eighteenth century, blaming political intellectuals for the decline of authority has been a constant theme of modern conservative doctrine. See Nisbet (1979) pp. 116–20.

law. In England, this issue was sharply posed after the 'Glorious Revolution' of 1688, when a new balance of power between the monarchy and Parliament required that the relationship between the authority of the sovereign and the liberty of enterprise and conscience be clarified. In the decades following Hobbes's death, constitutional developments in England tended to look to the law to check the tendency towards the arbitrary exercise of power, attempting 'to deprive the sovereign power of the two main instruments by which despotism becomes possible – control of armed forces of the state and of finance'.[2]

Hostility to absolutist government was motivated by the desire to limit its arbitrary and intrusive character. The demand was for strong institutions that enforced the rule of law.

The social, political and above all, intellectual revolution that occurred in the eighteenth century had a profound impact on the way that authority was perceived, represented and experienced. This historical moment, tucked in between the overthrow of King James II in England in 1688 and the French Revolution of 1789, is frequently characterised by historians as the Age of Reason. In the centuries to follow, this era of the Enlightenment is generally represented as the point at which the very idea of authority was called into question. The intellectual temper of the time insisted that 'men were to be taught to rely on evidence provided by nature or reason not on the arguments supplied by tradition'.[3] The significance that eighteenth-century thinkers attached to reason, scientific research and experimentation meant that they celebrated their cultural achievements as superior to those of their ancestors. Previous generations of thinkers sought to legitimise their ideas through validating them with the wisdom of the ancients; by contrast, 'enlightened modernity viewed itself as a historical rupture without precedent'.[4] In effect the cultivation of the sensibility of continuity gave way to the valuation of change and novelty.

The emerging tension between the reason and unquestioned authority has led numerous interpreters of this period to provide an unmediated depiction of this relationship. The Enlightenment is sometimes represented as a time when reason sought to overthrow authority. According to one account of the 'antipathy to authority' in the eighteenth century, 'all forms of traditional authority were suspect' and 'nothing was to be taken on trust'.[5] This point is echoed by the political scientist Carl Friedrich, who concludes that 'ever since the eighteenth-century revolt,

---

[2] Laski (1936) p. 101.   [3] Cragg (1964) p. 2.
[4] Sternhell (2010) p. 37.   [5] Cragg (1964) pp. 2–3.

freedom-loving intellectuals and their following have viewed authority with hostility'.[6]

To be sure, a growing body of influential philosophers developed arguments promoting the liberation of the individual and criticised the authority of traditional beliefs. Such sentiments were expressed by Locke's *Second Treatise of Government*, Kant's *Reply to the Question: What is Enlightenment?* and Rousseau's *Discourse on the Origin of Inequality*. The attitude of the *philosophes* (who did not think of themselves as philosophers, but as enlighteners) was explained in Diderot's *Encyclopedie* as one who, 'trampling on prejudice, tradition, universal consent, authority, in a world, all that enslaves most minds dares to think for himself'. Kant explicitly challenged custom and insisted that its unthinking acceptance was a sign of moral immaturity. Whereas previously the authority of the father was used to legitimate the necessity for obedience to the ruler, Kant used the 'imagery of paternal authority' to heap scorn on it. As one summary of Kant's contention outlines, 'accepting guidance from another was to remain at the level of the child; short of intellectual deficiency, the only reason for doing so were lethargy and cowardice'.[7]

However, eighteenth-century society could not do without some form of authority; so the renunciation of the customs and traditions of the past coincided with attempts to revive authority in a new modernising form. The new self-acclaimed enlightened elites had little hesitation about putting themselves forward as a virtuous leadership, who could prepare and educate the untutored masses for exercising their freedoms.

As an idea, authority was often associated with what was dismissed as the unthinking traditions of the past, and had an uneasy relationship with the prevailing intellectual climate. Stirk and Weigall claim that 'the attack upon the idea of authority which is reflected in Kant's paean to enlightenment was in large measure successful' and that therefore the 'idea of authority became increasingly difficult to defend'.[8] The pertinence of this observation was most vividly expressed in France, where even the monarchy found it increasingly difficult to justify its supreme status. The era, which opened with the autocracy of Louis XIV, ended with the unprecedented social and political upheaval unleashed by the French Revolution. As a historical event, the French Revolution represented a singular moment in the modernisation of authority. Unlike previous 'pre-modern revolts', where the 'justification of social and political change invariably invoked theological *fundamental*, customary law, and veneration of tradition', modern revolts like that of 1789 'quintessentially

---

[6] Friedrich (1972) p. 45.   [7] Stirk and Weigall (1995) p. 42.
[8] Stirk and Weigall (1995) pp. 42–3.

legitimize themselves in terms of, and depend on, non-traditional, and newly introduced, fundamental concepts'.[9]

In retrospect, the road from the cultural demotion of the status of authority to the outbreak of the French Revolution appears relatively straightforward. Arendt asserts that the 'loss of authority of the body politic had been a well-known phenomenon in Europe and the colonies ever since the seventeenth century'.[10] More than 40 years before the French revolution, Montesquieu was 'so haunted by the fear that the absolute monarchy had so undermined the traditional constitution of France that liberty had become forever impossible'.[11] Sensitive to the declining influence of custom and tradition, Montesquieu feared that without their restraining influence, some form of despotism would prevail; that once people became estranged from their habit and custom, obedience to authority could no longer be taken for granted. Arendt claimed that,

what Montesquieu, was only the first to predict explicitly, was the incredible ease with which governments would be overthrown; and the progressive loss of authority of all inherited political structures which he had in mind became plain to an increasing number of people everywhere throughout the eighteenth century.[12]

The revolution in ideas, which gained a powerful momentum with the ascendancy of the Cartesian worldview in the late seventeenth century, 'questioned all criteria of legitimacy based on past authority, knowledge and practice'. However, as Jonathan Israel observes, the new empiricist and mechanistic outlook was not welcomed by all; 'Most men had no desire to discard traditional reverence for established authority and idealized notions of community' or 'their belief in magic, demonology and Satan'. Moreover, even the more scientifically minded thinkers were hesitant about using the new criterion of truth to explain all phenomena according to mechanistic and mathematical logic.[13] So Descartes had his 'two-substance dualism' which 'created a reserve area for spirits, angels, demons and miracles'; Boyle and Locke 'ring-fenced' core Christian beliefs 'so the intellectual elites of Europe mostly sought one or another intellectual expedient for having it both ways'. In effect they sought to reconcile their rationalism not only with religion, but also with social norms regarding 'education, society and politics based on custom, usage, and existing law as well as social hierarchical principles'.[14]

---

[9] Israel (2006) p. 3.   [10] Arendt (2006) p. 107.   [11] Sabine (1961) p. 552.
[12] Arendt (2006) p. 108.   [13] Israel (2006) p. 10.   [14] Israel (2006) p. 10.

The reluctance of leading Enlightenment thinkers to rely solely on rationality expressed the presentiment that whatever reservations they possessed about the status of custom and tradition, society simply could not function without drawing on some of the norms and values that influenced everyday life. One reason for this hesitancy was the premonition of disorder. That is why the late seventeenth-century French sceptic Pierre Bayle, no less than the German philosopher Immanuel Kant, opted for the enlightened rule of the absolute king. The eighteenth-century concept of 'enlightened despotism' indicated that for some, 'enlightenment belonged with despotism as at once its necessary condition and transcendent control'.[15] That some could associate the Enlightenment with a dependence on a despot indicated the hesitant and partial manner with which the new freedoms were enunciated.

The anti-traditionalist ideas that emerged in the Age of Reason were tempered by the intuition that the loss of authority invited disorder. Hence this period saw the re-emergence of the problem of order – but unlike in Hobbes's era, the danger was not seen to be religious conflict but the threat posed by 'uneducated opinion'. That is why the philosophical criticism directed at traditional forms of authority was motivated by the aspiration for more freedom for only the small groups of educated professionals and entrepreneurs. What drove Enlightenment critics of the old order was not the impulse of democratisation, but the aspiration to replace the old elites with own rule.

Writers on the Enlightenment point out that many of the new movements from below, for example in Bohemia in 1775 or Pugachev's revolt in Russia in 1773, 'took the form of a protest by the educated against their exclusion from political power by privileged minorities who based their claim to govern on tradition and prescription'.[16] Typically these movements represented a relatively narrow constituency. In France, until the autumn of 1788 it consisted of sections of the nobility and legal profession; the social movements in England, the Netherlands and Geneva did not identify themselves with democracy and 'represented the views of the educated but unprivileged men who considered themselves unjustly barred from a share of political power'.[17] Hampson indicates that these movements were not so much against Divine Right monarchs 'but against oligarchies whose claim rested on tradition alone'. This was the orientation of the moderate English movement for parliamentary reform, which began around 1779 and whose target was a franchise 'defended in the name of traditional rights'.[18] However, the questioning of the authority

[15] Krieger (1975) pp. 88–9.   [16] Hampson (1982) p. 181.
[17] Hampson (1982) p. 181.   [18] Hampson (1982) pp. 182–3.

of tradition threatened the prevailing order. The outbreak of the Gordon Riots in London 1780 reminded the elites of the threat posed by the urban masses, stalling the movement for reform in England and fostering a more conservative attitude towards political change.

The Gordon Riots moved the French statesman Turgot to exclaim, 'To what stage [of civilisation] has the human race advanced when in this century we see such fanaticism in London itself?'[19] In France it was more difficult to reconcile the aspirations of the educated middle-class reformers with the traditional order. The call for social equality in a 'limited sense of the equality of gentlemen and nobles' in France sought to establish conditions comparable to those of Britain. But whereas in Britain, such attitudes 'could be defended in the name of tradition', in France this required the 'rejection of tradition in the name of abstract principle'.[20] The necessity for mobilising opinion around principle rather than precedent opened up the question of consent and authority to public scrutiny. In such circumstances the claim to equality could not be easily monopolised by a minority. Gradually, the movement for reform was transformed into a revolutionary one.

In the case of France, the concept of popular consent was so politicised that it became incompatible with the monarchical principle. Consent conveyed the idea of an agreement made by equals and implicitly contradicted the idea of subordination to a superior. 'The French revolution of 1789 was the principal turning point in the transition from the authority of kings to the mandate of the people', states the sociologist Reinhardt Bendix.[21] The event also raised what at times appeared as the insoluble problem of how to reconcile authority founded on popular consent with the maintenance of order. During the century to follow, the question of how to represent the people's will, or what came to be known as public opinion, became the central question to those preoccupied with the project of modernising authority.

Conflicts of interest frequently crystallised around the question of how to define the relationship between authority and power. The previous problematic of how to conceptualise the relationship between different forms of authority was displaced by a new question about the relationship between individual freedom and authority. According to liberal philosophers such as Locke, individual freedom (as experienced in the state of nature) was logically prior to the constitution of authority; therefore the burden of justifying restrictions on liberty was upon those who sought to uphold authority. These thinkers developed a strategy that recognised

---

[19] Cited in Cavanaugh (1969) p. 57.   [20] Hampson (1982) p. 255.
[21] Bendix (1978) p. 321.

the predominant status of authority in the political sphere while claiming that liberty had to prevail in the economic and cultural spheres.

The emerging, modern conception of authority sought to answer the question of 'what was the boundary of the common interest for which the exercise of power was collectively recognised'.[22] However, even within the political sphere, the tension between individual liberty and authority as justified power persisted. Throughout the eighteenth and nineteenth centuries, competing groups and theories upheld the 'primacy either of authority or liberty', with all sides assuming an inverse relationship between the two. Attitudes to this relationship served to define the two leading modern political orientations of the eighteenth century:

> the liberals sketched out a large sphere for political rights and civil liberty and a small sphere for responsible authority, and the conservatives sketched out a large sphere for aristocratic – that is, independent – authority and a small sphere for freedom of enterprise and liberty of conscience; but both sides acknowledged some role for both the authoritarian and the liberal principle.[23]

In a sweeping generalisation, Marx contrasted the eleventh century, whose dominant historical character was the 'principle of authority', with the eighteenth century, defined by the 'principle of individualism'.[24] Outwardly this was indeed the century where individual became an object of veneration. As Sternhell notes, the 'Enlightenment wished to liberate the individual from the constraints of history, from the yoke of traditional unproven beliefs'.[25] Historians of the eighteenth century frequently represent the rise of liberalism as the political expression of the principle of individualism. According to one such account:

> The political liberalism, the religious liberalism, and the economic liberalism of the eighteenth century were merely separate manifestations of one and the same attempt to break down the older institutional forms and set free human energies and allow satisfaction to human aspirations that could no longer find expression in those forms. Liberalism in all its manifestations was essentially a doctrine of the rights of the individual, and a criticism of the claims of existing institutions to regulate his activity. Individual liberty, in politics, in religion, in industry, was felt to be the first and sometimes the only thing necessary for the introduction of a better social and political order. Other ages have perhaps appreciated more fully the meaning of individuality, but no age ever desired or fought for it with greater zeal than the century of Voltaire, Rousseau, and Adam Smith.[26]

While the philosophers endorsed the principle of individuality they were by no means unambiguously hostile to the principle of authority. For

---

[22] Krieger (1977) p. 254.   [23] Krieger (1977) p. 255.   [24] Marx (1955) p. 125.
[25] Sternhell (2010) p. 7.   [26] Morrow (2007) pp. 325–6.

most eighteenth-century philosophers and commentators, the relation-ship between these two principles was fraught with tension and ambiguity. The distinguished American historian Robert Palmer remarks that Jean-Jacques Rousseau (1712–1778) 'revolutionized the nature of authority since he denied the existence of authority apart from the individual over whom it was exercised'.[27] Yet his view of the individual was profoundly pessimistic and he looked to a benevolent educator to give people direc-tion. Rousseau's affirmation of the authority of the individual co-existed with its subordination to what he characterised as the General Will, which in turn was personified through a Great Legislator. Rousseau sought to reconcile his radical denunciation of the subordination of the individual to the institutions of society with his deification of a powerful charismatic leader, who was charged with the task of educating an otherwise ignorant people.

The French revolutionary leader Maximilien de Robespierre shared Rousseau's reservations about the intellectual capacity of the multitude, regarding individuals as powerless to resist the influence of prejudice and of social pressure. 'Human authority can always be attacked by human pride', claimed Robespierre, taking the view that people lacked the capacity to reason and therefore they needed to be instructed by 'the religious sense by which the soul would is impressed with the idea of a sanction given to moral principles by a power superior to man'.[28] That a radical leader of the French Revolution would embrace a 'power superior to man' illustrated the hesitant and selective manner with which the Age of Reason dealt with the relationship between individual liberty and authority. Optimistic beliefs about the capacity of education to set the individual free existed alongside the conviction that individuals in the here and now were likely to be 'wildly wrong'.[29]

The liberal reaction to Hobbes

Hobbes's pioneering and realistic theorisation of the modern problem of authority laid bare its conventional character. This was one of its main strengths, but because Hobbes 'went so far in the direction of emanci-pating the rules of politics nominally from prior sanctions as to deny the validity of the "notions of Right and Wrong, Justice and Injustice,"' he exposed authority to permanent political scrutiny.[30] Hobbes's empha-sis on the absolute power of the ruler left open the question of how to

---

[27] Palmer (1969) p. 114.   [28] Cited by Palmer (1969) p. 128.
[29] Israel (2010) p. 1.   [30] Krieger (1975) p. 3.

reconcile the exercise of supreme sovereignty with the exigencies of commercial and a market-dominated society.

In Hobbes's account, once authority is transferred to the supreme ruler it becomes entirely political. According to this scenario, political authority dominates society to the point that, as Minogue puts it 'the people are never allowed any real existence'.[31] John Locke (1632–1704) is often counterposed to Hobbes as someone who was more interested in justifying resistance to 'the illegitimate authority of the king' than in elaborating a concept of strong authority'.[32] This influential representative of the Enlightenment offered arguments that were 'directed towards providing an account of the nature and limits of authority'.[33] According to some of his interpreters, Locke was more interested in questioning authority than in upholding it. Locke's 'great message was to set us free from the burden of tradition and authority both in theology and knowledge', states one study.[34]

Heineman argues that 'Locke's reluctance to provide a clear, comprehensive rationale for the strong governmental authority that he and his contemporary English readers assumed began a degenerative process in the theoretical foundations for authority that was to culminate in liberalism's current quandary as to its conceptual basis'.[35] Certainly many conservative opponents of the Enlightenment and the democratisation of public life denounced Locke as the enemy of order and of traditional authority. The Victorian essayist Thomas Carlyle observed that Locke 'had paved the way for banishing religion from the world', while the French conservative commentator, Joseph de Maistre attacked him as the evil genius of the 'theophobia' of the eighteenth century.[36]

Yet Locke, like most liberal thinkers of the time, was more ambivalent about the status of religion and authority than his detractors imply. Locke's political philosophy expressed a self-conscious rejection of the authority of tradition and of the past, on the basis that what mattered was reason. As one of his interpreters contends, Locke gave up historical arguments for ancient liberties because he believed that reason was 'a far more powerful foundation for government by consent and firmer foundation for the fundamental rights of life, liberty and property'.[37] But contrary to accusations of theophobia, Locke claimed that reason, as expressed through the law of nature, is ultimately an expression of God's will. As the political theorist John Dunn wrote, for Locke 'all legitimate authority' exercised 'by one human being over another is an authority conferred upon him ultimately by God'.[38]

[31] Minogue (1963) p. 134.   [32] Ashcraft (1994) p. 227.   [33] Ashcraft (1994) p. 228.
[34] Aarsleff (1994) p. 252.   [35] Heineman (1994) p. 40.   [36] Aarsleff (1994) p. 279.
[37] Resnick (1984) p. 102.   [38] Dunn (1975) p. 127.

His ambivalence towards the role of religion notwithstanding, Locke took a decisive step towards undermining the status of tradition as a source of authority. One of the distinct contributions of Locke to political theory was his reluctance to use the past to validate authority. Skinner argues that 'the absence of an appeal to the traditional liberal constitutionalist arguments of the seventeenth century represents Locke's intention to reject and repudiate one of the most prestigious forms of political argumentation of his day'.[39] Locke's attempt to repose the concept of authority on a rational foundation undermined arguments for obeying the sovereign rule that appealed to the precedent of the past. The disconnection of tradition from authority lent the latter a distinctly political character.

Arguably, one of the most significant contributions that Locke made to the modernisation of political theory was to set boundaries around the purview of the political. While Hobbes politicised authority, Locke sought to segregate it from the economic and social spheres. According to one account, Locke attempted to posit the State as a 'distinct entity', one that was dependent on 'the wishes of the people' but separate from it.[40] This compartmentalisation of politics was important for its modernisation, since it helped consolidate the distinction between the domain of (political) authority and (economic) freedom. Through the formalisation of the distinction between the two spheres, the ruler's authority became limited outside of the political jurisdiction.

Locke also argued for restraining the influence of the state over matters of individual conscience and moral life. He thought that through the exercise of moral judgment, individuals could influence prevailing sentiments about virtue and vice, which would acquire force through the emergence of public opinion. Consequently as Koselleck asserts, it is 'no longer the sovereign' but the 'citizens who constitute the moral laws by their judgment, just as merchants who determine a trade value'.[41] In a sense, by freeing morality from its subordination to the authority of the state, Locke extended the domain where individual freedom could be exercised. At the same time, the protection offered to conscience and judgment had the potential for empowering the status of an alternative source of authority. As Koselleck asks, 'Which authority decides? The moral authority of the citizens or the political authority of the State?'[42]

In effect, Locke's differentiation of economic from political power and the space he reserved for individual moral judgment provided a powerful argument for restraining the role of the state in social and economic

---

[39] Cited in Resnick (1984) p. 98.   [40] Minogue (1963) p. 134.
[41] Koselleck (1988) p. 56.   [42] Koselleck (1988) p. 58.

life. Laski's account of the historical emergence of liberalism stated that what it actually represented was 'the attempt to curb the political power of the state', adding that liberalism 'has sought, almost from the outset of its history, to limit the ambit of political authority, to confine the business of government within the framework of constitutional principle; and it has tried, therefore, fairly consistently to discover a system of fundamental rights which the state is not entitled to invade'.[43] This interpretation emphasises less Locke's promotion of liberty and freedom than his attempt to restrain the arbitrary power of the state, amounting to a regime of limited liberty in the domain of the political co-existing with the freedom of conscience and enterprise. Through this formula, claims Laski, 'Locke reconciled the contradiction between authority and freedom in such a way as to offer the rising middle class exactly the ideas they were seeking'.[44] Writing in a similar vein, Wolin observes that 'Lockean liberalism was fully as much a defense against radical democracy as an attack on traditionalism'.[45] It offered protection against threats to security and order, and freedom of enterprise.

However one interprets Locke's political agenda, his *Second Treatise on Government* outlined a powerful argument for the centrality of popular consent to the exercise of political rule. In this text, Locke put forward a modernised version of *auctoritas*, making a distinction between power and authority and arguing that tyranny was the exercise of the former without the latter. He characterised tyranny as the 'exercise of power beyond Right', and defined it as the 'use of force without Authority'.[46] Through distinguishing between force and authority, Locke offered a powerful argument for the right of resistance against a tyrannical ruler. Since, for Locke, the source of authority was the consent of the people, its exercise is limited by consent.

Unlike Hobbes's absolute ruler who makes his own law, the authority of Locke's sovereign is subject to the limits of constitutionally enacted laws. This conception of authority exercised through and limited by law provided one of the defining themes of eighteenth-century liberalism. Conversely, freedom was represented as the 'right of doing whatever the law permits'.[47] It is at this point that the law – an impersonal and rational power – acquired significance as a source of legitimacy. The decline of traditional, including monarchical, authority is paralleled by the emergence of demands to institutionalise popular consent.

The liberal interpretation of the law as an institution through which freedom could be preserved against the intrusion of the state resonated

[43] Laski (1936) p. 15.   [44] Laski (1936) p. 118.   [45] Wolin (2004) p. 264.
[46] Cited in Ashcraft (1994) p. 228.   [47] Manent (1995) p. 60.

with the experience of eighteenth-century England, where the law possessed a unusual degree of influence and played a crucial role in validating order and peace. As the historian E. P. Thompson argues, at this time the law was a 'central legitimizing ideology, displacing the religious authority and sanctions of previous centuries'. Thompson writes that the,

> hegemony of the eighteenth century gentry and aristocracy was expressed, above all, not in military force, not in the mystifications of priesthood or of the press, not even in economic coercion, but in the rituals of the study of the Justices of the Peace, in the quarter sessions, in the pomp of the Assizes and in the theatre of Tyburn.[48]

To some extent, the apparent disassociation of the law from any sectional interests was accomplished through the self-conscious autonomisation of the political from economic power. While political authority was depicted as an institution possessing coercive powers, the compulsion of economic forces was represented as a necessity-imposed fact of life.[49] Why? Because property rights came to be seen as 'essentially prior to the institution of society, independent of others' consent or political law'. As Manent reminds us, unlike political authority, 'property' appeared as 'natural and not conventional'.[50] In this way the conflict between authority and freedom was confined to the autonomous sphere of politics and the power of extra-political coercion was exempted from the connotation of illegitimate domination. Wolin concludes that 'equating of government with physical compulsion' was the other side of the coin to the 'willingness to accept compulsion from an impersonal source'.[51]

The social contract tradition initiated by Hobbes and pursued by Locke and other liberal theorists deployed this device in an attempt to develop an explanation of how order was possible. It offered an account of political authority and obligation whose foundation was provided by the consent of the governed. This tradition insisted that political conventions were the product of the voluntary accord of free and equal individuals. 'On this view, legitimacy and duty depend on a concatenation of voluntary individual acts, and not on "natural" political authority, patriarchy, theocracy, divine right necessity, custom, convenience or psychological compulsion', writes Riley.[52]

The liberal interpretation of the social contract tended towards an anti-political direction; as Laski contends, 'it sought to limit political intervention to the narrowest area compatible with the maintenance of

---

[48] Thompson (1977) p. 262.   [49] See the discussion in Wolin (2004) pp. 278–81.
[50] Manent (1995) p. 42.   [51] Wolin (2004) p. 280.   [52] Riley (2010) p. 82.

public order'.[53] The French political philosopher Michel Foucault has accurately described the political economy of the eighteenth century as an expression of the tendency towards the 'self limitation of governmental reason':[54] it took the view that liberty, including the freedom of commerce and trade, depended on the inviolability of the law. James Steuart (1713–1780) warned that liberty was precarious when it relied on 'the ambulatory will of any man or set of men', and regarded the protection of the rule of law as the guarantor of freedom.[55]

One of the most influential arguments for constraining the authority of the political ruler was outlined in Montesquieu's *Spirit of the Laws* (1748). He was preoccupied by the threat posed by the arbitrary rule of an absolutist monarchy, and devised a system of division of power underpinned by the rule of law. He argued that the restraint of the sovereign, through institutionally checking his power, provided space for freedom to flourish. 'Liberty is produced through the neutralization of the political,' comments Manent.[56] Political economists extended Montesquieu's approach, through counterposing the efficacy of the economic to the potentially destabilising consequences of the political activity.

One important outcome of the neutralisation of the political was that order and its maintenance were no longer contingent on the will and the act of political authority. Eighteenth-century Scottish political economy often represented order as the spontaneous and even natural accomplishment of history. Adam Smith's *Wealth of Nations* (1776) argued against political intervention in economic life through developing the claim that it was through the pursuit of individual self-interest that the prosperity of the nation was realised. However, the same argument was used to contend that it was through the interaction of individual interests that order is established. As one exposition of Smith's doctrine of self-interest claimed, what is offered is a 'conception of a rational or natural social order, in which there is a complete reconciliation of the interests of the individual and the interests of the society'.[57] This reconciliation is realised through the working of the market. As the Russian political economist I. I. Rubin wrote, 'the basic proposition of Smith's *theoretical* system states that *economic phenomena possess an inherent, "natural", law determined regularity*, which exists independently of the will of the state and is based on the immutable "natural" inclinations of the individual'.[58]

Smith believed that the potential for the realisation of this natural social order could be disrupted through inept and disruptive political intervention. As Morrow points out, Smith conceived of order as an

[53] Laski (1936) p. 15.   [54] Foucault (2010) p. 13.   [55] Cited in Berry (1997) p. 128.
[56] Manent (1995) p. 60.   [57] Morrow (2007) p. 332.   [58] Rubin (1979) p. 172.

actuality 'existing in every society, though not fully realized in his day because of the unwise restrictions of governments'.[59] Smith's solution was to restore the conditions necessary for the operation of natural liberty through removing these restrictions: he wrote that 'all systems of preference or of restraint, therefore, being thus completely taken away, the obvious and simple system of natural liberty establishes itself of its own accord'.[60]

The characterisation of order as 'natural' also conveyed the impression that it was superior to the arrangement achieved artificially through political means. From Smith's perspective, the principal role of political authority was to create the conditions where the spontaneous process through which natural order is forged is protected from external disruption.[61]

The belief that natural order is spontaneously formed was systematically promoted by Smith's friend, the Scottish historian and social philosopher Adam Ferguson (1723–1816). His writings offered a historical account of the process through which people's subordination to authority and order was forged, representing the acceptance of order and obedience as the result of spontaneous and unconscious historical process. Ferguson wrote that,

we follow a leader, before we have settled the ground of his pretensions, or adjusted the form of his election; and it is not till after mankind have committed many errors in the capacities of magistrate and subject, that they think of making government itself a subject of rules.[62]

Ferguson's theory of a spontaneously evolved regime of order offered an idealised account of the relationship between the individual pursuit of interest and its unintended but benevolent consequence. For Ferguson it is not human intention or human effort but what Lisa Hill has characterised as Providential Functionalism that is responsible for securing social order;[63] thus, the role of human intervention and political intercession is redundant in this task.

The conceptualisation of the spontaneous formation of order through the pursuit of individual interests was closely linked to a utilitarian interpretation of the workings of society. This approach asserted that what benefits the interest of the individual is also good for all. As Smith argued in *The Theory of Moral Sentiments*: 'society may subsist among different men, as among *different merchants*, from a sense of its utility, without any

---

[59] Morrow (2007) p. 332.   [60] Cited in Morrow (2007) p. 332.
[61] See Long (2006) p. 291.   [62] Ferguson (1980) p. 63.   [63] Hill (1986) p. 209.

mutual love of affection'.[64] Such calculations also influenced how and why individuals obey authority. The Scottish philosopher John Millar (1735–1801) argued in his *The Origin of the Distinctions of Ranks* (2006) that 'authority has legitimacy when it is used to efficiently satisfy needs'.[65]

For his part, Adam Smith presented obedience as a habit acquired through the passage of time; an act based on the internalisation of custom and tradition. The tendency to defer to another on account of the superior person's age or wealth or ability was characterised by Smith as 'the principle of authority'. As against the habitual obedience induced by the principal of authority, Smith also proposed the principal of utility, which 'induces men to obey the civil magistrate'. According to this principle, obedience of the sovereign power is essential 'to preserve justice and peace in the society' and for 'upholding the security of the individual'.[66] In this way, the habit or disposition to obey is 'mitigated by a sense of calculation' based on a 'utilitarian judgment as to costs and benefits to ensure good order'. Through the recognition that all have an interest in the maintenance of institutions that enforce justice, an acceptance of order is realised; 'It is the sense of public utility, more than of private, which influences men to obedience'.[67]

The utilitarian orientation of thinkers associated with the Scottish Enlightenment did not engage with pre-existing attempts to provide a foundational theory of authority and obedience. Implicitly, the questions raised by the search for a normative foundation for political order were displaced by projecting utility as the point of reference for authority. The need to balance political authority with the utility principle endowed order with a pragmatic quality. The tendency to displace political teleology with a more rationalist and utilitarian stance towards public life was motivated in part by the need to weaken pre-existing political values that could serve as obstacles to the working of commercial society.

Although utilitarian theories of authority are usually associated with liberalism, in the eighteenth century they influenced political thinkers across the ideological divide. When the French encyclopaedist Denis Diderot stated that 'good princes know that they are holders of power only for the happiness of the state', he affirmed the co-existence of the principle of authority and of utility.[68] A similar standpoint was put forward by the eighteenth-century Prussian Cameralist Johann Heinrich Gottlob von

---

[64] See http://knarf.english.upenn.edu/Smith/tms223.html (accessed 30 April, 2013).
[65] See Knud Haakonssen's introduction to Millar (2006) p. xvi.
[66] This idea is developed by Adam Smith in his *Lectures on Jurispridence*, http://oll.libertyfund.org/?option=com_staticxt&staticfile=show.php%3Ftitle=196&chapter=55640&layout=html&Itemid=27 (accessed 30 April 2013).
[67] Long (2006) p. 292.   [68] Diderot is cited in Krieger (1975) p. 53.

Justi, who declared that 'the best government will ever be that which most completely satisfies the final end for which men live in commonwealths', adding that 'no one can govern rational and free beings except through the purpose of promoting their welfare and making them happy'.[69] In France the principle of utility was also adopted by political commentators who wished to find new forms of validation for the monarchy, and promoted through advocates of what came to be known as enlightened despotism. As the era of absolute monarchy in France was coming to its end, its supporters even embraced the authority of science to preserve the Old Regime, playing an active role in supporting scientific institutions in order to modernise the monarchy's image and gain legitimacy for its rule.[70]

The adoption of the principle of utility as a source of validation for governmental rule was one of the key innovations of eighteenth-century modernisers of authority. This utilitarian focus expressed an important revision in the way that authority was justified. For many Enlightenment thinkers, it was the capacity to promote public welfare rather than simply an *a priori* claim to authority that justified obedience. The *philosophe* Paul-Henri d'Holbach (1723–1789) claimed that there was a direct relationship between an authoritative sovereign and the capacity to protect the welfare of the public, writing that 'the citizen obeys the law, the public will, the sovereign authority' because 'he hoped that they will guide him more surely toward durable happiness than his own desires do'.[71]

Holbach's emphasis on the duty of the sovereign to secure public welfare illustrates the tendency to validate authority through its effects. Krieger believes that there occurred a 'shift in political thinking from considerations of origins to considerations of ends, from justification by cause to justification by effect', and contends that this shift, 'which underlay the more graduated expansion of the security function to include the welfare dimension – was a principled reorientation which betokened a changed attitude toward the whole realm of human relations'.[72] The modernising impulse articulated by utilitarian-minded philosophers had as its premise the belief that the role of government was to realise public welfare through acting on the laws of nature.

As noted previously, acting in accordance with the laws of nature required that a government knew its limits and refrained from interfering with the working out of these laws. At the same time, government was expected to secure the public's welfare. For proponents of this modernised form of authority, the legitimacy of a government was based on its capacity to secure the happiness and security of the people. Foucault

---

[69] Cited in Krieger (1975).   [70] See Baker (1994) Chapter 7.
[71] Cited in Krieger (1975) p. 54.   [72] Krieger (1975) p. 55.

points out that at this point in time, 'success or failure' replaces the 'division between legitimacy and illegitimacy'.[73] Foucault's counterposition of success to legitimacy is possibly too unmediated; the problem of legitimation remained one of the principal issues of the eighteenth century. However, increasingly one of the means through which legitimacy came to be claimed was through the idiom of success. Governments could now lay claim to legitimacy through demonstrating competence, and showing that their rule worked to improve the welfare of the public.

But of course not all governments were successful at securing the public's welfare and certainly not all of the time. Despite attempts to limit or neutralise the role of the political, there were times when the extraordinary power of the sovereign would be called upon to create the conditions necessary for the preservation of order.

The socialisation of authority

The shift in emphasis from the legitimacy of authority to its effects was reflected through the institutionalisation of new bureaucratic and administrative instruments for implementing policy. The actions of the ruler were now justified by their capacity to enhance the well-being of the people, rather than their consistency with a normative foundation of government. This reorientation towards a utilitarian conception of government was matched by a perceptible tendency towards the *socialisation of authority*.

The discussion surrounding authority gradually widened its focus from the political to society. In political and cultural thought, society was conceptualised as a site where, through the working out of natural laws, a modern rational set of social interests could evolve. In France, physiocrats and political commentators gave voice to this trend through insisting that the role of government was to uphold social interests – the most important of which was property. This sentiment was elaborated through a 'social theory of representation', which had as its premise the view that the 'entity that is to be represented is *society*, understood as an association of individuals engaged in the common production and enjoyment of economic and social values, and that its articulation takes the form of the expression of social *interests*'.[74] At this point in time, social interests were principally identified with the 'existence and ownership of property'. The narrative of French political modernisers challenged the Old Regime by endorsing 'property versus privilege, as the principle of representation; election versus cooptation, as the means for the selection of

---

[73] Foucault (2010) p. 16.   [74] Baker (1994) p. 241.

representatives; vote by head versus vote by order, as the basis for their deliberation'.[75]

The tendency to give meaning to the fundamental role of property ownership through the relatively novel concept of society was influenced by the anti-political ethos of eighteenth-century liberalism. Particularly in France, politics was associated with the subordination of property to privilege and with non-rational arbitrary institutions. The necessity for rationalising 'social decision making' was even recognised by modernising advisors of the monarch Louis XVI.[76] However, it was the opponents of the Old Regime who most consistently promoted the authority of society. This perspective was eloquently expressed by Emmanuel-Joseph Sieyes (1748–1836), one of the key theorists of popular sovereignty and the French Revolution. In his 1788 *Essai sur les priviliges*, his denunciation of privilege was based on the argument that it was incompatible with the free pursuit of economic activity in civil society, where 'there is no subordination but a continual exchange'. For Sieyes, the privileges of the Old Regime represented an obstacle to the realisation of reason in society.[77]

The discovery of society as a site where the pursuit of individual interests culminates in the realisation of public welfare and order gave emphasis to the superiority of the operation of the law of nature over political intervention. Many philosophers were deeply suspicious of the role of politics and were therefore drawn towards the project of depoliticising authority. David Hume (1711–1766), one of the early precursors of utilitarianism, made a significant contribution to this project. His writing, like that of Hobbes, can be seen in part as a reaction to the English Civil War: he was no less concerned than Hobbes about the destructive power of religious fanaticism, and regarded political conflict, particularly when fuelled by ideologically influenced opinion, as dangerous. But he did not share Hobbes's faith in the politicisation of authority. Writing at a time when the growth of the press and of the public lent opinion an unprecedented significance, he regarded the management of this unpredictable force as one of the main challenges facing government. Influenced by Scottish political economy, Hume's tendency to depoliticise public life was linked to his admiration for the workings of commercial society.

It was Rousseau who expressed the eighteenth-century reaction against politicised authority in the most consistent fashion. He insisted that the distinction between the political state and civil society was 'possible because both terms have their source and foundation in a third term incorporating both of them'. Manent writes that Rousseau was 'the first

---

[75] Baker (1994) p. 240.   [76] Baker (1994) p. 242.   [77] Baker (1994) p. 245.

to bring out in all its clarity the third term, which he christens with a name that will last: "society"'.[78] From this point onwards, knowledge about society would become essential for securing order.

Today, when the concept of society is often associated with theories of social construction and radical conventionalism, it is easy to misunderstand its usage in the eighteenth century. Although social conventions were often interpreted as the result of the spontaneous interaction of individual interests and were frequently contrasted to the traditional notions of unchanging customs, they were nonetheless represented as the natural products of the forces of nature. That is why, despite his criticism of those who looked for the source of authority in the past, Hume could regard custom as one of the important institutions through which authority was maintained. In *A Treatise on Human Nature*, Hume argued that 'time *and custom* give authority to all forms of government and all succession of princes', and claimed that even governments that were constituted through 'injury and violence' become 'in time legal and obligatory'.[79]

At this point in time, the concept of society possessed a weak sense of individual subjectivity and of the social. Even Rousseau, who drew a sharp contrast between nature and society, identified with 'natural man' rather than a social one. Rousseau regarded the state of nature as one where people lived in a state of virtue, and feared that society's influence corrupted what was virtuous in humanity. His disenchantment with society led him to develop an intensely fatalistic version of what would later be characterised as social determinism. Rousseau's individuals were incapable of resisting the corrupting influence of society and therefore required the guidance of Great Legislature to gain freedom.

Liberal thinkers tended to depict obedience to superiors as natural habits underwritten by customs. So when Adam Smith wrote that 'superior age, superior abilities of body and of mind, ancient family, and superior wealth seem to be the four things that give one man authority over another', he provided an account of social authority that was distinctly naturalised.[80] Smith criticised the idea that obedience to authority was based on a pre-existing contract, writing:

Ask a common porter or day-labourer why he obeys the civil magistrate, he will tell you that it is right to do so, that he sees others do it, that he would be punished if he refused to do it, or perhaps that it is a sin against God not to do it. But you will never hear him mention a contract as the foundation of his obedience.[81]

---

[78] Manent (1995) p. 78.   [79] Berry (1997) p. 34.

[80] See http://oll.libertyfund.org/?option=com_staticxt&staticfile=show.php%3Ftitle=196&chapter=55640&layout=html&Itemid=27 (accessed 30 April 2013).

[81] http://oll.libertyfund.org/?option=com_staticxt&staticfile=show.php%3Ftitle=196&chapter=55640&layout=html&Itemid=27 (accessed 30 April 2013).

The American sociologist Charles Camic insists that utilitarian theory of society contained a powerful moral impulse. In this model of society, individuals appear to possess a kind of reverent attitude towards authority. Camic writes that Smith 'perceives' the relevance of normative rules to the problem of order – general rules of conduct 'are felt as "sacred", are regarded with "awe and respect" and regulate the action of even the selfishly motivated'. He believes that for Smith, 'human society . . . would crumble into nothing if mankind were not generally impressed with reverence for these important rules of conduct'.[82]

Although Adam Ferguson insisted that order was spontaneously constructed, he took the view that social stability was maintained through habit and custom. In *Principles of Moral and Political Science*, Ferguson claimed that custom helped stabilise institutions because 'key social institutions are supported through "habits of thinking"' so in government 'habit engenders stability through shared authority values'.[83] Though habits are social they gain their force through their reproduction over time and acquire an influence analogous to a tradition. This tendency to reinvent tradition in the form of a social habit can be interpreted as way of reintroducing custom as the source of order and authority. As the British social theorist Alan Swingewood argues, for eighteenth-century sociology, social consensus was accomplished through the 'factors of habit and custom'; and 'the Scots treated habit as a social factor' which 'constituted a significant part of social action'.[84]

In the writings of Hume, Smith, Ferguson and Millar, custom works as a form of social convention that 'acts as external constraints on individual action' and which 'over a period of time' comes to be 'accepted as the correct way of doing things'.[85] At this point in time, the social overlapped with the natural. The authority of society was assumed to be eternal – but in this model it is ratified less by God than by the nature of socio-economic power. 'It is obvious, that some mode of subordination is as necessary to men as society itself; and this, not only to attain the ends of government, but to comply with an order established by nature', wrote Ferguson.[86] In the new natural/sociological accounts of subordination, domination is based on socioeconomic power; and for Ferguson 'there was a direct causal connection between property and the "distinction of ranks" in society'. A similar sentiment was held by Millar, who believed that property was the 'natural source of influence and authority' in society.[87]

[82] Camic (1979) p. 533.   [83] Cited in Hill (1986) p. 214.
[84] Swingewood (1970) p. 165.   [85] Swingewood (1970) p. 165.
[86] Ferguson (1980) p. 63.   [87] Cited in Swingewood (1970) p. 171.

Because of the strong linkage drawn between authority and the exercise of political force, the impersonal compulsion of the market and of social constraint could be represented as non-coercive and as consistent with the pursuit of individual freedom. 'Hence what was truly radical in liberalism was its conception of society as a network of activities carried on by actors who knew no principle of authority', observes Wolin, adding that 'society represented not only a spontaneous and self-adjusting order, but a condition untroubled by the presence of authority'.[88] This observation was not entirely right. Authority continued to have a presence – but a discrete one. It was confined to the sphere of the political, and faced competition with other principles, such as that of utility.

According to Wolin's analysis of the socialisation of authority, the depoliticisation of power is paralleled by its re-composition as social domination. An early variant of social determinism lent domination a modern soon to be familiar character. As Wolin astutely remarks, eighteenth-century liberalism 'conceived the issue as of reconciling freedom and authority, and they solved it by destroying authority in the name of liberty and replacing it by society, but only at the cost of exposing freedom to society's controls'.[89]

Reflections on the authority of society were not confined to attempts to validate the practices associated with the newly emerged commercial economies. The exploration of the history and role of custom and habit was complemented by discussions of public opinion. Public opinion was interpreted in a variety of ways. It was defined as a form of belief that influenced people's attitude towards the conduct of their affairs. Significantly, it was often depicted as a force that possessed a degree of autonomy from the dominant institutions of eighteenth-century Europe. Governments had to learn to act in accordance with, manage it and represent it. In numerous accounts of the time, public opinion was interpreted as a form of social pressure, whose power exercised great force over individuals and rulers alike: according to one study, in France public opinion was seen as one of the decisive influences on government.[90] This was a force that was 'distinct from political power or legal authority'.[91]

The influence and power of opinion had been widely discussed and acknowledged by thinkers since the sixteenth century. Shakespeare described opinion as the 'mistress of success', Pascal represented it as the 'queen of the world', and Bentham would later associate it with an imaginary tribunal that would hold Government to account. Early attempts to interpret the workings of the newly emerging modern society often

---

[88] Wolin (2004) p. 270.   [89] Wolin (2004) p. 314.
[90] See Gunn (1995).   [91] Wolin (2004) p. 308.

referred to the significance of opinion in influencing behaviour. John Locke's *Essays Concerning Human Understanding* drew attention to the 'law of fashion' and the 'law of opinion or reputation', with its power to gain conformity, and argued that 'no Man' who 'offends against' opinion, '[e]scapes the Punishment and Censure' of the 'company he keeps'.[92] Locke conceptualised the role of opinion as a form of social pressure and introduced the 'liberal's note of suspicion of the attitudes of the mass', seeking to uphold the rights of the individual 'above the claim of collective will'.[93] Locke's association of opinion with the constitution of a powerful force of social pressure would be elaborated by eighteenth-century liberal thinkers and developed further by social commentators in the nineteenth century.

Locke's law of 'opinion and reputation' posits opinion as potent form of social pressure that dominates the behaviour of the individual. Unlike the power of legal domination, the law of opinion was depicted as possessing a powerful moral immediacy on individual behaviour. Koselleck wrote that, 'It exists and works by praise and blame alone, but in fact, in the results it achieves, it is much more effective' than formal laws.[94] Hume's analysis of opinion elaborated the psychology of social pressure, which he took to be based on 'the human urge to be respected'.[95] In line with the prevailing consensus, Hume regarded opinion – by which he meant belief – to be the foundation of government. Implicit in this interpretation of the power of belief was the notion that opinion had become the most significant source of authority. In *Essays Moral, Political and Literary*, Hume wrote:

Nothing appears more surprising to those who consider human affairs with a philosophical eye than the easiness with which the *many* are governed by the *few*; and the implicit submission with which men resign their own sentiments as passions to those of their rulers. When we inquire by what means this wonder is effected, we shall find that . . . the governors have nothing to support them but opinion. It is, therefore, on opinion only that the government is founded; and this maxim extends to the most despotic and most military governments as well as to the most free and popular.[96]

Adam Smith, too, believed that it was the opinion of society that shaped individual conscience and behaviour, and that this was a force which no government could ignore. As we shall see, the discussion on how to engage with public opinion would become the dominant underlying theme of nineteenth- and twentieth-century debates on the subject of authority.

[92] Locke (2008) p. 224.   [93] Minar (1960) p. 35.   [94] Koselleck (1988) p. 59.
[95] See discussion in Noelle-Neumann (1979) p. 146.   [96] Hume (1963) p. 29.

The tendency towards the depoliticisation of power and the socialisation of authority should not be interpreted as simply a response to the inability of political philosophy to deal with the problematic. The rise of capitalism created a demand for the restraint of political intervention in economic and social life. At the same time, the growth of civil society and public life meant that a new force, that of social opinion had to be taken into account. One way of dealing with this situation was to demonstrate that government was looking after the security and well being of its citizens. However, utilitarian-minded thinkers did not believe that the support of social opinion for order could be gained on its own accord. They recognised that social opinion could play an important role in gaining the conformity of the public, but felt that something else had to done. As Wolin observes, 'social norms' were 'not only to be accepted but exploited and manipulated'.[97]

---

[97] Wolin (2004) p. 309.

10   The limits of the authority of the rational

From the moment of its 'discovery', public opinion was portrayed as an all-powerful force that no ruler could ignore. In France, discussions surrounding the fate of the Old Regime adopted a tone of reverence towards public opinion; the lawyer and minister Chretien-Guillaume Malesherbes (1721–1799), in his maiden speech to the Académie Française in 1755, expressed the widely held sentiment that a 'tribunal has arisen independent of powers and that all powers respect, that appreciates all talents, that pronounces on all people of merit'.[1] This view that public opinion was the highest court in the life of the nation communicated the idea that henceforth only those who could represent or give voice to this new force could claim to possess real authority. Strictly speaking, the eighteenth-century idea that 'opinion rules' should be understood as the recognition of an important development, in which the validation of opinion becomes increasingly essential to the capacity to govern.

At first sight it is difficult to understand why public opinion was assigned such power by political thinkers. To be sure this era saw the expansion of the educated and professional classes, particularly in Western Europe, and the growth of printing and the press created a public that could develop its beliefs and ideas through accessing alternative sources of knowledge and information. However, despite its influence on intellectual and cultural life, public opinion was as much a construction of claim-makers as feature of material reality. The precondition for delineating opinion as an independent source of authority was the autonomisation of ideas and beliefs from established traditional sources. Belief could no longer be monopolised in circumstances where the contestation of knowledge had become the norm; and since opinion could not be taken for granted it had to be discovered, voiced and represented.

Competing claims to speak on behalf of or to represent public opinion played an important role in the social construction of this power. In his study of the discovery of public opinion in pre-revolutionary France,

[1] Ozouf (1988) p. 9.

Baker remarks that 'suddenly it designated a new source of authority, the supreme tribunal to which the absolute monarchy, no less than its critics, was compelled to appeal'.[2] He contends that competing claims for authority were mediated through a political struggle to define who constituted the public and what defined its role and character. Noting that 'sociologically, the nature of this entity remained ill defined', Baker suggests that 'one can understand the conflicts of the Pre-Revolution as a series of struggles to fix the sociological referent of the concept in favour of one or another competing groups.'[3] Through the struggles to gain political hegemony, 'the notion of the "public" came to function as the foundation of a new system of authority, the abstract source of legitimacy in a transformed political culture'.[4]

Assessments of the role of public opinion were influenced by whether it was seen, on balance, as a constructive or as a destructive force. Such observations were based on perceptions of the moral and intellectual competence of the people. Most eighteenth-century philosophers were ambivalent at the very least about the power of the force of opinion, and some were openly fearful. Rousseau represented opinion as a corrupting influence from which children had to be protected.[5] Like many of his contemporaries, he was preoccupied with how to influence and guide opinion in a constructive direction, and this led to his call for strong press censorship. According to one of his most influential interpreters, Hume believed that the 'formation of sound political opinion is the most basic political activity', and his writings were devoted to understanding and managing it.[6] In line with the dominant mood of European political thought, Hume's disposition towards the power of opinion became increasingly defensive and weary, as indicated by his anxieties about the influence of the press. Initially Hume adopted a pragmatic approach towards press freedom. Although he had little sympathy for the 'people', he believed that the authority of their rational intellectual superiors could exercise influence over the direction of their thinking:

A man reads a book or pamphlet alone and coolly. There is none present from whom he can catch passion by contagion . . . The liberty of the press, therefore, however abused, can scarce ever excite popular tumults . . . the *people* are no such dangerous monster as they have been represented, and in every respect better to guide them, like rational creatures, than to lead or drive them like brute beasts.[7]

When Hume published his essay 'Of the Liberty of the Press' in 1741, he maintained the hope that it could act as a welcome counter-balance to the

---

[2] Baker (1994) p. 168.   [3] Baker (1994) p. 186.   [4] Baker (1994) p. 186.
[5] Shklar (2001) p. 160.   [6] Haakonssen (1994) p. xxvii.
[7] Cited in Porter (2000) p. 192.

arbitrary power of the monarch, and he defended the press as central to the maintenance of civil liberty. However, disturbances in England during the 1760s and 1770s, in particular the Wilkes riots, undermined Hume's confidence in an institution that he previously regarded as central to a 'free and independent government'. So when this essay was republished in 1770, Hume replaced the positive assessment of the liberty of the press in his original concluding paragraphs and added a final sentence that decried it as 'one of the evils' that the nation had to live with.[8] His radical change of attitude towards the press was motivated by the presentiment that public opinion was likely to be led astray by dangerous demagogues.

As noted earlier, liberal thinkers looked to the law both to limit arbitrary rule and to protect individual freedom. But in face of an unpredictable and volatile public opinion, was the institution of the law sufficient to uphold the authority of the sovereign? Foucault contends that the theorists of sovereignty sought to demonstrate 'how power can be constituted, not exactly in accordance with the law, but in accordance with a certain basic legitimacy that is more basic than any law and that allows laws to function as such'.[9] Arendt echoes the point when she writes that for the thinkers associated with the American and French Revolutions, the need for a 'higher law' or an 'absolute' as the source of authority became a key issue.[10] Rousseau argued that the law was 'psychologically ineffective' for guiding people in the desired direction, believing that the law could only touch external behaviour, whereas public opinion and custom could influence the internal life of individuals.[11]

As discussed in the previous chapter, ambivalence regarding the capacity of the law to legitimate political rule and motivate behaviour was clearly communicated through Adam Smith's writing. Smith believed that the rule of law was essential for the protection of individual freedom, but that social consensus and order required other forms of cultural support.[12] What Weber was to characterise as rational-legal legitimation appeared far too precarious to Adam Smith. Thus Smith assigned a crucial role to religion in the maintenance of social order, writing that religion 'even in its rudest form, gave a sanction to the rules of morality'.[13] He asserted that 'habitual reverence' for moral customs and duties was essential for the maintenance of social order, and claimed that through religion, public opinion internalised a reverence for order which in turn

[8] Haakonssen (1994) p. 5.   [9] Foucault (2004) p. 44.
[10] See Arendt (2006) pp. 174–6.   [11] Shklar (2001) pp. 160–80.
[12] See Kersting (2006) p. 1061.
[13] See Smith (2010), Chapter 8, 'The Relation of Religion to Morality'.

naturalised the act of obedience and adherence to norms. Smith wrote that,

when the general rules which determine the merit and demerit of actions, come thus to be regarded as the laws of an All-Powerful Being, who watches over our conduct, and who, in a life to come, will reward the observance, and punish the breach of them; they necessarily acquire a new sacredness from this consideration.

In this way the deification of the law renders it persuasive to the individual.

The project of moralising the law was pursued relatively effectively in eighteenth-century Britain. As the sociologist John O'Neill explains:

Although the law was used to enact severe and terrible punishments for crimes against rural and urban property, it nevertheless seems to have been employed also to teach lessons of mercy and a universal sense of order. In other words, the bourgeois state tempered the force of law with the ideology of respect for the Law.[14]

Religious belief played an important role in providing the law with moral force. 'It is in this manner that religion enforces the natural sense of duty: and hence it is, that mankind are generally disposed to place great confidence in the probity of those who seem deeply impressed with religious sentiments', argued Smith.[15] Despite the belief that order was the outcome of the spontaneous forces of nature, Smith took it for granted that society still needed religion to remind individuals of their 'obligations of morality', pointing out that the 'world' placed a 'double confidence in the rectitude of the religious, man's behaviour'.[16]

In the decades following the Revolution, when French liberals became extremely wary of the power of public opinion, they looked wistfully to the capacity of religion and tradition to influence public behaviour in the past. Leading French political commentator Benjamin Constant (1767–1830) warned that many supporters of revolution 'failed to appreciate the potential dangers of popular opinion and to consider sufficiently the constraints of historical traditions'.[17] Constant sought to remedy this by attempting to construct a tradition based on 'best ideals of the

---

[14] O'Neill (1986) p. 52.
[15] See 'Of the influence and authority of the General Rules of Morality, and that they are justly regarded as the laws of the Deity' in *Theory of Moral Sentiment*, www.marxists. org/reference/archive/smith-adam/works/moral/part03/part3c.htm (accessed 30 April, 2013).
[16] See www.marxists.org/reference/archive/smith-adam/works/moral/part03/part3c.htm (accessed 30 April 2013).
[17] Vincent (2000) p. 623.

Revolution, that is popular sovereignty and civil liberty'.[18] He was an
enthusiastic modernist who looked to commerce and trade to assist the
progressive development of humanity. However, following Adam Smith,
Constant argued that 'commerce alone was not a sufficient guarantee of
the existence of liberty and that liberty itself was grounded on and was
sustained by religious sentiment'.[19]

Reliance on the rule of law was perceived as a problem when the lower
classes could not be relied on to adhere to the prevailing arrangements.
Political thinkers tended to look upon the uneducated lower orders as
steeped in the old irrational ways of the past; thus many adherents of the
Enlightenment, who personally regarded religion as an outdated prejudice, nevertheless prescribed it as essential for containing the unpredictable behaviour of the people. For example, as Laski writes, Voltaire
'hates religious fanaticism; but he is certain that religion is necessary for
the people if the rich are not to be murdered in their beds'; and 'the God
of Voltaire is a social necessity for the maintenance of order; without him
there would be no restraint upon the behaviour of men'.[20]

The Age of Reason was selective in the way it applied its principles.
Even in the midst of revolting against the traditions of the past, it lacked
confidence in the capacity of the authority of rationality and its institutional expressions to maintain order and stability. In the end, even some
of the most radical leaders of the French Revolution concluded that a
religion was necessary to secure the loyalty of the masses, and opted to
invent a new religion. On 7 May 1794, the Convention declared that 'the
French people recognizes the Supreme Being and the immortality of the
soul' and called for the 'Worship of the Supreme Being'. The President
of the Convention, Maximilien de Robespierre, believed that his newly
invented religion would provide a focus of unity to the citizens of France
'whatever private religious views they might entertain'.[21] Robespierre
regarded reason as far too fragile an instrument to inspire ordinary citizens, and warned that 'human authority can always be attacked by human
pride'. Therefore, the limitation of human reasoning required that it be
'supplemented by the religious sense by which the soul is impressed with
the idea of a sanction given to moral principles by a power superior to
man'.[22]

Despite the intensely polarised political climate of the late eighteenth
century, supporters and opponents of the French revolution agreed on
the point that some kind of religion was required to guide public conduct. Conservative opponents of the Revolution shared this instrumental

[18] Vincent (2000) p. 625.   [19] Jennings (2009) p. 72.
[20] Laski (1936) pp. 213–14.   [21] Palmer (1969) p. 127.   [22] Palmer (1969) p. 128.

approach with their radical foes. Palmer observes that for Joseph de Maistre and Edmund Burke, 'the importance of religion lay in the inculcation of moral principles, that is, in a doctrine of attitudes and duties towards one's fellow man, and one's own place in society', and concludes that this 'clash was less between religion and irreligion than between the cults, respectively, of an idealized aristocratic and idealized democratic world'.[23]

According to one important study, a small minority of Enlightenment thinkers attempted to rely entirely on the authority of reason but the 'moderate mainstream' opted for combining reason with 'faith and tradition'.[24] Even Baron d'Holbach, whose *System of Nature* (1773) gained him a reputation for atheism and was denounced by Voltaire as too extreme, believed that a system of morality was needed to serve as an alternative to the Christian religion that he had so forcefully challenged. Holbach shared his fellow intellectuals' scepticism of the reliability of public opinion. His text *Social System* (1773) insisted that only men of property could be relied upon to serve as the representatives of the people: order relied on men who were 'bound to the state by their possessions and interested to conserve them as much as to maintain liberty'. His anxiety regarding the role of opinion was founded on the belief that a significant section of society – those without property – lacked the moral and intellectual characteristics necessary for enlightened behaviour. But he set great store by the capacity of education to enlighten a significant section of society and, in line with prevailing intellectual consensus, assigned this task to the reforming sovereign ruler.[25]

In the decades following the Revolution, French liberals became extremely fearful of the power of public opinion and decried the loss of the capacity of religion and tradition to influence public behaviour. The question of who could tame public opinion would continue to dominate political debate in the century to follow.

The great legislator

Eighteenth-century political thinking on opinion frequently remarked on its capacity to compel and even coerce. This power seemed to possess its own inner dynamic and resistance to political or moral influence by those who governed society. Public opinion was at once perceived as the source of authority and as its antithesis. Its independent and non-institutionalised quality highlighted the relative decline of previous forms of tradition and authority. When Hobbes raised concerns about

[23] Palmer (1969) p. 128.   [24] Israel (2006) p. 11.   [25] See Sabine (1961) pp. 569–70.

the necessity for the sovereign ruler to subordinate conflicting opinions to a moral consensus, he knew that this was a challenge that had yet to be tackled. The question was, how?

Retrospectively, Foucault wrote how the emerging logic of the modern state 'must act on the consciousness of people' to 'create belief in their own legitimacy', reasoning that 'this work of public opinion will be one of the aspects of the politics of truth in *raison d'Etat*'.[26] One of the most consistent arguments for promoting utilitarianism to gain public support for government was provided by Claude Adrien Helvetius (1715–1771) in his development of a programme for a reforming legislator, who was assigned the role of utilising 'the mechanism of human motives to bring private happiness and public welfare into the most complete accord'.[27] Helvetius, like many contemporary liberals and utilitarians, came to the conclusion that one of the ways that authority of reason could be recast in a form that harnessed the feelings and imagination of the public was through communicating it through the person of a Legislator or a Leader.

A variety of philosophers, commentators and political economists assigned the Legislator or the Lawgiver the role of enlightening and educating the public. Enlightenment required the application of the wise leadership of the Legislator to this task, since the public could not be expected to develop its capacity to reason on its own. The French scholar Louis de Jaucourt (1704–1779) insisted that an enlightened monarch would ensure that government was carried out in 'rational conformity to the law'.[28] From this perspective even enlightened despots, who were 'systematically trained and actively rationalizing – rulers' had a decisive role to perform.[29]

The role that Helvetius assigned to the legislator was the relatively modest one of protecting the 'natural operation of economic laws' from interference.[30] Other political thinkers were less convinced that order could enforced through the operation of natural law, and were prepared to allocate the legislator a far more ambitious role. At this time, the liberal predilection for the impersonal force of the market and the law co-existed with the opposite tendency to reintroduce personalised authority through the wise legislator. Indeed it was the very recognition of the limited capacity of impersonal rules to motivate obedience that disposed so many key Enlightenment figures to look to the influence of personal authority for guiding society.

The authorisation of the legislator was also encouraged by the importance that eighteenth-century intellectuals attached to science and

[26] Foucault (2007) p. 275.   [27] Sabine (1961) p. 564.   [28] See Krieger (1977) p. 86.
[29] Krieger (1977) p. 55.   [30] Sabine (1961) p. 564.

knowledge as the basis of an enlightened government's actions. Adam Smith regarded political economy as not simply a subject to be confined to the university lecture hall but as a 'branch of the science of a statesman or legislator'.[31] Smith, too, looked to a legislator to endow the institutions of the state with moral authority.[32] In anticipation of Weber's distinction between the unprincipled demagogue and the leader with a vocation, Smith contrasted the politician to the legislator. In *Wealth of Nations* published in 1776, he distinguished between a politician and legislator by depicting the latter as 'governed by general principles which are always the same' as opposed to 'that insidious and crafty insidious animal' who is guided by 'momentary fluctuations of affairs' and constantly swayed by pressure.[33] Adopting what would in subsequent centuries be described as a technocratic approach to governance, Smith offered a 'strategy of persuasion' for 'bringing science to bear on the conduct of legislators'. Smith's technocratic inclinations were tempered by his suspicion of what he called the 'man of system' – a leader whose ideological commitments to a system leads to the loss of political realities.[34]

Smith's version of the modern legislator was a moderate and pragmatic leader, who had to avoid the temptation of using force and violence to achieve his objective. He had both to accommodate to the prevailing state of opinion and also to educate it. Smith's legislator was a 'man whose public spirit is prompted altogether by humanity and benevolence';[35] he was an educator who would 'do his best to accommodate public arrangements to the confirmed habits and prejudices of the people'. Smith's ideal of a sober and pragmatic legislator was the Athenian law-giver Solon: when the legislator 'can't establish the right' he 'won't be too proud to ameliorate the wrong', and like Solon, 'when he can't establish the best system of laws he will try to establish the best that the people can bear'.[36]

Although Smith's legislator is characteristically pragmatic and realistic, he is also a powerful leader whose 'finest hour' comes at times of 'crisis and threatening anarchy', in which circumstances 'he may assume the greatest and noblest of all characters, that of the reformer and legislator of a great state'.[37] Smith's legislator was influenced by the principles of natural justice and exercised authority through the rule of law. 'By grounding the science of the legislator in the universal norms of justice, Smith intended to provide a mechanism capable of elevating statesmanship above the politics of interest characteristic of his insidious and crafty

---

[31] Winch (1983) p. 501.   [32] See Kersting (2006) p. 1061.
[33] Cited in Winch (1983) p. 502.   [34] Winch (1983) pp. 503–4.
[35] Smith (2010) p. 124.   [36] Smith (2010) p. 124.   [37] Smith (2010) p. 123.

"politician"', states Hanley.[38] The humility and pragmatism of Smith's legislator is not quite the charismatic leader of Weber, but both play the role of the great leader demanded by the imperative of personalising authority.

Smith's investment of hope in the leadership of the reforming legislator was rooted in the conviction that the enlightenment of the public relied on the guidance of the already enlightened, and he was assigned a comparatively modest and restrained role. A far more powerful and ambitious version was offered by Rousseau, whose legislator is at once the initiator and founder of a new society, the Mortal God of Hobbes, and the charismatic leader that would be invoked by Weber in the aftermath of World War I. This legislator is described by Rousseau as the figure that undertakes an 'enterprise too difficult for human powers',[39] and his authority is clearly constituted through a supra-human source. His is an 'authority that is no authority' and has as its task the transformation of the people. He seeks to 'annihilate the prejudices that Smith is concerned to respect'.[40] His project of freeing people from the prejudicial influences of society requires that individuals assign their right to liberty to a single authority, which he calls the General Will. But the idea of the general will is so mysterious and spiritual that, as Krieger observes, it is 'embodied in no earthly institution'.[41]

Rousseau's lack of clarity about the institutionalisation of personalised authority stands in contrast with his confidence about why personalised authority was necessary. Since Rousseau concluded that effective authority needed to penetrate people's internal life, the inspiration and leadership of the Great Legislator was called upon to create the moral climate conducive to the acceptance of the law.[42] Rousseau believed that through his charisma and personality, the Great Legislator could educate opinion to accept the law as their own.[43] His charismatic leader possesses a religious appeal: he 'must have recourse to another order of authority, which can win over without violence and persuade without convincing'.[44] In an allusion to Moses, Rousseau indicates that 'he sees religion as the major tool of the legislator's persuasion'.[45] Legislators need to 'attribute their own wisdom to the Gods' and can only do so if they already possess the special quality of leadership. In this way the Legislator's words acquire a prophetic quality and his words are rendered sacred:

---

[38] Hanley (2008) p. 221.
[39] See *Social Contract* Book 2, Chapter 7, 'The Legislator' in www.classicreader.com/book/615/18/ (accessed 30 April, 2013).
[40] Hanley (2008) p. 221.   [41] Krieger (1977) p. 263.   [42] Shklar (2001) pp. 160–80.
[43] Shklar (2001) p. 181.   [44] Rousseau (1968) pp. 87–8.   [45] Kelly (1987) p. 324.

'The lawgiver's great soul is the true miracle which must vindicate his mission'.[46]

Rousseau's characterisation of effective authority as one that needed to 'persuade without convincing' demonstrates its reliance on quasi-religious resources. It also confirms his scepticism towards the power of reason and his lack confidence in the capacity of rational calculation to gain consent.[47] Although he claimed that in principle, the people ought to be the 'authors' of the law to which they were subject, Rousseau did not think that they had the 'foresight' necessary for this task, asking: 'How can a blind multitude, which often does not know what it wants, because it seldom knows what is good for it, undertake by itself an enterprise as vast and difficult as a system of legislation?'[48]

Rousseau could not disregard the growing consensus that there was 'something inherently improper about compelling a person to do anything against his will'.[49] Yet despite his acknowledgement of the 'natural freedom' of all, he believed that the 'blind multitude' required the authoritative intervention of the Great Legislator to direct it towards freedom. Thus Rousseau's thinking combines a rejection of traditional authority, particularly that of the parent, with an embrace of the moral authority of the Great Legislator. What was remarkable about Rousseau was that he proposed a radically individualistic critique of forms of authority that curbed the free and spontaneous activities of the individual while upholding a coercive moral authority that 'radiates from great men'.[50] His very denial of the 'existence of authority apart from the individual over whom it was exercised' co-existed with his demand that 'all members of a community had to obey the General Will'.[51]

Rousseau's legislator is portrayed as a charismatic figure whose source of power and authority is his personality. 'It is the force of a magnetic personality alone that forces a character on a disoriented multitude', observes Shklar.[52] This allows the Great Legislator to perform 'a task which is beyond human powers', which is to give expression to the General Will.[53] During the course of the French Revolution, Robespierre's search for transcendent source of authority led him to develop the idea of an 'Immortal Legislator', a divine leader who could lend authority to the new regime.[54]

The historical tendency to look for salvation in the 'extraordinary figure, the philosophical king, who would break through the dilemma to

[46] Rousseau (1968) p. 87.   [47] Kelly (1987) p. 324.   [48] Rousseau (1968) p. 85.
[49] Lewis (1974) p. 354.   [50] Shklar (2001) p. 155.   [51] See Palmer (1969) p. 122.
[52] Shklar (2001) p. 183.   [53] Rousseau (1968) p. 86.
[54] See the discussion in Arendt (2006) pp. 176–84.

improve men by his example and life by his power' is evident as far back as the antiquities. One of the recurring themes in historical sociology of authority is that at times of crisis there is perceptible tendency to look to a great legislator to restore and maintain order. The investment of so much hope in the Great Legislator in the eighteenth century indicates that the support that impersonal and rational institutions enjoyed was inconsistent, and qualified by the presentiment that they lacked the capacity to maintain order. This represented an implicit acknowledgement that authority could only be effectively communicated through a personal form.

Authority itself becomes a subject of investigation

Eighteenth-century contributions to the science of the legislator can be interpreted as attempts to constitute a viable and authoritative system of political rule. Unlike the 'Mirror For Princes' textbooks of the Middle Ages and the Renaissance, which advised and instructed kings and princes on how to conduct their affairs and how to behave, the literature on the science of legislation was concerned with broader issue of how to give meaning to authority. Its new focus of concern was how to manage public opinion. This required an understanding of the phenomenon and a realistic strategy for dealing with it. Despite his idealisation of the Great Legislator, Rousseau understood that even this omnipotent figure had to act in a manner that did not offend and alienate the sensibilities of his subjects. Although often described as a utopian and idealist, he adopted a self-consciously pragmatic, even instrumental stance towards law-making:

Just as an architect who puts up a large building first surveys and tests the ground to see if he can bear the weight, so the wise law giver begins not by laying down laws good in themselves, but by finding out whether the people for whom the laws are intended is able to support them.[55]

Rousseau's ideal of what people need was tempered by his belief about what was possible. His point of departure was the prevailing consciousness of the people, and he believed that the law gains its authority through its relation with public opinion; thus, clarity about the behaviour of the people, their beliefs and attitudes, became an essential component of his thought. Rousseau's exploration of the workings of authority is sociologically directed, in that society, and its stage of maturity and development, is seen to determine the work of the Legislator. This

[55] Rousseau (1968) p. 88.

represents both an opportunity for and an obstacle to the enlightened legislator:

Nations, like men, are teachable only in their youth; with age they become incorrigible. Once customs are established and prejudices rooted, reform is a dangerous and fruitless enterprise: a people cannot bear to see its evils touched, even if only to be eradicated; it is like a stupid, pusillanimous invalid who trembles at the sight of the physician.[56]

At times Rousseau retains a belief that the legislator can play the role of liberating the people to realise their own freedom. But more frequently, his implicit concern with the problem of order leads him in a more authoritarian direction. In circumstances when society faces disturbances and the 'state falls apart', Rousseau recommends that 'what is needed is a master, not a liberator'; and he criticised Peter the Great for trying to civilise the Russian people when 'he ought rather to have drilled them'.[57] It is not always clear whether Rousseau assumes that the problem lies with the customs and institutions of society, or with the people that have internalised prevailing values. He appears to argue that the people need to be saved from the destructive influence of social customs, and this requires that they be immunised from the influence of public opinion. That is the main reason why he is hostile to the authority of the father and the mother, for 'parents are the agents who transmit false traditions and habits from one generation to the next'.[58] The powerful and wholly evil influence of society can only be countered by an extraordinary power: in effect, as Shklar states, the 'Great legislator is a god'.[59]

Rousseau's sociological account of the problem of order assumed that the active intercession of the law-giver was indispensable for the realisation of social conformity. Other, less radical minds tended to present conformism as a natural imperative that was the outcome of spontaneous influences such as self-interest or custom. Hume was no less concerned with gaining social conformity than Rousseau but he drew the opposite conclusion, arguing that enlightened self-interest provided an effective foundation for co-operation and for gaining obedience to authority.[60]

Despite his modernising leanings, Hume relied on the force of tradition and custom to motivate obedience to order. Thus he argued that the '*Long Possession* of power is the strongest and most common source of authority', which 'was dramatically demonstrated in Britain by the continuing influence of the Stuarts long after they had exhausted most other

---

[56] Rousseau (1968) p. 89.   [57] Rousseau (1968) pp. 89–90.
[58] Shklar (2001) p. 170.   [59] Shklar (2001) p. 179.   [60] See Kersting (2006) p. 1061.

sources of authority, including that of present possession'.[61] For Hume, continuity with the past served as a guarantor of order: 'time and custom give authority to all forms of government, and all successions of princes; and that power, which at first was founded only on injustice and violence, becomes in time legal and obligatory'.[62] In his theory, the claim that tradition legitimates authority is combined with the more liberal contention that self-interest disposes individuals to support and maintain order. Smith, like Hume, offered a synthesis of a utilitarian account of self interest with a naturalistic interpretation of the disposition to obey authority. For Millar, the force of habit was 'the great controller and governor of our actions'.[63] One important theme that emerged from the tentative sociological accounts of these Scots was, as noted previously, the spontaneous tendency towards order.

Despite some important differences in emphasis, the conservative reaction to the upheavals of the eighteenth century shared many of the assumptions of liberal thinkers. They sought to represent order as a natural state of being, representing obedience to authority as the natural deference of the inferior to the superior. Krieger writes that that this conservative attitude 'stressed the voluntary and even spontaneous commitment of subordinates to their authorities, and contrasted it to the potential reality of a democratic dictatorship which made the enforcement of equal liberty an aspect of political power'.[64] Sir William Blackstone (1723–1780), the pre-eminent judge and Tory politician, wrote in his famous *Commentaries on the Laws of England* that it was the sense of 'weakness and imperfection that keeps mankind together; that demonstrates the necessity of this union; and that therefore is the solid and natural foundation, as well as the cement, of society'.[65]

The question that was rarely explicitly posed but which preoccupied both liberal and conservative minds was that, if order was the natural or spontaneous outcome of custom and self-interest, how was one to account for the instability that surrounded it? In historical accounts, the impact of the French Revolution on traditional European societies is often presented as the point at which order was conceptualised as something that had to be rescued, restored or affirmed. However, although the Revolution helped concentrate the mind, anxiety about order was evident in the preceding decades. What gave the problem a sense of immediacy was the trend towards the democratisation of public life.

Edmund Burke (1729–1797), whose *Reflections on Revolution in France* constituted what Nisbet has described as 'the very foundation of modern

---

[61] Cited in Haakonssen (1994a) p. 364.   [62] Cited in Haakonssen (1994a) p. 365.
[63] Cited in Berry (1997) p. 107.   [64] Krieger (1968) p. 152.
[65] Cited in Kersting (2006) p. 1058.

philosophical conservatism', was concerned about the threat posed by political change years before the revolution. As far back as 1769, he expressed concern about proposals to enlarge the electorate and feared that if people got the idea that 'our constitution is not so perfect as it ought to be', the authority of Parliament could be undermined.[66] Palmer argues that Burke's opposition to the reform of Parliament was principally 'directed against the democratization of government even by peaceful means'.[67] However it was conceptualised, public opinion represented a challenge to tradition and prevailing forms of authority.

At times, liberal public figures took the view that they could advance their cause if they could speak on behalf of public opinion. Charles James Fox, a leading Whig politician, in 1770 denied the value of consulting people, only to insist in 1783 that 'no ministers who acted independently of public opinion, ought to be employed'. He went on to state that 'public opinion alone' was the basis 'on which an administration should be formed.[68] During the final decades of the Old Regime in France, all sides of the debate appealed to public opinion and claimed to speak for it.[69] But such enthusiastic claims made on behalf of public opinion co-existed with a profound insecurity about the unpredictable trajectory of this force.

Authority's uneasy relation with the people

The Enlightenment, particularly in its French version, provided a powerful cultural affirmation of liberty and the freedom of the individual. In this historical era, the moral, intellectual and religious foundations for authority lost their compelling influence, and in its relationship to freedom, authority was often depicted as the inferior principle. What divided competing philosophies and political factions was the balance of emphasis that they placed on the relative value of these two principles. Liberals tended to represent authority as a necessary political evil which was 'inevitably opposed and normatively inferior to individual freedom', while conservatives 'stressed the voluntary and even spontaneous commitment of subordinates to their authorities' and portrayed unregulated liberty as a recipe for chaos.[70]

Despite profound differences on the relationship between the principles of authority and liberty, it was generally recognised that both had a legitimate role to play. David Hume wrote that,

---

[66] Cited in Palmer (1969) p. 312. See Nisbet (1974) p. 409.
[67] Palmer (1969) p. 316.   [68] Gunn (1983) p. 281.   [69] Baker (1994) p. 172.
[70] Krieger (1968) p. 153.

In all governments, there is a perpetual intestine struggle, open or secret, between AUTHORITY and LIBERTY, and neither of them can ever absolutely prevail in the contest. A great sacrifice of liberty must be made in every government; yet even the authority, which confines liberty, can never, and perhaps ought never, in any constitution, to become quite entire and uncontrolable.[71]

In line with the spirit of the times, Hume stated that 'it must be owned, that liberty is the perfection of civil society'. However, he swiftly added, 'but still authority must be acknowledged essential to its very existence: and in those contests, which so often take place between the one and the other, the latter may, on that account, challenge the preference'.[72]

The very fact that political thinkers wrote about authority as distinct, stand-alone principle indicated that it no longer possessed its previous extraordinary transcendental power. As noted earlier, formal authority was increasingly confined to the political sphere, while the socialisation of authority displaced its moral power and relocated it in society. Increasingly it was the people and public opinion that were charged with the moral power to authorise.

The socialisation of authority helped mediate the tension between its relation to freedom. It allowed critics of political authority to adhere to what were projected as legitimate forms of non-coercive authority – in this way, Locke 'implicitly accepted the temporary intellectual authority of men who show the way to truth through their exemplary use of the "natural faculties" common to all over those who first receive such truths as "imperfect and unsteady notions"'.[73] Through the affirmation of the intellectual and moral qualities of these men, the potential for a new hierarchy was elaborated with a view to acquiring the status of representatives of the opinion of the people.

One of the challenges facing this enlightened elite was how to turn the abstraction of public opinion, which they claimed to represent, into a foundational source of authority. The most adequate form for expressing the general will was the community, and at a certain point in the eighteenth century the authority of the people mutated into that of the nation. This shift was indicated by the fact that in the French Revolution, the citizen emerged as the central category of political discourse. Through the construction of the modern citizen, individuals became detached from one another and re-inscribed as members of a new family. What the revolution aimed to achieve was to fundamentally alter the prevailing relations of authority. As Lucien Jaume argues,

[71] David Hume 'Of the origin of government' in Haakonssen (1994a) p. 22.
[72] David Hume 'Of the origin of government' in Haakonssen (1994a) p. 23.
[73] Krieger (1968) p. 153.

The Revolution sought to fundamentally detach the individual from allegiances to all forms of social grouping and hierarchy in order to place him under the sole authority of the law; for a horizontal membership of traditional communities, the Revolution substituted a vertical allegiance to the law, which as stated in the Declaration of the Rights of Man and of the Citizen, was 'the expression of the general will'.[74]

The form through which the general will came to be expressed was the nation. This principle was enshrined in the Constitution of 1791, which stated that 'sovereignty is one, indivisible, inalienable and imprescriptible' and which 'belongs to the Nation; no one section of the people, no one individual can claim the right to exercise it'.[75]

During the era of the French Revolution, the sovereignty of the people/nation was depicted as the moral opposite of authority based on divine decree or on heredity and tradition. The triumph of the people over the Old Regime and the destruction of the power of the Church and nobility ensured that this new form of sovereignty was backed up by the verdict of history. Article 3 of the 1789 *Declaration of the Rights of Man and of the Citizen* stated that the 'sources of all sovereignty resides essentially in the nation; no body, no individual can exercise authority that does not proceed from it in plain terms'. This invocation of the nation as the source of all sovereign authority was paralleled by an outburst of enthusiasm for human liberty and individual rights. For a brief moment, the American and the French Revolutions, and the growing influence of liberal and humanitarian ideals, helped to strengthen the 'new principle that all sovereign authority emanates from the nation as a whole and that the central government is the only legitimate executor of that authority'.[76]

However, the shift from the traditional order to that of the people raised important questions about how a sovereignty, whose source was the nation or the people, was to be expressed, how authority was to be represented, and by whom. As Cowans observes, in France, 'this problem had its roots in the transition from royal to national (or popular) sovereignty, which involved shifting sovereignty from a human being capable of coherent speech to an abstraction unable to utter complete sentences'.[77] The translation of the abstract category of 'the people' into the homogenous category of 'the citizen' provided only a provisional solution to the quest for the constitution of a popular form of authority. The sociological reality of a heterogeneous public with its conflict of interest meant that, in practice, authority would be exposed to contestation. As Arendt argues, the 'so-called will of a multitude' is 'ever-changing by definition' and a

---

[74] Jaume (2010c) p. 156.   [75] Cited in Jaume (2010c) p. 157.
[76] Bendix (1978) p. 596.   [77] Cowans (2001) p. 186.

'structure built on it as its foundation is built on quicksand'.[78] The question of how public opinion would be voiced, represented and directed was also left unresolved. The recognition that the people were the source of sovereignty did not necessarily mean that this new force could always be called upon to validate it.

Looking back on the post-Reformation era, Hegel's 1830–31 lectures on history opined that 'authority has much greater weight in determining men's opinions than people are inclined to believe'. He observed that 'there are certain fundamental principles which men are in the habit of receiving on the strength of authority'.[79] But what about the future? For Hegel, the question of sustaining the 'strength of authority' led directly to the deification of the state. Lack of faith in the workings of popular sovereignty would lead others to look to a virtuous elite for guidance. In a sense, the problem of authority had mutated into that of order – the challenge was how to manage the people and ensure that the individuals who comprise society identify with their authority.

What is often represented as the intellectual revolution of the Enlightenment also had the profound consequence of radically transforming the authority of knowledge. The ascendancy of the new science did not simply mean the replacement of one form of knowledge with a new one; nor was it simply a shift from religious and secular way of knowing. It also meant a reorientation from the received wisdom of tradition to the constantly re-evaluated and fluid knowledge of empirical science. The new knowledge was communicated through the powerful medium of public opinion. By the end of the eighteenth century, at least from a sociological perspective, public opinion had become the modern successor to traditional belief. By the time Emile Durkheim penned his classic study of the sociology of religion in 1912, his statement that opinion 'is a source of authority, and it might be even asked whether all authority is not the daughter of opinion' was an uncontroversial one.[80]

Alongside opinion, society was conceptualised as central authorising institution. The attribution of authority to public opinion in the eighteenth century was in part fuelled by the aspiration to lend intellectual coherence to a potentially important source of validation. Through its elaboration, public opinion also served to legitimise the status of those individuals who interpreted it, expressed its goals and represented it. At times, public opinion was represented as susceptible to the influence of enlightened individuals and leaders; at others, as an object to be tamed and managed. It was in relation to opinion that the inconsistent and selective sensibility of Enlightenment rationalism is most apparent.

---

[78] Arendt (2006) p. 154.   [79] Hegel (2004) p. 420.   [80] Durkheim (1968) p. 208.

Enlightenment thinkers were far more consistent in applying reason and science against the traditions of the past than in dealing with the problems of their times. As noted earlier, there was little confidence in the capacity of science, reason or the rule of law to motivate the masses, and hope was invested in religion or in the charisma of the Legislator to harness the power of opinion towards constructive ends. The socialisation of authority meant that the moral authority of society was now interpreted as the successor to the spiritual power of the Church. But whereas religion was founded upon a doctrine and embodied a system of norms, society lacked a coherent system of values that could be used to validate the status of the sovereign power.

In the period between the publication of *Leviathan* and the era of the French Revolution, the tension between political authority and freedom hardened, and the two principles began to appear as irresolvable opposites. By the early nineteenth century, the idea that the origin of authority was based on free consent and that freedom was its supposition had given way to the sentiment that these were directly antithetical principles. For the first time, a significant section of society 'rejected the very principle of authority as the dominant value of the human community'.[81]

[81] Krieger (1968) p. 150.

11 Taming public opinion and the quest for authority

The nineteenth century was frequently perceived as an era of transition between the relatively stable world of pre-revolutionary Europe and an uncertain age where the outlines of what authority would look like in the future was difficult to discern. This was a question that preoccupied political commentators and also dominated the agenda of the emerging discipline of sociology.

For public commentators associated with the rising middle class in the nineteenth century, the notion of public opinion was central to a narrative through which both the problem of authority and its potential solutions could be conceptualised. In the aftermath of the upheavals of the previous century, traditional arguments about the sanctity of hierarchy and authority lost much of their capacity to motivate society. In any case, the aspirations of the urban middle classes were inconsistent with a hierarchy based on birth. Many of them sought to consolidate their status through claiming moral and intellectual leadership over public opinion. However, the project of influencing opinion constantly raised questions about its relationship to authority.

At the outset of the nineteenth century, liberal and utilitarian thinkers were reasonably optimistic about their capacity to harness the authority of public opinion to their wider objectives. By the 1850s, optimism gave way to apprehensions about the unpredictable and potentially threatening trajectory of public opinion. Such sentiments were a sublimated expression of elite concerns about the management of the growth of democratic aspirations and the enfranchisement of the majority of citizens. The narrative of public opinion expressed its ambivalence towards democracy through a critique of mass politics.

The era of transition

In a remarkable series of lectures on socialism and the work of the French social theorist Henri Saint Simon, delivered between November 1895 and May 1896, Emile Durkheim characterised his era as one of transition between the loss of the authority of the old and the construction, in the future, of the new. Following Saint-Simon's conceptual distinction between a critical and organic era – the former being one of questioning and destruction, while the latter is characterised by a constructive mood of consensus and obedience – Durkheim held out the hope that it was now possible to 'reorganise society'. Durkheim took the view that this was 'vital', arguing that the 'work of criticism has reached its last stop – everything is destroyed and must be reconstructed'. He chose the word 'reconstruction' so as not to give the impression that the order that prevailed before the French Revolution could be simply restored. Durkheim recognised that in a modern industrial era, 'reconstruction cannot consist of a simple restoration of the ancient edifice' – 'it must be built on new foundations'.[1]

Saint-Simon, who considered himself a survivor of the French Revolution, was 'obsessed with the need to re-establish social order on a new basis'.[2] Unlike conservative politicians and thinkers, Saint Simon believed that it was not possible to restore past forms of authority. He claimed that since the fifteenth century, when the medieval era gave way to early modern society, Europe had faced a crisis of transition, and that the destruction of the old order did not lead to the construction of a new social equilibrium. Durkheim, who regarded Saint-Simon as the founder of positivist philosophy and sociology, shared this interpretation of a crisis of transition. Although more than 70 years had passed between Saint-Simon's diagnosis of a transitional crisis and Durkheim's lecture, the resolution to the question of what would constitute the 'new foundations' for order remained a subject of contestation and debate. Durkheim argued,

What is needed if social order is to reign is that the mass of men be content with their lot. But what is needed for them to be content is not that they have more or less, but that they are convinced they have no right to more. And for this, it is absolutely essential that there be an authority whose superiority they acknowledge and which tells what is right.[3]

For Durkheim, the prerequisite for social order was a 'moral power' whose 'superiority' was recognised. In pre-modern times, religion and royal authority played this role; however, this 'same function could not be exercised today in the same manner or spirit as formerly'.[4]

For Durkheim, the constitution of moral authority represented the fundamental question facing sociology. In *The Elementary Forms of the*

---

[1] Durkheim (2009) p. 135.   [2] Lyon (1961) p. 55.   [3] Durkheim (2009) p. 126.
[4] Durkheim (2009) p. 127.

Religious Life, his classic text published two years before the outbreak of
the First World War, he noted that the 'problem of sociology – if we can
speak of a sociological problem – consists in seeking among the different
forms of external constraint, the different forms of moral authority corresponding to them and in discovering the causes which have determined
these latter'.[5] The sociological problem of reconstituting moral authority required a conversation with history about its working in the past:
'The past not only helps us to pose the problem – it also indicates the
direction in which the solution should be sought'. Asking what, in fact,
were the temporal and spiritual powers that for so long moderated industrial activity, his answer was effectively a restatement of the problem.
Such authority was exercised through the 'moral ascendancy' of what
he termed 'collective forces'. In other words, society itself created the
moral resources necessary to subordinate the behaviour of individuals to
a supreme force: 'society, through the moral regulation it institutes and
applies', plays the 'same role that instinct fills with respect to physical
existence'.[6]

The idea of society directly serving as the foundation for authority
was far too unmediated to be plausible even to its author. In his lectures on Saint-Simon, Durkheim asked the pertinent question of 'where,
today, are the moral forces capable of establishing, making acceptable,
and maintaining the discipline?', before pointing to an institution that 'if
transformed, could suit our present state'. What he had in mind were
professional intermediate organisations and corporations who, through
representing the interest of their members, could also morally regulate
their behaviour.[7] Now and again Durkheim came back to elaborate his
idea of institutionalising moral regulation through developing new occu-
pational corporations.[8] However, what strikes the reader of his account
is the striking contrast between the force of his historical presentation of
the role of the corporation in ancient Rome and Middle Ages Europe,
and its tentative and exhortative argument for its relevance for modern
times.

Saint-Simon and, to a lesser extent, Durkheim, interpreted authority
through the prism of the experience of medieval Europe. Durkheim con-
curred with Marx, who depicted the eleventh century as the high point
of the principle of authority, when 'spiritual and temporal powers were
definitively established; never was the authority of clergy and lords more

[5] Durkheim (1968) p. 208, fn. 4.   [6] Durkheim (2009) p. 127.
[7] Durkheim (2009) pp. 127 and 128.
[8] Most famously in the Introduction to the second edition of his *The Division of Labour in
Society,* Durkheim (1984).

undisputed'.[9] By contrast, the nineteenth century was characterised by a sense of authority lost.

Saint-Simon's ideas and those of his follower, the French positivist Auguste Comte, about social evolution resonated with the intellectual climate of the first half of the century. In 1831, the English philosopher J. S. Mill published a series of articles entitled *The Spirit of the Age*. Mill, who was impressed by the diagnosis of his time as an era of transition, sought to spell out its implications through formulating a rudimentary sociology of authority. In the first half of his article, he explained that,

> the times are pregnant with change; and that the nineteenth century will be known to posterity as the era of one of the greatest revolutions of which history has preserved the remembrance, in the human mind, and in the whole constitution of human society.[10]

In this 'age of transition', mankind has 'outgrown old institutions and old doctrines, and have not yet acquired new ones'. The old maxims, argued Mill, have become irrelevant and people have ceased to defer to their influence, yet,

> Now, it is self-evident that no fixed opinions have yet generally established themselves in the place of those which we have abandoned; that no new doctrines, philosophical or social, as yet command, or appear likely soon to command, an assent at all comparable in unanimity to that which the ancient doctrines could boast of while they continued in vogue.[11]

For Mill, 'this intellectual anarchy' was symptomatic of the disorganisation of its elites: 'divisions among the instructed nullify their authority – and as a result the multitude are without a guide'.[12] Time and again, Mill reiterated his concern about the fragile foundation of intellectual authority.

As Pateman observes, it is likely that these articles on *The Spirit of the Age* represent the first phase of Mill's attempt to elaborate a 'theory of rational authority'.[13] It was his concern with ensuring the 'deference on the part of some persons to the moral and political beliefs of others' that led Mill to search for a way of 'justifying authority in the realm of beliefs'.[14] As the political theorist Richard B. Friedman points out in his excellent essay on this subject, Mill's project of developing such an

---

[9] Durkheim (2009) p. 71.   [10] Mill (1831).   [11] Mill (1831).   [12] Mill (1831).
[13] Pateman (1978) p. 60.   [14] See the discussion in Friedman (1968).

authority represented a 'reaction' against the eighteenth century and the utilitarian philosophy of his father, James Mill, and his mentor, Jeremy Bentham.

According to Friedman, *The Spirit of the Age* contained the first 'public statement of Mill's doctrine of authority'.[15] But a close inspection of these essays indicates that what Mill offers is not so much a doctrine of authority as a lament of its absence. Mill counsels his readers against becoming obsessed with novel forms of authority and, at times, appears to find it difficult to avoid celebrating the authority of the past. He wrote that the 'great authority for political doctrines' in past governments 'was the wisdom of ancestors: their old laws, their old maxims, the opinions of their ancient statesmen', and reminded his sceptical modernist audience that 'this may sound strange to those who have imbibed the silly persuasion, that fickleness and love of innovation are the characteristics of popular government', but that it is a 'matter of authentic history'.

Pointing to the French Revolution as the point at which Europe 'entered into the state of transition', Mill warned about the tendency to 'disregard of the authority of ancestors, which characterise an age of transition'.[16] That Mill, who was no traditionalist, could reflect so wistfully on the authority of the past indicates the seriousness with which he regarded the absence of a recognised form of moral authority. Nine years after writing this article, Mill's essay on Coleridge asserted the necessity for a source of unquestioned authority, arguing that in 'all political societies which have had a durable existence, there has been some fixed point; something which men agreed in holding sacred', but when these 'fundamental principles' are habitually questioned the 'state is virtually in a position of civil war'.[17] He criticised the *philosophes* of the eighteenth century for 'ignoring the conditions necessary for the stability of society', and put forward a plea to reformers 'to be sensitive to whatever values may reside in old institutions and beliefs, and not to destroy everything which is regarded as bad without at the same time being able to replace it with something else'.[18]

---

[15] Friedman (1968) p. 388.

[16] J. S. Mill, 'The Spirit of the Age IV', *Examiner*, 3 April, 1831, pp. 210–11, http://oll. libertyfund.org/title/256/50848 (accessed 30 April, 2013).

[17] Cited in Ten (1969) pp. 58–9. Later this passage was altered to give it a wider more liberal tone but the emphasis was essentially the same as before. This essay can be accessed on http://oll.libertyfund.org/?option=com_staticxt&staticfile=show.php% 3Ftitle=241&chapter=21494&layout=html&Itemid=27 (accessed 30 April, 2013).

[18] Cited in Ten (1969) p. 60.

Although Mill would go on to devise numerous proposals through which a rational form of authority could be institutionalised, he, like Durkheim, found it easier to conceptualise its working in the past than to elaborate an equivalent institution for his time.

The reaction to the legacy of the eighteenth century

The unease with which Durkheim and Mill looked back upon the eighteenth century was widely shared by liberal and conservative thinkers and public figures. Mainstream European and American thought reacted to the dramatic destruction of the old order with dread and turned implacably hostile to the legacy of the French Revolution. Although it was not possible to simply dismiss the intellectual and cultural legacy of the Age of Reason, it became increasingly common to differentiate between the moderate Enlightenment of Locke and the 'pernicious' Enlightenment of the subversive *philosophes*.[19]

In retrospect, the criticism directed at the eighteenth century had the quality of an intense reaction to the immediate past. As we noted in the previous chapter, despite its rationalist and secular anti-authoritarian tendencies, most of the key figures of the Enlightenment were sensitive to the destabilising potential of change. Often radical thinkers proved to be moderate, even conservative, in their political imagination. They were certainly far more hesitant about promoting radical change than their caricatured representation in the nineteenth and twentieth centuries would imply. Their intellectual challenge to the old order did help to foster a climate of radicalism, but the disintegration of the old order was an outcome of important historic changes, of which the revolution of the mind was only one important factor. The French Revolution was the dramatic event through which the consequences of the unravelling of authority imprinted itself on the modern mind, but the event itself was the result of the protracted disintegration of prevailing institutions of authority.

Much of the reaction against the eighteenth century at the beginning of the nineteenth was motivated by the belief that the French Revolution represented a beginning of a process of social disorganisation. This revolution only anticipated the development of mass politics: it began under the leadership of elite opponents of the Old Regime, and gradually created a situation that would lead to the mobilisation of the people or at least the urban masses. In the nineteenth century the urban proletariat would prove to be a far more formidable force, one that regularly called

---

[19] See Israel (2010) especially his 'Conclusion'.

into question the legitimacy of the prevailing political arrangements. This was the case even in relatively stable Britain, where the 'essence of the challenge' posed by the working class 'between 1815 and 1848 lay in their denial of the legitimacy of the social and political order'. In contrast to most plebeian movements that preceded it, this challenge was not simply a response to 'immediate deprivation' but 'rested on solid intellectual foundations', as popular radicalism could draw on the anti-authoritarian principles of the previous century.[20]

That the leaders of radical movements could so readily appropriate this intellectual legacy and recast it in a democratic form represented a threat to the stability of industrialising Europe. As Horkheimer observed, 'the mainstream of bourgeois philosophy down to the beginning of the nineteenth century, despite its internal contradictions, is marked by a recurring rejection of authority-motivated behaviour'.[21] Despite the reaction against the French Revolution, the claims of reason and science continued to exercise a powerful influence over European intellectual life, and the rejection of beliefs that depended on tradition and authority remained part of the self-consciousness of the post-French Revolution and Napoleonic era. Yet the sharp opposition between reason and authority served to remind the governing elites that their power to influence the attitudes and opinions of the public had become problematic, and the attempt to soften this conceptual opposition became a recurring theme.

Alan Kahan's study of nineteenth-century aristocratic liberalism points out that the response of key social theorists such as J. S. Mill, the Swiss-German historian Jacob Burckhardt, and the French political thinker Alexis de Tocqueville to the eighteenth century was 'largely an exercise in historical pathology'.[22] From their vantage point, the radicalism of eighteenth-century intellectual life went too far in its deification of reason and its hostility to the past. According to Burckhardt's verdict, there emerged 'in state, education, a sudden attack against everything inherited from the Middle Ages; hatred for the historical, trust in an ideal of absolute progress'.[23] He believed that hostility towards tradition encouraged an anti-historical orientation that coincided with a naive optimism about human perfectibility and the inevitability of progress.

Mainstream liberal and conservative commentators tended to blame the new ideas that freed public opinion from its subordination to traditional authority for the destructive powers unleashed by the French Revolution and the subsequent disorganisation of society. Critics of public opinion warned about its homogenising influence, and the threat it

---

[20] Tholfsen (1971) p. 58.   [21] Horkheimer (2002) p. 73.   [22] Kahan (2001) p. 15.
[23] Cited in Kahan (2001) p. 19.

represented to minority views. Mill warned that mass opinion had the potential to crush individuality and create the conditions for the flourishing of tyranny and despotism.[24] Burckhardt lamented that 'for a long time I have been aware that the world is pushing forward to the alternative between universal democracy and absolute despotism both without law and right'. He warned that the future would bring governments of 'total domination' and that 'Europe will be the victim of such new tyrants as a consequence of unleashing the masses to compete for key positions of control'.[25] Fear towards the tyranny of the majority was underwritten by the belief that the destructive force of egoistic individualism had been unleashed, and the cultural validation of individual authority was interpreted as a recipe for anarchy and disorder. In his analysis of the response of the founders of sociology to the eighteenth century, Nisbet echoes their views with the observation that 'when men become separated, or feel themselves separated, from traditional institutions, there arises, along with the spectre of the lost individual, the spectre of lost authority'.[26]

By the middle of the nineteenth century, it was increasingly common to attribute social disorganisation to the anarchy created through the process of individuation. When Comte characterised individualism as 'the disease of the Western world', he gave voice to a widespread sentiment.[27] Hostility to individualism was justified on the grounds that its corrosive impact on community and intermediate institutions created a condition of social atomisation. Without the guidance of such institutions, it was believed, individuals became part of an indistinct mass and opinion became homogenised, threatening those with more refined views. It was also suggested that in the absence of any countervailing institutions, the state could acquire despotic powers,[28] and that when mass opinion became public opinion, the tyranny of the majority could also turn into a despotic demon.

As an emerging corpus of knowledge, sociology sought to counter the sentiments promoting social fragmentation. 'Sociology arose in the first instance as a deeply conservative movement,' contends Nisbet.[29] In its origins, sociology represents a reaction to the eighteenth century, and took the form of criticising the loss of authority brought about by the French Revolution and ensuing war. But its criticism was also directed

---

[24] See his discussion on the tyranny of the majority in his essay *On Liberty*.
[25] Burckhardt is cited by Salomon (1940) pp. 425–6.   [26] Nisbet (1979) p. 108.
[27] Comte is cited in Nisbet (1944) p. 320.
[28] These arguments for what would eventually provide the foundation for the theory of mass society are discussed in Kahan (2001) pp. 61–5.
[29] Nisbet (1943b) p. 161.

at the rationalising and secularising trends of modern society and the cultural valuation of the individual and individualism. Often the decline of authority was portrayed as the loosening of the moral restraint on individual behaviour.

Wolin writes that 'preoccupation with social disorganisation persisted because of industrialism, which was quickly recognised to be a revolution, came to play the same disturbing social role that 1789 had for an earlier generation'.[30] Social commentators from the reactionary de Maistre to the republican Durkheim were hostile to the Enlightenment's optimistic representation of humanity. Durkheim was no less critical of human pride and individualism than de Maistre, 'who had inveighed against the eighteenth century for undermining all forms of authority and thereby leaving human passions without control'.[31] Durkheim's important sociological concept of *anomie*, a state of social disintegration, captured the anxious sensibility with which the process of historical transition was viewed. Wolin explains,

In his description of a society ridden by *anomie* Durkheim provided his age with an up-to-date version of the Hobbesian state of nature: it was the same authorityless condition; without effective moral or legal controls; the same riot of egoism.[32]

Although the nineteenth-century reaction against the authority of the individual took many forms, one of its principal targets was the cultural authority enjoyed by individual rationality. This hostility was explicitly expressed by reactionary, conservative and romantic advocates of the restoration of the past. Their rediscovery of custom, tradition and religion, and their sacralisation of nation and community, was directed at demoting the role of the authority of the individual. Such criticisms of individualism were particularly directed at individual subjectivity, and often couched as an attack on the arrogance and ambition of Enlightenment rationality. Anti-Enlightenment thinkers such Burke and de Maistre 'set out to demonstrate the insignificance of men',[33] claiming that as against society, the individual person is nothing. From Burke's perspective, society constitutes a fact of life that has always existed and 'it can neither be created nor refashioned according to the needs of the individual'.[34]

One of the unexpected outcomes of the critique of the eighteenth century's celebration of the status of the individual was the deification of the authority of society. The French restorationist social philosopher, Louis de Bonald (1754–1840), articulated a yearning for the past

---

[30] Wolin (2004) p. 357.   [31] Wolin (2004) p. 357.   [32] Wolin (2004) p. 358.
[33] Sternhell (2010) p. 187.   [34] Sternhell (2010) p. 189.

where medieval traditional and religious values would underwrite an unquestionable supreme authority. He argued that in the final analysis the origin of all authority is God, but in line with the secular sensibilities of the nineteenth century, this supreme power was vested in society itself. He was resolutely hostile to the 'primacy of the individual' and in response advocated the 'doctrine of the absolute primacy of society'.[35]

Bonald's insistence on the primacy of society, though inspired by religious motives, would gradually gain intellectual coherence through the emerging secular discipline of sociology. Many of the early social theorists believed that they were rehabilitating society and community against the 'arrogant' claims of individual egoism. According to one sympathetic account of this process, 'the great achievement of the early sociologists was to rephrase the problem of order in such a way as to bring to the fore not only the ethical importance of the intermediate groups but their theoretical value in the study of man'. In other words, in shifting the focus to family, community and nation, sociology helped to endow the individual with an undistinguished status.[36]

Georg Iggers remarks that the Saint-Simonian movement's 'critique of the "philosophy of the eighteenth-century" . . . rested heavily on the writings of the catholic counter-revolutionary thinkers'. Iggers argues that this theory of society constituted a radical rejection of the revolutionary belief in liberty and equality and its replacement by a cult of authority'.[37] However, the aspiration for the constitution of a 'cult of authority' was easier to envisage in theory than in practice. Hannah Arendt's analysis of the loss of eighteenth-century authority focuses on 'troublesome problem' of the search for absolutes. So for example, Robespierre opposed atheism because he realised that a legislator had to rely on a 'religious sentiment which impresses upon the soul the idea of a sanction given to the moral precepts by a power greater than a man'.[38]

Arendt notes how the Preamble of the American Declaration of Independence contains an appeal to 'nature's God', 'which relates to transcendent source of authority for the laws of the new body politic. In this respect Jefferson's famous words "We hold these truths to be self-evident" clearly gives voice to a truth that is not a product of reasoning. It is beyond debate and discussion. Agreement is with a truth 'that needs no agreement since, because of its self-evidence, it compels without argumentative demonstration of personal persuasion'. Moreover,

---

[35] Koyre and Cohen-Rosenfeld (1946) p. 60.   [36] Nisbet (1943b) p. 160.
[37] Georg Iggers (1958) p. 38.   [38] Robespierre cited in Arendt (2006) p. 184.

by virtue of being self-evident, these truths are pre-rational – they inform reason but are not its product – and since their self-evidence puts them beyond disclosure and argument, they are in a sense no less compelling than 'despotic power' and no less absolute than the revealed truths of religion or the axiomatic verities of mathematics.[39]

Arendt claimed that, while the new American constitution provided a provisional solution to the problem of foundation, there were very few truths left in Europe that were held to be 'self-evident'.

The search for legitimacy

The self-consciousness with which the Saint-Simonian movement attempted to construct a new cult of authority was the outcome of its recognition that society desperately required some form of validation of authority. Saint-Simon, Comte and their disciples often boasted of their scientific, objective and progressive stance towards dealing with the problems of society, yet at the same time they were prepared to harness the power of spiritual and religious forces – some even advocating the establishment of a non-rational Saint-Simonian Church led by a Supreme Father. Despite their embrace of science and reason they believed that authority had to be restored at all cost. That is one reason why they were deeply suspicious of democracy, liberty and equality: 'despite their avowal of human progress, their utopia resembled a New Middle Ages in which faith, social cohesion and hierarchy would be restored'.[40]

The problem of order dominated French political and social life throughout the nineteenth century. Attempts to restore a monarchy and the power of the Roman Catholic Church competed with democratic movements devoted to the establishment of an egalitarian republic. The July days of 1830, the Revolution of 1848, the establishment of the empire under Louis Napoleon in 1852, the Paris Commune of 1871, and numerous attempts at regime change through coups, are reminders of the depth with which the problem of order was experienced in France, and indicate why some of the most strident and eloquent counter-revolutionary and restorationist theories were developed by French thinkers.

The term *legitimacy*, with its connotation of the justifiability of relations of power, entered the modern political vocabulary in response to the French Revolution, which had created a demand for a new way of characterising the validation of authority. It was after the rise and fall of Napoleon and the Bourbon Restoration that royalists in France began to refer to themselves as 'legitimist'. Holmes explains that under the

[39] Arendt (2006) p. 184.   [40] Iggers (1958) p. 183.

Old Regime this concept was unnecessary because 'hereditary succession had been a custom'; however, when it 'ceased to be taken for granted' it became necessary to develop a doctrine of legitimacy.[41] According to Richter, Burke was among the first to 'combine theory of legitimacy with an attack on democracy'.[42] In his case religion, custom, precedent and tradition were mobilised to justify monarchical rule. However, once the power of the monarchy was broken, arguments for the legitimacy of hereditary succession could no longer be convincingly justified. This was not only a problem for traditional monarchy: the wily Austrian diplomat, Prince Metternich, wrote that the 'one thing' that Napoleon 'always regretted extremely was that he could not invoke the principle of legitimacy as the basis of his power'. Metternich continued, 'few men have been so profoundly conscious as he was that authority deprived of this foundation is precarious and fragile, and open to attack'.[43]

In Germany, the search for foundational norms turned towards the nation and the state. Under the influence of Johann Herder and other romantic historians and philosophers, tradition and custom were converted into the intellectual foundation of an anti-rationalist nationalism. The development of the cultural idea of a nation, which defined a people's character and an individual's source of identity, provided an important resource on which authority could draw. Hegel later developed a political version of nationalism, but he was much more concerned to provide authority with a foundation that possessed spiritual and even transcendental qualities. Hegelian philosophy recast the state as the realisation of the development of the 'world spirit' and as the embodiment of the authority of the truth.[44] One legacy of this tradition is that in Germany the issue of authority tended to be interpreted as directly interconnected with the legitimacy of the state.

Even England, which enjoyed far greater stability and prosperity than most European nations, was confronted with the loss of the old order. One study writes of the 'sudden collapse of the English *ancien régime*'.[45] Astute commentators like J. S. Mill and Thomas Carlyle were critical of the 'traditional ruling classes, who 'had either abdicated their power to influence opinion or were stripped of it'.[46] In his 1829 essay *Sign of the Times*, Carlyle portrayed his epoch in the following terms: 'the King has virtually abdicated; the Church is a widow, without jointure; public principle is gone; private honesty is going; society, in short, is fast falling in pieces; and a time of unmixed evil is come on us'.[47]

[41] Holmes (1982) p. 166.   [42] Richter (1982) p. 188.   [43] Holmes (1982) p. 171.
[44] Marcuse (2008) p. 59.   [45] Webb (1992) p. 3.   [46] Webb (1992) p. 11.
[47] This essay is available on www.victorianweb.org/authors/carlyle/signs1.html (accessed 30 April, 2013).

Despite the problems outlined by Carlyle, the rising British middle class felt reasonably confident that it possessed the political and cultural resources to maintain order. Whereas in France the problem of order was bound up with the issue of legitimacy, in England it was focused on the subject of deference. During the second half of the eighteenth century, deference to rank played an important role in the stabilisation of order, as did paternalist ideology. 'Those at the summit of society, exercising their authority within the context of widely recognized paternalist values were able thereby to secure the endorsement of their power and thus the legitimacy of their authority,' contends O'Gorman.[48]

The nineteenth-century Anglo-Irish historian W. E. H. Lecky explained the relationship between the traditional authority of the aristocracy and the deference to it in the following terms:

For the essence of an aristocracy is to transfer the source of honour from the living to the dead, to make the merits of living men depend not so much upon their own character and actions as upon the actions and position of their ancestors; and as a great aristocracy is never insulated, as its ramifications penetrate into many spheres, and its social influence modifies all the relations of society, the minds of men become insensibly habituated to a standard of judgment from which they would otherwise have recoiled.[49]

However, by the early nineteenth century it became increasingly difficult to justify deference on these traditional grounds. With the exception of a relatively small body of reactionaries, British elite opinion recognised that 'natural deference' to authority would have to be replaced by a new form of subordination to the outlook of the superior section of society: that which Bagehot would describe as 'intellectual deference'.[50] For the leading parliamentary reformer and Whig prime minister, The Earl Grey, it was essential to 'gain the affection and confidence of the governed'.[51] But how was deference to be achieved in age where, as Bagehot noted, the electors 'easily found themselves committed to "anti-aristocratic" sentiments' and when 'their collective action may be bitterly hostile to rank'?[52]

Deliberation on the subject of deference in nineteenth-century Britain represents an important point of transition in the way that the validation of authority was tackled. Unlike the alternative projects of inventing or reinventing or restoring new sources of authority, the British political class was drawn towards the project of gaining what would be called ideological hegemony. By the mid-nineteenth century, deference was regarded as the outcome of public interaction, education and debate.

[48] O'Gorman (1984) p. 398.   [49] Cited in Kriegel (1980) p. 269.
[50] Spring (1976) pp. 524–31.   [51] Cited in Kriegel (1980) p. 277.
[52] Cited in Spring (1976) p. 531.

The most interesting response to this challenge was the attempt by liberal and utilitarian thinkers to reconstitute deference on a new rational foundation. In his 1820 essay *Government*, James Mill outlined a theory of political deference that had as its premise the capacity of the new middle class to exercise moral authority over the lower orders, through influencing public opinion in general.[53] Mill wrote:

> The opinions of that class of the people, who are below the middle rank, are formed, and their minds directed by that intelligent and virtuous rank, who come most immediately in contact with them, to whom they fly for advice and assistance in all their numerous difficulties, upon whom they feel an immediate and daily dependence, in health and in sickness, in infancy, and in old age: to whom their children look up as models for their imitation, whose opinion they hear daily repeated, and account it their honour to adopt.[54]

James Mill's optimism about the ascendancy of middle-class hegemony was based on his belief in the superior public virtues of this group. Mill praised this class for giving 'to science, to art and to legislation itself, their most distinguished ornaments, the chief source of all that has exalted and refined human nature', and sought to reassure those who doubted the capacity of middle-class opinion to influence of the behaviour of urban workers and the poor: 'Of the people beneath them, a vast majority would be sure to be guided by their advice and example'.[55]

More than 40 years after James Mill penned his essay *Government*, his son John returned to the question of deference in his treatise *Representative Government* (1861). J. S. Mill believed that the power of persuasion was the most effective way of avoiding instability and conflict, writing that the 'only hope from class legislation in its narrowest, and political ignorance in its most dangerous form would lie in such disposition as the uneducated might have to choose educated representatives and defer to their opinion'.[56] Mill's argument for deference had as its foundation a belief in the authority of the knowledge of the expert. Although he was inclined to be more democratic than most of his liberal contemporaries, he allocated a central role for elected expert representatives in the drafting of legislation,[57] insisting that it was 'so important that the electors should choose as their representatives wiser men than themselves, and should consent to be governed according to that superior wisdom'.[58]

For utilitarian and liberal thinkers, the rationalisation of deference demanded that the opinion of the intellectual and scientific community should be upheld as authoritative by society. One of the earliest attempts to develop a utilitarian theory of authority was provided by the

[53] See Pateman (1978).   [54] Mill (1820) p. 32.   [55] Mill (1820) p. 32.
[56] Mill (1861) p. 383.   [57] Kahan (2001) p. 71.   [58] Mill (1861) p. 378.

legal philosopher John Austin in *The Province of Jurisprudence Determined* (1832). In these lectures, Austin argued that deferring to an opinion whose source is widely accepted by a body of intellectual and scientific knowledge represents the voluntary acceptance of authority. This use of individual reasoning to rely on the superior knowledge of others is, for Austin, an act of voluntary deference. 'For Austin, then, the distinguishing feature of the authority relationships is not compulsion, but the voluntary abdication of one's "private judgement" and the acceptance of someone else's judgement as a reason for believing,' explains Richard Friedman.[59]

Austin thus combined his justification of rational deference with an attack on the practice of blindly deferring to tradition and custom. These old sentiments, which rely 'upon brute custom' and which 'have been taken from preceding generations without examination', are described as the 'productions of childish and imbecile intellect',[60] and contrasted to the reasonable deference of people to the authority of the expert. Austin's argument for voluntary rational deference was also directed against reliance on traditional authority. Through establishing rational authority, Austin hoped that 'the multitude' could be 'freed from the dominion of authority, from the necessity of blindly persisting in hereditary opinions and practices'.[61]

Austin' arguments were elaborated Sir George Cornewall Lewis, whose book, *On the Influence of Authority in Matters of Opinion*, first published in 1849 attempted to reconcile rationality with authority. He sought to accomplish this objective through developing an argument for treating deference as an act of voluntary consent, writing that there are many circumstances where reasoning for oneself is not a more rational course of action than a 'recourse to the authority of others'. Lewis concluded by stating that frequently 'reason does not forbid, but prescribes a reliance on authority.'[62] In other words, the very refusal to defer to the opinion of an expert is as irrational, if not more so, than deference to custom and tradition.

Lewis was aware that rational deference could work only if there was trust and belief in the authority of the different domains of cultural and public life, and that in the modern world deference had to be earned. Whatever deference is 'justly due to the great names and competent judges, they are not to be regarded as infallible – as the oracles of a scientific religion – or as courts of philosophy without appeal', he remarked.[63]

---

[59] Friedman (1968) p. 397.   [60] Austin (1832) pp. 67, 76–7.
[61] Cited in Friedman (1968) p. 397.   [62] Lewis (1974) p. 64.
[63] Lewis (1974) p. 367.

Nevertheless, he believed that if there was one unique source of rational authority it was that of science, and he hoped that the authority enjoyed by science could re-created or developed in other domains of public life, particularly in the sphere of morality:

That there is a strong inclination to the adoption of the opinion of competent judges, when competent judges can be clearly discerned to exist, is plain from the deference which is universally paid to the authority of the great luminaries of physical science. If there was a body of authority upon moral and political subjects, equally fulfilling the conditions which entitle it to public respect; if the choice of the people was not distracted by the wide divergence of opinions upon fundamental questions in this department of knowledge; it may be presumed that they would be equally inclined to place themselves under that guidance.[64]

Despite his relatively optimistic prognosis about the positive influence that can be exercised through rational authority, the author of *Influence of Authority in Matters of Opinion* was sensitive to its limits. A careful reading of this text indicates that the quest to establish a source of moral or religious authority was unlikely to be resolved. 'All Christians, whatever might be their creed, would be glad to find any living persons, or body of persons, whom they could conscientiously recognise as an infallible organ and exponent of religious truth', stated Lewis. However, his review of the history of Christianity convinced him that 'no one church can justly make any claim to authority in matters of religious belief, upon the grounds on which opinion in matters of science acquire authority'.[65] Implicitly, the acceptance of authority in matters of belief was likely to be confined to matters related to science: in religion, the contestation of authority would prevail, as Christians recognised and obeyed 'different' authorities.

Through drawing attention to the divergent patterns of relations of authority in science and religion, Lewis drew attention to a problem that would constitute the main obstacle to the working of rational-legal legitimation – the absence of a normative foundation. It also anticipated one of the central questions raised in Weber's sociology of religion, to do with the way in which the rational pursuit of knowledge, through becoming an end in itself, leads to the disenchantment of religion. In such circumstances, religion not only ceases to play a role in legitimating secular knowledge and power – its values and beliefs lose meaning as it attempts to justify itself on rational grounds. This is particularly the case with Protestantism. As Gane observes, 'Protestantism effectively *devalued* or *disenchanted* itself, for in its attempt to prove its own intrinsic rationality

---

[64] Lewis (1974) p. 400.   [65] Lewis (1974) pp. 64 and 97.

through non-religious means it affirmed the value of science, and with this laid itself open to the charge of irrationalism and to attack from the outside from "rational", secular forms of this-worldly legitimation'.[66]

The attempt to develop a theory of rational deference was in part an attempt to deal with the uncertainties surrounding society's ability to maintain order. In particular the theory sought to reconcile what Lewis called the 'numerical principle' – majority voting and the extension of the franchise – with the ability of a small minority of competent authorities to influence events. Time and again Lewis questioned the value and truth of mass opinion, asserting that a 'majority of voices is no conclusive proof of rectitude'. Moreover, decisions taken by a majority tend to be 'opposed to the principle of judgment, which reason and usage equally prescribe'.[67] Yet gaining the assent of the majority was essential for legitimising the social order.

Lewis regarded the expansion of the franchise as a necessary evil for endowing governing with legitimacy. His view on democracy was influenced by Tocqueville's aristocratic liberal suspicion of the rule of the majority, and he claimed that 'the secret of a free constitution' was the capacity of the 'principle of special fitness' to counteract the influence of the morally inferior 'numerical principal'.[68] From this standpoint, the best way of containing the power of the majority was to subject it to the influence of elite opinion. The recognition of the co-existence of equality of participation with the inequality of knowledge constituted the premise for the 'necessity' for rational deference.[69] J. S. Mill also based his arguments for democratic representative government on the assumption that there was a difference in the knowledge and opinion of the 'few' and those of the many. In his review of Tocqueville's classic, *Democracy in America*, Mill stated that for 'the formation of the best public opinion, there should exist somewhere a great social support for opinions and sentiments different from those of the mass'.[70]

Reconciling the principle of majority rule with deference would constitute one of the central problems of modern liberalism; but it was recognised as a fundamental issue by a variety of political and intellectual currents. Saint-Simon, who constructed an elaborate theory justifying social hierarchy, nevertheless recognised that a bargain had to be struck with the 'claims of equality' because 'no order could be maintained except on a mass basis'.[71] Francois Guizot, a leading conservative-liberal political figure in post-Napoleonic France, upheld the sovereignty of reason and advocated the rationalisation of authority. Like J. S. Mill, he

[66] Gane (2002) p. 21.   [67] Lewis (1974) p. 240.   [68] Lewis (1974) p. 279.
[69] Pateman (1978) p. 93.   [70] Mill (1840) p. 45.   [71] Wolin (2004) p. 338.

sought to legitimate the leadership of the liberal elite on grounds of capacity and fitness to rule; he opposed universal franchise on the grounds that it 'would reward ignorance and prejudice instead of knowledge and reason'.[72] But despite his suspicion of mass politics, Guizot regarded elections as an indispensable institution of authorisation.

Guizot was prepared to make concessions to the numerical principle because he believed that publicity, through the working of a free press and public debate, would help create the conditions for the forging of order and consensus. He wrote in 1818 that 'where publicity is lacking, there might be elections, assemblies and deliberations, but people do not believe them and they are right not to do so'.[73] His recognition of the legitimating power of public opinion echoed the issues raised by liberal and utilitarian thinkers across the Channel. Benjamin Constant adopted a similar pragmatic approach towards public opinion, arguing that no government could ignore public opinion without risking its isolation but that it was a potentially dangerous force that had to be contained. Constant believed that though government required the legitimation of public opinion, it needed to be insulated from its direct pressure.[74]

In theory, the rationalisation of deference offered the possibility of reconciling the principles of democratic franchise with authority. In practice, the cultural and political elites were less than confident about their capacity to maintain order in a non-coercive manner, through exercising authority over the beliefs of the people. The premonition that something more was needed was, to a greater or lesser extent, shared by all sections of the political class. As we shall see in the next chapter, this was an era when virtually every possible source of authority was examined with a view to testing its potential for providing the prevailing order with legitimacy.

An evasive debate on public opinion

The discussion of deference was closely knitted to, and directly parallel with, the shifting conceptualisation of public opinion. The term 'deference' – 'submission to the acknowledged superior claims, skill, judgment, or other qualities of another' – suggests a non-coercive act of obedience to authority,[75] and was frequently coupled with terms such instinct, custom and habit.[76] The phrase 'deference to public opinion' spoke to the

---

[72] Craiutu (2003) p. 270.   [73] Craiutu (2003) p. 275.   [74] Vincent (2000) pp. 623–4.
[75] *OED Second edition*, 1989; online version March 2012. www.oed.com.chain.kent.ac.uk/view/Entry/48816 (accessed 24 May, 2012).
[76] The OED cites Coleride in 1833 remarking on 'that voice of authority to which he would have paid most willing deference'.

ascendancy of a new modern form of authority.[77] This phrase had a variety of connotations. It was frequently used to imply people's willingness to accept the superior wisdom of the elites, presuming the intellectual and moral hegemony of the educated middle class or cultural elite over the wider public. But it was also used to signify the formidable power of public opinion – to the point that everyone, including the educated elite, would have to defer to it. In 1819, a public meeting held in Manchester protesting against the Corn Bill agreed to send a petition denouncing the Government to the King, which pointed out that,

Had Charles the First and James the Second shown a becoming deference for public opinion and a little decent respect for liberties of their subjects – the one would not have lost their head on the scaffold, not the other have been driven from the throne by an insulted and justly enraged people.[78]

The petitioners were clearly not deferential to their social superiors. Their demand that government defer to public opinion expresses a diametrically opposite conception to the traditional usage of the term 'deference'.

When a newspaper reported in January 1806 that Government had demonstrated 'respect for the feelings of their Sovereign and a laudable deference to the public opinion', it implicitly drew attention to a new source of authority.[79] The point was reiterated in 1825 in *The Edinburgh Magazine*, when an essayist wrote that the 'Christian nations have almost all arrived at that point of social elevation in which the government is compelled to pay some deference to public opinion'.[80] Some commentators expressed the hope that public opinion could be regulated and its subversive potential curbed through governments managing their response to it. This was the burden of the argument put forward in the *Blackwood's Edinburgh Magazine*, by a commentator who stated that 'the only free constitution which can exist practically applicable to human wants and properties, is that which is governed in its deliberations and measures by a temperate and regulated deference to public opinion'.[81]

Numerous essays on public opinion failed to clarify its relationship to deference. Sometimes there is distinctly evasive quality about the author's reluctance to elaborate the concept of public opinion. Kahan has remarked that 'aristocratic liberals did not feel any need to define

---

[77] See OED for examples of the usage of the term 'deference to opinion', *OED Second edition*, 1989; online version March 2012. www.oed.com.chain.kent.ac.uk/view/Entry/48816.
[78] 'Manchester Metting' in *Liverpool Mercury*; 29 January, 1819.
[79] 'Weekly Summary', *York Herald*, 18 January, 1806.
[80] *The Edinburgh Magazine and literary miscellany*; April 1825, vol. 93, p. 46.
[81] *Blackwood's Edinburgh Magazine*; January 1824, p. 46.

rigorously what they meant by public opinion'.[82] The vague and diffuse status of public opinion was commented on by contemporary observers: an edition of the London-based literary journal *The Atheneum* in 1828 remarked that 'it is remarkable, that in a country, perhaps the only one in Europe, where the executive and Parliament are bound and controlled by the unseen, irrefragable, though not unfelt, bond of Public Opinion, no efforts have been hitherto made to define the progress of a power to which Kings and Ministers are forced to yield a reluctant obedience'.[83] Arguably, the elites' lack of motivation to dwell on this concept was influenced by an awareness that public opinion was a force that could call into question the legitimacy of their status.

The classical liberal theories of public opinion that emerged during the Enlightenment regarded it as a counterweight to the exercise of absolutist authority. The utilitarian ideal of public opinion and of the free press promoted by James Mill and Jeremy Bentham presumed that it both held authority to account and provided it with legitimacy. Jeremy Bentham 'championed public opinion', conveying a sense of confidence 'that in the long run the truth wins out and the public will make the right choices'.[84] Although in his early writings Bentham regarded public opinion as an instrument of social control, he eventually came to regard it as a 'chief safeguard against misrule and as the characteristic mark of a democratic state'.[85] Conservative attitudes towards public opinion tended to be far more critical about its moral and intellectual status. In 1820, the Conservative statesman Sir Robert Peel dismissed 'that great compound of folly, weakness, prejudice, wrong feeling, right feeling, obstinacy and newspaper paragraphs, which is called public opinion'.[86]

Hegel shared Peel's reservations towards this new force, regarding the insights afforded through public opinion as lacking the objectivity that politics required. He believed that public opinion had to be pragmatically accommodated to provide an outlet for the energies of the public, but that politics had to be 'insulated from its influence',[87] and the institutions of the state organised in a way that prevented 'individuals from having the appearance of a mass or an aggregate and so from acquiring an unorganized opinion and volition and from crystallizing into a powerful bloc in opposition to the organized state'.[88]

[82] Kahan (2001) p. 65.
[83] 'Review of Books, Rise, Progress, and State of Public Opinion' in *The Atheneum*; 21 March 1828, p. 257.
[84] Cutler (1999) p. 339.   [85] See Palmer (1967) pp. 243–5.
[86] Bryce (1895) vol. 2, p. 255.   [87] Minar (1960) p. 41.
[88] From *Philosophy of Right*, Oxford University Press: Oxford, 1949, p. 197.

The first serious study of public opinion published in Britain was relatively optimistic about the ability of the educated middle class to reign in the passions of their less cultured brethren. The 1828 study, by the liberal Conservative politician William MacKinnon, argued that the development of public opinion was paralleled by the rise of the educated middle class, and defined by its outlook:

public opinion may be said to be, that sentiment on any given subject which is entertained by the best informed, most intelligent and most moral persons in the community, which is gradually spread and adopted by nearly all persons of any education or proper feeling in a civilized state.[89]

MacKinnon contrasted a morally authoritative public opinion with what he labelled as 'popular clamour', a force he identified with the passions of the multitude. He explained the distinction between the two forces in the following terms:

Public opinion may be said to be powerful in proportion as its requisites are possessed by the individuals in a community; that is, in proportion as such community is well-informed, possessed of proper religious feeling, facility of communication, &c., . . . popular clamour, on the contrary, is powerful in proportion as the lower class is ignorant and numerous, when compared to the other classes.[90]

While MacKinnon regarded popular clamour as an object of moral contempt and a threat to the stability of governments on the European continent, he felt that in England it was effectively contained by the influence of the middle class.

MacKinnon's interpretation of public opinion as synonymous with the views of the middle class allowed him to depict it as a positive source of legitimacy of government. He went on to claim that a government 'in a country where public opinion is powerful, must be directed by such public opinion, and follow its dictates',[91] and concluded on an optimistic note with the statement that 'that public opinion renders the government liberal, and establishes freedom'.[92] Jeremy Bentham and other utilitarian commentators adopted a similar approach, grounding their support for democratic reform in their belief that the wisdom of the middle class could shape and guide public opinion. As far as they were concerned, 'the public to be trusted was the English middle class, which in England

---

[89] MacKinnon (1971) p. 15. His book, *On the Rise, Progress and Present State of Public Opinion In Great Britain and Other Parts of the World* has as its premise an optimistic presumption of an educated middle class guiding civilisation towards greater and greater progress.
[90] MacKinnon (1971) p. 17.   [91] MacKinnon (1971) p. 25.
[92] MacKinnon (1971) p. 341.

was viewed as the most rational political class that had ever appeared in history'.[93]

Shifting discourse on opinion

As we noted in the previous chapter, in the aftermath of the French Revolution public opinion was widely regarded as the force that any governing elite had to contend with. Napoleon's statement that 'opinion rules everything' was endorsed by statesmen throughout Europe.[94] In 1808 Metternich, Austria's envoy to Napoleonic Paris, wrote to his foreign minister that public opinion was 'the most powerful force' because 'like religion, it penetrates the most hidden recesses where administrative measures have no influence'. Metternich believed that since public opinion influenced people's beliefs and influenced their internal lives, it was itself a new source of authority. 'To despise public opinion is as dangerous as to despise moral principles', he wrote, before pointing out that 'the newspapers are worth to Napoleon an army of three hundred thousand men'.[95] The French diplomat Charles Maurice de Talleyrand reported from the Congress of Vienna in 1815 that whereas 'the secular power could derive support from the authority of religion; it can no longer do this, because religious indifference had penetrated all classes and become universal'. 'The sovereign power', wrote Talleyrand, 'can only rely upon public opinion for support, and to obtain that it must seek to be one with that opinion'.[96]

By the 1830s it is possible detect a shift of emphasis in the discourse on public opinion. Political reforms and technological change increased the cultural and political weight of the public, and the same process – particularly the growth of the media and of the electorate – also enhanced the insecurity of the ruling class. 'More and more, public opinion became the supreme power, strengthened by the general diffusion of knowledge, the growth of the press, and the increasingly public nature of government actions and decision-making process', notes Kahan.[97] It sometimes seemed as if the great power attributed to public opinion was a way of expressing elite insecurities towards a force that it could no longer be certain of managing. The tone of the discussion became increasingly defensive and pessimistic, as numerous commentators recycled the classical pathologies of the multitude – ignorance, susceptible to corruption, envious of other's status and wealth – and coupled public opinion with the peril posed by the tyranny of the majority. The concept of the tyranny

---

[93] Wilson (1955) p. 488.   [94] Napoleon cited by Dicey (1920) p. 1.
[95] Jaeger (2010) p. 30.   [96] Jaeger (2010) p. 30.   [97] Kahan (2001) p. 66.

of the majority conveyed the anxious prognosis that the authority of the many would lead to the de-authorisation of the few.

The pessimistic swing in the evaluation of public opinion is illustrated by the example of John Stuart Mill. A study on the evolution of his thinking on this topic states that initially, Mill 'regarded public opinion as a great check on any interference with individual liberty'. His 'Speech on Perfectibility', delivered to the London Debating Society in 1828, stressed the positive influence that the public character of opinion would have over sectional interests and sentiments.[98] But whereas in the 1820s 'he was fearful of any power that might be exercised without the control of public opinion', during the next decade he became concerned of what would happen if general opinion was not influenced by 'enlightened doctrines propounded by more cultivated minds'. Mill's focus was now on the question of how the influence of the educated clerisy could shape and direct public opinion, and his concern regarding the tyranny of the majority was compounded by his suspicion that 'even wise men are capable of being corrupted'.[99]

Mill's shift in attitude was influenced by Tocqueville's analysis of public opinion in the United States. As Habermas points out, both Mill and Tocqueville 'treated public opinion more as a compulsion toward conformity than as a critical force'.[100] Tocqueville's expansive vision of the power and influence of public opinion in America seems to be linked to his concern about the erosion of aristocratic authority in Europe. America served as a warning to the threat posed by Europe's accommodation to pressure for majority rule. Tocqueville warned how, in the United States, 'the power of the majority surpasses all the powers with which we are acquainted in Europe', writing that once the majority has made a decision 'everyone is silent, and the friends as well as the opponents of the measure unite in assenting to its propriety'. Tocqueville claimed that the power of the majority is far greater than that of an absolutist monarch, since 'no monarch is so absolute as to combine all the powers of society in his own hands and to conquer all opposition, as a majority is able to do, which has the right both of making and of executing the laws'.[101]

Tocqueville's dramatic rendition of the power of opinion makes Hobbes's absolutist ruler appear relatively impotent. In Tocqueville's imagination, whereas 'the authority of a king is physical and controls the actions of men without subduing their will', public opinion can overwhelm the internal life of people. Tocqueville argued that the authority

---

[98] Ten (1969) p. 67.   [99] Ten (1969) p. 67.
[100] Habermas (1992) p. 133.   [101] Tocqueville (1998) p. 103.

of public opinion was so formidable that a 'man who raises his voice in the cause of truth' has less protection in the United States than he would even in an absolutist state.[102] It should be noted that some American commentators were bemused by the unrestrained language used to describe their countrymen's deference to opinion: one article, published in *Harper's Magazine* in 1858, noted that Americans have 'often been taunted by foreigners, as well as by their own writers, with an excessive deference to public opinion'.[103]

Tocqueville's warnings about the power of public opinion in America captured the European elite's unease with the growing influence of the 'many' and the uncertain and contingent status of its own authority. While Tocqueville may have been more hostile to this power than those of more liberal or radical inclinations, the sense of omnipotence he attributed to it was integral to the conventional wisdom of the era. Not for nothing was public opinion anointed as the new religion of industrial Europe. The German historian Barthold Georg Niebuhr expressed this sentiment when he declared,

Public opinion is that opinion which in spite of the difference in individuals and of the very different conditions or situations in which they are placed, is so unanimously expressed, and merely represented by one man after another, that it may be taken as the utterance of universal truth and reason, and even as the will of God itself.[104]

Niebuhr's representation of public opinion as a modern equivalent of an utterance of divine will resonated with the temper of the times. Some of the most important pioneers of sociology – Emile Durkheim, E. A. Ross, Herbert Spencer, Ferdinand Tonnies – perceived public opinion as the supreme influence on social behaviour. Durkheim argued that opinion 'is a source of authority', and noted that 'it might be even asked whether all authority is not the daughter of opinion'.[105]

By the end of the nineteenth century, public opinion was regularly perceived more as a threat to than a source of authority. It was depicted as a 'power and influence' that literally forces politicians and statesmen to act against their better judgment. Often this destructive influence was blamed on the press, which both gave voice to and shaped this force. As a result, wrote a commentator in the conservatively inclined *National Review*, 'leading statesmen grow more and more into opportunists, and are more and more compelled to say, not what they themselves think

---

[102] Tocqueville (1998) p. 104.
[103] 'War Against Public Opinion', *Harper's Magazine*, 1858, vol. 16, p. 830.
[104] Cited in Shepard (1909) p. 42.   [105] Durkheim (1968) p. 208.

ought to be said, but what, in their judgment, the audience they address would like to have said'.[106]

There were differences of emphasis and interpretation between competing arguments of the status of public opinion, but all saw it as the principal source of legitimacy.[107] Some nineteenth-century social commentators, such as Durkheim, postulated a model of public opinion that served as the modern equivalent of tradition and custom.[108] But of course public opinion was not comparable to a tradition or custom, because it did not provide a recognised foundational doctrine or norms of behaviour. The public's opinion could not be taken for granted; and since authority could be only exercised through public opinion, what mattered was the relationship between what the public thought and who influenced those beliefs. Ultimately, even the authority of the expert required the recognition of public opinion; and calls for political reform and expanding the electorate created a situation where 'questions of intellectual and political authority were explicitly connected'.[109]

Thus public opinion emerged as one of the principal sources of validation in the modern era. The claim to represent it or speak on its behalf now became a warrant for authority.

Unlike other forms of validation, public opinion was perceived as an inherently unstable and therefore unpredictable force which not only legitimated but also threatened authority. Yet as a sublimated expression of the democratisation of public life, it was a phenomenon that could not be ignored. With the passing of time commentaries on public opinion were increasingly and instinctively drawn towards the project of seeking to de-authorise its influence. In his path-breaking study, *The Structural Transformation of the Public Sphere*, Habermas argued that by the late nineteenth century there was a perceptible tendency to divest public opinion of its normative link with political and constitutional life and turn it into 'an object of social-psychological research'.[110]

Arguably, the pathologisation of mass psychology was never far from the surface of public opinion discourse. Premonitions of the crisis of authority were sublimated through the discourse of public opinion, and the language through which inferences about public opinion were communicated contained coded references to the threat of the masses and elite apprehensions about the durability of civilised cultural norms. At the same time, characterisations of public opinion helped to establish distinctions between the educated elite and the gullible masses, and assisted

---

[106] P. H. Colomb 'The Patriotic Editor in War', *National Review*, April 1987, p. 253.
[107] Gordon (1992) p. 883.   [108] Durkheim (1984) p. 82.
[109] Yeo (1984) p. 44.   [110] Habermas (1992) p. 240.

the consolidation of a sense of self-conscious superiority towards easily manipulated subjects. By the end of the nineteenth century, the problem raised by Lewis – of how to elaborate a mark of authority over public opinion and ensure that the masses defer to it – gave way to the cynical quest of how to tame public opinion through manipulating its ignorance.

12   Nineteenth-century authority on
the defensive

The defensive discourse on public opinion offered a medium through which anxieties about the cultural and moral devaluation of authority could be communicated. In the nineteenth century the loss of cultural support for authority was shown by the fact that it was increasingly presented as a principle that was inferior to freedom. Moreover, the couplets of Authority versus Truth and Authority versus Reason cast doubts on its moral and intellectual credibility. The erosion of cultural valuation for authority was captured rhetorically through concepts such as 'the principle of authority' and 'authoritarian'.

The language through which authority was expressed had become ambiguous and evasive. This trend was exemplified in the nineteenth century through the concept 'principle of authority', which, though frequently used in public discussions and the press, was rarely defined. For example, London's *The Times* referred to the principle of authority in a manner that suggested its readers would readily understand the term.[1] In France, the term *la principe d'authorité* was used by the leading anarchist Proudhon, and in Germany, the word *Autoritätsprinzip* was widely used by theologians and social commentators. Friedrich Engels referred to it in his article 'On Authority' and Rudolph Sohm, who influenced the development of Weber's theory of charisma, used the term in his 1892 discussion of charismatic authority.[2]

The use of the term 'the principle of authority' often conveyed a sense of insecurity about the challenge posed by other principles, such as those of reason, liberty or individualism. Often it was through the contrast drawn between the principle of authority and its counter-principle that its meaning crystallised. 'There are, then two principles in the world – the principle of authority and the principle of liberty, the principle of

---

[1] In my search for this term in this newspaper in the nineteenth century, I was struck by the frequency with which the term was used as an idiom that spoke for itself.
[2] I am grateful to the Weber scholar Dr Christopher Adair-Toteff for the reference to Rudolph Sohm's *Kirchenrecht*. Leipzig: Verlag von Duncker and Humblot, 1892.

society and the principle of individualism', claimed a textbook on the history of philosophy published in 1890.[3] The political and social views of commentators and journalists determined their attitude to the principle of authority, but all assumed that it existed in an uneasy relation to alternative principles. An editorial in *The Times* coupled the principle of authority with 'respect for tradition upon which an hereditary aristocracy must mainly rely';[4] while at a meeting of the British Medical Association in July 1890 Sir Walter Foster, a doctor and Member of Parliament, contrasted the 'modern spirit of doubt and scientific research' to the principle of authority.[5] Tocqueville, like most serious commentators, used the concept to convey the idea of the recognition of obedience or deference, and contrasted it with what he called the principle of equality.[6]

Advocacy of the principle of authority often conveyed an assertion of order, respect for government and obedience. For example, the French General Purtouneaux was cited as demanding that it was mandatory for the National Guard to 'maintain in a complete manner discipline, hierarchy, and the respect due to the principle of authority'.[7] A London *Times* correspondent reported from France in August 1852 on a group of local dignitaries praising Louis Napoleon for the 're-establishment of the principle of authority' and the 'repression of anarchical elements'.[8] One journalist complained about the 'impotent and ridiculous' behaviour of Italian policemen in Pisa, and concluded that 'respect for the Government, which is the true principle of authority, gained nothing'.[9] In a similar vein, the principle of authority was cited as the antidote to disorder. Sir Robert Peel was praised because, as leader of the Opposition, he did not forget 'that he represented ideas of order and the principle of authority and for this reason lent his assistance to the Government under the most important circumstances'.[10] In his essay *Culture and Anarchy* (1869), the conservative cultural critic Matthew Arnold argued that 'we have got a much wanted principle, a principle of authority, to counteract the tendency to anarchy which seems to be threatening us'.[11]

The concept sometimes served as a counterpoint to the free and independent formation of opinions and attitudes. So an article that compared French and German schools with those in England warned about

---

[3] Flint (1894) p. 34.   [4] 'Editorial', *The Times*; 20 February, 1856, p. 6.
[5] 'The British Medical Associaton', *The Times*; 1 August, 1890, p. 3.
[6] See Chapter 2 'Of the Principal Source of Belief Among Democratic Nations' in Tocqueville (1998).
[7] 'Discipline of the National Guard in France', *The Times*; 3 May, 1851, p. 8.
[8] 'From Our Correspondent', *The Times*; 26 August 1852, p. 5.
[9] 'Express from Paris', *The Times*; 1 July 1857, p. 4.
[10] 'Ministerial Crisis in England', *The Times*; 12 June 1841, p. 6.
[11] Arnold (1966) p. 82.

the 'systematic substitution of the principle of authority for the spirit of independence'.[12] An editorial supporting Liberal proposals on a new Reform Bill observed that the 'Tory represents the comfortable principle of authority and the graciousness of patronage, – the Whig troublesomeness of reason and the harshness of self-exertion; the Tory sufferance and submission – the Whig independence and progress'.[13] A similar counterposition was provided in an editorial on France on the day of Voltaire's centenary, which noted that 'on the one side are the people who rely on personal freedom; on the other are those who trust the principle of authority; and the principle of authority is upheld by the rule of the Catholic Church'.[14] The Liberal social commentator Sedley Taylor distinguished the principle of authority from that of private judgment.[15]

The principle of authority was invariably associated with traditionalism, religion and conservatism. The Catholic newspaper *The Tablet* offered guidance on whom to support in a forthcoming election, and arguing that 'so far as the Tory Party go with us in upholding and defending against Whiggism, Liberalism, Radicalism and Democracy the principle of authority, and the great principles which we should upheld and defend . . . we go with them'.[16] The Scottish theologian Robert Flint represented the Tory party as the political expression of the principle of authority and the Liberals as representing that of liberty.[17]

'One of the essential differences between Liberals and Conservatives lies in the attitude which they respectively assume towards the principle of authority', wrote Sedley Taylor in his flattering counter-position of the former to the latter. According to his account, the history of the Liberal Party 'is essentially the history of a long struggle for mental freedom', whereas that of the Tories is 'the history of persistent efforts to hinder the emancipation of the human intellect'. Yet on closer inspection it becomes evident that since 'both owe their political opinion to authority', the distinction between the two parties' attitude towards the principle was not totally clear cut.[18]

Since authority-rejecting behaviour resonated with the prevailing climate of the nineteenth century, it is not surprising that liberal and radical

---

[12] See 'Editorial', *The Times*, 30 July 1857, p. 8.

[13] 'The Dissolution of Parliament', *The Times*, 7 July 1865.

[14] 'Editorial', *The Times*; 30 May 1878, p. 9.

[15] Sedley Taylor 'On the Principle of Authority in Matters of Opinion', *Macmillan's Magazine*, May 1873, p. 9.

[16] Cited in 'The Roman Catholics and the Coming Elections', *The Nottinghamshire Guardian*, 7 July, 1865.

[17] Flint (1894) p. 34.

[18] Sedley Taylor 'On the Principle of Authority in Matters of Opinion', *Macmillan's Magazine*, May 1873, p. 9.

commentators favourably contrasted the values of independence and reason to the principle of authority. However, most of the comments in the mainstream press, such as *The Times*, communicated a sense of anxiety about its erosion. Thus one editorial concerned about the growing activism of the 'working man' was concerned lest the 'principle of authority and veneration of law should be destroyed, and no curb should remain strong enough to rein in the headlong course of democratic passion'.[19]

The very fact that authority was conceived as one principle among many indicates that it expressed an ideal upheld by some, rather than a sturdy feature of everyday social reality. One of the rare attempts to define this concept explicitly was made by Lewis, who explained his understanding of it as the 'principle of adopting the belief of others, on a matter of opinion, without reference to the particular grounds on which that belief may rest'.[20] However, possibly the most extensive discussion of the principle of authority was provided by one its fervent opponents, the French anarchist leader Pierre-Joseph Proudhon. Proudhon's *General Idea of the Revolution in the Nineteenth Century* (1851) contained a chapter devoted to this concept, which he represented as the opposite to the idea of Revolution. Proudhon anticipated twentieth-century theories of the authoritarian family, in his argument that 'the principle of authority and government has its source in the dominating attitude of the family'; and his review of the history of this concept suggested that authority was a term of mystification, which in his era had become discredited and exposed: 'no authority, no government, not even popular, that is the Revolution'.[21]

Commentators who used the concept often failed to recognise its historically specific character. At times they presented the tension between the principles of authority and freedom as a trans-historical conflict that has its origins in the beginning of time. *The Tablet* in July 1865 claimed that the 'the principles in whose name men have opposed one another since the world began and will oppose another till the world ends, are the principles of authority and the principle of liberty'.[22] A similar analysis was put forward by the German theologian Julius Kaftan, who wrote that the 'conflict in the two principles, authority and reason is almost as old as Christian theology'.[23] In Flint's account of the past, historical

[19] 'Editorial', *The Times*; 12 April, 1860, p. 8.   [20] Lewis (1974) p. 7.

[21] 'Fourth Study. The Principle of Authority' in Pierre-Joseph Proudhon, *General idea of the Revolution in the Nineteenth Century* (1851) http://fair-use.org/p-j-proudhon/general-idea-of-the-revolution/ (accessed 3 May, 2013).

[22] Cited in 'The Roman Catholics and the Coming Elections, *The Nottinghamshire Guardian*, 7 July, 1865.

[23] Kaftan (1900) p. 676.

progress assumes the form of the gradual ascendancy of the principle of reason against that of authority, which led him to argue that in medieval times,

> The principle of authority was maintained in the Church and the State, in science and practice, in such a way as to discourage and condemn the hope that reason might achieve great triumphs in the future; and study and reflection were mainly confined to theology and philosophy, the provinces of knowledge in which progress is least visible. Still the idea was never completely lost.[24]

Through reading history backwards in this way, the very distinct medieval conceptualisation of authority and reason was conflated with its nineteenth-century variant. Through universalising this conflict of principles, commentators avoided tackling a difficult problem that was actually a unique feature of their time.

The representation of the relation of authority to reason as polar opposites spoke to a degree of individualisation that simply did not exist pre-modern times. The construction of a new abstract concept of the principle of authority implicitly recognised that there was something distinct about the taken-for-granted acceptance of another person's command and opinion: whereas in pre-modern societies authority is 'hardly recognised as having separate on even distinguishable identity', it now had to self-consciously recast as an explicit autonomous principle.[25] As Nisbet pointed out, in a pre-modern setting 'authority is so closely woven into the fabric of tradition and morality as to be scarcely more noticeable than the air men breathe'.[26]

The rhetorical strategy of presenting authority in a self-conscious and explicit form as principle was testimony to the uncertain foundation on which it rested in nineteenth-century society. It sought to establish a claim for the acceptance of authority at least in some domain of social experience. Most often it was deployed to legitimate the authority of the elite over the opinions of the masses, where unexamined assent to a superior wisdom was presented as an illustration of the working of the principle of authority.[27] Through this usage it was acknowledged that on its own this principle was insufficient to maintain stability and order. The necessity for his principle to co-exist with another source of legitimation was increasingly seen as essential for a modern society. Thus a *Times* article advocating the necessity of vaccinating the public against smallpox in 1859 argued that since 'complete security' against this scourge 'can only be attained by universal vaccination it is of the highest importance to

---

[24] Flint (1894) p. 101.   [25] Nisbet (1979) p. 107.
[26] Nisbet (1979) p. 108.   [27] See Gladstone (1877) p. 902.

278   Nineteenth-century authority on the defensive

bring the influence of reason, authority and if need be compulsion to bear upon the small remnant of recusants'.[28]

For their part, theologians sought to reconcile the principle of authority demanded by their religious doctrine with that of reason. Kaftan argued that the 'principle of authority' can 'be taken as the natural principle of theology' and 'justified in a scientific way'.[29] To substantiate this thesis he pointed to Thomas Aquinas's distinction between dogmas that 'even reason is capable of knowing', and those 'dogmas which transcend the range of reason and which are accessible only in the church on the ground of revelation'. Only the latter doctrines have to 'submit to authority', stated Kaftan.[30] Thus a harmonious balance is established for the two opposing principles within the sphere of religion.

The coupling of the concept of the principle of authority with the obedience to order tended to ascribe to it the conservative function of maintaining the *status quo*. That is why in the nineteenth century, especially in its first half, the unqualified affirmation of authority tended to be advocated by religious leaders and conservative commentators. Liberal and radical commentators developed an attitude towards this principle that relied on a 'categorical distinction between the conservative function of authority which subordinates it to the needs of any established power and the innovative function of authority which subordinates the executive powers to its own transcendent design'.[31] In this vein, Proudhon and Marx adopted a 'compound concept of authority', and made a distinction between what they interpreted as the oppressive, conserving role of the authority principle and its positive, transformative role in the creation of a utopian or classless society. Marx wanted to free 'the worker' from believing in authority and stated that 'the main thing is to *teach him to walk by himself*'. At the same time he upheld the transformative role of political authority of a dictatorship of the proletariat.[32] Liberals, too, allocated a role for the transformative or innovative role of this principle, in their theory of rational authority exercised through an intellectual elite.

That even radical political thinkers like Proudhon and Marx could not entirely abolish the principle of authority in their own thinking indicated that the question at stake was the balance between competing principles. Few were prepared entirely to dispense with one or the other of the competing principles in case this led to either the re-emergence of a coercive hierarchy or its opposite – a state of anarchy. The danger in one

---

[28] 'Smallpox and Vaccination', *The Times*; 29 March 1859.   [29] Kaftan (1900) p. 676.
[30] Kaftan (1900) p. 676.   [31] Krieger (1968) p. 154.
[32] See 'Letter from Marx to Schweitzer', London, 13 October, 1868, in Marx and Engels (1988) p. 132.

principle crushing the other was highlighted by Flint, who argued that 'order and progress' are secured when the two principles both co-operate with and counteract one another.[33]

By the end of the nineteenth century, conservative and religious parties experienced a profound sense of unease about the status of the principle of authority. Political change, uncertainty and disorder were diagnosed as symptoms of the parlous condition of this principle. In September 1901, the assassination of the American President William McKinley was seized upon by the Vatican as proof that licence and liberty threatened to engulf the principle of authority. For the Pope this was proof that McKinley was the 'victim' of the 'unrestricted liberty that prevailed in the United States': 'It is this clear that the hatred of the sectaries aims at destroying the principle of authority and that no *regime*, however free it may be, will satisfy the brutal passions of the enemies of society'. Hinting at conflicts to come, the Pope asserted that in the 'perils of Socialism, Freemasonry, Judaism and Anarchism, we must multiply our endeavours'.[34]

Competing visions of authority

Thomas Carlyle personified the desperate yet pragmatic quest for authority in the nineteenth century. More than most, he felt the loss of the reassuring influence of transcendental authority, yet his writings are dominated by the presentiment that a return to the pre-industrial medieval past was foreclosed. Unlike Burke and Coleridge, his fellow romantic conservative critics of a modernising social order, Carlyle believed that traditional religious and political institutions had become irrelevant to industrial society. Through his essays, he expressed 'in a particularly acute form, the Victorian desire both to recapture the transcendental idyll and to remain on the battlefield of history'.[35] At different times, his vision of authority attached itself to the emergence of a great hero like Oliver Cromwell or Frederick the Great, a new transcendental myth, or the moral authority of the man of letters. Towards the end of his life he became increasingly drawn towards relying on coercion to maintain order, indicating that he had failed in his quest for a moral validation of authority.[36]

Competing visions of authority expressed themselves through contrasting claims about the *source* of authority. Although often cast in a

---

[33] Flint (1894) p. 34.
[34] 'The Pope and the Anarchists', *The Times*, 21 September, 1901, p. 5.
[35] Vanden Bossche (1991) p. 10.
[36] For a fascinating account of Carlyle's quest see Vanden Bossche (1991).

doctrinaire form, these claims tended to be tempered by a pragmatic recognition that what was required was a form of validation for order that worked. Both liberal and conservative thinkers were conscious of the tension between the principle of authority and of liberty and sought to minimise the contradiction between them. Thus, deliberations on authority were often resolved through compromise, and some of the most influential statements on the subject sought to validate order through establishing a balance between different principles of legitimation.

The essayist Walter Bagehot, whose books *The English Constitution* (1867) and *Physics and Politics* (1872) were focused on the problem of how to gain and maintain obedience to order, offered an eloquent argument for compromise between the competing principles of authority and freedom. While he recognised the virtues of the 'age of free discussion', he also feared its unpredictable and potentially destabilising consequences. Bagehot's solution upheld the authority of tradition and custom while acknowledging the important contribution that free discussion and debate made to the efficient conduct of government.[37] A similar orientation was taken by Benjamin Constant: although he possessed robust modernist liberal attitudes towards reforming French political life, he claimed that something more than reason was needed to guarantee liberty, and believed that 'liberty itself was grounded on and was sustained by religious sentiment'.[38]

Tradition and religion vied with nationalism, the cult of the leader or the expert and with public opinion in an attempt to give authority meaning in the nineteenth century. It is to these competing visions of authority that we now turn.

Authority of the past

Conservative and reactionary theorists were particularly sensitive to the necessity of establishing authority on a firm and unquestioned foundation, and were at the forefront of attempting to restore or re-create forms of traditional and non-rational norms with which to validate it. Edmund Burke, arguably the intellectual father of modern conservatism, outlined his traditionalist orientation in a speech to the House of Commons in May 1782:

Our constitution is a prescriptive constitution whose sole authority is that it has existed time out of mind...Prescription is the most solid of titles, not only to property, but, which is to secure that property, to government...It is

---

[37] See Spring (1976).   [38] Jennings (2009) p. 72.

accompanied with another ground of authority in the constitution of the human mind – presumption. It is a presumption in favour of any settled scheme of government against any untried project, that a nation has long existed and flourished under it.[39]

Burke insisted that the 'wisdom' of prejudice built up over centuries was a far more reliable guide than an individual's 'own private stock of reason'.

Burke sought to depict the principles of authority and liberty as complementary. People's loyalties to their traditional institutions expressed a balance between liberty and constraint; the authority of established institutions encouraged loyal assent and its 'power' was rendered 'gentle' by the support of 'ancient opinions and rules of life'. Burke recognised that rendering power 'gentle' required a sensibility that was inconsistent with the modern mind. His frank acknowledgement that 'pleasing illusions' were necessary for rescuing tradition is testimony to his instrumental avowal of its mystery. Yet when he warned about the danger of casting off the illusions of tradition – 'all the decent drapery of life is to be rudely torn off' – he pointed his finger at the 'sophisters, economists and calculators' for their instrumental behaviour.[40] It is not surprising that one of his twentieth-century disciples could argue that the source of authority for Burke was 'tradition tempered by expediency'.[41]

The attempt to resurrect the authority of tradition also drew on the resources of religion, which Burke, Herder, de Maistre and other restorationist thinkers regarded as fundamental for securing order. Louis De Bonald argued that the ultimate source of all authority was religion;[42] the Spanish Catholic theorist Donoso Cortes proposed a form of political theology that looked to the Church and Christianity to legitimate the rule of an authoritarian dictator.[43]

Herbert Marcuse wrote that Burke, Bonald, Maistre, August Schlegel and Adam Muller elaborated a 'consciously irrationalist and traditionalist theory'.[44] Insofar as these theories were explicitly directed at discrediting human rationality, Marcuse's emphasis on conscious irrationalism is apposite. Marcuse observed that for these theorists, 'the principle which upholds state and society is not the truth as arrived at through human insight, but faith: prejudice, superstition, religion and tradition are celebrated as the essential social virtues of man'.[45] Such attempts to evoke a

---

[39] Edmund Burke, 'Speech on the Reform of the Representation of the Commons in Parliament', 7 May 1782, www.econlib.org/library/LFBooks/Burke/brkSWv4c2.html (accessed 3 May 2013).
[40] See Burke (2009) pp. 76–7.   [41] Kirk (1953) p. 374.
[42] Koyre and Cohen-Rosenfeld (1946) p. 60.
[43] See discussion on Donoso Cortes in Spektorowski (2002).
[44] Marcuse (2008) p. 67.   [45] Marcuse (2008) p. 77.

source of transcendental authority relied on the mystification of a power beyond human creation and reason. This approach was formulated by de Maistre in the following terms:

To put it briefly, the mass of the people has absolutely no part in any political creation. It only respects the government itself because the government is not its own work. This feeling is engraved deeply into its heart. *It bends beneath the sovereign power because it feels that this is something sacred which it can neither create nor destroy.*[46]

To maintain the illusion of the sacred, de Maistre insisted that those who rule should be separated from the masses – for,

if the opinion of the people does not place a barrier between itself and authority, if the power is not out of its reach, if the crowd who are governed can believe they are the equal of the small numbers who actually govern, *government no longer exists.*[47]

The project of sacralising the institution of authority led to a challenge against the conventionalist representation of state and society as the rational will of humans. Instead, restorationst theories depicted state and society as 'indirectly or directly, as divine institutions whose authority beyond this is derived either from its mere existence or mere permanence', or from some mystical power.[48] Burke's idea of 'tradition tempered by expediency' contained a fundamental contradiction. Expediency implies a motive that involves action based on calibrated choice rather than principle; it instrumentalises tradition and signals the idea that customs and values that were once sacred have become objects of human construction. Since expedience involves a non-traditional criterion for decision-making, it calls into question the inviolability of tradition and custom. Its very reliance on a non-traditional form of calculation exposes tradition's incapacity to generate foundational norms for authority.

Authority of religion

It is in their attitude towards religion that the pragmatism of conservative thinkers like Burke often matches that of their liberal counterparts. Sternhell wrote that Burke's attitude to religion was 'highly ambiguous': he seemed to 'recognize the existence of a divine order and of a religiously revealed truth', but he also regarded '"the spirit of the gentleman and the spirit of religion" to be the two mainstays of order and conservation, and it generally seems that the function of religion is above all to serve as a tool'.[49] In this respect Burke's attitude was similar to those of

---

[46] Cited in Marcuse (2008) p. 73.   [47] Cited in Marcuse (2008) p. 74.
[48] Marcuse (2008) p. 68.   [49] Sternhell (2010) pp. 191–2.

Herder, Barres, Maurras and Spengler, all of whom who believed that 'religion was no longer a revealed truth but a means of cohesion and social well-being'.[50]

Some interpreters of Burke contend that he did not have a pragmatic theory of religion. 'Burke duly emphasizes the benign consequences of religion, but he explicitly rejects the functional treatment of religion adopted by many political thinkers,' argues Richard Boyd. Boyd recognises that 'Burke calls attention to the possibility that functional justifications are not incompatible with religion's underlying goodness and truth', but qualifies this statement with the observation that 'to suggest that religion is good for political life does not necessarily imply one's insincerity or that religion is not also good for its own sake'.[51] The real issue at stake is not the sincerity of Burke's conviction but his recognition of the functional benefit of religion. In this respect, the conservative Burke shared some of the instrumental sentiments expressed by J. S. Mill's essay, *Utility of Religion*.

In his account of the attitude to religion held by the traditionalist anti-Enlightenment movement, Sternhell observes that, 'with the exception of Herder, a Protestant preacher' none of the key critics had 'faith' but 'they all saw religion as a tremendous civilizing force, an important element in social stability, and a source of moral strength'.[52] It is noteworthy that many of the leading liberal social theorists praised the social role of religion, even though they were not Christians: a study of the political thought of Burckhardt, Mill and Tocqueville notes that all these thinkers 'believed that religion has a potentially positive role to play in society'.[53]

Tocqueville argued that one of the merits of religion was that it 'imposes a salutary restraint on the intellect'. He believed that without the influence of this power, people would become confused and disorganised. 'When there is no longer any principle of authority in religion any more than in politics, men are speedily frightened at the aspect of this unbounded independence' he wrote. Tocqueville's instrumental approach towards religion was clearly communicated in his approval of the pragmatic behaviour of the American clergy, which he praised for its capacity for flexibility and accommodation to prevailing opinion. Through adapting to 'democratic tendencies', wrote Tocqueville, 'religion sustains a successful struggle with that spirit of individual independence which is her most dangerous opponent'.[54]

For Tocqueville, it was the capacity of religion to constrain individual passion and bind people together around a common consensus that

---

[50] Sternhell (2010) p. 192.   [51] Boyd (1999) pp. 472–3.
[52] Sternhell (2010) p. 207.   [53] Kahan (2001) p. 108.   [54] Tocqueville (1998) p. 120.

merited its support. The imperative of restraining the behaviour of the democratically influenced public endowed religion with the task of helping provide moral support for the maintenance of order. While for traditionalist and conservative writers, religion was an essential for the exercise of moral authority, more liberal thinkers regarded it as a useful supplement to other sources of authority. Advocates of rational-technocratic authority, like the early sociologists Saint-Simon and Comte, actively promoted the founding of a new religion. Saint-Simon invented a religion because he felt that science alone could not provide the foundation for a common belief in the legitimacy of the prevailing order,[55] while Comte, who was concerned that the masses would not acquiesce to the wisdom of his technocratic rulers, sought to strengthen the appeal of this technocracy through harnessing the spiritual power of religion.[56]

The declining influence of traditional beliefs and the weakening of religious faith were experienced by conservatives and liberals alike as a symptom of the erosion of authority. The real difference of opinion was on the best way of re-creating a measure of moral cohesion. Whereas traditionalists opted for the revival of old-style Christianity, liberals and radicals advocated new secular faiths, which were often closely linked to science, as an alternative. Even some scientists and philosophers who lacked religious faith themselves were reluctant to allow their scepticism to undermine the faith of the masses, fearing that it might contribute to the erosion of social stability. The Social Darwinist Benjamin Kidd, whose 1894 text *Social Evolution* stressed the role of religion and other non-rational influences in enhancing social cohesion, expressed a sentiment held widely within the scientific community.

Nineteenth-century sociology, too, regarded religion as indispensable for the working of moral authority. For Durkheim the need for religion was eternal, though its specific expression could change with the evolution of society. His was a pragmatic approach that was open to the idea that new more secular forms of collective sentiments could serve as the functional equivalents of traditional religion:

what essential difference is there between an assembly of Christians celebrating the principal dates of the life of Christ, or of Jews remembering the exodus from Egypt or the promulgation on the Decalogue, and a reunion of citizens commemorating the promulgation of a new moral or legal system or some great event in the national life.[57]

---

[55] Wolin (2004) p. 328.   [56] See Stirk and Weigall (1995) p. 40.
[57] Durkheim (1968) p. 427.

Durkheim recognised that reasoning individualism weakened the moral foundation of religion. However, he drew back from thinking through the logic of his analysis, and sought to reconstitute religion in a more secular and rational form. It was left to Weber to spell out the inconsistency of the rationalisation of moral life with the legitimation of secular authority.

The authority of nationalism

One of the most important ideological innovations pursued by traditionalists and conservatives was the elaboration of the nation and a national cultural identity. In the works of Moser and Burke, the cultural idea of the nation served to provide a sense of permanent identity through people's organic link with the past.[58] The cult of the national past and the traditions associated with it were mobilised against the universalistic claims of rational authority. So in the nineteenth century, tradition gains its definition through a nationalism that had a predominantly anti-rationalist form, as opposed to the liberal nationalism of the French Revolution.

Drawing on the resources of custom, tradition and religion, nationalism provided a modern doctrine for the recreation of community. Through the idealisation of the nation the bonds of tradition could be reaffirmed, if not quite rescued. The German liberal philosopher Johan Fichte (1762–1814) expressed this sentiment in his 1806 address 'To the German Nation' in the following terms:

> The first, original, and truly natural boundaries of states are beyond doubt their internal boundaries. Those who speak the same language are joined to each other by a multitude of invisible bonds by nature herself, long before any human art begins; they understand each other and have the power of continuing to make themselves understood more and more clearly; they belong together and are by nature one and an inseparable whole.[59]

Nationalism came to play a significant role in the provision of moral validation for the nation state. Romantic nationalism emphasised the mystical cultural connections that bound people together in a common political community. Its reference to the 'soul of the nation' conveyed a sense of the sacred that attached itself to the institutions of state and society. National culture was represented as mysterious and awe-inspiring, and therefore not susceptible to rational analysis or debate. Yet for all its emphasis on the mysterious and the sacred, the promoters of the myth of the nation were surprisingly open about the instrumental agenda driving their project. The French nationalist historian Ernest Renan argued

---

[58] Krieger (1970) p. 234.   [59] Kelly (1968) pp. 190–1.

that the construction of a national myth was a necessity, noting that 'forgetting' and even 'historical error are an essential factor in the creation of nation'. As a result, he warned that 'progress in historical studies is often a danger to nationality'.[60] For Renan, the 'wish of nations is, definitely the sole criterion of legitimacy', the normative source for authority.[61]

The myth of the nation served as a model for the different brands of myth-makers in the nineteenth century. One important reason why nationalism proved to be an important source of legitimacy was because it had the capacity of linking the legacy of the past to a community of people. The leaders of the French Revolution recognised its potential and justified their action and appealed to the nation as 'the highest object of allegiance and ultimate source of authority'.[62] Although their nationalism was not a traditionalist one – it appealed to universal democratic values – its capacity to mobilise the people demonstrated its potential for harnessing the appeal of *La Patrie* to legitimate social order. The conservative traditionalist reaction against the legacy of the French Revolution often took the form of recasting nationalism into an anti-liberal particularistic ideology.

In his quest for moral authority, Durkheim tended towards the sacralisation of society, writing that the 'ideas of society is the soul of religion'. In the end this soul gained definition through the nation, which Durkheim came to characterise as the most important social unit of all, representing it as a 'psychic being', which possessed great moral power over the behaviour of the individual. In this way the collective consciousness mediated through a national culture came to provide 'the only solid basis of the state'.[63]

The authority of the Great Leader

In retrospect, one is struck by the frequency of attempts to resolve the difficulties surrounding authority-related controversies through the search for a Great Leader. This trend has been noted in our discussion of the eighteenth century and in relation to the inter-war crisis; in the nineteenth century, the heroic leader often emerged as a kind of *deus ex machina* who, through his personality, united authority and power in the institutions of the state. Such sentiments often assumed a virulently anti-democratic form by elitist thinkers who regarded the law, rational deliberation and public opinion as a restraint on their freedom. Friedrich Nietzsche, the

---

[60] Renan Cited in Abizadeh (2004) p. 292.   [61] See Abizadeh (2004) p. 292.
[62] Palmer (1940) p. 96.   [63] Durkheim cited in Mitchell (1931) p. 96.

German philosopher of irrationalism, forcefully argued that authority was founded on natural inequality and hierarchy, and looked to charismatic leaders like Napoleon for restoring and maintaining the legitimacy of the prevailing order.[64]

Around the years 1805–6, Hegel had become wary of disorder and was 'seduced by the idea of a strong leader' – a Napoleon of the Germans. In his reflection on the experience of Rome, he spelled out his vision for the construction of authority for his own time: 'the elevation of one majestic individual to the apex of all-encompassing power'. According to one of his interpreters, Hegel drew the conclusion that 'since everything done and everything actual is inaugurated and brought to completion by the single decisive act of a leader', what is required is Caesar or a Bonaparte, for only they 'know how to rule'.[65]

In France, the cult of the Great Leader had as its focus the two Napoleons. French historians frequently used the appellation *caesarism* as a synonym for Bonapartism. The 1850 text *Era of the Caesars*, by the anti-democratic and reactionary polemicist Francois-Auguste Romieu, summed up his aspiration for a charismatic leader who could maintain law and order.[66] Romieu regarded the rationalism of Enlightenment and the rise of liberal constitutionalism as the source of France's problem of order. Unlike many of his peers he did not think that 'any traditional idea of legitimacy' could be restored; he preferred a powerful Caesar, who could hold society together by force to the weak regimes of his era.[67] At more or less the same time, the more radical Saint-Simonian movement proposed a government constituted by their Church and led by a 'great man' or 'father'.[68]

Thomas Carlyle's lectures, *On Heroes and Hero-Worship*, attempted to confront the problem of order by envisioning a new form of heroic authority. An important study on this essayist outlined that 'through the figure of the hero, Carlyle attempted to resolve the tension between transcendence and history'.[69] Despite his elitist assumptions, Carlyle hoped to frame his advocacy of hero worship in a way that reconciled the Great Leader's authority with the principles of freedom. His definition of freedom included the statement: 'surely of all rights of men the right of the ignorant man to be guided by the wiser, to be, gently or forcibly, held in the true course by him is the indisputablest'. Carlyle insisted that 'if Freedom has any meaning it means enjoyment of that right'.[70]

[64] Cristi (2010) pp. 4–5.   [65] Cristi (2005) p. 142.
[66] See discussion in Yavetz (1971) p. 189.   [67] See Baehr (1998) pp. 106–19.
[68] See Iggers (1958).   [69] Vanden Bossche (1991) p. 98.
[70] Carlyle is cited in Vanden Bossche (1991) p. 144.

On Heroes and Hero-Worship influenced a great deal of nineteenth-century history writing, and Weber's charismatic leader arguably represents a continuity with this line of argument.[71] Yet Carlyle's vision of an authoritative hero required him to plunder history to find a credible candidate for the role. History suggests that heroes do not wait to be discovered by essay writers: as Mommsen notes, despite his best efforts, Carlyle 'cannot show us how to find or recognize a hero'.[72]

The ideas that led to the emergence of the totalitarian Leader of the twentieth-century inter-war era were already in circulation in the early nineteenth century. As Neumann reminds us, 'the emergence of a Caesar from the womb of democracy has been predicted time and again by French, German and Spanish counter-revolutionaries'. Their prophecy was based on the conviction that man is 'utterly corrupt, ignorant, wicked and incapable of freedom',[73] and that the threat posed by mass society and democratic passions could only be contained by the power and authority of a Great Leader. Considerable hope was invested in the cult of the leader in the nineteenth century because of its promise to overcome the contradiction between the principle of authority and freedom. Charismatic leadership, in the form of apostolic authority, was perceived by many of its advocates as an unanswerable alternative to claims of reason and rationality.

One of the most interesting contributions to the elaboration of apostolic authority was made by the Danish philosopher Søren Kierkegaard. Overwhelmed by what he saw as the spiritual illness of his age, Kierkegaard looked to salvation through the one true authority based on the 'eternal, essential, qualitative difference between God and man', which is exercised only 'when God appoints a particular man to have divine authority'.[74] The authority of this apostle is beyond question and demands obedience. Apostolic authority refers to a divine calling which is unrelated to the personal – intellectual and moral – characteristics of the individual concerned. Since such individuals are chosen according to criteria which are 'not comprehensible to mortals, we cannot judge or doubt the justification of their authority'.[75] The revelations of an apostle are not empirically verifiable by facts, because they refer to a different order of truth. According to one study of Kierkegaard's vision of authority, 'if revelatory claims in particular, are to be affirmed as truths, they must be personally commended and obediently received, not as objectively adjudicable hypothesis but as existence communications'.[76] The

---

[71] See Gerth and Mills (1958) p. 53.   [72] Vanden Bossche (1991) p. 99.
[73] Neumann (1963) p. 195.   [74] Kierkegaard (1966) pp. 112–17.
[75] See Kronflic (2005) p. 27.   [76] Whittaker (1999) p. 85.

authority of an individual with a divine calling appeared to some as the only way of reconciling the human aspiration for meaning with order.

During the second half of the nineteenth century, a powerful Romantic reaction against the trends towards rationalisation and massification led a significant section of the European intelligentsia towards the personalisation of authority. The emergence of the Romantic cult of the genius often converged with a search for political salvation. This aspiration was forcefully articulated by Lecky in 1867:

> There arise from time to time men who bear to the moral condition of their age much the same relations as men of genius bear to its intellectual condition . . . the magnetism of their perfection tells powerfully upon their contemporaries. An enthusiasm is kindled, a group of adherents is formed, and many are emancipated from the moral conditions of their age.[77]

Weber's subsequent construction of the charismatic leader bore the influence of this Romantic revolt against the rationalisation of life.[78]

As noted previously, the search for the personification of authority through an individual is a reoccurring theme in history; and as the examples of Hobbes's Mortal God and Rousseau's Great Legislator indicate, the attempt to find salvation through an individual leader was no less compelling in the modern era than in ancient times. Rousseau's Legislator is a 'heaven sent person' who, like Kierkegaard's Apostle, speaks with divine authority.[79] Sohm's concept of charismatic organisation stressed the importance of 'reverence for authority': according to one account, 'Sohm was fired by a mortal fear of plebeian radicalism, which he feared the ruling class would underestimate'.[80]

The authority of the expert

The representatives of the newly industrialising European societies invested considerable hope in the effectiveness of new institutions of intellectual and, in particular, scientific authority. In some cases, advocates of science actually sought to present their doctrine as a modern progressive religion. Saint-Simon, who was preoccupied with the erosion of social consensus in the aftermath of the French Revolution, regarded science as a political vehicle for the forging of new foundational norms for the exercise of authority. According to one study, what interested Saint-Simon was the 'therapeutic function of science'.[81] Saint-Simon adopted a functional approach to science and sought to use its prestige

---

[77] Cited in Potts (2009) p. 114.   [78] See Chapter 6 in Potts (2009).
[79] On Rousseau's charismatic Legislator see Lewis (1978).
[80] Smith (1988) pp. 38, 40, and 43.   [81] Lyon (1961) p. 55.

to reinforce the social order. It is likely that Saint-Simon 'believed in the usefulness, rather than the validity of scientism';[82] however, his vision of a society managed and co-ordinated by 21 experts spoke to a new technocratic impulse towards rationalising order.

At a time when traditional sources of legitimation appeared exhausted, science appeared to possess a singular capacity to provide society with an authoritative guide to the future. As noted in the previous chapter, this sentiment was confidently articulated by G. C. Lewis, who believed that scientific authority possessed a unique capacity to enjoy the kind of deference absent in moral and political life. Lewis's enthusiastic embrace of the authority of science was shared by liberal and utilitarian-influenced commentators. John Austin argued that science represented a unique source of authority, writing that in 'the mathematical and physical sciences, and in the arts which are founded upon them, we may commonly trust the conclusions which we take upon authority'. However, he was far less positive about the status of other fields of knowledge. He stated that 'unhappily' the natural sciences were 'different to 'the important science of ethics, and also with the various sciences which are related to ethics', because those involved in the sphere of ethics 'have rarely been impartial' and therefore 'have differed in their results'. He concluded that the people participating in the field of ethics were 'advocates' rather than 'inquirers', and hence their 'testimony is not to be trusted'.[83] The belief that the statements of the sciences were uniquely trustworthy was widely held, and helped to validate the claims of rational authority.

The ascendancy of scientific expertise was inextricably linked to the crisis of traditional authority in nineteenth-century Europe. By the end of this century, even theologians attempted to justify their doctrine as a science. Julius Kaftan wrote that 'in theology religion and science meet' and that 'at whatever else theology may be, it is at all events the science of theology'.[84]

The vanishing of tradition was an invitation to the reconstitution of authority in a new form. In an era of scientific and technological progress, the project of reconstituting authority was drawn inevitably towards the status enjoyed by technical expertise and specialised knowledge. But unlike traditional authority, which touched on every dimension of the human experience, the authority of the expert was confined to that which could be exercised through reason. Joseph Raz writes that the 'authority of the expert can be called theoretical authority, for it is an authority about what to believe'.[85] However, in the nineteenth century, claims to

[82] Lyon (1961) p. 65.   [83] Austin (1832) pp. 65–6.   [84] Kaftan (1900) p. 673.
[85] Raz (1990) p. 2.

expert authority were also mobilised to settle the question of *whom* to believe. The question of which individuals could be trusted and who bore the 'mark of authority' was a subject of serious discussion in the Victorian era.[86]

Politicians and the educated elite drew on the authority of science to legitimate their own knowledge claims. They devoted considerable energy towards constructing their authority as the possessors of knowledge, wisdom and superior insight. The question at issue was whether their knowledge would be recognised as authoritative by the rest of society. Those of a conservative disposition tended to be pessimistic about the capacity of the elites to maintain cultural and intellectual authority. In 1865, Matthew Arnold predicted that,

the very absence of any powerful authority amongst us, and the prevalent doctrine of the duty and happiness of doing as one likes, and asserting our personal liberty, must tend to prevent the erection of any very strict standard of excellence, the belief in any very paramount authority of right reason.[87]

Tocqueville expressed similar concerns and argued that the influence of an egalitarian ethos led to rejection of the 'authority of learned elites'.[88]

Distrust towards the opinion of the people led positivist thinkers like Comte to adopt a coercive approach to public debate and discussion. For Comte, the necessity for citizens to defer to experts was self-evident Although J. S. Mill shared some his concerns, he opted for a version of clerisy that distanced itself from the Comte's 'spiritual despotism'. In a letter to his wife in 15 January 1855, Mill wrote that: 'opinion tends to encroach more & more on liberty & almost all the projects of social reformers of these days are really *liberticide* – Comte's particularly so'.[89]

Mill's writings on the capacity of a clerisy or the expert rulers to influence public opinion tended to fluctuate between a mood of restrained optimism and one of sober concern. Writing in the *Westminster Review* in April 1849, he defended the 1848 Revolution but argued that the legislative activity should be reserved for 'the intellectual elite of France': in line with his previous views, Mill suggested that,

it is not for the people to govern, but only to choose a well-qualified assembly to govern for them; it is not for the assembly to make laws, but only to see that they are made by a panel of experts.[90]

Yet, less than a year later, he expressed serious doubts about both the moral authority of the expert rulers and the integrity of the masses,

---

[86] See the discussion on this subject in Lewis (1974).   [87] Arnold (1966) p. 109.
[88] Yeo (1984) pp. 6–7.   [89] Cited in Ten (1969) p. 51.
[90] Mill is cited in Burns (1968) p. 315.

writing that 'progress even of a political kind is coming to a halt, by reason of the low intellectual and moral state of all classes, and of the rich as much as of the poorer classes'.[91] In this respect, his views echoed the wider tendency of liberal opinion towards doubt and uncertainty, discussed in the previous chapter.

With the exception of a relatively small group of positivists and intellectuals, the claim to expert authority was rarely expressed in an undiluted technocratic form. So although Lewis stated that 'the advantage of taking professional advice, on certain classes of practical subjects, is so generally recognised as not to require proof', he recognised that there were clear limits to the purview of expertise: 'The only admissible substitute for self-judgment, in domestic affairs and questions of private conduct, is the advice of relations and trustworthy friends'. More significantly, Lewis recognised that there is no expertise of governing.[92] The one question that could not be avoided was whether a clerisy or any other variant of expert authority could actually succeed in preserving order. Ultimately this tension between the technocratic-utilitarian claim for authority and that of democracy expressed the contradiction between the principles of authority and liberty in a different guise.

Doubts about the influence that expertise could exercise over public life co-existed with the conviction that its authority was indispensable for maintenance of order in a modern society. The turn towards expertise had the effect of transforming moral questions into technocratic ones. In this way scientism – the politicisation of science – helped to depoliticise the question of authority. Of all the nineteenth-century visions of authority, this one would leave the most lasting legacy.

The authority of public opinion

From a sociological perspective it is the discussion surrounding the relationship between authority and public opinion that is most fascinating. As we noted in the previous chapter, public opinion was conceptualised as both a powerful source of legitimacy and a threat to authority. Apprehension about the 'principle of numbers' or the 'tyranny of the majority' grew during the period under consideration. So although it was recognised as a powerful force – and by many as *the* most important source – of legitimacy, because of its disruptive potential public opinion had relatively few enthusiastic advocates. On balance, even the more liberal commentators on this subject believed that its power had to be contained before it could be harnessed to support the social order.

[91] Cited in Burns (1968) p. 317.   [92] Lewis (1974) pp. 119 and 121.

Public opinion often served as a code through which ideas and concerns about the problem of order were communicated. Not infrequently, statements about the role of public opinion expressed the preoccupation of its author about the relationship of the masses to their rulers. As political and cultural life became more public, governments and reigning elites were forced to account for their actions to a larger and more heterogenous public. In such circumstances the exercise and meaning of authority appeared to be inseparable from the beliefs and behaviour of the public.

The often-repeated statement that 'All Government is Based on Opinion' conveyed the sentiment that the exercise of authority required the validation of public opinion. The key question posed in the nineteenth century was that of who influenced and directed this opinion. The assumption that public opinion was the subject of competing influences and that its allegiance had to be fought for ensured that attitudes towards it would not be complacent. Certainly by the 1880s and 1890s, the question of authority and its preservation was consistently linked to the effective management of public opinion. As the Liberal politician James Bryce reminded his readers, it was 'only by rare exception that a monarch or an oligarchy has maintained authority against the will of the people'.[93]

By its very nature, the authority of public opinion had a potential for containing the influence of political authority. This paradox was recognised by Bryce, whose historical account of the relationship between ruler and ruled suggested that public opinion disrupted the political equilibrium. So when he wrote that 'belief in authority and the love of established order, are among the strongest forces in human nature' and 'therefore in politics', what he had in mind was the pre-modern era. According to Bryce, this era is succeeded by an intermediate stage when conflicts and revolutions erupt because 'people are awakening to the sense that they are truly the supreme power in the State, but when rulers have not yet become aware that their authority is delegated'. Finally a new stage was reached, when rulers and governments respond to public opinion and seek to actively control it.[94]

In retrospect, the late nineteenth-century literature on opinion implies that it possessed a legitimacy that other institutions lacked. Even expert authority depended on its validation.[95] That is why a significant section of the scientific and intellectual elites regarded public opinion as threat to their status, believing that 'with the rise of the industrial middle classes and the emergence of public opinion as a political force, there

[93] Bryce (1895) p. 255.   [94] Bryce (1895) pp. 255–8.
[95] See the excellent discussion in Yeo (1984).

was a danger that the criterion of popularity would come to decide the acceptability, and even the truth of ideas'.[96]

A pragmatic quest

Arguably one of the main legacies of nineteenth-century thought was the emergence of an uneasy relationship between anti-authoritarian sensibilities and the demand for order. At a time of rapid social and economic transformation and cultural change, the pragmatism with which the advocates of competing visions of authority pursued their argument is understandable. Although in theory advocates of different sources of authority – tradition, religion, the nation, the great leader, the expert, public opinion – argued that theirs was the true foundation for order, in practice they were often prepared to compromise and accept that there were multiple types of validation. Despite their grand rhetorical statements about the principle of authority, conservative thinkers understood that concessions had to be made to the growing demand for democracy and participation. For their part, liberal and utilitarian public figures realised that their attempt to construct a regime of rational authority required the support of the majority of citizens. Whatever the views put forward about the principle of authority, the principle of numbers could not be ignored.

The principle of authority, with its connotation of expressing the interest of established political power, had lost much of its majesty and cultural support. The insecure cultural foundation on which authority rested is demonstrated by the fact that for the first time the very idea of authority – any kind of authority – was disparaged in European public life. The idea that authority was inherently anti-democratic and the negation of freedom enjoyed a degree of influence among more libertarian and radical sections, and the denunciation of the state by anarchist publicists resonated with younger educated radicals, particularly in France and Italy. Certainly at the level of rhetoric, anarchism influenced liberal discourse on the subject which frequently counterpoised Authority to Freedom.[97] At the end of 1870, Friedrich Engels wrote to Paul Lafargue, Marx's son-in-law, that among the Bakuninists, the term authority had become something of a swear word: 'As soon as something displeases the Bakuninists, they say: it's *authoritarian* and thereby imagine they have damned it forever'.[98]

---

[96] Yeo (1984) p. 7.   [97] See Draper (1990) p. 133.
[98] Cited in Draper (1990) p. 136.

It is at this point in time that the term 'authoritarian' became widely used, as an adjective to describe someone who is 'favourable to the principle of authority as opposed to that of individual freedom'. The *Oxford English Dictionary* cites the *Daily News* in June 1879 writing about 'men who are authoritarian by nature', who 'cannot imagine that a country should be orderly save under a military despotism'. Another definition offered is 'favouring imposed order over freedom'. As a noun, the meaning of this word was 'one who supports the principle of authority'.[99]

The coupling of terms like 'despotism' and 'imposition' with authority signified the erosion of its moral content. In this context, the term 'principle of authority' had become estranged from the idea of *auctoritas* and non-coercive influence and power. Certainly the qualities implied by concept of 'authoritarian' were seen as directly antithetical to those of freedom and consent. By the end of the century, the tension between the principle of authority and that of freedom had arguably become more difficult to manage than at its beginning. The theologian Julius Kaftan, at the turn of the twentieth century, wrote that 'the word "authority" has no attractive sound for modern ears, at least where religious conviction and scientific knowledge are concerned', remarking that external forms of authority had given way to 'the prevailing impression that piety is genuine only when it rests on inward personal conviction and has its mainspring, not in submission to authoritative traditions, but in the experience of our own heart and conscience'.[100]

But the cultural devaluation of authority ran in parallel with rehabilitating it as a practical necessity. From the middle of the nineteenth century there is a perceptible tendency for the 'reluctant acceptance' of this principle, 'even by those liberals and radicals who had originally shunned it'.[101] This respect was particularly directed towards the intellectual authority of the expert or intellectual elite. Even the most radical wing of European intellectual life did not entirely reject the principle of authority. In 1873, Engels took it upon himself to polemicise against a 'number of Socialists [who] have latterly launched a regular crusade against what they call the *principle of authority*', arguing that 'it is absurd to speak of the principle of authority as being absolutely evil, and of the principle of autonomy as being absolutely good'. Engels's thesis was that the relationship between authority and autonomy depended on its historical context. His famous remark – 'revolution is certainly the most authoritarian thing there is' – expressed the sentiment that

[99] See www.oed.com.chain.kent.ac.uk/Entry/13344 (accessed 13 January 2011).
[100] Kaftan (1900) p. 673.   [101] Krieger (1977) p. 265.

the exercise of authority was the precondition for a post-revolutionary freedom.[102]

Proudhon, too, found a place – albeit limited – for the principle of authority in his vision of a future society. In his outline of what future anarchist society would look like, written in 1864, he attempted to integrate authority into his model of federalism:

Anarchy, if I can express myself in this manner, is a form of government or constitution in which public and private conscience, formed by the development of science and of law, alone suffice to maintain order and guarantee all liberties; where, by consequence, the principle of authority, the institutions of police, the means of prevention or of repression, officialdom, taxation, etc., find themselves reduced to their simplest expression; much more, where monarchical forms, extreme centralization, disappear and are replaced by federative institutions and communal customs.[103]

Hostility to prevailing institutions of authority thus co-existed with a reluctance to imagine a world that was entirely without it.

Alternative visions of validating authority often led to a form of competitive claims-making. The Latin scholar Henry Nettleship observed that 'there are as many claimants for authority as there are moral and intellectual aspirations demanding it'.[104] Attempts to reconcile different visions of authority inevitably led to the elaboration of self-consciously constructed models of its different forms. For Leslie Stephen, authority had two meanings, 'not only different, but often so related that the greater the authority in one sense, the less it is in another'. He wrote that 'authority, when I speak as a historian or a man of science, is a name for evidence', whereas when the term is 'used by a lawyer, is a name for coercion, whether physical or moral'.[105] Others proposed more elaborate models of authority.

By the end of the century, rational authority was on the defensive. The mood of cultural pessimism was palpable, leading many, to 'fall back on guidance on the irrational elements in life'.[106] However, non-rational accounts of authority also lacked the moral resources to capture the public's imagination. Nettleship directly addressed the question of how authority can be validated by asking the question of whether the various accounts of authorities 'rest upon any permanent principle': his answer was that it had to be based on 'the moral feeling or conviction of the society which they affect'. This argument was qualified by the awareness that in a modern society, such a moral consensus is unlikely to

---

[102] See Engels (1873) p. 422.   [103] Cited in George (1922) p. 533.
[104] Nettleship (1892) p. 218.   [105] Stephen (1891) p. 188.
[106] Nettleship (1892) p. 219.

be permanent and that the only 'absolute authority for the individual is his conscience'. Nettleship suggested that in practice, individuals required the guidance of a wider moral consensus, and that the tension between individual and society can be resolved through a struggle for 'harmonious expression'.[107]

Nettleship was critical of nineteenth-century liberal philosophers for failing to provide a positive foundation for authority, and his contribution attempted to 'take up a more positive ground than was occupied by the liberal philosopher of thirty years ago'. To this end, he developed a model of authority based on four different types: the authority of law, the authority of religious institutions, the authority of society or public opinion, and the authority of great men. The effectiveness of the law depends on the influence of the foundations that underpin it, and laws which 'represent the oldest moral feeling of the community' possess the greatest authority. In a language that echoed Durkheim's sociology, Nettleship stated that it is the 'general moral sense of society which gives to law its permanent authority'.[108] But what is this moral sense that validates the law? Nettleship's analysis indicates that religion is unlikely to exercise significant influence on secular life, and therefore does not appear to be a promising source of moral validation.

In line with the sentiments of the late nineteenth century, Nettleship argued that the authority of public opinion is actually greater than either that of religion or the law. He regarded the authority of public opinion and that of society as interchangeable entities. Though public opinion is 'the strongest available force which can be invoked in the cause of humanity' he is clearly uncomfortable with its conformist imperative: public opinion expresses the mediocrity of the masses and its authority is often directed against the 'high aspirations' of the cultural elites.[109] The 'most fatal error which any community can commit it to crush its men of genius', he warned.[110] Nettleship's preference was for the authority of great men:

There is, however, a power, which in the long run proves itself stronger even that of public opinion, and which public opinion is constantly, though in vain, endeavouring to crush, – that of great men, the leaders of moral feeling and intellectual activity.[111]

Salvation is to be realised through the power of the great men, whose personal qualities help society transcend its crisis of authority. 'Great or

[107] Nettleship (1892) p. 221.   [108] Nettleship (1892) p. 224.
[109] Nettleship (1892) pp. 227–8.   [110] Nettleship (1892) p. 230.
[111] Nettleship (1892) p. 228.

leading men are distinguished by general power and insight, by a force which in the mind seems analogous to physical force in the body, a force which imposes itself at once, the faculty of command', wrote Nettleship, in this fantasy of charisma.[112]

What is interesting about this late nineteenth-century attempt to provide a conceptual framework for authority is that it only comes alive through the persona of the great leader. Other forms of authority appear as if they are emptied of a vital force:

> The position and authority of a great man is the absolute reverse of that which belongs to law and to general opinion. The man goes forward, and represents the future; law, and to a great extent social opinion, represent the past.[113]

The situating of the authority of law and opinion in the past renders explicit what is generally implicit in the late nineteenth century discourse on this subject which was its difficulty in giving a contemporary meaning to it. At this point in time very few could bring themselves to acknowledge the fact that authority was vanishing.

The construction of the idiom 'principle of authority' contained the implication of an ideal on the defensive. This was a principle whose foundation was rarely reflected upon and which provided a foundation to authority that was mainly rhetorical. It is worth noting that the quest for authority failed to make much progress. This is particularly striking in relation to the two spheres of potential authorisation that were relevant to the modern era – science/expertise and public consent/opinion – where no significant headway was made in transforming expert knowledge into a moral authority, or harnessing consent and opinion to the validation of secular rule. The discipline of sociology came forward as a body of knowledge to assist the quest.

[112] Nettleship (1892) p. 228.   [113] Nettleship (1892) p. 230.

13   Authority transformed into sociology's cause

Sociology emerged at a time of moral hiatus. It was dominated by the consciousness of transition from the certain traditions of the past to uncertain beliefs that were not yet formed. Emile Durkheim was intensely conscious of transition, and a keen interest in the shift in moral sensibility pervaded his work. He wrote of a world where 'the old gods are growing old or are already dead, and others are not yet born', and criticised Comte for his vain attempt 'artificially' to revive the 'old historic souvenirs', because 'it is life itself, and not the dead past' that 'can produce a living cult'. As if to try to reassure himself, Durkheim wrote that,

this state of incertitude and confused agitation cannot last forever. A day will come when our societies will know again those hours of creative effervescence, in the course of which new ideas arise and new formulae found which serve for a while as a guide to humanity.[1]

Outside of Europe Franklin Henry Giddings, one of the founders of American sociology, remarked that though 'the speculative theories of causation embodied in religious systems have fallen into discredit', nevertheless 'the convictions of human need, of the supremely desirable ends of life, of what ought to be, that religious systems have fostered and transmitted have been and in the main are still vitally true'.[2]

The recognition of the need for belief expressed a consciousness of authority lost. This sensibility was more than a reaction to apprehensions about the threat of disorder from below; it touched on existential questions to do with meaning and moral guidance. But recognition of such an absence only highlighted the elusive character of the problem. 'To endow a government with the authority it requires, it is not enough to feel the need for this', warned Durkheim: 'we must address ourselves to the sole sources from which all authority is derived: the establishment of traditions, a common spirit, etc'.[3] For Durkheim, science and

[1] Durkheim (1968) pp. 427–8.   [2] Giddings (1906) p. 2.
[3] Durkheim (1992) p. 120.

299

rationalised forms of authority could help give guidance but not provide the normative foundation for a 'common spirit'.

As Gouldner's review of the rise of sociology in the nineteenth century states, 'utilitarianism has a built-in tendency to restrict the sphere of morality' and it bred a culture that is estranged from moral norms. Consequently, a rationalised utilitarian culture possesses a '"natural" or built-in disposition towards moral normlessness', a tendency that Durkheim characterised through his concept of *anomie*.[4] This concept refers to a historical moment 'when society is disturbed by some painful crisis or by beneficent but abrupt transitions'. In such moments 'the scale is upset; but a new scale cannot be immediately improvised', and therefore 'time is required for the public conscience to reclassify men and things'.[5] Rational authority can do little to counteract this weakening of 'public conscience' because it does not speak the language of moral norms.

Gouldner writes that the 'soil on which sociology grew was manured by a pervasive anomie', at a time when 'the old patterns of legitimacy were losing or had lost their potency, while the emerging locus of power, the new bourgeoisie, had only the thinnest and most dubious legitimacy'.[6] What was important about sociology was its consciousness of this process, which lent the problem of the loss of authority a distinct modern dimension. It was no longer a question of a contest between two competing variants of authority – political versus religious or reason versus tradition – but the intimation that authority would be contested constantly, often to the point that its legitimacy could not be taken for granted. The fragile foundations on which authority appeared to rest were refracted through sociological theories that stressed its transient character. Saint-Simon and Comte expressed this dynamic through distinguishing between an organic and critical eras; others, such as Ludwig Stein, interpreted the history of authority through cycles that reflected the struggle between universalistic and individualistic norms.

The emergence of the new discipline of sociology can be interpreted as a response to the nineteenth century's quest for certainty and authority in an era of transition. Edward Ross, another founding figure in American sociology, reflected,

No doubt, as history shows us, there are times when every timber in the old house of order which has sheltered so many generations of men endures as if for a thousand years; and again there are seasons when one after another props settle, sills rot, beams crack, and the business of repair engages all minds. It would seem that in this century society is passing through such a season; and amid the decay

---

[4] See Gouldner (1973) p. 67.   [5] Durkheim (2002) p. 213.
[6] Gouldner (1973) p. 103.

of old authorities, reverences, and illusions in the critical atmosphere of our time many look for the roof and walls of the social order to come crashing upon our heads.[7]

Ross, a theorist of social control, was far more optimistic than most, believing that order could be maintained through enlightening 'the leaders of opinion'. In that way, 'the control of society over its members ought to become more conscious and effective than it now is, and the dismal see-sawing between change and reaction that has been the curse of this century ought to disappear'.[8] This statement of elitist/technocratic thinking expressed the aspiration of the emerging Anglo-American managerial imagination and, as Wolin argues, it encouraged the response of an ethos of organisation to the problem of order.[9] However, technocratic solutions avoided the fundamental issues to do with the moral power of authority, and existed in an uneasy relationship with the cultural influence of disenchantment.

Sociologists, like political philosophers and social commentators, regarded the principle of authority as an important subject for their disciplinary reflection. Their comments on the subject echoed the wider conversation about negotiating the tension between the principle of authority and of liberty. The Hungarian/German philosopher and sociologist Luwig Stein claimed that 'the principle of authority was permanent', but that the motives 'upon which it was based change'.[10] Giddings also reflected on the contrast between the 'the principle of liberty' and the 'principle of authority'.[11] Leonard Trelawny Hobhouse, who became the first full professor of sociology in Britain, wrote about the role of the principle of authority in establishing the 'elements of outward order'.[12]

The emerging sociological theories of authority overlapped with the ideas that were already in circulation, discussed in the previous chapter; in practice, they accepted the unstated definition of the principle of authority as expressing a certainty that stood in sharp contrast to the uncertainties posed by the democratisation of society. Sociologists attempted to elaborate all the questions raised by the decline of traditional and religious authority – the problem of order, the question deference, the role of public opinion – in a more systematic and, as they argued, 'scientific' manner than had been accomplished previously. In his study of the professionalisation of sociology, Haney asserts that the

---

[7] Ross (1898) pp. 827–8.   [8] Ross (1898) p. 821.
[9] See Wolin (2004) Chapter 10.
[10] His book on authority, published in 1902 is discussed in *Notes and Abstracts* (1902) pp. 419–20.
[11] Giddings (1896) p. 730.   [12] See his essay on *Liberalism* (1911).

'nineteenth-century social scientist perceived the scientific identity as the means to the preservation of traditional moral authority'.[13] However, despite their interest in the reconstitution of moral authority, most leading social scientists understood that it could not be achieved through its traditional form.

Although many of its pioneers believed that sociology constituted a distinct discipline with its own intellectual agenda, the problems it engaged with were integral to the public debates of the time. For example, Franklin Henry Giddings wrote at length about the different dimensions of the problem of order. His article 'The Nature and Conduct of Political Majorities' (1892) investigated the influence of majority rule on public life: although he believed that 'undisciplined public opinion at first so easily goes wrong', he predicted that with experience and education political progress could correct such mistakes.[14] Giddings's prognosis of the future fate of majority rule was based on the conviction that 'however republican in spirit a community may be, and however intelligent its members, its public opinion is moulded by a few leading minds'.[15] Such sentiments provided a relatively optimistic alternative to the arguments of earlier aristocratic liberal theorists such as Tocqueville. His subsequent writing was directed towards the management of 'majority absolutism', and he contrasted circumstances where the 'mob-crowd bent of vengeance' prevails with a situation where 'individuals in general defer' and 'respect and obey' a rationally founded 'collective opinion'.[16]

Durkheim, too, regarded the management of public opinion as a key challenge facing sociology. For Durkheim, authority required its acceptance by public opinion. From this perspective, legal and moral precepts are founded upon 'public consciousness': 'If that opinion ceased to feel the weight of their authority, then that authority would be as if it no longer existed', since 'it would no longer act upon conscience'. At a debate held in 1908, Durkheim told his audience to be on 'guard against the derogatory sense which is often given to the word "opinion"': the prevailing association of opinion with 'mindless prejudice or fanciful feelings', according to him, was only 'one of its aspects', and was the 'end result of the experiences of people over the centuries – and that had imparted authority to it'. For Durkheim, 'morality and opinion are closely intertwined realities'.[17]

Durkheim's views on morality and opinion were strongly influenced by those of Comte, who 'laid stress upon the value of public opinion as an

---

[13] Haney (2008) p. 9.   [14] Giddings (1892) p. 131.
[15] Cited in Ross (1896) p. 765.   [16] Giddings (1906) pp. 11 and 25.
[17] 'Debate on Political Economy and Sociology' in Durkheim (1982) pp. 233–4.

effective agent of social control'. Comte believed that opinion was 'practically the sole guaranty of public morality', which in the future was likely to become the 'great regulator of society'.[18] This point was developed at length by the German sociologist Ferdinand Tonnies in his classic study, *Gemeinschaft und Gesellschaft* (1887). Tonnies regarded public opinion as a product of modernity; one that played a role analogous to religion in a traditional setting. His contrast between community (*Gemeinschaft*) and society or association (*Gesellschaft*) corresponded to a parallel shift from traditional religion to public opinion. Tonnies wrote that it is 'public opinion' that brings the morality of *Gesellschaft* into 'rules and formulas'; nevertheless, he was concerned that public opinion could pass 'easily from the demand for freedom' to 'that of despotism'.[19]

As has been widely noted, the sociological response to the problem of order had as its focus the threat from below. Tonnies warned that the 'class struggle' is 'unconditional' and 'it recognizes no estates, no natural masters'.[20] But the problem of authority was not confined to the question of how to gain the deference of the masses. Georg Simmel, whose writings on the corrosive impact of rationalisation on moral and cultural life retain their vitality to this day, explained how the problem of authority also undermined the solidarity of the ruling elites.[21] Simmel's discussion of the 'calculating character of modern times' pointed to the crucial development of the cleavage between political/economic power and morality, which means that the ethos of rationalisation finds it difficult, if not impossible, to convert power into authority.

The principal response of sociology to the dissonant relation between power and morality was to develop an account of society as itself the source of authority. As we noted previously, this approach was vigorously pursued by traditionalist and conservative critics of modernity. As one survey of the history of sociology notes, this legacy of 'sociologistic positivism was passed from reactionary philosophers such as Bonald and De Maister, through Saint-Simon and Comte through to Durkheim and other modern sociologists'.[22] Krieger contends that sociologists tried to work out an autonomous role for social authority 'consonant with the autonomy of the social science which they were establishing'.[23] In the early stage of its development, one of the main accomplishments of social science was to crystallise ideas about society as the site of authority.

---

[18] Comte is cited in Becker and Barnes (1961) pp. 590–1.
[19] See Tonnies (1955) p. 269.   [20] Tonnies (1955) p. 25.
[21] See Simmel (1990) pp. 441–2.   [22] Becker and Barnes (1961) p. 498.
[23] Krieger (1968) p. 156.

Social authority

Throughout the nineteenth century, there was a manifest tendency to divest authority from its political connotations and to reformulate it as a social force. Giddings took the political concept of sovereignty and reformulated it as 'social fact of sovereignty'.[24] Simmel tended to interpret domination as a coeval with the emergence of society and as a presupposition of the process of socialisation:

For we must observe that superiority and inferiority is by no means a formation necessarily subsequent to the existence of 'society'. It is one of the forms in which 'society' comes into being. It is one of the manifold interactions between individuals, the sum of which we designate as the socialization of the individuals concerned.[25]

In his historical investigation of the different forms of subordination, Simmel wrote that the 'relationships of superordination and subordination', which 'play an immense role in social life' have a spontaneous character. The subordinate 'participates in a sociological event which requires his spontaneous cooperation.'[26] Simmel's analysis of subordination, which has echoes of Hegel's master-slave dialectic, placed emphasis on spontaneous cooperation in the act of obedience to authority,[27] writing that 'what is called "authority" presupposes, in a much higher degree than is usually recognized, a freedom on the part of the person subjected to authority'.[28]

Simmel's statement that 'even in the most oppressive and cruel cases of subordination, there is still a considerable measure of freedom' was in line with the conceptions of mainstream twentieth-century sociology.[29] Krieger points out that 'the great pioneers of sociology assiduously recast authority into a social relation signifying a voluntary or conventional interaction categorically detached from its political connection with coercive power'.[30] Of course the sociological accounts of the authority of society acknowledged its power to compel, and ideas of spontaneously formed social solidarity ran in parallel with the recognition that society possessed significant resources required to dominate the individual. This idea was developed at length by Durkheim: in the programmatic statement where he claimed to delineate 'the exact field of sociology' as the study of social facts, he wrote that 'a social fact is identifiable through the power of external coercion which exerts or is capable of exerting

---

[24] Giddings (1906) p. 11.   [25] Simmel (1896) p. 169.   [26] Simmel (1971) pp. 98–9.
[27] For a discussion of dominion and bondage in Hegel see Chapter 2 of Shklar (1976).
[28] Simmel (1971) p. 98.   [29] Simmel (1971) p. 97.   [30] Krieger (1968) p. 156.

upon individuals'.[31] Compulsion exercised in this depoliticised form was contrasted to the coercive power of the political, and represented as an inevitable fact of life.

Like Durkheim, *fin-de-siècle* sociology embraced the authority of society as the foundation of order. Society was frequently represented as possessing the power to forge conformity to custom and laws, and help establish consensus about norms, values and social solidarity. In his review of the state of his discipline Lester Ward, the first president of the American Sociological Association, pointed to the numerous recently developed concepts through which the compelling power of society was represented. His sociology of coercion stressed the moral dimension of what he characterised as 'social constraint':

Quite a school of sociologists has recently arisen which holds, under varying forms and with a varying terminology, that the principal social fact is an unconscious coercion of the members of society to do, or refrain from doing, certain things. This coercion is never physical, but always moral, i.e., psychic.[32]

In this presentation of a veritable *Who's Who* of world sociology, Ward drew attention to the French sociologist Gabriel Tarde and his concept of 'imitation', going on to review the work of the physiologist William Carpenter and the English philosopher and evolutionary sociologist, Herbert Spencer. Both Carpenter and Spencer wrote about the role of impersonal compulsion of 'social influences',[33] and Spencer used the concept of public opinion to signify a source of authority that can 'exercise a coercion'. Ward's review alluded to the work of the French philosopher Alfred Fouille, who developed the concept of 'collective determinism' and to the category of 'social imperative' elaborated by Ludwig Stein. Noting that 'social imperative is among the happiest contributions to sociological terminology',[34] Ward went on to praise Edward Ross's concept of 'social ascendancy' for illuminating the workings of social control and social influence'.[35] These variants of the concept of social control had as their presupposition the idea of a socially constructed authority either acting in lieu of political power or buttressing it.

What distinguished Marx from the other founders of sociology was his emphasis on the coercive dimensions of social power: he regarded the domination exercised through social power as no less despotic than that of the political state. In the nineteenth century, the main exception to the representation of the association of social authority with a non-despotic

---

[31] Durkheim (1982) p. 56.   [32] Ward (1902) p. 754.   [33] Ward (1902) pp. 753–7.
[34] Ward (1902) p. 757.   [35] Ward (1902) p. 758.

and voluntary dimension of subordination is to be found in the writings of Marx.

Marx's critique of capitalist society has as one of its principal objectives the demystification of the working of political power and authority. His theory of capitalist domination is based on the idea that the separation of economic from political compulsion obscures the social character of domination. This occurs because property in the form of capital acquires an independent form where its material properties, not its relationship to labour, appear as its distinctive character: 'social action takes the form of action of objects, which rule the producers instead of being ruled by them'.[36] As a result the social character of productive activity confronts individuals as autonomous power.

Marx contends that capital as social power not only confronts and dominates the working class, but also compels individual capitalists to behave in accordance with its dictates. These are social relations that work behind people's backs, and the fact that capital dominates does not mean that individual entrepreneurs are able to rule or regulate the process of production. Thus the capitalist holds power as the personification of capital;[37] he 'does not rule over his labourer through any personal qualities he may have, but only in so far as he is "capital", and his domination is only that of materialised labour over living labour'.[38] The tendency towards the materialisation of social relations is captured by Marx's concept of commodity fetishism. This concept, relating to the personification of things and the materialisation of persons, is central to Marx's sociology of authority.

One of the main arguments of Marx's sociology is that since capitalist relations are spontaneously reproduced through the market, it is only in rare instances that capital appears as what it really is – a relation of domination. Marx's representation of the spontaneous reproduction of social relations can be seen as development of the arguments advanced by eighteenth- and early nineteenth-century political economy. Scottish political economists like Adam Smith, and liberal and utilitarian thinkers, frequently claimed that the pursuit of individual interests would lead to the spontaneous formation of order. One important difference between classical political economy and Marx is the interpretation of the pursuit of individual interests. Marx claimed that the social relations of production only appear to be free and voluntary, and that the free and voluntary relationship of producers is subject to the domination of capital. But since domination is usually perceived as a political act – one that often

---

[36] Marx (1974) p. 79.   [37] See Marx (1971) p. 264.   [38] Marx (1969) p. 390.

appears to fly in the face of the freedoms formally upheld by society – its social coercive character is obscured.

The separation of the social from the political lends authority, in its modern market-related form, a distinct historical character. Marx wrote that,

> the authority assumed by a capitalist as the personification of capital in the direct process of production, the social function performed by him in his capacity as manager and ruler of production, is essentially different from the authority exercised on the basis of production by means of slaves, serfs, etc.[39]

This difference is due to the fact under capitalism, domination is exercised in a relatively spontaneous manner and is not typically enforced through politics or through a system of fixed hierarchy. So authority is not exercised through 'political or theocratic rulers as under earlier modes of production'; its powers 'assert themselves as an overwhelming natural law in relation to free will'.[40]

Marx's characterisation of capital as a form of coercive power emphasised the social as opposed to the political aspects of domination. But having considered the paradox of formal equality co-existing with social compulsion, Marx did not go deeply into the sociological and cultural aspects of authority; and despite his radical inclinations, his reaction to nineteenth-century anarchism indicated that he was concerned with what he perceived as a simplistic counterposition of authority to autonomy. Marx's major contribution was to call into question theories that treated order as the unproblematic consequence of spontaneous forces. In contrast to Marx, the theories of social authority that emerged sought develop a harmonious relationship between society and order. Comte's aphorism of 'Order and Progress' indicated that authority was not only a subject of study but sociology's cause; Durkheim provided the most coherent argument in favour of this cause.

Of all the sociologists, Weber went furthest in conceptualising the relationship between domination and authority. Unlike Durkheim he made a clear distinction between social domination and authority. He interpreted domination as a much broader exercise of power than that which is mediated through authority. According to Weber domination 'can be produced' through 'exchange relations' and through pre-eminent cultural institutions of society. His interest was in a narrower form of domination, which was 'identical with '*authoritarian power of command*' – a 'command that is accepted as a "valid" norm'.[41]

---

[39] Marx (1971) p. 881.   [40] Marx (1971) p. 881.   [41] Weber (1978) pp. 945 and 946.

The reconciliation of modernity with moral authority

Durkheim's 1897 masterpiece, *Suicide* possesses a well-deserved reputation for being a pioneering exemplar of modern sociology. It is also of fundamental importance for providing one of the most important sociological statements on the problem of authority or, more specifically, the consequences of its absence. In this study Durkheim investigated some of the psychological and sociological processes that encourage deference to custom and tradition on the one hand, and public opinion on the other.[42] His aim was to establish if there is a relationship between cultures of authority and rates of suicide. His contrast between the Roman Catholic Church's 'hierarchical system of authority', with the greater emphasis on the 'religious individualism' of the Protestant, led Durkheim to conclude that the 'proclivity of Protestantism for suicide must relate to the spirit of free inquiry that animates this religion'.[43]

For Durkheim, an increase in the rate of suicide was a symptom of the erosion of the authority of tradition over individual behaviour. He assumed that a 'highly developed traditionalism always more or less restricts the activity of the individual', and the 'greater the number of dogmas and precepts the interpretation of which is not left to individual consciences, the more authorities are required to tell their meaning: moreover, the more numerous these authorities, the more closely they surround and the better they restrain the individual'.[44] Durkheim suggested that the 'progressive weakening of collective and customary prejudices produces a trend to suicide'.[45] For Durkheim suicide represented a marker of social disorganisation. Through his focus on suicide, Durkheim sought to explore the consequences of the weakening of authority over individual behaviour in modern society.

What is significant about Durkheim's exploration of authority is that his attention is directed at grasping its foundational norms. What renders a relationship authoritative is that it is based on shared belief, common practices and an 'intense collective life'. He argued that the 'more numerous and strong these collective states of mind are, the stronger the integration of the religious community, and also the greater its preservative value'.[46] Durkheim's *Suicide* is also a study of the inter-relationship between the loss of the restraining influence of traditional authority and the moral pathology of its individualising effects. His is the cause of social integration and, at times, his exaltation of society conveyed a sense

[42] Durkheim (2002) pp. 75–82.   [43] Durkheim (2002) p. 112.
[44] Durkheim (2002) pp. 115–16.   [45] Durkheim (2002) p. 116.
[46] Durkheim (2002) pp. 124–5.

of missionary zeal. He claims that societies that are strongly integrated restrain the destructive behaviour of individuals. But when people refuse to accept as 'legitimate' the supremacy of society, it 'no longer possess the requisite authority to retain them in their duty if they wish to desert; and conscious of its own weakness, it even recognises their right to do freely what it can no longer prevent'.[47]

Durkheim claimed that individualisation and social disintegration created a mood of moral malaise. This sense of aimlessness has an impact on society itself – 'society cannot be conscious of its own decadence without feeling' that much of its activity is 'purposeless'. Perversely, as the sense of cultural pessimism gains resonance, it itself develops an authority over the behaviour of the individual to 'drive him more vigorously on the way to which he is already inclined by the state of moral distress directly aroused in him by the disintegration of society'.[48]

Durkheim's concern about the pathology of 'excessive individualisation' was linked to a wider preoccupation with its tendency to encourage social unrest and conflict. In a sense, the diminishing capacity of society to restrain behaviour expressed itself in the problem not unlike that of the problem of deference, discussed on the other side of the Channel. Durkheim believed that human appetites and desires can only be restrained by a 'limit they recognise as just', which must come 'from an authority which they can respect, to which they yield spontaneously'. Who possesses such an authority? Durkheim's answer was unequivocal:

Either directly and as a whole, or through the agency of one of its organs, society alone can play this moderating role; for it is the only moral power superior to the individual, the authority of which he accepts.[49]

From this perspective, through the moral authority it enjoys, society can develop a consensus of what constitutes the common interests to which individual ambition must defer.

For deference to work, people need to understand that the rules of society are just and that all must make 'sacrifices and concessions' to the 'public interest'. Durkheim believed that 'moral pressure' is indispensable and that 'moral discipline' is essential to 'make those less favoured by nature accept the lesser advantages which they owe to the chance of birth'. But though 'authority is necessary to impose this order on individuals', the power of domination 'must also be obeyed through respect, not fear'.[50] What Durkheim feared was the coincidence of a social crisis

---

[47] Durkheim (2002) p. 168.   [48] Durkheim (2002) p. 173.
[49] Durkheim (2002) p. 210.   [50] Durkheim (2002) pp. 211–12.

with cultural disorientation; more specifically, the concurrence of the rising aspiration of the lower classes with the loss of authority of traditional rules.[51]

Durkheim was certain that the authority of past traditions cannot be brought back to life, writing that 'religions will no longer be able to exert very deep or wide sway on consciences'.[52] And unlike many traditionalist thinkers, he did not blame the advance of science and knowledge for the loss of social cohesion: rather, it was precisely because tradition had lost its force and faith was already deeply shaken that the new modern ideas were able to triumph. Science was the most suitable instrument for replacing the 'authority of vanished traditions':

Once established beliefs have been carried away by the current of affairs, they cannot be artificially re-established; only reflection can guide us in life, after this. Once the social instinct is blunted, intelligence is the only guide left us and we have to reconstruct a conscience by its means.[53]

While such an undertaking was 'dangerous', there was no alternative.

In the event Durkheim, as previously noted, looked to the past for inspiration and invested hope in professional corporations as the potential focus for authority. He claimed that such institutions could, through the exercise of 'moral discipline', force the powerful to moderate their ambitions and prevent the weak from 'endlessly multiplying their protest'. He observed that 'standing above its own members, it would have all necessary authority to demand indispensable sacrifices and concessions imposed upon them'.[54]

From the vantage point of today, Durkheim's observations on the resurrection of authority through professional corporations appears almost as an afterthought to a serious exploration of the problem of moral authority. Yet there was a clear logic driving this abstract proposal, which was the recognition that the prevailing institutions dominating society were far too distant from people to provide moral guidance. Durkheim believed that with the decline of religion and traditional institutions the State had become over-burdened with the task of moral regulation, which it was too distant from people's lives to exercise, and that what was required were intermediary institutions to influence individual behaviour.[55] Authoritative institutions required a normative foundation: 'nothing but a moral power can set a law for men', and what was required was a moral authority that was relevant to the times.[56]

---

[51] Durkheim (2002) pp. 213–14.   [52] Durkheim (2002) p. 341.
[53] Durkheim (2002) p. 124.   [54] Durkheim (2002) p. 350.
[55] Durkheim (2002) pp. 346–57.   [56] Durkheim (2002) p. 351.

Five years after the publication of *Suicide*, Durkheim delivered a series of lectures on Moral Education at the Sorbonne. Durkheim's interest in moral education and the socialisation of children was linked to his continuing apprehension regarding the state of moral authority. In contrast to his earlier work, he adopted a more explicitly critical stance towards prevailing cultural trends and advocated the virtues of moral discipline to counter them. He at times adopts a moralising narrative, and is clearly drawn towards societies that possess 'the self-mastery, the power of inhibition, the authority over themselves that is developed by the performance of duty' such as that of the era of 'Louis XIV or that of Augustus'.[57] These are historical moments 'when society has come to be quite fully integrated'. He contrasted these heroic moments with his own epoch in the following terms:

Indeed, history records no crisis as serious as that in which European societies have been involved for more than a century. Collective discipline in its traditional form has lost its authority, as the divergent tendencies troubling the public conscience and the resulting general anxiety demonstrate.[58]

Durkheim's sociology of authority has as its focus the historical relationship between foundational moral norms and their capacity to influence and restrain human behaviour, and gain deference to the prevailing moral order. Like most other sociologists of the time, Weber in particular, he was sensitive to the potential for disorientation caused by the rationalisation of morality. His concern with the decoupling of a normative foundation from a rationalised morality was explicitly expressed in his discussion of moral education. He was certain that 'historical development' dictated that schools had no choice but to offer a 'completely rational moral education', which excluded 'all principles derived from revealed religion'. At the same time he warned about the tremendous challenge involved in this reorientation towards a rationalised morality. Durkheim noted that historically, the 'essential elements of morality' were never 'expressed save in a religious guise'. Consequently, the danger was, that 'if we begin to eliminate everything religious from the traditional system without providing any substitute, we run the risk of eliminating essential moral ideas and sentiments'.[59] According this analysis, a rational morality could never entirely dispense with religion.[60]

Yet the process of rationalisation and the ascendancy of the authority of science contained an anti-religious imperative. Science undermined faith and the speculative dimension of religion, but the authority of

[57] Durkheim (1973) p. 101.   [58] Durkheim (1973) p. 101.
[59] Durkheim (1973) p. 19.   [60] Durkheim (1974) p. 48.

the rules of science does not stem 'uniquely from their objective value' because:

> In the last resort, the value which we attribute to science depends upon the idea which we collectively form of its nature and role in life, that is as much as to say that it expresses a state of public opinion. In all social life, in fact, science rests upon public opinion.[61]

Science as a form of social authority requires the validation of society, which is mediated through public opinion. The task of the young discipline of sociology was to transform public opinion into a subject of science and make it more conscious of its role. 'It is undoubtedly true that this opinion can be taken as the object of a study and a science made of it; this is what sociology principally consists in', Durkheim concluded.[62]

Like numerous nineteenth-century social commentators, Durkheim raised the importance of finding a 'substitute' for, or functional equivalent of, traditional religion. However, he went further than his contemporaries in examining the difficulties involved in this enterprise. He was aware that the shift from a religion and tradition based morality to one that was founded on reason had a very different content – a 'rational morality cannot have the same content as one that depends upon some authority other than reason'.[63] His analysis indicated that rationalism was paralleled by the development of a heightened sense of individual consciousness and a 'refinement in moral sensitivity', which disposes people to regard many hitherto taken-for-granted ideas about rights and obligations as 'unjust'. As a result, the 'new authority of reason' can turn on those traditions that still persist; and he warned that 'we must take care lest we impoverish morality in the process of rationalizing it' and 'anticipate' its consequences.[64]

In his last major work, *The Elementary Forms of Religious Life* (1912), Durkheim attempted to reconcile the demand for rational morality informed by science with morals that have a wider meaning. His project was directed towards society, which, because it possesses the 'most powerful combination of physical and moral forces', is capable of directing its members towards a 'higher life'. He concluded by stating that 'sociology appears destined to open a new way to the science of man' and provide humanity with access to a new morality of society.[65]

Unlike most of his contemporaries, who withdrew from grappling with the problem of elaborating a moral foundation for rational authority,

---

[61] Durkheim (1968) p. 438.   [62] Durkheim (1968) p. 438.
[63] Durkheim (1973) p. 19.   [64] Durkheim (1973) p. 20.
[65] Durkheim (1968) p. 446.

Durkheim sought to reconstruct it through studying its basic forces and sentiments. His investigation of the historical variations of religious and moral norms led him to the conclusion that it is social pressure, expressed through a variety of rules and rituals, that both creates and regulates moral life. He claimed that society moulds people, inculcates them with moral sentiments, and prescribes how they should behave. It is almost as if society by itself spontaneously produces the moral resources necessary to validate authority: 'Our moral conscience is its product and reflects it'.[66] At times, Durkheim appears to endow the 'collective consciousness' of society with a quasi-sacred character, observing that 'the collective consciousness is the highest form of psychic life, since it is the consciousness of the consciousness'.[67]

In investing of society with a 'remarkable authority', Durkheim reaches the limits of his attempt to find a 'substitute' for religion. The erosion of the distinction between the social and the moral, and between society and authority, appears outwardly as a product of social determinism. However, the unproblematic rendering of this relationship between society and authority lends morality an almost naturalistic character. This provides Durkheim with a provisional solution, albeit at a high level of abstraction: 'Not only is society a moral authority . . . but there is every reason to consider it the type and the source of all moral authority'.[68] Society is, in Durkheim's words, an 'imperative authority'.[69]

Durkheim's conflation of the moral and the social was accompanied by an explicit anti-individualist orientation. Unlike Weber, Durkheim is dismissive of the 'Great Leader' theory of charismatic authority, claiming that it is society that recognises and endows man with their greatness. It is from 'society that all authority emanates' and provides the 'prestige that 'elevates the persons possessing it beyond themselves'.[70] His generic concept of authority is distinct from any specific (including political) institution; it is a simple but abstract idea that represents the moral power exercised through the 'collective being' of society:

Authority is a quality with which a being, either actual or imaginary is invested through his relationship with given individuals, and it is because of this alone that he is thought by the latter to be endowed with powers superior to those they find in themselves.[71]

This account offers not so much a definition of authority as a statement about its subjective quality. Thus 'it is of no importance' whether 'these

---

[66] Durkheim (1973) p. 90.   [67] Durkheim (1968) p. 444.
[68] Durkheim (1973) p. 90.   [69] Durkheim (1973) p. 93.
[70] Durkheim (1973) p. 91.   [71] Durkheim (1973) p. 88.

powers are real or imaginary'; what matters is that 'they exist as real in people's minds'. Belief 'exists in minds, not things' and that is 'why authority is called moral'.[72] Moral authority constitutes a pure form in that it must be obeyed out of 'respect for it and for this reason alone'; it exists independently of political calculation or instrumental reasoning, and 'to the extent that any other element enters into conduct, to that extent it loses its moral character'.[73]

Durkheim's analysis of the power of collective beliefs overlaps with the nineteenth century's fascination with the power of public opinion. He regarded 'collective sentiments' and 'the condition of public opinion as forces that are 'quite as real and active as the forces that fill the physical world',[74] and from this perspective the pressure public opinion serves as a moralised species of discipline. Indeed, 'the fundamental element of morality is the spirit of discipline'.[75] Durkheim was an unapologetic advocate of moral discipline. He criticised Bentham and utilitarian thinkers because they regarded morality as a 'pathology', and *laissez-faire* political economists and 'socialist theoreticians' alike because of their critical stance towards the regulation of society. Durkheim wrote scathingly how 'the notion of an authority dominating life and administering law seemed to them to be an archaic idea, a prejudice that could not persist', and warned that 'it is life itself that makes its own laws'.[76] His comments regarding his opponents' celebration of the infinite were derisive: 'Here we have the lofty sentiments par excellence, since by means of it man elevates himself beyond all limits imposed by nature and liberates himself at least ideally, from all restrictions that might diminish him'.[77] Durkheim was certain that people should be discouraged from being drawn towards a 'limitless horizon'; what was required was moral discipline and deference.

For Durkheim, effective moral authority and discipline serve as guarantors of a healthy society. His preoccupation with the destructive potential of moral disorientation led him to adopt a suspicious stance towards claims for expanding freedoms and rights. As he put it, 'the theories that celebrate the beneficence of unrestricted liberties are apologists for a diseased state'. This hostility towards the call for greater liberties was fuelled by his conviction that his was an era where 'authority is usually weakened through the loss of traditional discipline – a time that may easily give rise to a spirit of anarchy'.[78] His concept of *anomie* refers to a condition where

---

[72] Durkheim (1973) p. 88.   [73] Durkheim (1973) p. 30.
[74] Durkheim (1973) p. 92.   [75] Durkheim (1973) p. 31.
[76] Durkheim (1973) p. 36.   [77] Durkheim (1973) p. 36.
[78] Durkheim (1973) p. 54.

the 'lack of collective force' is too weak to restrain individual egoism.[79] In this condition, the pursuit of individual liberation has the character of what Comte described as the 'disease of the Western world'. Such individuals 'are not free because they are chained to their own inexhaustible desires'.[80]

Authority naturalised

Durkheim's elevation of society to the status of an all-pervasive determining force appears as the opposite to the more naturalistic evolutionary theories of Herbert Spencer. However, at times his social determinism comes across as the equivalent of a natural force: 'If the principle of determinism is solidly established to-day in the physical and natural sciences, it is only a century ago that it was first introduced into the social sciences and its authority there is still contested'.[81] The task is for social science is thus to adopt the 'laborious methods of the natural sciences to gradually scatter the darkness'.[82]

A highly deterministic epistemology was a characteristic feature of early modern sociology. It was a determinism that was outwardly anti-individualistic, but whose dominant target was human subjectivity and its exercise of agency. Marx's theory of subjectivity represented a counterpoint to this trend. Although Marx is often accused of going too far down the road of social determinism, he also emphasised the history-making potential of human subjectivity. He was critical of the nineteenth century's fascination with Social Darwinist theories of history and society, criticising the 'intellectual laziness' of the idea that 'all history must be subsumed in one single great natural law'. Marx's objection was premised on the view that teleological views exclude human beings from history; 'thus life appears as non-historical, while the historical appears as something separated from ordinary life, something extra-superterrestrial'.[83]

Sociological thought in the late nineteenth century possessed a strong teleological view of change, and its invective against individualism often had as its target the belief in human agency. Albion Small of the University of Chicago, the founder of the first Department of Sociology in the United States, expressed this sentiment in the first article to be published in the first issue of the *American Journal of Sociology*, in 1896. The article, titled 'The Era of Sociology', justified the need for a new discipline in

[79] Durkheim (2002) p. 350.   [80] Giddens (1978) p. 117.
[81] Durkheim (1968) p. 27.   [82] Durkheim (1968) p. 27.
[83] See 'Marx to Kugelman', 27 June 1870, in Marx and Engels (1988) p. 527, and Marx (1976) pp. 50 and 55.

these terms: 'Modern thought assumes that the fixed factors in human conditions are insignificant as compared with the elements that may be determined by agreement'. Small wrote scathingly about how 'popular judgment is just now intoxicated with the splendid half truth that society is what men choose to make it', and indicted 'popular social philosophy' for its 'speculation about institutional rearrangement without due estimate of human limitations'.[84]

It is likely that the criticism levelled against the idea that 'society is what men choose to make it' was influenced by the presentiment of conflict and instability to come. Statements that reflected on the uncertainties of an era of transition were typically coupled with reassuring declarations about the compelling power of social authority. This argument was systematically developed by Herbert Spencer, who coined the term 'survival of the fittest'. Having located authority as natural fact of life in the animal kingdom, Spencer extended his analysis to the prevalence of what he described as the 'consciousness of authority' in human society. Spencer argued that although this consciousness of authority can assume a variety of historical forms it always possesses the capacity for coercion.[85] Spencer's concept of 'consciousness of authority' suggested that the internalisation of authority-responsive attitudes had a natural quality.

'The tendency to the constructing of authority may be traced back to the animal kingdom', argued Stein's evolutionary rendering of the history of authority. Writing of the 'struggle for existence', Stein claimed that 'discipline is the soul of struggle and authority is the soul of discipline'. In this way, human survival becomes contingent on the discipline it provides. What's interesting about these quasi-biological interpretations of authority is that they rarely lose sight of blending it with a moral dimension. So although Stein claims that the 'first ground of authority, lies in its natural growth', he also claims that it requires a moral and cultural dimension: 'nature commands a subjection to the principle of authority, she does not proclaim the kind of authority to be established'.[86]

In the United States, the sociology establishment was drawn towards a notion of order and authority that was the outcome of social and natural imperatives. Lester Ward looked forward to discovering its secret in what he called the 'sociological laboratory':

---

[84] Small (1895) p. 3.
[85] Spencer (1978) Accessed from http://oll.libertyfund.org/title/333/40653 on 2012–06–08.
[86] See 'Notes and Abstracts' (1902) pp. 419–20.

Further researches in this fruitful direction will doubtless carry the principles back toward the biological plane and show that a large part of social control is or once was a true selection, and that much of the spirit of submission to social imperatives has become constitutional through a long process of elimination of the unfit, i.e., the unsocial.[87]

During the first decade of the twentieth century, sociology attempted to strengthen the authority of the social by providing with an evolutionary foundation.

In his discussion of social control, Giddings wrote that society 'by its instinctive and by rational effort, carries further and brings to greater precision that process which in its unconscious mode we call natural selection'.[88] From this perspective order, authority and discipline are not simply moral accomplishments, but are the outcomes of an evolutionary imperative of the 'struggle for existence'.[89]

Giddings was not totally reassured by his synthesis of social control and natural selection. Although he wrote that 'differences of mental ability and of moral power' mean that 'inferior men will continue to defer to their superiors', he looked to the political intervention of an intelligent elite to correct the anti-authoritarian cultural temper of his time. 'The destinies of political democracy will, therefore, be determined ultimately by the character of the aristocracy that rules the state behind the constitution', he predicted. He was critical of 'the democracy that has rebelled against the traditional modes or forms of authority'.[90]

Even sociologists who were intellectually distant from the project of interpreting society through the prism of the principles of evolution tended to present social authority as a necessity for disciplining society. Simmel wrote that,

Occasionally, the consciousness of being under coercion, of being subject to a subordinate authority, is revolting or oppressive – whether the authority be an ideal or social law, an arbitrarily decreeing personality or an executor of higher norms. But, for the majority of men, coercion probably is an irreplaceable support and cohesion of the inner and outer life.[91]

In this way, the psychological need for coercion reconciled the exercise of external power with moral discipline.

The tendency to naturalise the need for authority, like the argument for the spontaneous formation of order, had to contend with powerful currents of anti-authoritarian sentiment. Plebeian political movements

---

[87] Ward (1902) p. 759.   [88] Giddings (1909) p. 574.
[89] Giddings (1909) p. 579.   [90] Giddings (1896) p. 729.
[91] Simmel (1971) p. 34.

appeared to be gaining wide support, and those in authority seemed confused about how to exercise their power. In such circumstances, it was not sufficient to assert the omnipotence of social authority; it was also essential to explain its normative foundation. Nor did it suffice to attribute to society itself the capacity to self-generate a collective consciousness that could validate authority.

Sociology and rationalisation

The fatalistic sensibility associated with the naturalisation of authority was also expressed through theories that emphasised the coercive power of impersonal forces. This idea was most systematically developed by Marx, who claimed that the compelling power of the social relations embodied in capital operate as if they are the forces of nature. The inherently dominating power of capital is mediated by free economic relations, which make political authority appear as autonomous from society. The impersonal forces of social domination has a tendency to extend and stabilise itself beyond its origins, leading to what Marcuse has described as the 'reification of authority',[92] which develops through the consolidation of the legal system and its institutionalisation in the state. Lukàcs wrote that 'the organs of authority harmonise to such an extent with the (economic) laws governing men's lives, or seem so overwhelmingly superior that men experience them as natural forces, as the necessary environment for their existence'; and 'as a result they submit to them freely'.[93]

In his path-breaking investigation of the sociology of impersonal domination, Lukàcs developed the concept of reification – the objectification of social relations and their subsumption to rational criteria. In this essay, the influence of Max Weber and his study of the theory of rationalisation is clearly evident.[94] The process of rationalisation – the rise of an impersonal order, where domination is exercised through legal-rational forms through an instrumentally driven nation state and the bureaucratisation of social life – represents a dominant theme of Weber's historical sociology, providing important insights into the corrosive relationship between the ascendancy of an impersonal regime of instrumental calculation and religion. Rationalisation not only devalues cultural and religious values – it also alters the very meaning of religion, as every increase of rationalism in empirical science 'increasingly pushes religion from the rational to the

---

[92] Marcuse (2008) p. 93.
[93] Lukàcs (1920) 'Legality and Illegality in Lukàcs (1971) p. 257.
[94] See Lukàcs (1923) 'Reification and the Consciousness of the Proletariat' in Lukàcs (1971).

irrational realm'.[95] In this way, rationalisation neutralises the potential of religion to provide the moral resources required for the validation of authority.

The tendency towards the expansion of rationalised authority and its institutionalisation through bureaucracy is one of the dominant features of modernity. Its ethos of calculating instrumentality has had the effect of estranging people from the institution of bureaucracy. Nietzsche's reaction – 'State is the name of the coldest of all cold monsters'[96] – was based on what he perceived as the tendency of the process of rationalisation to devalue culture. Influenced by Nietzsche, Weber regarded the trend towards the rationalisation of society as a corrosive force that devalues meanings and values, and developed his concept of an impersonal form of domination exercised through the law and administration. However, the transformation of legal-rational domination into moral authority is fraught with tension. As Gane notes, 'it gives rise to an impersonal order of social relations or "external life" in which personal or ultimate values and beliefs are subordinated increasingly to rational considerations of wordly conduct'.[97] Distanced from ultimate values, it is difficult to reconcile legal-rational domination with the exercise of moral authority.

The limits of legal-rational domination were evident to Tonnies, arguably the first sociologist to explore the implication of rationalisation for relations of authority. Tonnies noted the 'veiled hatred and contempt' of the modern rationalised state towards the customs and traditions of community life, describing a 'revolution in social order', which led to the contract becoming the foundation of the new system where the 'rational will of *Gesellschaft*' dominates institutional and cultural life. Tonnies noted that depth of moral life diminishes as religion and traditional values are displaced by science.[98] Paradoxically, the very process of rationalisation deprives the state of the fundamental moral values that it requires for validation, and Tonnies predicted that it was 'highly improbable' that the state could invent or construct a morality that would provide its authority with a normative foundation.[99] The rationalised modern state, he concluded, 'means the doom of culture itself'.[100]

Paradoxically, early sociological thinkers responded to the apparent failure of rational authority to provide communities with meaning by adopting a counter-rationalist approach. If by rational authority we understand a form of authority that 'derives from conscious and

[95] Weber (1915a) p. 351.   [96] Nietzsche (1969) p. 70.
[97] Gane (2002) p. 24.   [98] Tonnies (1955) pp. 263–5.
[99] Tonnies (1955) pp. 268–9.   [100] Tonnies (1955) p. 270.

calculated effort to make the authority correspond to the express needs of the situation and to the norms of reason and logic', it can be argued that someone like Durkheim sought to assimilate science and instrumental reasoning to his concept of moral authority.[101] Durkheim, who went further than any other sociologist in his investigation of the moral foundation of society, never fully accepted the contradiction between a rational utilitarian ethos and one capable of providing society with meaning. His openness to the construction of a useful religion is testimony to his status as at once a moralist and reluctant utilitarian.

Utilitarian and rational forms of authority depend on their effectiveness in securing stated objectives and contributing to the well-being of individuals.[102] However, such forms of authority lack the moral power to motivate and to give meaning to the relationship of command and obedience. In this respect, the key sociological thinkers of the turn of the century – Durkheim, Simmel and Weber – understood that authority was not simply about the power of persuasion but also about giving meaning to human existence. Simmel in particular was interested in engaging with the modern individual's quest for existential authority, writing of an aspiration to deal with our 'disorderly, fragmentary and confused first perceptions of an object by distinguishing a stable and essential substance from the flux of movements, colours and accidents that leave the essence unchanged'. To resolve this tension, people look within themselves to find 'a being whose existence and character is centred in ourselves, a final authority which is independent of the outside world'. According to Simmel the search for ascertaining truth 'must have somewhere an ultimate basis, a supreme authority' that 'provides legitimation' without 'needing legitimation itself'.[103]

Simmel sought to resolve the problem of truth seeking by attempting to posit an open-ended orientation to authoritative knowledge that would restrain the corrosive influence of either scepticism or dogmatism:

If we admit that our knowledge may have somewhere an absolute norm, a supreme authority that is self-justifying, but that its content remains in constant flux because knowledge progresses and every content suggests another which would be more profound and more appropriate for the task, this is not scepticism; any more than it is scepticism when we admit, as is generally done, that while natural phenomena are subject to universal laws, these laws have to be corrected continually as our knowledge increases, as their content is always historically conditioned, and that they lack the absolute character that the concept implies.[104]

---

[101] See Nisbet (1970) p. 122.   [102] See Gouldner (1973) pp. 72–3.
[103] Simmel (1990) pp. 101 and 103.   [104] Simmel (1990) p. 104.

Simmel's discussion was directed towards a form of authority that was based on absolute norms, which were at the same time specific to the state of knowledge of the times. In this way, the changing character of life could be captured through a form of authority that could yield to new experience.

The question that Simmel left unanswered was what, in modern society, could serve to provide the content of authority. Simmel, like Durkheim and others sought to engage with the problem through exploring the historical variations of authority. His interest in the 'historico-psychological origin of those forms in which interactions take place between human beings' led him to develop a three-fold classification of the way that superiority or authority can be exercised: by an individual; by a group; or by an 'objective principle higher than individuals'.[105] His analysis points to the growing shift from personal to impersonal domination and its objectification.

Nisbet has argued that Simmel's analysis of objectivism 'can also mean transfer of power from person or group to social *norms*'. Nisbet thought that the 'objectification of power is revealed by such conceptions as the supremacy of the law, of the office, of the command, of abstract moral commandment'. The burden of this argument was to suggest that Simmel's analysis of the shift from the personal to the impersonal 'supplies the lasting element of the authority that inheres even in objective circumstances'.[106] However, experience indicates that it is precisely the objectification of human customs and relationships that denudes it of its original moral content. Thus while Simmel observed that 'subordination to the law' in ancient Athens appeared 'thoroughly adequate' precisely because it is 'free from any personal characteristics', he also noted that Plato believed that in the 'ideal state, the insight of the ideal ruler stands above the law'.[107] One important historical detail that Simmel did not discuss was that the impersonal law of ancient Greece was inseparable from its living custom and traditions. In contrast, a modern system of impersonal, procedure-based law lacks the motivational content of moral norms. It is worth noting that nowhere in Simmel's writing is there an example of a modern, spontaneously crafted form of impersonal but still meaningful type of authority: all his examples of effective authority are drawn from history.

Simmel's example of the 'primary form of the superior and inferior relation' is the monarchical principle: 'monarchy is so expressive and effective' in that its functions survive in a modern parliamentary

[105] Simmel (1896) pp. 167 and 172.   [106] Nisbet (1979) p. 172.
[107] Simmel (1971) p. 115.

constitutional setting.[108] Tonnies, too, found it easier to detail with the mechanism of traditional authority in the past than to capture it in *Gesellschaft*:

There is a contrast between a social order which, being based upon consensus of wills, rests on harmony and is developed and ennobled by folkways, mores, and religion, and an order which based upon a union of rational wills, rests on convention and agreement, is safeguarded by political legislation, and finds its ideological justification in public opinion.[109]

There is little that is ennobling in rationalisation. Tonnies stated that 'convention maintains at least the appearance of morality', and that 'it is still related to the folkways, mores and religious and aesthetic feeling, although this feeling tends to become arbitrary and formal'.[110]

To be sure there were strands of sociological thinking that regarded some of the impersonal power released through rationalisation as useful for solving the problem of order. Giddings, who defined sociology as the 'science of the phenomena of discipline', regarded rationalisation of domination as the goal of history since the beginning of time, and that society is 'an organization for the promotion of well-being and efficiency by means of standardization and discipline'.[111] The rationalisation of impersonal coercive power was also expressed through technocratic and liberal theories of society. In his study of the history of the nineteenth century, the Liberal philosopher Bertrand Russell argued that the 'opposition and interaction' of the principle of organisation with that of freedom was one of the 'two main causes of change in the nineteenth century'. Russell contrasted the belief in Freedom 'which was common to Liberals and Radicals' with the 'necessity' for Organisation 'which arose through industrial and scientific technique'.[112]

The ideals of organisation and administration were to play an important role in an age of rationalisation – not least because they promised to provide an administrative solution to the problem of order. However, it is important to note that the concepts of rational, expert and scientific authority only came into their own during the early twentieth century. In the late nineteenth century, such ideas remained relatively underdeveloped and were asserted as practical necessities more than moral imperatives.

---

[108] Simmel (1896) p. 178.   [109] Tonnies (1955) p. 261.
[110] Tonnies (1955) p. 269.   [111] Giddings (1909) pp. 579–80.
[112] Russell (2010) p. viii.

Facing the past

In common with political theory and philosophy, sociology was troubled by its failure to discover in the modern era the foundational resources for validating authority. The two potential sources of modern authority – democratic consent/public opinion, and expertise/science – were rarely elaborated to the point where their capacity to legitimate was conceptually elaborated with force and conviction. Science exercised influence and appeal but could not generate the norms required for establishing moral commitment; and despite its widely recognised role as a validator of political rule, it was feared that public opinion was too troublesome and divisive to serve as a reliable source of ultimate authority.

A recurrent feature of sociological thinking was to dwell on the contrast between the traditional and modern societies. Tonnies

associated tradition with 'consensus' and 'harmony' and contrasted it with the modern which required 'ideological justification'.[113]

Tonnies's contrast of the different foundations of traditional and modern order contains an implicit preference for the former. An authority qualified with terms like 'harmony' and 'enobled' is implicitly more coherent than one that needs to be 'safeguarded' and ideologically justified. Similarly, Tonnies's discussion of authority is far more compelling in his discussion of *Gemeinschaft* than in his survey of *Gesellschaft*, and the conceptual distinction between the authority of age, the authority of force and the authority of wisdom or spirit in pre-modern societies is more nuanced than his discussion of parallel concepts in *Gesellschaft*.

Beyond Tonnies, ideas about power, the nature of government, and authority were developed through exploring the insights provided by history and its representation through philosophy and political theory. The writings of Simmel, Durkheim and Weber testify to these thinkers' constant conversation with the historical past, in which concepts and ideas that pertain to the past often come across with a greater intensity and passion than those that relate to modern times. As McCarthy notes, 'Durkheim returns to the Greeks for a better picture of the nature of society as a whole – its order, unity and solidarity – which he counterbalances to the anomie, social disruption and physical suffering in a modern economy'.[114]

Durkheim's sociological thought conceptualised authority as the cultural accomplishment of the legacy of the past. The experiences that

[113] Tonnies (1955) p. 261.   [114] McCarthy (2003) p. 158.

are codified in thought, taken-for-granted practices, customs and local knowledge provide the resources for the genesis of a collective consciousness. He accepted that experiences that are 'common to the present generation' also contribute to this consciousness, but claimed that the 'authority of collective consciousness is therefore made up in large part of the authority of tradition'.[115] Durkheim wrote at length about the inexorable tendency for the influence of the authority of tradition to diminish. His (ultimately unsuccessful) attempt to invest the modern division of labour with the capacity to produce an organic solidarity capable of generating the foundation of authority presupposed a model of the past, drawing on the corporation of Cicero's Rome to argue the case for recasting solidarity through professional groups.[116] Saint-Simon advocated the social imperative for an organised society by upholding the virtues of feudal times. He complained that,

we affect a superb scorn for the centuries called the Middle Ages, we see there only a time of stupid barbarity and ignorance, of disgusting superstition, and we do not understand that it is the only time when the political system of Europe was founded on a true base, on a general organization.[117]

Krieger argued that the 'sociologists' atavistic definition of social authority received a precise terminological confirmation from Max Weber'. He states that, in his exposition of the three legitimate bases for domination, Weber 'applied *Autorität* to the charismatic and traditional types of authority but only *Herrschaft* to the legal bureaucratic'.[118] The conclusion drawn from this observation is that a 'distinctive connotation of authority' which was associated with past forms had lost its force in the modern era. The conceptualisation of authority as an atavistic ideal was even more forcefully spelled out by Britain's pre-eminent sociologist and rationalist philosopher L. T. Hobhouse, who confined the principle of authority to a distinct stage of history, which was superseded by the principle of citizenship in modern times.[119]

The main alternative to dominant atavistic orientation of sociological theories of authority were attempts to neutralise the concept altogether. From the standpoint of American and British liberal supporters of progress, rational and scientific organisation could serve as an alternative to traditional authority. For his new model of authority, the American liberal philosopher John Dewey looked to the application of the scientific method to what he referred to as the 'control of organized intelligence'

---

[115] Durkheim (1984) p. 233.
[116] See discussion in 'Preface to Second Edition' in Durkheim (1984).
[117] Cited in Carlisle (1974) p. 447.   [118] Krieger (1968) p. 157.
[119] Hobhouse (1994) pp. 137–8 – originally published in 1906.

as the 'working model of the union of freedom and authority'.[120] Hobhouse's *Morals in Evolution* (1906) assumed the evolving rationality of society and its organisation of social life. He contrasted a community which rests on authority to the modern state, 'which rests upon consent', and described this shift as an outcome of social evolution from the 'fiat of authority' to a more enlightened stage of the 'organic legislation of the modern world', one 'in which at its best, there is an effort to determine social progress in accordance with rational ideal'.[121] This evolution was captured by Hobhouse through his categories of the three principal forms of social organisation – kinship, authority and citizenship. The distinction between the historical stage represented by the ideal type of authority and of citizenship expresses a dramatic reversal in the way that the relationship between the socio-political order and people are conceptualised. According to one interpreter of Hobhouse, in 'this third type of political order' – citizenship – 'the relations of governed and governing, as compared with conditions in the previous stage of authority and force, are reversed'.[122] Authority becomes a servant of the people rather than an institution of domination.

Once society is organised according to the principle of citizenship, Hobhouse argued, the impersonal power of the law serves to organise and co-ordinate public life and mediate people's rights and duties.[123] Hobhouse's optimistic harmonisation of rights and duties of liberty and authority has as its premise an idealistic belief in moral progress and the assumption that 'the rationalization of the moral code' will lead to deepening of 'spiritual consciousness' and the purging of the 'ethical order' of its confusions.[124] Rather than emptying moral values of meaning, the rationalisation of life gives it greater consistency, clarity and universality.[125]

Theories that identified the rationalisation of society with moral progress were not concerned about the ascendancy of impersonal power and the consequent emergence of instrumentally oriented values and institutions of domination. Dewey and Hobhouse sought to reconcile impersonal organisation with democratic consent; others, like the Italian social scientist Vilfredo Pareto, presented their theories of organisation as arguments for elitist domination. However, although theories advocating different forms of rationalised institutions – legal system, impersonal bureaucratic administration, scientific organisation – continue to flourish and influence the technocratic rule-making and management of society, they have never succeeded in developing the foundational norms required

---

[120] Dewey (1936).   [121] Hobhouse (1951) pp. 278–9.   [122] Barnes (1922) p. 460.
[123] Hobhouse (1951) p. 60.   [124] Hobhouse (1951) p. 34.   [125] Hobhouse (1951).

for legitimate authority. That is why time and time again Weber's theory of domination – the most systematic critique of rationalisation – continues to serve as the point of reference in this debate.

Sociology's cause

In retrospect it is possible to interpret early modern sociology's relationship with authority as something of an intellectual cause. Durkheim personified the sociologist in search of a cure for the ills of society. His quest for moral solidarity inspired many of his foundational essays on solidarity and religion, and his sociology was devoted to the project of harnessing the authority of science to the construction of moral norms through the study of society. Durkheim drew back from claiming that ultimate values could be derived directly from social facts, opting instead for the more modest strategy of relying on science to provide general guidance for protecting normalcy and avoiding the pathological. He famously wrote that,

> For societies, as for individuals, health is good and desirable; sickness, on the other hand, is bad and must be avoided. If therefore we find an objective criterion, inherent in the facts themselves, to allow us to distinguish scientifically health from sickness in the various orders of social phenomena, science will be in a position to throw light on practical matters, while remaining true to its own methods.[126]

Drawing on science's capacity to help establish an objective criterion for diagnosing social pathology, Durkheim proposed for the pursuit of health as the norm for endowing policy with authority. Through establishing what is normal in a particular socio-historical context, science helps sustain a healthy collective life. The norm of health cast through a medical metaphor is Durkheim's sociological equivalent of the Hobbesian concepts of security and order; but instead of the absolute ruler of the Leviathan, Durkheim offered the rule of the very practically minded Physician-Statesman:

> The duty of the statesman is no longer to propel societies violently towards an ideal which appears attractive to him. His role is rather that of the doctor: he forestalls the outbreak of sickness by maintaining good hygiene, or when it breaks out, seeks to cure it.[127]

Durkheim explicitly presented his argument as non-ideological and scientific – yet his sacralisation of normalcy and health can be seen as a pioneering justification for the politicisation of expert authority.

[126] Durkheim (1982) p. 86.   [127] Durkheim (1982) p. 104.

Unlike Durkheim, Weber expressly distanced his writings from judgments of value. A joint statement with his fellow editors announcing the orientation of their journal stated that 'we are of the opinion that it can never be the task of a science of empirical experience to determine binding norms and ideals from which practical prescriptions may then be determined.'[128] Weber's principled attempt to separate empirical facts from values did not mean that he was less interested than Durkheim in the role of foundational norms in the constitution of authority: it expressed the conviction that rather than generating values, the pursuit of scientific knowledge had the effect of emptying them of meaning.

[128] Weber (1904) p. 102.

14   The rise of negative theories of authority

In the nineteenth century, authority was conceptualised as an institution founded on society. From the turn of the twentieth century, a turn in the thinking about this subject becomes evident. This shift was most vividly expressed in influential theories asserting that consent provided an irrational foundation for authority.

The 1890s is frequently represented as a turning point in attitudes towards modernity, industrialism, technological progress and the future. This period is often portrayed as one of crisis, which 'changed the intellectual physiognomy of Europe' and whose destructive consequences had, by 1914, ensured that 'nothing remained of the proud structure of European certainties'.[1] Radical syndicalist and socialist ideas competed with New Liberal social engineers for the soul of public life; culture reacted against previous ideals of rationality, and new doctrines stressing the role of intuition and the unconscious resonated with the mood of the times.

Although many practising sociologists, such as Hobhouse, Ward and Ross, possessed the social engineering ambitions of turn-of-the-century modernisers, the leading theoreticians of this discipline had internalised a cultural critique of modernity. As we noted in the previous chapter, conceptions of authority drawn from the past appeared to have greater meaning than those drawn from industrialised society. The contrast that Tonnies drew between community and society had echoes of a Romantic sensibility, in which his sense of the vitality and life of a community stood in sharp contrast to the dehumanising forces of change.[2] In this era, theories highlighting the antithesis of culture and civilisation gained a significant audience, and technical, scientific and economic advances were frequently contrasted to cultural decline

Ninety years after Tonnies developed his conceptual antithesis between cultural and economic developments, Daniel Bell wrote in his *Cultural Contradictions of Capitalism*:

---

[1] Rouanet (1964) p. 45.   [2] Tonnies (1955) p. 270.

The traditional bourgeois organization of life – its rationalism and sobriety – has few defenders in the serious culture; nor does it have a coherent system of cultural meanings or stylistic forms with any intellectual or cultural respectability. What we have today is a radical disjunction of culture and social-structure, and it is such disjunctions which historically have paved the way for the erosion of authority, if not social revolution.[3]

The connection that Bell drew between the cultural contradictions of capitalism and the erosion of authority derive from the thesis of rationalisation that came to the fore during the *fin de siècle*. The tendency to counterpose rationalisation to the loss of authentic meaning in life had important implications for the way that authority was conceptualised. Weber's thesis of the displacement of pre-modern forms of legitimate authority by impersonal, bureaucratic domination signified a very important difference in the way that authority is validated.

In his discussion of bureaucratic and patriarchal domination, Weber noted that the 'meaning of norms is fundamentally different under the two forms of domination': bureaucratic domination is underwritten by 'enacted' norms, whereas patriarchal domination it is guaranteed by norms, which are 'sanctified by tradition'.[4] An authority founded on enacted norms has a very different meaning than one based on tradition. The contrast between personal and impersonal domination or, in Weber's terminology, between value-rational and instrumental-rational, directly touches on the prevailing system of meaning. The devaluation of norms through the dominant imperative of rationalisation has decoupled authority from a system of moral meaning, leading to what Jürgen Habermas characterised as a legitimation crisis. Writing more of less at the same time as Bell penned his thesis on the cultural contradictions of capitalism, Habermas stated that 'while organizational rationality spreads, cultural traditions important for legitimation are undermined and weakened.'[5]

Cultural traditions are not only weakened, but fragmented. Weber stated that the 'various value spheres of the world stand in irreconcilable conflict with each other', and science cannot make pronouncements about the virtues of different cultural values'.[6] As Nicholas Gane commented in his interpretation of Weber, 'in the absence of a divine, transcendental authority there no longer exist ultimate grounds upon which value-conflicts may be resolved, meaning in turn that modern culture is necessarily conflict-ridden'.[7] Accordingly, the authority of science and knowledge is confined to what can be rationally known, but its postulates are always subject to dispute.

---

[3] Bell (1980) p. 302.   [4] Weber (1978) p. 1006.   [5] Habermas (1976) p. 47.
[6] Weber (1919a) pp. 147–8.   [7] Gane (2002) p. 35.

By the turn of the century it was evident that the cultural traditions necessary for the validation of authority were not being replaced
by their moral equivalent. It was this exhaustion of the moral foundation of authority that Hannah Arendt had in mind when she stated
that 'authority has vanished'.[8] Although social and political theorist frequently addressed the parallel development of technological advance and
the diminishing of moral meaning, the implication of these trends for
authority and order was inconsistently pursued. Even Weber, who dwelt
at length on the rationalisation-disenchantment couplet, did not consistently extend his insight to his sociology of domination. It is in his
sociological study of religion that the relationship between meaning and
legitimation is most interestingly explored. Discussing the 'reason of the
state', Weber describes how 'calculating politics' empty political life of
passion and emotion; however, in conditions of war, the 'pathos and a
sentiment of community' is forged:

> War thereby makes for an unconditionally devoted and sacrificial community
> among the combatants and releases an active mass compassion and love for
> those who are in need.[9]

Writing in the early stages of the First World War, Weber argued that
a community of solidarity created on the battlefield provided meaning
and motivation comparable to the experience of religious brotherhood.
He stated that a 'war does something to a warrior which, in its concrete
meaning, is unique', because 'it makes him experience a consecrated
meaning of death which is characteristic only of death in war'. Unlike
normal death, which in a rationalised world has no special meaning, in
war and '*only* in war, the individual can *believe* that he knows he is dying
"for" something'.[10] The sacralisation of an individual's sacrifice of life
has implications for the community as a whole, as it gives meaning not
just to death but to life.

The moral rehabilitation of community through war is ultimately
inconsistent with the religion of brotherliness. But as Weber suggests,
'the very extraordinary quality of brotherliness of war, and of death in
war', which is 'shared with sacred charisma and the experience of communion with God', is an important component of the legitimation of
force: 'The location of death within a series of meaningful and consecrated events ultimately lies at the base of all endeavours to support the
autonomous dignity of the polity resting on force'.[11] Writing at a time
when militaristic nationalism appeared to provide the resources essential

---

[8] Arendt (1958) p. 91.   [9] Weber (1915a) p. 335.
[10] Weber (1915a) p. 335.   [11] Weber (1915a) pp. 335–6.

for solidarity and order, Weber did not elaborate its implications for the legitimation of the authority of the nation state.

Other thinkers regarded the cultivation of violent heroism as the missing ingredient for the consolidation of authority. Georges Sorel's *Reflection on Violence*, published six years before the outbreak of the First World War, proposed that myths were essential for the morals of heroism. Sorel regarded heroism as ethically superior to reasoning, for it inspired a total devotion to a transcending principle: 'lofty moral convictions' never 'depend on reasoning or on any education of the individual will, but on a state of war in which men voluntarily participate and which finds expression in well-defined myths'.[12]

Sorel's apotheosis of myths represented his attempt to counter the consequences of rationalisation through the self-conscious construction of a new morality. What was interesting about Sorel's *Reflection* was not his fantasy of myth-making as his critique of the attempt of social scientists and philosophers to develop what he called a 'sovereign force' through the application of reason and intellect[13] – a criticism that was not entirely misplaced.

Sorel's attempt to forge a community through a myth, like Weber's hint at the capacity of nationalism and militarism to motivate acts of solidarity, were integral to a wider search for non-rational and irrational cultural resources for dealing with the social consequences of rationalisation. This quest was motivated by the intuition that irrationalism constituted a more sturdy foundation for authority than did rationalism, its polar opposite. Weber regarded his typology of charismatic authority as the most effective antidote to the threat posed by bureaucratisation, and through his emphasis on the cultivation of democratically elected charismatic leaders he shows a degree of voluntarist belief in the capacity of the individual subject to transcend the limits posed by a rationalised society. As Weber reminded his reader, 'charismatic authority is sharply opposed to rational, and particularly bureaucratic authority', and 'charismatic authority is specifically irrational in the sense of being foreign to all rules'.[14]

Weber's interest in an irrational form of authority resonated with the temper of his time. To a considerable extent, the psychology of irrationalism constituted a defensive response to the uncertainties posed by mass-based democratic political life. Sohm, who invented the modern concept of charisma, stressed 'reverence' for authority, also regarded charismatic authority as an alternative to popular sovereignty.[15]

---

[12] Sorel (1950) p. 234.   [13] Sorel (1950) p. 250.
[14] Weber (1978) p. 244.   [15] Smith (1988) pp. 38 and 40.

Rationalisation as a critique of the masses

The thesis of rationalisation conveys a profound sense of unease with the working of human reason. The wider socio-economic trends associated with modernisation, such as bureaucratisation, standardisation and calculation, were diagnosed as forces that imposed a regime of moral disorientation on an increasingly homogeneous but atomised mass of people. Commentaries on the disheartening consequences of rationalisation not only touched on the cultural mood of disenchantment, but also its tendency to create a new mass of demoralised and atomised people. The impact of disenchantment on the human mind is seen to be 'ultimately, reason destroying'.[16]

By the late nineteenth century, many social and political thinkers began to have doubts about the capacity of rational authority to deal with the problem of order. During the earlier part of the century liberal and representative institutions were perceived as 'the guarantors of order and rationality in society';[17] however, with the expansion of the franchise, the growth of public pressure on parliaments and assemblies and the radicalisation of political life, disillusionment with radical institutions gained momentum. At the same time it was evident to most commentators that popular sovereignty would continue to constitute the fundamental principal of politics. The tension between the recognition that some form of democratic principle would continue to dominate public affairs and a deep-seated anxiety towards it underpinned much of the discourse on the question of authority at this point in time.

One of the most interesting expressions of the disappointment towards liberal institutions was the utilisation of the authority of science to call into question the capacity of the people to assume the role of responsible citizens. The emerging discipline of psychology, through its theories of the 'crowd', played an important role in providing a narrative through which the alleged mismatch between rational institutions and an irrational public were most systematically expressed. Roger Geiger's review of three pioneering crowd theorists – Gabriel Trade, Scipio Sighele and Gustave Le Bon – provides a compelling account of the way that their theories sought to provide a psychological explanation and a solution to the problem of order.

As we noted previously, the pathologisation of human reasoning was already an important feature of the eighteenth- and nineteenth-century reaction to the French Revolution. 'Man's cradle must be surrounded by dogmas and when his reason awakens he must find all his opinions

---

[16] See Nisbet (1979) p. 294.   [17] Geiger (1977) p. 47.

already made', insisted Joseph de Maistre.[18] This argument, central to the conservative imagination, claimed that without the faith and certainty provided by religion and prejudice, people become the helpless and confused fodder for rabble-rousers. By the middle of the nineteenth century, concern with the crowd was transformed into a theory that depicted an atomised collection of people, detached from their communities, as gradually transformed into an undifferentiated mass.

Whereas reactionary ideologues were alarmed about the threat posed by the rabble, the mid-nineteenth-century liberal theories of mass culture were preoccupied with the disintegration of social solidarity. From this standpoint it was modernity itself, with its imperative towards equality and democracy, that was responsible for the disorientation and disorganisation of social life. Theories of rationalisation took these insights a step further and claimed that the undifferentiated masses were susceptible to the influence of an irrational logic. Arguments about the irrationalism of the masses were further elaborated with the assistance of a new science, as crowd psychologists diagnosed the new collectivities of the masses in a language that 'contrasted unfavourably with the liberal ideas of the rational and conscious human individual'.[19] The psychology of collective irrationality became an expression of both the conservative and the liberal reaction to the democratisation of public life. As Nye states, 'collective psychology thus articulated a liberal critique of democratic tendencies in industrial societies with a facade of "scientific" and clinical terminology that lent a certain respectability to its pronouncements'.[20]

Crowd psychology played a significant role in influencing a new corpus of elite theories that emerged during the last two decades of the nineteenth century. Some of the key figures associated with this political sociology were the Italian legal scholar and social theorist Gaetano Mosca; the well-known Italian economist Vilfredo Pareto, who turned his attention to the study of society in the mid 1890s; and the sociologist Robert Michels. These political sociologists integrated the insights of crowd psychology into a theory that had as its premise the assumption that politics represented 'an eternal struggle of the few for rule over the many'.[21] They regarded the masses as morally dissolute, dominated by irrational sentiments and a threat to civilisation and culture. At the same time, since the threat posed by the crowd was neutralised by its incapacity to control its destiny, its destructive power could be managed by a competent elite. This group of elite theorists promoted the reassuring message that their knowledge could be used to manage the masses.

---

[18] Cited in Giner (1976) p. 40.   [19] Nye (1977) p. 12.
[20] Nye (1977) p. 13.   [21] Therborn (1976) p. 191.

Robert Michels, author of the theory of the 'iron law of oligarchy', proclaimed that an effective leader is someone who understands how 'to use the laws of psychology' and can therefore respond to the 'latent yearning for the heroic type of leader which lies concealed in the subconscious of the masses'.[22] Mosca wrote that 'for many years it has been my conviction that there is only one way for man to control' his 'passions and to improve his lot – through the study of individual and collective psychology'.[23] Michels, along with Mosca and Pareto, insisted that he was using a scientific method to uncover the power of the irrational. Pareto developed a veritable system which claimed to promote value-free objective sociology to interpret the impact of irrational factors on human behaviour. His categories of logical and non-logical action assumed that the former characterised the behaviour of social scientists, while the latter captured the irrational behaviour the masses.

Crowd psychology provided elite theories with coherent 'scientific' arguments for the indispensability of strong leadership. From the standpoint of crowd psychology, the 'leaders stood in the same authoritarian relationship to the crowd as the hypnotist to his passive subject'.[24] This pathologisation of the crowd implicitly called into question the rationality of democratic political life, and the legacy of crowd psychology was implicitly to neutralise the role of popular consent as the legitimate foundation for authority. If popular sovereignty was an unreliable foundation for order, then there was no alternative but to look to an enlightened elite to assume responsibility for the future of society.

A negative theory of authority

The remarkable influence that crowd psychology exercised over public life in the early twentieth century testified to apprehensions towards the consequences of mass democracy. In most Western societies, the ideals of a democratic public life could not be outwardly repudiated. As Westel Woodbury Willoughby, one of the founders of American political science, stated in 1917: 'the political philosophy of England since 1688 at least, of France since 1789 and of the United States since its foundation, is squarely committed to the proposition that all political authority comes from the people, and is not vested in the rulers as an original or inherent right'.[25] The rhetorical affirmation of popular sovereignty was rarely matched by a willingness to expound a genuinely democratic system of political authority. Popular sovereignty was frequently posed as a fact of

---

[22] Cited in Beetham (1977) p. 175.   [23] Mosca is cited by Nye (1977) p. 48.
[24] Nye (1977) p. 12.   [25] Willoughby (1917) p. 635.

life in a democratic era, and the public's participation in political life was depicted as an inconvenience whose destructive potential had to be managed by the ruling elites. The 1909 lectures on public opinion given by Abbot Lawrence Lowell, President of Harvard University, expressed this sense of disdain; and his editor praised Lowell for seeing 'more clearly than others' that 'the future of popular government would likely depend on how well the role of public opinion was defined in relation to its capabilities'. That meant not demanding the 'mass electorate to do more than it was capable of doing, to ask it to answer questions beyond its competence' which would 'be as unwise as to ignore its opinions altogether'.[26]

The validation for authority was often cast negatively, with theories making little attempt to justify themselves on any positive normative foundations. Elite theorists devoted their energy to cynically debunking previous and current foundational norms for authority. As Marcuse wrote,

It is the enemy who prescribes the position of the theory. It has no ground of its own from which the totality of social phenomena could be understood. All its basic concepts are counter-concepts.[27]

Most important counter-concepts uniting elite theorists were based on the premise that social behaviour was predominantly irrational, and the necessity for containing the moral corruption of the masses provided the principle justification for their conception of authority. Nye contends that, 'it can be persuasively argued that the legitimacy claimed for elite rule by these theorists follows from the particular nature of the mass rather than the elite'.[28]

One of the earliest exponents of the paradigm of negative authority was Hippolyte Taine, whose work demonstrated a change of focus 'within Liberalism from rationalism towards the emphasis on the power of the unconscious'.[29] His historical study elaborated the idea of the credulous crowd, led astray by the wild fantasies promoted by revolutionary leaders. According to an interesting study by Pitt, Taine's censure of crowd behaviour motivated by unconscious resentment served as a psychological critique of radical democracy and socialism, and continues to be used by critics of mass society to the present day.[30] Taine's criticism of the 'delirium' of democracy and his condemnation of the incompetence of the masses was expressed through a liberal narrative that claimed to defend rational individualism. But according to this narrative, the basis

---

[26] See introduction by Harwood L. Childs to Lowell (1969) p. vi.
[27] Marcuse (2008) p. 101.   [28] Nye (1977) p. 8.
[29] Pitt (1998) p. 1035.   [30] Pitt (1998) p. 1049.

for the authority of the elites was not so much their claim to expertise as the necessity for protecting the masses from themselves and from would-be manipulative militant ideologues.[31] Taine's discussion of the French Revolution and the despotism of the mob constituted the premise for his argument for the limitation of the franchise in the France following the Paris Commune. As with other elite theorists, the moral devaluation of the people – not ready for the franchise – provided the principal argument against democracy. In effect, the classical arguments about the need for the few to govern the many were recast in a narrative that justified itself through the language of science.

What distinguished the work of Mosca and the other so-called New Machiavellian theorists, Michels and Pareto, was the realistic and cynical manner with which they set out to provide a theory of negative authority. Mosca, Michels and Pareto delved deep into history to prove their claim that no matter what the form of political rule – monarchical, aristocratic, democratic – authority was always exercised by a small oligarchy. Outwardly their theories presented themselves as a confident and reassuring affirmation of the inevitability of elite domination. However, a closer inspection of their doctrine indicates that beneath the surface of an arrogant celebration of elite rule lurked a sense of defensive insecurity.

Mosca

Drawing on Taine, Mosca's writings in the 1880s and 1890s warned Italy's rulers about the dangers of enlarging the franchise and providing the resentful and envious masses with more influence over public affairs. His writings revealed apprehension about the capacity of the Italian elite to work as a cohesive force, and he tended to interpret the crisis of authority at the end of the century as integral to the disorganisation and incoherence of the ruling class.

Mosca's main objective was to provide a critique of democratic theory to call into question the moral legitimacy enjoyed by representative government. His point of departure was the assumption that every form political authority is exercised through a ruling class, and from the outset he presented the relationship between rulers and ruled as an unalterable fact of life that renders democracy into a facade for elite domination. Mosca argued that in 'all societies' the necessity to mediate the relation between these two classes of people represents the key question facing political science,[32] and in his historical account the perpetual reconstitution of the ruling class appears to have the force of natural

---

[31] See Nye (1977) p. 11 and Pitt (1998).   [32] Mosca (1980) pp. 50–1.

necessity. Regardless of the nature of the prevailing institutional arrangement – absolute monarchy or parliamentary democracy – behind the
scenes, 'the dominion of an organized minority, obeying a single impulse,
over the unorganized majority is inevitable'.[33] The domination of a
minority – posed as a technical, natural or psychological necessity –
is one of the recurrent themes of the project of neutralising the problem
of authority.

The inevitability of elite domination is underwritten by the thesis of
the incompetent mass. Mosca's metaphor of the 'common herd' served
to devalue both the moral integrity of the people and the system of parliamentary democracy.[34] He warned about the threat of the institutions
of the state falling prey 'to the irresponsible and anonymous tyranny of
those who win in the elections and speak in the name of the people',[35]
arguing that democratic ideas stir 'the most base passions' and 'most bes-
tial instincts' of the plebeian masses, which could result in government
'by the ignorant crowd'.[36] Mosca regarded mass elections as dangerous
also because of their corrosive influence on the integrity and behaviour of
the political elites. He claimed that electoral politics forced members to
debase themselves through accommodating the emotions of the 'common
herd'; consequently, the most qualified individuals who possess integrity
and honour will leave politics, while a disproportionate number of those
versed in the arts of intrigue will enter the ruling class.[37]

Despite the contention of the inevitability of elite rule, Mosca also
understood that this form of domination could only be effective if it possessed moral authority; and he was concerned about how to counteract
the historical tendency for the dominant ruling classes to decline and
lose their way.[38] His interest in the legitimation of elite rule led him to
develop the concept of 'political formula', and his elaboration of this concept indicates that he was clearly focused on the necessity of addressing
the problem of foundation.

Mosca asserted that every organised political society has its 'political
formula', a doctrine or body of belief that legitimises the political struc-
tureand the authority of the ruling class. The doctrines of divine right or
democracy are examples of political formulae. Since a ruling class could
not run society through the use of force or violence alone, Mosca argued
that it needed to demonstrate its intellectual and moral pre-eminence.
Mosca characterised the political formula as the 'legal and moral
basis, or principle, on which the power of the political class rests'. He

---

[33] Mosca (1980) p. 53.   [34] Mosca (1980) p. 155.   [35] Mosca (1980) p. 157.
[36] Mosca is cited in Nye (1977) p. 17.   [37] See Zuckerman (1977) p. 340.
[38] Mosca (1980) p. 65.

indicated that others had used the term 'principle of sovereignty' to convey a similar meaning; however, the concept of popular sovereignty has a principled and transcendental quality that the term 'political formula' lacks. Mosca's term 'political formula' lacked any intrinsic moral content and had an unprincipled and self-serving character, self-consciously aiming to provide a juridical justification for the exercise of power.

One of the conclusions that Mosca derived from history was that the maintenance of order depended on the internal coherence of the elite, which in turn was contingent on its belief in the prevailing foundational norms for authority:

> The majority of a people consents to a given governmental system solely because the system is based upon religious or philosophical beliefs that are universally accepted by them. To use a language that we prefer, the amount of consent depends upon the extent with which, the class that is ruled believes in the political formula by which the ruling class justifies its rule.[39]

Mosca concluded from his study of history that the precondition for the exercise of effective moral authority was the elite's belief and commitment to the ideals through which it exercised its rule.

Mosca distinguished between political formulae founded upon supernatural beliefs and those founded upon rational or apparently rational ones. However, he tended to treat both types as simply justifications rather than as moral or scientific truths. Mosca qualified his Machiavellian interpretation of the political use of beliefs by warning against seeing 'political formulas' as 'mere quackeries aptly invented to trick the masses into obedience'. Why? Because they are a necessary response to the need for authority: the 'truth is that they answer a real need in man's social nature', and moreover,

> this need, so universally felt, of governing and knowing that one is governed not on the basis of mere material or intellectual force, but on the basis of a moral principle, has beyond any doubt a practical and a real importance.[40]

It is this psychological 'need' for a political formula, rather than its intrinsic moral qualities which serves as justification for this version of negative authority. He explicitly counselled against the adoption of a formula that was absolute or sacred on the grounds that institutions built on such a doctrine became, like the Hindu caste system, rigid and unable to respond flexibly to change.[41]

Through his historical account of different political regimes, Mosca drew the conclusions that the 'very ancient political formulas', which

---

[39] Mosca (1980) p. 296.   [40] Mosca (1980) p. 71.
[41] See discussion in Macpherson (1941) p. 97.

have the 'sanction of ages', were particularly successful in 'making their way into the lowest strata of human societies'. The implication of this argument was that with rapid 'flow of ideas' and change, the task of developing a 'spiritual unity' among all social classes became more complicated.[42] Developments such as the growing specialisation of public life, growing public debate and the rise of the free press encouraged the contestation for moral authority. Mosca argued that a number of 'moral forces' – the Church, social democracy, nationalism – have 'long striven to upset the juridical equilibrium in Europe'.[43]

To counter the destabilisation of the juridical equilibrium, Mosca developed his concept of *juridical defense*. This can be described as a form of moral regulator that disciplines people's conduct through the rule of law.[44] The development of juridical defense is most effectively promoted by honest government and the integrity of elites. In institutional terms, the most favourable system for its cultivation is a mixed government, where checks and balances ensure that the 'absolute preponderance of a single political force' is avoided. Mosca expanded on Aristotle and Polybius's arguments on mixed governments, and held up the Greek city state as an example of such arrangements. Here an ancient monarchy 'resting on its sacred character and on tradition', along with the 'demos, based on money, mobile wealth and numbers and the mob balanced each other'.[45] In a Burkeian fashion, Mosca advocated the separation of powers in order to provide opportunities for the participation of different social groups.

Echoing some of the views of nineteenth-century aristocratic liberalism, Mosca argued that juridical defense involved the cultivation of institutions and processes that protected individual freedom, order and the rule of law. His hostility to the expansion of the franchise and the call to restore parliamentary initiative to the Italian monarch in the late 1890s were justified on the grounds of protecting the juridical defense of his society.[46] Mosca's orientation towards juridical defence was pragmatic, realistic and manipulative: what mattered was not the truth but the appearances, and his begrudging acceptance of a representative political system was justified on grounds of *realpolitik*. He declared that 'just as we do not combat a religion because its dogmas seem far fetched, so long as it produces good results in the field of conduct, so the application of a political doctrine may be acceptable so long as they result in an improvement in juridical defense, though the doctrine itself may easily be open to attack from a strictly scientific standpoint'.[47]

[42] Mosca (1980) p. 107.   [43] Mosca (1980) p. 146.   [44] Mosca (1980) p. 126.
[45] Mosca (1980) p. 137.   [46] See Nye (1977) pp. 19–20.   [47] Mosca (1980) p. 258.

Nye writes that Mosca, like other contributors to elite theory, tends to opt for a psychological interpretation of authority, in which authority stems 'from the *appearance* of power which the political class "must have, or in any case be presumed to have" by virtue of the prevailing criteria for the bestowal of "prestige" and "respectability" in a given time or place'.[48] Mosca's concern with appearances and his readiness to support the manipulation of the masses indicated how the claim to promote a rational political science could be so easily reconciled with a willingness to harness instruments of irrationality to maintain order.

Michels

One of the most influential modern classics of elite theory is Robert Michels's study, *Political Parties*. In this book, Michels devoted his considerable sociological skills to analysing the tendency towards the bureaucratisation of social movements, from which he developed his theory of the iron law of oligarchy and offered a systematic argument for the inevitability of elite domination. But Michels's objective was not so much to celebrate the superior qualities of the elites as to de-authorise the legitimacy of mass-based democratic politics. His systematic focus on the absence of any redeeming qualities in mass participation has as its objective the negative authorisation of the oligarchy.

Written in 1911, *Political Parties* offers a self-consciously cynical Machiavellian interpretation of the way that the ethos of democracy was manipulated by conservative, aristocratic and liberal politicians to legitimate their own narrow class and social position. Like other New Machiavellian thinkers, Michels understood that in an era of mass-influenced parliamentary politics, the elites need to play the democratic card. His account assumed that the authority of the few – in its present or past form – had been lost and that it required authorisation from a principle that contradicted its oligarchical ambitions. Instead of dwelling on the problem of validating authority explicitly, Michels opted for neutralising it.

Michels offered an unusually cynical portrayal of elite domination, where democracy functions as a medium of elite manipulation of a gullible and subservient public. He wrote that 'the aristocrat is constrained to secure his election in virtue of a principle which he does not himself accept, and which in his soul he abhors'; however, the aristocrat 'recognises that in the democratic epoch by which he has been overwhelmed' he has no choice but to 'dissemble his true thoughts'. So conservative-minded politicians are forced to wear a 'specious democratic

[48] Nye (1977) p. 16.

mask'; while for liberals 'the masses pure and simple are no more than a necessary evil'.[49] He summarised his argument by stating that 'in modern party life aristocracy gladly presents itself in democratic guise, while the substance of democracy is permeated with aristocratic elements'. To clinch his case, he pointed to the bureaucratisation of social democratic parties. That even parties who are hostile to aristocratic values become subject to domination by elites serves as 'conclusive proof of the existence of immanent oligarchical tendencies in every kind of human organization which strives for the attainment of definite ends'.[50]

Although the focus of *Political Parties* was the social democratic movement, Michels's arguments about the inevitability of oligarchical domination are presented as relevant for society as a whole. His claim regarding the imperative of bureaucratisation strikes a Weberian note, and anticipates the arguments of the soon-to-emerge field of organisation theory:

It is indisputable that the oligarchical and bureaucratic tendency of party organization is a matter of technical and practical necessity. It is the inevitable product of the very principle of organization.[51]

The logic of organisation, in turn, creates technical and administrative demands as well as tactical ones, which require not just a strong organisation but also a powerful leadership.

According to Michels's interpretation, the logic of organisation is inconsistent with the ethos of democracy. So whatever the defects of democracy in the past, its criticism is 'applicable above all in our own days, in which political life continually assumes more complex forms'.[52] Complex organisation and technical specialisation create a need for 'what is called expert leadership', and Michels argued that the authority enjoyed through the claim to expertise led to the emancipation of leaders from the party membership.[53] The principle of oligarchy trumping that of democracy is based on the logic of complex organisation: 'The most formidable argument against the sovereignty of the masses is... derived from the mechanical and technical impossibility of its realization'.[54]

But Michels did not simply rely on technical arguments for supporting his thesis. His central proposition is that the Many will inevitably defer to the Few. He adopted the trans-historical perspective which claimed that the moral inferiority of the masses is a natural fact, justified on the psychological ground that the masses have an innate need to be led: 'Man as individual is by nature predestined to be guided, and to be guided all the more

[49] Michels (1968) p. 47.   [50] Michels (1968) p. 50.   [51] Michels (1968) p. 72.
[52] Michels (1968) p. 76.   [53] Michels (1968) p. 70.   [54] Michels (1968) p. 65.

in proportion as the functions of life undergo division and subdivision'.[55] This argument is based on the claim that there are 'innate human tendencies' such as that towards deference: 'The incompetence of the masses is almost universal throughout the domains of political life, and this constitutes the most solid foundation of the power of the leaders'.[56] So in the first instance, it is the 'incompetence' of the mass that 'furnishes the leaders with a practical and to some extent a moral justification' for their position.

The explicit linkage between the incompetence of the masses and the foundation of leadership is methodically pursued throughout Michels's study. It not only provides a negative foundation for elite authority but also a critique of democracy. He is unequivocal on this point: 'the democratic masses are thus compelled to submit to a restriction of their own wills when they are forced to give their own leaders an authority which is in the long run destructive to the every principle of democracy'.[57]

During the first two decades of the twentieth century, Michels's cynical attitude towards mass democracy was widely shared in sociological and political literature. He could readily draw on a consensus that, aside from radical democrats, anarchists and Marxists, embraced virtually the whole ideological spectrum. His psychological diagnosis of the mental incompetence of the masses inevitably hints at the positive role of manipulation to manage mass behaviour. He wrote of superstition and reverence as the foundation for 'mass support of leaders', and cited with approval the English anthropologist James Frazer, who asserted that 'the maintenance of the order and authority of the state' is to a large extent dependent upon the superstitious ideas of the masses.[58] The inference that authority is maintained by superstition and other irrational forms of manipulation flows from his diagnosis of the pathology of the masses, as does the conclusion that political leadership involved the art of deception and trickery. Citing similar claims made by Mosca, Michels quoted with approval H. G. Wells's statement that 'an electoral system simply places power in the hands of the most skilful electioneers'.[59]

Charles Austin Beard, one of the most influential American historians of the first half of the twentieth century, responded to *Political Parties* by stating that 'from this point of view, all that conservatives have to do is to regard the radicals with calm indifference and to buy the powerful among them with ribbons, titles, honors, nominations, benefices, positions – and money'.[60] Michels's negative theory of authority may

[55] Michels (1968) p. 376.   [56] Michels (1968) p. 111.   [57] Michels (1968) p. 111.
[58] Michels (1968) p. 93.   [59] Michels (1968) p. 76.   [60] Beard (1917) p. 155.

have been transmitted in a cynical tone but it also sounded reassuring to those concerned about the unpredictable trajectory of mass democracy. However, as events in the 1920s and 1930s were to show, those preoccupied with the problem of order were unlikely to be 'calm and indifferent'.

Pareto

Of all the New Machiavellian theorists, Pareto offered the most ambitious and systematically elaborated theory of negative authority. Like Mosca, Pareto stressed the inevitability of elite domination; and like Michels, Pareto regarded the masses with contempt. But Pareto's contribution to the elaboration of a negative theory of authority is in a class of its own. His was an ambitious project of elaborating a grand system for the study of social behaviour, which recast normal human behaviour as mainly irrational and non-logical, and he conceptualised irrational sentiments as the arguments on which authority is founded. Pareto's construction of a social equilibrium based on the 'stability of domination and being dominated' is founded on irrational factors, most importantly the non-logical behaviour of people.[61] All forms of foundational norms for authority – Christianity, socialism, nationalism – are portrayed as religions and reduced to 'varying forms of a single substance': merely historical variants of irrational sentiment. Pareto treats problem of authority as one that is susceptible to a psychological solution.[62]

Pareto's four-volume study *Mind and Society; A Treatise on General Sociology* is, as Zeitlin notes, as 'much a study of antiquity as of contemporary society'.[63] Pareto uses history to substantiate his thesis that human behaviour was and continues to be invariably subject to powerful irrational and non-rational influences. He dismisses religious, philosophical and political ideals and beliefs as stories that cultures use to justify their practices and behaviour, and argues that most of the time people attempt to rationalise their irrational behaviour by inventing theories to justify their conduct. Thus, most knowledge claims are merely attempts to rationalise a pre-existing agenda – 'derivations', which 'merely satisfies that hankering for logic which the human being feels'.[64] Pareto's history eternalises social conduct to the point where the sentiments that influences it are depicted as unchanging.

Pareto's discussion of authority was sometimes developed through a relentless questioning of human rationality and the reasonableness of opinion. His assessment of the authority of public opinion provides a

[61] Marcuse (2008) p. 106. [62] Pareto (1935a) p. 1144. [63] Zeitlin (1997) p. 258.
[64] Pareto (1935a) p. 1201.

striking contrast with G. C. Lewis's study of the subject, which, by comparison, comes across as optimistic about the possibility of trustworthy authority guiding public opinion. Pareto calls into question the very integrity of a claim to the authority of opinion and belief, and appears to be far more interested in discrediting the authority of public opinion than in elaborating an alternative to it. In his discussion of the relationship between authority and opinion, the former is regarded in a one-sidedly ideological manner: 'merely as an instrument for logicalizing non-logical actions and the sentiments in which they originate'.[65]

Pareto uses history to assert that there is no substantive difference between the status of different claims to moral and intellectual authority:

> The Protestant who sincerely accepts the authority of the scriptures and the Catholic who defers to the pope pronouncing *ex cathedra* are both doing the same thing under different forms. So also the humanitarian who swoon over a passage of Rousseau; so the socialist who swears by the Word of Marx or Engels as a treasure-store of all human knowledge; and so further, the devout democrat who bows reverent head and submits judgment and will to the oracles of suffrage, universal or limited . . . Each of such believers of course considers his own belief rational and other beliefs absurd.[66]

In this sociology of history, all forms of intellectual authority are reduced to a matter of arbitrary subjective preference: there is little room for objective or disinterested viewpoints. Pareto's presentation of how claims to authority serve as rationalisations for certain forms of behaviour implicitly accuses claims-makers of self-deception.

From Pareto's perspective, the principle of authority in matters of belief is based on sentiment and prejudice. He rejected claims based on an alleged consensus or on the opinion of large numbers of people: 'Experience by no means shows that when a very large number of people have an opinion that opinion corresponds of reality'. Moreover, unlike nineteenth-century elitist theorists of public opinion, Pareto is dismissive even of the consensus of 'competent' individuals, stating that the 'history of science is the history of the errors of experts'.[67] Although Pareto is prepared to accept that some statements are scientific and verified by experience, he seems to suggest that opinions about matters of belief rarely fall into that category, characterising them as 'articles of faith'.[68] His is a 'value-free' science that attempts to demote all norms to the status of a prejudice.

Pareto attempted to engage with the problem of foundational norms for authority through his theory of derivations. This theory has as its point

---

[65] Pareto (1935) p. 173.   [66] Pareto (1935) p. 351.
[67] Pareto (1935) pp. 357–8.   [68] Pareto (1935) p. 384.

of departure the psychological observation that people have a 'need' to 'make their nonlogical conduct appear logical'. As a result people resort to using 'pseudological' accounts of their conduct, and actually believe that their narrative of self-justification is the cause of their conduct.[69] Pareto argued that to rationalise their essentially non-logical, sentiment-driven actions – to make the non-logical appear logical – people often employ ostensibly logical derivations. Pareto named four principal classes of derivations: (1) derivations of assertion; (2) derivations of authority; (3) derivations that are in agreement with common sentiments and principles; and (4) derivations of verbal proof.

In his typology of derivations in the *Treatise*, Pareto labelled authority as a Class II derivation, which serves as a 'tool of proof and a tool of persuasion'. The constant theme of his outline of the different type of authority – individual, divine, traditional, people – is to expose them as fictitious.[70] He is particularly dismissive of the moral status of a claim to authority based on the consent of the people: citing the example of a conflict between a claim to divine authority by the Kaiser and one based on the will of the people, he wrote that 'both were calculated to stir emotions, for there is no other way of catching the ear of the masses at large'.[71] The implication of this statement is that both claims were irrational assertions, which relied on inciting an emotional response.

According to Pareto, appeals to authority are persuasive insofar as they are based on individual or collective sentiment. Pareto is far from precise in his conceptualisation of sentiment: some have interpreted his concept of sentiment as meaning values, but it is probably more useful to understand it as 'unchanging, instinctual, biopsychic forces'.[72] In part, sentiments pertain to unconscious psychic states that are mediated through cultural values and expressed through non-logical conduct. Derivations are thus attempts both to rationalise such sentiment-driven conduct and endow it with meaning.

Pareto's psychologically dominated theory of authority is explicitly oriented towards the management of the psychic state of the masses. The task of the elite is to harness mass sentiments towards the realisation of positive objectives. Through drawing on the experience of the Roman Empire and of British Rule in India, he emphasised the importance of respecting people's sentiments, no matter how irrational they prove to be. Pareto's theory of domination is based on the psychological management of irrational behaviour. He argued that 'the art of government lies

---

[69] See Zeitlin (1997) pp. 277–82.   [70] Pareto (1935a) pp. 899–923.
[71] Pareto (1935a) pp. 972–3.
[72] This is Zeitlin's interpretation of sentiments. See Zeitlin (1997) p. 265.

in finding ways to take advantage' of the sentiments of the masses, and that so long as a ruling elite was free of such sentiments they 'would be in the position of utilising the sentiments of other people' for their 'own ends'. His advice to the ruling elite was straightforward: 'the statesman of the greatest service to himself and his party is the man who himself has no prejudices but knows how to profit by the prejudices of others'.[73]

Pareto's exhortation to 'profit by the prejudices of others' communicates the idea that the persuasion of the public is realised through a combination of psychological manipulation and opportunistic mobilisation of prejudice. This is an authority that depends on the credulity of the masses and the exploitation of its irrationality, where what matters is not ideals or truths but effectiveness. Impressed by 'the great power and great effectiveness of the two forces, morality and religion, for the good of society', Pareto claimed that 'no society can exist without them', because these derivations are effective in gaining the obedience of the masses. What truly mattered for Pareto is obedience: 'it is advantageous to society that individuals not of the ruling classes should spontaneously accept, observe, respect, revere, love, the precepts current in society'.[74] This cynical realism assumed that truth was not always useful to society and that irrational prejudice was not necessarily harmful.

Arguably, the most significant contribution that Pareto made to development of a negative theory of authority was to reconcile rationalisation with irrationality. His is a self-consciously rational utilitarian theory that advocates the management of the irrational as the solution to the problem of order. His erudite historical account of political domination posits authority as a response to the psychological need for leadership. From this perspective it is a psychological constant – the need for non-logical behaviour to rationalise itself as logical – that causes the construction of norms and ideologies. The conceptualisation of domination as the outcome of a need is one of the constant claim made by proponents of theories of negative authority.

Numerous commentators have drawn attention to Pareto's influence over American intellectual life in the inter-war period. The Harvard 'Pareto Circle' of influential social scientists and philosophers drew on Pareto's sociological system to develop their own ideas and theories of organisation. Pareto's emphasis on the tendency of social systems towards equilibrium was attractive to academics who were apprehensive about the reality of social disequilibrium during the 1930s,[75] 'because of its politically conservative conception of society which was based on a

---

[73] Pareto (1935a) p. 1282.   [74] Pareto (1935a) p. 1345.
[75] For a discussion of the Pareto Circle see Keller (1984).

mechanical – system model that incorporated the concept of stable equilibrium'.[76]

However, although Pareto clearly influenced the emerging field of organisational theory, his most valued contribution was his endeavour to develop a social theory that, while claiming to be value-free and scientific, emphasised the importance of non-rational norms in the upholding of society. It is worth noting that, of all the theorists discussed by Talcott Parsons in *The Structure of Social Action*, it is with Pareto that he most identified. It is likely that it was Pareto's willingness to provide a critical and positive role for irrational values that attracted the attention of someone interested in the normative foundation of order. Parsons reiterated Pareto's warning about the danger of subjecting 'value questions' to scientific scrutiny in order to avoid undermining prevailing prejudices, and cited with approval Pareto's statement, 'discussions of ethical questions can be harmful to a society and even destroy its foundations'.[77] R. K. Merton's functionalist framework sought to 'weld together an anti-rationalistic sociology and a rationalistic view of science'. Following Pareto, Merton's is a 'sociology of the unconscious motivations of social behaviour and of its unanticipated consequences, a sociology that renders non-logical behaviour intelligible by studying it in a context not appreciated by the actor'.[78] Through this synthesis Merton, like Pareto, was able to 'reinstate the beliefs and practices dismissed as irrational' and reconstitute a role for them in the validating of social order.

Sociology's turn to psychology

Sociology had to account for the fact that 'social authority was a characteristic product of the declining, pre-industrial stage of Western civilization and yet that authority in some form remained a prominent feature of the industrial age'.[79] It was evident that tradition, religion, custom and community had lost much of their capacity to validate authority. At the same time rational-legal forms of validation appeared as an unreliable instrument of legitimation. In such circumstances, questions such as why people obeyed, what the source of authority was, and how order could be preserved, posed a serious intellectual challenge for social theorists of the early twentieth century.

Sociological accounts of authority tended to adopt a strategy not dissimilar to that of the New Machiavellian elite theorist. On the one hand, social domination was interpreted as the consequence of the impersonal

---

[76] Keller (1984) p. 194.   [77] Parsons (1968) p. 276.
[78] King (1971) p. 7.   [79] Krieger (1968) p. 158.

forces of rationalisation. Theories of bureaucratisation, the necessity for hierarchy, and expert rule were presented as explanations for the inevitability of elite domination, and arguments regarding the complexity of organisation and bureaucracy served to validate expert authority. The fatalistic manner with which the imperative of technical authority was asserted was most eloquently presented in the writings of Weber. As Mészáros outlines, Weber 'managed to formulate a critique of *bureaucracy and technological rationality* while simultaneously declaring them – and on their account capitalism as a socioeconomic and political order – to be fundamentally *untranscendable*'.[80]

Theories focusing on the different dimensions of rationalisation served to render social hierarchy as a technical and organisational accomplishment. In a similar manner it tended to naturalise the role of an oligarchy. The argument regarding the inherent necessity for a ruling technocratic elite, which was eloquently pursued by Saint-Simon in the nineteenth century, acquired a more politicised form in response to perceived threats to social peace in the early twentieth century. However, technical arguments for rational authority lacked the capacity for moral persuasion, leading to a perceptible tendency to look for non-rational and irrational solutions to the problem of order. During the decades leading up to the outbreak of the World War II, rational theories of authority were trumped by their irrational counterparts. As the leading American political scientist Harold Lasswell asserted in *World Politics and Personal Insecurity* (1935), the 'consensus on which order is based is necessarily nonrational'.[81]

As we discuss in the next chapter, one form of non-rational authority that emerged at this time was that of the leader. The quest for a personified form of authority was coherently expressed through Weber's concept of charismatic leadership, whose authority is legitimated through election by a 'plebiscitary democracy'.[82] The charismatic emotional bond between leader and the irrational masses became a recurrent theme in a new literature on mass societies. This sentiment was also communicated through radical and left-wing psychological theories that sought to explain the need of the masses for leaders as an expression of the anxiety and insecurity of ordinary people. Social theorists associated with the Frankfurt Institute for Social Research developed a critical anti-capitalist theory which accepted that authority was a response to a psychological need. Max Horkheimer shifted the focus from the exercise of authority to its acceptance by an 'authority-oriented character'. Horkheimer claimed that the cultivation of such character occurred through the family:

[80] Mészáros (1989) p. 87.   [81] Cited in Lyon (1961) p. 63.   [82] Weber (1978) p. 268.

childhood 'becomes an habituation to an authority which in an obscure way unites a necessary social function with power over man'.[83]

By the inter-war period, negative theories of authority had succeeded in influencing the outlook of even radical social theorists. As a result, crowd psychology's insistence on the gullibility of the masses and its susceptibility to manipulation were integrated into the mainstream of twentieth-century social and political thought. Sociology had come under the influence of theories about the power of the unconscious. Thus Karl Manheim regarded the gullibility of the masses to be an 'aspect of the irrational thirst of the modern populace for "wish fulfilment"', which led to the acceptance of the political fantasies of a totalitarian age.[84]

The need to obey became interpreted as a character trait that existed independent of a particular system of social domination. Mass men needs not only 'community and belief' but also 'hierarchy and social order'. In this way the need for order was rendered both a natural and a psychological fact of life. According to this view, 'mass men are, by definition, so weak that they cannot stand on their own and are therefore naturally submissive or, what amounts to the same thing in their case, naturally authoritarian'. This line of thought proposed the thesis that authoritarianism is 'not just an attitude of certain rulers but also an attitude of many people who desire to be ruled and to obey commands without questioning them'.[85] This period saw the rise of theories of authoritarian personality, which claimed to have discovered the formation of an authoritarian character through the socialisation process. The outcome of this form of socialisation is that the masses become psychologically dependent on charismatic paternalistic leaders, 'who in turn manipulate the unconscious fears and insecurities of the masses for their personal or ideological ends'.[86]

What distinguished these arguments from those of the New Machiavellians was their unease with the manipulation of the irrational for the purpose of consolidating an authoritarian order. However, the psychological theories of authoritarian personality type had much in common with the openly elitist doctrines that they criticised. By shifting the focus onto the psychological deficits of individuals and masses, they reinforced the influence of a negative conception of authority over public life.

---

[83] Horkheimer (2002) p. 108.   [84] Cited in Giner (1976) p. 141.
[85] Giner (1976) p. 142.   [86] Nye (1977) p. 40.

15   By passing authority through the rationalisation of persuasion

It is worth recalling that modern utilitarian and liberal theory emerged in the eighteenth century on the supposition that the 'foundation of order in society is reason in individuals'.[1] The belief that persuasion rather than force constituted the foundation of order had as its premise the belief that, through free speech and communication, the public could be influenced to act in accordance with reason and their interest. Moreover, the liberal utilitarian theories of the eighteenth century regarded the 'development of public opinion as a constituent component of social order'.[2] Such optimistic sentiments towards the role of public opinion were antithetical to the subsequent psychological turn in political thought, and its claim that order was founded on irrational and non-rational sentiments.

In sociological theories the problem posed by the power of irrational forces was linked to an interpretation of the process of modernisation, or rationalisation. The disruptive impact of the erosion of tradition was linked to a state of *anomie* or normlessness, which in turn fostered a climate of existential insecurity. As Weber's own theory indicated, rationalisation has a corrosive effect on the foundation on which authority is exercised. This insight was developed by Talcott Parsons in the 1930s and 1940s to explain both the perilous threat facing liberal democracies and the influence of authoritarian power. After pointing out that the very development of 'rational-legal patterns' undermined 'many of the values which have played an important part in our past history', Parsons warned that the erosion of these traditional sources of authority represents 'one of the most important sources of widespread insecurity'.[3]

Unlike many of his peers, Parsons recognised that the problem of authority could not be evaded and that a positive conception of its role had to be elaborated. This chapter reviews the discussion of the inter-war politicisation of the irrational and concludes with the Parsonian response of a rationalised theory of authority.

---

[1] Mayhew (1984) p. 1285.   [2] Mayhew (1984) p. 1282.   [3] Parsons (1942b) p. 160.

Liberal democracy on the defensive

The significant degree of affirmation and legitimacy currently enjoyed by the ideal of democracy is of very recent vintage. In the inter-war era democracy was regularly depicted as the source of society's problem, rather than as its solution; and throughout most of the first half of the twentieth century democracy was regarded in highly ambiguous terms, even by its supporters. Arguably it was the devastating experience of fascism and Stalinism which has 'given the concept an appeal even its supporters would not have expected in the 1920s and 1930s.'[4] The ambivalence about democratic politics that characterised much of the twentieth century had a significant impact on the conceptualisation of authority.

In its most elementary sense, modern democratic theory is characterised by its belief in majority rule: it upholds the 'fullest participation of the interested parties and the greatest possible accountability of the institutions involved in the process'.[5] However, the unpredictable dynamic of mass participation posed a problem for democratic theory. It has been widely noted that from the 1870s onwards, conservative and liberal thinkers expressed serious doubts about the capacity of the multitude to play the role of responsible citizens; what has been less noted is that from the 1920s onwards, a loss of faith in the moral integrity of the multitude also characterised the mood of a significant section of the left. Erich Fromm combined his critique of capitalist rationality with pessimistic diagnosis of 1930s public life: 'We have been compelled to recognize that millions in Germany were as eager to surrender their freedom as their fathers were to fight for it'.[6] The political philosopher and social reformer John Dewey tended to regard the psychological attitudes of the masses as a threat to democracy in the United States. 'The serious threat to our democracy', he asserted, 'is not the existence of foreign totalitarian states', but the 'existence within our personal attitudes and within our own institutions of conditions which have given a victory to external authority, discipline, uniformity and dependence upon The Leader'.[7]

The crisis of liberal democracy was intimately linked to the difficulty it had in elaborating a normative foundation for its authority. This dilemma was most acutely evident in the debate surrounding the construction of a new constitution in Germany in the immediate aftermath of the First World War. As one account notes, 'first and foremost came the

---

[4] Bronner (1999) p. 17.   [5] Bronner (1999) p. 24.   [6] Fromm (1965) p. 3.
[7] Cited in Fromm (1965) p. 3.

theoretical problem of what the "foundation" or "source" of the system was'.[8] A failure to find a convincing solution to this problem exposed the authority of the new parliamentary constitution to continual questioning. Following the War, 'there was a critical revision of modern mass democracy' by political theorists and policy makers. At this point Europeans 'critically re-examined the idea of democratic citizenship, which traditionally was based on the rational capacity of participation and decision on the part of the citizen'.[9] Public opinion was represented as a synthesis of irrational myths and prejudice. This argument was forcefully presented by the American commentator Walter Lippmann in his influential 1922 study, *Public Opinion*, which declared that the proportion of the electorate that is 'absolutely illiterate' is much larger than one would suspect, and that these people who are 'mentally children or barbarians' are the natural targets of manipulators. The belief that the public was dominated by infantile emotions was widely echoed in the social science literature of the inter-war period, often conveying the assumption that public opinion does not know what is in its best interests. As one American sociologist noted in 1919, 'public opinion is often very cruel to those who struggle most unselfishly for the public welfare'.[10]

Harold Lasswell, one of the pioneers of the psychological turn of American political science, expressed a scepticism that characterised his discipline's attitude towards democratic public life. 'Familiarity with the ruling public has bred contempt', he stated, and reminded his readers that the 'public has not reigned with benignity and restraint'. Lasswell denounced people with democratic inclinations for 'deceiving themselves', and claimed that the power of propaganda to manipulate the masses called into question 'the traditional species of democratic romanticism'.[11] Throughout Europe and America, pessimism directed towards democratic institutions pervaded public life. Graham Wallas, a leading member of the British Fabian Society and author of *Human Nature in Politics*, provided a powerful critique of the capacity of a democratic electorate to behave rationally.[12]

With the rise of fascism and the ascendancy of Stalin's regime, the loss of faith in the public intensified. It was from this perspective that Walter Shepard, President of the American Political Science Association asked in 1935, 'who are the People'? In reply, he argued that 'we have been impressed, more than we care to admit, with the practical failure

---

[8] Caldwell (1997) p. 2.   [9] Frezza (2007) p. 128.
[10] Lippmann (1922) p. 68 and Paget (1929) p. 439.   [11] Lasswell (1927) p. 148.
[12] Wallas (1929) p. xi. 'Preface to 1920 edition'.

of democratic government in Europe'; and pointing to the 'spread of fascism and the success of the communist experiment in Russia' and the 'breakdown of the capitalistic system and the prolonged economic depression', he suggested that Americans had become a 'nation of political skeptics'.[13]

Shepard wrote as a matter of fact that 'the idea that government springs from and is dependent upon the will of the people cannot withstand the analysis of modern criticism'.[14] Although he recognised that the 'electorate has its role to play in modern government', that role was a matter of 'practical expediency' to be decided on pragmatic grounds, for, 'Is it not evident that the theory of popular sovereignty, the central idea of democratic ideology, cannot stand up under an objective critical analysis and must be frankly abandoned?'[15] What Shepard proposed was a technocratic political system, based on planning and education and run by men with 'brains'. His goal was to 'lose the halo' surrounding the electorate, calling for 'a system of educational and other tests which will exclude the ignorant, the uninformed, and the anti-social elements which hitherto have so frequently controlled elections'. His vision was of a modern technocracy run by experts. 'We must frankly recognize that government demands the best thought, the highest character, the most unselfish service that is available'.[16]

Disappointment towards democratic politics was reflected through an intensification of the tendency to pathologise public opinion. As one important study of this trend points out, 'the experience of the World War intensified the tendency to emphasize the non-rational forces involved in the formation or manipulation of public opinion, and it promoted a deep and wide-spread scepticism as to the validity of democratic theory in general and the competence of public opinion in particular'.[17] By the mid 1930s, democracy itself was held responsible for unleashing the destructive and irrational powers sweeping the world. In his 1933 essay 'The Democratization of Culture', Karl Mannheim asserted that it was democracy itself that created the terrain for the flourishing of totalitarian movements:

Dictatorships can arise only in democracies; they are made possible by the greater fluidity introduced into political life by democracy. Dictatorship is not the antithesis of democracy; it represents one of the possible ways in which a democratic society may try to solve its problems.[18]

[13] Shepard (1935) pp. 9–10.   [14] Shepard (1935) p. 6.   [15] Shepard (1935) p. 8.
[16] Shepard (1935) pp. 18–19.   [17] Palmer (1967) p. 252.
[18] Cited in Borch (2012) p. 175.

The classical representation of the multitude as an 'unreliable' and easily corruptible entity resurfaced as commentators tried to make sense of the apparently inexplicable attraction of a new wave of powerful dictators. Mussolini's statement that to 'speak of the sovereign people is to utter a tragic jest' transcended the inter-war ideological divide.[19]

Mainstream commentaries on the role of democratic consent adopted the pragmatic attitude that this was a fact of life that one had to deal with. Morris Ginsberg's 1921 classic *The Psychology of Society* exemplified this pragmatism, in drawing attention to the significance of public opinion 'for the simple reason that it is an existent fact of the greatest magnitude and that to defy it would certainly lead to disaster'. When he asserted that 'government must be by consent', he did not refer to liberal democratic political theory for affirmation but to Aristotle: 'Aristotle pointed out long ago, to exclude any large number of people from a share in government is exceedingly dangerous'.[20] Ginsberg's statement that, whatever view one adopted towards public opinion, its consent was essential for the validation of authority, was shared by commentators on the subject. With some reservations, it was generally recognised that in the twentieth century the validation of public opinion was essential for the constitution of political authority. For many commentators the management of public opinion represented the key challenge facing a democratic political order. The social psychologist George Catlin voiced this sentiment in 1930: 'the question of how public opinion may be manipulated is now receiving that attention which it deserves in an age when democracy has made it of leading importance'.[21]

Weber's dilemma

Max Weber's sociology of domination evolved in the context where scepticism about the possibility of reconciling mass politics with order co-existed with the recognition that its consent was essential for the legitimation of authority. That is why in the early twentieth century, the discipline of sociology became so interested in investigating the relationship between social control and mass opinion.[22]

In his report to the first meeting of the German Sociological Society in 1910, Weber called for the launch of a major research project to

---

[19] Cited by Stewart (1928) p. 852.
[20] Ginsberg (1964) p. 129. Forty years after the publication of his book, Ginsberg echoed his disenchantment with democracy. 'As to democratic institutions, no one could write of them now with the Mazzinian enthusiasm', in Ginsberg (1964) p. xix.
[21] Cited in Palmer (1967) p. 23.
[22] On Weber's attitude to public opinion see Furedi (2011a).

study the influence of the press upon public opinion.[23,24] He described his proposed study as necessary for tackling one of the 'great cultural problems of the present',[25] and one of his principal research themes was the 'production of public opinion by the press'. From the outline of this proposal it is evident that Weber regarded opinion as a target of manipulation, and the press as the key influence on the constitution of cultural and moral attitudes. He believed that the German working class was politically 'infinitely less mature than the clique of journalists who would like to monopolise its leadership would have it believe';[26] and that newspapers moulded and shaped 'mass judgments and mass beliefs'.[27]

Yet despite his interest in the development of mass society and the sociology of domination, Weber wrote very little about the sociology of public opinion and did not really address many of the fundamental questions to do with the role of public consent in the exercise of authority. He was far more worried about the failure of German political leadership than with the threat from below, and his writings indicate that he perceived the problem of order through his preoccupation with the disorientation of Germany's ruling elites and the impact of bureaucratisation. Weber took the view that the question of how a few rule the many depends on the integrity and quality of the elite.[28] In his political journalism, he stated that only the individual leader was capable of heroic deeds, and that the most useful contribution that the masses could make was to acclaim and elect such charismatic figures. Weber had no doubts that Caesarism was 'virtually inevitable under democratic conditions',[29] and in his sociology of domination, the rule of a charismatic leader over the masses was taken as axiomatic.

Weber's remarks and asides indicate that he regarded the *demos* as unstable and volatile because they were dominated by irrational emotions. But unlike crowd psychologists and classical elite theorists such as Mosca and Pareto, Weber regarded the masses and the propertied with equal contempt. Writing about threats facing Germany after the First World War, he wondered whether 'the emotional effect of the blind fury of the masses will activate the equally emotional and senseless cowardice of the bourgeoisie'.[30] Weber had an ambiguous relationship to the democratisation of German political life: he regarded democratisation as the precondition for modernising Germany's political system, based on

[23] Whimster (2010) p. 132.   [24] Weber (1998).   [25] Weber (1998) p. 111.
[26] Kelly (2003) p. 343.   [27] Weber (1998) p. 119.
[28] Cited in Therborn (1976) p. 217.   [29] See Baehr (1999) p. 340.
[30] Weber (1978) p. 1461.

the pragmatic assumption that this was the most suitable institution for legitimating and cultivating effective and charismatic leaders.

Weber advocated the 'Caesarist transformation of leadership selection' even, as Mommsen observes, 'at the cost of rationality and objectivity in the formation of public opinion', because he believed that this was the only way to 'bring about rule by independent and genuinely qualified leaders'. Drawing on his understanding of the taming of the *demos* in ancient Athens by a demagogic figure, Weber stated that 'mass democracy' had 'always bought its successes since Pericles time with major concessions to the Caesarist principle of leadership selection beginning at the times of Pericles'.[31] Thus like most sociological theorists, Weber was forced to turn back to the past to rescue a concept of authority. While many thinkers during the inter-war period turned to the Roman Empire for an exemplar, Weber chose to embrace the Athenian statesman, Pericles.

In Weber's idealised account, Pericles personified the Caesarist political leader with a calling. Weber's commitment for cultivating charismatic leaders who possessed intellectual integrity stands in sharp contrast to his indifference to the wider public's level of political culture. Weber believed that although plebiscitarian leadership leads to the 'soullessness' of their following and their 'intellectual proletarianization', this is 'simply the price paid for guidance by leaders'.[32] Weber looked to the force of charismatic authority exercised either by an individual leader, or through the ascendancy of a new spiritual aristocracy, in a half-hearted attempt to create a focus for the obedience of the public. Weber simply did not countenance the possibility that a democratic public ethos could provide a stable foundation for social order: as the German political sociologist Carl Offe states, for Weber the proper selection of political leadership is the key problem of parliamentarianism and democratisation.[33]

Weber's estrangement from a democratic ethos was fuelled by his concern with the power of bureaucratisation and rationalisation to deprive public life of any meaning. Influenced by Nietzsche's diagnosis of the death of God, he came to interpret 'the process of secularisation' as one 'which has rendered human existence meaningless'.[34] At times overwhelmed by the sensibility of cultural pessimism, he seemed to imply that in a disenchanted world the project of constructing a new ultimate source of meaning can only result in 'monstrosities'.[35] It is likely that Weber sensed that rationalisation had eroded the old order and its values, and that the new values associated with an instrumentalist

---

[31] Mommsen (1984) pp. 186–7.   [32] Weber (1958) p. 113.
[33] Offe (2005) p. 54.   [34] Turner (1992) p. 188.   [35] Villa (2001) p. 241.

orientation lacked the capacity to motivate obedience of authority. He had little faith in the capacity of mass democracy to foster a culture that could provide enlightened norms and values that would provide foundation for genuine political authority. Hence, from this perspective, public opinion could only serve as an unwelcome reminder of the scale of problem confronting authority.

In the inter-war era, widespread political insecurity encouraged anti-democratic ideals in which many people invested their hope in salvation through a decisive leader. It was in this context that ideas about charismatic leadership gained traction. It is worth noting that despite his formidable sociological grasp of the world, Weber himself adopted an increasingly psychological orientation towards the political challenges faced by his Germany, and could only imagine authority in a personalised form.

The problem of leadership

Weber's reluctance to attribute positive qualities to mass opinion, his rejection of the ethos of liberal democracy, and his deification of leadership expressed views that were widely disseminated by intellectuals, scholars and other public figures in Western societies, and would have been familiar to an educated middle-class public at the time. As Richter explains, an emphasis on leadership and the devaluation of the masses was 'far from exceptional in the Germany of his time',[36] and such ideas were not confined to Germany.

Around the same time that Weber developed his argument about the necessity for a new Pericles, Sigmund Freud was working on his study *Group Psychology and the Analysis of the Ego*. This study sought to explain the relationship between the 'function of the leader' and the 'group mind', and claimed that members of a group submit to the leader through forging a psychological bond whereby the image of the leader is put in the place of the individual's own ego. Freud suggested that the common quality binding a group together is mediated through the psychological process of *identification* with the leader, observing that 'the mutual tie between members of a group' is 'based upon an important emotional quality; and we may suspect that this common quality lies in the nature of the tie with the leader'.[37]

Freud's interest in the 'nature of the tie' that bound groups with their leader was shared by a wide constituency of political thinkers, who, like Weber, drew the conclusion that the maintenance of order required the

[36] Richter (1995) p. 69.   [37] Freud (1985) p. 137.

supervision of an authoritative person. With the rise of dictators in many parts of Europe, interest in the role of leaders as authority-substitutes gained momentum. For many political thinkers the Leader offered a promising medium through which authority could gain definition. The emergence of a new science of leadership in the United States represented an attempt to capitalise on the potential of this road to authority through the rationalisation of leadership: 'We need leaders in the professions, in education, in business, in the church' exhorted a text published in 1935.[38]

Since the maintenance of order was seen to be so closely intertwined with sound leadership, it became a subject in its own right. In Western democracies, particularly in the United States, the focus on leadership often diverged from the Weberian charismatic type towards a model of an enlightened technocratic elite. Organisational theory was directed towards the cultivation of an enlightened administrative elite in both industry and political life. Elton Mayo insisted that whichever country first learns to develop a method for training effective leaders would 'outstrip the others in the race for stability, security, development'.[39] However, by the mid 1930s, the examples of the cult of leadership surrounding Hitler and Mussolini created a growing interest in the irrational and emotional factors involved in the rise of authoritarian regimes.

Paul Pigors's classic, *Leadership or Domination* (1935), focused on the apparent ease with which leaders succeeded in dominating the public. 'In a critical period such as ours thoughtful observers cannot help but marvel at the ease with which certain people acquire ascendancy over their fellow men', noted Pigors.[40] One American sociologist represented the modern demagogue as 'the "leader of the people" and the "substitute for institutions" in a time of transition',[41] predicting that 'It is the historical hour of the demagogue'. Significantly, the demagogic leader was represented as the product of mass democracy: that a 'contradictory feature of modern demagogical rule is found in its militant leadership and its democratic foundation.'[42]

Leadership as authority substitute

'The emergence of a Caesar from the womb of democracy has been predicted time and again by French, German and Spanish counter-revolutionaries' wrote Franz Neumann in his classic study of the nature

---

[38] See Paul Pigors's *Leadership or Domination*, cited in Frezza (2007) p. 158.
[39] See Frezza (2007) p. 151.   [40] Pigors is cited in Frezza (2007) p. 161.
[41] Neumann (1938) p. 487.   [42] Neumann (1938) p. 487.

of National Socialism.[43] Written in the dark hours of the early 1940s, before the outcome of the war was clear to this German émigré author, Neumann places great emphasis on the highly personalised form of Nazi rule. He asserts that in Germany, the Leader not only runs but has literally displaced the state; that 'political power rests in the leader, who is not the organ of the state but who *is* the community, not acting as its organ but as its personification'.[44] The unification of independent powers of more or less equal strength – the party, the army and the state bureaucracy – are not 'institutionalized but only personalized'.[45] Neumann stated that 'except for the charismatic power of the Leader, there is no authority' that co-ordinates these powers, 'no place where the compromise between them can be put on a universal valid basis'.[46]

While Neumann's emphasis on the role of the personal power of the leader underestimated the role of institutions of domination, it drew attention to the unprecedented status gained by the Leader in an industrial society. This development has been interpreted as proof of the potential for the emergence of a charismatic leader. However, the necessity for investing so many resources in the deification of the Leader can be more fruitfully interpreted as a symptom of the depth of the crisis of authority in the inter-war period.

Arguments in favour of resolving the crisis of authority through its personification in supreme leader impressed political thinkers throughout the Western world. Commentators often contrasted the alleged merits of efficient totalitarian societies to the state of disorganisation of democracies. So after noting that the 'old foundations of authority are left without loyalty', the American political scientist Francis Wilson explained that democratic institutions had become ineffective in the new era:

> Most thinkers admit that some changes must be made if democracy is to survive, and one solution which seems to be gaining more adherents than the others is that some elements of fascist organization and authority must be carried over into democratic liberalism.[47]

Wilson's proposal for a form of 'democratic authoritarianism' was based on the premise that order and efficiency required the expansion of the intervention of the state. In a similar vein, Shepard proposed to reorganise democratic institutions on the basis that, 'if this survey of a possible reorganization of government suggests fascism, we have already recognized that there is a large element of fascist doctrine and practice that we must appropriate'.[48] Although Shepard was careful to qualify his remark by

---

[43] Neumann (1963) p. 195.   [44] Neumann (1963) p. 469.
[45] Neumann (1963) p. 469.   [46] Neumann (1963) p. 470.
[47] Wilson (1937) p. 14.   [48] Shepard (1935) p. 19.

affirming his commitment to American freedoms, his statement reflected a wider tendency to attempt to resolve the crisis of authority through authoritarian solutions.

The turn towards self-consciously authoritarian solutions indicated that negative theories of authority could make only a limited contribution to the stabilisation of order. At a time of global economic and political crisis, the consolidation of order created a demand for a more positive version of authority. The rise of inflated concepts of authority through the construction of authoritarian political solutions represented what now appears as a desperate attempt to deal with the problem. The German political theorist Carl Schmitt advanced a conception of personal authority that transformed representation into a fiction.[49] To accomplish this project, Schmitt was forced to re-politicise authority to the point that it totally prevailed even over the law: the 'sovereign is highest legislator, judge and commander simultaneously', and he also served as 'the final source of legality and the ultimate foundation of legitimacy'.[50]

One can debate the different interpretations of Schmitt's intellectual and political role in inter-war Germany and his relationship with the ascendancy of National Socialism and the Nazi regime. However, there is little doubt that he provided a systematic anti-liberal political theory of authoritarianism. His authoritarian conception of political rule was linked to a negative theory of authority that was well within the mainstream of political thought; Schmitt described Walter Lippmann's condemnation of public opinion as 'very shrewd', and his dismissal of public debate was consistent with the views put forward by mass society theorists.[51]

Schmitt was acutely sensitive to the absence of a normative foundation for authority. His concept of political theology is premised on the necessity for the construction of a form of legitimation that does not have to justify itself in rational terms. According to one interpretation, 'Schmitt's political existentialism looks very much like the radicalization of Weber's conception of charisma as the antidote to the age of rationalization and value neutrality'.[52] In fascist theory the sovereign ruling through the authoritarian state required no external validation: this was a form of authority that claimed to be its own foundation, and the authority of the ruler was thus endowed with Hobbesian absolute powers. In effect, Schmitt attempted to provide a solution to the problem of foundation through providing an entirely subjective theory of authority. As Krieger argues, 'in totalitarian fascism the

---

[49] See Kelly (2004).   [50] Schmitt (2004) pp. 5–6.
[51] Schmitt (1988) p. 6.   [52] Tregenza (2002) p. 360.

principle of authoritative power became the principle of the entire human world'.[53]

Schmitt's radical expansion of the concept of charisma should not be interpreted in isolation from the wider discussion on mass society and public opinion. The very fragility of the inter-war political order and the apparent weakening of liberal-democratic institutions encouraged a disposition towards non-rational modes of motivating the public. This was a moment when Western society found it difficult to give meaning to legal or any other form of impersonal authority. John Dickinson of Princeton University insisted that a 'large part of the effectiveness of authority is due to psychological motives of sentiment, loyalty, reverence, which are most likely to attach to a concrete visible person or institution'. This belief was based on the argument that the ordinary members of the public lacked the 'intellectual development' necessary for identifying with an abstract impersonal cause. He added that 'men in general seem to conceive the degree of sentiment which is capable of overriding selfish interests only toward a person or object which appeals immediately to some of their senses – Pope or Kaiser or the *fasces* of the Roman lictor'.[54]

Dickinson's allusion to Mussolini spoke to a sense of defensiveness regarding the capacity of parliamentary democracy to mobilise the kind of public support apparently enjoyed by this new Dictator of Rome. With the subsequent rise of Hitler it appeared that the cult of leadership had acquired its own independent dynamic. According a study of the so-called 'charismatisation' of European politics, the Mussolini experiment 'provided a pool of inspiration for a generation of political leaders', many of whom – Horthy, Metaxas, Pilduski, Franco, Salazar – were traditional dictators with little charisma but nevertheless served to confirm the view that this was the era of the leader. Although these dictatorships had disparate origins, the 'leadership cult' has 'generally been regarded as one of the most striking common elements of political rule in the period between the two world wars'.[55]

At the time, fascination with the magnetic powers of the Leader influenced the thinking of otherwise sober political thinkers. The German political philosopher Karl Lowenstein wrote that the new cohort of dictators were 'undoubtedly possessed by the lust of power'; they were motivated by 'the metaphysical impulse of a vocation which is a strange mixture of personal ambition and super-personal patriotism, and in which the individual passion for power may be an underlying, but by no means the decisive, motive'. Lowenstein described their conduct as one of *deo excitatus* – action inspired by god.[56] This portrayal of 1930s

[53] Krieger (1977) p. 255.   [54] Dickinson (1929) pp. 604–5.
[55] Kallis (2006) p. 32.   [56] Lowenstein (1935) p. 572.

dictators as exemplars of Weber's charismatic authority – the leader with a vocation – was influential in the social sciences. Hans Gerth, who was responsible for translating Weber into English, described the new Leader as not unlike 'the great prophets who have protested against orthodoxy in ecclesiastical organization and in theological doctrines', and Hitler as a 'revolutionary who does not accept the existing order but sets up instead an order of his own'. Gerth wrote that Hitler's 'authority is not a delegated authority but one residing in himself'.[57]

Although the imposition of dictatorial rule on numerous European societies exposed the lack of legitimacy of their political institutions, the rise of these authoritarian regimes was often misconstrued as the re-emergence of authority. So Wilson wrote in 1937 that the 'predominant note in the pragmatic age in which we live is the resurgence of authority' and added, 'the use of this authority for the planning of economic and social well-being is generally accepted as a valid end of government'.[58] Some observers were more sceptical, noting that the ascendancy of authoritarian political movements coincided with disorder and a crisis of legitimacy. In his diagnosis of the early 1920s, Merriam pointed to the paradox of the growing influence of authoritarian doctrines at a time when 'political obligation is least firmly rooted'.[59] One reason why the rise of dictatorships was interpreted as the re-emergence of authority was due to a tendency to lose sight of the distinction between authority and power, and between the terms 'authority' and 'authoritarian'. For example in the writings of Erich Fromm, 'attachment to and awe of authority' is represented as a marker of an authoritarian personality: the 'simultaneous love for authority and the hatred against those who are powerless are typical traits of the "authoritarian character"'. Although Fromm made a distinction between what he characterised as 'rational' as opposed to 'inhibiting' authority, his theory tended to elide the difference between these concepts and that of authoritarianism; as he argued, the 'difference between rational and inhibiting authority is only a relative one'.[60]

In a fascinating essay written in the late 1940s, the American sociologist Jeremiah Wolpert reinterpreted the inter-war cult of leadership as less a product of the resurgence of authority than a symptom of its dramatic absence. He linked the problem of foundation and its separation from moral and metaphysical imperatives to what he saw as exaggerated attempts to restore authority, writing that 'paradoxically, with the increased *instability* of authority, there was a corresponding emphasis, in grandiloquent terms, upon its timelessness'. As examples he pointed

[57] Gerth (1940) p. 518.   [58] Wilson (1937) p. 25.
[59] Merriam (1921) p. 179.   [60] Fromm (1965) pp. 82–3 and 162–4.

to 'Mussolini's evocation of a new Roman Empire and Hitler's boast of the thousand-year Reich'.[61] What Wolpert appeared to suggest was that the obsessive cultivation of leadership was itself symptomatic of a culture of insecurity and defensiveness towards a ruler's capacity to gain obedience. He linked the growing significance attached to technique of leadership as an indication of the decline of authority, writing that 'when the core of authority suffers erosion, when its ethical justification dissolves, manipulative techniques, become all the more necessary, and the stability of social relationships suffers accordingly'.[62] Moreover, argued Wolpert, this instrumentalisation of leadership 'has contributed considerably toward calling into question authority as such'.[63] One of the most important insights offered by Wolpert was that, contrary to the perception of the inter-war era as a renaissance of authority, 'too often, "authority" has been confused with "authoritarian" which is merely a particular type of authority'.[64]

The rationalisation of persuasion

Throughout history there have been attempts to manufacture authority through the construction of its outward symbols, myths and customs. However, the first three decades of the twentieth century saw an unprecedented interest in the development of techniques that could be used to cultivate the outward manifestations of authority. A sensibility of authority's absence encouraged a move towards issues linked to psychology and techniques of influence over public opinion. This psychological turn was motivated by the conviction that techniques of persuasion, rather than the exercise of moral authority, provided the key to gaining obedience and maintaining order.

A special issue of the *Annals of the American Academy of Political and Social Science* in 1935 on the subject of propaganda indicated that dictatorial regimes did not possess a monopoly on the use of thought control and techniques of psychological manipulation. In his introduction to this collection of essays, Harwood Childs was blunt in his warning that the 'struggle for power, domestically and internationally, is in large part a struggle for control over the minds of men'. Success in this struggle did not depend on the force of ideas but on the technical sophistication of propagandists. Childs argued that 'the groups which excel, whether official or unofficial, will be those most effectively implemented with the

---

[61] Wolpert (1950) p. 683. [62] Wolpert (1950) p. 681.
[63] Wolpert (1950) p. 686. [64] Wolpert (1950) p. 680.

techniques and tools of opinion leadership' – 'their ideals will constitute the value-patterns of the future'.[65]

Child's statement on the struggle for 'control over the minds of men' was in part a reaction to the apparent effectiveness of dictatorial regimes in developing techniques of mass manipulation. His aim was to win the argument for accepting propaganda as a rational technique of governance. This point was strongly promoted by the social psychologist Leonard Doob, who wrote a series of monographs advocating the virtues of propaganda. He claimed that 'propaganda is neither better nor worse than "rational" discourse'; 'the simple emotional appeal, like statistical and dialectical arguments, may be put to good purposes as well as to bad'.[66] Doob's affirmation of techniques of persuasion was justified on the ground that moral and ethical truths lacked the authority to prevail against falsehoods, and he wrote, with Edward Robinson:

Whether one looks upon the psychological problem of modern social life as that of securing complete control over the sources of psychological influence, or whether one accepts the conception that only limiting controls should be exercised to define areas of free expression, there is no longer any possibility of escaping the problem on the ground that when truth and falsehood are turned loose against each other, truth will necessarily triumph. Too much of such 'truth' is the dogma of those who have the power to issue decrees.[67]

Scepticism about the authority of the truth was more than matched by the conviction that the control of the public's mind through propaganda techniques constituted a legitimate solution to the problem of order.

The embrace of techniques of psychological manipulation was justified in part by the claim that a public that was moved only by irrational drives needed the guidance of rational expertise. Disillusionment with democracy in the 1930s encouraged the search for technical and psychological solutions to the problem of governance. However, it was the challenge posed by the Soviet Union, Nazi Germany and Fascist Italy that intensified the demand for techniques of mass persuasion, as the apparent success of totalitarian regimes in gaining the obedience of their citizens was frequently attributed to the success of their propaganda. Authoritarian public figures regarded myth-making and psychological manipulation as legitimate instruments for maintaining order. For Carl Schmitt, mythology provided a superior alternative to rational authority: he wrote that 'the theory of myth is the most powerful symptom of the decline of the relative rationalism of parliamentary thought', and praised 'anarchist

---

[65] Childs (1935) p. xi.   [66] Doob and Robinson (1935) p. 89.
[67] Doob and Robinson (1935) p. 94.

authors' who discovered the importance of the mythical from an 'opposition to authority and unity' for, inadvertently, helping to establish 'the foundation of another authority, however unwillingly', an authority based on the 'new feeling for order, discipline and hierarchy'.[68]

Mussolini's embrace of the cult of Augustus was regarded by many foreign observers as a uniquely effective manipulation of a symbol of authority. For some commentators, Mussolini's success served as evidence of the potential role of techniques of manipulation and propaganda. Writing from Harvard in 1926, William Y. Elliott described Mussolini as the 'Prophet of the Pragmatic Era in Politics'. His choice of terminology – the coupling of prophet and pragmatism – expressed the prevailing sentiment that modern politics required a rational calculating approach towards the management of irrationality. It is unlikely that Elliott had either read Weber or was familiar with the concept of charisma, but his was an era where modern political 'prophets' appeared to occupy the centre stage of public life. Liberal democracy was on the defensive: as Elliott commented, 'Italy and Russia have cast the die', and 'Spain and the Balkans have followed their lead, while Germany and Central Europe waver on the verge'[69]. Elliott wrote that 'by creating a myth of patriotism and embodying that myth in the figure of Mussolini, Fascism may succeed for a time in imposing what Plato would have called "a noble lie" upon Italy'.[70]

As someone who believed that the 'consent of the governed' possessed a moral authority that the 'techniques of myths, advocated by Plato' could not match, Elliott stood up for constitutional government. Nevertheless, one of the lessons that he drew from his experience of the 1920s was the need to subject representative democracy to the influence of the expert: 'The necessity of more independent expert administration and advice is obvious'.[71] Elliott, a future counsellor to several American Presidents and a member of Roosevelt's 'Brains Trust', recognised the uneasy relationship between consent and the attempt to use myths to manufacture it.

The 1920s brought a pragmatic orientation towards adopting techniques of persuasion. This standpoint was most coherently expounded by Harold Lasswell, who argued that the drive of irrational forces constituted one of the principal problems confronting public life. He praised the 'contribution of psychoanalysis' for throwing light on unconscious mass processes and believed that as a result 'the possibility of controlling mass insecurity by manipulating significant symbols has been put in

---

[68] Schmitt (1988) p. 76.   [69] Elliott (1926) pp. 163–4.
[70] Elliott (1926) p. 189.   [71] Elliott (1926) p. 185.

new perspective'.[72] Lasswell's focus was the power of political manipulation: the 'modern division of labour includes persons who are specialised creators of symbols', and the 'management of masses by propaganda has become one of the principal characteristics of our epoch'. In this era, rulers who depend on bread and circuses are 'superseded by rulers who are adept at diverting, distracting, confusing and dissipating the insecurities of the mass by the circulation of efficacious symbols'.[73]

For Lasswell the emotions of the masses become the focus for political intervention and psychiatry serves as the instrument of enlightened governance and the prevention of war. He wrote of the 'special province of political psychiatrists who seek to develop and to practice the politics of prevention' through 'devising ingenious expedients capable of discharging accumulated anxieties as harmlessly as possible', and claimed that 'the political psychiatrist' now assumed responsibility for the 'task of mastering the source and mitigating the consequences of human insecurity in our unstable world'.[74]

Manipulation by experts was the most effective instrument for maintaining order: 'The prerequisite of a stable order in the world is a universal body of symbols and practices sustaining an elite which propagates itself by peaceful methods and wields a monopoly of coercion which is rarely necessary to apply to the uttermost'. Lasswell added that 'the consensus on which order is based is necessarily nonrational; the world myth must be taken for granted by most of the population', and that 'efficacious symbols' with the capacity to gain 'deference to permit the elite to recruit its successors with a very minimum of violence was essential for world order'.[75] Lasswell's advocacy of the rationalisation of techniques of persuasion led him to emphasise the role of public ceremonies in the symbolic validation of authority. In his 1935 study *Propaganda and Promotional Activities*, he wrote:

In many times and places the symbols that sustain the existing distribution of values are transmitted with a minimum of premeditation, since they are deeply implanted in the culture. Under such conditions the ceremony is one of the most potent means of preserving the traditional order . . . The ceremonial is a reminder of continuity and permanence, offering the individual another opportunity to identify his own destiny with the imperishable.[76]

His promotion of the instrumental use of ceremonies became of interest to 'those involved with the study of public opinion and the means necessary for conditioning it'.[77]

[72] Lasswell (1965) p. 19.   [73] Lasswell (1965) p. 19.   [74] Lasswell (1965) pp. 19–20.
[75] Lasswell (1965) p. 181.   [76] Lasswell is cited in Frezza (2007) p. 167.
[77] Frezza (2007) p. 167.

The advocacy of techniques of rationalising persuasion often expressed an anti-democratic creed that regarded propaganda, advertising techniques, and the use of psychology as a legitimate way of gaining consensus. In the United States a fine line separated public education from propaganda. In 1932 the psychologist Horace B. English observed that social consensus could be easily forged 'by using the current psychological techniques of mass persuasion', and that 'if the right catch-words are used, a group of emotions with a corresponding complex of ideas is so effectively aroused that reflection becomes impossible'.[78] However, despite the bold claims made on behalf of techniques of mass persuasion, it became evident that these lacked the moral force associated with the rule of authority. Lasswell concluded that 'under democratic conditions' the 'long-run effect of this resort to propaganda is to undermine the basic loyalties upon which democratic institutions depend, and to prepare the way for impulsive revolt against them'.[79] He feared that whatever its short-term advantages, governance through propaganda threatened to make the situation worse. Techniques of persuasion could not serve as effective substitutes for moral authority.

Forty years later, Lasswell's insights were further developed by Habermas, who warned that the administrative use of propaganda would fail to motivate the public and that the instrumental manipulation of myths and symbols was likely to exacerbate the problem of meaning.[80] His conclusion was certainly backed up by the experience of the inter-war period. The cumulative effect of the different attempts to manufacture consent was to breed cynicism towards public life. In the end, the various attempts to bypass the problem of order through mobilising the forces of irrationality only served to highlight the fragility of authority.

The Parsonian attempt to reconcile rationalisation with meaning

At a time when a sensibility of the triumph of the irrational dominated the Western mind, the attempt by Talcott Parsons to rescue the idea of rational authority stood out as an exceptional attempt to give meaning to what many others considered a lost cause.

Parsons's major work, *The Structure of Social Action*, was published in 1937; a time when the consequences of global depression, the Russian Revolution and the growing influence of fascism had forced on the defensive the eighteenth- and nineteenth-century ideals associated with

---

[78] Cited in Frezza (2007) p. 139.   [79] Lasswell (1935) p. 188.
[80] Habermas (1976) pp. 70–1.

the Enlightenment and liberal and utilitarian thinking.[81] He claimed that the problem which his massive two-volume *opus* set out to answer was why the 'positivistic-utilitarian tradition' had lost its influence and died.[82] But fundamentally, he was wrestling with the failure of utilitarian conceptions of rationality to provide a normative foundation for authority. His work can be interpreted as an attempt to provide this form of authority with moral meaning through his engagement with the problem of order. Parsons regarded the Reformation as the key moment when what he calls the 'atomistic tendency', expressed through the 'very deep-seated individualism' of European culture, came to assume a dominant position in the intellectual life of the West. The principal philosophical expression of this trend 'has been a concern for the ethical autonomy and responsibility of the individual, especially as against authority'.[83]

Parsons claimed that the long-term cumulative outcome of the sanctification of religious freedom was the erosion of the intellectual foundation of authority. This dramatic shift in the historical evolution of authority was underlined in his declaration that, whereas the 'arguments for freedom from authority tended to become predominantly normative', the:

arguments for limitation on freedom of the individual tended to become empirical and factual, emphasizing the inexorable conditions of human life in society and the numerous ways in which a freedom gained in the name of religion could be perverted so as to endanger the stability of society itself.[84]

In this contrast drawn between the normative foundation for freedom and the pragmatic justification for restraining it, Parsons alluded to the loss of the moral foundation of authority; and this is the development that lies at the centre of his historical-logical representation of the problem of order.[85]

Parsons credits Hobbes with attempting to provide a utilitarian solution to the problem of order. But his is a precarious solution because there cannot be 'stability without the effective functioning of certain normative elements'.[86] He is drawn towards Pareto and Durkheim for their attempts to provide a sociology of order,[87] and approves of Durkheim's critique of Spencer for overlooking the cultural support that legal rules, for example contract, need in order to be binding. Following Durkheim, who stressed the 'importance of a system of regulatory, normative rules'

---

[81] 'A revolution of such magnitude in the prevailing interpretations of human society is hardly to be found occurring within the short space of a generation unless one goes back to about the sixteenth century', wrote Parsons (1968) p. 5.
[82] Parsons (1968) p. 3.   [83] Parsons (1968) p. 53.   [84] Parsons (1968) p. 88.
[85] Parsons (1968) p. 88.   [86] Parsons (1968) p. 92.   [87] Parsons (1968) p. 307.

in his critique of utilitarian theories of contract, Parsons wrote that legal rules are 'supplemented by a vast body of customary rules, trade conventions and the like which are in effect, obligatory equally with the law, although not enforceable in the courts'.[88,89]

Parsons's analysis of the history of authority can be interpreted as an elaboration of the insights provided by Weber. However unlike Weber, Parsons did not regard rationalisation and disenchantment as insurmountable obstacles to the endowing rational authority with meaning. He sought to develop a modernist form of impersonal authority that could provide the foundation for social order. It is in his writing on the role of the professions that his argument for the rationalisation of authority took shape.

In a monograph published in 1939, Parsons put forward the bold claim that professional or expert authority offered the model of a distinct principle of capitalist social organisation. Parsons sought to provide this authority with a normative foundation, one that recast the rational as a form of impersonal but universal normative principle of organisation. The impulse for developing a theory of professional authority was an attempt to engage with the highly charged 1930s debates about the nature of capitalism. Through drawing a moral equivalence between the ethos of the professional and that of business, Parsons sought to neutralise the prevailing anti-capitalist sentiments. Carrying on where Durkheim's critique of individualism left off, Parsons concluded that in a well-integrated society the corrosive impact of the pursuit of individual interests would be contained.

Parsons argued that it was the axial role played by the professions that defined modern society. Unlike the prevailing consensus, which would characterise 'capitalism' or 'free enterprise' as the most significant feature of modern Western civilization, Parsons insisted that it was the professions who played that role. Parsons also questioned the tendency to depict the disinterested professional as 'mere survival of the medieval guild' in a world wholly dominated by the pursuit of self-interest,[90] arguing that the contrast between business and the professions was less significant than the 'elements common to both'.

Through extending Weber's analysis of rationalisation, Parsons contended that the imperative of science and technology dominates all forms of human activity and orients it towards the normative standard of 'objective truth'. The norms of scientific work and investigation are 'independent of traditional judgments'. What counts is not how something was

---

[88] Parsons (1968) p. 313.   [89] Parsons (1968) pp. 314–15.
[90] Parsons (1939) pp. 457–8.

done in the past but objectively given facts. The loss of the normative authority of tradition affects business no less than the professions, and both are 'under continual and subtle social pressures to be rational, critical, particularly of ways and means'. Through its institutionalisation, rationality creates a 'mode of orientation' that dominates behaviour of business and the professions alike.[91]

Parsons developed his theory of rational authority through analysing its inner working in the professions, from which he highlighted three fundamental and distinct features of expert authority; that is, an authority based on 'technical competence'. Firstly, authority based on technical competence is limited to a 'particular technically defined sphere' – this is a *functionally specific* form of authority. In a statement that has echoes of G. C. Lewis's earlier discussion of this subject, Parsons wrote that 'a professional man is held to be "an authority" only in his own field'; thus, a doctor has no authority outside his specialism any more than biologist can claim authority over the handling of a legal dispute. Through extending the concept of functional specificity to the world of commerce, Parsons was able to claim that authority is exercised in a similar manner by administrators and business people working for a company, where authority is 'not enjoyed by virtue of technical competence' but by the functionally specific office that an individual holds.[92] Rationalisation promotes the institutionalisation of functional specificity throughout the professions and business.

Unlike diffuse relationships between friends and family members, functionally specific relationships can be captured by formal objective categories. The relation of client and customer or doctor and patient are impersonal and objectively defined. It is not family bonds or sentiment that influences such relationships but objectively and universally accepted criteria. Thus the second distinctive feature of authority based on technical competence is it is based on *universalistic* standards. Parsons argues that the role of universalism 'is by no means confined to the professions', but is equally significant to the management of administrative office and contractual relationships. The reintroduction of universalism as a foundational principle of professionalism represented a bold move to re-appropriate a foundational norm associated with authority in the past. However, as Gouldner points out, the universalistic standards of the professional do not represent a claim for transcendental or moral values but serve as the organisational imperative for impersonal institutions.[93]

---

[91] Parsons (1939) pp. 459–60.   [92] Parsons (1939) pp. 461.
[93] Gouldner (1973) p. 155.

The universalistic foundation on which rational authority is based limits the role of informal and particularistic considerations in the making of important decisions. Parsons pointed out that this was especially significant for the 'judgment of achievement in the occupation field'. The institutionalisation of universal criteria of judgment means that people advance and are rewarded on the basis of their achievement rather than on other criteria. This third element of rational authority – that it is based on the merit of *achievement* – is also one that is not confined to the professions.[94]

Parsons qualified his outline of modern professional authority by suggesting that it applied 'literally only to a well-integrated situation'. He feared that lack of integration could lead to the emergence of practices that ran counter to rationalised institutional patterns. For example, pressure from family and other particularistic loyalties could undermine the impersonal, objective and universalistic-based allocation of resources. Implicitly drawing on the distinction that Durkheim made between the pathological and the normal, Parsons regarded social strains as an aberration that could be fixed. The argument that the cultivation and institutionalisation of rational authority could provide an antidote to the disruptions caused by the 'strains' of the 1930s Depression had a minimal impact at the time; it was only after the experience of World War II that it would find a wider hearing.

Parsons's theory of the role of the professions sought to develop a limited, functionally specific form of technical authority. Through its emphasis on the institutionalisation of rationality, the theory severely limited the role of individual motivation and self-interest in the management of relations of authority. Universalism appeared to provide a normative basis for decision-making, and authority was underpinned by impersonal, scientific and objective criteria. The introduction of achievement as the basis on which authority roles were allocated could assists their legitimation. From this standpoint, the technical imperatives of objectivity mediated through an achievement-oriented institutional culture and based on universalism could claim the authority of science and the moral force possessed by disinterested universal norms.

The main instrument through which professional expertise could assist the rationalisation of authority was psychology. As Larry Carney noted, Parsons's advocacy of professional and expert intervention as agents of rationalisation led him to opt for policies of social engineering as early

---

[94] Parsons contends that what drives professionals and businessmen is not so much self interests but the twin objective of 'objective achievement and recognition'. See Parsons (1939) p. 464.

as 1942, in his proposal for dealing with defeated fascist powers.[95] He looked to 'rationalized forms of political interventions' to deal with threat of Nazism and the 'inevitable "strains" and group-specific psychological insecurities in modernizing and modernized societies'.[96] In his 1942 article 'Propaganda and Social Control', published in *Psychiatry: Journal of Inter-Personal Relations*, Parsons outlined an argument for justifying the role of professionals and their mass therapy as a form of impersonal authority. Whereas in medieval and early modern times political theorists drew on the model of patriarchal authority to elaborate their argument for absolutist rule, Parsons looked to the authority of the doctor and therapist. It is evident that Parsons was impressed by the authority that a medical doctor enjoyed over his patient and he sought to replicate this relationship in a wider social context. He observed that the medical profession possesses a 'very important kind of authority'. A doctor is in a position to exercise 'great influence even though his "orders" are not, in the usual sense, backed by coercive sanctions'.[97]

Parsons regarded the therapeutic relationship between doctor and patient as one through which an unusual degree of trust is invested in the authority of the therapist. Although confidence is essential in all forms of technical competence, it is 'doubly important in the medical case because all schools of psychiatry seem to be agreed that it is essential to psychotherapy, in any form, conscious or unconscious'.[98] Parsons was interested in the potential of the therapeutic relationship for validating authority in a wider social setting: just as therapy could manage the unconscious drives of individual behaviour, he believed it could do the same on a wider social scale.

In Parsons's presentation, propaganda was represented as the functional equivalent of individual therapy: 'It is the principal thesis of this paper that the structure of Western society in its relation to the functions of social control provides an extraordinary opening for the deliberate propaganda of reinforcement as an agency of control'.[99] He explained the connection between professional therapy and propaganda in the following terms:

it can safely be said that consideration of the role of the propaganda agency as analogous to that of the psychotherapist is more than a mere analogy. Social control in the sense of this discussion is after all in the last analysis a process of influencing, through psychological mechanisms, first the behaviour, more deeply, through the process of socialisation especially, the character structure of humans.

---

[95] Carney (1994) p. 472.   [96] Carney (1994) p. 472.   [97] Parsons (1942c) p. 155.
[98] Parsons (1942c) p. 159.   [99] Parsons (1942c) p. 173.

In its non-deliberate functional significance the institution of medical practice is an integral part of a far more generalized institutional structure and system of social control.[100]

Parsons attempted to depict 'propaganda policy as a kind of "social psychotherapy"' that worked 'directly in accordance with the essential nature' of the social system.'

Unlike some of his colleagues, Parsons was not embarrassed to praise the virtues of propaganda, which, he wrote, 'is essentially a technique which is capable of use in the service of any goal'. He depicted propaganda as an instrument for reinforcing stability and order, with a formidable potential for strengthening attachment to 'basic institutional patterns and cultural traditions of the society and deliberately and systematically counteracting. . . important existing deviant tendencies'.[101] His analysis of propaganda was designed to provide intellectual support for the American way of life in the middle of a global war, and thus he could confidently declare that,

few would question that this is the direction that propaganda should take in relation to the internal situation since, in this great crisis, it is fundamentally preservation of continuity with the great traditions and institutional patterns of Western society which is at stake.[102]

Parsons's advocacy of the role of the professional expert should not be interpreted as merely another attempt to embrace science for the legitimation of authority. His argument on the predominant role of professional expert authority has as its focus the relationship between doctor/therapist and patient. As Gouldner points out, 'Parsons placed considerably less emphasis on science as a source for elite legitimation and social integration; instead he gave a new emphasis to "professionalism"'.[103] Professionalism, with its moral connotation of a calling and what Gouldner characterises as the 'moral exercise of competence on behalf of public interest', provides rationality with a moral dimension.[104]

Reconciling the rational with the moral was at the heart of the Parsonian project of promoting therapeutic authority. After noting that 'it is essential to establish a position of impersonal authority', Parsons stated that in the case of medicine this 'involves primarily two elements, technical competence and moral integrity'.[105] It is significant that his model

---

[100] Parsons (1942c) pp. 174–5.   [101] Parsons (1942c) pp. 171–2.
[102] Parsons (1942c) p. 172.   [103] Gouldner (1973) p. 155.
[104] Gouldner (1973) p. 156.   [105] Gouldner (1973) p. 175.

was the therapist, not the scientist nor the administrator. Therapy, with is promise to engage the public's emotion and gain its trust, appeared to Parsons to be the most promising institution for reinforcing the influence of the social order over individual behaviour. The synthesis of rational professional with therapeutic guidance expressed a trend that Foucault would characterise decades later as the mutation of pastoral power into a medical form.[106]

Like Parsons, Foucault regarded the Reformation as representing a decisive moment in the transformation of authority and power. Foucault argued that pastoral power, a specific and autonomous authority in the Christian world, was 'unknown to any other civilization'.[107] As discussed previously, this separation of moral and political power was challenged by the Reformation; arguably, it was the subsequent loss of influence of an autonomous sphere of pastoral power that provided the historical context for the modern theory of authority. Parsons, who had grasped this legacy of the Reformation, was acutely sensitive to disorienting consequences of the absence of an independent sphere of moral authority. That is why he did not merely advocate the virtues of a professional ethos but also its insulation from politics. He argued that propaganda should avoid domestic political engagement and 'involvement in any of the internal struggles for power of partisan groups'; it should be 'as close as possible to the ideal of an impartial judiciary'.[108] Mass therapy and professional social engineering had to assume a neutral, depoliticised form if it was to gain the trust of the public.

Parsons's call to use propaganda to help 'connect Americans with the continuity of their institutional and cultural heritage' was justified as a legitimate exemplar of the use of rational professional and expert authority. This statement combined Machiavellian realism with the new techniques of psychological manipulation. But Parsons was no cynic. What he attempted to accomplish was to construct a system of 'impersonal authority', one where the expertise of 'social psychiatry' and of 'social science' could exercise a central role. Looking ahead, he stated that,

since there is as yet in society no professional group which has come to be defined to the public in general as possessing technical competence in 'social psychiatry' – perhaps someday some of the social sciences will achieve this – the next best seems to be the deliberate cultivation of a reputation for scrupulously truthful reporting of information, the sources of which the public cannot have direct access to.[109]

---

[106] Foucault (2007) p. 199.   [107] Foucault (2007) p. 149.
[108] Parsons (1942c) p. 174.   [109] Parsons (1942c) p. 174.

In effect, Parsons acknowledged that the cultivation of impersonal authority had to wait for a more propitious time in the future. He thereby anticipated an important development in the way that society would conceptualise the question of authority and the problem of order in the aftermath of the World War II – which hinged on the problem of *trust*.

16   In the shadow of authoritarianism

In the immediate aftermath of World War II, the revulsion against Nazism tended to intensify the sentiments of suspicion and hostility towards authority. This reaction fostered a climate of estrangement from authority, which was frequently interpreted as merely a milder version of authoritarianism. In this historical context the practice of obedience itself was often associated with negative and potentially pathological form of behaviour.

Antagonism towards authority was more than matched by antipathy towards mass culture and the emotions it fostered. The emotional deficits of the masses were depicted as one of the forces responsible for the scourge of authoritarian dictatorships, and reflections on the problem of authoritarianism frequently took the form of deprecating the capacity of the masses for informed consent. Whereas in the early part of the twentieth century elite theories of mass society tended to be authored by conservative and right-wing ideologues, in the post-World War II era they were more likely to express the disappointment of liberal and left-wing commentators. In 1950, the radical social critic Theodor Adorno echoed Robert Michels, the theorist of the iron law of oligarchy, in observing that 'throughout the ages', ever since the oligarchy arose in Greece, 'the majority of the people frequently act blindly in accordance with the will of powerful institutions or demagogic figures, and in opposition both to the basic concepts of democratism and their own rational interest'.[1]

Nevertheless, scepticism towards people's capacity for consent had to co-exist with the acceptance of some form of democracy as an essential principle for the organisation of a modern society. Adorno's response to this quandary was to argue for bypassing the problem of consent by relying on a democratic oligarchy to define the best interest of the public. He wrote that a democratic leadership must make the people 'conscious of their own wants and needs as against ideologies which are

---

[1] Adorno (1950) p. 418.

hammered into their heads by the innumerable communications of vested interests'.[2]

The traumatic events of the 1930s and the global war helped to foster a climate where the idea of authority was compromised by its association with authoritarianism. In this context, the conspicuous absence of a positive theorisation of authority is understandable. Indeed, one reason why Weber's sociology of domination continued to exercise such influence over the social sciences was because it was almost the last rigorous endeavour to take the subject of authority seriously, while, as Barbara Misztal remarked in the 1990s, 'Talcott Parsons was probably the last of the great sociologists who placed the problem of order at the centre of his concern'.[3] Parsons's functional conceptualisation of authority had a significant influence on the way that this subject was discussed in the social sciences in the post-war era. Parsons considered authority to be the 'the institutionalized code within which the "language of power" is meaningful',[4] and he claimed that this capacity to give meaning to power can be found in a variety of institutional settings. From this vantage point, he was able to represent the authority of the profession as the functional equivalent of religion.

Authority was frequently defined by its motivational function of gaining obedience, a representation that was particularly influential in organisation theory. Chester Barnard wrote that 'authority is another name for the willingness and capacity of individuals to submit to the necessities of cooperative systems'.[5] From this stance authority worked as a function of the imperative of organisation. Such formal or technical interpretations emphasised the contrast between authority as a role –'being in authority' – with its subjective manifestation – 'being an authority'. In her 1954 pioneering essay 'What is Authority?', Arendt observed of the social sciences that 'their concern is only with functions, and whatever fulfils the same function can, according to this view, be called the same'. She wrote that 'the same argument is frequently used with respect to authority: if violence fulfils the same function as authority – namely, make people obey – then violence is authority'.[6] Arendt rightly assumed that this functionalist approach would lead to the project of inventing authority substitutes, and that a moral equivalence would be claimed between the different ways of gaining consent.

Once authority is interpreted as a function serving the project of social co-ordination through the gaining of obedience, it acquires a technical and non-normative status. From a functionalist position, techniques for

[2] Adorno (1950) p. 420.   [3] Misztal (1996) p. 65.   [4] Parsons (1963) p. 250.
[5] Barnard (1962) p. 184.   [6] Arendt (2006) p. 102.

gaining obedience are presumed to constitute instruments of authorisation. The American political scientist David Easton expressed this position by arguing that 'both in the case where the legitimacy of the rulers
is accepted and where the rulers are obeyed only because they possess a
predominance of effective, violent sanctions, the rulers can be described
as authorities'.[7] In effect, functional theories render the issue of authority
unproblematic – acts of obedience serve as proof of its existence. The
question of its legitimacy is immaterial, for what matters is compliance
to a command; and the distinctions between legitimate authority, power
and the use of force are lost.

Arguments in favour of interpreting authority as a technique for gaining obedience served to depoliticise its relationship to obedience. As
Nancy Rosenblum wrote, the post-war generation of analytic philosophers debated authority as a concept that was detached from any specific
historical or political context. She observed that their 'studies tend to be
apolitical, strikingly so and that they contemplate the meaning of authority apart from questions of acquisition, legitimacy, purpose, effectiveness
and institution'.[8] Functionalist and abstract theories of obedience to
authority carried on the previously established practice of ignoring the
question of how to represent democratic consent as the ultimate source
for political authority. During the 1940s and 1950s, the rhetorical acclamation of democratic consent was rarely followed through to its elaboration into a liberal democratic validation of authority, and this tension
between rhetoric and reality continues to this day.

Thus in the 1980s the political philosopher Joseph Raz asserted that
although the 'idea that the legitimacy of government rests on consent
is deeply embedded in Western thought', it could not account for the
exercise of governmental power, because,

if consent to authority is consent to respect the claim the authority makes for
itself, then it is hard to see what justification there can be for the binding force
of consent to the authority of governments, given the extremely extensive powers
modern governments claim to have.[9]

For Raz, consent constitutes a relatively modest role in legitimating
authority: it has 'an independent, but auxiliary and derivative, place as a
source of legitimacy'.[10] What he seems to claim is that trust in authority is independent of consent and is only 'exceptionally formed by it
or expressed through it': trust, respect and obligation to obey are 'normally formed not through deliberate decisions, let alone formal acts of

---

[7] Easton (1958) p. 180.   [8] Rosenblum (1987) p. 102.   [9] Raz (1987) p. 86.
[10] Raz (1987) p. 93.

consent, but through normal habit-forming processes of education and habituation'.[11]

Raz's derivation of consent from the process of habit formation echoes the arguments advanced by Hume and the eighteenth-century Scottish political economists. He concludes by arguing that consent 'represents the deliberate and relatively formal end' of the spectrum of acts that lead to trust in government; consent 'can have no more than a marginal ceremonial, as well as an auxiliary and derivative role', a matter that Hume understood 'better than Locke'.[12] This interpretation of consent as possessing little intrinsic normative or moral content, and confining its role to that of formalising an act, can be seen as a post-war variation of the approach taken by Weber, in whose model of 'leadership democracy' the role of elections is to formalise charismatic authority with legitimacy.[13] Leadership is 'indirectly' based on the consent of the ruled, but this consent ceases to possess an intrinsic significance in the post-plebiscite era.

Once consent was portrayed as instrument of formalisation, its role was taken for granted, and what mattered was adherence to rules and processes. In this model consent became indistinguishable from compliance. By the 1950s, a 'shift of emphasis from substantive to procedural sources of authority' was evident in Western societies.[14] Furthermore, while liberal theories that emerged with the rise of modernity sought to ground authority 'in the rational consent of agents who agree (or promise) to obey rules and officials according to proper procedures',[15] with the psychological turn, the 'theory of consent, is haunted by the corollary appearance of theories of the unconscious and personal identification'.[16] The concept of consent was implicitly neutralised or negated by a new post-war consensus that both questioned people's capacity to consent and called into question the cultural value of obedience.

The devaluation of obedience

The negative theories of authority that emerged in the early part of the twentieth century claimed that the passivity and irrationality of the masses led inexorably to the rise of oligarchical domination. Following World War II, one of the distinct manifestations of the 'crisis of authority' was that the very act of obedience was derided as a marker for a psychological malaise. Frequent references to the willingness of the civilian population to obey its totalitarian leaders communicated the sentiment

---

[11] Raz (1987) p. 93.   [12] Raz (1987) p. 93.   [13] Mommsen (1981) p. 114.
[14] Spiro (1958) p. 54.   [15] Connolly (1987) p. 13.   [16] Connolly (1987) p. 14.

that obedience was inconsistent with a democratic form of public life. By the time Stanley Milgram published his classic *Obedience to Authority: An Experimental View* in 1974, the idea that obedience was a dangerous and dysfunctional form of behaviour enjoyed considerable cultural and intellectual support.

Milgram's experiment on obedience to authority represented a self-conscious attempt to account for the ease with which a significant proportion of the civilian population acquiesced to the inhuman commands of the Nazi regime. To this day, it is upheld as a cautionary story about the perils of authority. When, in the late 1980s, Nancy Rosenblum reminded her readers that 'Stanley Milgram's experiments remind us of what we know, or fear, about ourselves', she could confidently assume that her sentiments would resonate with a university-educated public.[17] The willingness of Milgram's study participants to obey an authority figure who commanded them deliver a high-voltage electrical shocks that appeared to cause significant physical pain on other people has become a widely disseminated moral tale about the dangers of deferring to authority. Milgram directly contributed to the construction of this narrative, writing,

> With numbing regularity good people were seen to knuckle under the demands of authority and perform actions that were callous and severe. Men who are in everyday life responsible and decent were seduced by the trappings of authority, by the control of their perceptions, and by the uncritical acceptance of the experimenter's definition of the situation, into performing harsh acts.[18]

Although his focus was on the psychology of obedience, Milgram drew a clear link between the act of individual command and the influence of legitimate authority. He defined legitimate authority in both psychological and inter-personal terms, writing that someone who is 'perceived to be in a position of social control within a given situation' constituted an authority figure, and qualified this focus on individual control by conceding that 'the power of an authority stems not from personal characteristics but from his perceived position in a social structure'.[19] He also wrote of the 'antecedent conditions' that dispose individuals to obey authority: the 'individual's familial experience, the general social setting built on impersonal systems of authority and extended experience with a reward structure in which compliance with authority is rewarded and failure to comply is punished'.[20] The socialisation of people, which leads to the internalisation of prevailing cultural norms regarding the social hierarchy, underwrites individual power.

[17] Rosenblum (1987) p. 112.   [18] Milgram (1974) p. 74.
[19] Milgram (1974) pp. 138–9.   [20] Milgram (1974) p. 138.

Milgram's emphasis on inter-personal relationships renders the concept of authority almost banal. He acknowledged that 'authority need not possess high status in the sense of "prestige"' and illustrated this point with the example of an 'usher at a theatre', who is the 'source of social control to whom we ordinarily submit willingly'.[21] Regarding the influence of legitimate authority, he argued that it is through controlling the way that people 'interpret the world' that their behaviour can be manipulated, and pointed to the role of propaganda and ideology in motivating people to perform 'extraordinary action'. This is accomplished through the capacity to define people's everyday reality: 'There is a propensity for people to accept definitions of action provided by legitimate authority', so that 'although the subject performs the action, he allows authority to define its meaning'.[22]

Previously, authors such as Harold Laski had questioned the virtues of obedience in order to support the ethos of freedom.[23] Milgram, by contrast, was more interested in exposing the dark side of obedience, and in this respect he succeeded in providing a powerful stimulus for its cultural devaluation. Through forging a causal connection between the willingness to obey authority figures and the Nazi experience, the very willingness to accept authority was reframed as problematic behaviour.

Milgram's influential indictment of obedience represented the elaboration of a corpus of work that evolved as a critique of the mass psychology of fascism. The work carried out by the Frankfurt School of Social Research and by social scientists influenced by the Freudian tradition made a significant impact on the way that public life was conceptualised by the middle of the twentieth century. Erich Fromm's 1941 study, *Escape from Freedom*, which was influenced by Horkheimer's study of the patriarchal family, served as a paradigm for other works that sought to draw attention to the destructive potential of the obedient personality.[24] Theodor Adorno's *The Authoritarian Personality*, published in 1950 was more influential still. *The Authoritarian Personality* claimed to uncover the traits in individuals that disposed them towards the acceptance of fascistic and authoritarian influences. According to this text, the problem was not simply the dysfunctional character traits of the individual, but a wider society that encouraged obedience to authority. This point was highlighted in an earlier contribution by Adorno and Horkheimer, when they expressed a sense of despair towards enthusiastic obedience 'to mass culture';[25] and later elaborated by Daniel Bell, who explained that the problem of 'democratic leadership is shaped by the fact that

---

[21] Milgram (1974) p. 139.   [22] Milgram (1974) p. 145.   [23] See Laski (1936).
[24] See Borch (2012) p. 213.   [25] Adorno and Horkheimer (1944) p. 120.

while we live in a society of political democracy, almost all basic social patterns are authoritarian and tend to instil feelings of helplessness and dependence'.[26]

Adorno's critique of the authoritarian personality and the subsequent literature it influenced contributed to an important shift, from the problematisation of the exercise of authoritarianism to the alleged need of the masses for authority figures. As the sociologist Richard Sennett explains, Adorno's contribution led a reorientation from Weber to Freud. Whereas Weber construed that people's action were shaped by a prevailing sense of legitimacy, Adorno underlined the importance of people's 'own need to believe', arguing that it is the psychological need for a strong authority figure in childhood that creates the demand for authoritarian domination.[27]

During this era, obedience was frequently qualified by the term 'unquestioned', conveying the implication that this was an act carried out by essentially unthinking and uncritical people. Such sentiments were particularly influential in intellectual life and the sphere of education. Even a child's obedience to parent and teacher were regarded as the precursor for more dangerous forms of deference to authority. For example, a paper delivered to the American Educational Research Association in 1975, warned that 'The danger is that too many citizens, as Stanley Milgram has demonstrated in *Obedience to Authority*, are quite prepared to unquestioningly obey the instructions of any authority they recognize as legitimate'.[28] The author went on to argue that 'authority relationships in American classrooms' were 'mirror images of authority relationships in the larger society', which were either 'authoritarian or bureaucratic in character'; she concluded that in 'either case, they are both politically and socially, regressive'.[29]

The questioning of obedience in pedagogical and psychological literature co-existed with a wider tendency to challenge relations of authority in everyday life. This was particularly striking in relation to the family. An American study of changes in traits desired in children between the years 1924 and 1978 showed a marked decline in the valuation of obedience to the family and church and an increase in the affirmation of individual independence. Preferences for 'strict obedience' fell from 45 per cent in 1924 to 17 per cent in 1978, and preferences for 'loyalty to the church' fell from 50 per cent to 22 per cent. By 1978, the 'most important traits desired in children were *independence* and *tolerance*'.[30] Similar trends were observed in Britain. One educationalist declared that

---

[26] Bell (1950) p. 406.   [27] Sennett (1981) p. 25.   [28] Montgomery (1975) p. 1.
[29] Montgomery (1975) p. 2.   [30] Alwin (1988) p. 42.

'nothing is so characteristic of twentieth-century man as his critical questioning approach to all traditional forms of authority':

It can be seen in all parts of life. It can be observed in the family, where children have a liberty to challenge their parents' demands that would have shocked our grandparents; where women are far less dependent, financially and emotionally on their husbands than was the case at the turn of the century.[31]

Although often represented as an expression of the democratisation of family life, it is more useful to interpret this trend as an expression of the difficulty that Western cultures had in giving meaning to authority itself. What had brought this about was not a revolt against authority so much as the exhaustion of society's capacity to motivate obedience. As one prescient account written in 1957 indicated, 'the alteration of attitude has taken possession not only of those who take orders but of those who give them: the one side has become more hesitant as the other has become more clamorous'.[32] In effect, authority had become a sort of embarrassment to those who were called upon to exercise it – a subject best avoided.

Instead of demanding obedience, people were now encouraged to cultivate relationships of trust. Trust is fundamentally a subjective act based on an individual's assessment of an institution, profession or an individual. Unlike claims to authority, relations of trust make no claim to permanence, universality or duty. Trust relations are provisional and open to negotiation. Moreover, the call to trust yourself, your doctor, priest, government or father, implies a different meaning and context and is rarely founded on a shared narrative.

Arguably, the emergence of a discourse of trust should be conceptualised as an expression of the shift from the authority of the past towards the search for guidance for engaging with the future. As Connolly explains, 'modern projects are designed to realize an anticipated future more than to maintain or restore a pure condition located in the past'. This involves investing hope in the capacity of currently authoritative procedures and norms to realise their promise: 'If the secularisation of authority means that faith is translated into trust, it also installs the future as the interconnecting link between trust and authority'.[33]

However, as shown by the rapid decline of trust in Parsons's ideal of professional authority, this link is inherently fragile.[34] From the 1960s onwards, the legitimacy of the professions faced constant questions, and by the 1980s it was evident they were facing a significant erosion of

[31] Collier (1957) p. 283.   [32] Collier (1957) p. 283.   [33] Connolly (1987) p. 14.
[34] See Chapter 'Who Can You Trust?' in Furedi (2006).

trust. Social scientists pointed to the 'bureaucratisation and proletarianization of professional work', with one study characterising the
loss of the moral status of the professional as the 'deconstitution of
professional authority'.[35] Habermas argued that the politicisation of
professional activity through the expansion of state activity 'produces
a universal pressure for legitimation in a sphere that was once distinguished precisely for its power of self legitimation'.[36] This crisis of legitimacy is strikingly evident in relation to the sphere that once served as
the exemplar for Parsons's theory of professional authority – the American medical profession. According to research carried out in the early
1990s, the erosion of 'professional legitimacy in American medicine was
far more pronounced than that experienced by other social institutions':
surveys indicated that over a 30-year period, American medicine went
from being perhaps the most trusted to being one of the least trusted
social institutions'.[37]

Narratives on authority

In retrospect, there appears a considerable degree of continuity in the
way that the problem of authority was managed and interpreted during
the twentieth century. The inter-war era, which saw the politicisation
of authority, marked an interlude that contrasted with the previous and
subsequent phases that were characterised by the tendency to depoliticise it. Throughout most this century, negative conceptions of authority
tended to displace its more positive affirmation. During the early part
of the century, mass pathology was used by conservative and right wing
theorists to account for the threat to authority from below; by the 1940s
and 1950s, theories of the psychological deficits of the masses served to
implicate their authoritarian behaviour in the ascendancy of totalitarian
and xenophobic dictatorships.

The period following World War II brought the emergence of competing claims about the nature and status of authority. Of these, the
four most significant narratives can be characterised as those of *evasion*,
fear, *loss* and *expertise*. Although these narratives often overlapped and
were often used by claims-makers in conjunction with one another, they
resonated with different constituencies of people.

Narrative of evasion

The evasive tendency, to depoliticise authority and render it technical and abstract, was rarely elaborated through a self-consciously

---

[35] See Esquith (1987) p. 255.   [36] Habermas (1976) p. 71.
[37] Schlesinger (2002) p. 189.

formulated argument. For example, the shift from a concern with substantive and normative questions towards process and rules was both experienced and justified as a necessity posed by the technical imperatives of a complex society. This was facilitated by the great political, moral and social upheavals culminating in World War II, after which Western liberal democracies and the 'way of life' they represented were able enjoy a degree of legitimacy. The moral contrast between the Allies and the Axis powers served to consolidate the valuation of democracy, providing at least a temporary solution to the problem of political authority during the years leading up to the 1960s. Moreover, the negative example of the Soviet bloc lent credibility to the claim of Western governments that they represented the 'free world', and the very necessity to defend society from the threat of totalitarianism and nuclear conflict displaced substantive questions surrounding the nature of consent and the source of authority.

The significance of the Cold War for underwriting the moral authority of Western governments was spelled out in 1953 by Douglas Copland, a Jesuit writer, in the following terms:

We live in a totalitarian age when, in a moment of crisis, we are prepared to enlarge and trust authority in order to defeat those who would wish to impose their authoritarian order upon us. We do this because we have sufficient belief in the inherent capacity of a free society to concede control to authority, when all are agreed that the challenge to freedom must be met by a united effort.[38]

Despite this statement's rhetorical flourish, there is little doubt that threat of totalitarian aggression provided governments with a significant measure political support. Although a 'crisis of legitimacy' resurfaced in the 1960s, it was not until the end of the Cold War that the scale of the problem of authority became visible.

Indeed, the contribution that the Cold War made to the displacement of authority as a central political problem only became evident after the disintegration of the Soviet Union. The collapse of the 'Soviet Threat' and the suspension of Cold War rivalries in the 1980s brought to the fore problems of legitimacy that were obscured by the intensity of a highly ideological superpower conflict. At this time, the externalisation of domestic problems ceased to be an effective formula for avoiding them, and the problem of order and of legitimacy re-emerged in the form of a loss of cultural cohesion, meaning and identity.[39]

The stability and sense of order experienced during the Cold War was also underwritten by the unprecedented expansion of capitalist

[38] Copland (1953) pp. 275–6.
[39] These points are discussed in Furedi (1992), Chapter 4.

economies during the era known as the 'post-war boom'. Until the late 1960s this growth of economic activity led to a steady increase in living standards and the expansion of the Welfare State. When on 20 July 1957, the British Prime Minister Harold Macmillan famously told his fellow Conservatives that 'most of our people have never had it so good', he knew that his words would resonate with the prevailing national mood. Prosperity and a sense of unparalleled security helped to neutralise and hence evade the problem of authority. As Douglas Copland stated,

> there is little doubt that the growth of authority and control in free societies has been accompanied by great progress in production, in living standards, in security against many of the hazards of personal life and in elevating the status of the individual in the community.[40]

In reality the mood of economic optimism co-existed with nagging doubts about the meaning of life and of the future. The historian Eric Hobsbawn wrote that this was:

> a crisis of the beliefs and assumptions on which modern society had been founded since the Moderns won their famous battles against the Ancients in the early eighteenth century – of the rationalist and humanist assumptions, shared by liberal capitalism and communism, and which made possible their brief but decisive alliance against fascism, which rejected them.[41]

However, the eighteenth-century model of the displacement of the Ancients by the Moderns was not to be replicated in the mid-twentieth century. This was the moment widely characterised as 'The End of Ideology', and in decades to come the end word would be attached to a variety of concepts – end of history, end of the author or the end of geography – signifying a mood of cultural pessimism. Although this sense of terminus was occasionally punctuated by the emergence of counter-tendencies, there was little demand for the constitution of a modern or novel version of foundational norms for validating authority.

This crisis of belief, or what Connolly characterised as the loss of *telos*, called into question the workings of cultural authority. That is why even at the height of the post-war boom American thinkers of virtually all shades of political opinion were deeply concerned about the absence of any positive vision of the future. 'No one could ignore the avalanche of works with such titles as "whither modern man?" or "good-bye to the West" or the "destiny of European culture"', wrote Judith Shklar in 1957.[42] Ironically, the crisis of belief was frequently perceived as an argument for bypassing the problem of authority. The absence of agreement about the

---

[40] Copland (1953) p. 276.   [41] Hobsbawn (2004) p. 11.   [42] Shklar (1957) p. vii.

purpose of life was often interpreted as an unavoidable fact of modern life, which, in turn, provided a justification for the renunciation of the need for a substantive and normative foundation for authority.

With the rise of so-called post-modern cultural and intellectual currents came an implicit notion of *post-authority*.[43] So precisely at a time when the exhaustion of the conjunctural influences of the Cold War and the post-war boom made more visible the absence of a normative foundation for authority, influential intellectual currents called for the bypassing of the problem on the grounds that it was irresolvable.

Insofar as attempts were made to recognise this absence, the solutions offered tended to have a hesitant, pragmatic and technical character. William Connolly wrote that *telos* 'in any strong sense of the word, cannot be restored to modernity, but the practice of modern authority is possible without a restoration'.[44] Connolly's response was to opt for a form of authority that is at once ambiguous and pragmatically oriented towards co-ordination: 'Authority, rightly instituted, is a mode of coordination that treats individuals with the respect due them without requiring each to possess an impossibly high level of civic virtue'. Emphasising his pragmatic premise, he stated that 'it is an appropriate mode of coordination in societies where social knowledge is specialized, interests are diverse, and the requirements of common action are relatively high'.[45] Connolly's advocacy of an 'ambiguous orientation to authority' was motivated by his reluctance to give it too much scope to influence life. He was clearly concerned about the danger of people deferring too much:

> The most ominous danger confronting modern authority is that our experience of its fragility, in conjunction with the anxiety that experience evokes, will impel too many to concede too much to it, to suppress awareness of the dangers and injustices that accompany its successful exercise.[46]

In social theory the absence of teleological unity was often represented as the inexorable consequence of modern or 'post-modern' life. Nancy Rosenblum celebrates the consequent pluralisation of authority and explicitly rejects attempts to posit a single foundational norm as the validation of authority. 'Official policy often cannot be traced to an identifiable source or justified with a single rationale, or even with several noncontradictory ones', she claims, in support of her argument that 'Weber's classic typology simply does not suffice even as an introduction to this diversity'.[47] The displacement of authority with a pluralised concept of *authorities* turns it into a problem that, at least in its

---

[43] See Kumar (1986) p. 193.   [44] Connolly (1987) p. 10.
[45] Connolly (1987) p. 19.   [46] Connolly (1987) p. 22.   [47] Rosenblum (1987) p. 103.

classical form, has ceased to exist. This argument has been advanced most forcefully by Zygmunt Bauman, in his discussion of the 'gradual, but consistent fading of the "legitimation discourse"'.[48]

Bauman argues that the pluralisation of modern society inexorably leads to the fracturing of authority, contending that the 'rationalization process has brought in its wake an extreme fragmentation of the sites of authority'. The only link that binds together otherwise autonomous sites of authority is the market. This argument, which was clearly anticipated by eighteenth-century political economists like Adam Smith, has in its recent guise served to explain how order can co-exist with the absence of its legitimation: 'In the absence of systemic legitimation, the market becomes as well the principal mechanism of social integration'.[49]

Bauman goes so far as to argue that the issue of authority has ceased to be a problem for the state. In his historical account of debates around the 'sources of legitimacy', he asserts that the problem 'simply lost its significance as the modern state grew in confidence as to the efficacy of policing, surveilling, categorizing, individualizing and other methods of modern bureaucratic administration'. According to Bauman, 'having lost its relevance to the practical business of politics, the problem became, uncontestedly the private property of philosophers'.[50] He concludes that 'the state is not necessarily weaker from this demise of authority' for it has 'found better, more efficient ways of reproducing and reinforcing its power; authority has become redundant, and the category specializing in servicing the reproduction of authority has become superfluous'.[51] The argument that new techniques of control have led to the 'gradual displacement of ideological legitimations' is in places qualified by the intuition that the problem has been postponed, rather than solved.[52]

It is difficult to avoid the conclusion that Bauman and others have opted for interpreting the absence of a serious challenge to the prevailing order as proof that modern society has come up with a technical solution to the problem of authority. Such conclusions could draw on Foucault's discussion of biopower, where he outlined the rise of a 'new type of power' in the context of the decline of sovereignty. Foucault wrote that 'this non-sovereign power, which is foreign to the form of sovereignty, is "disciplinary" power', which is a power that 'cannot be described or justified in terms of the theory of sovereignty'.[53] That power ceased to be

---

[48] Bauman (1987) p. 190.   [49] Bauman (1987) p. 188.
[50] Bauman (1987) p. 106.   [51] Bauman (1987) p. 122.
[52] Bauman recognises the importance of legitimacy for public life when he argues that the 'legitimation of the social system must again be made a matter of public debate'. Bauman (1987) pp. 159–60 and 191.
[53] Foucault (2004) p. 36.

justified through the theory of sovereignty or through other foundational norms does not mean that a solution to the problem of legitimacy has been found: simply that it can be evaded.

In current sociological contributions on the problem of social solidarity, trust and order, the issue of authority is self-consciously bypassed. Barbara Misztal's study of trust disassociates authority from social order, writing that Hobbes's attempt to develop an answer to the problem of order was a 'pessimistic evaluation of the chance to obtain social order without political authority'.[54] The assumption conveyed is that reliance on political authority is inconsistent with genuine relations of trust. Following Anthony Giddens, Misztal argues that, 'the fragility of the modern trust relationship, left without external support of kinship ties, local community, traditions or authority of religion, and the less satisfying nature of abstract trust have increased the importance of trust in our societies', and thus 'more than ever, trust needs to be actively built', by opening ourselves up to others through a form of self-directed therapy.[55] In effect, the problem of order is interpreted through inter-personal relations of trust.

Giddens argues that contemporary society is subject to competition between 'multiple authorities'. In such circumstances, those who seek solace in overarching authority risk giving up their capacity for critical thought, for 'taking refuge in a dominant authority' is 'essentially an act of submission'.[56] Giddens's representation of obedience as a conformist act of submission speaks to the narrative of evasion, but also overlaps with the narrative of fear.

Narrative of fear

In the post-World War II era, insecurity about the dangers of fascist authoritarianism was reinforced by anxieties regarding the Soviet threat. But what endowed this narrative with a sense of urgency and intensity was the conviction that mass culture in democratic societies tended to produce people who were vulnerable to authoritarian influences. Nineteenth-century versions of the idea of the suggestibility of the masses were recycled through narratives that emphasised the subliminal powers of hidden persuaders, operating through advertising, public relations, propaganda, the media or mass culture. Despite their difference of emphasis, these theories expressed an intense sense of foreboding towards manifestations of conformist patterns of mass behaviour.

[54] Misztal (1996) p. 27.   [55] Misztal (1996) p. 91.   [56] Giddens (1991) p. 196.

From the 1940s onwards, the narrative of fear dominated the conceptualisation of authority among cultural critics, academia and wider intellectual life, and was often directed towards a *narrative of prevention*. The English biologist and philosopher Julian Huxley expressed this sentiment in a restrained form in his 1950 lecture to the Royal Anthropological Institute of Great Britain and Ireland, in which he diagnosed people's need for authority as a psychological problem inflicted by a 'burden of guilt' resulting from 'having to repress the impulses of aggression in the primal infantile conflict of hate and love for the parents'. Huxley advised that the search for the certainty was, in any case, a futile one, since 'the provision of dogma, whose absolute truth is buttressed by authority or guaranteed by revelation' is likely to break down 'in the face of the accumulation of new facts and new knowledge.'[57]

Others expressed the narrative of fear in a far more interventionist form. One of the most eloquent and well argued examples was provided in a collection of essays, *Studies in Leadership; Leadership and Democratic Action*. Published in 1950 and edited by Alvin Gouldner, the volume contains contributions by some of the most influential commentators on the subject – Theodor Adorno, Daniel Bell, Kurt Lewin, William Whyte, Seymour Lipset, Jeremiah Wolpert and Reinhard Bendix – which, taken together, reveal a tendency for the concept of authoritarianism to blend in with that of authority. Though rarely stated explicitly, this conceptual synthesis was informed by the premise that the gaining of obedience is likely to be the accomplishment of mass manipulation, which works to the advantage of an authoritarian agenda and to the detriment of democratic authority.[58]

Gouldner's essay 'Manipulation and Authoritarian Leadership' sought to define 'some of the characteristics of authoritarian and democratic leadership', on the grounds that 'it is vital to know the former for diagnostic purposes and for judging when some sort of therapy or remedy is required'. Throughout this essay, understanding the nature of leadership is presented as vital for assisting the task of therapeutic intervention against authoritarianism. Gouldner asserts that finding the answer to his question could provide the data to 'guide our remedies, making them less of a trial-and-error-procedure', stating elsewhere that such answers have 'certain prognostic value' and that this knowledge is 'useful for therapeutic purposes'.[59] Gouldner understood that his call for therapeutic

---

[57] Huxley (1950) p. 22.
[58] It is worth noting that even someone as sensitive to the nuances surrounding the meaning of authority tended at times to use the term authoritarian as not just a cognate but as a variant of the concept of authority. See Arendt (1958) p. 83.
[59] Gouldner (1950) p. 389.

intervention was no less manipulative than those of his foes, and to his credit raises the question of whether democrats ought to counter authoritarian manipulation with their own version. Grasping the inconsistency between an ethos of democracy and the tactic of manipulating public behaviour he expresses the sentiment that 'somehow, the injuries which manipulation does to a democratic group's chances for survival must be both avoided or minimized'.[60]

Adorno's critique of authority and of mass psychology was far more assertive and far-reaching. In an era where 'the spell of a thought-controlling mass culture has become almost universal', it was 'utopian' and 'naively idealistic' to assume that the containment of authoritarian trends 'could be achieved through intellectual means alone'. In other words, the countering of a 'heavily libidinized' mass culture required the use therapeutic counter-manipulation rather than intellectual arguments. In a section titled 'Vaccines Against Authoritarianism', Adorno advocated enlightening the attitudes of the masses through 'making the best possible use of the insights of depth psychology', adding that it was important to understand the techniques of the enemy since one 'might derive from them, as it were, vaccines against antidemocratic indoctrination'.[61]

The twin themes of fear and prevention that dominated this narrative had as their premise the belief that the psychological deficits of the masses significantly diminished the potential for the emergence of a democratic form of authority. This apprehension was expressed with considerable force by Jeremiah Wolpert, who argued that rationalisation breeds 'personality malfunctions' which diminish influence of rationality on human behaviour'. As a result, people are pushed 'towards actions over which they have no conscious control; actions which are compensatory for the frustrations which an impersonal schematized order brings in its train'. According to Wolpert, this development led to a 'counterfeit' hero worship and declared that 'modern pseudo-charisma is a product of very conscious rationality'.[62]

Wolpert's solution to the danger of authoritarian rationalisation was therapeutic intervention, to cultivate a more democratically inclined personality; he called for a 'concerted effort at building the type of personality which will secure, self-sufficient and self-insightful'.[63] His focus was challenging the relations of authority within the family, since intervention in this institution 'provides much more promising results for enduring change than an isolated frontal attack upon given political and economic institutions'. He called for the targeting of the middle class, since it is

---

[60] Gouldner (1950) pp. 391–2.   [61] Adorno (1950) pp. 420 and 429.
[62] Wolpert (1950) pp. 680–1.   [63] Wolpert (1950) p. 700.

'much more receptive to changes in child rearing than lower-income groups', and concluded,

If sufficient numbers of individuals are raised in an atmosphere in which the ambivalent attitude toward authority, which expresses itself in the need for love and the fear of its withdrawal, is muted, *while constant efforts at changing political and economic institutions are going on*, there will be a nucleus from which the total social pattern may be changed.[64]

Wolpert's call to reconstruct the family along more enlightened lines was explicitly oriented towards the objective of modifying the foundation of authority. He argued that such intervention 'seems to be the only positive way toward reshaping the bases of authority'.[65]

The literature of the 1960s and 1970s often conveys a sense of ambivalence about the devaluation of authority. A text devoted to expounding the meaning of authority warned that 'when a person enters a situation of obedience and accepts authority, he enters into a binding relationship which is difficult to break without questioning the competence, status and wisdom of authority, all of which creates anxiety, fear, embarrassment and inner doubt': thus, 'a great deal of courage and determination is required to defy authority which has previously been accepted and obeyed'.[66]

In recent decades, the narrative of fear has become more influential, particularly in social theory. Richard Sennett's 1980 study *Authority* expresses this sentiment in the assertion that 'we have come to fear the influence of authority as a threat to our liberties, in the family and in society at large'.[67] In its more a radical interpretation, authority is presented as a pathology to be avoided. According to one interpretation of the association of authority with the abuse of power,

those who in a previous era held positions of power, responsibility and authority – parents, teachers, doctors, priests, day care workers, nurses, scout leaders, etc. – have been 'unmasked' as unworthy of the trust placed in them via the 'revelation' that many have been found guilty of child abuse.[68]

Narrrative of loss

In mainstream social life, concern about the estrangement of society from authority is frequently expressed through a narrative of loss. This narrative appealed to people who felt disoriented by the consequences of what appeared to them as a relentless process of social and cultural change.

---

[64] Wolpert (1950) p. 700.   [65] Wolpert (1950) p. 700.   [66] Dominian (1976) p. 20.
[67] Sennett (1981) p. 15.   [68] Scott (2008) p. 16.

Despite the difficulty that society had in giving a positive meaning to authority, the demand for guidance, co-ordination and leadership continued at all levels of society. However, the more coherent and systematic constructions of the narrative of loss tended to be advocated by commentators concerned with the problem of order as well as conservative and religious thinkers preoccupied with the erosion of traditional forms of authority.

The narrative of loss often acknowledged that authority had become a focus of suspicion. 'The theoretical problem is that authority as a concept and as a phenomenon is often confused with power, force or coercion', wrote one political scientist.[69] One of the most influential attempts to rehabilitate the concept of authority in the 1940s was the contribution of the French Thomist political philosopher Yves Simon, whose essay *The Nature and Functions of Authority* attempted to reconcile authority with modern aspiration for freedom. He directed his arguments against those who assumed that the 'progress of liberty' and 'social progress' implied the 'decay of authority'.[70] Simon's work is remarkable for its defensive and pragmatic tone. Despite his theological and philosophical convictions, he makes little attempt to rescue traditional religious authority, arguing instead, in line with the prevailing climate, for authority on functional grounds. Simon declared that this 'essential function' was to 'assure the unity of action of a united multitude', adding that 'a multitude aiming at a common good which can be attained through a common action, must be united in its action by some steady principle' and that 'the principle is precisely what we call authority'.[71] Simon's version of the principle of authority lacks a *telos* or a normative foundation. Its justification is the pragmatic need for social co-ordination.

Arguments in the 1940s and 1950s on behalf of the 'need for authority' often had a tentative and abstract character. Participants in a 1956 meeting of the American Society for Political and Legal Philosophy were convinced that this topic was of 'vital importance' but could not find the words with which to justify the rehabilitation of the ideal of authority. 'Whenever philosophy even glances at this question nowadays, it seems to have eyes only for freedom and ignores authority', complained one.[72] While most participants struggled to rescue a version of meaningful authority, Hannah Arendt argued that it had become 'almost a lost cause'. Arendt's paper spoke to the past and was self-consciously titled 'What Was Authority?' She stated that 'authority has vanished from the modern world, and that if we raise the question what authority is, we

---

[69] Cochran (1977) p. 546.   [70] Simon (1948) p. 5.
[71] Simon (1948) p. 7.   [72] Hendel (1958) p. 7.

can no longer fall back upon authentic and undisputable experiences common to all'.[73] Arendt's narrative of loss left little room for retaining illusions that authority in its classical form could survive.

Arendt drew attention to a dramatic development in the 'gradual breakdown', 'the authority of parents over children, of teachers over pupils and, generally of the elders over the young'.[74] She observed that this is 'the one form of authority' that existed in 'all historically known societies', as it is 'required as much by natural needs, the helplessness of the child, as by political necessity'. But:

ours is the first century in which this argument no longer carries an overwhelming weight of plausibility and it announced its anti-authoritarian spirit more radically when it promised the emancipation of youth as an oppressed class and called itself the 'century of the child'.

Arendt was less interested in the implosion of generational authority itself as in the extent to which it signified 'to what extremes the general decline of authority could go, even to the neglect of obvious natural necessities'.[75]

The devaluation of adult authority pointed to an important development, which was the failure to give meaning to the authority of authority. Arendt intuited that the devaluation of authority had spread beyond the political sphere to capture all domains of social and cultural experience. This trend was expressed through the powerful counter-cultural moment of the 1960s. At the time, the so-called crisis of legitimation tended to be perceived as a political problem afflicting the state. However, as Eric Hobsbawn noted almost four decades after Arendt's 1956 contribution, the loss of authority was principally a cultural phenomenon. In his account of what he called the 'cultural revolution', he wrote of 'the breaking of the threads which in the past had woven human beings into social textures'. Echoing Arendt's point about the far-reaching effect of the loss of pre-political authority, Hobsbawn stated that 'what children could learn from parents became less obvious than what parents did not know and children did'.[76]

References to the loss of 'respect for authority' since the 1960s have tended to constitute a statement about a cultural attitude rather than about the status of any specific authority. Take the following letter published in the London *Times* in December 1967:

Mr David Frost asks Mr Ray Gunther, 'What is the malaise affecting the English people?' I can tell him. It is the lack of respect towards those in authority, and the failure to inspire respect and to exert authority by those who are expected to do

---

[73] Arendt (1958) p. 81.   [74] Arendt (1956) p. 403.
[75] Arendt (1956) p. 404.   [76] Hobsbawn (2004) pp. 327 and 334.

so. When a Cabinet Minister in a supposedly serious television discussion allows a television entertainer to call him 'Ray' and responds by calling the entertainer 'David', no wonder no one takes any notice of him.[77]

This trivial example of resentment was a response to the realisation that authority was not only rejected, but held in contempt.

Since the 1970s, the narrative of loss has been preoccupied with the development of a counter-authority culture. In the introduction to *Authority: A Philosophical Analysis*, the American R. Baine Harris notes that 'institutions are no longer respected just because they are institutions', adding that 'one of the factors contributing to the current unrest in our society is the breakdown of respect for authority'. He writes that 'authorities are now being challenged in all areas of human life': 'church, the school, the family, the state – those traditional bastions of authority – have lost a large amount of the respect that was formerly accorded to them'.[78] The 'loss of respect' for authority conveys concern with an attitude that disdains it. The focus of the narrative is youth, since 'in almost every country of the world, the young question the views of their elders to a degree never done before';[79] and what is 'at issue is a change in our way of thinking about the basic nature and function of *authority itself*'. For Harris, society was now witnessing a 'challenge to the very *idea* of authority', and engaging in the 'reconsideration of the *meaning* of authority'.[80]

One of the clearest statements of the narrative of loss of cultural authority was provided by the conservative sociologist Robert Nisbet, who warned that the 'revolt against authority has already reached a higher point than in any other period in the West since perhaps the final years of the Roman Empire'. Like most laments of authority lost, Nisbet pointed the finger of blame at the rise of individualism and the authority of the self: 'Clearly, the individual seeking, through every possible means, escape from authority is one of the central realities of our age in American society'.[81] Unlike Arendt, Nisbet and most other authors of the narrative of loss could not reconcile themselves to a world where authority appeared merely as a historical phenomenon. However, they were also aware that of the failure of attempts to revive cultural support for authority. That is why the elusive quest for cultural authority invariably leads to the embrace of science, as the one authority that still possesses the capacity to validate claims and decisions.

[77] See Letter signed by Anthony Prince in *The Times*; 15 December 1967.
[78] Harris (1970) p. 1.   [79] Harris (1970) p. 1.
[80] Harris (1970) p. 1.   [81] Nisbet (1972) pp. 3, 4 and 12.

The narrative of expertise

In different ways, the narratives of evasion, of fear and of loss are far too negative to provide the moral and intellectual resources necessary for the validation of authority. Yet Arendt's stark claim that 'authority has vanished' could not be the end of the story for society, especially a complex modern one requiring authoritative guidance and moral direction. As noted previously, the processes of rationalisation and modernisation worked to diminish and ultimately corrode the normative foundation on which authority was constituted. However, rationalised forms of authority – legal, bureaucratic, scientific – often lacked the moral depth necessary for legitimating the exercise of power.

The late nineteenth-century reaction to rationalism and the turn to psychology were often associated with disillusionment about the authority of science. However, the progressive rationalisation of society meant that science and expertise always had a presence and could be called upon to authorise decisions and actions. Moreover, as older forms of legitimation lose their salience, society becomes increasingly dependent on expert guidance. In his prescient 1969 study *Toward a Rational Society*, Habermas observed that in the post-war period, technology and science worked as a quasi-ideology: he wrote of the 'scientization of political power' and argued that politicians had become increasingly dependent on professionals.[82] The hope that Parsons invested in the influence of professional authority appeared prophetic.

Yet twenty-first-century society cannot exist without the exercise of reason and science. Despite Western culture's disenchantment with rationality, competing parties in the key controversies of our era continually appeal to the authority of science, and the narrative of expertise represents the most influential validation of authority of our times.

In policy debates about social and public issues the evidence provided by the experts is used by all parties to validate their arguments, and even constituencies who are motivated by moral, religious and political concerns adopt a technocratic, rationalised and scientific narrative. In recent decades, environmentalists who were formerly suspicious of science and anti-abortion activists who were inspired by a religious ethos have embraced the authority of scientific expertise to justify their cause. This pragmatic, arguably opportunistic, embrace of the authority of science has been pointed out by Steve Yearley in relation to the environmental movement. This movement 'has a profound dependence on scientific evidence and scientific expertise', but 'at the same time, many within

---

[82] Habermas (1987) p. 63.

the green movement are distrustful of scientific authority and fruits of technology.'[83]

That moral discourse is frequently communicated through the language of science is testimony to the authoritative status of the latter. As one American commentator observes, arguments framed in the language of science trump those expressed through a grammar of morality:

It is especially interesting that both religious and environmentalist voices – voices that in the United States culture often adopt similar rhetoric regarding the inherent wrongness of altering the natural or God-given order – tend to be quieted, especially in comparison to voices that make explicit reference to science or to its use and effects, bad or good. This makes sense in light of the observation that in the United States culture, science is a very special form of authority.[84]

Science is arguably the one form of authority that has remained resistant to the corrosive influence of rationalisation.

The contemporary definition of an expert as 'one whose specialist knowledge or skill causes him to be regarded as an authority' is directly associated with the role of the 'specialist' and specialisation.[85] As the sociologist Michael Schudson observes, 'an expert is someone in possession of specialized knowledge that is accepted by the wider society as legitimate'. This knowledge includes specific, technical skills 'based on some wider appreciation of the field of knowledge in question'.[86] Unlike traditional authority, which touched on every dimension of the human experience, the authority of the expert was confined to that which could be exercised through reason. Joseph Raz writes that the 'authority of the expert can be called theoretical authority, for it is an authority about what to believe'.[87]

Raz observes that unlike political authority, which 'provides reason for action', theoretical authority 'provides reason for belief'.[88] However, while it is valid to draw a conceptual distinction between these two forms of authority, historical experience suggests that expertise becomes politicised easily. With the passage of time, the distinction between these two forms of authority becomes blurred, and the very fragility of political authority encourages a process whereby politicians outsource their power to experts. 'Governments find expert advice to be an indispensable resource for formulating and justifying policy and, more subtly, for removing some issues from the political domain by transforming them into technical questions', writes Stephen Hilgartner.[89]

---

[83] Yearley (1992) p. 511.   [84] Priest (2006) p. 210.
[85] Cited in *OED*, see entry 'Expert'.   [86] Schudson (2006) p. 499.
[87] Raz (1990) p. 2.   [88] Raz (1990) p. 5.   [89] Hilgartner (2000) p. 146.

Terrence Ball suggests that the potential for the politicisation of expertise can be understood through understanding the distinction between epistemic and epistemocratic authority. Epistemic authority is 'that which is ascribed to the possessor of specialized knowledge, skills, or expertise'. For example, this form of authority works through deference to doctors on medical matters and lawyers on legal affairs. Epistemocratic authority, 'by contrast, refers to the claim of one class, group, or person to rule another by virtue of the former's possessing specialized authority not available to the latter'. Ball argues that,

[E]pistemocractic authority is therefore conceptually parasitic upon epistemic authority. Or, to put it slightly differently, epistemocratic authority attempts to assimilate political authority to the non-political epistemic authority of the technician or expert.[90]

Ball claims that the conceptual distinction between political rule and expert authority in modern society becomes 'blurred if not meaningless'. In effect, the epistemocratic imperative extends the claim of expertise to the domain of political and public life, assimilating moral and political issues to 'the paradigm of epistemic authority' and asserting that 'politics and ethics are activities in which there are experts'.[91] The influence exercised by epistemocratic authority today is shown by the constant slippage between scientific advice and moral and political exhortations on issues as diverse as global warming and child-rearing. The influence of managerial and technocratic ideals on public life indicates that epistemocratic ideal is one 'to which political reality in some respects increasingly corresponds'.[92]

Creating a demand for expert authority

The status of experts requires that their knowledge and skill is recognised as authoritative by the public, and the ascendancy of the expert depended on the institutionalisation and professionalisation of their skills. As Thomas Haskell points out, by the mid-nineteenth century, the 'man of science' gave way to the 'scientist', representing a shift from gentlemanly vocation to a profession.[93] Haskell's book, *The Emergence of Professional Social Science*, provides a convincing account of the campaign 'to establish professional authority on a firmer base and to extend professional performance into new areas'. He writes that the 'word "scientific"

---

[90] Ball (1987) p. 48.   [91] Ball (1987) p. 51.
[92] Ball (1987) p. 51.   [93] Haskell (2000) p. 68.

then seemed to epitomize the very essence of professional idea – expert authority, institutionally cultivated and certified'.[94]

Although influenced by self-interest, the professionalisation of expertise also represented an attempt to respond and overcome the crisis of traditional authority. Haskell perceives the trend towards professionalisation as part of a 'broad movement to establish or re-establish authority in the face of profoundly disruptive changes in habits of casual attribution' and 'changes in the very notion of truth itself'. He adds,

> [P]rofessionalization in the nineteenth century was not merely a pragmatic and narrowly self-seeking tactic for enhancing occupational status, as it often is today: instead it then seemed a major cultural *reform*, a means of establishing authority so securely that the truth and its proponents might win the deference even of a mass public, one that threatened to withhold deference from all men, all traditions, and even the highest values.[95]

Back in the nineteenth century, the professionalisation of expertise can be seen as representing the constitution of a new focus for public deference. At a time of disruptive change and moral and intellectual confusion, the professional expert, who represented the personification of reason and science, served as a reassuring figure of authority. This form of authority claimed to represent objective scientific truth. As a possessor of this truth the expert could claim a moral status that was superior to the rest of society. 'Precisely because there were truths that no honest investigator could deny, the power to make decisions had to be placed in the hands of experts whose authority rested on special knowledge rather than raw self-assertiveness, or party patronage, or a majority vote of the incompetent', writes Haskell.[96]

'What is it about modern society that causes men to rely increasingly on professional advice?' asks Haskell,[97] and 'under what circumstances do men come to believe that their judgment, based on common sense and the customary knowledge of the community, is not adequate?' A useful concept for understanding this situation is that of the *crisis of causality*. The prerequisite for the rise of the expert was the erosion of traditional authority and the diminishing salience of custom and traditional truths, leaving a cultural climate where little could be taken for granted. The world of the nineteenth century appeared increasingly complex, and traditional notions of cause and effect could do little to illuminate the problems brought about by industrialisation, rapid social change and the

---

[94] Haskell (2000) p. 88.   [95] Haskell (2000) p. 65.
[96] Haskell (2000) p. 87.   [97] Haskell (2000) p. 28.

rise of an inter-connected world economy. As Haskell puts it, 'causation' threatened to 'evaporate altogether'.

Since the nineteenth century, expertise has thrived on the crisis of causality. Uncertainty about the world encouraged the birth of the social sciences, a field in which experts often justify their existence by insisting that the world is far too complex to be understood by ordinary folk. As David Haney points out, the discipline of sociology sought to legitimise its expertise by drawing attention to the complexity of modern society, an argument eloquently promoted by Talcott Parsons. Haney observes that 'in an argument consistent with those of earlier generations of social scientists', Parsons asserted that 'the very fact of modernity, with its complexity and resultant confusion, required the expertise of social scientist'. A technological era, in his view, required 'scientifically trained personnel'.[98]

The tendency to render reality complex is one of the distinct features of the politicisation of expertise. Critics of technocracy's propensity for an elitist anti-democratic orientation to public issues are often dismissed as naïve. Writing in this vein, Michael Schudson dismisses the romanticism of those who fear that reliance on experts may be incompatible with democracy: such a standpoint 'fails to see not only the complexity of democracy but the democracy of complexity'.[99] Schudson adds that 'in a world too complex for any one person or agency to comprehend, there is no governing without colleagues, consulting, committees and compromise'. Nevertheless, the authority of science and expertise is inherently unstable and ambivalent. It possesses the power and authority to weaken traditional attitudes and beliefs, but as Habermas argued, also sets the very standards by which its own claims can be undermined.[100] The open-ended and provisional quality of scientific claims means that they can be adapted and used to support competing and conflicting interests.[101]

A major limitation of science is that it cannot endow human experience with meaning. However, this limitation has not stopped advocates of specific causes from framing their appeals to the authority of science through a normative narrative: Robert Lackey points out that policy and scientific preferences often blend together, and that the moralisation of scientific claims has become a regular feature of public life. Lackey noted that in the USA 'the use of normative science cuts across the ideological

---

[98] Haney (2008) p. 34.   [99] Schudson (2006) p. 504.   [100] Habermas (1976) p. 84.
[101] See Sarewitz (2004) for a discussion of the opportunistic use of conflicting facts in environmental debates.

spectrum': 'it seems no less common coming from the political Left or Right, from the Greens or the Libertarians'.[102]

Despite its pre-eminent role as an all-purpose source of authorisation, the authority of science is continually scrutinised and sometimes subject to a powerful moral anti-scientific critique. So called scientific advice is frequently questioned and attacked for allegedly serving a nefarious agenda. Vitriolic moral denunciation is often present in discussions about stem cell research, GM food and technology, climate change, cloning and a variety of other topics. As Hilgartner writes, although 'science advice is a ubiquitous source of authority in contemporary Western societies':[103]

Most of the drama surrounding science advice consists of efforts to expose, disclaim, or disavow putative interests, as competing performers present conflicting assessments of the character of the advisor. Judgments about the credibility of advice thus cannot be separated from moral judgments about the people and institutions that produce it.[104]

From the standpoint of our investigation of authority in history, we would conclude that the current ascendancy of scientific authority has far less to with its intrinsic attributes. It is likely that its pre-eminent status is principally an outcome of the discrediting of other forms of authorisation. In other words it is the one form of authorisation that is still left standing. That is why even movements who are profoundly suspicious of science nevertheless seek to appropriate its authority. The embrace of creation science by some fundamentalist religious groups is symptomatic of this trend. As the author of a text on the politicisation of science notes, 'where religious conservatives may once have advanced their pro-life and socially traditionalist views through moral arguments, they now increasingly adopt the veneer of scientific and technical expertise'.[105]

The formidable influence of scientific authority encourages claims-makers on all sides to embrace it 'with the ironic outcome that the demand for legitimation results in the process of delegitimation'.[106] Liftin adds that 'once science enters the political fray, especially for a high-stakes issue like global climate change, it risks being perceived as contaminated and thereby losing its authority.'[107]

Attempts to moralise science represent an often unstated and unrecognised search for authority. As I have discussed elsewhere, there are powerful cultural pressures towards transforming scientific claims into non-negotiable truths.[108] Terms such as 'scientific consensus' are used to acclaim the 'truth', and the recently constructed term 'The Science' is a

---

[102] Lackey (2007) p. 15.   [103] Hilgartner (2000) p. 4.   [104] Hilgartner (2000) p. 15.
[105] Mooney (2006) p. 75.   [106] Liftin (2000) p. 122.   [107] Liftin (2000) p. 122.
[108] Furedi (2011) pp. 186–8.

deeply moralised and politicised category. Those who claim to wield the authority of The Science are demanding the kind of submission historically associated with Papal Infallibility. However, such claims lack the normative foundations to prevent the inevitable rise of counter-claims. Ultimately, science lacks the unquestioned moral status needed to provide a solution to the problem of authority.

Conclusion: final thoughts

Authority has never been entirely a taken-for-granted institution. Even during the Middle Ages, often described as an epoch of tradition and religion, competing claims to authority had a significant impact on public life. Yet the questions raised by medieval claims-makers appealed to a shared religious and cultural legacy and did not fundamentally query the authority of authority. In the centuries to follow, the range of issues subjected to competing claims has both expanded and assumed a more profound quality. Claims-making has always been a competitive enterprise; but this competition has become complicated by the fact that the authority or authorities it appeals to today are also intensely contested. Who speaks on behalf of the child or the victim? Whose account of global warming is authoritative? Those in authority look for the authorisation of others to validate their claims. Scientists and advocacy organisations seek alliances with authoritative celebrities. Governments appeal to the evidence of experts to justify their policies, as illustrated in the way that government initiatives are usually accompanied by 'new research' that legitimises such policies. As Giddens notes, in the absence of 'determinant authorities', there 'exist plenty of claimants to authority – far more than was true of pre-modern cultures'.[1]

The proliferation of competing claims-making is a symptom of the difficulty that society has in elaborating a shared narrative of validation. Historically, the question of how to validate and give meaning to authority has been posed and answered in different ways. The contrast between the explicit assertion of *auctoritas* by Augustus or Pope Gregory, and the current tendency to evade the question, highlights the transformation of the workings of authority over the centuries. The last historical moment that there was an explicit attempt to recover and assert a politicised conception of foundation for authority – the inter-war era of the 1920s and 1930s – led to its 'revival' in the caricatured form of authoritarianism. The

---

[1] Giddens (1991) p. 194.

experience of these decades continues to haunt discussions of authority, and shape the way that it is conceptualised in public life.

One of the symptoms of the devaluation of authority is that, instead of being paired with the concept of legitimacy, it is often perceived as its opposite. The incongruous concept of 'illegitimate authority' is used even by social scientists. Richard Sennett writes of the 'dilemma of authority in our time' and the 'fear it inspires', because 'we feel attracted to strong figures we do not believe to be legitimate'. In his discussion of 'illegitimate authority', Sennett acknowledges that this concept 'would be a contradiction in terms to Weber'.[2] It certainly would; and it would also be incomprehensible to leading thinkers on this subject throughout most of history. Yet although the concept of illegitimate authority is an oxymoron, it captures a cultural orientation towards this subject. It suggests that authority exists in an uneasy relationship with legitimacy, and also expresses the presentiment that societies today are confused about how to speak the language of legitimation.

Weber intuited the potential dissonance between authority and legitimation. His sociology of domination sought, in part, to minimise the obstacles to the realisation of an authority that was legitimate. He was particularly concerned with the political dimension of authority, of how those who rule can gain the acquiescence of the masses. Weber's focus was on 'legitimate domination' – how rule can justify itself. His concept of legitimate authority raises questions about whether authority can be anything other than legitimate. Our contention is that an authority that ceases to be legitimate can no longer act authoritatively. In this context it is important to draw attention to the confusions created by Parsons's attempt to clarify this matter. Parsons defined legitimacy as 'having a "right" to exercise authority over others and claim obedience as a duty, as distinguished from merely compelling it by *force majeure*'. He adds that it is this claim which 'distinguishes "authority" (legitime Herrschaft) from Herrschaft in general'.[3] This formulation leaves open the question of whether it is possible to have *illegitimate* forms of authority.

Weber himself did not attempt to elaborate a concept of illegitimate authority. However, his fascinating historical review of political conflict in ancient and medieval city-states has as its focus what he characterises as *non-legitimate domination*. Typically he associates non-legitimate domination with popular and plebeian movement and leaders who contest the prevailing formal hierarchy of authority. So in his discussion of the evolution of the Roman *tribune plebis* – the elected heads of the non-noble Roman citizenry – who fought for plebeian interests, Weber remarks that

[2] Sennett (1981) pp. 26–7.   [3] Parsons (1942a) p. 65.

they did not 'possess legitimate authority of office'. But what his study exposes is not so much the rise of an 'illegitimate authority' as the contestation of the prevailing forms patrician and aristocratic authority from below. As Weber remarked, 'numerous claims to authority stand side by side, overlapping and often conflicting with each other'.[4] In the context of such a contest, it is more useful to characterise the activities of emerging movements as representing *alternative* claims to authority, rather than illegitimate claims to authority.

Weber's concern with legitimate order and the process of legitimation – that is, how order is rendered valid – is influenced by the realisation that power can only be effectively exercised if people accept its commands as binding. Even appeals to self-interest are unlikely to provide stability: 'An order which is adhered to from motives of pure expediency is generally much less stable than one upheld on a purely customary basis through the fact that the corresponding behaviour has become habitual'. Weber adds that even habit turns out to be 'much less stable' than an order which 'enjoys the prestige of being considered binding', that is where 'belief in legitimacy' is achieved.[5]

Although authority is always a problem, as the experience of the ancient world indicates, it was in the post-Reformation era that the question of what constituted its foundation became a critical issue. The Reformation did not merely undermine the religious foundation of authority but also that of tradition and the past. This desacralisation of authority led to its politicisation and its reconstitution as a product of human convention. Conventional accounts of authority invited competing claims, and not even Hobbes's *Leviathan* could put an end to such disputes. Hobbes's solution of the problem of foundation was a negative one, where it was fear and insecurity that drove individuals in the state of nature to authorise an absolute sovereign. His solution anticipated the crystallisation of the negative theories of authority that dominated the twentieth century. In the eighteenth century, attempts to depoliticise authority ultimately led to the constitution of society as its foundation. Sociology emerged in the nineteenth century as a constituent part of the process of endowing society as the source of authority. In turn sociology embraced authority as its cause, and attempted to develop a narrative that could contain the disorienting effects of the problem of order.

The tendency towards the rationalisation of authority, identified by Weber, came up against two difficult challenges. The first challenge pertained to the capacity of modern society to give meaning to authority. The quest of providing a normative foundation for authority has

---

[4] Weber (1978) pp. 1251 and 1308.   [5] Weber (1978) p. 31.

proved to be an elusive one, and secular rational responses have typically opted to rely on rules and procedures. However, the authority of rules lacks the moral depth to give meaning to human experience. Consequently it leaves all the big questions about the nature of the good life unresolved.

The second challenge confronting rational authority was how to reconcile democratic consent, or the principle of majority rule, with what used to be called the principle of authority. Consent has lurked in the background since Roman times, and notions of consent to rule emerged in a limited sense in the medieval era. By the fourteenth century, custom as an expression of consent represented an important dimension of legitimation. Despite his absolutist inclinations, Hobbes still found a role for consent; and from the seventeenth century onwards, consent in the form of public opinion was increasingly projected as the source of authority. In the nineteenth century, the necessity for harmonising the authorising role of public opinion with authority was the principal problem facing liberalism. This issue was to dominate public life up to the present time. In a world where public opinion was accorded an authorising role, it was essential that authority could rely on its acquiescence.

Our study suggests that despite the problems associated with the legitimation of authority through popular consent in the past it provides the only plausible model for modern authority. Fukuyama argued that there is 'no universal principle of legitimacy other than the sovereignty of the people'.[6] But the difficulty of giving practical meaning to this universal principle has led to a tendency towards adopting evasive theories of negative authority. Negative theories of authority served to negate the moral status of consent by calling into question the capacity of the public to make intelligent choices.

Since the Cold War negative theories of authority have tended interpret domination as a tendency immanent in modernity. Theories of the press, media, propaganda, consumption and rationalisation contend that domination is a spontaneous outcome of the process of modernisation and rationalisation. Theories of total domination were eloquently elaborated by theorists working in the tradition of the Frankfurt school. Even Arendt came to possess 'the grounding conviction that total domination (*totale Herrschaft*) is a distinctively modern pathology'.[7] The idea of spontaneous domination minimises the role of authority since obedience and compliance are now interpreted as the outcome of impersonal forces of domination.

[6] Fukuyama (1992) p. 45.   [7] Villa (2008) p. 215.

The shift from positive affirmation to a negative conception of authority is one of the most significant developments in the cultural history of modernity. Yet this is a subject that is rarely discussed and insofar as it constitutes a subject of reflection, it tends to be considered indirectly. At least implicitly authority has been displaced by the constitution of domination. The vast literature on propaganda, the media, advertising, consumption and mass society all allude to a form of domination that diminishes the significance of voluntary and conscious consent. Indeed frequently the very possibility of conscious choice making is called into question by contemporary theories of domination. Nevertheless the question of consent and legitimacy continually intrudes on public life. It indicates that the questions raised by the historical problem of authority domination cannot be displaced by domination.

Weber was aware of the limited potential that legal-rational rules have to inspire belief in the legitimacy of the political order. Indeed one reason why Weber's theory of domination is unconvincing is because he could not convince himself that the modern state could draw on foundational authority. His concept of legal-rational legitimacy lacks plausibility as a force for authorising political rule. As one of Weber's critics writes, he had 'great difficulties in pinning legal legitimacy down to beliefs and normative compliance, partly because procedural regularities in legal decision making do not provide a satisfactory alternative to substantive justice and natural law'.[8] The rational-legal lacks the cultural and moral resources possessed by tradition to motivate and influence the public. As one legal sociologist observes, the law is 'rather cold and bloodless' and 'cannot replace traditional authority in the expressive, emotional sense'; he adds that it 'is possible to worship the idea of law; but law does not hold authority in the modern world because of its grip on the emotions'.[9] Weber was all too aware of the limited capacity of rational legal norms to inspire the public.

Compared with firm beliefs in the positive religiously revealed character of a legal norm or in the inviolable sacredness of an age – old tradition, even the most convincing norms arrived at by abstraction seem to be too subtle to serve as the bases of a legal system.[10]

Moreover, the law itself needs to draw on cultural resources external to itself to render it not just valid but morally compelling. As Beetham claims, there are 'substantive and moral questions about the content

---

[8] Turner (1992) p. 200.   [9] Friedman (1994) pp. 112 and 118.
[10] Weber (1978) p. 874.

and justification of law itself'.[11] He has gone as far as to claim that the failure to 'provide any account at all of the normative (as opposed to the juridical) legitimation of the law' actually 'invalidates Weber's account of legitimacy'.[12] Legality is 'not sufficient to justify supreme authority', so 'some substantive principle is required'.[13] This point was further addressed by Habermas in his 1986 lecture, titled 'How is legitimacy possible on the basis of legality?' He argues, 'Despite all the authority that the sciences have been able to muster in modern societies, legal norms still cannot achieve legitimacy merely by the fact that their language is made precise, their concepts explicated, their consistency tested, and their principles unified'.[14] Habermas adds that Weber's assumption that an independent, morally neutral rationality intrinsic to law counts for the legitimating force of legality has not stood up'.[15] Indeed, Habermas has argued that the emergence of a 'law-based state' depends on 'the binding of all state activity to a system of norms legitimated by public opinion'.[16] In this case, legal norms are themselves required to draw on the legitimacy of public opinion.

However, as our historical review of the uneasy relationship between public opinion and authority indicates, what some see as the source of authority others imagine as a fundamental threat to it. Experience indicates that it is far easier to claim the authority of public opinion than it is to institutionalise consent. Yet democratic public life cannot live without some form of authority; which is why the quest for an authority that is perceived as genuinely legitimate will continue into the indefinite future. Whatever the outcome of this quest, it will have to engage with the thorny question of consent and its relationship to the legitimation of authority.

In light of its demise some may be tempted to ask the question of 'what remains of authority'. However, history shows that authority is not so much a finite resource that has been depleted but an accomplishment of cultural and social interaction and contestation. How relations of authority are constituted and challenged in the twenty-first century is one of the big issues facing the social sciences.

One final point. During the past two centuries authority was frequently contrasted to freedom. The authority-freedom couplet conveyed the idea that a relation of conflict existed between the two. The theme of Authority versus Freedom was frequently communicated in public life. It is worth

---

[11] Beetham (1991a) p. 5.   [12] Beetham (1991) p. 40.
[13] Spencer (1970) p. 130.   [14] In Habermas (1986) p. 226.
[15] Habermas (1986) p. 241.   [16] See Habermas (1992) p. 82.

noting that the current demise of authority has not been paralleled by a greater cultural affirmation for freedom. The historic tension between authority and freedom lost much of its relevance. Indeed both ideas seem to have lost much of their meaning. Why this is so is the fascinating problem that emerges from our study of the history of the problem of authority.

Bibliography

Aarsleff, H. (1994) 'Locke's Influence' in Chappell (1994).

Abizadeh, A. (2004) 'Historical truth, national myths and liberal democracy: on the coherence of liberal nationalism', *The Journal of Political Philosophy:* vol. 12, no. 3, pp. 291–313.

Adair-Toteff, C. (2005) 'Max Weber's Charisma', *Journal of Classical Sociology*, vol. 5, no. 2, 189–204.

Adorno, T. W. (1950) 'Democratic leadership and mass manipulation' in Gouldner, A. (ed.) *Studies In Leadership; Leadership and Democratic Action*, Harper & Brothers: New York.

Adorno, T. and Horkheimer, M. (1944) 'The culture industry: enlightenment as mass deception', in Adorno, T. and Horkheimer, M. (1979) *Dialectic of Enlightenment*, Verso: London.

Agamben, G. (2005) *State of Exception*, The University of Chicago Press: Chicago.

Allen, J. W. (1964) (1928) *A History of Political Thought in the Sixteenth Century*, Methuen: London.

Alwin, D. F. (1988) 'From obedience to autonomy: changes in traits desired in children, 1924–1978', *The Public Opinion Quarterly*, vol. 52, no. 1, pp. 33–52.

Arendt, H. (1956) 'Authority in the twentieth century', *The Review of Politics*, 18, no. 4, pp. 403–17.

Arendt, H. (1958) 'What is authority?' in Arendt, H. (1966) *Between Past and Future*, Penguin Books: London.

Arendt, H. (1970) *On Violence*, Harcourt Publishers: New York.

Arendt, H. (2004) (originally published 1990) 'Philosophy and politics', *Social Research*, vol. 71, no. 3, p. 453.

Arendt, H. (2005) 'The tradition of political thought' in Arendt, H. *The Promise of Politics*, Schocken Books: New York.

Arendt, H. (2005a) *The Promise of Politics*, Schocken Books: New York.

Arendt, H. (2006) *Between Past and Future*, Penguin Books: London.

Arendt, H. (2009) *The Origins of Totalitarianism*, Benediction Classics: Milton Keynes.

Armitage, D. (2009) *The Ideological Origins of the British Empire*, Cambridge University Press: Cambridge.

Arnold, M. (1966) (originally pub. 1869) *Culture and Anarchy*, Cambridge University Press: Cambridge.

Ashcraft, R. (1994) 'Locke's political philosophy' in Chappell (1994).

Atherton, I. (2003) 'The press and popular political opinion' in Coward, B. (2003) (ed.) *A Companion to Stuart Britain*, Blackwell: Oxford.

Austin, J. (originally pub 1832) *The Province of Jurisprudence Determined*, downloaded from HeinOnline, http://heinonline.org.

Baehr, P. (1998) *Caesar and the Fading of the Roman World*, Transaction Publishers: New Brunswick.

Baehr, P. (1999) 'An "ancient sense of politics"? Weber, Caesarism and the republican Tradition', *European Journal of Sociology*, vol. 40, pp. 333–50.

Bagehot, W. (1993) (originally published in 1867) *The English Constitution*, Fontana Press: London.

Baker, H. (1952) *The Wars of Truth: Studies in the Decay of Christian Humanism in the Earlier Seventeenth Century*, Harvard University Press: Cambridge, MA.

Baker, M. K. (1994) *Inventing the French Revolution*, Cambridge University Press: Cambridge.

Ball, T. (1985) 'Hobbes' linguistic turn', *Polity*, vol. 17, no. 4, pp. 739–60.

Ball, T. (1987) 'Authority and conceptual change' in Pennock and Chapman (1987).

Ball, T., Farr, J. and Hanson, R. (1989) (eds) *Political Innovation and Conceptual Change*, Cambridge University Press: Cambridge.

Balsdon, J. (1960) 'Auctoritas, Dignitas, Otium', *The Classical Quarterly, New Series*, 10, no. 1, pp. 43–50.

Barker, E. (2009) *Entering the Agon; Dissent and Authority in Homer, Historiography and Tragedy*, Oxford University Press: Oxford.

Barlow, F. (1980) 'The King's evil', *The English Historical Review*, vol. 95, no. 374, pp. 3–27.

Barnard, C. (1962) (originally published in 1938) *The Functions of The Executive*, Harvard University Press: Cambridge, MA.

Barnes, H. E. (1922) 'Some typical contributions of English sociology to political theory', *American Journal of Sociology*, vol. 27, no. 3, pp. 289–324.

Barraclough, G. (1964) 'The Investiture Contest and the German Constitution' in Williams (1964).

Bauman, Z. (1987) *Legislators and Interpreters: On Modernity, Post-Modernity and Intellectuals*, Polity Press: Cambridge.

Beard, C. A. (1917) 'Review of political parties: a sociological study of the oligarchical tendencies of modern democracy, by Robert Michels,' *Political Science Quarterly*, vol. 32, no. 1, pp. 153–5.

Becker, H. and Barnes, H. E. (1961) *Social Thought From Lore To Science, Vol. 2*, Dover Publications, Inc.: New York.

Beetham, D. (1977) 'From socialism to fascism; the relation between theory and practice in the works of Robert Michels', *Political Studies*, vol. 24, no. 2, pp. 161–81.

Beetham, D. (1991) 'Max Weber and the legitimacy of the modern state', *Analyse & Kritik*, no. 13, pp. 34–45.

Beetham, D. (1991a) *The Legitimation of Power*, Macmillan: Houndmills, Basingstoke.

Bell, D. (1950) 'Notes on authoritarian and democratic leadership' in Gouldner, A. (ed.) *Studies in Leadership; Leadership and Democratic Action*, Harper & Brothers: New York.

Bell, D. (1976) *The Cultural Contradictions of Capitalism*, Heinemann: London.

Bell, D. (1980) *Sociological Journeys: Essays 1960–1980*, Heinemann: London.

Bendix, R. (1978) *Kings or People; Power and the Mandate to Rule*, University of California Press: Berkeley.

Benson, R. (1991) 'Political renovatio: two models from Roman antiquity', in Benson, R. and Constable, G. (eds.) *Renaissance and Renewal in the Twelfth Century*, University of Toronto Press: Toronto.

Berman, H. J. (1983) *Law and Revolution; The Formation of the Western Legal Tradition*, Harvard University Press: Cambridge, MA.

Berman, H. J. (1987) 'Some false premises of Max Weber's sociology of law', *Washington University Law Quarterly*, vol. 65, pp. 759–70.

Berry, C. J. (1997) *Social Theory of the Scottish Enlightenment*, Edinburgh University Press: Edinburgh.

Bertman, M. (1997) 'Sociology and Hobbes', *Hobbes Studies*, vol. 12, pp. 90–102.

Best, J. (1999) *Random Violence: How We Talk About New Crimes and New Victims*. University of California Press: Berkeley, CA.

Borch, C. (2012) *The Politics of Crowds: An Alternative History of Sociology*, Cambridge University Press: Cambridge.

Borot, L. (2006) 'History in Hobbes's thought', Sorrel, T. (ed.) *The Cambridge Companion to Hobbes*, Cambridge University Press: Cambridge.

Bostock, D. (1989) 'The interpretation of Plato's Crito', *Phronesis*, vol. 1, p. xxxviii.

Bourdieu, P. (1984) *Distinction: A Social Critique of the Judgment of Taste*, Routledge and Kegan Paul: London.

Boyd, R. (1999) '"The unsteady and precarious contribution of individuals": Edmund Burke's defense of civil society 2, *The Review of Politics*, vol. 61, no. 3, pp. 65–491.

Bronner, S. E. (1999) *Ideas in Action; Political Tradition in the Twentieth Century*, Rowman & Littlefield Publishers: Lanham, Maryland.

Brooke, Z. N. (1928) 'The effect of Becket's murder on Papal authority in England', *Cambridge Historical Journal*, vol. 2, no. 3, pp. 213–28.

Brooke, Z. N. (1964) 'Lay investiture and its relation to the conflict of Empire and Papacy' in Williams (1964).

Bryce, J. (1895) *The American Commonwealth, Vol. 2*, Macmillan and Co.: London.

Burger, T. (1977) 'Talcott Parsons, the problem of order in society, and the program of an analytical sociology', *American Journal of Sociology*, vol. 83, no. 2, pp. 320–39.

Burke, E. (2009) *Reflections on the Revolution in France*, Oxford University Press: Oxford.

Burke, K. (1966) *Language as Symbolic Action*, University of California Press: Berkeley.

Burke, P. (1998) 'Two crises of historical consciousness', www.culturahistorica.es/peter_burke/historical_consciousness.pdf.

Burns, J. H. (1968) 'J. S. Mill and democracy' in Schneewind, J. B. (1968) *Mill; A Collection of Critical Essays*, Macmillan: London.

Burns, J. H. (1991) (ed.) *The Cambridge History of Medieval Thought*, c350–c1450, Cambridge University Press: Cambridge.

Burns, J. H. (2008) (ed.) *The Cambridge History of Political Thought, 1450–1700*, Cambridge University Press: Cambridge.

Caldwell, P. (1997) *Popular Sovereignty and the Crisis of German Constitutional Law*, Duke University Press: Durham.

Camic, C. (1979) 'The Utilitarians Revisited', *The American Journal of Sociology*, vol. 85, no. 3, pp. 516–50.

Canning, J. P. (1991) 'Law, sovereignty and corporation theory, 1300–1450' in Burns (1991).

Canning, J. (1996) *The History of Medieval Political Thought; 300–1450*, Routledge: London.

Carlisle, R. B. (1974) 'The birth of technocracy: science, society, and Saint-Simonians', *Journal of the History of Ideas*, vol. 35, no. 3, pp. 445–64.

Carlyle, A. J. (1913) 'The sources of medieval political theory and its connection with medieval politics', *The American Historical Review*, vol. 19, no. 1, pp. 1–2.

Carlyle, R. W. and Carlyle, A. J. (1957) (originally pub. 1903) *A History of Mediaeval Political Theory in the West, Vol. 1*.

Carlyle, R. W. and Carlyle, A. J. (1957a) *A History of Mediaeval Political Theory in the West, Vol. 2*.

Carlyle, R. W. and Carlyle, A. J. (1962) *A History of Mediaeval Political Theory in the West, Vol. 4*, W. Blackwood and Sons: Edinburgh and London.

Carlyle, R. W. and Carlyle, A. J. (1962a) *A History of Mediaeval Political Theory in the West, Vol. 5*, W. Blackwood and Sons: Edinburgh and London.

Carney, L. (1994) 'Sociology in the throes of fascism: Parsonian Meliorism in the myths of triumphalism', *International Journal of Politics, Culture and Society*, vol. 7, no. 3, pp. 469–83.

Carter, J. M. (1983) 'Augustus down the centuries', *History Today*, vol. 33, no. 3, pp. 10–15.

Cavanaugh, J. G. (1969) 'Turgot: The rejection of enlightened despotism', *French Historical Studies*, vol. 6, no. 1, pp. 31–58.

Chappell, V. (1994) (ed.) *The Cambridge Companion to Locke*, Cambridge University Press: Cambridge.

Cheyette, F. (1963) 'Case law, and medieval "constitutionalism": A re-examination', *Political Science Quarterly*, vol. 78, no. 3, pp. 362–90.

Childs, H. L. (1935) 'Introduction to pressure groups and propaganda', *Annals of the American Academy of Political and Social Science*, vol. 179, pp. xi–xii.

Cicero (2008) (translation by Niall Rudd) *The Republic and The Laws*, Oxford University Press: Oxford.

Clark, G. N. (1947) *The Seventeenth Century*, Oxford University Press: Oxford.

Cochran, C. (1977) 'Authority and community: The contributions of Carl Friedrich, Yves, R. Simon, and Michael Polanyi', *The American Political Science Review*, vol. 7, no. 2, pp. 546–58.

Coleman, J. (2000) *A History of Political Thought: From the Middle Ages to the Renaissance*, Blackwell Publishers: Oxford.

Collier, K. G. (1957) 'Authority, society and education', *Journal of Educational Sociology*, vol. 30, no. 6, pp. 283–8.

Connolly, W. E. (1987) 'Modern authority and ambiguity', in Pennock, J. R. and Chapman, J. W. (eds.) *Authority Revisited*, New York University Press: New York.

Constable, M. (1994) 'Genealogy and jurisprudence: Nietzsche, Nihilism and the social scientification of law', *Law And Social Inquiry*, vol. 19, pp. 554–8.

Cook, F. (2003) 'Agamemnon's test of the army in Iliad Book 2 and the function of Homeric *akhos*', *American Journal of Philology*, vol. 42, no. 167, pp. 165–98.

Cooper, J. M. (1997) *Plato; Complete Works*, Hackett Publishing Company: Indianapolis.

Copland, D. (1953) 'Authority and Control in a Free Society', *Studies: An Irish Quarterly Review*, vol. 42, no. 167, pp. 275–92.

Cowans, J. (2001) *To Speak for the People; Public Opinion and the Problem of Legitimacy in the French Revolution*, Routledge: New York.

Cragg, G. R. (1964) *Reason and Authority in the Eighteenth Century*, Cambridge University Press: Cambridge.

Craiutu, A. (2003) 'Guizot's elitist theory of representative government', *Critical Review*, vol. 15, nos. 3–4, pp. 261–84.

Cristi, R. (1997) 'Carl Schmitt on Sovereignty and Constituent Power', *Canadian Journal of Law and Jurisprudence*, vol. 10, no. 1, pp. 189–201.

Cristi, R. (2005) *Hegel on Freedom and Authority*, University of Wales Press: Cardiff.

Cristi, R. (2010) 'Nietzsche on authority and the state', *Animus*, vol. 14 www.swgc.mun.ca/animus.

Curran, E. (2002) 'A very peculiar Royalist. Hobbes in the context of his political contemporaries', *Kent Academic Repository* – http://kar.kent.ac.uk.

Cutler, F. (1999) 'Jeremy Bentham and the public opinion tribunal', *Public Opinion Quarterly*, vol. 63, pp. 321–46.

Damaska, M. (1985) 'How did it all begin?', *The Yale Law Journal*, vol. 94, pp. 1807–24.

Davies, R. E. (1945) *The Problem of Authority in the Continental Reformers: A Study in Luther, Zwingli and Calvin*, The Epworth Press: London.

Davis, C. T. (2007) 'Dante and the empire', in Jacoff, R. (ed.) *The Cambridge Companion to Dante: 2nd Edition*. Cambridge University Press, 2007. Cambridge Collections Online. 23 June, 2011, http://cco.cambridge.org/uid=7780/extract?id=ccol0521844304_CCOL0521844304_root.

Davis, J. C. (2003) 'Political thought during the English revolution' in Coward, B. (2003) (ed.) *A Companion to Stuart Britain*, Blackwell: Oxford.

Dawe, A. (1970) 'The two sociologies', *The British Journal of Sociology*, vol. 21, no. 2, pp. 207–18.

Dawson, C. (1964) 'Monastic reform and Christian culture' in Williams (1964).

De Grazia, S. (1959) 'What authority is not', *The American Political Science Review*, vol. 53, no. 2, pp. 321–31.

De Jouvenel, B. (1945) *On Power: The Natural History of its Growth*, Liberty Fund: Indianapolis.

De Ste. Croix, G. E. M. (1981) *The Class Struggle in the Ancient World; from the Archaic Age to the Arab Conquests*, Duckworth: London.

Dewey, J. (1936) 'Authority and Freedom', *Survey Graphic*, November, p. 605.

Dicey, A. V. (1920) (1st edn 1905) *Lectures on the Relation between Law & Public Opinion in England During the Nineteenth Century*, Macmillan and Co.: London.

Dickinson, J. (1929) 'Social order and political authority', *The American Political Science Review*, vol. 23, no. 3, pp. 593–632.

Dio, Cassius (1987) *The Roman History: The Reign of Augustus*, Penguin Classics: London.

Docherty, T. (1987) *On Modern Authority: The Theory and Condition of Writing. 1500 To the Present Day*, The Harvester Press: Brighton.

Dominian, J. (1976) *Authority*, Burns & Oates Limited, London.

Donlan, W. (1970) 'The foundation legend of Rome: an example of dynamic process', *The Classical World*, vol. 64, no. 4. pp. 109–14.

Donlan, W. (1973) 'The tradition of anti-aristocratic thought in early Greek poetry', *Historia Zeitschrift fur Alte Geschichte*, vol. 22, no. 2, pp. 145–54.

Donlan, W. (1979) 'The structure of authority in the Iliad', *Arethusa*, vol. 12, no. 1, pp. 51–70.

Doob, L. W. and Robinson, E. S. (1935) 'Psychology and propaganda', *Annals of the American Academy of Political and Social Science*, vol. 179, pp. 88–95.

Draper, H. (1990) *Karl Marx's Theory of Revolution: Critique of Other Socialisms, Vol. 4*, Monthly Review Press: New York.

Dunn, J. (1975) *The Political Thought of John Locke*, Cambridge University Press: Cambridge.

Durkheim, E. (1968) *The Elementary Forms of the Religious Life*; George Allen & Unwin: London.

Durkheim, E. (1973) *Moral Education: A Study in the Theory and Application of the Sociology of Education*, The Free Press: New York.

Durkheim, E. (1974) *Sociology and Philosophy*, The Free Press: New York.

Durkheim, E. (1982) *The Rules of Sociological Method and Selected Texts on Sociology and its Method*, Macmillan: London.

Durkheim, E. (1984) *The Division of Labour in Society*, The Free Press: New York.

Durkheim, E. (1992) *Professional Ethics and Civic Morals*, Routledge: London.

Durkheim, E. (2002) *Suicide: A Study in Sociology*, Routledge: London.

Durkheim, E. (2009) (originally pub. 1928) *Socialism and Saint-Simon* (edited and introduced by Alvin Gouldner), Routledge: London.

Easton, D. (1958) 'Authority in socio-political perspective', in Friedrich, C. J. (1958) (ed.) *Authority, Nomos 1*, Harvard University Press: Cambridge, MA.

Eck, W. (2003) *The Age of Augustus*, Blackwell: Oxford.

Eder, W. (1993) 'Augustus and the power of tradition: the Augustan principate as binding link between republic and empire', in Raaflaub and Toher (1993).

Eder, W. (2005) 'Augustus and the power of tradition' in Galinsky, K. (2005) (ed.) *The Cambridge Companion to The Age of Augustus*, Cambridge University Press: Cambridge.

Edwards, C. (1999) (ed.) *Roman Presences; Receptions of Rome in European Culture, 1789–1945*, Cambridge University Press: Cambridge.

Edwards, R. (2003) *Divus Augustus Pater: Tiberius and the Charisma of Augustus*, Ph.D. Thesis, Department of Classical Studies, Indiana University.

Eksteins, M. (1980) 'All quiet on the Western Front and the fate of war', *Journal of Contemporary History*, vol. 15, no. 2, pp. 345–65.

Elliott, W. (1926) 'Mussolini, prophet of the pragmatic era in politics', *Political Science Quarterly*, vol. 41, no. 2, pp. 161–92.

Elton, G. R. (1973) *Reformation Europe; 1517–1559*, Fontana: London.

Engels, F. (1988) (originally published in 1873) 'On authority', in *Karl Marx-Friedrich Engels Collected Works, Vol. 23*, Lawrence and Wishart: London.

Esquith, S. L. (1987) 'Professional authority and state power', *Theory and Society*, vol. 16, no. 2, pp. 237–362.

Euben, J. P. (1997) *Corrupting Youth; Political Education, Democractic Culture, and Poltical Theory*, Princeton University Press: Princeton, NJ.

Feldman, A. (1947) 'The apotheosis of Thersites', *The Classical Journal*, vol. 42, no. 4, pp. 219–21.

Ferguson, A. (1980) *An Essay on the History of Civil Society*, Transaction Books: New Brunswick, NJ.

Ferguson, J. (1973) *Utopias of the Classical World*, Thames and Hudson: London.

Figgis, N. (1960) *Political Thought from Gerson to Grotius, 1414–1625*, Harper Torchbooks: New York.

Finer, H. (1935) *Mussolini's Italy*, Victor Gollanz: London.

Flathman, R. E. (1973) *Political Obligation*, Croom Helm: London.

Flathman, R. E. (1997) 'Hobbes, premier theorist of authority', *Hobbes Studies*, vol. 10, pp. 3–22.

Flint, R. (1894) *Historical Philosophy in France, French Belgium and Switzerland*, C. Scribner & Sons: New York.

Flower, H. (2004) 'Introduction' in Flower, H. (ed.) *The Cambridge Companion to the Roman Republic*. Cambridge University Press: Cambridge.

Foucault, M. (2004) *Society Must Be Defended*, Penguin Books: London.

Foucault, M. (2007) *Security, Territory, Population; Lectures at the College de France 1977–78*, Palgrave Macmillan: London.

Foucault, M. (2010) *The Birth of Biopolitics; Lectures at the College de France, 1978–1979*, Palgrave Macmillan: London.

Fox, P. W. (1960) 'Louis XIV and the theories of absolutism and Divine Right', *The Canadian Journal of Economics and Political Science/Revue canadienne d'Economique et de Science politique*, vol. 26, no. 1, pp. 128–42.

Freud, S. (1985) (originally published 1921) 'Group psychology and the analysis of the ego', in Freud, S. (1985) *Civilization, Society and Religion; Group Psychology, Civilization and its Discontents and Other Works*, Penguin Books: London.

Frezza, D. (2007) *The Leader and the Crowd: Democracy In American Public Discourse, 1880–1941*, University of Georgia Press: Athens, GA.

Friedman, R. B. (1968) 'An introduction to Mill's theory of authority', in Schneewind, J. B. (ed.) (1968) *Mill; A Collection of Critical Essays*, Macmillan: London.

Friedman, R. B. (1987) 'Authority' in Miller, D. (ed.) *The Blackwell Encylopedia of Politican Thought*, Basil Blackwell: Oxford.

Friedman, R. B. 'On the concept of authority in political philosophy', in Raz, J. (1990) (ed.) *Authority*, Basil Blackwell: Oxford.

Friedman, L. (1994) *The Republic of Choice' Law, Authority and Culture*, Harvard University Press: Cambridge, MA.

Friedrich, C. J. (1958) (ed.) *Authority, Nomos 1*, Harvard University Press: Cambridge, MA.

Friedrich, C. J. (1972) *Tradition and Authority*, The Pall Mall Press: London.

Fritz von, K. (1941) 'Conservative reaction and one man rule in Ancient Greece', *Political Science Quarterly*, vol. 56, no. 1, pp. 51–83.

Fromm, E. (1965) (originally published 1941) *Escape From Freedom*, Henry Holt and Company: New York.

Fukuyama, F. (1992) *The End of History and the Last Man*, The Free Press; New York.

Fukuyama, F. (2011) *The Origins of Political Order*, Profile Books: London.

Furedi, F. (1992) *Mythical Past, Elusive Future; History and Society in an Anxious Age*, Pluto Press: London.

Furedi, F. (2006) *The Culture of Fear Revisited*, Continuum Press: London.

Furedi, F. (2009a) *Wasted: Why Education Isn't Educating*, Continuum Press: London.

Furedi, F. (2011) *On Tolerance: A Defence of Moral Independence*, Continuum: London.

Furedi, F. (2011a) The Authority of Public Opinion – why Weber declined to take part in the conversation. *Max Weber Studies*, vol. 11, no. 1, pp. 119–39.

Galinksy, K. (1996) *Augustan Culture: An Interpretive Introduction*, Princeton University Press: Princeton, NJ.

Galinsky, K. (2005) (ed.) *The Cambridge Companion to the Age of Augustus*, Cambridge University Press: Cambridge.

Gane, N. (2002) *Max Weber and Postmodern Theory; Rationalization versus Reenchantment*, Macmillan: London.

Garrett, W. R. (1987) 'Religion, law, and the human condition', *Sociological Analysis*, vol. 47, pp. 1–34.

Geiger, R. L. (1977) 'Democracy and the crowd: the social history of an idea in France and Italy, 1890–1914', *Societas – A Review of Social History*, vol. 7, no. 1, pp. 47–71.

Gentile, E. (1990) 'Fascism as political religion', *Journal of Contemporary History*, vol. 25, no. 2/3, pp. 229–51.

George, E. H. (1922) 'Proudhon and economic federalism', *Journal of Political Economy*, vol. 30, no. 4, pp. 531–42.

Gert, B. (1967) 'Hobbes and psychological egoism', *Journal of the History of Ideas*, vol. 28, no. 4, pp. 503–20.

Gerth, H. (1940) 'The Nazi Party: its leadership and composition', *American Journal of Sociology*, vol. 45, no. 4, pp. 517–41.

Gerth, H. and Wright Mills, C. (1958) *From Max Weber: Essays in Sociology*, Galaxy Books: New York.

Giddens, A. (1978) *Capitalism and Modern Social Theory: An Analysis of the Writings of Marx, Durkheim and Max Weber*, Cambridge University Press: Cambridge.

Giddens, A. (1991) *Modernity and Self-Identity: Self and Society in the Late Modern Age*, Polity Press: Cambridge.

Giddens, A. (1994) 'Living in a post-traditional society', in Beck, U., Giddens, A. and Lash, S. (2004) *Reflexive Modernization: Politics, Tradition, Aesthetics in the Modern Social Order*, Polity: Cambridge.

Giddings, F. H. (1892) 'The nature and conduct of political majorities', *Political Science Quarterly*, vol. 7, no. 1, pp. 116–32.

Giddings, F. H. (1896) 'The destinies of democracy', *Political Science Quarterly*, vol. 11, no. 4, pp. 716–31.

Giddings, F. H. (1906) 'Sovereignty and government', *Political Science Quarterly*, vol. 21, no. 1, pp. 1–27.

Giddings, F. H. (1909) 'Social self-control', *Political Science Quarterly*, vol. 24, no. 4, pp. 569–88.

Giner, S. (1976) *Mass Society*, Martin Robertson & Company Limited: London.

Ginsberg, M. (1964) (originally 1921) *The Psychology of Society*, Methuen: London.

Giorgini, G. (2009) 'Radical Plato: John Stuart Mill, George Grote and the revival of Plato in nineteenth-century England', *History of Political Thought*, vol. 30, no. 4, pp. 617–46.

Gladstone, W. E. (1877) 'On the influence of authority in matters of opinion', *Nineteenth Century*, vol. 1, no. 1, pp. 2–22.

Goldie, M. (2008) 'The reception of Hobbes' in Burns (2008).

Gordon, D. (1992) 'Philosophy, sociology, and gender in the enlightenment conception of public opinion', *French Historical Studies*, vol. 17, no. 4, pp. 882–911.

Gouldner, A. (1950) (ed.) *Studies In Leadership: Leadership and Democratic Action*, Harper & Brothers: New York.

Gouldner, A. (1965) *Enter Plato: Classical Greece and the Origins of Social Theory*, Basic Books: New York.

Gouldner, A. (1971) *Enter Plato: Classical Greece and the Origins of Social Theory*, Part 2, Harper Torchbooks: New York.

Gouldner, A. (1973) *The Coming Crisis of Western Sociology*, Heinemann: London.

Grant, M. (1949) 'The Augustan "Constitution"', *Greece and Rome*, vol. 18, no. 54, pp. 97–112.

Gray, P. W. (2007) 'Political theology and the theology of politics: Carl Schmitt and medieval Christian political thought', *Humanitas*, vol. 20, nos. 1–2, pp. 175–200.

Grote, G. (1857) *A History of Greece, Vol. 2*, John Murray: London.

Gunn, J. A. W. (1983) *Beyond Liberty and Property: The Process of Self-Recognition in Eighteenth-Century Political Thought*, McGill-Queen's University Press: Kingston and Montreal.

Gunn, J. A. W. (1995) *Queen of the World: Opinion in the Public Life of France from the Renaissance to the Revolution*, Voltaire Foundation: Oxford.

Guthrie, W. K. C. (1971) *The Sophist*, Cambridge University Press: Cambridge.

Haakonssen, K. (1994) (ed.) *Hume: Political Essays*, Cambridge University Press: Cambridge.

Haakonssen, K. (1994a) 'The structure of Hume's political theory' in Norton (1994).

Haakonssen, K. (2006) (ed.) *The Cambridge Companion to Adam Smith*, Cambridge University Press: Cambridge.

Habermas, J. (1976) *Legitimation Crisis*, Heinemann: London.

Habermas, J. (1986) 'Law and morality', *The Tanner Lectures on Human Values*, delivered at Harvard University, October 1 and 2, 1986.

Habermas, J. (1987) *Toward a Rational Society*, Polity Press, London.

Habermas, J. (1992) *The Structural Transformation of the Public Sphere*, Polity: Cambridge.

Hammer, D. (1997) '"Who shall readily obey": Authority and politics in the Illiad', *Phoenix*, vol. 51, no. 1, pp. 1–24.

Hammond, P. (1965) 'The sincerity of Augustus', *Harvard Studies in Classical Philology*, vol. 69, pp. 139–62.

Hampson. N. (1982) *The Enlightenment: An Evaluation of its Assumptions and Values*, Penguin Books: London.

Haney, D. P. (2008) *The Americanization of Social Science: Intellectuals and Public Responsibility in the Postwar United States*, Temple University Press: Philadelphia, PA.

Hanley, R. P. (2008) 'Enlightened nation building: The "science of the legislator" in Adam Smith and Rousseau', *American Journal of Political Science*, vol. 52, no. 2, pp. 219–34.

Hanley, R. P. and McMahon, D. M. (2010a) *The Enlightenment; Critical Concepts in Historical Studies, Vol. 3*, Routledge: London.

Hanley, R. P. and McMahon, D. M. (2010b) *The Enlightenment; Critical Concepts in Historical Studies, Vol. 4*, Routledge: London.

Hanley, R. P. and McMahon, D. M. (2010c) *The Enlightenment; Critical Concepts in Historical Studies, Vol. 5*, Routledge: London.

Hannigan, J. (2nd edn, 2006) *Environmental Sociology: A Social Constructionist Perspective*, Routledge: London.

Harris, R. B. (1970) (ed.) *Authority: A Philosophical Analysis*, The University of Alabama Press: Alabama.

Harrison, P. (1994) *The Disenchantment of Reason: The Problem of Socrates in Modernity*, State University of New York Press: Albany, NY.

Haskell, T. L. (2000) (originally pub. in 1977) *The Emergence of Professional Social Science: The American Social Science Association and the Nineteenth-Century Crisis of Authority*, The John Hopkins University Press: Baltimore, MD.

Hathaway, R. (1968) 'Cicero, De Re Publica II, and his Socratic view of history', *Journal of the History of Ideas*, vol. 29, pp. 3–12.

Havelock, E. A. (1957) *The Liberal Temper in Greek Politics*, Jonathan Cape: London.

Hazard, P. (1973) (originally pub. 1935) *The European Mind; 1680–1715*, Penguin: Harmondsworth.

Hegel, G. W. F. (2004) (originally pub. in 1837) *The Philosophy of History*, Dover Publications, Inc.: Mineola, NY.

Heineman, R. (1994) *Authority and the Liberal Tradition*, Transaction Publishers, New Brunswick, NJ.

Hendel, C. W. (1958) 'An exploration of the nature of authority', in Friedrich, C. J. (1958) (ed.) *Authority, Nomos 1*, Harvard University Press: Cambridge, MA.

Hilgartner, S. (2000) *Science on Stage; Expert Advice as Public Drama*, Stanford University Press: Stanford, CA.

Hill, C. (1986) 'The problem of authority' in Hill, C. (1986) *The Collected Essays of Christopher Hill, Vol. 2*, The Harvester Press: Brighton.

Hobbes, T. (1998) *Leviathan*, Oxford University Press: Oxford.

Hobhouse, L. T. (1951) (originally pub. in 1906) *Morals in Evolution: A Study in Comparative Ethics*, Chapman & Hall: London.

Hobhouse, L. T. (1994) *Liberalism and Other Writings*, Cambridge University Press: Cambridge.

Hobsbawn, E. (1992) 'Introduction; Inventing Traditions' in Hobsbawn, E. and Ranger, T. (1992) (eds) *The Invention of Tradition*, Cambridge University Press: Cambridge.

Hobsbawn, E. (2004) *The Age of Extremes: The Short Twentieth Century, 1914– 1991*, Abacus Books: London.

Holmes, S. (1982) 'Two concepts of legitimacy: France after the Revolution', *Political Theory*, vol. 10, no. 2, pp. 165–83.

Homer (1987) *The Iliad* (translated by M. Hammond), Penguin Classics: London.

Hopfl, H. M. (1991) (ed.) *Luther and Calvin on Secular Authority*, Cambridge University Press: Cambridge.

Hopfl, H. M. (1999) 'Power, authority and legitimacy', *Human Resource Development International*, vol. 2, no. 3, pp. 217–34.

Horkheimer, M. (2002) 'Authority and the family', in Horkheimer, M. (2002) *Critical Theory: Selected Essays*. Continuum: New York.

Huet, V. (1999) 'Napoleon I: A new Augustus?' in Edwards, C. (1999) (ed.) *Roman Presences; Receptions of Rome in European Culture, 1789–1945*, Cambridge University Press: Cambridge.

Hume, D. (1963) *Essays Moral, Political and Literary*, Oxford University Press: Oxford.

Huntington, J. (2007) 'Saintly power as a model of royal authority: "the royal touch" and other miracles in the early vitae of Edward The Confessor', in Bolton, B. and Meek, C. (eds) *Aspects of Power and Authority in the Middle Ages*, Brepols Publishers: Bejinhof.

Hurstfield, J. (1965) 'Introduction: The framework of crisis' in Hurstfield, J. (ed.) *The Reformation Crisis*, Edward Arnold: London.

Huxley, J. (1950) 'New bottles for new wine: ideology and scientific knowledge' *The Journal of the Royal Anthropological Institute of Great Britain and Ireland*, vol. 80, no. 1/2, pp. 7–23.

Iggers, G. (1958) *The Cult of Authority: The Political Philosophy of The Saint-Simonians, A Chapter In The Intellectual History Of Totalitarianism*, Martinus Nijhoff: The Hague.

Inge, W. R. (1944) 'Religion: Luther is to blame' in *Time Magazine*; 6 November 1944, www.time.com/time/magazine/article/0,9171,803412,00.html#ixzz1iU0H3lGw (accessed 30 April, 2013).

Inglis, D. and Robertson, R. (2004) 'Beyond the gates of the *Polis*, reconfiguring sociology's ancient inheritance', *Journal of Classical Sociology*, vol. 4, no. 2, pp. 165–89.

Israel, J. (2006) *Enlightenment Contested: Philosophy, Modernity, and the Emancipation of Man 1670–1752*, Oxford University Press: Oxford.

Israel, J. (2010) *A Revolution of the Mind: Radical Enlightenment and the Intellectual Origins of Modern Democracy*, Princeton University Press: Princeton, NJ.

Jaume, L. (2010c) 'Citizen and state under the French Revolution', in Hanley and McMahon (2010c).

Jaeger, H. (2010) 'Before "world opinion": "public opinion" and political community before the twentieth century', *Paper presented at the SGIR 7th Pan-European International Relations Conference*, Stockholm, 9–11 September, 2010.

Jennings, J. (2009) 'Constant's idea of modern liberty' in Rosenblatt, H. (2009) (ed.) *The Cambridge Companion to Constant*, Cambridge University Press: Cambridge.

Johnson, J. (1958) 'The Meaning of "Augustan"', *Journal of the History of Ideas*, vol. 19, no. 4, pp. 507–22.

Jouvenel, de B. (1957) *Sovereignty: An Inquiry into The Political Good*, Cambridge University Press: Cambridge.

Kaftan, J. (1900) 'Authority as a principle of theology', *The American Journal of Theology*, vol. 4, no. 4, pp. 673–733.

Kahan, A. (2001) *Aristocratic Liberalism: The Social and Political Thgought of Jacob Burckhardt, John Stuart Mill and Alexis de Tocqueville*, Transaction Publishers: New Brunswick, NJ.

Kallis, A. (2006) 'Fascism "charisma" and "charismatisation": Weber's model of "charismatic domination" and interwar European fascism', *Politics, Religion & Ideology*, vol. 7, no. 1, pp. 25–43.

Kamen, H. (1976) *The Iron Century: Social Change in Europe 1550–1660*, Sphere Books: London.

Kantorowicz, E. (1997) *The King's Two Bodies: A Study in Mediaeval Theology*, Princeton University Press: Princeton, NJ.

Keen (1967) *A History of Medieval Europe*, Routledge and Kegan Paul: London.

Keller, R. T. (1984) 'The Harvard "Pareto Circle" and the Historical Development of Organization Theory', *Journal of Management*, vol. 10, no. 2, pp. 192–203.

Kelley, D. R. (1984a) 'The prehistory of sociology: Montesquieu, Vico, and the legal tradition', in Kelley, D. R. *History, Law and the Human Sciences: Medieval and Renaissance Perspectives*, Variorum Reprints: London.

Kelley, D. R. (1984b) 'An essay on the very young Marx', in Kelley, D. R. (1984) *History, Law and the Human Sciences: Medieval and Renaissance Perspectives*, Variorum Reprints: London.

Kelly, C. (1987) '"To Persuade without Convincing": The language of Rousseau's Legislatoe', *American Journal of Political Science*, vol. 31, no. 2, pp. 321–35.

Kelly, D. (2003) 'From moralism to modernism: Robert Michels on the history, theory and sociology of patriotism', *History of European Ideas*, vol. 29, no. 3, pp. 339–63.

Kelly, D. (2004) 'Carl Schmitt's political theory of representation', *Journal of the History of Ideas*, vol. 65, no. 1, pp. 113–34.

Kelly, G. A. (1968) *Johann Gottlieb Fichte, Thirteenth Address, Addresses to the German Nation*, Harper Torch Books: New York.

Kennedy, L. (1988) 'Introduction', in Schmitt, C. (1988) *The Crisis of Parliamentary Democracy*. The MIT Press: Cambridge, MA.

Kerferd, G. B. (1981) *The Sophistic Movement*, Cambridge University Press: Cambridge.

Kersting, W. (2006) 'Politics', in Haakonssen, K. (2006) (ed.) *The Cambridge History Of Eighteenth-Century Philosophy*, Cambridge University Press: Cambridge.

Khalil, E. (2005) 'An anatomy of authority: Adam Smith as political theorist', *Cambridge Journal of Economics*, vol. 29, pp. 57–71.

Kierkegaard, S. (1966) *On Authority and Revelation*, Harper Torchbooks: New York.

Kimbrough, R. (1964) 'The problem of Thersites', *The Modern Language Review*, vol. 59, no. 2, pp. 173–6.

King, M. D. (1971) 'Tradition, and the progressiveness of science'. *History and Theory*, vol. 10, no. 1, pp. 3–32.

Kirk, R. (1953) 'Burke and the philosophy of prescription' *Journal of the History of Ideas*, vol. 14, no. 3, pp. 365–80.

Koselleck, R. (1988) *Critique and Crisis: Enlightenment and the Pathogenesis of Modern Society*, Berg: Oxford.

Koyre, A. and Cohen-Rosenfeld, L. (1946) 'Louis De Bonald', *Journal of the History of Ideas*, vol. 7, no. 1, pp. 56–73.

Kraynak, R. (1982) 'Hobbes' Behemoth and the argument for absolutism', *The American Political Science Review*, vol. 76, no. 4, pp. 837–47.

Kriegel, A. D. (1980) 'Liberty and Whiggery in early nineteenth-century England', *The Journal of Modern History*, vol. 52, no. 2, pp. 253–78.

Krieger, L. (1968) 'Authority', in Wiener, P. (1968) *Dictionary of the History of Ideas; Studies of Selected Pivotal Ideas*, Charles Scribner & Sons: New York.

Krieger, L. (1970) *Kings and Philosophers 1689–1789*, Weidenfeld and Nicolson: London.

Krieger, L. (1975) *An Essay on the Theory of Enlightened Despotism*, The University of Chicago Press: Chicago.

Krieger, L. (1977) 'The idea of authority in the West' *The American Historical Review*, vol. 82, no. 2, pp. 249–70.

Kronflic, R. (2005) 'New concepts of authority and citizen education' in Ross, A. (ed.) *Teaching Citizenship*, CiCe: London.

Kumar, K. (1986) *Prophecy and Progress*, Penguin: Harmondsworth.

Lackey, R. (2007) 'Science, scientists, and policy advocacy', *Conservation Biology*, vol. 21, no. 1, pp. 12–17.

Ladner, G. B. (1947) 'Aspects of medieval thought on Church and State', *The Review of Politics*, vol. 9, no. 4, pp. 403–22.

Lake, P. and Pincus, S. (2006) 'Rethinking the public sphere in early modern England', *The Journal of British Studies*, vol. 45, no. 2, pp. 270–92.

Lancaster, R. (2010) From custom to rule: the mechanism of authority in the medieval English Church, available at: www.chicagobooth.edu/socialorg/docs/Lancaster-MedievalEnglishChurch.pdf (accessed 8 May, 2013).

Laski, J. H. (1919) *Authority in the Modern State*, Yale University Press: New Haven, Conn.

Laski, J. H. (1936) *The Rise of European Liberalism*, George Allem & Unwin: London.

Lassman, P. and Speirs, R. (2008) (eds) *Weber; Political Ideas*, Cambridge University Press: Cambridge.

Lasswell, H. D. (1927) *Propaganda Techniques in the World War*, Alfred, A. Knopf: New York.

Lasswell, H. D. (1935) 'The person: subject and object of propaganda', *Annals of the American Academy of Political and Social Science*, vol. 179, pp. 187–93.

Lasswell, H. D. (1965) (originally published in 1935) *World Politics and Personal Insecurity*, The Free Press: New York.

Launderville, D. (2003) *Piety and Politics: The Dynamics of Royal Authority in Homeric Greece, Biblical Israel and Old Babylonian Mesopotamia*, William B. Eermans Publishing Company: Grand Rapids, Michigan.

Le Goff, J. (1994) *Medieval Civilization*, Basil Blackwell Ltd: Oxford.

Leithart, P. J. (2003) 'The Gospel, Gregory VII, and Modern Theology', *Modern Theology*, vol. 19, no. 1, pp. 5–28.

Letwin, S. R. (2008) *On the History of the Idea of Law*, Cambridge University Press: Cambridge.

Lewine, A. (2008) 'Ancient Rome in modern Italy: Mussolini's manipulation of Roman History in the Mostra Augustea della Romanita', *Studies in Mediterranean Antiquity and Classic*, vol. 2, no. 1, p. 8.

Lewis, E. (1954) *Medieval Political Ideas, Vol. 1*, Routledge & Kegan Paul: London.

Lewis, E. (1954a) *Medieval Political Ideas, Vol. 2*, Routledge & Kegan Paul: London.

Lewis, G. C. (1974) (originally published 1849) *An Essay on the Influence of Authority in Matters of Opinion*, Arno Press: New York.

Lewis, H. D. (1978) 'Freedom and authority in Rousseau', *Philosophy*, vol. 53, no. 205, pp. 353–62.

Lincoln, B. (1994) *Authority: Construction and Corrosion*, University of Chicago Press: Chicago.

Liftin, K. (2000) *Environment, Wealth, and Authority: Global Climate Change and Emerging Modes of Legitimation*, International Studies Association, 2000.

Lippmann, W. (1991) *Public Opinion*, Transaction: New Brunswick, NJ.

Lively, J. and Reeve, A. (1991) (eds) *Modern Political Theory From Hobbes to Marx*, Routledge: London.

Lloyd, S. A. (2002) *Ideals as Interests in Hobbes's Leviathan; the Power of Mind over Matter*, Cambridge University Press: Cambridge.

Locke, J. (2008) *An Essay Concerning Human Understanding*, Oxford University Press: Oxford.

Long, D. (2006) 'Adam Smith's politics' in Haakonssen, K. (2006) (ed.) *The Cambridge Companion to Adam Smith*, Cambridge University Press: Cambridge.

Lovin, R. W. (1984) 'Review of law and revolution', *Journal of Law & Religion*, vol. 2, pp. 206–11.

Lowell, A. L. (1969) (originally 1913) *Public Opinion and Popular Government*, Johnson Reprint: New York.

Lowenstein, K. (1935) 'Autocracy versus democracy in contemporary Europe', *The American Political Science Review*, vol. 29, no. 4, pp. 571–93.

Lukac De Stier, M. (1997) 'Hobbes on authority, De Cive and Leviathan: A comparison', *Hobbes Studies*, vol. 10, pp. 51–67.

Lukàcs, G. (1920) 'Legality and illegality', in Lukàcs, G. (1971) *History and Class Consciousness*, Merlin Press: London.

Lukàcs, G. (1923) 'Reification and the consciousness of the proletariat', in Lukàcs, G. (1971) *History and Class Consciousness*, Merlin Press: London.

Lukàcs, G. (1980) *The Destruction of Reason*, The Merlin Press: London.

Lukes, S. (1979) 'Power and authority', in Bottomore, T. and Nisbet, R. (1979) (eds) *A History of Sociological Analysis*, Heinemann: London.

Luscombe, D. E. (1991) 'Introduction; the formation of political thought in the west', in Burns (1991).

Luscombe, D. E. and Evans, G. R. (1991) 'The twelfth-century renaissance', in Burns, J. H. (1991) (ed.) *The Cambridge History of Medieval Thought*, c350–c1450, Cambridge University Press: Cambridge.

Lyon, P. V. (1961) 'Saint-Simon and the origins of scienticism', *The Canadian Journal of Economics and Political Science*, vol. 27, no. 1, pp. 55–63.

Macdonald, A. J. (1933) *Authority and Reason in the Middle Ages*, Oxford University Press: London.

MacIntyre, A. (2007) *After Virtue: A Study in Moral Theory*, Duckworth: London.

MacKinnon, W. A. (1971/1828) *On the Rise, Progress and Present State of Public Opinion In Great Britain and Other Parts of the World*, Irish University Press: Shannon, Ireland.

Macpherson, C. B. (1941) 'Review of "The Ruling Class"' *The Canadian Journal of Economics and Political Science*, vol. 7, no. 1, pp. 95–100.

Mahaffy, J. P. (1925) (originally pub. in 1874) *Social Life in Greece: From Homer to Menander*, Macmillan: London.

Malcolm, N. (2008) 'Hobbes and Spinoza' in Burns (2008).

Manent, P. (1995) *An Intellectual History of Liberalism*, Princeton University Press: Princeton, NJ.

Marcuse, H. (2008) (originally published 1936) *A Study on Authority*, Verso: London.

Marius, R. (1985) *Thomas More: A Biography*, J. M. Dent & Son: London.

Marks, J. (2005) 'The Ongoing *Neikos*: Thersites, Odysseus, and Achilleus', *American Journal of Philology*, vol. 126, no. 1, pp. 1–31.

Markus, R. A. (1991) 'The Latin fathers' in Burns (1991).

Marx, K. (1955) *The Poverty of Philosophy*, Prometheus Books: New York.

Marx, K. (1969) *Theories of Surplus Value, Part 1*, Lawrence & Wishart: London.

Marx, K. (1970) (originally pub. 1851) 'The eighteenth brumaire of Louis Bonaparte', in *Marx-Engles Selected Works*, Lawrence and Wishart: London.

Marx, K. (1971) *Capital, Vol. 3*, Lawrence & Wishart: London.

Marx, K. (1974) *Capital, Vol. 1*, Lawrence & Wishart: London.

Marx, K. (1975) (originally written 1835) 'Does the reign of Augustus deserve to be counted among the happier periods of the Roman Empire?', in *Karl Marx Frederick Engels Collected Works, Vol. 1, 1853–1843*, Lawrence & Wishart: London.

Marx, K. (1975a) (originally published 1844) 'Contribution to the critique of Hegel's philosophy of law. Introduction', in *Karl Marx Frederick Engels Collected Works, Vol. 4*, Lawrence & Wishart: London.

Marx, K. (1976) 'The German Ideology' (originally published 1855), in *Karl Marx Frederick Engels Collected Works, Vol. 5*, Lawrence & Wishart: London.

Marx, K. (1988/1870) 'Marx to Kugelman', 27 June 1870, in *Karl Marx Frederick Engels Collected Works, Vol. 43*, Lawrence & Wishart: London.

Marx, K. and Engels, F. (1988) *Karl Marx Frederick Engels Collected Works, Vol. 43*, Lawrence & Wishart: London.

Mason, H. (1965) 'The sincerity of Augustus', *Harvard Studies in Classical Philology*, vol., pp. 139–62.

Mayhew, L. (1984) 'In defense of modernity: Talcott Parsons and the utilitarian tradition', *American Journal of Sociology*, vol. 89, no. 6, pp. 1273–305.

McCarthy, G. (2003) *Classical Horizons; The Origins of Sociology in Ancient Greece*, State University of New York Press: Albany.

McCready, W. (1973) 'Papal Plenitudo Potestatis and the Source of Temporal Authority in Late Medieval Papal Hierocratic Theory', *Speculum*, vol. 48, no. 4, p. 655.

McCready, W. (1975) 'Papalists and antipapalists: Aspects of the Church/State controversy in the later middle ages', *Viator*, vol. 6, pp. 241–73.

McCutcheon, R. R. (1991) 'The *Responsio Ad Lutherum*: Thomas More's inchoate dialogue with heresy', *Sixteenth Century Journal*, vol. 22, no. 1, pp. 77–90.

McGlew, J. (1989) 'Royal power and the Achaean assembly at Iliad 2.84–393', *Classical Antiquity*, vol. 8, no. 2, pp. 283–95.

McIntosh, D. (1970) 'Weber and Freud: on the nature and sources of authority'. *American Sociological Review*, vol. 35, pp. 901–11.

Meier, C. (1993) 'Caesar Divi filius and the formation of the alternative in Rome', in Raaflaub, K. and Toher, M. (1993) (eds) *Between Republic and Empire: Interpretations of Augustus and His Principate*, University of California Press: Berkeley.

Melograni, P. (1976) 'The Cult of the Duce in Mussolini's Italy', *Journal of Contemporary History*, vol. 11, no. 4, pp. 221–37.

Melve, L. (2006) 'The revolt of the medievalists. Directions in recent research on the twelfth century renaissance', *Journal of Medieval History*, Vol. 32, pp. 231–52.

Merivale, C. (1896) *History of the Romans Under the Empire, Vol. 3*, Longman, Green, and Co.: London.

Merriam, C. E. (1921) 'The present state of the study of politics', *The American Political Science Review*, vol. 15, no. 2, pp. 173–85.

Mészáros, I. (1989) *The Power of Ideology*, Harvester Wheatsheaf: New York.

Michels, R. (1927) 'Some reflections on the sociological character of political parties', *The American Political Science Review*, vol. 21, no. 4, pp. 753–72.

Michels, R. (1965) *First Lectures in Political Sociology*, Harper Torchbooks: New York.

Michels, R. (1968) *Political Parties: A Sociological Study of the Oligarchical Tendencies of Modern democracy*, The Free Press: New York.

Milgram, S. (1974) *Obedience to Authority*, Harper Collins: New York.

Mill, J. S. (1820) 'Government', in *Essays on Government, Liberty of the Press, and Law of Nations*, London, J. Innes (ed.) (1825), [reprint edition] 1986: New York.

Mill, J. S. (1831) 'The Spirit of the Age', *Examiner*, 9 January, p. 20, http://oll. libertyfund.org/title/256/50800 (accessed 30 April, 2013).

Mill, J. S. (1840) 'Democracy in America', *Edinburgh Review*, vol. 63, pp. 1–47.

Mill, J. S. (1861) 'Considerations On Representative Government', in Mill, J. S. (2008) *On Liberty and Other Essays*, Oxford University Press: Oxford.

Mill, J. S. (1978) (ed. Robson, J. M.) *Collected Works of John Stuart Mill, Vol. 11*, University of Toronto Press: Toronto.

Millar, J. (2006) *The Origin of the Distinction of Ranks*, Liberty Fund: Indianapolis.

Miller, D. (ed.) (1987) *The Blackwell Encyclopedia of Politican Thought*, Basil Blackwell: Oxford.

Minar, D. W. (1960) 'Public opinion in the perspective of political theory', *The Western Political Quarterly*, vol. 13, no. 1, pp. 31–44.

Minogue, K. R. (1963) *The Liberal Mind*, Methuen & Co Ltd: London.

Misztal, B. (1996) *Trust in Modern Societies: The Search For the Bases of Order*, Polity Press: Cambridge.

Mitchell, M. (1931) 'Emile Durkheim and the philosophy of nationalism', *Political Science Quarterly*, vol. 46, no. 1, pp. 87–106.

Mommsen, W. J. (1981) 'Max Weber and Roberto Michels: An asymmetrical partnership', *European Journal of Sociology*, vol. 22, pp. 100–16.

Mommsen, W. (1984) *Max Weber and German Politics, 1890–1920*, University of Chicago: Chicago.

Montgomery, T. J. (1975) 'Authority, the American Liberal Tradition, and the Classroom' Paper presented at the Annual Meeting of the American Education Research Association (Washington, DC, April 1975).

Mooney (2006) *The Republican War on Science*, Basic Books: New York.

Morrow, G. (2007) 'Adam Smith: moralist and philosopher' *Journal of Political Economy*, vol. 35, no. 3 (Jun., 1927), pp. 321–42.

Mosca, G. (1980) (originally pub. 1916) *The Ruling Class*, Greenwood Press Publishers: Westport, CT.

Mulgan, R. G. (1979) 'Lycophron and Greek theories of social contract', *Journal of History of Ideas*, vol. 40, no. 1, pp. 121–22.

Murvar, V. (1967) 'Max Weber's concept of hierocracy: A study in the typology of Church-State relationships', *Sociological Analysis*, vol. 28, no. 2, pp. 69–84.

Munn, M. (2000) *The School of History: Athens in the Age of Socrates*, University of California Press: Berkeley.

Nederman, C. J. (2005) 'Empire and the historiography of European political thought: Marsiglio of Padua, Nicholas of Cusa, and the medieval/modern divide', *Journal of the History of Ideas*, vol. 66, no. 1, pp. 1–15.

Nelis, J. (2007) 'Constructing fascist identity: Benito Mussolini and the myth of "Romanita"', *The Classical World*, vol. 100, no. 4, pp. 391–415.

Nettleship, H. (1892) 'Authority in the sphere of conduct and intellect', *International Journal of Ethics*, vol. 2, no. 2, pp. 217–32.

Neuman, F. (1963) *Behemoth: The Structure and Practice of National Socialism 1933–1944*, Harper & Row: New York.

Neumann, S. (1938) 'The rule of the demagogue', *American Sociological Review*, vol. 3, no. 4, pp. 487–98.

Nicol, D. M. (1991) 'Byzantine political thought' in Burns (1991).

Nielsen, D. A. (1988) 'Rationalization in medieval Europe: The inquisition and sociocultural change', *Politics, Culture and Society*, vol. 2, no. 2, pp. 217–41.

Nietzsche, F. W. (1969) *Thus Spoke Zarathustra: A Book for Everyone and No One*, Penguin Books: London.

Nietzsche, F. W. (2007) *The Twilight of the Idols*, Wordsworth Editions Limited: London.

Nisbet, R. A. (1943b) 'The French Revolution and the rise of sociology in France', *American Journal of Sociology*, vol. 49, no. 2, pp. 156–64.

Nisbet, R. A. (1944) 'DeBonald and the concept of the social group', *The Journal of the History of Ideas*, vol. 3, pp. 315–31.

Nisbet, R. A. (1970) *The Social Bond: An Introduction to the Study of Society*, Alfred A. Knopf: New York.

Nisbet, R. A. (1972) 'The Nemesis of Authority', *The Intercollegiate Review*, Winter–Spring, pp. 3–13.

Nisbet, R. A. (1974) *The Social Philosophers: Community and Conflict in Western Thought*, Heinemann: London.

Nisbet, R. A. (1979) *The Sociological Tradition*, Heinemann: London.

Noelle-Neumann, E. (1979) 'Public opinion and the classical tradition: a re-evaluation', *The Public Opinion Quarterly*, vol. 43, no. 2, pp. 143–56.

Norton, D. (1994) (ed) *Cambridge Companion to Hume*, Cambridge University Press: Cambridge.

Notes and Abstracts (1902) (signed as EM) in *American Journal of Sociology*, vol. 8, no. 3, pp. 419–20.

Nye, R. A. (1977) *The Anti-Democratic Sources of Elite Theories: Pareto, Mosca, Michels*, Sage Publications: London.

Oakeshott, M. (1975) *Hobbes On Civil Association*, Basil Blackwell: Oxford.

Oakeshott, M. (2006) *Lectures in the History of Political Thought*, Imprint Academic: Exeter.

Oakley, F. (2004) *The Conciliarist Tradition: Constitutionalism in the Catholic Church 1300–1870*, Oxford University Press: Oxford.

Ober, J. (1998) *Political Dissent in Democratic Athens; Intellectual Critics of Popular Rule*, Princeton University Press, Princeton, NJ.

Offe, C. (2005) *Reflection on America: Tocqueville, Weber and Adorno in the United States*, Polity Press: Cambridge.

O'Gorman, F. (1984) 'Electoral Deference in "Unreformed" England: 1760–1832', *The Journal of Modern History*, vol. 56, no. 3, pp. 391–429.

O'Hear, A. (1977) 'Guilt and shame as moral concepts', *Proceedings of the Aristotelian Society, New Series*, vol. 77, pp. 54–73.

Olafson, F. (1991) 'Nietzsche's philosophy of culture: a paradox in the will to power', *Philosophy and Phenomenological Research*, vol. 51, no. 3, pp. 557–72.

O'Neill, J. (1986) 'The disciplinary society: From Weber to Foucault', *The British Journal of Sociology*, vol. 37, no. 1, pp. 42–60.

Ostwald, M. (1990) 'Nomos and Phusis in Antiphon's Peri Aletheias', Retrieved from www.escholarship.org/uc/item/7kg1w5zm, 10 December 2009.

Ozouf, M. (1988) '"Public opinion" at the end of the old regime', *Journal of Modern History*, vol. 60, p. 2.

Paget, E. H. (1929) 'Sudden changes in group opinion', *Social Forces*, vol. 7, no. 3, pp. 438–44.

Palmer, P. (1967) 'The concept of public opinion in political theory', in Witke, C. (1967) (originally 1936) (ed.) *Essays in History And Political Theory: In Honor Of Charles Howard McIlwain*, Russell & Russell: New York.

Palmer, R. R. (1940) 'The national idea in France before the Revolution', *Journal of the History of Ideas*, vol. 1, no. 1, pp. 95–111.

Palmer, R. R. (1969) *The Age of the Democratic Revolution: The Struggle*, Princeton University Press: Princeton, NJ.

Pareto, V. (1935) *The Mind and Society; A Treatise on General Sociology, Vols. 1 & 2*, Dover Publications: New York.

Pareto, V. (1935a) *The Mind and Society; A Treatise on General Sociology, Vols. 3 & 4*, Dover Publications: New York.

Parker, D. (1973) *The Making of French Absolutism*, Edward Arnold: London.

Parsons, T. (1939) 'The professions and social structure', *Social Forces*, vol. 17, no. 4, p. 457.

Parsons, T. (1942a) 'Max Weber and the contemporary political crisis: 1. The sociological analysis of power and authority structures', *The Review of Politics*, vol. 4, no. 1, pp. 61–76.

Parsons, T. (1942b) 'Max Weber and the contemporary political crisis: 2', *The Review of Politics*, vol. 4, no. 2, pp. 291–314.

Parsons, T. (1942c) 'Propaganda and social control', in Parsons, T. (1964) *Essays in Sociological Theory*, The Free Press: Glencoe.

Parsons, T. (1954) 'The problem of controlled institutional change' in Parsons, T. (1954) *Essays in Sociological Theory*, The Free Press: New York.

Parsons, T. (1963) 'On the concept of political power', *Proceedings of the American Philosophical Society*, vol. 107, no. 3, pp. 232–62.

Parsons, T. (1963a) 'Christianity and modern industrial society', in Tiryakian, E. A. (1963) (ed.) *Sociological Theory, Values, and Social-Cultural Change*, The Free Press: New York.

Parsons, T. (1968) *The Structure of Social Action, Vol. 1*, Free Press: New York.

Parsons, T. (1974) 'The life and work of Emile Durkheim', in Durkheim, E. (1974) *Sociology and Philosophy*, The Free Press: New York.

Pateman, T. (1978) *How is Political Knowledge Possible?*, M.Phil. Thesis: University of Sussex: Brighton.

Pennington, K. (1991) 'Law, legislative authority and theories of government, 1150–1300', in Burns (1991).

Pennock, J. R. and Chapman, J. W. (1987) (eds) *Authority Revisited*, New York University Press: New York.

Pitt, A. (1998) 'The Irrationalist Liberalism of Hippolyte Taine', *The Historical Journal*, vol. 41, no. 4, pp. 1035–53.

Pocock, J. G. A. (1985) 'Authority and property: the question of liberal origins', in Pocock, J. G. A. (1985) *Virtue, Commerce, and History; Essays on Political Thought and History, Chiefly in the Eighteenth Century*, Cambridge University Press: Cambridge.

Pocock, J. G. A. (2003) *The Machiavellian Moment; Florentine Political Thought and the Atlantic Republican Tradition*, Princeton University Press: Princeton, NJ.

Porter, R. (2000) *Enlightenment: Britain and the Creation of the Modern World*, Allen Lane: London.

Poslethwaite, N. (1988) 'Thersites in the Iliad', *Greece & Rome*, vol. 35, no. 2, pp. 123–36.

Potts, J. (2009) *A History of Charisma*, Palgrave Macmillan: Houndmills, Basingstoke.

Preus, J. (1972) 'Theological legitimation for innovation in the middle ages', *Viator*, vol. 3, pp. 1–26.

Priest, S. H. (2006) 'Public discourse and scientific controversy: a-spiral-of silence analysis of biotechnology opinion in the united state', *Science Communication*, vol. 28, no. 1, pp. 195–215.

Raaflaub, K. and Toher, M. (1993) (eds) *Between Republic and Empire: Interpretations of Augustus and His Principate*, University of California Press: Berkeley.

Rankin, H. D. (1972) 'Thersites the Malcontent, a discussion', *Symbolae Osloenses*, vol. 47, part 1, pp. 36–60.

Rawson, E. (1985) *Intellectual Life in the Late Roman Republic*, John Hopkins University Press: Baltimore, MD.

Raz, J. (1990) (ed.) *Authority*, Basil Blackwell: Oxford.

Raz, J. (1987) 'Government by Consent' in Pennock, J. R. and Chapman, J. W. (1987) (eds) *Authority Revisited*, New York University Press: New York.

Resnick, D. (1984) 'Locke and the Rejection of the Ancient Constitution', *Political Theory*, vol. 12, no. 1, pp. 97–114.

Richter, M. (1982) 'Toward concept of political illegitimacy; Bonapartist dictatorship and democratic legitimacy', *Political Theory*, vol. 10, no. 2, pp. 185–214.

Richter, M. (1995) *The History of Political and Social Concepts: A Critical Introduction*, Oxford University Press: Oxford.

Richter, M. (2004) 'Tocqueville and the two Bonapartes' in Baehr, P. and Richter, M. (2004) (eds) *Dictatorship in History and Theory: Bonapartism, Caesarism and Totalitarianism*, Cambridge University Press: Cambridge.

Riley, P. (2001) (ed.) *Cambridge Companion to Rousseau*, Cambridge University Press: Cambridge.

Riley, P. (2001a) 'Rousseau's general will', in Riley (2001).

Riley, P. (2010) 'Social contract theory and its critics', Hanley, R. P. and McMahon, D. M. (2010a) *The Enlightenment; Critical Concepts in Historical Studies, Vol. 3*, Routledge: London.

Roberts, J. T. (1994) *Athens on Trial: The Antidemocratic Tradition in Western Thought*, Princeton University Press: Princeton, NJ.

Robin, C. (2004) *Fear: The History of a Political Idea*, Oxford University Press: New York.

Robinson, I. S. (1978) '"Periculosus Homo": Pope Gregory VII and episcopal authority', *Viator*, vol. 9, pp. 103–31.

Robinson, I. S. (1979) 'Pope Gregory VII, the princes and the Pactum 1077–1080', *The English Historical Review*, vol. 94, no. 373, October, pp. 721–56.

Robinson, I. S. (1991) 'Church and papacy', in Burns (1991).

Rocco, A. (1926) *The Political Doctrine of Fascism*, International Conciliation, no. 223.

Rose, P. (1988) 'Thersites and the plural voices of Homer', *Arethusa*, vol. 21, no. 1, pp. 5–25.

Rosenblatt, H. (2009) (ed.) *The Cambridge Companion to Constant*, Cambridge University Press: Cambridge.

Rosenblum, N. (1987) 'Studying authority: keeping pluralism in mind', in Pennock, J. R. and Chapman, J. W. (1987) (eds) *Authority Revisited*, New York University Press: New York.

Ross, E. A. (1896) 'Social control II. Law and public opinion', *The American Journal of Sociology*, vol. 1, no. 6, DOI: 10.1086/210569.

Ross, E. A. (1898) 'Social control XIII. The system of social control', *American Journal of Sociology*, vol. 3, no. 6, pp. 809–28.

Rouanet, S. P. (1964) 'Irrationalism and myth in Georges Sorel', *The Review of Politics*, vol. 26, no. 1, pp. 45–69.

Rousseau, J. J. (1968) *The Social Contracti*, Penguin Classic: London.

Rubin, I. I. (1979) *A History of Economic Thought*, Ink Links: London.

Runciman, W. G. (1971) *Social Change and Political Theory*, Cambridge University Press: Cambridge.

Russell, B. (1947) *A History of Western Philosophy*, George Allen and Unwin Ltd: London.

Russell, B. (2010) (originally pub. 1934) *Freedom and Organization, 1814–1914*, Routledge: London.

Sabine, G. (1961) *A History of Political Theory*, Henry Holt and Company: New York.

Salmon, E. T. (1956) 'The evolution of Augustus' Principate', *Historia: Zeitschrift fur Alte Geschichte*, vol. 5, no. 4, pp. 456–78.

Salmon, J. H. M. (2008) 'Catholic resistance theory, Ultramontanism, and the royalist response, 1580–1620', in Burns (2008).

Salomon, A. (1940) 'Crisis, history and the image of man', *The Review of Politics*, vol. 2, no. 4, pp. 413–37.

Sarewitz, D. (2004) 'How science makes environmental controversies worse' *Environmental Science & Policy*, vol. 7, pp. 385–403.

Saxonhouse, A. W. (1978) 'Nature and convention in Thucydides' history', *Polity*, vol. 10, no. 4, pp. 461–87.

Saxonhouse, A. W. (2008) *Free Speech and Democracy in Ancient Athens*, Cambridge University Press: Cambridge.

Schlesinger, M. (2002) 'A loss of faith: The sources of reduced political legitimacy for the American medical profession', *Milbank Quarterly*, vol. 80, no. 2, pp. 185–235.

Schmitt, C. (1988) *The Crisis of Parliamentary Democracy*. The MIT Press: Cambridge, MA.

Schmitt, C. (2004) *Legality and Legitimacy*, Duke University Press: Durham, NC.

Schmitt, C. (2008) *The Leviathan in the State Theory of Thomas Hobbes*, The University of Chicago Press: Chicago.

Schneewind, J. B. (ed.) (1965) *Mill's Essays on Literature and Society*, Collier Books: New York.

Schneewind, J. B. (1968) *Mill: A Collection of Critical Essays*, Macmillan: London.

Schochet, G. J. (1975) *Patriarchalism in Political Thought*, Basil Blackwell: Oxford.

Schudson, M. (2006) 'The trouble with experts – and why democracies need them', *Theory and Society*, vol. 35, pp. 491–506.

Scott, C. (2008) 'Relationships; Ethics committees and research' in Piper, H. and Stronach, I. (eds) (2008) *Don't Touch!; The Educational Story of a Panic*, Routledge: London.

Scott, K. (1932) 'Mussolini and the Roman Empire', *The Classical Journal*, vol. 27, no. 9, pp. 645–57.

Scott, J. and Marshall, G. (2005) *A Dictionary of Sociology*, Oxford University Press: Oxford.

Sedley, D. L. (1998) 'Sublimity and Skepticism in Montaigne', *Publications of the Modern Language Association of America*, vol. 113, no. 5, pp. 1079–92.

Seligman, A. (1990) 'Moral authority and Reformation religion: On charisma and the origins of modernity', *International Journal of Politics, Culture, and Society*, vol. 4, no. 2, pp. 159–79.

Sennett, R. (1981) *Authority*, Vintage Books: New York.

Shepard, W. J. (1909) 'Public opinion', *The American Journal of Sociology*, vol. 15, no. 1, pp. 32–60.

Shepard, W. J. (1935) 'Democracy in transition', *The American Political Science Review*, vol. 29, no. 1, pp. 1–20.

Shils, E. (1981) *Tradition*, The University of Chicago Press: Chicago.

Shklar, J. (1957) *After Utopia: The Decline of Political Faith*, Princeton University Press: Princeton, NJ.

Shklar, J. (1976) *Freedom and Independence: A Study of the Political Ideas of Hegel's Phenomenology of Mind*, Cambridge University Press: Cambridge.

Shklar, J. (2001) 'Rousseau's images of authority' (Especially in *La Nouvelle Heloise*) in Riley (2001).

Shotter, D. (2005) *Augustus Caesar*, Routledge: London.

Simmel, G. (1896) 'Superiority and subordination as subject matter of sociology', *The American Journal of Sociology*, vol. 2, no. 2, pp. 167–89.

Simmel, G. (1971) *On Individuality and Social Forms*, The University of Chicago Press; Chicago.

Simmel, G. (1990) *The Philosophy of Money*, Routledge: London.

Simon, Y. (1948) *The Nature and Functions of Authority*, Marquette University Press: Milwaukee.

Skinner, Q. (1989) 'The state' in Ball, T., Farr, J. and Hanson, R. (eds) *Political Innovation and Conceptual Change*, Cambridge University Press: Cambridge.

Skinner, Q. (1998) *Liberty Before Liberalism*, Cambridge University Press: Cambridge.

Skinner, Q. (2004) *The Foundations of Modern Political Thought, Volume 2, The Age of Reformation*, Cambridge University Press: Cambridge.

Skinner, Q. (2006) 'Hobbes on persons, authors and representatives', in Springborg, P. (ed.) *The Cambridge Companion to Hobbes*, Cambridge University Press: Cambridge.

Skinner, Q. (2009) *The Foundations of Modern Political Thought: Volume 1, The Renaissance*, Cambridge University Press: Cambridge.

Small, A. W. (1895) 'The era of sociology', *American Journal of Sociology*, vol. 1, no. 1, pp. 1–15.

Smith, A. (2010) *Theory of Moral Sentiment*, Penguin Classics: London.

Smith, D. (1988) 'Faith, reason, and charisma: Rudolf Sohm, Max Weber and the theology of grace', *Sociological Inquiry*, vol. 68, no. 1, pp. 32–60.

Smuts, M. (2003) 'Political thought in early Stuart Britain', in Coward, B. (ed.) *A Companion to Stuart Britain*, Blackwell: Oxford.

Sommerville, J. P. (1999) *Royalists and Patriots: Politics and Ideology in England 1603–1640*, Longman: London.

Sophocles (1973) *Antigone* (R. E. Braun, trans.), Oxford University Press: Oxford.

Sorel, G. (1950) *Reflection on Violence*, Free Press: Glencoe.

Sorell, T. (1996) (ed.) *The Cambridge Companion to Hobbes*, Cambridge University Press: Cambridge.

Southern, R. (1967) *The Making of the Middle Ages*, Pimlico: London.

Spektorowski, A. (2002) 'Maistre, Donoso Cortes, and the legacy of Catholic authoritarianism', *Journal of the History of Ideas*, vol. 63, pp. 283–302.

Spellman, W. M. (1998) *European Political Thought 1600–1700*, Macmillan Press: London.

Spencer, H. (1978) *The Principle of Ethics*, 2 Vols. Liberty Classics: Indianapolis.

Spencer, M. (1970) 'Weber on legitimate norms and authority', *The British Journal of Sociology*, vol. 21, no. 2, pp. 123–34.

Spiro, H. J. (1958) 'Authority, values, and policy', in Friedrich (1958).

Spring, D. (1976) 'Walter Bagehot and deference', *The American Historical Review*, vol. 81, no. 3, pp. 524–39.

Springborg, P. (2006) (ed.) *The Cambridge Companion to Hobbes*, Cambridge University Press: Cambridge.

Stanton, T. (2010) 'Authority and freedom in the interpretation of Locke's political theory', www.york.ac.uk/media/politics/documents/resourcesyork/teaching/resources/Authority%20and%20freedom%20in%20the%20interpretation%20of%20Locke's%20political%20theory.pdf, February 2010 (accessed, 20 January 2012).

Starr, C. G. (1952) 'The perfect democracy of the Roman Empire', *The American Historical Review*, vol. 58, no. 1, pp. 1–16.

Stefanson, D. (2004) *Man as Hero: Hero as Citizen. Models of Heroic Thought and Action in Homer, Plato and Rousseau*, Thesis submitted for the degree of Doctor of Philosophy, The University of Adelaide: Adelaide.

Stein, P. G. (1991) 'Roman Law', in Burns (1991).

Stein, P. (1995) 'Custom in Roman and medieval civil law', *Continuity and Change*, vol. 10, no. 3, pp. 337–44.

Stephen, L. (1891) 'Cardinal Newman's Scepticism', *Nineteenth Century*, vol. 29, pp. 179.

Sternhell, Z. (2010) *The Anti-Enlightenment Tradition*, Yale University Press: New Haven.

Stewart, W. K. (1928) 'The mentors of Mussolini', *The American Political Science Review*, vol. 22, no. 4, p. 411.

Stirk, P. and Weigall, D. (1995) *An Introduction to Political Ideas*, Pinter: London.

Stone, L. (1986) *The Causes of the English Revolution 1529–1642*, ARK: London.

Stone, M. (1999) 'A flexible Rome: Fascism and the cult of romanita', in Edwards, C. (1999) (ed.) *Roman Presences; Receptions of Rome in European Culture, 1789–1945*, Cambridge University Press: Cambridge.

Strauss, L. (1966) The political philosophy of Hobbes: Its basis and its genesis. The University of Chicago Press: Chicago.

Strayer, J. (1970) *On the Medieval Origins of the Modern State*, Princeton University Press: Princeton, NJ.

Strong, T. (1993) 'How to write scripture: Words, authority, and politics in Thomas Hobbes', *Critical Inquiry*, vol. 20, no. 1, pp. 128–59.

Stuurman, S. (2004) 'The voice of Thersites: Reflections on the origins of the idea of equality', *Journal of the History of Ideas*, vol. 65, no. 2, pp. 171–89.

Swanson, R. N. (1999) *The Twelfth-Century Renaissance*, Manchester University Press: Manchester.

Swingewood, A. (1970) Origins of sociology: the case of the Scottish Enlightenment. *The British Journal of Sociology*, vol. 21, pp. 164–80.

Syme, R. (2002) (1939) *The Roman Revolution*, Oxford University Press: Oxford.

Takacs, S. (2003) 'The *res gestae* of Augustus', in Eck, W. *The Age of Augustus*, Blackwell: Oxford.

Ten, C. L. (1969) 'Mill and liberty', *Journal of the History of Ideas*, vol. 30, no. 1, pp. 47–68.

Thalmann, W. G. (1988) 'Thersites: Comedy, scapegoats, and heroic ideology in the *Iliad*', *Transactions of the American Philological Association*, vol. 118, pp. 1–28.

Therborn, G. (1976) *Science, Class and Society: On the Formation of Sociology and Historical Materialism*, New Left Books: London.

Tholfsen, T. R. (1971) 'The intellectual origins of Mid-Victorian stability', *Political Science Quarterly*, vol. 86, no. 1, pp. 57–91.

Thompson, E. P. (1977) *Whigs and Hunters: The Origin of the Black Act*, Penguin Books: Harmondsworth.

Tierney, B. (1982) *Religion, Law, and the Growth of Constitutional Thought*, Cambridge University Press: Cambridge.

Tocqueville, de A. (1998) *Democracy in America*, Wordsworth Editions: London.

Tonnies, F. (1955) *Community and Association*, Routledge & Kegan Paul Ltd: London.

Toulmin, S. E. (2008) *The Uses of Argument*, Cambridge University Press: Cambridge.

Tregenza, I. (2002) 'Leviathan as myth: Michael Oakeshott and Carl Schmitt on Hobbes and the critique of rationalism', *Contemporary Political Theory*, vol. 1, pp. 349–69.

Trevor-Roper, H. (1959) 'The general crisis of the 17th century', *Past & Present*, vol. 6, no. 1, pp. 31–64.

Tuck, R. (1972) 'Why is authority such a problem?' in Laslett, P., Runciman, W. G. and Skinner, Q. (eds) *Philosophy, Politics and Society*, Basil Blackwell: Oxford.

Tuck, R. (1974) 'Power and authority in seventeenth-century England', *The Historical Journal*, vol. 17, no. 1, pp. 43–61.

Turner, B. (1992) *Max Weber: From History to Modernity*, Routledge: London.

Turner, F. (1986) 'British politics and the demise of the Roman Republic: 1700–1939', *The Historical Journal*, vol. 29, no. 3, pp. 577–99.

Turner, F. (1993) *Contesting Cultural Authority: Essays in Victorian Intellectual Life*, Cambridge University Press: Cambridge.

Turner, S. (2000) (ed.) *The Cambridge Companion to Weber*, Cambridge University Press: Cambridge.

Ullmann, W. (1961) *Principles of Government in the Middle Ages*, Methuen & Co Ltd: London.

Ullmann, W. (1975) *Law and Politics in the Middle Ages: An Introduction to the Sources of Medieval Political Ideas*, Sources of History Limited: London.

Van Caenegem, R. (1981) 'Law in the medieval world', *Tijdschrift voor Rechtsgeschiedenis*, vol. 49, pp. 13–46.

Van Caenegem, R. (1991) 'Government, law and society', in Burns (1991).

Vanden Bossche, C. (1991) *Carlyle and the Search for Authority*, Ohio University Press: Colombus, OH.

Van Krieken, R. (2003) 'Beyond the "Parsonian Problem of Order": Elias Habit and contemporary sociology', paper delivered, 30 June 2003. Macquarie University, Sydney.

Villa, D. (2001) *Socratic Citizenship*, Princeton University Press: Princeton, NJ.

Villa, D. (2008) *Public Freedom*, Princeton University Press: Princeton, NJ.

Vincent, K. S. (2000) 'Benjamin Constant, the French Revolution, and the origins of French romantic liberalism', *French Historical Studies*, vol. 23, no. 4, pp. 607–37.

Visser, R. (1992) 'Fascist doctrine and the cult of the Romanita', *Journal of Contemporary History*, vol. 27, no. 1, pp. 5–22.

Wallas, G. (1929) *Human Nature in Politics*, Constable & Co.: London.

Walton, D. (1997) *Appeal To Expert Opinion; Arguments From Authority*, The Pennsylvania University Press: University Park.

Ward, L. F. (1902) 'Contemporary sociology III'. *American Journal of Sociology*, vol. 7, no. 6, pp. 749–62.

Watanabe, M. (1972) 'Authority and consent in church government: Panormitanus. Aeneas Sylvius, Cusanus', *Journal of the History of Ideas*, vol. 33, no. 2, pp. 217–326.

Waterfield, R. (2009) *Why Socrates Died; Dispelling the Myths*, Faber and Faber: London.

Watt, J. A. (1991) 'Spiritual and temporal powers', in Burns (1991).

Webb, R. (1992) 'A crisis of authority: Early nineteenth-century British thought', *Albion: A Quarterly Journal Concerned with British Studies*, vol. 24, no. 1, pp. 1–16.

Weber, M. (1904) 'The "objectivity" of knowledge in social science and social policy', in Bruun, H. H. and Whimster, S. (2012) *Max Weber: Collected Methodological Writings*, Routledge: London.

Weber, M. (1915) 'The social psychology of the world religions' in Gerth, H. and Wright Mills, C. (1958) *From Max Weber: Essays in Sociology*, Galaxy Books: New York.

Weber, M. (1915a) 'Religious rejections of the world and their directions' in Gerth, H. and Wright Mills, C. (1958) *From Max Weber: Essays in Sociology*, Galaxy Books: New York.

Weber, M. (1918) 'Parliament and democracy in Germany' in Lassman, P. and Speirs, R. (2008) (eds) *Weber: Political Ideas*, Cambridge University Press: Cambridge.

Weber, M. (1919) 'The profession and vocation of politics', in Lassman, P. and Speirs, R. (2008) (eds) *Weber: Political Ideas*, Cambridge University Press: Cambridge.

Weber, M. (1919a) 'Science as vocation' in Gerth, H. and Wright Mills, C. (1958) (eds), *From Max Weber: Essays in Sociology*, Oxford University Press: New York.

Weber, M. (1958) 'Politics as a vocation' in Gerth, H. and Wright Mills, C. (1958) (eds), *From Max Weber: Essays in Sociology*, Oxford University Press: New York.

Weber, M. (1978) (eds Roth, G. and Wittich, C.) *Economy and Society; An Outline of Interpretive Sociology, Vols. 1 & 2*, University of California Press: Berkeley.

Weber, M. (1998) (originally 1909) 'Preliminary report on a proposed survey for a sociology of the press', *History of the Human Sciences*, vol. 11, no. 2, pp. 107–20.

Weimann, R. (1996) *Authority and Representation in Early Modern Discourse*, The Johns Hopkins University Press: Baltimore, MD.

Wells, J. (1966) 'The Spirit of Republican Rome', Chapter 58 in *Universal History of the World*, vol. 3, p. 1712.

Whimster, S. (2010) 'Book review of Max Weber, Briefe 1915–1917', *Max Weber Studies*, vol. 10, no. 1, pp. 125–37.

White, D. S. (1936) 'The attitude of the Romans toward peace and war', *The Classical Journal*, vol. 31, no. 8, pp. 465–78.

Whittaker, J. H. (1999) 'Kierkegaard on the concept of authority', *International Journal for Philosophy of Religion*, vol. 46, pp. 83–101.

Wiecker, F. (1981) 'The Importance of Roman Law for Western Civilization and Western Legal Thought', *Boston College International and Comparative Law Review*, vol. 4, no. 2, pp. 257–81.

Wilken, R. (1999) 'Gregory VII and the politics of the spirit', *First Things*, vol. 89, January, pp. 26–32.

Williams, S. (1964) (ed.) *The Gregorian Epoch. Reformation, Revolution, Reaction?*, D.C. Heath and Company: Boston, MA.

Willoughby, W. W. (1917) 'The Prussian theory of monarchy', *The American Political Science Review*, vol. 11, no. 4, pp. 621–42.

Wilson, B. (2009) *What Price Liberty?*, Faber and Faber: London.

Wilson, F. (1937) 'The prelude to authority', *The American Political Science Review*, vol. 31, no. 1, pp. 12–27.

Wilson, F. G. (1955) 'Public opinion and the middle class', *The Review of Politics*, vol. 17, no. 4, pp. 486–510.

Winch, D. (1983) 'Science and the legislator: Adam Smith and After', *The Economic Journal*, vol. 93, no. 371, pp. 501–20.

Wirszubski, M. A. (1950) *Libertas as a Political Idea at Rome During the Late Republic and Early Principate*, Cambridge University Press: Cambridge.

Wolff, H. J. (1987) *Roman Law: An Historical Introduction*, University of Oklahoma Press: Norman.

Wolin, S. (2004) (1960) *Politics and Vision*, Princeton University Press: Princeton, NJ.

Wolpert, J. F. (1950) 'towards a sociology of authority', in Gouldner, A. (1950) (ed.) *Studies In Leadership: Leadership and Democratic Action*, Harper & Brothers: New York.

Wood, E. M. (1991) *The Pristine Culture of Capitalism*, Verso: London.

Wood, E. M. (2008) *Citizens to Lords: A Social History of Western Political Thought from Antiquity to the Middle Ages*, Verso: London.

Wood, N. (1968) 'Some reflections on Sorel and Machiavelli', *Political Science Quarterly*, vol. 83, no. 1, pp. 76–91.

Wrong, D. (1979) *Power; Its Forms, Bases and Uses*, Basil Blackwell: Oxford.

Wrong, D. (1995) *The Problem of Order: What Unites and Divides Society*, Harvard University Press: Cambridge, MA.

Wyke, M. (1999) 'Screening ancient Rome in the new Italy', Edwards, C. (ed.) *Roman Presences; Receptions of Rome in European Culture, 1789–1945*, Cambridge University Press: Cambridge.

Yates, F. (1985) *The Imperial Theme in the Sixteenth Century*, ARK Paperbacks: London.

Yavetz, Z. (1971) 'Caesarism, and the historians', *Journal of Contemporary History*, vol. 6, no. 2, pp. 184–201.

Yearley, S. (1992) 'Green ambivalence about science: Legal-rational authority and the scientific legitimation of a social movement', *British Journal of Sociology*, vol. 43, no. 4, pp. 511–32.

Yeo, R. (1984) 'Science and intellectual authority in mid-nineteenth-century Britain: Robert Chambers and Vestiges of the natural history of creation', *Victorian Studies*, Autumn, vol. 28, no. 1, pp. 5–31.

Zaller, R. (1998) 'Breaking the vessels: The desacralization of monarchy in early modern England', *The Sixteenth Century Journal*, vol. 29, no. 3, pp. 757–78.

Zaret, D. (1989) 'Religion and the rise of liberal-democratic ideology in 17th-century England', *American Sociological Review*, vol. 54, no. 2, pp. 163–79.

Zaret, D. (1996) 'Petitions and the "invention" of public opinion in the English revolution', *The American Journal of Sociology*, vol. 101, no. 6, pp. 1497–555.

Zeitlin, I. (1997) *Ideology and the development of sociological theory*, Prentice Hall: Englewood Cliffs, NJ.

Ziolkowski, J. (2009) 'Cultures of authority in the long twelfth century', *Journal of English and Germanic Philology*', vol. 108, no. 4, pp. 412–48.

Zuckerman, A. (1977) 'The Concept "political elite": lessons from Mosca and Pareto', *The Journal of Politics*, vol. 39, no. 2, pp. 324–44.

Zweig, S. (2006) *Tersites – Jeremias. Zwei Dramen*, S. Fischer Verlag: Frankfurt.

Index